THE UNITED NATIONS SYSTEM and its FUNCTIONS
selected readings

EDITED BY ROBERT W. GREGG
AND MICHAEL BARKUN

Maxwell School of Citizenship and Public Affairs
Syracuse University

D. VAN NOSTRAND COMPANY, INC.
Princeton, New Jersey Toronto   London   Melbourne

Van Nostrand Regional Offices: *New York, Chicago, San Francisco*

D. Van Nostrand Company, Ltd., *London*

D. Van Nostrand Company (Canada), Ltd., *Toronto*

D. Van Nostrand Australia Pty. Ltd., *Melbourne*

Library of Congress Catalog Card No. 68-20917

PRINTED IN THE UNITED STATES OF AMERICA

Preface

THE functional approach we have taken in this volume is somewhat different from the customary approach to international organizations, which are all too often seen simply as agencies self-consciously pursuing the purposes elaborated in their charters. The functions identified in this book are all performed, with varying degrees of effectiveness, by the United Nations and affiliated bodies; some are consciously, others less consciously, discharged. These functions are, in effect, generic categories of things which international organizations do. By using this approach, we hope that the important functions of Communication, Aggregation, and Socialization will not be lost to view, and that Peace-Keeping and Economic Development may be placed in their proper context as facets of larger Conflict Management and Redistribution functions.

Although the several selections were chosen with an eye to clarifying a particular function of the UN system, virtually all selections will shed light on other functions as well; this is particularly true of those selections which are case studies. None of the authors was writing within the somewhat procrustean structural-functional framework employed here. We have sought, in Paul Appleby's felicitous phrase, to make a mesh of things.

Obviously the activities of the United Nations are not neatly compartmentalized. The functions of the system are mutually reinforcing and we hope that the chapters of this book will be, too. Some functions are instrumental in discharging others—Aggregation, for example, in discharging the Conflict Management and Redistribution functions. Moreover, there is an obvious interdependence among such functions as Socialization and Integration. In terms of specific selections, the essays by Haas under Articulation and Aggregation of Interests and Citrin under Conflict Management shed light on Integration. Alger's essay under Communications is pertinent to an understanding of Socialization, and Friedheim's and Horowitz's case studies under Redistribution are illustrative of Articulation and Aggregation of Interests. The net effect should be the impression, not of functional compartmentalization, but of a web of interrelated activities.

The twenty-five essays in this volume do not cover every issue before the United Nations, nor were they intended to. They *do* illustrate the

iii

six functions which we have identified and taken together they *do* provide an interesting mosaic of the UN political process. Although the primary consideration in their selection was their contribution to an understanding of the functional typology, there were other considerations.

One of the most important was a desire to introduce students to some of the most imaginative contemporary scholarship on the UN system in particular and international organization in general, including examples of model-building, quantitative analysis, and depth interviewing. The essays vary in their level of difficulty and the brief introductory passages have been included to make the material accessible to undergraduates.

Another factor in determining what to include was a belief that a range of disciplinary perspectives would contribute to a more balanced assessment of the place of the UN system in contemporary international politics, and we have in fact included sociologists as well as political scientists, practitioners as well as academicians, and students of international law and comparative politics as well as of international organization *per se*. Where possible, we have chosen essays with a comparative dimension, drawing upon the literature of domestic politics and regional international organizations for analogy and perspective.

This is not a collection of snippets, a series of essays edited to the bare bone. Enough different works and approaches have been used to convey a feeling for the variety of the subject matter and of contemporary scholarship, but not so many that depth has been sacrificed to eclecticism. Most selections have been printed virtually in their entirety, and provide full development of the author's ideas; they include the notes which reflect the range of his inquiry and the tables and figures which support and illustrate his findings.

There are many ways to study the phenomenon of international organization. The one employed in this volume is quite compatible with others in wider use. We believe that it will supplement and enrich any other approach, be it historical, legal, policy-oriented, or whatever. And it will certainly suggest answers to the question so often raised by the UN's friends and foes alike when that organization seems immobilized or inadequate in the face of mounting problems: Why the United Nations? This is what the United Nations does; these are the functions of the United Nations system.

ROBERT W. GREGG
MICHAEL BARKUN

Contents

Chapter IV: CONFLICT MANAGEMENT — 241

Chapter V: REDISTRIBUTION — 333

Chapter VI: INTEGRATION — 399

Introduction

PERHAPS the most unfortunate thing about the study of international organizations is that it has too often been isolated from its natural milieu, international politics. International organizations may be of some intrinsic importance, but not very much. They have a very limited claim upon the attention of students of international relations unless they are placed in some larger frame of reference. This larger frame of reference can be supplied by the adaptation of systems theory and structural-functional analysis to the world of global inter-state relations and to the place of the United Nations and its affiliated agencies in that world.

Controversy continues to swirl around the literature of systems theory, and it is not the purpose of the editors of this volume to enlist in that controversy. In suggesting that the UN ought to be viewed in the context of the international system, we are not claiming—as systems theorists who consciously borrow from biology and physics sometimes do—that the world is homeostatic (i.e., that like the human body or a heating system with a thermostat it possesses some propensity for self-preservation through adaptive adjustments in the face of extremely destabilizing threats). There may be a grain of truth in the characterization of the world as a system in the homeostatic sense. It can also be argued that the very existence of the United Nations, as well as the general acceptance of "rules" (e.g., no first use of nuclear weapons) in the waging of both hot and cold war, reflects a shared concern for ultra-stability. However, the word *"system"* is used in this volume in a much more modest sense. In the first place, we simply wish to avoid the use of expressions such as "world community," which suggest a non-existent consensus. This leads us to the adoption of the comparatively value-neutral expression "international system." In the second place, the concept of system is useful because it suggests actors interacting within environmental constraints, and this is precisely the picture which we wish to conjure up.

The world, moreover, is a *political system,* the interactions among its actors being preeminently political. Some of the more widely quoted definitions of "political system" would seem to preclude the application of the term to the world or indeed to virtually any set of interstate relations. Easton, for example, defines political system in terms of the "authoritative allocation of values";[1] Almond calls it "the legitimate,

---

[1] David Easton, *The Political System* (New York: Alfred A. Knopf, Inc., 1953), pp. 130 ff.

order-maintaining or transforming system in the society";[2] and Dahl sees it as "any persistent pattern of human relationships that involves, to a significant extent, power, rule, or authority." [3] Each of these definitions is more apposite when applied to the state than when used in reference to the global system. In order to avoid this definitional problem, a political system is simply presumed to exist for the purposes of this volume wherever and whenever a group of actors are caught up in a nexus of relationships, both conflictual and cooperative, generated by common problems and the need to deal with them. Such a definition avoids linking politics to concepts such as compulsion, authority, legitimacy, and power. Politics is rather the processing of issues, which are problems that have crossed the threshold of the political system.

There are many levels and kinds of political system, including the Soviet Union, the German state of Bavaria, the city of London, the House Rules Committee in the U.S. Congress, and the Teamsters Union. The world is another, albeit one in which power is conspicuously decentralized and authority largely lacking. Interaction among actors on the world stage, most of them nation states, is preeminently political. Although there may be no world community, there is at least a universal awareness of participation in a political process. The name of the game is international politics, and it is played at the United Nations as well as elsewhere in an almost infinite variety of bilateral and multilateral relationship patterns.

In addition to the international system, reference is frequently made in the following pages to the *United Nations system*. This latter phrase has two meanings and, inasmuch as the authors whose essays are represented in this volume did not have a common theoretical framework in mind, they have used the two meanings interchangeably. The UN system may simply be a shorthand for the UN *and* the specialized agencies, taken collectively. It may also refer to a political system comprising those actors who may be observed to interact at UN (and specialized agency) sessions and sites within the somewhat elastic strictures of Charter and *Realpolitik*. In this latter sense, the United Nations system may be regarded as a subsystem of the international political system or as a structure (or complex of structures) of that system. It is thus both a kaleidoscopic pattern of conflictual and cooperative relationships, universal in both the number of states involved

[2] Gabriel A. Almond, "Introduction: A Functional Approach to Comparative Politics," in Gabriel A. Almond and James S. Coleman, eds., *The Politics of the Developing Areas* (Princeton: Princeton University Press, 1960), p. 7.

[3] Robert A. Dahl, *Modern Political Analysis* (Englewood Cliffs, N.J.: Prentice-Hall, Inc., 1963), p. 6.

and in the scope of subject matter, and a setting wherein the issues which are the substance of that pattern of relationships are processed. In Wolfram Hanrieder's concise definition, an international organization is "an institutionalized arrangement among members of the international system to solve tasks which have evolved from systemic conditions;"[4] the UN and the specialized agencies are such.

At this point the concepts of *system* and of *structure* and *function* both come into focus. Systems theorists speak of *functions* of a political system, i.e., of those generic categories of activities which are performed within any political system. In other words, if one identifies a given set of relationships as a political system, one has, *ipso facto*, identified the existence of a set of functions. It should be possible to exactly specify what these functions are, but there is little consensus in the literature of functional theory. Almond a few years ago developed a seven-fold classification: four input functions—political socialization and recruitment, interest articulation, interest aggregation, and political communication; and three output functions—rule making, rule application, and rule adjudication.[5] More recently he has identified three levels of system functions: capabilities, conversion functions, and system maintenance and adaptation functions, with the "original" seven functons now distributed between conversion functions and system maintenance functions.[6] Other authors have other lists, with Spiro suggesting four irreducible "existential" functions of political systems: formulation, deliberation, resolution of issues, and solution of problems.[7] At the risk of contributing to a further proliferation, we shall argue that there are six discrete UN system functions.

When we speak of "the functions of the United Nations system" we are identifying those things which the UN system, defined as structure and subsystem of the international political system, actually does. They may very well not be conscious acts or phases of the UN political process, and should be distinguished from the *purposes* of the United Nations. Purposes, according to Ernst Haas, are action patterns consciously willed by the actors, whereas functions are the results of those actions.[8] It is usually possible to ascertain the purposes for which an international organization has been created or for which it is being

---

[4] Wolfram Hanrieder, "International Organizations and International Systems," *The Journal of Conflict Resolution*, Vol. X, No. 3, p. 297.   [5] Almond, *op. cit.*, p. 17.

[6] Gabriel A. Almond and G. Bingham Powell, Jr., *Comparative Politics: A Developmental Approach* (Boston: Little, Brown and Company, 1966), pp. 27-30.

[7] Herbert J. Spiro, *World Politics: The Global System* (Homewood, Ill.: The Dorsey Press, 1966), p. 51.

[8] Ernst B. Haas, *Beyond the Nation-State* (Stanford, California: Stanford University Press, 1964), p. 81.

used by reading the constitutional documents and annotating them by perusal of the organization's record. According to the Charter of the United Nations, for example, the purposes of that organization include maintenance of international peace and security, development of friendly relations among nations based on respect for principles of equal rights and self-determination, and achievement of international cooperation in solving economic, social, and other problems. A general purpose, such as the maintenance of peace and security, acquires specificity when, as in the Indo-Pakistani conflict of 1965, the United Nations makes it its purpose to achieve a peaceful settlement of the particular dispute and adopts strategies which have that end in view. But the *functions* performed in the process of pursuing this purpose are another matter. They are, of course, related to purposes, and may in some cases be only more abstract renderings of generalized purposes. But they are on the whole less consciously willed and less frequently verbalized.

The six functions of the United Nations system which are analyzed here are:

1. articulation and aggregation of interests
2. communication
3. socialization and recruitment
4. conflict management
5. redistribution
6. integration

Why these six? It is conceivable that the UN does other things, but we believe that this list of functions subsumes all activities consciously and unconsciously performed within the system. It will immediately be apparent that these functions bear some resemblance to Almond's original typology; at least the input functions are the same. But Almond developed his initial scheme, and indeed his subsequent one, to facilitate comparative study of developed and developing countries. It would not, for example, be particularly helpful to an understanding of the functions of the United Nations system to insist upon rule functions, as he does. The UN does, of course, adopt and apply rules for its own internal functioning, and it is possible to speak of "the law of the United Nations." [9] Moreover, the UN contributes, albeit modestly, to the limited body of rules governing inter-state behavior external to the UN. But it has seemed preferable not to dwell on rule making or law making by the UN, but rather on areas of recurrent UN system activity

[9] See for example, D. W. Bowett, *The Law of International Institutions* (London: Stevens and Sons, 1963), or the monumental work by Rosalyn Higgins, *The Development of International Law Through the Political Organs of the United Nations* (London: Oxford University Press, 1963).

in which there is some impact, even if few authoritative and enduring rules are laid down. Thus our functions include *conflict management* and *redistribution,* which resemble the system capabilities (especially the regulative, distributive, and symbolic capabilities) of Almond's later typology,[10] and *integration,* which is the ultimate function of the United Nations system.[11] These are generic task areas in which the UN system is continuously engaged. It is because the UN is presumed to have capabilities in these areas that the UN is a setting for *articulation and aggregation* of interests within the international system. The *communication* function is instrumental in the performance of the other functions; it is the lubricant of the system. *Socialization and recruitment,* a system maintenance and adaptation function in the later Almond scheme,[12] is also instrumental for UN system survival.

Articulation and aggregation of interests are certainly the primary UN system functions. If the uses to which the UN system is put were arranged along a spectrum from minimal to maximal, the minimal use (i.e., the one to which most states could most readily subscribe and in which they almost reflexively join each day) would be that of a permanent conference machinery. Here states make their demands, express their fears, seek support; here they articulate their interests and through a process of aggregation seek to maximize their chances of getting what they want and avoiding what they do not want. The UN is a complex of structures for the performance of these functions.

Communication is a function which pervades all others. Although the interaction necessary for politics to exist does not guarantee that those interacting are also communicating effectively, it is difficult to conceive of a political system to which communication is not important if the actors in conflict are to discipline or channel those problems the existence of which is at the root of the phenomenon we have termed the political system. International organization sites and the many-faceted multilateral diplomacy which takes place at those sites make for a rather special kind of communications pattern to supplement other, more traditional ones, and international organizations are also themselves transmitters of messages—their words, their deeds, and even their omissions—to the environment within which they operate.

Socialization and recruitment are closely related functions. The

---

[10] Almond and Powell, *op. cit.,* pp. 190–203.

[11] See Haas, *op. cit.,* who suggests that "the historical purpose of the UN is to encourage the evolution of a world community beyond the minimal level of cooperation represented by a permanent conference of governments; to reach a stage at which the organization can act autonomously for constructive and universal ends . . ." (p. 124).

[12] Almond and Powell, *op. cit.,* pp. 22–25, 47–48, 64–66.

former is "the process of induction into the political culture," [13] the latter the process whereby persons are brought out of parochial sub-systems and given roles in the larger political system. Among nation states there is little loyalty to or identification with the UN system, but one of the functions of the system is to infect those who participate in it with a larger perspective so that what they value has universal, rather than exclusively national, referents. International officials are by definition supposed to be system-oriented; participants in international organizations are supposed to abide by institutional rules, many of them uncodified. That they are not, and do not, in every case is perhaps less surprising than that some changes in outlook and behavior are in fact wrought by the existence of the UN system.

Conflict management is probably the most obvious of UN system functions. Although the UN may wistfully be viewed by some as a possible vehicle for eliminating conflict among states, and occasionally may even be successfully employed for resolving conflict, its function is much more accurately described as that of conflict management. Conflict is ubiquitous; without it there is no politics. To eliminate it is impossible—but to bring it under some control, to keep it within tolerable bounds, is necessary. Every issue on the UN's agenda is evidence of a conflictual relationship in which the UN has become involved. The UN's involvement may signify that the conflict is being waged symbolically within the UN, that some semblance of a cooperative effort is being made to regulate the conflict, or both.

Redistribution is a UN system function because all participants in the system make claims and demands with respect to the allocation of scarce resources such as wealth, power, status, and influence. The UN is confronted with *de facto* configurations of power and influence and patterns of wealth and poverty. Expectations exist in some quarters that the UN can effect a redistribution of these commodities. But even when the United Nations is not subject to conscious pressure of this sort, it contributes, by the very fact of its existence and the nature of its mode of operation, to the reallocation of intangible resources such as status and prestige, to the legitimization of values, and to the conferral of attention.

Integration is a UN system function because the cooperation essential to the performance of the other functions may contain the seeds of increased future authority and cohesiveness. The further growth of a global web of transactions and an increase in the authority and legitimacy of institutions, such as those of the UN itself, are thought to be

[13] Almond, *op. cit.*, p. 27.

by-products of UN activities. Integrative potential is latent in virtually all that the UN system does, and indeed in the very existence of that system. Although the UN has not thus far been very effective either as a vehicle or as a catalyst for integration, and although the UN may even have a disintegrative impact on occasions, it is necessary to include in any list of UN system functions a category which embraces both the functionalist thrust of the United Nations and the specialized agencies and an occasional manifestation by the system of incipient "supranationalism."

These, then, are the functions of the UN system. They are functions performed in part by the UN for the international system, viewed as the UN system's environment, and in part for the UN system itself. It ought to be observed that the international system has many structures or relationship patterns, of which the United Nations is only one. Other systemic structures (sub-systems) would include: "the balancing operations of the 'classical' balance-of-power system, nuclear deterrence postures, the procedures and restraints of international law, the interdependencies of international trade, alliances, the routines of diplomatic communications. . . ." [14] These, too, perform these functions, although they do not perform them in just the same way.

The UN system brings to the performance of these functions a combination of attributes which is unique in contemporary international politics. The actors are concentrated, physically, and they are both very numerous and diverse. Many of their interactions are conspicuously public, but the opportunities for certain kinds of private interaction are unparalleled. The interaction is highly institutionalized and periodic. The procedures and rules employed in the processing of conflict and canalizing of cooperation are peculiar to the UN system. The agenda is virtually unlimited and issues of initially limited interest quickly become universal issues. A system-oriented bureaucracy exists to assist in disseminating information, bringing issues into focus, and implementing agreements. An aura of idealism attaches to UN deliberations, even when they are most narrowly interest-oriented, which is absent in other relationship patterns of the international system.

But these distinguishing characteristics add up only to a different style of international politics. The United Nations system is still very much a part of international politics. What distinguishes it from other patterns of international political relationship is interesting and important, but not so important as what it has in common with them, namely the performance of certain system functions.

---

[14] Hanrieder, *op. cit.,* p. 297.

Chapter I

ARTICULATION AND AGGREGATION OF INTERESTS

1. Political Influence in the General Assembly by Robert Owen Keohane
2. The United Nations and Some African Political Attitudes by Ali A. Mazrui
3. Toward A Model of Competitive International Politics by Bruce M. Russett
4. Discovering Voting Groups in the United Nations by Bruce M. Russett
5. Beyond the Nation-State: Programming and Organizational Ideology by Ernst B. Haas

I. Articulation and Aggregation of Interests

THE concept of national interest is familiar to all students of international relations. It is a convenient if frequently criticized shorthand for that complex of attitudes and policy preferences which characterize a state's relationships with other states and the international environment. We say that a given country wants regional hegemony, more favorable terms of trade, dependable allies, borders which embrace fellow nationals, prestige and status which are its due, military parity with neighbors, the opportunity to export its ideology, the luxury of being left alone. Such general interests are usually supplemented by, or translated into, more specific demands in individual cases and crises: cessation of border incursions, establishment of a capital development fund, a treaty to stop proliferation of nuclear weapons, and numerous other demands touching upon such diverse subjects as apartheid in South Africa, diversion of the Jordan River, the status of the Western garrison in Berlin, commercial fishing off the coast of Ecuador, and the world price of coffee. All states have things which they seek to achieve, possess, avoid, and influence, and they are continually addressing themselves to those objectives. What they are doing, of course, is articulating their interests, and the United Nations is one of the places where they do so.

In a famous definition, Harold Lasswell argues that politics is who gets what, when, and how.[1] Nation states and such other actors as nationalist groups in dependent territories, insurgents, and international officials are the "who" in the international version of the Lasswell definition. The interests whose satisfaction and frustration are at issue, the values and resources whose allocation is in dispute: These are the "what." The UN political process is part of the "how." It is, in effect, a conversion process, whereby inputs, i.e., the claims made by states on behalf of their interests, are transformed into outputs. It would be in-

[1] Harold Lasswell, *Politics: Who Gets What, When, How* (New York: McGraw-Hill Book Co., 1936).

accurate to say that the UN is the center of gravity of the international system. Several other system structures are probably more important, including the military postures of the superpowers and the more traditional patterns of bilateral diplomacy, and the processing of claims through these structures may well produce more significant outputs than does the UN. However, in no place is the articulation of interests and their subsequent aggregation more highly visible than at the United Nations. Moreover, the near universality of membership and the long agenda are testimony to the importance attached to the UN system as a channel for the articulation and satisfaction of interests.

Nation states are then, in a sense, the interest groups of the international system. They are not the only representatives of the genus, of course, and they differ from each other to such a great extent as to suggest that they are not really of the same species, even if convention and international law would have it so. Nevertheless, the nation state is to world politics what interest groups are to American national politics. Although states *qua* interest articulators have some of the characteristics which Almond identifies either with institutional or with associational interest groups, especially organization and continuous representation, in an important sense they are communal interest groups, reflecting the fact that the international system is a relatively primitive system.[2] Most articulators at the UN speak for national (read communal, tribal, ethnic, linguistic) interests. For the most part we hear Ghanaians, Poles, and Chileans, rather than educators, agronomists, and all manner of other functional specialists.

There are, to be sure, other than nation state voices at the UN. Unique opportunities are afforded by the UN to petitioners on behalf of nationalist groups in dependent territories such as Southwest Africa, Angola, and the Pacific Islands. The expression of transnational functional interests through non-governmental organizations (NGOs) such as the World Federation of Trade Unions and the Chamber of Commerce has been facilitated. Indeed, the UN system has pioneered in the provision of channels for interest articulation by actors other than states, the International Labor Organization having even gone so far as to provide representation in its principal organs to national employers' and workers' groups as well as to governments. The most important actors engaged in interest articulation through the United Nations

---

[2] For a discussion of different kinds of interest group structures, see Gabriel A. Almond and G. Bingham Powell, Jr., *Comparative Politics: A Developmental Approach* (Boston: Little, Brown and Company, 1966), pp. 74–79.

(other than nation states), however, are international officials. The Secretary-General of the UN, the Directors-General of the specialized agencies, and countless lesser officials are presumed by virtue of office and sometimes of reputation to be spokesmen for the organization as a whole, urging institutional interests in competition with the many advocates of national interests.

The United Nations tends to be an arena in which interests articulated elsewhere are amplified and directed to a wider audience. Thus border incidents, demonstrations, diplomatic exchanges, and all manner of threats and appeals are echoed in the UN, which is often acoustically suited to interest articulation even when there is little or no prospect that claims can be converted into authoritative decisions. There are, moreover, instances in which the very existence of an international organization forum helps to make manifest demands which might otherwise remain latent and dictates the channel as well as the style of interest articulation. Who can doubt that the articulation of demands for self-determination, human rights, and racial justice have been affected markedly by the availability of the United Nations? In sum, the UN may be viewed as a complex of structures through which a variety of conflicting and sometimes converging interests are expressed with the aim of influencing attitudes and behavior.

If the UN agencies provide more opportunities for more actors to state their positions on more issues, so do they generate pressures for interest aggregation. The demands of 120 nation states, not to mention those of other interests, are, in their crude, unaggregated form, too numerous and usually too diffuse to permit the UN to be much more than a modern day Babel. In any political system a need exists to convert the many demands upon decision-makers into general policy alternatives. This process we may term interest aggregation. Narrow expressions of interest are combined and more general expressions of interest are formulated. Much of the activity taking place at any given time at the site of an international organization is aggregative; except for the ceaseless articulation of demands and claims, the most commonly observed phenomenon at the UN is the continuing quest for support through persuasion and accommodation. This activity, continuous with articulation but distinct from it, is aggregation; it is usually a necessary condition for the conversion of inputs into outputs.

Just as interest articulation is related to and subsumes the activity of interest groups, so interest aggregation is related to and subsumes the activity of political parties. There is in fact a tendency, both journalistic and scholarly, to view the UN General Assembly as a parliament and the various blocs and groups within it as nascent parties. Although these analogies are based upon superficial resemblances and should not be too rigorously insisted upon, the UN system does promote the development of aggregative structures which might otherwise not exist and which perform some of the functions of political parties in more highly developed political systems. These "parties" have been created for the purpose of bringing about a convergence and synthesis of otherwise conflicting or unrelated interests in order that a general policy line may be adapted, thereby increasing the influence of the combined interests. The most conspicuous example of such structures is the caucusing group. True, this label covers a variety of different entities, some large and some small, some highly visible and some barely visible, some permanent and others *ad hoc,* some comparatively formal and others decidedly informal. But all contribute to the development of patterns of consultation, bargaining, consensus formation, and role assignment within international organizations and, in some cases, outside them as well—as when these patterns prove to have a continuing or more widely applicable utility.

Interest aggregation in the UN system leads to another level of interest articulation. Thus parochial views with which states approach an issue in the General Assembly are synthesized to some extent through the activities of a caucus, such as the so-called Afro-Asian bloc, which holds regular meetings and seeks to define a common substantive policy or to agree upon procedural tactics. The resultant interest is in turn articulated and then aggregated, perhaps with the Soviet bloc on self-determination issues or with the Latin American bloc on economic development issues, in a new round of coalition formation. Thus is produced the "UN position" in the form of a resolution approved or a resolution defeated. Some UN resolutions may be said to be a form of institutional interest articulation, as when the Security Council or General Assembly makes demands upon combatants in a local war or upon participants in a disarmament conference. The UN then becomes, in a very crude sense of the word, an actor in the international system as well as a set of structures in which other actors meet and bargain.

This process is hardly as neat a stairstep sequence as is suggested here, nor for that matter are articulation and aggregation easily identified and attributed to particular structures in any system. International secretariats, for example, may also aggregate interests (i.e., formulate policy alternatives), and the "blocs" referred to are only among the

more visible and systematic of the relationship patterns which aggregate. The road to a UN resolution is more frequently subterranean,
passing through numerous bilateral and multilateral relationships. But
the process is an aggregative one, nonetheless.

The United Nations is obviously a special kind of structural complex,
one which gives its own distinctive shape to interest articulation and
aggregation. This is the theme of Keohane's essay, which is nothing
less than a *tour d'horizon* of the UN political process. The UN is unlike
other patterns of relationship within the international system, both in
the number, variety, and concentration of the participants and in the
decision-making methods employed. This leads to the universalization
of all issues, with all states addressing themselves to all subjects and all
joining in the bargaining and decision making process. As Keohane
makes quite clear, it is not only the principal powers which exercise influence at the UN, although their influence is still paramount. Unique
opportunities are afforded other states and groups of states to persuade
and manipulate in this most visible and equalitarian of arenas for the
conduct of international politics. The result is that on some occasions
the United Nations appears to reflect the power realities of international
politics, while on others it seems not so much to mirror the world as
distort it.

For the super-powers and perhaps for certain other large states, the
United Nations is an organization which is often useful for the enunciation of policy, sometimes useful as an agent of that policy, and on occasions a source of annoyance because it seems to require public defense of policies which they might prefer not to talk about. In any event,
the UN is not central in the policy planning of these powers; their size
and power guarantee that they shall command attention and exercise
influence—with the UN or without it. Not so with many smaller states,
for whom the United Nations is necessary if they are to focus attention
on "their issues." Mazrui discusses this special relationship between the
United Nations and the African states, who have become the largest
single pressure group within the UN and who regard that organization
as a vehicle for the realization of many of their aspirations.

The international system since World War II has usually been characterized as bipolar, with the two polar powers engaging in a competition for the allegiance of uncommitted states. This relationship has been
reflected in bargaining and voting within the UN. Russett, observing
this phenomenon, turns to the theoretical literature about competitive
national political systems for ideas which may be useful in the develop-

ment of a model of competitive international politics. He asks us to hypothesize a two-party system (i.e., a Communist and a Western party) competing for the allegiance of new voters (i.e., new states), then proceeds to explore their relationships within the UN in terms suggested by the analogy with national politics. Thus interest articulation and aggregation at the United Nations are viewed in terms of competition for support of neutrals, consensus with regard to the limits of this competition, evidence of movement from ideological to pragmatic bargaining styles, and the impact of "enfranchisement of new voters" on the distribution of voters' preferences in the UN.

Discussion of UN blocs has tended to have a Mercator-projection orientation. Thus we hear much about the Afro-Asian bloc, the Latin American bloc, and the Western European bloc. Even when geography is compromised by ideology, as in the case of the Communist bloc, Cuba's inclusion in an otherwise Eastern European grouping is an anomaly which many students of UN affairs find aesthetically disturbing. Because UN votes are one of the most obviously quantifiable of international political data, a number of the mathematically inclined students of international politics have turned their attention to the UN and have used vote analysis to attack the facile identification of bloc with geographical area. Using factor analysis, and more precisely Q-analysis, Russett eschews prior specification of groups and "discovers" a number of blocs based upon similar voting patterns. Although the resulting profile of bloc politics in the UN is not shocking in its identification of strange bedfellows, it does provide statistical evidence that some eastern countries (such as Japan) are Western in their voting habits, for example, and that Yugoslavia is in a sense an Afro-Asian state.

As noted previously, although nation states are the most important actors in the United Nations system, international officials may play important roles as articulators of institutional interests and may contribute to aggregation of interests in organizations characterized by a multitude of purposes and a wide variety of member interests. Haas, writing in the context of a study of functionalism and integration, analyzes briefly the organizational ideologies of five leaders of international bureaucracies and assesses their load-bearing qualities as vehicles for institutional growth and adaptation. He suggests canons for an effective ideology which would infuse each instance of interest articulation and aggregation by the Secretary-General or the Director-General with a content that lifts it out of the category of mere survival policies and simultaneously saves it from utopian excesses. The place of the international official in policy formulation is assured by the inability of international parties and parliaments to reach consensus at a level of high specificity; but this failure of consensus also extends to support for the Secretary-General himself, thereby making of his opportunity to lead a test of his political skills and acumen.

1. Political Influence in the General Assembly*

ROBERT OWEN KEOHANE

THE United Nations General Assembly is an organization of more than 100 sovereign states, but the arena of international politics in which it exists is militarily dominated by a small number of powerful nations, particularly the United States and the Soviet Union. Since it exists in a world of tension and frightening destructive power, the General Assembly is extremely sensitive to the impact of external events and decisions, particularly if great powers are involved. The weakness of the General Assembly compared to the modern superstate reduces its potential autonomy and sharply defines the limits of its influence.

Yet it cannot properly be said that the actions of the General Assembly merely reflect the power realities of international politics. On the contrary, the quasi-parliamentary nature of the organization gives the small and poor states, over thirty of which have become independent only since 1960, an arithmetical advantage in its internal political process. Thus the politics of the General Assembly reflect an interplay between the forces of pluralism, legal equality, and diversity on the one hand, and those of political and military inequality and bipolarity on the other. The organization's behavior cannot be satisfactorily explained either in its own terms, as expressed in the "one state—one vote" rule, or by reference to the outside world alone. It is in the interaction between international politics and parliamentary politics that an understanding of the General Assembly must be found.

The subject here is political influence in the General Assembly, that is, the ability of a state or group of states to achieve its ends by altering the behavior of other states without the exertion of physical force. This discussion of political influence will be divided into . . . sections: (1) the framework of influence—the patterns of political agreement and cooperation in the Assembly; (2) the exercise of influence—how states attempt to achieve their ends; (3) the sources of influence—those characteristics that tend to make a state influential . . .

The diversity of these approaches to the problem of political influence reflects the difficulties in studying an organization such as the General Assembly, which probably remains something of an enigma to everyone involved in it, participants as well as scholars. Whereas the former may lack objectivity, analytical techniques, and time

* From *International Conciliation*, No. 557, March 1966. Reprinted by permission.

for research, the latter are hampered by second-hand information and lack of personal involvement. The participants suffer from being too close, the scholars from not being close enough.

Faced with these difficulties, the student of the General Assembly must be eclectic. He can afford to discard neither the skills of the statistician nor the experiences of the working diplomat. His analysis of the formal structure of the organization and its officially recorded actions must be supplemented by insights into its half-hidden and informal activities, whether these insights can be gained by the analysis of voting records or by interviews with participants. The following discussion, therefore, is based on these separate techniques: study of the formal record, voting analysis, and interviews with a large number of delegates in New York.

Regional Groups

The diversity of the United Nations is obvious. The size of the Organization makes some form of regularized cooperation among states necessary, yet its diversity insures that such cooperation will remain essentially limited in nature. Although most states in the General Assembly are members of regional groups, their first loyalties are to their own national interests, which may differ considerably from those of other states in the same region. Thus the most striking feature of the regional groups is their weakness. Not only do the groups fail to make authoritative policy, but often they do not even reflect the real patterns of political coalition in the organization. Therefore, while they are undoubtedly important, their significance can easily be overemphasized.

The major regional groups may be defined as those that nominate candidates (states or individuals, as the case may be) for offices of the General Assembly. There are six such groups:

Western European, Latin American, East European,[1] African, Asian, and African-Asian. Africa and Asia are included separately as well as together; states in these regions belong to their respective groups as well as to the broader one. Since these six groups are functioning entities rather than mere geographic expressions, certain discrepancies exist between group membership and geography. China, Cuba, Israel, and South Africa, for example, do not attend meetings of the caucusing groups for their geographic regions.

These six major groups do not exhaust the group structure of the Assembly. On the contrary, within and across group lines there are more or less well-organized subgroups arranged along political, historical, ethnic, or special-interest lines. For example, the thirteen Arab states and the five Nordic countries are merely the most cohesive examples of subregional groups operating in the Assembly. A large array of developing states (known as the Seventy-Five) acts as an intra-Assembly interest group working for favorable trade and development policies. Even the Commonwealth states meet occasionally, although they are politically divided and no longer have a significant joint role in nominating candidates for Assembly offices.

Little is known about the actual operations of the East European group, which will therefore be excluded from this analysis. It is difficult to determine in what ways interaction and consultation take place within this group. Nevertheless, its high degree of voting cohesion should be noted. One may as-

---

[1] As a regional group in the General Assembly, it includes the following states: Albania, Byelorussia, Bulgaria, Czechoslovakia, Hungary, Poland, Romania, Ukraine, and USSR. Cuba and Mongolia now also form part of the group. See Sydney D. Bailey, *The General Assembly of the United Nations* (Rev. ed.; New York: Frederick A. Praeger, 1964), p. 32.

sume that there are more discussions and fewer commands in the group now than ten or fifteen years ago.

The scope of group action for the other five associations varies considerably. The Asian and Western European groups function almost exclusively as mechanisms for decisions on candidacy and related problems. Neither group, however, plays a significant role in the process by which substantive resolutions are adopted. Both are too divided politically to discuss effectively important issues in group meetings. In addition, the Western European group suffers under the handicap of having France and the United Kingdom as co-chairmen; the French and British delegations do not depend as heavily on group consultation and common action as their smaller colleagues.

The African, African-Asian, and Latin American groups meet regularly and often while the Assembly is in session to discuss a large variety of issues. Even in these groups, however, the scope of decision-making is limited. The African group has so far primarily discussed questions directly related to Africa, leaving broader issues to the joint African-Asian group. Yet the latter group also does not discuss the entire range of issues before the Assembly. According to one Asian representative, "The African-Asian group does not discuss such matters as nuclear tests and disarmament. It only discusses matters on which there is a common interest—such as colonial questions, *apartheid,* and economic matters." [2]

Whether or not this statement is literally true, it illustrates an important point. Controversial issues that would raise or exacerbate conflicts within the diverse African-Asian group are usually considered in informal consulta-

tions or in non-regional associations of states with similar viewpoints. Thus a number of African and Asian states, along with Yugoslavia, have formed a "non-aligned" group in which they can work together within a framework of common interest and attitudes. Diversity is particularly great within the African-Asian group; in the Latin American group—Cuba being excluded—political outlooks are more similar on non-hemispheric issues, and the scope of discussion therefore is broader.

Even within their areas of effective operation, the regional groups by no means act as nascent political parties or real decision-making units. On the contrary, they are principally means of consultation and communication among states with certain similarities of aims and attitudes, tenuous though these affinities may be. They provide a continuing forum for discussion and an organizational structure, within which occasional common action may be planned.[3] The reasons for regional group weakness are not hard to discern. Composed of states with independent decision-making processes rather than—as in national legislatures —of politicians dependent to some extent on their political parties for re-election, the groups possess little power vis à vis recalcitrant members. If a unanimously accepted compromise cannot be reached, no official group action is taken. None of the groups makes decisions by majority vote that are binding on all members. Even an overwhelming majority is relatively powerless to impose its will on one or a few dissenters; it is limited to exhortation, persuasion, and appeals to group solidarity.

The chief business of the groups is, therefore, to create a consensus within the limitations imposed by independ-

---

[2] Quotations without sources are from the author's interviews with delegates, whose comments specifically were not for attribution.

[3] For the uses to which groups can be put by states, see pp. 31–34. For a historical and procedural discussion of groups, see especially Bailey, *op. cit.,* Chapter 2.

TABLE I

AGREEMENT SCORES FOR REGIONAL GROUPS
IN THE 15TH AND 18TH GENERAL ASSEMBLY SESSIONS

	15th Session			18th Session		
	mean	low	high	mean	low	high
Eastern Europe	99.4	98.8	100.0	98.9	95.8	100.0
Latin America	83.7	68.4	95.4	91.1	78.9	100.0
Western Europe	79.2	57.8	98.4	83.5	60.9	98.6
Africa	78.9	55.1	97.9	88.1	68.8	100.0
Asia	77.6	52.6	96.2	82.4	55.0	97.6
Africa-Asia	76.5	48.1	98.1	85.2	54.1	100.0

ent sovereignties and intra-regional diversity. Thus drafting committees may be appointed to formulate compromise resolutions that will be generally acceptable, but their recommendations remain subject to the approval of each member of the group. In some instances, negotiating committees will be formed to deal with other groups. However, there is no assurance that agreements reached will be acceptable to the group as a whole. The process is often frustrating and its results frequently vapid.

These difficulties reach their quintessence in the African-Asian group. Its members number more than sixty and range geographically, culturally, economically, and politically from Japan to Guinea, from the Philippines to Ethiopia. This array of states is so diverse that it may even be questioned whether the African and Asian states can act effectively as a group on significant as opposed to ritualistic issues. The recent movement among African delegations to emphasize the importance of the African group rather than the joint one indicates that perhaps it cannot. Size may confer more the semblance than the reality of political power.

With this background, it is not surprising that the regional groups, excluding the East European one, do not act as voting blocs in the sense of rigidly disciplined units. Table I provides evidence for this conclusion by presenting agreement scores for the fifteenth and eighteenth sessions, 1960–61 and 1963, respectively. These agreement scores measure the frequency of voting similarities between any two states according to a formula that takes into account abstentions and absences. Complete disagreement would be represented by a score of zero; complete agreement by a score of 100. The first column shows the mean agreement scores of all states in each group with all others of the group; the second column gives the lowest intra-group score; and the third indicates the highest score between two group members.[4]

[4] Only roll-call votes were used in the analysis, with whatever limitations that may imply. Of the roll-call votes, two types were excluded: unanimous votes and votes that directly duplicated later ones. Therefore, when an identical resolution was considered in a committee and later in the Assembly, the former was excluded unless significant changes in voting alignments took place. A large number of votes were used: 190 for the 15th session, 152 for the 16th, and 63 for the 18th,

This table points to a dual conclusion. The occurrence of low intragroup scores indicates that there is considerable dissension within most of the regional groups. On the whole, however, the regional groups maintained greater cohesion than the mean for the Assembly, although the differential was not strikingly large.

To some extent the improvement in group unity in the eighteenth session —indicated by higher agreement scores both within and between regions—is the result of diminished controversy in the Assembly that year. It may also be significant that the African and Latin American groups increased their cohesion about twice as much as did the Asian and Western European groups; furthermore. the lowest scores in the African and Latin American groups rose by at least ten points each compared with minimal gains for the two other regions. Since it was in the African and Latin American groups that members tried hardest to increase group unity between 1960 and 1963, these differences may indicate that their efforts met with some success.

When voting patterns in the eighteenth session are analyzed independently of regional affiliations, however, it becomes clear that cross-regional cooperation and cleavage remained important in 1963. Specifically, crossgroup coalitions of African, Asian, and Latin American states are evident. A number of states in each of these groups agreed more often with certain states in the two other groups than with members of their own group. As will be shown below, many of the Assembly's voting patterns have regularly

been based on intra-regional and interregional coalitions rather than strict adherence to regional group boundaries. The use of the term 'bloc voting" should not obscure an awareness of this reality.

Voting Alignments

If a clear understanding of actual voting patterns in the General Assembly is to be gained, the voting data must be analyzed not only in regional group terms, but also without reference to the regional groups. An analysis focusing on regional groups and their cohesion cannot determine to what extent significant cross-regional coalitions exist and is therefore likely to obscure rather than illuminate many important features of voting in the Assembly.[5] Thus the analyst who merely studies the cohesion of caucusing groups cannot detect the presence, on a given issue, of a high degree of agreement among such geographically diverse but politically congenial states as Austria, Brazil, Denmark, Iceland, Iran, Malaysia, Norway, Pakistan, the Philippines, Sweden, and Thailand; yet such a coalition did exist in the fifteenth and sixteenth sessions on the issue of disarmament.

To determine voting patterns by using actual voting data, Assembly votes for either a session or a particular issue can be evaluated in terms of agreement scores. In one such analysis, agreement scores were calculated separately for the fifteenth, sixteenth, and eighteenth sessions, and for six issue-areas of the fifteenth and sixteenth sessions taken together.[6] The six issue-areas were: disarmament, peacekeeping, colonialism, other political issues, economic and social issues, and legal issues. This analysis indicated that re-

which was shorter and less controversial. For a further discussion, see Arend Lijphart, "The Analysis of Bloc Voting in the General Assembly: A Critique and a Proposal," *American Political Science Review,* Vol. 57 (Dec. 1963), pp. 902–917; and Robert O. Keohane, "Political Practice in the United Nations General Assembly" (Ph.D. thesis, Harvard Univ., 1965), Chapter 1. Unpublished.

[5] See Thomas Hovet, Jr., *Bloc Politics in the United Nations* (Cambridge: Harvard Univ. Press, 1960); see also the critique by Lijphart, *op. cit.*
[6] See Keohane, *op. cit.,* Chapters I, II.

gional groups in the Assembly do not necessarily act as unified and disciplined blocs.

In all six issue-areas and in the three Assembly sessions, significant divisions were apparent within the major regional groups except for the East European one. The African-Asian group was divided on all occasions into a number of subgroups: usually, the anti-Western states, the moderate African states, the Western-allied Asian states, and the French-speaking African states. The Western European group was often split between the Nordic states and neutrals on the one hand, and the NATO-allied continental countries, frequently joined by the United States, on the other. Divisions among Latin American states were also omnipresent, although the lines of cleavage were not as consistent as they were for the other regions.

Moreover, cross-regional coalitions were very much in evidence on a number of issues. This was particularly true of those relating to disarmament, but was also true of votes on peacekeeping, colonialism, other political issues, and social and economic questions. The composition of cross-regional coalitions varied, but participating states were usually more moderate (closer to the political center of the Assembly) than most other members of their regional groups. Thus Nordic states and other European nations with neutralist inclinations, such as Austria and Ireland, often voted with pro-Western Asian and African states, such as Iran, Japan, Liberia, Malaysia, Nigeria, Pakistan, Thailand, and Tunisia. At the eighteenth session, voting agreement was quite pronounced between Latin American states, such as Bolivia, Costa Rica, Haiti, Mexico, and Uruguay, and moderate African and Asian states, such as Gabon, Liberia, Madagascar, Malaysia, and Thailand.

This evidence for cross-regional cooperation should not be taken as a suggestion that rigid cross-regional cleavages exist in the Assembly. The "voting coalitions" that can be defined are far from being distinct blocs sharply set apart from one another, and often include states having very high agreement scores with states in other voting clusters. Such interrelationships are symptoms of a fluid political process characterized by ad hoc coalitions, independent decision-making by states, and the absence of any effective system to coordinate voting among large numbers of countries.

Quite a variegated pattern thus presents itself to the observer of voting in the General Assembly. Allies on one issue may be opponents on another. Yet coalitions do operate within certain fairly well-defined political boundaries. Although Thailand may find itself in sympathy on peacekeeping issues with the United States, on disarmament with Sweden, and on decolonization with Ecuador, it is hardly likely to be allied on a major group of issues with Guinea, Mali, or the Soviet Union.

Political Position and the Balance of Power

The General Assembly is faced most frequently with two types of questions: those concerning relationships between the two great-power blocs (cold war issues) and those primarily affecting the relations between established, economically developed states and economically less-developed states, many of which have attained sovereignty only recently. On both sets of issues, the United States and the Soviet Union have usually found themselves in opposition to one another. In the eighteenth session, for example, the lowest over-all agreement-scores in the Assembly occurred between the Warsaw Pact states and NATO members.

Within the framework set by frequent East-West opposition, however, a good deal of variation has occurred; different issues produce different voting coalitions. Instead of viewing political positions as distributed along an East-West line, it is useful, therefore, to consider separately positions on issues related to the cold war and on those of concern to the developing nations. Thus the United States and its European allies are pro-Western and relatively unsympathetic to African and Asian demands, whereas the USSR and some African and Asian states take the opposite stand. Other African and Asian states are more pro-Western but remain sympathetic to the aspirations of the developing states, whereas certain European states, such as the Scandinavian countries, are less pro-Western on cold war issues, but also less sympathetic to African and Asian proposals.[7]

Within this context, which states most often hold the balance of voting power in the Assembly? States that frequently vote in the majority tend to be in the majority so often because it is their weight on either side of the scale that tips the balance. Thus an investigation of which states vote most frequently with the majority of the Assembly will indicate those delegations whose support is usually essential to the passage of major Assembly resolutions.

The states most often found in the majority for the fifteenth, sixteenth, eighteenth sessions were moderate African and Asian states and other countries not firmly members of any one regional group. They tended to be slightly more pro-Western than pro-Soviet Union in cold war attitudes, but sympathetic to aspirations for self-determination and economic development. Listing particular states, Liberia and Malaysia were among the ten states with highest majority-agreement scores for all three sessions; Cyprus, Haiti, and Iran were the only other

[7] See Hayward R. Alker, Jr., and Bruce M. Russett, *World Politics in the General Assembly* (New Haven: Yale Univ. Press, 1965), Chapter 6.

states in this category more than once. Iran, Liberia, and Malaysia are all African-Asian group members with powerful cross-pressures pulling them toward the West. Cyprus and Haiti, on the other hand, both have ties to more than one group: Cyprus to Africa-Asia and Western Europe (it is a member of both caucuses); Haiti to Latin America geographically and to Africa ethnically. By contrast, the United States and the USSR, along with Western European and communist states in general, had relatively low majority-agreement scores for the sessions under consideration.

No regional or voting group can succeed in dominating the Assembly consistently on the whole spectrum of issues before it. Therefore the attitudes of those African, Asian, and Latin American states that take independent and moderate courses in General Assembly politics are crucial. Moreover, the balance of power shifts somewhat with the issues being considered, even though certain states, such as those mentioned above, tend to have high majority-agreement scores in every area of Assembly activity. This dual pattern can be seen more clearly by examining majority-agreement results for a number of separate issues in the fifteenth and sixteenth sessions taken together.

Moderate Western predominance characterized the patterns for peacekeeping questions concerning United Nations forces and their financing. Malaya, New Zealand, Nigeria, Pakistan, Sweden, and the United States were among those most often in the majority, whereas the communist states were consistently in opposition, and many non-aligned states occupied a middle position on the scale of majority agreement. This Western predominance in part reflected the inability of non-aligned African and Asian states to collaborate on a common position. With respect to colonialism, the more anti-Western African and Asian states did better, and the Soviet Union was in the majority more often than the United States. In this situation, states such as Iran, Lebanon, Malaya, Nigeria, the Philippines, and Tunisia were also all near the top of the list. On disarmament issues, the great powers and their allies were quite strikingly isolated from the mainstream, which was occupied by a coalition of moderate states including Brazil, Malaya, Norway, and Sweden. Clearly no "mechanical majority" currently exists, except possibly on questions of colonialism and *apartheid*. It is the small and moderate states rather than the large and purposeful ones that most often succeed in identifying themselves with the decisions of the Assembly as a whole.

Therefore, "winning" in the General Assembly requires not merely the solid support of one's own regular allies and supporters, but the assistance of other members as well. This has meant that African and Asian states with moderately but not slavishly pro-Western governments have generally held the balance of power. However, when a two-thirds majority has been required to pass a resolution, the Soviet Union and the African and Asian states particularly opposed to the status quo must attract support from states even less sympathetic to their general outlook, especially from the liberal European states and Latin American countries; the Western allies must gain adherents among non-aligned and anti-colonial African and Asian states in order to accomplish similar objectives. States in the political center will attempt to attract support for their proposals from both sides. Since no group can be assured of victory on a consistent basis, except on a few particularly favorable and often ritualistic issues, compromise and bargaining must be engaged in continually by all sides to obtain the best possible terms. This lack of control over the Assembly by any group of states, as well as the ab-sence of large and cohesive groups, means that a powerful force for compromise—the necessity to acquire uncommitted votes—is added to whatever self-restraint may be practiced by representatives for other reasons.

To exercise leadership in the General Assembly, a state must be willing to do so. This statement is not as tautological as it may sound: many governments do not wish to be active in the discussion of certain issues. As a result, very large powers with important interests to defend and states that want to upset the international status quo tend to dominate Assembly debates. Other characteristics that encourage a state to be active in the General Assembly are: a broad interpretation of national interests, high evaluation of the importance of the United Nations for the state's foreign policy, desire for prestige and publicity, and a foreign policy independent of the great powers. Whether a state will in fact be influential depends, however, on other significant characteristics that will be discussed later.[8] We will consider here only the methods used in the search for influence.

Pressure

To those who revel in the cynical amorality of *realpolitik,* the phenomenon of "pressure" in the General Assembly must be one of the organization's most fascinating aspects. Despite the United Nations' commitment to the use of rational and deliberative procedures, states attempt to coerce one another to support their positions. Yet even the most "realistic" observer of the General Assembly will quickly realize that attempts to achieve results by using extra-parliamentary threats—for instance, the threat to reduce foreign aid—are almost entirely limited to the two great powers. Nowhere is bipolarity more marked. The United

[8] See pp. 29–41 of this study.

States and the Soviet Union each possesses three means of influence held by no other power: the ability to make convincing and meaningful threats and promises directly to many other states; the capacity, on a large range of issues, to obstruct United Nations efforts to implement General Assembly resolutions objectionable to them; and the capability to disrupt the United Nations and the peace of the world through unilateral action. Endowed with these attributes—each a means of pressure—a superpower is a formidable adversary in the General Assembly.

Direct bilateral pressure is exercised in many ways, more often subtly than crudely. Perhaps the most usual disguise is the appeal for good relations. A common approach, described by one delegate, is to ask whether the other state attaches "importance to the sentiments of our people and to good relations with our country." In this situation, if the government being appealed to does not vote "correctly," the government making the appeal will be entitled to assume that the former does not attach "importance to good relations" with the latter. Such an appeal may therefore constitute a hint that, in the absence of cooperative action, the friendship may be in danger.

This suggestion may become a painfully acute form of pressure if it is exercised by great powers and directed toward states that depend on them for aid or support. Clearly, if the United States were inclined to make Nicaragua's vote on a particular issue a test of Nicaraguan concern for "the sentiments of the American people and good relations with the United States," Nicaragua would be reluctant to refuse to cooperate. In this context, the comments of a Central American delegate are revealing.

We believe strongly in the necessity for the United States to have hegemony of advice in the American continent. We cannot afford to have another nation in a better position than the United States. We try to harmonize our policy with the United States point of view, in the interests of regional solidarity.

The more insistent the great power is in its persuasive attempts and the more forcefully it presses its arguments, the stronger is the implication that adverse consequences will result if the smaller country casts its vote against the great power's wishes. Threats of retaliation of one sort or another—reducing foreign aid, for example—usually need not be made explicit. Often it is sufficient that the smaller state is aware that "Big Brother" is watching. A delegate from a state friendly to and quite dependent on the United States expressed his attitude as follows: "The United States may come up to us and ask what we propose; if the United States says, 'We don't like that,' that is pressure. Then we have to decide whether or not the issue is important enough to pick a quarrel about."

The threat of retaliation or warning of adverse consequences can be defined as the essence of pressure. Not content with trying to convince a state that its own interests dictate that it cooperate, the state applying pressure asserts or implies that its attitude should also be taken into account in the former's calculation of national interests. If it is somewhat difficult to point out exactly where persuasion ends and pressure begins, it is nevertheless generally agreed by delegates that threats and warnings are most effective when employed by great or near-great powers toward states that depend on them in some way. Thus the bipolar aspects of General Assembly politics are strengthened. The United States and the Soviet Union possess such great economic and military resources that many states must carefully weigh statements and actions of the superpowers before deciding on their own policies.

Certain states in the Assembly are very susceptible to bilateral pressure, no matter how subtle its application may be. The more dependent a state is on a great power for trade, aid, or protection. the more responsive it is likely to be pressure. It would be remarkable, for example, if Bulgaria, Malaysia, and Israel did not defer somewhat to the positions of the Soviet Union, the United Kingdom, and the United States, respectively. Certain states in special situations, such as Austria and Finland, may often be constrained from voting as their inclinations suggest for fear of retaliation by the Soviet Union.

Bilateral pressure, or "arm-twisting," is probably not as important now as it may have been in the past.[9] Delegates at the United Nations agree that bilateral pressure is not a continuing and major factor in General Assembly decision-making, although it does exert a peripheral effect. While at certain times of crisis such pressure may be exerted, great-power control of the actions of other states is strictly limited. In fact, in recent years both the United States and the Soviet Union have found themselves less often in the majority on roll-call votes than about three-quarters of the other members.

This decline in the efficacy at least of United States pressure can be attributed largely to the changes in the composition of the United Nations, which have taken place during a period of great-power competition. Almost one-third of the Assembly's current membership joined in 1960 or thereafter; most of these states, along with a number of others, are assertively and self-consciously independent, with no strong ties to either of the great

powers. Taking advantage of great-power divisions, these states have developed policies of non-alignment and corollary techniques at the United Nations to avoid the impact of pressure from either the Soviet Union or the United States.

Apart from the extreme competitiveness of the contemporary international situation, these states have been assisted in their efforts to preserve their independence by the inherent limitations on the exercise of pressure. To be effective, the threat of warning behind an attempt to exert pressure must obviously be credible; the state on the receiving end of the message must be convinced that the warning or threat might be implemented. Most decisions of the General Assembly, however, are not important enough to United States interests for it to threaten convincingly to alter the level of aid or support that it is giving, or to exercise other forms of pressure, all of which have their costs, for the sake of gaining a few more votes in the United Nations. The costs of exercising pressure therefore tend to be too high for the marginal gains, particularly in view of the resentment and long-run antagonism that pressure can produce. It is only on very important issues, such as the Article 19 crisis, that bilateral pressure becomes worthwhile for the great powers.

In these situations, the non-aligned states have developed two main defenses to counter great-power pressure. The first is the doctrine of non-alignment itself, which has gained great prestige in Africa and Asia. A state that cannot be considered non-aligned is regarded as being on a lower level of independence and self-respect than one whose purity remains unblemished. Although the manifestations of non-alignment may seem silly at times, the doctrine has important functions. In particular, a non-aligned state can resist great-power blandishments with the argument that acquiescence would cause it to lose prestige and authority

[9] For a discussion of pressure in the General Assembly, based on research done in 1955, see Robert E. Riggs, *Politics in the United Nations: A Study of United States Influence in the General Assembly* (Urbana: Univ. of Illinois Press, 1958). Illinois Studies in the Social Sciences, Vol. 41.

within its own region. Thus when the representative of a leading African state declared that "nobody can put any pressure on us or approach us with any idea of pressure," he was making a statement with important implications for the prestige of his country. By making a public commitment to non-alignment, a state improves its bargaining position with those using pressure to influence its actions.

The second major technique employed by small states is to play off the great powers against each other and perhaps increasingly against the spector of communist China. A small state can exploit great-power competition negatively and achieve immunity from from pressure by threatening to request help from the other superpower if a great-power threat is implemented. In certain extremely unusual circumstances, the small power may employ this tactic positively and threaten to move toward the other camp or become neutral, as the case may be, if the great power does not actively work on its behalf. This technique probably can be effective only when the vital interests of the small state are strongly involved.

If bilateral pressure does not promise to be sufficiently effective, the great power may turn to more generalized uses of its strength. In particular, threats to obstruct measures voted by the Assembly may be successful, as illustrated by two recent controversies over economic development. In the debate in 1960 on a proposal for a United Nations capital development fund, only a few Western powers, including the United States, were actively opposed to the plan in the face of overwhelming majority sentiment for it. The fact that the establishment of such a fund was only accepted "in principle" was a triumph for the United States and its allies.[10] Since the capital development

fund depended on the support of economically developed states, economic power became an effective substitute for voting strength in the General Assembly.[11]

The debate in 1962 on the proposed United Nations Trade and Development Conference was characterized by a similar great-power cleavage: Western powers versus everyone else. A joint African–Asian–Latin American resolution, calling for a conference to meet by September 1963, was adopted by a vote of 73-10-23 in the Second Committee, after Western amendments had been voted down.[12] The opposition of France, the United Kingdom, and the United States served as a warning that compromise was necessary, and concessions were made by the sponsors to certain Western objections before the nearly unanimous Assembly vote. In this situation, Western economic power brought only a partial success. Since UNCTAD could have functioned without the advanced industrial states, the United States and its allies could not merely apply an effective veto, but had to make some concessions of their own as well.

The efficacy of this type of great-power pressure within the Assembly

[11] Although the Soviet Union did not publicly oppose this fund in 1960, its failure to make an offer of financial assistance implied that it was not enthusiastic about the plan. According to one observer, a USSR offer to contribute at a critical juncture of negotiations would have put the United States in a politically impossible position, forcing it to agree to the establishment of the fund. Thus United States opposition did not defeat the fund single-handedly. See Alvin Z. Rubinstein, "Soviet and American Policies in International Economic Organizations," *International Organization*, Vol. 18 (Winter 1964), pp. 29–52.

[12] The resolution was subsequently adopted by the General Assembly (91-0-1); see General Assembly Res. 1785 (XV), 8 Dec. 1962. For committee action and amendments, see General Assembly Official Records (GAOR): 17th Sess., 1962, Annexes, Agenda items 12, 34–37, 39, and 84 (A/5316), pp. 24–28.

[10] General Assembly Res. 1521 (XV), 15 Dec. 1960.

clearly depends on the attitudes of the other states. If these countries had decided to "establish" a capital development fund in 1960, they probably could have done so, thus nullifying attempts of the Western powers to use their economic power as a bargaining counter within the organization. If this had happened, however, the capital development fund would have been ineffective, and the net result would probably have been to increase strains between the developed and developing areas of the world. On issues of colonialism and economic development, the anti-colonial and pro-development majority is often faced with this same dilemma: to enact its preferences into ineffective resolutions, or to make the best possible compromise with the powerful minority. The choice is neither an easy nor a happy one to make.

A great power may wield its strength in yet another way if it can effectively threaten to disrupt the United Nations or the peace of the world by its response to General Assembly action. The Article 19 crisis provides the best example of this phenomenon. As a fragile structure built upon the smoldering volcano of international politics, the General Assembly is understandably sensitive to rumblings from below that could foreshadow volcanic eruptions.

The great powers are therefore extremely important in the General Assembly, yet their influence is not all-determining. Each superpower must operate within the context of bipolar conflict, which may reduce the efficacy of its influence; each must also maneuver within the confines set by the attitudes of other states, including those which are small and relatively powerless. Both superpowers together could not induce the Assembly to adopt a resolution favoring colonialism or opposing economic development, even if they so desired. In general, great-power influence tends to vary directly with the importance of the issue to them, and inversely with its importance to other members of the Assembly. Furthermore, the influence of each great power vis à vis the other (if they are in conflict on the issue) depends on the relative importance of the issue to the one as compared with the other, and the extent to which their attitudes are in conformity with, or run parallel to, attitudes held independently by most states in the General Assembly.

Thus if the United States were deeply involved in an issue in which neither the Soviet Union nor the vast majority of Assembly members were interested, United States influence on the issue would probably be high. Conversely, on an issue such as *apartheid,* where its attitude is ambivalent in the face of a consensus, the United States can hardly expect to find its influence at a peak. In a situation of bipolar conflict, the superpower with the greater interest gains its advantage from its greater willingness to commit itself and to incur costs in gaining its objective.

It is obvious that being sympathetic with a widely held point of view will be helpful; more subtly, similar advantages may be gained if the interests of the great power run parallel to those of a majority of states. For example, many small states may not care how a great-power conflict is solved, but only that it be solved. In such a situation, even though these states may be unconcerned or unsympathetic with the objectives of either great power or divided among themselves in their sympathies, their desire for a solution may lead them to take actions that improve the position of one great power of the other. The Article 19 crisis provides an example of this phenomenon.

Persuasion and Maneuver

States that are not able to exercise pressure, or that do not choose to exercise pressure on a given issue, are not necessarily without influence in the General Assembly. On the contrary, delegations may attempt to influence each other in three ways without applying pressure: by taking initiatives that structure the parliamentary situation and limit the effective alternatives of others; by persuasion; and by the use of the *quid pro quo,* that is, parliamentary "logrolling." Effective use of these techniques is essential to any delegation aspiring to maximize its influence in the politics of the Assembly.

Initiatives are taken in the General Assembly in the form of both draft resolutions and amendments. States sponsoring resolutions have a chance to create the framework for subsequent debates, to define the issues, and to express ideas and grievances in a forcible and widely publicized way. Introduction of a resolution may give its sponsors momentum while potential opponents are placed on the defensive. In the contemporary General Assembly, African and Asian states, usually acting in concert, almost completely dominate the process of initiating resolutions. In the eighteenth session, for example, the thirty states sponsoring the largest number of resolutions were either African or Asian (except for Yugoslavia); Nigeria and Ghana each sponsored fifty-five resolutions, whereas the United States sponsored only thirteen, and the Soviet Union, nine. It has become increasingly common for the United States or the Soviet Union to find smaller states to co-sponsor resolutions, or even to act as the sponsors with the great power remaining in the background.

To exercise influence through resolution sponsorship, it is desirable, therefore, to be a prominent member of the African-Asian group. This is not necessarily the case when it comes to altering resolutions. Most resolutions offered in the General Assembly go through a series of changes that are promoted through informal suggestion and, more rarely, through formal amendment. For example, of the sixty-eight resolutions on economic development introduced between 1960 and 1963, fifty-nine were revised at least once before final passage in the Second Committee. However, whereas 128 revised drafts of resolutions were submitted by sponsors, usually in response to formal or informal suggestions, only thirteen changes were made through amendments voted on in committee.

It is therefore clear that much effective negotiation in the General Assembly goes on informally before a proposal has "jelled." A good deal of effort is spent in maneuvering to ensure that the proposal finally voted on will be as favorable to one's interests as possible. In this process, which combines making proposals for compromise with persuasion, countries politically in a middle position in the Assembly are advantageously situated. A Western delegate remarked, for example, that when he had changes to propose in an African-sponsored resolution, he would call first on the Scandinavians, present his objections to them, and hope that they could work out a mutually satisfactory arrangement. Serving as "honest brokers" in an effort to find compromise ground, moderate powers such as the Scandinavian states may be able to exert considerable influence.

The delicacy of many situations in the General Assembly, where large groups of African and Asian states often face smaller coalitions of Western powers on particular issues, makes the quality of a delegation's diplomacy extremely important. Imagination in finding mutually acceptable solutions, a feeling for when to concede a point and when to press an advantage, and a delicate sense of timing are all necessary in a situation in which emotions, when controlled, are just beneath the surface. In particular, where it is necessary to persuade African and Asian states of the value of one's proposal, it is clearly essential to cultivate an image of constructive assistance rather than of opposition turning into grudging acceptance of compromise when it is already too late.

Despite the extensive compromise, which is a feature of General Assembly action and which often produces resolutions that extensively repeat phrases in former ones, the fate of many proposals rests in the end on a trial of strength, that is, formal votes in a committee or in the Assembly. What cannot be achieved through compromise must be decided by traditional parliamentary methods. At this point, the exercise of influence becomes less a matter of securing prominent consideration of favorable and widely supported proposals, and more a matter of persuading other states to support advocacy of or opposition to a particular draft resolution. On closely contested issues, the adoption of a resolution or one of its controversial passages may be at stake; on others, the question may be whether or not the resolution will achieve a decisive and overwhelming majority.

Arguments on the basis of the issues involved and on one's own avowed principles are the first and most straightforward weapons used in this struggle. These arguments are made behind the scenes as well as in public. Crucial to the success of such a persuasive attempt are the prestige of the persuading delegation and the compatibility of its position with the prejudices and values of other Assembly members. It would be quixotic for most delegates to attempt to oppose anti-colonialism, economic development, and disarmament. Certain opinions, if held, are best kept private. For example, as one delegate pointed out, anyone who has an extenuating word to say for South Africa is immediately suspect.

States may attempt to use common group membership or ideological ties as reasons to support their positions in the Assembly. Among the more closely-knit groups, particularly the African and Latin American ones, an appeal not to disrupt group unity may occasionally be effective. Other types of affiliations are also invoked; the United States, for example, may stress the concept of the "free world." A delegate from an authoritarian Latin American state assured the author that his government was careful to consult closely with the "other democratic nations" before voting on important issues.

In considering the problems of persuasion in the General Assembly, it must be realized that not all delegates are thoroughly informed and responsible. The following incident, related by a United Nations delegate, illustrates this point.

A representative of a new country happened to sit beside me, and always asked what the subject was on which the committee was going to vote. I was very helpful, and explained the questions to him, but he always voted opposite from me. And, in fact, he occasionally voted against his own interests and the interests of the Afro-Asian group. Once, in conversation, he asked, "Do you know how I am voting?" I replied that I thought he was voting the opposite way from me. He said no, that he merely looked at Portugal and South Africa to see how they were voting, and voted the opposite way.

Whether literal or apocryphal, this story illustrates an important feature of General Assembly politics: many states just cannot afford delegations large enough to keep up with Assembly business, both formal and informal. Thus a number of small states are not well-informed on many issues arising in the organization. This situation enhances the political influence of large states and of regional groups, both of which act as sources of information for smaller delegations. Since most small states probably place their confidence chiefly in their regional groups, alert and active members of the African, Asian, and Latin American regions can use their positions in the network of group relationships to educate their less informed colleagues. This process increases the influence of the well-informed states in two ways: it allows them to be the first to present the issue to their colleagues; and it builds up relationships of confidence and mutual contact that can be of continuing benefit. Thus India, for example, may have ties with a number of smaller states that look to it for advice as well as information.

Delegations must often go beyond appeals to general interests and principles and get down to the "concrete interests" of other states. Even here the formal arguments may dwell on the benefits of a particular proposal to the United Nations or to the world. Fortunately for the diplomats who engage in this sort of camouflage, almost any self-interested scheme can be plausibly presented as a contribution to international well-being. In the words of one delegate, "the *quid pro quo* is served up on a tray of universal principles."

The *quid pro quo* may take the classic form of an explicit, although unwritten, agreement by which one state trades its vote on an issue for another state's vote on a different question. Frequently, however, the process of mutual accommodation is of a continuing nature. Each party to the agreement attempts to cooperate whenever possible with its associates when the latter's interests are directly affected, without a specific undertaking to trade one's vote on a particular resolution. Thus the Moslem states are likely to assist one another in disputes in which one of their number is involved with a non-Moslem state.

Vote trading is probably most frequent on those issues that affect some states very deeply but on which many others are indifferent; few states are likely to trade their votes on an issue of general importance. In the issues of specific concern to only a few states, vote trading may be tacit as well as implicit. An example of such interaction was given by the representative of a state (state *a*) faced with one overwhelmingly important issue. His delegation would watch closely the behavior of another state (state *b*), which was obsessed with another issue affecting its vital interests. If state *b* voted against the position of state *a,* the latter would in turn oppose the former. Conversely, favorable action by state *b* would bring a similar response by state *a* in its wake. According to this delegate, "Why should we support [state *b*] if they won't support us?"

Thus the exercise of influence at the General Assembly is both many-sided and subtle. Delegates must not only be adept at debate and discussion, they must be sensitive as well to the unsaid word and the nuance of expression. In view of the intricacies of bargaining at the Assembly, a keen sense of strategy and tactics is also a prerequisite to an effective use of one's resources. Only those delegations whose members possess these qualities and whose governments hold other sources of influence will become leaders in the General Assembly.

The overwhelming importance of the United States and the Soviet Union in the General Assembly indicates that the physical resources of states are crucial in defining their potential capabilities for influence in the organization. Except in the ethereal world of legal formalism, no one can entertain illusions that the United Nations is a society of equals. Even apart from the superpowers, it is clear that large states such as Argentina, Brazil, France, India, and the United Kingdom have usually been important in the politics of the Assembly.

However, it is not possible merely to list states according to their physical resources and power to determine which delegations are most influential at the United Nations. After the first rank of the two superpowers and the second rank of other particularly large or powerful states, the General Assembly contains a number of states that are neither strong enough economically nor militarily for their physical strength to be a significant factor in the Assembly's politics. Some of these states, however, are clearly more important in the organization than others, despite their common military and economic impotence. The following question thus arises: within the framework provided by international political reality and national power, what determines how influential a small or medium-size state will be in the General Assembly?

Some clues to the answer are contained in the preceding discussion on exercising influence. In general, the characteristics that make a state influential will be those that allow it to negotiate and maneuver effectively. In terms of negative requirements, for a state to wield much influence in the General Assembly, three minimal conditions must be met. It must have no enemies more influential than itself; its attitudes and actions must not consistently violate deeply held positions of a great majority of states; and its internal political situation must be relatively well-defined.

The current situations of Israel and the Republic of China illustrate the relevance of the first principle. China never co-sponsors resolutions because of the negative effects such action would have on their prospects, and it also does not take a leading role in bargaining and negotiating. Since the

legal validity of China's claim to sovereignty is challenged by a large number of Assembly members, it is to a great extent a pariah in the organization. Its exclusion since the beginning of 1961 from the Economic and Social Council, and its failure to be appointed to the 33-nation committee on peacekeeping questions established at the end of the nineteenth session indicates how low its status has fallen.

Israel, which has many of the qualities of an effective small power in the Assembly, is seriously hampered by the bitterness of the Arab-Israeli quarrel, particularly since the Arabs command thirteen votes to Israel's one. However, contacts do take place between Israel and many African and Asian states as well as Western and Latin American states. Nevertheless, the handicap imposed by the dispute with the Arabs is very real. One indication of this is that Israel seldom introduces resolutions in the Assembly.

As a consequence of their involvement in issues affecting their very survival, the diplomatic activities of Israel and China must concentrate on their areas of vital interest. The need of these states for support from others on the one overwhelmingly important issue restricts their freedom of action on other significant questions, and their diplomatic efforts, which might otherwise contribute to their general influence in the Assembly, must be devoted to mustering support on crucial votes. In view of its handicaps, Israel has been quite successful in this endeavor. Support for its position among African states, particularly the former French colonies, has been considerable. Referring to Israeli aid programs, a representative of a small and poor country mentioned that his delegation supports Israel in the United Nations because "Israel is a good friend to my country." Yet this Israeli effort, effective though it is, does not and cannot serve to make Israel a leader in United Nations activities.

A state that espouses principles or policies that others find repugnant also labors under a handicap in the Assembly. Portugal and South Africa, for example, are treated as outcasts. If a state other than a great power is to exercise significant leadership in the United Nations, its attitudes must conform in some degree with the viewpoints of an overwhelming majority of the world community on emotionally charged issues.

A third crippling liability for an ambitious delegation is disunity or governmental uncertainty at home. If a country appears to be disunited or if radical changes in its government are likely, its opinions will generally carry less weight in the Assembly than if it presents a united front. In addition, the activity of the delegation of a disunited country is likely to be reduced if the delegation is not certain of strong support from home for its initiatives.

Three national attributes are of fundamental importance in determining to what extent a small or medium-size state without particular liabilities can exercise leadership in the General Assembly: political position, prestige, and the quality of its diplomacy. Less crucial, but also of some significance, are the offices that a state or its representatives may hold in the organization and the positions of tactical advantage or disadvantage in which a state may find itself. The impact of each of these qualities depends somewhat on the types of issues being discussed and the attitudes taken by General Assembly members.

Political Position

Although regional groups are not monolithic, their importance in the political process of the General Assembly is considerable, particularly as a chief focus of diplomatic activity. A member of a large group can participate in meetings and attempt to exercise leadership within its own region. An Af-rican state, for example, has access to about sixty African and Asian countries within the African-Asian group, more than thirty-five of which also belong to the African group. Ambitious delegations can take advantage of group membership to exercise their persuasive powers before governmental attitudes have become firmly established. In this way, it may sometimes be possible to mold the "consensus" of a region to one's will. Common policies commonly arrived at may often bear the distinctive stamps of the most active, prestigious, and ambitious states of the region.

It is less desirable to belong to a large and powerful group, however, if a state's policy is not politically compatible with that of a majority of members. An African, Asian, or Latin American delegation that is unable to take effective leadership within its own group is unlikely to be influential in the General Assembly. The strong attachments of Japan to the West, for instance, weaken what would otherwise be a strong position in the African-Asian group on the basis of population, economic and military capabilities, and diplomatic finesse. Japan cannot speak for any large number of Asian states because it is too highly developed economically and too conservative politically, and it cannot act as a leader of the West because it is Asian. Caught between the political and geographic realities, Japan must play a rather quiet role at the United Nations.

Although the political position of a state with respect to the attitudes of its regional group is extremely important, the significance of political position for influence in the General Assembly can be analyzed in more general terms. If a state's viewpoint is accepted in the United Nations as worthy of serious consideration (this excludes South Africa's views on *apartheid,* for example), a major question is whether it can make itself a prominent spokesman for a distinctive point of view, preferably one shared by a number of other states. Since much of the diplomatic effort in the Assembly is devoted to building the greatest possible degree of support for a resolution, the position of each distinctive set of countries must be taken into account. To the extent that a state or group of states can determine that it holds a reasonable position in terms of the range of attitudes acceptable to the majority, and that is own position is not dependent upon those of other Assembly members, it can establish itself as a bargaining unit. It may then be able to require that its spokesmen participate in negotiations and that its views be taken into account. The degree of influence that the state or group exercises will naturally depend on its size, power, and prestige, as well as on the diplomatic skill of its representatives and the tactical situation in the organization.

The dilemma of a small state in this context often takes the form of a choice between merging its views with those of a large group of states, in which case the group may be effective without the state's representatives being influential, or by taking an independent position, perhaps with a few associates, and hoping that its support will be needed. The latter course entails the risk of being ignored entirely, and a state that is not in a particularly good position on the issue, by virtue of its prestige, leadership of a number of other states, or tactically crucial parliamentary position, will be likely to act as a minor member of a large coalition. In contrast, large states can avert the dilemma either by acting alone (they must be listened to) or by dominating regional groups. As a result, large states are often less attached than their smaller associates to their regional groups, regarding them more as useful devices through which to exert influence and less as exclusive and sacred agencies of General Assembly action.

Thus the position of a state that is generally recognized as a leader of an established regional group—for example, Brazil, India, or the United Arab Republic—is primarily a corollary result of the general principle that leadership of a group with a distinctive point of view is the best way for a state that is not a great power to exercise influence in the Assembly. The regional group's leader works with a continuing organization. This may enable him to construct coalitions with more regularity than if the group did not exist.

Leadership possibilities in the General Assembly tend to be more open for small states toward the political center of the organization than for those in the camp of either superpower. The states closely associated with either great power must often "follow the leader" on issues of political importance, since they can hardly hope to speak for the other states that share their views. On the other hand, more opportunities may exist in the political center, since neither great power holds sway. Thus the Ivory Coast can speak on certain issues for a group of moderate African states, and Uruguay may represent liberal Latin American and associated countries in negotiations. Bulgaria, however, is not likely to take independent leadership and neither is Guatemala when it is in a coalition with the United States.

Prestige

The effectiveness with which a state can speak for a particular point of view in the General Assembly depends to a great extent on its prestige in the organization, that is, the esteem in which it is held by other member states, apart from its physical power resources. High prestige may derive from a state's domestic political system or the popularity of its leadership as well as from its foreign policy attitudes. Whatever the issue, the prestigious state finds that its opinions are listened to more closely, its support solicited more often, and its distinctive positions respected more fully than they would be otherwise. Prestige is essential if a small or medium-size state is to be influential in the Assembly.

Prestige may result from the particularly distinctive or even anomalous political position of a state, which may stand out precisely because it is not a member of any Assembly political grouping. Yugoslavia provides a prime example of this phenomenon. Its sociopolitical system endears it to many one-party states striving for rapid industrialization through state ownership; its occasional defiance of the Soviet Union has impressed the West; and its "rugged independence" appeals to a broad variety of other governments. Yugoslavia has turned what might otherwise be a liability—alienation from its regional group—into an asset by using its flexibility and prestige to move closer to the African-Asian group. It has in fact become a leader among the non aligned states, which has increased its influence in the Assembly. It is very often the only non-African-Asian co-sponsor of resolutions backed by the African-Asian group; it votes with the most anti-Western of the African and Asian states; it consults intimately with these delegations; and its representatives have received African and Asian support in contests for office. In short, Yugoslavia's independent communism allows it to enjoy the "rites of the Church without the commands of the Pope"; it is "progressive" without being subservient. As the East European group becomes less monolithic, however, the uniqueness of Yugoslavia's position, and the prestige thus conferred, may decline. For example, Romania's emerging independence may work in this direction.

States that take positions more acceptable to the majority in the Assembly than to most members of their regions may also gain prestige. Norway

and Sweden, and to some extent Canada and Ireland, have acquired reputations as liberals on issues as *apartheid* and as moderates on cold war issues. These states are also not directly connected with colonialism. One African delegate stated that he trusted the Scandinavian states more than other Europeans because they have no "ax to grind." Thus, when an emotional issue arises, the African states may defer to the opinions of Norway or Sweden more than to those of powerful but less highly respected Western states. The discussion of a resolution in the eighteenth session condemning the South African trial of nationalist leader Nelson Mandela is a good example. The delegate of Guinea leading the African forces was ready to override United States objections to his draft resolution. But when the Norwegian delegate expressed some reservations, he agreed to a recess for "informal consultation" because he

> could not remain indifferent to a suggestion made by a representative of the Scandinavian countries, which had expressed a desire to join with the African and Asian countries in seeking a satisfactory solution to the problem posed by the policy of *apartheid*.[13]

Norway and Sweden are in the uniquely favorable position of possessing high prestige in the West as well as in Africa and Asia. Here their historical traditions of peacefulness as well as their support of United Nations peacekeeping efforts are probably important factors. The effect of this prestige is that even if the African states did not really hold Norway and Sweden in any particular esteem, they would be well-advised on occasion to accede to Scandinavian objections and to associate Norway and Sweden with

[13] GAOR: 18th Sess., Special Political Cmtte., 381st Mtg., 10 Oct. 1963, para. 19.

their resolutions, thus helping to increase the impact of their ideas on the West. Since most General Assembly resolutions apply only moral pressure, sponsors must be aware of the advantages of associating their ideas with prestigious states and must weigh these advantages against the costs of concessions required to assure this wider support.

The strictly internal affairs and leadership of a state can also affect its prestige in the General Assembly. A charismatic leader may attract international attention to a state and increase, at least for a period of time, its importance in the eyes of others. A whole nation may take on certain prestige for its deeds. The long Algerian war for independence, for instance, endowed that country with a revolutionary mystique that contributed to its emergence as an important member of the African group.

Recent developments in Brazil illustrate dramatically the impact that national leadership changes may have on prestige and, therefore, on Assembly influence. Until the military *coup d'état* in early 1964, Brazil occupied a preeminent place among Latin American states, both because of its size and its independence from United States foreign policy. By the autumn of 1964, however, Brazil no longer held this exalted position. The successor military government did not enjoy the respect of the former regime in Africa and Asia. Although the power and resources of Brazil did not diminish between the spring and autumn of 1964, the reputation of its government and, consequently, its influence in the General Assembly suffered.

A certain international social code thus exists in the microcosm of the General Assembly; certain types of governmental and international behavior are more acceptable than others. Independence of statement and action are highly regarded, along with "progressive" economic systems and adherence to a common set of ideals in the Assembly. With the numerical dominance of newly emergent states, the peculiar atmosphere of the Assembly reflects, to a great extent, their values. Social norms may be said to exist and to affect the influence of states, even if they are not very effective in controlling international political behavior.

Delegation Effectiveness

To be influential in the General Assembly, a state must have policy-makers and delegates who are sophisticated in the ways of international politics. Beyond the range of real incompetence, however, it is extremely difficult to assess the impact of the quality of personal representation on a state's influence. Clearly, every state will benefit by having representatives who combine the traditional diplomatic virtues with those of the legislative politician; any country's influence will suffer if its representatives are stupid, inarticulate, or lazy. Yet, given the limits set by power, political position, and prestige, how much difference can an able or incompetent representative make?

In the highly informal and often intricate diplomacy of the Assembly, personal contacts and friendships may at crucial moments count heavily in securing access to negotiations, if not as direct bargaining assets. A distinction must be drawn, however, between large and small states in the Assembly. The great powers and a few other large states command respect in their own right; whether liked or disliked, they must be listened to. On the other hand, a small state may be ignored quite readily if its delegation does nothing to distinguish itself from the scores of similar entities. Thus the quality of a great power's delegation may determine the extent of its influence within certain limits, whereas the ambassador of a small state may determine whether or not his delegation's views are considered.

Furthermore, some representatives of small and new states have more freedom of action than delegates from larger entities, particularly since they are less closely instructed by their foreign offices. In specific terms, this means that the policies of certain African and Asian states may be influenced heavily by what their representatives think. The process of persuasion within the African and African-Asian groups thus becomes quite important. An able African or Asian delegate may be able to carry a number of group members with him and thereby transform his delegation from follower to leader within the group.

It is impossible to be precise, however, about the effect of the delegate's ability. In certain favorable circumstances, a particularly able delegate may be able to exert considerable personal influence in the General Assembly. It must be borne in mind, however, that effective representation at the United Nations is not an accidental personal factor. Ambitious, internationally-minded, and dynamic governments are more likely to send able men to the United Nations than are more inward-looking and retiring states. Therefore, whatever the exact effect on leadership of a representative's personal competence, this ability is not an independent variable, but largely a function of other characteristics of his state and government.

Office in the Assembly

Formal positions of authority in the General Assembly, such as committee chairmanships, usually confer little political influence themselves, although the prestige and prominence associated with them may be useful to their occupants. Chairmen of the seven main committees are members of the General Committee and meet weekly with Secretariat officials to discuss Assembly business. They tend to be servants of the committees rather than their masters. However, chairmen of the special ad hoc committees, such as the Committee of 24 on decolonization, may wield more effective power.

Since chairmanships of regional groups rotate on a monthly basis in the African-Asian and Latin American groups, any influence conferred by these positions must be temporary. In general, the significance of these positions lies in their potential visibility. In a difficult situation, the committee or group chairman may become the focal point of an attempt to negotiate a satisfactory settlement. Thus in the Article 19 crisis, the fact that the Permanent Representative of Afghanistan was Chairman of the African-Asian group at a crucial time allowed him to seize the initiative and a certain amount of effective influence for a limited period of time.

Membership in the Security Council may also be important. By election to the Council, a small and otherwise insignificant state may be catapulted into a more prominent position. Security Council membership may lift the state above the mass of similar entities, call attention to it, and contribute to its parliamentary position in the Assembly, as well as involve it in Council actions. In particular, the state may come to serve as an intermediary between its regional group and the Security Council, transmitting information and ideas in both directions and acting as a spokesman for the point of view of the group, or a section of the group, in the Council. In contributing to the flow of communication, the state can to some extent put its own emphasis on the group's attitudes. Recently, for example, the Ivory Coast appears to have gained slightly greater influence in the Assembly as a result of its Security Council membership.

Positions of Tactical Advantage

In any particular General Assembly situation, certain delegations will be in more favorable tactical positions than others and therefore able to exercise influence more effectively. Sponsors of resolutions are often in a strong tactical position insofar as they determine the framework for debate and raise issues for discussion. This is particularly true when strong emotional support exists for the general position upheld by the sponsors. In this situation, sponsoring delegations may be able to use the general sentiment to endorse their own distinctive proposals. Militant powers, which can demand more forceful resolutions than moderate states, may benefit from strong emotional feeling on issues such as colonialism by seizing leadership on the issue. If consensus is strong in one direction but the more moderate states are reluctant to conduct a crusade on behalf of their positions, leadership may fall to other delegations that will work aggressively for a solution. On *apartheid,* for example, even moderate African and Asian states may be unable to withhold support for an anti-*apartheid* resolution of any kind. Therefore initiators of a resolution calling for especially forceful action may effectively control the types of choices open to others.

If militancy can confer influence in certain situations, so can moderation in others. States holding a position between two contesting factors in the Assembly often are in a favorable position, provided that at least one of two conditions applies: (1) the voting situation is so close that the votes of moderate states are needed for passage of the resolution; or (2) the sponsors of the proposal need the prestige associated with the moderate states for the impact of their action to be felt. Moderate states will be in strong bargaining positions in either case. As noted earlier, Sweden and Norway, among others, often benefit from being in this middle position.

The states most often mentioned as "influential" in the General Assembly fall into several categories according to the sources of their influence. In the first rank are the two super-powers. Other large states, such as Argentina, Brazil, France, India, Nigeria, the United Arab Republic, and the United Kingdom, are also universally conceded to be important. Among smaller states, delegates in the winter of 1964–65 most often mentioned Ghana, Guinea, and Mali—outspoken opponents of the status quo—on the one hand, and Norway and Sweden on the other. The pluralism and fluidity of the General Assembly precludes the possibility of a rigorous status ordering, even if appropriate means could be devised. Beyond the great powers, political influence in the Assembly is limited, temporary, and insecure.

Decline of Influence: The Case of India

Just as the study of political failure may contribute to the understanding of political success, an analysis of the decline of a particular state's influence may provide some clues as to the sources of influence in the General Assembly. Delegates at the Assembly in late 1964 and early 1965 volunteered India's name with striking consistency in answer to a question as to whether any states had suffered a decline in influence since 1960. An examination of the reasons for this trend may shed some light on the subject.

A major factor in the Indian decline was the rise of a large and coherent African group in the Assembly. Before the advent of substantial representation from sub-Saharan Africa, India could presume to speak for absent Africans as well as for itself in leading the anticolonial battle. Since the Africans now have voices of their own and the Asian states are hopelessly divided, India has in a sense become a "leader" without followers.

India might have been able to cope more effectively with this strategic shift had it not been for the border dispute with the People's Republic of China. This had three major effects, all of them adverse, on India's position in the Assembly. It put the Indians in opposition to what is clearly the most powerful Asian state. The Chinese success in the border conflict exposed India's essential weakness to the world; after the Chinese attacks, India could no longer claim to be a major military power. Finally, the quarrel with China drove the Indians somewhat reluctantly toward the West, and acceptance of United States aid against the People's Republic called into question India's non-aligned status. This was perhaps the most damaging aspect of the affair as far as India's role in the Assembly was concerned; it undercut India's claim to neutrality and the prestige associated with that position. Interestingly enough, as India's stock in the General Assembly fell, the status of Pakistan, which was loosening its ties with the West, appeared to rise.

Other events of this period failed to counteract, and rather reinforced, the tendency of Indian influence to decline. Since 1961 many non-aligned states have felt that India had lost its revolutionary fervor. Both the seizure of Goa, which briefly angered the United States, and the continuing quarrel with Pakistan have diminished India's prestige. Furthermore, the departure of Krishna Menon and the death of Nehru removed two experienced and influential Indian statesmen from the scene.

However, India is as large as it was in 1960, and its policies still command wide respect. For these reasons it continues to be, and will remain, one of the more important members of the General Assembly. Nevertheless, fundamental changes in the composition of the Assembly and in India's relations with the People's Republic of China, combined with lesser factors, have ended India's formerly preponderant position within the African-Asian group. . . .

2. The United Nations and Some African Political Attitudes*

ALI A. MAZRUI

WHAT constitutes "sovereign statehood"? Elaborate answers can be given under international law, under theories of international relations, under jurisprudence, and under general political philosophy. But from the point of view of African countries the empirical answer is perhaps the simplest. These countries know that it was not when they assumed control of their domestic affairs that they ceased to be colonies. As a matter of experience, many of

them found that the ultimate expression of sovereignty was not direct rule internally but direct diplomatic relations with other countries abroad. The very process of attaining independence might, in their case, be reduced to a single catch phrase—"from foreign rule to foreign relations." In other words, an African colony was said to have attained independence when it had moved from the status of being under foreign rule to the status of conducting foreign relations with full authority.

It must be admitted at once that there is an element of gross oversim-

* From *International Organization*, Vol. XVIII, pp. 499–520. Reprinted by permission. This essay received the 1964 Prize Award from *International Organization*.

plification involved in all this. But the essential point to grasp is that although African nationalism was born as a reaction to what was happening *within* an African country, it is seeking ultimate fulfillment by international participation *without*. The self-centered principle of self-determination has matured into a cult of participation in world affairs. And the whole outlook was helped and in part fostered by the very sequence of steps taken toward full independence.

Involved in African nationalism and in the aftermath of nationalism so far is a bundle of complexes, aspirations, fears, and values. These have an important bearing on how Africans view events in the world and how they react to those events. This point of rendezvous between a consciousness of events in the sense of mental perception and a consciousness of these events at the level of psychological response is the area of experience where attitudes are formed and then rationalized. This paper will examine not only African attitudes toward the United Nations but also the influence of the United Nations in the formation of African attitudes concerning other matters. But the paper will not stop here. It will seek to penetrate into the inner postulates of those attitudes and pursue some of their logical and political implications. The latter part of this exercise is here designated as the philosophical base of those African attitudes, though the discussion will be as much an examination of the *content* of the attitudes as it will be of the foundation which might be considered to underlie them.

But what is the place of the United Nations in all this? It may be useful to start here with a statement made by a British Colonial Secretary on the eve of the formation of the UN. Partly with that impending formation in mind, Oliver Stanley, then Secretary of State for the Colonies, said in March 1945:

I do not believe that any splinterization of the British Colonial Empire would be in the interests of the world. . . . Would the new machinery for world security, which is to be devised at San Francisco next month, be made any stronger by the substitution of these 40 [new] states for a cohesive Empire able to act as a strategic whole? [1]

In a sense, Oliver Stanley's question has not yet been answered. At best the syllables which will one day form the complete answer are now being assembled, and it will take a while before the effect is adequately intelligible. But there was one thing which Oliver Stanley did not allow for at the time. One of his fears expressed in the 1945 speech was that a disintegration of the British Empire might, among other things, jeopardize the very existence of the United Nations. In his capacity as Colonial Secretary he should perhaps have been more worried about a reverse possibility—that the existence of the United Nations might itself contribute toward the disintegration of the British Empire. The "machinery for world security," on whose behalf he seemed concerned, was to become a mechanism for the "splinterization" of empires. In principle, this reverse occurrence does not necessarily falsify Stanley's prediction. The United Nations' position as an accomplice in the dismemberment of empires might yet turn out to be a case of "suicidal murder"—i.e., that in destroying empires the UN was, all along, involved in a process of unconscious long-term self-destruction. All this is, in principle, a *prediction* and may or may not be vindicated. What should concern us, to begin with, is that which has already happened or is continuing to happen

[1] Speech of the Rt. Hon. Oliver Stanley to the American Outpost, London, on March 19, 1945. See *British Speeches of the Day* (London: British Information Services, 1945), pp. 318–320.

—the role of the United Nations in the momentous mid-twentieth century phenomenon of global decolonization. Predictive assessments should indeed be attempted—but only insofar as they are necessary for an adequate analysis of the implication of what is happening.

A useful approach will be to divide this paper into sections. We shall start by looking at the Charter of the United Nations as an ideology of decolonization. We shall go on to examine the Organization itself in relation to the influence of the new states on the future development of international law. We shall then proceed to an examination of the philosophical clash between the ideal of peace as the moral foundation of the United Nations in the view of the older Members, and the ideal of human dignity deemed as the foundation by the new Members. This clash will be examined first in relation to South Africa—but the ethical dichotomy itself underlies other issues studied in this paper. Just as legal principles in this analysis will lead to an examination of ethical values, so ethical values in turn will lead us to the process of decision making in relation to those values. More specifically, we shall examine the correlation between the voting system of the United Nations on the one hand and the ultimate purposes of the world Organization on the other. Included in that examination will be another correlation—the correlation between nonalignment and that moral dichotomy referred to earlier. The analysis will conclude with an examination of the possible role of the United Nations in an Africa at once dangerously divided and hopeful of unity.

The Charter of Decolonization

Partly with the experience of the League of Nations in mind, E. H. Carr argued in 1939 in the following vein:

Just as pleas for "national solidarity" in domestic politics always come from a dominant group which can use this solidarity to strengthen its own control over the nation as a whole, so pleas for international solidarity and world union come from those dominant nations which may hope to exercise control over a unified world.[2]

At first sight this seems to be borne out even by Oliver Stanley's arguments against the "splinterization" of the British Empire:

Would it really be an advantage to create another 40 independent states, all small? . . . Would the economies of the new world be made any easier by 40 more separate divisions, 40 more political obstacles; would it free the flow of world trade? [3]

And yet, although an empire may indeed consist of a multiplicity of nationalities, it is not in itself an instance of "internationalism." The logical extremity of Stanley's opposition to a multiplication of sovereignties is presumably a complete world union with a world government. And yet even a world government is, strictly speaking, inconsistent with internationalism. Demands for a world government are, in effect, demands that humanity should convert itself into a *single* global state —something quite distinct from the kind of *inter*-state relationships which are normally denoted by the term "internationalism." A world state would, in other words, be no more international than the British Empire was when Stanley was defending its unitary cohesion.

And yet Carr argues that "countries which are struggling to force their way into the dominant group naturally tend to invoke nationalism against the in-

[2] E. H. Carr, *The Twenty Years' Crisis* (London: Macmillan, 1948), p. 86.

[3] Stanley, *loc. cit.*

ternationalism of the controlling powers."[4] In the history of empires since the United Nations was formed, Carr's contention has been proved substantially wrong. The whole antithesis between "nationalism" and "internationalism" was exposed as decidedly superficial as soon as the Afro-Asian countries began to demand the right of participation in international affairs. For what inspired *nationalism* in those countries was, to a great extent, those very "universalist and humanitarian doctrines" which Carr identifies with the *internationalist's* stand.[5] It was, in short, the values of internationalism which awakened Afro-Asian national consciousness.

What Carr forgot was that there are, in effect, at least three categories of nations instead of his two. There are indeed those which are sufficiently strong to stand for internationalism—in the expectation that "international goodwill" is the best way of stabilizing and and perpetuating their dominant position. There may, in addition, be countries which are not yet quite "dominant" but near enough to dominance to invoke nationalism *instead* of internationalism as the paramount instrument for raising their status. Carr himself cited Germany up to World War II as a country which was at once nationalistic and opposed to internationalism. The category which Carr omitted altogether was that of a country which is quite incapable of attaining world dominance through its own nationalism but which is nevertheless nationalistic. In such a case a country might find itself needing a substantial degree of internationalism in order to start realizing its nationalistic aspirations at all. The best example of this category is that of those countries which based their case for parochial

independence upon universal values and now look upon the United Nations as the best hope for some of their national ambitions.

The central universal value in the search for parochial independence has been, of course, the principle of self-determination. From Africa's point of view the term "self-determination" as a slogan gained currency essentially in the late 1940's. It assumed an African significance not after World War I and Wilson's exuberance but during the course of World War II and following it. An important contributory factor to the popularity of the principle among African nationalists was the Atlantic Charter which President Franklin Roosevelt and Prime Minister Winston Churchill signed on August 14, 1940. The Charter, as a declaration of common Anglo-American principles, did not use the term "self-determination" as such. But it did say that the United Kingdom and the United States

> respect the right of all peoples to choose the form of government under which they will live; and they wish to see sovereign rights and self-government restored to those who have been forcibly deprived of them.[6]

This statement was taken by many people in the colonies as a promise of self-determination for them. But in the House of Commons Churchill was soon to disillusion attentive nationalists in Asia and Africa. Churchill said to the Commons:

> At the Atlantic meeting we had in mind, primarily, the restoration of the sovereignty, [and] self-government . . . of the States and Nations of Europe now under Nazi yoke . . . so that this is quite a separate

[4] Carr, *loc. cit.*

[5] *Ibid.* I have not overlooked the fact that internationalist values are sometimes invoked for tactical reasons rather than out of genuine conviction.

[6] "The Atlantic Charter," *United States Executive Agreement Series* No. 236 (Department of State Publication No. 1732) (Washington, D.C.: U.S. Government Printing Office, 1942).

problem from the progressive evolution of self-governing institutions in the regions and peoples which owe allegiance to the British Crown.[7]

But Churchill had already exposed himself to demands for an extension of the principle of self-determination to subject peoples elsewhere. The Atlantic Charter certainly stirred the national aspirations of politically conscious West Africans. In April 1943 the West African Students Union in London sent a demand to the Colonial Office for dominion status. A group of West African editors, with Azikiwe as leader, prepared a memorandum entitled *The Atlantic Charter and British West Africa,* visited Britain, and asked for substantial political reforms. And among the resolutions passed by the Pan-African Congress of Manchester in 1945 was one which demanded that "the principles of the . . . Atlantic Charter be put into practice at once."[8]

But in that year of 1945 a new Charter was born—and not long after, this new United Nations Charter effectively replaced the Atlantic Charter as the ultimate documentary confirmation of the legitimacy of African aspirations. It is probably safe to say that very few African nationalists had, in fact, read the United Nations Charter. And those who had were less interested in the specific procedures for assuring world peace than in the reaffirmation of "faith in fundamental human rights, in the dignity and worth of the human person, in the equal rights of men and women and of nations large and small."[9] But in spite of this limited or selective grasp of what the United

Nations Charter was all about, the Charter did become a kind of documentary expression of natural law and a global Bill of Rights. By 1955, when Asia had achieved its independence and Africa was at its most militant in the quest for its own, the nationalists of Asia and Africa were still basing their demands firmly on the Charter. As the final communiqué of the Bandung Conference put it in that year:

The Asian-African Conference declared its full support of the fundamental principles of Human Rights as set forth in the Charter of the United Nations and took note of the Universal Declaration of Human Rights as a common standard of achievement for all peoples and all nations.

The Conference declared its full support for the principles of self-determination of peoples and nations as set forth in the Charter of the United Nations and took note of the United Nations resolutions on the rights of peoples and nations to self-determination, which is a prerequisite of the full enjoyment of all fundamental Human Rights.[10]

The United Nations had by then become a liberating factor in practice as well as in principle. And it was involved in this process in two paradoxical capacities—in the capacity of a col-

[7] Speech to House of Commons, September 9, 1941. See Charles Eade (ed.), *War Speeches of Winston Churchill* (London: Cassell & Co., Ltd., 1952), Vol. 2, pp. 71–72.

[8] See the resolutions cited in Colin Legum, *Pan-Africanism* (London: Pall Mall, 1962), Appendix 2, pp. 135–137.

[9] Taken from the opening lines of reaffirmation of the United Nations Charter.

[10] Text given in Robert A. Goldwin with Ralph Lerner and Gerald Sourzh (ed.), *Reading in World Politics* (New York: Oxford University Press, 1959), p. 539. The interpretation of the Charter in moral terms is by no means peculiar to "the Bandung spirit." At the time of the Suez crisis Mr. Rodriguez-Fabregat of Uruguay described the Charter as "the deepest expression of human conscience." (General Assembly *Official Records* [first special session], p. 55, paragraph 115.) But what "the Bandung spirit" best illustrates is the emphasis on the proposition that colonial rule itself offended "human conscience" and was not adequately consistent with the Charter.

lective "imperialist" with "trusteeship" responsibilities of its "own" and in the capacity of the grand critic of imperialism at large. Indeed, as early as 1953 exasperated voices were already complaining that "perhaps the term 'self-determination' should be dropped, now that the United Nations is called upon to do the determining." [11]

Amending the Law of Nations

What has not yet been fully apprehended—not even by many of the Afro-Asian states themselves—is that the UN was becoming the nearest thing they had to a legislature which could gradually amend international law at their own persistent initiation. It cannot be repeated too often that the law of nations as it stands today is mainly the outcome of Western European practice and theory. It has, in the words of one analyst, "drawn its vital essence from a common source of European beliefs. . . . To this development no extra-European nation made any essential contribution. . . ." [12]

Verzijl noted in 1955 that the new nations which entered the international community adopted the rules of European origin which they found already

governing interstate relationships, and they based their own conduct and diplomatic procedure on these Western standards. As regard the future of international law, Verzijl concluded that

> it would seem very unlikely that any revolutionary ideas will appear as a result of the entrance of these new members which will have the power to challenge or supersede the general principles and customary rules of laws which have shown their vitality by standing the test of time and circumstance. [13]

It may indeed be unlikely that any of these new states would have the power to "challenge or supersede" international law, but their diplomatic pressure may lead to certain modifications in the rules of international conduct. Of course, not all rules of international conduct are, or need be, part of international law. But extralegal rules of behavior may influence interpretations of legal principles, and some may become legal themselves in the course of time. It is this latter consideration which makes Afro-Asian pressure in the United Nations relevant to the future development of international law. Until now the international community has been a community with a law but with no specific legislator. It is unlikely that the United Nations will in the foreseeable future become a global legislature. But to the extent that the United Nations influences new patterns of behavior and new attitudes, it must form a part of the long-term amending process of international law itself.

[11] See, for example, Clyde Eagleton, "Excesses of Self-determination," *Foreign Affairs,* July 1953 (Vol. 31, No. 4), pp. 592–604. He said, "If the decision on such a claim is made by the United Nations, it is no longer correct to speak of self-determination." He was sorry to see the United Nations becoming "the midwife of all groups desiring to be politically born." Up to 1964, however, it was possible for an article in an African newspaper to start with the words: "The United Nations is preparing to renew its annual campaign to end colonial rule throughout the world." See Gerald Ratzin, "The U.N. Fights Colonialism," *Uganda Argus,* January 25, 1964.

[12] J. H. W. Verzijl, "Western European Influence on the Foundation of International Law," *International Relations, 1955* (Vol. 1), pp. 137–146, cited in B. V. A. Röling, *International Law in an Expanded World* (Amsterdam: Djambatan, 1960), p. 10.

[13] *Ibid.* A similar conclusion is reached by G. van der Veen in his thesis *Aiding Underdeveloped Countries Through International Economic Cooperation* (Amsterdam, 1953). He points to the admission of technologically underdeveloped countries into the international community and remarks that "these entrances brought about no alteration of principle in the law of nations" (p. 16); cited in B. V. A. Röling, *op. cit.,* pp. 12–13.

"Colonialism is permanent aggression." This became an important theme in Afro-Asian argumentation mainly following India's annexation of Goa. When the question of defining "aggression" comes up again for discussion by a special General Assembly committee next year, "colonialism" will not necessarily form part of the definition.[14] But the more militant attitude toward colonialism which now characterizes the General Assembly both reflects and helps to consolidate

new attitudes toward that phenomenon. And even the criteria of what constitutes domestic jurisdiction and external intervention and interference may imperceptibly be undergoing a legal re-definition as the old principles are newly tossed around in the tussle of United Nations politics.

The issues of domestic jurisdiction and of the limits of intervention were given a dramatic setting in the Congo situation and the United Nations' involvement in it.[15] But a more persistent concern in world politics, and potentially more explosive than even the Congo proved to be, is the issue of South Africa. Racial equality is becoming a precept of increasingly significant international implications, and the law of nations may in time take greater cognizance of this principle. But with regard to South Africa the United Nations is, in African estimation, more than possible legislative machinery for outlawing *apartheid*. The United Nations moves from being the nearest thing to a world parliament to being the nearest thing to a symbolic embodiment of the world community

[14] Krishna Menon started invoking the concept of "permanent aggression" to reporters (the BBC broadcast the doctrine) even before he arrived at the United Nations to defend India's annexation of Goa. For a fuller discussion of the implications of this concept, see my article "Consent, Colonialism and Sovereignty," *Political Studies,* February 1963 (Vol. 11, No. 1), pp. 36–55. Professor W. H. Abraham of Ghana lent philosophical backing to Menon's approach by reaffirming that "colonialism is aggression." See his *Mind of Africa* (London: Weidenfeld and Nicolson, 1962), p. 152. This idiom may have started as a merely figurative use of the word "aggression." But it would not be the first instance in which a figurative use of a given term later took on a literal meaning as well.

The 21-member committee, which the General Assembly established in 1957 to advise it as to when to reconsider the question of defining aggression, held further meetings in 1962 but decided to adjourn its deliberations until April 1965. Among those who supported the adjournment were Kenneth Dadzie of Ghana and Nathaniel Eastman of Liberia. The Liberian delegate stressed that 22 new states—most of which were African—had joined the Organization since the committee's last session in 1959 and that they needed time to submit their views. For the same reason Ghana supported adjournment. Jan Polderman of the Netherlands favored a definition of aggression which would serve the interests of the small countries, particularly those which had recently attained independence. However, he did not think the circumstances were any more propitious for such a definition than they had been in 1959. For a brief description of the positions taken, see "Question of Defining Aggression," *United Nations Review,* May 1962 (Vol. 9, No. 5), pp. 14–16.

[15] The Congo story involved not just legal problems but also varying political issues touching on intervention. In spite of Dag Hammarskjöld's brave attempts to insulate the United Nations from the politics of the Congolese, the role of the United Nations gradually became interventionist, particularly after the resolution of February 1961 envisaging at last the possible use of force. But one of the political motives behind the United Nations' response to Lumumba's original invitation was, in fact, to avert the possibility of a clash of interventions by big powers in the Congo. The All-African Conference held in Leopoldville at the behest of Lumumba in August 1960 saw the United Nations' role not so much in terms of averting big-power intervention but in terms of ending Belgian intervention. The Conference passed a resolution commending the UN "for the work it is doing for peace in the Congo by effecting the withdrawl of the Belgian troops of aggression from the entire territory of the Republic of the Congo." (UN Document A/PV 860, p. 81.)

itself. And exclusion of South Africa from the world body and affiliated organizations begins to look like effective exclusion from the world community at large.

Executing the Law of Equality

The fate of "isolation" as envisaged for South Africa by the new African states rests on philosophical assumptions which have yet to be adequately analyzed. The old hazardous tendency to personify countries and then talk about them almost as if they were individual persons does sometimes affect people's entire attitude toward South Africa. Although it may be hazardous to treat countries as persons, it is nevertheless an exercise which can afford useful insights into the whole phenomenon of passing a moral judgment on another country's "behavior." Let us take the analogy of someone in a town who commits a crime and gets caught. That person may end up in jail. Now, a jail is a form of isolation. The criminal behind bars is isolated or at best confined to the compay of fellow criminals in a restricted area. Separation from the rest of society is itself seen as part of the pain inflicted upon the criminal.

These same assumptions now appear to be transposed onto the international scene. South Africa is viewed as an offender, if not of the law of nations, certainly of the canons of the new international morality. But the international society—unlike the society of, say, Great Britain or Tanganyika—has no jail to which it can send its worst offenders. South Africa may indeed be placed "before the bar of world opinion," but can she be put behind the bars of a world prison once judgment has been passed? This is where the penalty of isolation suggests itself in a new form—South Africa is to be sentenced not to the literal isolation of

a prison cell but to the limbo of international anomie.[16]

But what is the purpose of this isolation? As in the case of the individual criminal in our home town, three lines of reasoning are discernible. First, you isolate the criminal as retribution for his offense. Secondly, you seek to deter him from repeating the offense or to prevent him from continuing it. And, thirdly, implicit in the very idea of deterring him from doing it again, you attempt to reform the criminal to at least this negative extent.[17] In these attempts to isolate South Africa there lies, then, not only the vengeful aim of punishing her for her offense but also the reformative ambition of preparing her for a resumption on some future date of her place in international society. What the African states are involved in is, in other words, a search for a means of getting beyond a mere verdict of "guilty" pronounced on South Africa. They are seeking ways to make South Africa as a nation serve the nearest thing to a term of imprisonment— and become a better member of the international community.

But does imprisonment necessarily succeed in reforming an offender? Here again there is a direct analogy between an offending individual and an offending nation. Some individuals become hardened criminals as a result of imprisonment. Others make up their minds never to see the inside of a prison cell again. How can one be sure of the effect isolation would have on South Africa? After all, many would already argue that America's policy to isolate Communist China has aggravated, rather than mitigated, China's sense of grievance and thereby increased her aggressiveness.

This is where the whole issue of isolation touches that of qualifications for

[16] See my observations in the *Sunday News* (Dar es Salaam), November 24, 1963.
[17] This is quite apart from trying to deter others from doing the same.

membership in the United Nations. If the United Nations is, as most African states continue to regard it, the very center of the new international society, then exclusion from it is one of the more obvious methods of trying to isolate a country from that society. Communist China is outside the United Nations—should she be in? South Africa is in—should she really be out? These are the twin issues which have sometimes invited the charge of a double standard in the policies of some of the new nations. Madame Pandit, leader of India's delegation to the United Nations at the time, was confronted in September 1963 with such a charge in a television interview at the United Nations. India had suffered direct aggression at the hands of the Chinese and indirect racial humiliation from South Africa. Yet India was in favor of seating Communist China in the United Nations and of unseating South Africa altogether. How could Madame Pandit reconcile the two stands? Her own answer was simply the conviction that South Africa was worse than China.

But on what grounds can this assessment be based? This takes us right back to that Afro-Asian tendency to regard the United Nations not so much as an organization primarily designed to ensure peace and security—as the big powers intended it to be—but as an organization which should be primarily concerned with human rights at large. The actual framers of the Charter in 1945 first declared their determination to "save succeeding generations from the scourge of war" and then only secondly to "reaffirm faith in fundamental human rights, in the dignity and worth of the human person, in the equal rights of men and women and of nations large and small." [18]

[18] From the lines of reaffirmation opening the Charter.

But judging by their policies, attitudes, and stands, the new states of Africa and Asia would have reversed the order of affirmation; They would have reaffirmed, first, "faith in fundamental human rights [and] in the dignity and worth of the human person" and only secondly their determination "to save succeeding generations from the scourge of war."

This has an important bearing on qualifications for membership in the United Nations as viewed by, on the one hand, countries like the United States which are opposed to the "admission" of Communist China and, on the other, countries like Tanganyika which seek South Africa's expulsion from the world Organization. Those who are opposed to Communist China's "admission" have interpreted Article 4 of the United Nations Charter as restricting membership to those countries which are "peace-loving." This whole emphasis on peace is more characteristic of the big powers' conception of the United Nations' role than it is of the new, smaller powers' view.

This is not to deny the importance which some of the major powers attach to human rights. Historically, American foreign policy has been known to err on the side of "excessive" attachment to moral principles of this kind. And even today American pronouncements and rationalizations of political stands are often singularly humanistic and moralistic in tone.

On the other hand, it must not be assumed either that the new states are so preoccupied with demands for basic human rights that they have no time to worry about the problem of peace. On the contrary, these states revel in seeing themselves as peacemakers in the disputes of the giants.

Nevertheless, there does remain a significant difference in scale of values between the newer and older states. With regard to India's annexation of

Goa, for example, a major power may have argued that the very enjoyment of human rights presupposed a peaceful settlement of disputes. In a sense this line of reasoning makes peace more fundamental than those rights—at least to the extent that it makes it fundamental *to* those rights. But with that Goan experience in mind, the same great power may have become concerned that peace in western Africa would also be seriously disturbed if human rights were not extended to Angolans. In this second case it would at first appear that the major power was making human rights fundamental to peace rather than vice versa. And yet a good deal would depend upon whether this was an *ad hoc* calculation by the big power in regard to the particular situation or whether it was a basic, general postulate of its diplomatic reasoning at large. If, as is likely in this case, the calculation was *ad hoc,* then peace was still being deemed more fundamental than human rights—since the granting of human rights by Portugal in Angola was here regarded as *instrumental* in the promotion of peace. In general, it was more the new states than the older ones which supported India over Goa.[19] And it tends to be more the new than the old which are

[19] Hans J. Morgenthau has argued in these terms:

Our foreign policy since the end of the two World Wars has had the overall objective to prevent a change in the territorial status quo. The rationale for this policy is sound: a change in the status quo by force or likely to lead to the use of force can no longer be tolerated in the atomic age. The flaw which invalidates the policy is the refusal to recognize that not every status quo is inherently unstable and that it is the task of foreign policy to create a status quo which is defensible because the nations directly concerned with it consider it worth defending.

(Hans J. Morgenthau, *The Impasse of American Foreign Policy* [Vol. 2 of his *Politics in the Twentieth Century*] [Chicago: The University of Chicago Press, 1962]. p. 69.)

concerned about the rights of Angolans irrespective of the effect of such reforms on peace at large.

At times it is almost as if the new arrivals in international politics were reminding the older participants of the simple proposition that the importance of peace is, in the ultimate analysis, *derivative*. Taken to its deepest human roots, peace is important because "the dignity and worth of the human person" are important.

Once humanity is accepted in this way as a more fundamental moral concept than peace, membership in the United Nations might then be based not so much upon a test of being peace-loving as upon a test of being respectful of that "dignity and worth of the human person." And in African estimation—as in the estimation of India's Madame Pandit—*apartheid* is a more flagrant failure of that test than territorial aggrandizement by the Chinese. This is not necessarily a mitigation of the gravity of Mao Tse-tung's aggression; it is just a heightened condemnation of Verwoerd's arrogance. On this rests the determination of African states to sentence, if possible, Verwoerd's republic to something approaching solitary confinement.

In some ways this is a highly moralistic stand to take in international relations. And some African countries have yet to translate their moral indignation into specific polices of boycotting South Africa.[20] And yet, if

[20] Even such a militantly anti-*apartheid* country as Ghana was recently accused of not practicing the sermon of boycotting South Africa. South Africa's Eric Louw had claimed that Ghana still traded with South Africa. Ghana's Ministry of Trade issued a statement recalling that on February 16, 1961 a ban was imposed on the import of South African goods by the Ghanaian government and in October of the same year the open license for imports from South Africa was revoked. The statement continued: "The effect of these two measures was immediately reflected in the trade returns." The statistics showed that in 1960 Ghana imported goods valued at

moralism is irrelevant in international relations, emotionalism is not. And *apartheid* remains the most emotionally charged, single issue in the politics of the United Nations and perhaps of the world at large.

UN Purposes and the Voting System

But should these small countries be allowed to reverse the order of importance between peace and human dignity? This brings us to the whole issue of the voting system in the United Nations and to the significance of the growing power of a General Assembly based on a system of one state, one vote. On August 1, 1957, Sir Winston Churchill addressed the American Bar Association on the dangers arising from the new responsibilities which the General Assembly sought to assume. He said:

> We wish these new nations well . . . but it is anomalous that the vote or prejudice of any small country should affect events involving populations many times exceeding their own numbers, and affect them as momentary self-advantage may direct.[21]

In his preface to the 1957 edition of *War and Peace,* John Foster Dulles emphasized that the increase of United Nations membership since 1950 had accentuated the need for a reformed system of voting.[22] In 1962 Lord Home, then British Foreign Secretary, was exasperated enough with the militancy of the small powers in the United Nations to talk about a "crisis of confidence" as regards the future of the world Organization.[23]

It is safe to assume that these leaders were more polite in their public complaints than they might have been in their private thoughts. At any rate, certain sections of opinion in their countries have discerned a touch of absurdity in a situation in which little "tribes" have "the same say" or the same voting weight in the United Nations as some of the older giants have in international politics.

An African might retort that this whole way of thinking stems from the premise that the more powerful a country is, the greater should be not only its capacity but also its *right* to determine what ought to happen in the world. Its vote in the United Nations should count for more than the vote of a small country. This conclusion would certainly follow if the purpose of the United Nations were to make the powerful even more powerful. Any attempt to make the balance of influence in the United Nations commensurate with the ratio of strength outside the UN is not merely to make the Organization reflect the realities of the outside world but is to

---

£1,200,000 from South Africa as against her exports of £1,300,000. In 1961 the balance of trade fell to £10,000 for imports and £228,000 for exports. In 1962 the position changed "out of all proportion"—Ghana's imports from South Africa totaled only £33 and her exports to South Africa amounted to £50. The statement explained that the figures for 1962 comprised "personal effects of South African citizens resident in Ghana as well as the return to South Africa of spare parts previously bought." (*Ghana Today,* December 18, 1963 [Vol. 7, No. 21], p. 2.)

[21] Cited in Julius Stone, *Aggression and World Order* (London: Stevens and Sons Ltd. [under the auspices of the London Institute of World Affairs], 1958), p. 165, footnote 29.

[22] But for a more thorough discussion of this and of what reforms are needed, see Grenville Clark and Louis B. Sohn, *World Peace Through World Law* (Cambridge, Mass.: Harvard University Press, 1958).

[23] Home was probably worried not only about relations between the new and the old states in the United Nations but also about those relations in other areas of international life. I related Home's fear to African relations with the European Economic Community (EEC) in my article "African Attitudes to the European Economic Community," *International Affairs* (London), January 1963 (Vol. 38, No. 1), pp. 24–36.

give the big powers an *extra* arena of power. It is to *add* to the diplomatic influence which size and strength have already conferred upon them.

The argument continues that it would surely not serve the purposes of the United Nations to do this. The purpose of the UN should not be to make the powerful a little more influential; on the contrary, the United Nations should be concerned with moderating the immense capacity for independent initiative which power gives to the powerful. And in this task of moderation, a distortion of the vote in the UN to favor the smaller countries might be precisely what is needed. The distorted vote is certainly consistent with Dag Hammarskjöld's conception of the United Nations as, in the ultimate analysis, the hope of the small and weak countries.

But is this distorted vote consistent with a scale of values which puts the "dignity and worth of the human person" first and peace only second? Ambivalence is certainly involved in all this. In his fight for self-determination in his own country the African had declared his allegiance to the principle of "One Man, One Vote." In his fight for international participation through the United Nations he seems to stand for the principle of "One State, One Vote." And yet the premises on which the two principles stand are not always mutually consistent. The principle of "One Man, One Vote" seems to rest on the moral premise that no individual human being is to count for more than another human being. But the principle of "One State, One Vote" seems indifferent to equality as between *individual* human beings. A vote which represents less than 400,000 Gabonese is put on a par with a vote representing over 200 million Russians. As between the Gabonese and the Russian in the General Assembly, there can be no doubt that it is the Russian who is underprivileged. A remark of E. H. Carr's in 1939 has indeed now found a paradoxical substantiation—the claim that "the equality of man is the ideology of the underprivileged seeking to raise themselves to the level of the privileged." [24] In his nationalism, when contending with, say, British settlers, the African militant had been underprivileged and had stood for "One Man, One Vote." In his internationalism at the United Nations, he was later to leave the belief in numbers to people like Sir Winston Churchill, John Foster Dulles, and Lord Home since these leaders lamented the anomaly by which—to put it in Churchillian terms—"the vote or prejudice of any small country should affect events involving populations many times exceeding their own numbers." [25]

And yet, if this is a cry for the democratic principle of representation according to population size, the African might well wonder why the cry was not raised from the very inception of the United Nations, considering that nearly twenty of the original signatories of the UN Declaration were Latin American countries, including Panama with its population of less than a million. But then most of the Latin American votes were predictably Western. An African would be justified in wondering whether this was the factor which stilled the voices of the Churchillian prophets of proportional representation. In any case, even conceding that Africa is over-represented in the United Nations, it is easily established that Asia is *under*-represented. And if population were the criterion, many is an African who might in 1962 have settled for eight UN votes answerable to Mr. Nehru on the Katanga issue for every vote answerable to Lord Home. A few might even settle for, as it were, two Sukarnos for every de Gaulle on almost every issue discussed at the United Nations since 1960.

[24] Carr, *op. cit.*, p. 13.
[25] Quoted in Stone, *loc. cit.*

All the same, it remains true that in the United Nations, if nowhere else, the African prefers "sovereign equality" (as between states) to "human equality" (as between men). And if the rationale for this preference is that sovereign equality helps to moderate the power of the big states and to keep the peace, this is certainly one area of African ideology where peace is put first and the dignity and equal worth of the human person is put second.

UN Purposes and Nonalignment

But how is nonalignment itself related to these two ideals: peace on the one hand and equal dignity on the other? At first glance it would appear that the ultimate rationale for nonalignment must be the extent to which it promotes peace. The whole policy seems actually to *mean* a disengagement from the Cold War itself, though not from attempts to *end* the Cold War or to prevent its warming up. So important has this peacekeeping or meditating side of nonalignment been that even such a sincere friend of the nonaligned as Sir Hugh Foot has warned the nonaligned to beware lest they be accused of waiting first until the two blocs have expressed their opinions and then seeking a position in-between, expressed as the opinion of the nonaligned.[26]

In defense of the nonaligned, it can indeed be said that it is sometimes less important to have an independent categorical opinion than to remain sufficiently ambiguous to be acceptable to both sides as a potential mediator. In his famous rebuke of British aid to India, for example, Nkrumah must have felt that if everyone were to commit himself strongly on the rights and

wrongs of the Sino-Indian conflict, the chances of impartial mediation would diminish further. Nkrumah's position in that instance consisted in giving his opinion not on who was right in the dispute but on what was best from the point of view of settling it.[27]

But what was left on nonalignment in the face of that very conflict between China and India? Could it still be maintained that nonalignment as a disengagement from the Cold War was a practical proposition? Until the autumn of 1962 there was no ring of obsolescence in the idea of nonalignment. It was indeed often attacked in the West but on the mutually contradictory grounds that it was both "meaningless" and "untenable." With the Sino-Indian conflict the policy itself became exposed to the additional charge of sheer obsoleteness—of being a myth of the past already exploded along the Sino-Indian frontier.

It is, of course, true that the tenability of a policy of nonalignment varies according to the situation of each country. But if it were also true that the mere fact of being attacked by a member of one of the blocs invalidated nonalignment, Egyptian nonalignment would never have survived the Anglo-French attack of 1956. What has happened is that, in spite of all the prophecies that the attack would definitely tip Nasser into the communist camp, Egypt has remained as remarkably independent as ever. It is still not fully clear what long-term effect General Clay's report to the late President Kennedy on reducing foreign aid will have on Egypt's position, but at least at the outbreak of the Sino-Indian conflict Egypt was reportedly receiving more nonmilitary aid from the United States than almost any other Middle Eastern country, perhaps including Iran and Turkey, and more aid from the Soviet Union than any other African coun-

---

[26] Hugh Foot said this in, among other places, a BBC overseas program called "African Forum." The author of this paper was present when the program was recorded on December 14, 1962, in the BBC London Studios.

[27] For the text of Dr. Nkrumah's letters to Mr. Macmillan on the subject, see *Ghana Today*, November 7, 1962 (Vol. 6, No. 18).

try.[28] And in terms of initiative, President Nasser retained his own on a large number of issues.

It must be admitted, however, that Suez is not identical with the Sino-Indian conflict. But with regard to the question at issue, the differences just about even out. Against the fact that America was actively opposed to Britain and France in the Suez venture must be balanced the fact that it was America which precipitated the conflict in the first place—by an attempt to "teach Nasser a lesson" by withdrawing the Aswan Dam offer. The fact that Britain and America gave positive military aid to India in the Sino-Indian dispute must be balanced by the fact that Russia helped Nasser with pilots for the Canal in the Suez event —and added the flourish of threatening to convert the limited Suez conflict into a full-scale, rocket affair. And, of course, against the fact that China is a *big* member of the Eastern bloc must be balanced the fact that Britain and France were *two* members—and perhaps relatively as big—of the Western bloc.[29]

It is just possible that Indian nonalignment might not survive the Chinese invasion as Egyptian nonalignment survived Suez. It is even possible that, with the loss of India, nonalignment might gradually disappear altogether from the rest of Asia as well. But conceivably (though not at all with certainty) this could still leave Africa and the Middle East as the last and defiantly enduring bastions of nonalignment in the world, unless they

were joined by President de Gaulle's Europe newly converted to positive mediation between the United States and Russia.

And even if the Africans conceded that the Indian predicament was a case where nonalignment had not paid, they would have to see the Cuban predicament as a case where outright alignment had not paid either. When all is said and done the humiliation of Cuba in the autumn of 1962 arose out of permitting a foreign nuclear base on Cuban soil—a contravention of one of the basic tenets of Afro-Asian neutralism.

But was not the Cuban confrontation of the giants itself evidence of the futility of nonalignment in the sense of mediation by small countries? When it comes to the test, can either Russia or the United States be expected to pay the slightest attention to the protesting voices of little neutrals? In answer to this question, it might be pointed out that in the Cuban confrontation neither giant paid much attention to the little allies either. If, then, an African voice is going to be at best marginal within an alliance with either bloc, it might as well be marginal outside the blocs altogether—or perhaps marginal in influencing *both* blocs instead of only one.

And yet, important as these peacekeeping aspirations of nonalignment might be, it would be a mistake to assume that they constitute the ultimate reason for the existence of nonalignment. The attraction of nonalignment for the small countries does not rest primarily on the ideal of peace; it rests, in fact, on that other ideal of equal dignity. To be part of an alliance led by massive powers is to be overshadowed by those powers. An alliance involves an element of self-denial and self-discipline, but if you are a very small member of an alliance led by giants the "self-denial" and "self-discipline" might not be so self-imposed

[28] The United States Administration was understandably uncommunicative on American aid to the United Arab Republic. See interesting analyses in *The Daily Telegraph* (London), November 4, 1962, and *The Sunday Times* (London), January 6, 1963.

[29] I discussed this in a similar vein in a talk entitled "The Dress of African Thought," first broadcast on the BBC Third Program on August 19, 1963.

after all. In any event one thing surely holds—nonalignment gives small powers at least the *appearance* of independent initiative. To the extent that it involves fewer formal ties with big powers, nonalignment becomes the external extension of domestic self-government. It becomes, at any rate, an additional badge of independent status.

What makes such "independence" possible for countries which *are,* in some cases, absurdly small? Never in history have the voices of the weak been so strong in the councils of the world. How has this happened?

Of late the big powers have become more "enlightened" and tolerant in some respects. But this has not always been so. Afro-Asian neutrals sometimes speak as if they must be nonaligned in order to prevent the big powers from going to war. What is nearer to the truth is that the small powers can afford to be nonaligned precisely because the big powers are already afraid of going to war. It is not a case of nonalignment making peace possible—it is more a case of the fear of war making nonalignment possible. The voices of the weak have become strong because the strong are already afraid of one another. At any rate this is how it started. But although indulgence toward the weak may be the child of a mutual fear between the strong, that indulgence may already be changing into genuine respect. This respect would in turn make nonalignment more effective as a moderating influence on the big powers. The whole process has aspects of sheer circularity: fear of war among the big powers leads to toleration of presumptuous small powers; that toleration makes nonalignment possible; habit turns that toleration into a genuine respect; genuine respect makes the powers more responsive to the opinion of the nonaligned on at least some marginal issues; and nonalignment

thus at last vindicates the peace-seeking side of its existence.

The most important arena of articulation for nonalignment remains the United Nations. One measure of the policy's impact there is indeed the degree to which the big powers are prepared to respond to the arguments of the nonaligned. In positive terms this is the most important measure. But another indication of the influence of nonalignment is the number of UN members which are, in fact, nonaligned. And this takes us right back to the voting system of the General Assembly and the multiplicity of small powers within it. What must be examined now is something which can all too easily be overlooked—the extent to which the voting system of the United Nations encourages some of the small powers to *remain* small. In the African context this links the voting system of the United Nations not only to the effectiveness of nonalignment but also to the prospects for regional or even continental unification in Africa. Given the voting system of the United Nations and given that the influence of nonalignment is to be measured partly by the number of countries which are nonaligned in the General Assembly, nonalignment would stand to suffer if its adherents *ceased* to be so small. This is to postulate that ceasing to be small is to integrate with others into bigger territorial units. It is to postulate a situation where two or more small Members of the United Nations unite to form a new *single,* if bigger, Member. There are indeed forms of regional grouping which fall short of total political integration. The East African common market and common services organization has still left mainland East Africa with three seats in the UN instead of one. But assuming that East Africans are concerned with the effectiveness of nonalignment in the United Nations, future voting power is an important factor to take cautiously into account every time they talk about forming one bigger state.

The UN and Africa's Future

Yet, given our old premise that non-alignment is essentially an extra badge of independent status and of the dignity of independent initiative, Africans would, in fact, be generally less worried by the future of nonalignment itself than by the future of the status of Africa in the United Nations. Bigger African states would mean *fewer* African states and therefore fewer African votes in the United Nations. Symbols of sovereignty are important to countries which are newly sovereign. And a seat in the United Nations is sometimes regarded as the ultimate symbol of at least formal independence. A *collection* of seats becomes a symbol not just of sovereignty but also of influence; and the voting system of the United Nations is such that by this measurement Africa's influence would decline should Africa become stronger by uniting. Pan-Africanists often advocate full political integration between African states on the ground that this would among other things raise Africa's stature in the world. But the United Nations—which is so important as a means of giving the African a sense of stature since Africa is now weak and divided—is so constituted that it tends to lure some Africans away from the Pan-Africanist's goal. In short, raising Africa's world stature by reducing the African vote in the United Nations is a paradox of realism which has yet to be squarely faced.

When put in its historical context this factor has a touch of irony. The Rt. Hon. Oliver Stanley, in that speech in 1945, sought to protect the United Nations from a "splinterization" of the British Empire. Through its role in decolonization, the United Nations then helped to bring about that "splinterization" of empires. The irony of the present day is that the UN has temptations for small countries which may encourage them—however marginally—to *remain* in that state of splinterization. The idea of a multiplicity of African states in the General Assembly is, in fact, only one such temptation. The United Nations may also—with the best will in the world—help to mitigate difficulties which, if left unsolved by the Organization, might compel Africans to greater exertions toward unity.

Nations already sovereign will give up their sovereignty only if there are compelling needs which only such renunciation would meet. These needs may range from military insecurity to economic problems.

In spite of the recent events in East Africa, it is still true that the most important instance of military insecurity experienced so far by independent Africa revolved around the Congo situation. But the role of the UN in the Congo cannot be described as having been hostile to African unity. On the contrary, the Congo itself could hardly have been maintained as one country without UN exertion.[30]

It is, paradoxically, the less involved economic activities of the world Or-

---

[30] Although the significance of the Security Council has not formed a part of this paper, there are important implications in African demands for effective representation on that body. For one thing, the military insecurity sensed by individual African countries often arises out of relations with other African countries: Morocco and Algeria; Ethiopia and Somalia; Kenya and Somalia; Rwanda and Burundi. The Security Council can thus assume an intra-African significance when a crisis arises. Emperor Haile Selassie recently said in Addis Ababa that Africans were now prepared and able to settle African quarrels —but then went on to add that "the United Nations represents the best and perhaps the last hope for peace in the modern world." (*Uganda Argus* [Kampala], November 22, 1963.)

ganization which could inadvertently militate against greater union in Africa. This follows if we start from the premise that there are two possible unifying factors at stake in any significant program of foreign aid to Africa. One factor which might induce Africans to federate is their own poverty—and the hope that union would solve their economic inadequacies. To the extent that foreign aid helps to mitigate the inadequacies, does it make this particular federative inducement less and less compelling? Presumably this would partly depend upon the volume and kind of aid given. There may be some forms of economic aid which, while meeting some inadequacies, generate new demands—and perhaps spell out an even better case for federation. For example, even if it is accepted that foreign aid weakens the need for union, it may be argued that foreign *investment* strengthens it—at least to the extent that private investment often prefers larger markets. In spite of these qualifications, it remains true that some forms of aid militate against joint effort by Africans themselves. A country which can secure aid to establish and support its own university, for example, would be less inclined to seek ways and means of pooling resources with neighboring countries—and establishing a *joint* institution of higher learning in the area. What applies to joint or federal universities might apply to federalism at large.

Another potentially unifying factor at stake in foreign aid is related not to aid itself but to the *source* of the aid. In his list of reasons for which people seek federal unity, K. C. Wheare included "a desire to be independent of foreign powers." [31] Few will doubt that this is a desire of considerable persuasive force for many African coun-

tries. Indeed, now that most of Africa is *formally* independent, the Charter of the United Nations has become a Charter of neo-decolonization almost as much as it was a Charter of self-determination. At any rate, the term "neo-colonialism" has become a major debating concept in the General Assembly. In spite of the complaints of people like Mr. Spaak, the term "neo-colonialism," though vague, is certainly not meaningless.[32] Very often it signifies a fear of being so dependent on other powers as to become vulnerable to political manipulation by the benefactors. Translated in other terms, this fear can be understood as precisely what Wheare meant by "a desire to be independent of foreign powers." In order for this desire to lead to federation, Wheare himself postulated something else—"a realisation that *only* through union could independence be secured." [33] It is the applicability of this "only" which the United Nations could so easily put in doubt—particularly should the UN serve as the channel through which all aid, say, to Africa were extended. This would thereby reduce the threat of the "neo-colonialist" benefactor and, correspondingly, the impetus to union.

About three years before the United Nations was born E. H. Carr argued that the threat of military power to national self-determination and to the independence of small states was recognized by the peacemakers of 1919—and came to underlie the aspirations of the Covenant of the League of Nations. "But wedded as the peacemakers were to nineteenth century conceptions of *laissez faire* and of the divorce between economics and politics, they failed to detect the more recent and

---

[31] K. C. Wheare, *Federal Government* (3rd ed.; London: Oxford University Press [under the auspices of the Royal Institute of International Affairs], 1962), p. 37.

[32] Spaak complained at the United Nations about the lack of a clear-cut definition of "neo-colonialism." His intention was apparently to suggest that the term was meaningless. (*The Times* [London], October 2, 1962.)

[33] Wheare, *loc. cit.* Author's italics.

more insidious threat of economic power." [34]

The question which now arises is whether, firstly, the great powers would allow the UN to mitigate threats of economic as well as military power; and, secondly, whether such mitigation of the economic threat to self-determination is wholly desirable. Carr himself made a distinction between the principle of self-determination and the principle of nationality. The principle of nationality tended to be "one of disintegration," whereas self-determination did not necessarily entail that. "Men may 'determine' themselves into larger as readily as into smaller units," Carr said.[35] It is difficult to talk of the principle of "nationality" in the African context. But if we substitute for that the principle of territorial independence, we can almost say that the United Nations' role in Africa so far has promoted self-determination only in the sense of determining territorial independence. The point at issue now is what type of UN activities would increase or reduce the chances of a more integrative form of self-determination.

In general terms, African nationalism contains two fundamental elements. One concerns the relations of Africans with the outside world; the other pertains to the relations of Africans with each other. The former includes the fear of being manipulated by non-Africans; the latter comprehends the desire for greater unity among Africans. If the United Nations were to be the clearing house for all forms of aid to Africa, it might satisfy that element of African nationalism which fears foreign manipulation. But at the same time it might hamper that element of African nationalism which longs for greater unity in the continent. This is assuming that one factor which would encourage Africans to unite is precisely the fear of being externally manipulated if they remain divided. The UN would in this case be neutralizing that fear. In other words, if the most effective way of stripping foreign aid of the aura of "neo-colonialism" is to channel it through the United Nations, then the United Nations might also be the most effective instrument for depriving the cause of African federalism of the unifying services of neocolonial fears.

The story of the UN is, in a sense, one of growing *activity* in the promotion of some African aspirations. What might now be borne in mind is that there are other aspirations which can best be promoted by *inaction* on the part of the UN. And yet this is more easily put forward as an academic hypothesis than translated into an operative UN policy.

[34] E. H. Carr, *Conditions of Peace*. (London: Macmillan, 1942), p. 56.

[35] *Ibid.*, p. 60.

3. Toward a Model of Competitive International Politics*

BRUCE M. RUSSETT

I. A Two-Party System?

A NUMBER of attempts have been made in recent years to construct rigorous models of the international system, among which some of the more precise are various models of international equilibrium and other examples of systems analysis.[1] Most of these efforts have been directed to the application of models more or less directly derived from economics or the natural sciences.

It may be, however, that we have overlooked a number of possibilities from closely related aspects of political science. For example, there is a substantial body of theory about competitive national political systems which might profitably be applied to international politics. The relevance may not be immediately apparent. National systems are characterized by institutions empowered to make, execute, and interpret decisions binding on their citizens. Though these institutions are not entirely absent from the international system, they are undeniably weak. But in any society cooperative behavior results not only from the actual or potential threat of sanctions applied by authority. Nor would such institutions guarantee cooperation. In their comparative study of political integration Karl W. Deutsch et al. found the establishment of common governmental institutions and a "monopoly of violence" often more of a hindrance than a help.[2] Of the wars between 1820 and 1949 involving more than 31,000 casualties, at least half were internal rather than international.[3]

Rules of order are often followed, in both local and international society, because of social pressures. A reputation for morality and law-abidingness can be useful, and the contrary reputation damaging. In this respect the United States has an important asset not lightly to be squandered, for with most of its international audience America's word carries a certain presumption of sincerity. Similarly, rules may be followed to avoid reciprocal non-compliance by others with respect to common interests. Despite their hostility, the United States and the Soviet Union regularly avoid certain forms of threatening behavior (sinking "spying" trawlers, "spoofing" each others radar). On another level, interference with the regular channels of international commerce and postal exchange is generally avoided even though short-term gains might accrue from interference. If particular interference were countered from many sources, all parties might well lose.

Nor is even the threat of reciprocal sanctions all that restrains an actor. Co-operative behavior results from common values, and there are values, such as economic development, political autonomy, and equality, which

* From *The Journal of Politics*, Vol. XXV, No. 2, 226–247. Reprinted by permission.

[1] See especially George Liska, *International Equilibrium* (Cambridge, Mass., 1957) and Morton Kaplan, *System and Process in International Politics* (New York, 1957).

[2] *Political Community and the North Atlantic Area* (Princeton, 1957), p. 105.

[3] See Lewis F. Richardson, *Statistics of Deadly Quarrels* (Chicago and Pittsburgh, 1960), pp. 32–50.

seem to be held by virtually all governments (see below). Furthermore, what Talcott Parsons calls "an underlying structure of cross-cutting solidarities" produces restraint.[4] Even some firmly anti-Communist governments in Latin America refuse to apply sanctions to Castro—in part because of their established cultural and political ties with Cuba which cut across the Communist—non-Communist dimension. We shall discuss these and other sources of restraint in the following pages. It simply is erroneous to think of international politics as anarchic, chaotic, and utterly unlike national politics. Let us examine some of the similarities, as well as some differences, between national competitive systems and the international system.[5]

As a working hypothesis, consider the world as a political system in which the two power blocs, Communist and Western, are analogous to two parties which compete for the favor of the uncommitted "voters." Each party, including a leader and loyal party members or "partisans," tries to convince voters that it is best able to fulfill their needs and respect their normative prescriptions. At this stage of the analysis we shall consider a voter, whether neutral or partisan, as equivalent to the government of a particular nation. The United Nations is,

obviously, a major arena of the competition—it is the principle instance where the parties do vie for votes, and where the one-nation-one-vote principle holds. In fact, by providing an arena where the parties must participate in a continuing electoral competition for the allegiance of the neutrals the United Nations performs a major function in preserving the system's stability. But the United Nations is not the only arena for this kind of competition. By stretching the analogy somewhat we may extend the case to the competition for foreign military bases and allies. Those readers who are disturbed by the one-nation-one-vote simplification as applied to conditions outside the United Nations may imagine some kind of weighted "voting" system.

Note that we speak of a two-party rather than a multi-party system. While there may be some objection, it would seem that on the whole the present distribution of power is bi-polar, albeit in a "loose" rather than a "tight" bi-polar system.[6] Half of the world's independent political entities are at present militarily allied with one or the other of the two great blocs. More important, members of these alliances together account for over 70% of the world's population and nearly 90% of its income. Furthermore, as Thomas Hovet, Jr. has pointed out, even the "neutrals" do not form any really coherent grouping.[7] According to their voting records in the United Nations, they must be subdivided into "pro-Western," "pro-Eastern" and "neutral" neutrals. And if one goes on to distinguish different voting patterns on various issues, even the last subdivision loses much of its meaning.[8] On this basis it is difficult

---

[4] "Order and Community in the International Social System," in James N. Rosenau, ed., *International Politics and Foreign Policy* (New York, 1961), p. 126. Also see his article, "Voting and the Equilibrium of the American Political System," in Eugene Burdick and Arthur J. Brodbeck, eds., *American Voting Behavior* (Glencoe, 1959).

[5] Several recent pieces have examined the similarities of other political systems to international politics. For comparison with primitive societies and developing nations see Chadwick F. Alger, *Comparison of Intranational and International Politics,* paper delivered at the Annual Meeting of the APSA, September 1962, and Fred Riggs, "International Politics as a Prismatic System," *World Politics,* XIV (1961), pp. 141–81.

[6] Kaplan, *op. cit.*

[7] *Bloc Politics in the United Nations* (Cambridge, Mass., 1960). See also Arnold Wolfers, ed., *Neutralism* (Washington, 1961).

[8] Sydney D. Bailey (*The General Assembly of the United Nations,* New York, 1960, p. 28) refers in passing to an "embryonic"

to make a very convincing argument for the existence of a third party of a power and coherence comparable to that of either of the great power blocs. There are, of course, "independents" and "minor parties," and their existence is crucial to the functioning of the two-party system hypothesized, but that is quite a different matter.[9]

Naturally there are differences between national systems and the international model here suggested. First, the international electorate, with each nation considered as a single voter, is in this sense much smaller than any national electorate; each voter considers himself to have, and does in fact have, more influence on the parties' behavior than do single voters in the national systems. Thus in parts of the following analysis the similarity is more often between domestic blocs or interests and international "voters" than between single "voters" on both levels.

Second, and more important, there are no periodic elections at which the voters decide between the parties, and thus no long periods of relative quiescence during which the parties prepare for the next election. Instead, voting is practically continuous. Many major votes occur during every session of the General Assembly, and equally im-

portant opportunities for alignment arise outside the United Nations. Yet these are merely electoral skirmishes comparable to votes in a national legislature; complete victory for either side would imply the end of the electoral process, at least between those particular parties.

Because there is no powerful, permanent supranational government to gain control of, "victory" is likely to have meaning only as the destruction of the other party's power base. Similarly, the inability of a United Nations majority actually to enforce many of its decisions—the absence of much legislative power—encourages use of the Assembly as a propaganda forum rather than as an arena for close political bargaining. Many varied interests are represented, but often there is insufficient legislative power to force compromise for the achievement of a common parliamentary program.[10]

At least one institutional difference should be noted. Seymour Lipset suggests that a major contributor to the emergence of radical politics is the existence of effective channels of communication, informing voters of a potential community of interest and possibilities of joint action.[11] The United Nations, as a forum for promoting debate and the international exchange of ideas, certainly serves as an important means of facilitating communication among the underdeveloped nations. Yet the attitudes of individual voters are the subject of public communication in a way that they are not in democratic societies—on most issues the vote is open, not secret. The secret ballot protects a subordinate from reprisal by his superiors, and it equally protects him from social

---

party system in the Assembly, but then dismisses the idea on the grounds that because voting alignments differ so greatly on different classes of issues one cannot really call it a party system. Perhaps his conclusion is due to his greater familiarity with the relatively homogeneous British parties than with heterogeneous American parties where shifting alignments from one issue to the next are commonplace.

[9] We cannot at this stage dismiss entirely the possibility that in some respects a multi-party model would have a higher explanatory power in international politics than a two-party model. Its applicability is, however, a matter to be settled by empirical research, and one of the chief purposes of this paper is to indicate some of the questions which might be asked.

[10] See Arthur N. Holcombe, "The Role of Politics in the Organization of Peace," Commission to Study the Organization of Peace, 11th Annual Report, *Organizing Peace in the Nuclear Age* (New York, 1959), p. 79.

[11] *Political Man* (Garden City, 1960), p. 238.

ostracism by his fellows.[12] A laborer in the "reddest" mining area can vote conservative without his choice becoming known to his co-workers unless he chooses to make it known. Bloc members in the United Nations have no such protection.

II. Legitimacy and Consensus

In refering to some of the differences between national competitive systems and the international one we have, in the process, also alluded to some of the similarities. Let us now examine the similarities somewhat more systematically. We shall draw heavily on analyses of the American system, both because it has been intensively studied and because observers agree that it is characterized by much underlying diversity of opinion.

Most voters, including all the neutrals and even many of the partisans, regard continuing competition and the avoidance of a final resolution as the most desirable outcome. They probably have a preference as to the party they would wish to see win in a showdown, but it is far better for their self-perceived interests that neither party eliminate the other.[13] This is not only because of a fear that final victory would be achieved only by the

---

[12] See Stein Rokkan, "Mass Suffrage, Secret Voting, and Political Participation," *European Journal of Sociology*, II (1961), pp. 132–52.

[13] For evidence that this applies to neutrals as well as partisans see Lloyd Free, *Six Allies and a Neutral* (New York, 1959), pp. 33–56. Free cites numerous interviews with members of the Japanese Diet who affirm their attachment to the Western Alliance but nevertheless believe that the continuance of two-bloc competition serves Japanese interests best by making the Americans sensitive to Japanese needs. A similar situation surely applies to Poland, including many Polish Communists, who are well aware that even their limited independence is due to the existence of a rival to the Russians.

military destruction of at least one leader, with the concomitant destruction of many neutrals and partisans. More important, in a competitive world there are many potentialities to be exploited by the voters. Under many conditions competition between the parties is likely to produce concessions to the neutrals and the offer of substantial favors in the form of foreign aid, support for anti-colonial movements, and help in the achievement of other goals such as security from a local enemy. As we shall see below, conditions of competition may also serve to moderate the ideologies or platforms of the major parties; insofar as the original ideology of neither party appeals to the needs of a neutral, this moderating influence is likely to result in a nearer approximation of his wishes.

Not only does competition provide the neutral with parties who become eager suitors for his favor, it provides him with numerous opportunities actively to seek the fulfillment of his wishes. By the promise of his vote, or the implicit or explicit threat to give it to the other party, he may significantly influence the platform or performance of one or both of the parties in his favor. His influence may be dependent upon his ability to maintain his lobby in some kind of uncommitted position. This is analogous to a major question about interest group politics in national systems—under what conditions will a lobby be more influential as a partisan than with a foot in both camps? The partisan may, or may not, have substantial control over the politics of his leader; the uncommitted may, by playing his hand shrewdly, influence both leaders.

This is not very different from what goes on in democratic national politics, where neither the neutrals nor, in most cases, even the partisans will aid in the elimination of either party. No matter how deeply committed a party is to achieving final victory over its opponents, when it discovers that victory is not a real possibility for the foreseeable future it must become active in a different kind of politics. In Ernst Haas' terms, the result may be "a delicate negotiating process, with the world organization the forum, not of a community conscience or a concert of power, but of counterbalancing forces unwilling to seek a showdown, fearful of alienating friends or neutrals, and therefore willing to make concessions."[14]

Yet the system's stability may be quite fragile. Though neutral voters may much prefer a world where neither party wins final victory, even more vital may be the desperate necessity, in case one side *does* win, of being on the winning side. Thus if either side appeared to be winning one might witness an extremely powerful "bandwagon" effect far in excess of that in stable democracies where no one expects the victors to take drastic reprisals on their former opponents.

In domestic politics, of course, stability is maintained not only by a realization that the long term interests of most voters depend on the maintenance of an effective opposition, but by a normative element as well. Concepts of legitimacy as well as of interest restrain the partisans. Even Communist parties, in nations where they form a major part of the parliamentary Opposition, must at least pay deference to generally accepted norms.

If the idea of competition and the existence of competing forces is ever to be legitimized, it must be through the recognition that all voters share at least some interests in common. A principal mutual interest in the current international arena, though not the only one, is the avoidance of general war. Probably every government can conceive of some conditions to which

war is preferable, but also of many other outcomes which are definitely more desirable than war. Unavoidably there is considerable overlap of the views of the two sides, so that there are many circumstances both would prefer to general war. The balance of terror, if it remains stable over a long period, may eventually convince each side of its inability to destroy the other at an acceptable cost. From there, and recognizing their mutual interest in avoiding war, each may eventually develop a sense of the legitimacy of the opposition. One may not approve of the opposition's policies, but may grudgingly admit its right to exist and, within limits, to proselytize. Such a development would be aided by the above-mentioned conscious recognition by the neutrals and many of the partisans that their own interests are best served in a system where two or more opposing parties exist. Some such recognition seems to have occurred in England and America. The existence of the United Nations, and the "right" of the other side to take its case to the world body, may eventually contribute to some such development.

Even short-run stability, without the legitimization of conflict, depends on some degree of consensus on basic values as well as immediate interests. At present there is such a *limited* common "frame of reference" between East and West. Without such a consensus, in fact, the idea of competition for the favor of voters would make little sense. As Talcott Parsons has pointed out, both the Communist and Western ideologies place high value on each of the following: economic productivity, political autonomy, and equality.[15] What is more, the elites of the emerging nations, even when they are not confirmed believers in either

[14] "Regionalism, Functionalism, and Universal International Organization," *World Politics*, VIII, 2 (January 1956), p. 240.

[15] "Polarization and the Problem of International Order," in Quincy Wright, William Evan, and Morton Deutsch, *Preventing World War III* (New York, 1962).

Marxism or Western liberalism, usually accept these same values. This might not have been the case. Neither productivity nor equality is highly regarded in the traditional cultures of much of Asia and the Middle East, but in most countries those who are at least nominally committed to "modernization" are in power and not the traditionalists.

Obviously there are sharp limits to this basic consensus. Principally the conflict arises over two values: socialism vs. free enterprise, and the political freedoms of liberal democracy. Even here, however, the differences can be exaggerated. Western states have, in recent decades, abandoned or restricted free enterprise in many areas of their economies; free enterprise is often valued largely as an instrumental goal, a means of securing political freedom, rather than an aim in itself. Communist societies on the other hand, give a kind of defence to liberal democracy. However restricted political liberties may be at present, full freedom is promised for the day when the state withers away. Communist leaders are often highly cynical in discussing that day, but the acknowledgment that such a state is desirable does at least show that freedoms are *valued*. Every apparently liberal statement that they make tends, by encouraging popular hopes, to strengthen this very tenuous consensus.

A related factor which may promote system stability by narrowing the extremes of polarity is what Parsons calls "cross-cutting solidarities." Insofar as voters who adhere to one party belong to or are emotionally attached to organizations including many voters of the other party, this may reduce their demands for fear of losing those with cross-cutting solidarities or by causing disbelief in the ranks about the extremists' charges against the other party. There are rather few of these solidarities between the blocs at present, with the chief exception of Poland's cultural

and emotional predilections for the West and Cuba's ties to the Soviet bloc while remaining linked with many Latin American states. On the unofficial level such bonds as those of the Holy See with Roman Catholics in Eastern Europe also should not be ignored. Many more attachments exist, however, between neutrals and members of the two major blocs. They include formal organizations like the Nordic Council and the British Commonwealth, as well as non-governmental bonds such as Yugoslavia's Communist party ties, and links between neutralist and pro-Western Moslem nations. The role of these cross-cutting solidarities may well expand.

Yet another possible stabilizing factor might be the degree to which decision-makers develop broader institutional loyalties, as to the United Nations. One is reminded of the way Senators will rally to the defense of "the club." Does a similarity of background and profession common to many diplomats contribute to mitigating their conflicts? One would not expect this factor to have a very strong influence, but it ought not to be dismissed prematurely.

But any development of a consensus or sense of legitimacy in the international system is likely to be a fragile thing. The Soviets' defiance of "public opinion" to resume nuclear testing illustrates an important difference between democratic politics and the international system as presently constituted—there are, in international politics, sometimes major gains to be achieved by threatening to defy the consensus or destroy the stability of the system. By threatening to attempt a violent seizure of power one may promote a desire on the part of the independents to placate the violent party. Even this, however, sometimes applies in times of domestic crisis and impending revolution or civil war (e.g., the United States before 1861). The possibility of violence, from riot to coup d'état to social revolution, is never entirely absent from domestic politics.

III. Issues and Ideology

If the parties are to woo voters successfully they must be concerned both with making promises and seeing that their performances, their records, are such that their promises seem plausible. Each party may put a different emphasis on the two elements, and each may stress different aspects (the Soviet Union, for instance, was willing to accept a bad blot on its record of international action in its movement against Hungary), but both are nevertheless important. And if there is a substantial number of voters who do not share their ideological goals, the partisans' arguments are likely to turn increasingly away from ideological discussion in favor of particular pragmatic platforms and promises. Parties may become increasingly reluctant to commit themselves openly to the goals of a particular set of voters if there is another large set of voters whose goals are competitive (e.g., American reluctance to make an unequivocal commitment either to colonial powers or to anti-colonialists).

As ideologies are de-emphasized they are likely also to become more ambiguous. This may produce a split between an esoteric ideology for the inner party members which remains relatively pure and internally consistent and an exoteric, or public, ideology designed to appeal to or at least not to offend a wide variety of sentiments.[16] In recruiting new Party members American Communists, for instance, place little emphasis on the class-conflict elements of traditional Marxist thought but rather play to the desires of special groups wanting civil rights, civil liberties, or

the avoidance of "imperialist" war. Yet this difference between the esoteric and exoteric ideologies may cause a nearly intolerable strain producing either a weakening of even the leadership's attachment to the ideology or a situation where it is impossible for the party to hold most of its special-interest converts.[17] In the former case conflict between "revisionist" leaders and those who wish to hold fast to the basic ideology is certain. All these possibilities can be discerned both in the history of the American Communist Party and on the present-day international scene. Of course, in current international politics neither party seems really to anticipate the continued existence of both parties throughout the foreseeable future of the polity. The hope of final victory, eliminating the need for any subsequent elections, may circumscribe the true, as compared with the apparent, modification of ideology. Once "absolute power" was achieved the forces of ideology would reassert themselves. Yet a contrary hypothesis is also plausible—the real fear of annihilation may induce a party to jettison its ideology in the pursuit of survival.

The fear of alienating neutral voters may contribute to the formation of party platforms in other ways. In an effort to appeal to competing groups parties may make inconsistent promises, analogous to platforms which call both for more welfare spending and for lower taxes. Or a party may select only certain elements of its ideology for campaign emphasis. It is likely to ignore those issues which seem so divisive that almost any position the party might take would alienate more voters than it would attract. The United States government, which stands to antagonize someone whatever its position on colonialism, would surely be not unhappy to see the whole matter dropped. The Soviets, however, who depend upon quite a different set of partisans for their

[16] Gabriel Almond, *The Appeals of Communism* (Princeton, 1954), pp. 68–74, distinguishes between esoteric and exoteric communications.

[17] See George Liska, *The New Statecraft* (Chicago, 1961), pp. 48, 206–07.

basic support, stand to make a net gain by being anti-colonial, so they play up the issue as much as possible.

Any proliferation in the number of workable issues brought before the United Nations should also, in the long run, contribute to stabilizing the system. While the United Nations was used primarily as a forum for promoting Western security interests the independents and neutral-leaning partisans found themselves in a relatively weak bargaining position. But now, with the intrusion of economic development and colonialism as major issues in their own right, many nations have substantial freedom of maneuver. They may bargain and engage in log-rolling, exchanging support on security issues for votes against colonialism. As the authors of *The American Voter* declare,

If an electorate responds to public affairs in terms of one or a few well-defined and stable ideological dimensions on which there is little movement of opinion, political controversy will be relatively tightly bounded and the possibilities of party maneuver . . . relatively circumscribed. But if an electorate responds to public affairs in a less structured fashion, politics will be more fluid, party strategy will include or may consist primarily of exploiting new dimensions of opinion, and the likehood of party alternation in power will be greater.[18]

The emergence of new issues might eventually contribute to a sharp shift in alignments. Leaders and partisans of both major blocs may some day decide that they share a common interest in preserving their wealth from confiscation by an aroused underdeveloped bloc. This could conceivably produce the emergence of a new "have-not" party followed by the merger of the former opponents into a single party.

[18] A. Campbell, P. Converse, W. Miller, and D. Stokes, *The American Voter* (New York, 1960), p. 550.

Or it might mean simply that the voting alignment on some types of issues would be radically different from that on other matters.

The proliferation of issues contributes in other ways. A cumulative pattern of compromises and concessions can set up expectations of peace, stability, and co-existence which may constrain the leaders. Even if the leaders make concessions purely as temporary expedients and not out of any desire to promote such expectations, they are likely to give rise to hopes which it will be costly to disappoint.[19]

The intrusion of issues other than the military security one may make it possible for some partisans even of the tightly organized Communist bloc occasionally to deviate from the party norm. One can hardly conceive of the Soviets tolerating deviation on a major security measure in the near future, but on some other matters a vote against the bloc, or an abstention, might possibly be overlooked. By providing opportunities for deviation on issues which are not central to the Soviet Union's security we may contribute to a wholesome precedent. Once deviation is tolerated at all it may be difficult to stop it short of a certain fluidity even on rather vital matters.

The United States could conceivably gain in another way from the proliferation of issues, properly controlled. The West is in many ways a conservative group, seeking to restrain the pace and scope of economic and social change. Conservative groups traditionally have maintained themselves in part by yielding significantly to the program of their opponents, but also by promoting issues not directly bound up with class or status issues. Essentially conservative parties tend to emphasize "style" issues as efficiency in government or morality,

[19] Note, however, that to serve this function the issues must be ones about which there is *disagreement*. Matters about which there is consensus contribute in other ways. See Haas, *op. cit.*, p. 250.

or to stress personality in their campaigns.[20] To protect their own positions and to avoid disruption of the society they must prevent the lines of political division from becoming identical with those of economic cleavage. Both the Republicans and the British Conservatives expect to get about one-third of the working-class vote; their ability to do so both indicates and helps to maintain their societies' underlying consensus.

For these reasons it becomes vital to make a close analysis of current voting patterns in the United Nations. One would like to know at least the following: 1. How great a diminution has there been in the proportion of votes and debating time devoted to issues of East-West military security? 2. How high is the correlation between *per capita* income and voting with the Western Bloc? What other variables correlate with voting patterns?[21] 3. How greatly does the voting pattern on such issues as colonialism diverge from that on East-West relations?

Party competition not only may affect the issues chosen for stress and the positions taken, it may produce a tendency to avoid the explicit discussion of policy. Attention and effort may be concentrated on nominating politics and on electing men to office. Heterogeneous groups who could not be brought together on any explicit set of policy statements may nevertheless be able to combine for the purpose of winning elections and distributing offices. This too might be investigated by examining debates and votes in the United Nations. Is there more intra-bloc cohesion on such matters as admitting new nations ("convention credentials") than on most substantive issues?[22] Is the proportion of debate

time on such matters increasing over the years, indicating a tendency to avoid discussion of some divisive substantive matters?

We shall refer below to the effect of various distributions of attitudes among the population, but it is important also to recognize the effect of various *intensities* of preference. If those who hold the most extreme attitudes also hold them most intensely, a serious threat to the system's stability may exist, especially if the extremists are numerous.[23] Quite possibly the influx of new voters, the emergent nations, into the international arena has meant not only that most voters now prefer a "middle" solution to East-West problems, but that most voters are relatively apathetic in a particular sense. That is, the particular issues presented by the two parties' ideologies really have little appeal to them, so that they would not care greatly which was the victor. Their strong perferences are reserved for what are to them private matters— the development and modernization of their own countries, by whatever methods. They are thus not apathetic toward politics in general, but merely to the issues presented by the parties.[24] As noted above, in their eyes the achievement of their goals may depend upon the absence of a clearcut victory for either side. This necessity for two-party competition might, in the long run, be turned into a virtue, as the existence of the competitors took on important aspects of legitimacy in the neutrals' eyes.

One is here reminded of the argument by the authors of *Voting* about the role of the "independent" or, more

---

[20] Lipset, *op. cit.,* pp. 281–82.

[21] In the absence of high income, is some measure of "status" (white race, European culture) correlated with pro-Westernism?

[22] Party cohesion in legislative voting is higher on such issues than on more sub-

stantive matters. See Julius Turner, *Party and Constituency* (Baltimore, 1951), p. 53.

[23] See Robert A. Dahl, *A Preface to Democratic Theory* (Chicago, 1956), ch. 4.

[24] They may also share the attitude, rather widespread in some democracies, that politics is disreputable, and really played only by "professionals."

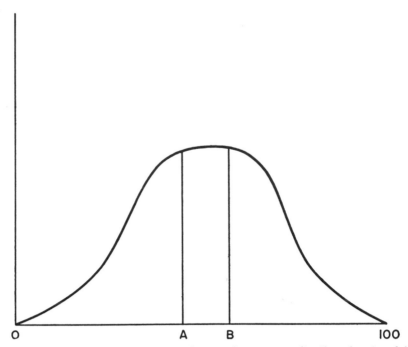

FIGURE 1: Two-party convergence when preferences are distributed unimodally.

accurately, the apathetic voter.[25] If the majority of voters held strong preferences the system might quickly become unworkable; only so long as most voters are relatively uninvolved in the ideological arguments of the partisans is the peaceful resolution of conflict possible.

IV. The Distribution of Preferences

Whether the two parties will become more or less extreme in their stands is a crucial question. Currently there is substantial evidence that the international party leaders have moderated their policies, at least those parts which are explicitly stated. Most of this can be seen as an attempt to win the support of neutrals and to hold that of the less extreme partisans. But whether

[25] Bernard Berelson, Paul Lazarsfeld, and William McPhee, *Voting* (New York, 1954), pp. 314–315.

these developments merely represent temporary tendencies, likely to be reversed in the near future, depends in large part upon the underlying distribution of voters' preferences. This leads to discussion of a variable which could promote system stability, but could also lead to the breakdown of the system and either to conflict or to the emergence of a polycentric system.

As Anthony Downs has shown,[26]

[26] *An Economic Theory of Democracy* (New York, 1957), p. 118. I owe to Downs' chapter 8 the method of presentation and many of the insights in the following paragraphs.

Donald E. Stokes has made a penetrating criticism of the Downs model (*Spatial Models of Party Competition,* paper presented to the Annual Meeting of the APSA, September 1962). Among his points are: 1. More than one dimension (issue) may be politically relevant, with different preference distributions for each dimension. 2. The salience of various dimensions may change over time.

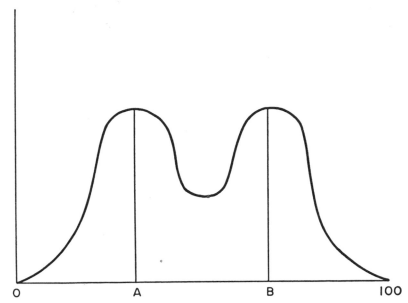

FIGURE 2: Two-party divergence when preferences are distributed bimodally.[27]

if most voters favor moderate or mid-
dle-of-the-road policies the two parties'

_____

3. Leaders, partisans, and neutrals all may
have different perceptions of salience and
preference distributions. These possibilities
were, however, dealt with in the previous
section of his article.

[27] In a digression, note the relevance of this
distribution to suggestions that if Southern
Negroes can get the right to vote, normal
party competition will force Southern politicians to modify their anti-Negro positions.
Assume for a moment that the mode at A
represents the advocates of integration, and
the mode at B represents the segregationists.
Assume further that most of the people near
mode A are at present disenfranchised, so
that both parties' policies naturally gravitate
toward mode B. If the A people gain the
right to vote, one party may well shift to
them, but given the basic distribution of
preferences *only* one party will make the
move, and there will be a wide gulf between
party policies as well as basic preferences. If
one assumes further that there really are
fewer people at A than at B—the mode is
lower—(not a bad assumption for the South,
where Negroes are substantially less than
50% of the population) the integrationists
are condemned to be a minority as long as
preferences remain unchanged.

will converge toward the center. The
possible loss of extremists will not deter their movement toward the center
and toward each other because there
will be so few voters to be lost at the
margin compared with the number to
be gained in the middle. This situation
is illustrated in the following figure.
The vertical axis measures numbers of
voters and the horizontal axis measures
degree of preference for some policy,
the extent to which economic control
ought to be centralized, for instance,
with zero representing no centralization and 100 complete central control.
If voters' perferences are such that
most voters are found at a single mode
around 50, then both party A and party
B will tend, over time, to move toward
that mode.

But if preferences are distributed bimodally, as in Figure 2, the outcome is
likely to be quite different. Attempted
shifts to the center may meet with the
refusal of extremists to support either
party if both become alike, or at least
similar. Since the potential loss at the
margin is so great, the parties may retain quite different programs.

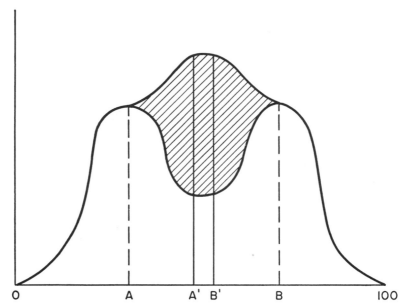

FIGURE 3: Two-party convergence with the creation of a single center made by the enfranchisement of new voters.

The recent moderation of some of the two international parties' policies might be traced to a world preference pattern like that indicated in Figure 1, which the parties have just now begun to recognize. But if we introduce a dynamic element, the moderation may be traceable to a shift in the world preference pattern caused by the "enfranchisement" of new voters. As the African and Asian countries have achieved independence and admission to the United Nations they have become new voters for whom the parties must compete. Whereas at the end of World War II preferences were distributed bimodally as in Figure 2, by the end of the 1950s the addition of new voters to the ranks had created another peak toward the center.

Figure 3 above illustrates one possible outcome of the enfranchisement of new voters. With the emergence of a new single mode at the center, the parties shift their policies from A and B to A′ and B′. But the result need not be that above, for the size of the center mode is crucial. If it were much smaller, not significantly higher than the modes at A and B and separated from each of the original peaks by a valley, the most likely outcome would be not the convergence of A and B but the creation of a third party, a "neutral bloc" C.

V. The Electoral System

Institutions also are relevant. It has often been said that single-member constituencies promote the emergence of two parties since small minorities in any district cannot hope, by themselves, to gain power. Do the "single-member districts" of the international system (one country, one government) make a similar contribution?

Federalism, it is sometimes alleged, contributes to the stability of a system which is threatened by many potential cleavages.[28] Nowhere in the American federal government is there a single locus of power, not even the Presidency, from which commands will receive obedience from officials everywhere. National leaders can control the nomination of local candidates only by enlisting the support of local leaders, and they are often unsuccessful. Federalism, reinforced by the electoral college, forces parties to have a decentralized structure appropriate for campaigning on a state-by-state basis. This encourages them to make contradictory promises, or at least to emphasize different aims in different areas. These factors reinforce the tendency noted above for the parties in a two-party system to concentrate on winning elections rather than on making explicit policy formulations. And the fact that national, state, and local elections are staggered is likely to prevent a party from getting complete control throughout the nation—there is always a new election taking place somewhere. To switch to the international arena, would it make any difference if all Free World elections were held simultaneously.

By forcing partisans to avoid great emphasis on issues which might divide the polity these institutional factors can contribute heavily to the long-run stability of the system, even if they sometimes exasperate the partisans. And the federal system, superimposed on a political system characterized by regional cleavages, contributes to the maintenance of long-run competition in another way. Just because there are various state elections as well as national ones, each party can depend on a safe "home base" from which it can hope to expand. Under competitive conditions the existence of safe regional bases may contribute to the moderation of

party policies. Because the leaders know their regional bases are secure they may tend to neglect their home interests in order to woo the uncommitted, and under many circumstances people in the regional bases may find there is little they can do to remedy the neglect. If regional demands should become too forceful, however, or should the leaders of either party despair of attracting the neutrals, these regional home bases could of course become disruptive forces leading to possible "civil" war.

VI. The Individual Voter

To this point we have for the most part been concerned with propositions about the international system as a whole, and broad trends in the behavior of voters in the mass. Yet it is also important to suggest hypotheses about the behavior of particular voters. One aspect of this problem is the relation between a single government's constituency and the policies it pursues in the international system. In trying to affect the behavior of another state one government may appeal either directly to another government or to the constituency beneath it. Thus the American government bargains directly with other delegations in the United Nations, and also uses the General Assembly as a propaganda forum to influence world opinion. To examine this we may draw upon some of the hypotheses advanced by students of legislative behavior.

Turner's study of Congressional voting noted that representatives from districts which are socio-economically most typical of their parties tend to show the highest degree of party loyalty on roll calls and those who come from districts atypical of their parties tend to cross party lines often.[29] Vot-

[28] Several of the hypotheses in this section I owe to Austin Ranney and Willmoore Kendall, *Democracy and the American Party System* (New York, 1956), pp. 490–99.

[29] Turner, *op. cit.* See, however, Samuel P. Huntington's conclusion ("A Revised Theory of American Party Politics," *Ameri-*

ing patterns in the United Nations should provide an excellent opportunity for testing this. "Typicality" might be measured in a number of ways. Several possible indices, as applied to members of the Western bloc, would be *per capita income,* "democratic" form of government, or perhaps some measurement of the degree to which each member shares the European cultural heritage. Different ways of making these indices operational should be experimented with, and several indices tried to see the patterns produced by each. One would expect party loyalty to be greatest where the member was typical on all dimensions, and diminish as he was atypical on one or more.[30]

Even if this hypothesis should hold generally true, one would nevertheless be required to explain a signficant number of exceptions. One interesting line of thought is suggested by Duncan McRae's finding that members of the Massachusetts state legislature whose previous election margins were close tended to reflect constituency socio-economic characteristics in their votes more closely than did those with wider margins.[31] He indicates that this may be due either to a heightened sensitivity to constituents' wishes resulting from anxiety about re-election or from a general rise in the level of interest in constituencies where there is a continuing political contest.

Quite the opposite conclusion is sug-

gested by Leon Epstein's examination of the characteristics of British M.P.s who defied their parties' stand on the Suez issue.[32] He found that constituency parties in safe districts were much more likely to retaliate against M.P.s who defied the party Whips than were the constituency organizations in marginal districts. It is generally felt in British politics that no candidate can add by his personal characteristics more than 500 votes to what any other candidate from the same party could poll. Thus the party organization in a safe constituency can win with any other candidate—its M.P.s need it more than it needs him. On the other hand, the constituency party of a marginal district may be loath to purge an M.P. and provoke an intra-party battle.

These contrary hypotheses might well be tested on United Nations voting. The equivalent of "closeness of election margin" might be measured either by some index of degree of "democracy" in a particular country or by the electoral margin of the government and/or the amount of party alternation in government. Did Britain vote more regularly with the Western Alliance than the Philippines (close margin, atypical)? Did the Dominican Republic (wide margin, atypical) vote more regularly with other members of the Alliance than Brazil (close margin, atypical)? These questions would have to be applied to all members of the bloc.

Part of the difference between the findings of MacRae on American politics and Epstein on British politics is surely explicable in terms of differences between the national systems. Local party organizations tend to be far more autonomous in the United States than Britain; a representative is better able to build up a local machine specifically for *his* support. The local party is more

---

can *Political Science Review,* XLIV, 3 [September 1950], pp. 669–77) that party differences in liberalism and conservatism are greatest where elections are closest.

[30] This would be consistent with Turner's findings, and also with the effect of demographic "cross-pressures" uncovered by the voting studies.

[31] Duncan R. MacRae, "The Relation Between Roll Call Votes and Constituencies in the Massachusetts House of Representatives," *American Political Science Review,* XLVI, 4 (December 1952), pp. 1046–55. See also MacRae, *Dimensions of Congressional Voting* (Berkeley and Los Angeles, 1958), p. 286.

[32] "British M.P.s and Their Local Parties: The Suez Cases," *American Political Science Review,* LIV, 2 (June 1960) pp. 374–90.

closely controlled by the central party organization, and thus more likely to reflect its views, in Britain than in the United States. Because he is more closely tied to the national party, a representative in the British system would be less likely to reflect the socio-economic characteristics of an atypical constituency than of a typical constituency, regardless of the "closeness" of his election.

On the international scene, governments most directly faced with a foreign-sponsored alternative to their rule —such as the divided states of China, Germany, Korea, and Vietnam—might be most dependent upon their alliances for support. Thus they might tend to be most extreme in the advocacy of their parties' policies. This does not mean that there would necessarily be great harmony between leader and partisan—both Chinas exemplify just the opposite—but that the dependence of the partisan on the strength of his party for protection would tend to make him at least as doctrinaire, and possibly more so, than his leader.

A somewhat different hypothesis is suggested by David Truman's finding that Congressmen who come from close districts and have low seniority tend to agree with the Democratic majority leaders.[33] That is, Congressmen who lacked power bases of their own followed the party leadership. The converse is shown by the fact that Republican Congressmen who were first elected in a Presidential year 1932–48 (i.e. against a strong Democratic national trend) were less likely to agree with the Republican House Leader than were Congressmen first elected in non-presidential years. Those with independent power bases tended to be either noticeably more conservative or significantly more liberal than G.O.P. Leader Martin.

VII. Toward a Model

The hypotheses suggested on these pages are all tentative, and need to be refined and tested. Not all are readily testable, but it would appear that data on voting patterns in the UN General Assembly would prove a uniquely valuable aid in the testing. In any case I certainly do not wish to suggest that propositions may be transferred eclectically and uncritically from one kind of political system to another. But I do hope that this exercise has indicated some of the fruits which might be obtained for international relations from awareness of the findings of studies of other systems. I have made rather extensive reference to such studies in order to suggest the wealth of material that is there. Perhaps as these hypotheses are tested more rigorously on national political systems—for their validity has not even been firmly established there—they may be tried out on the international system as well.

[33] The Congressional Party (New York, 1959), pp. 214–24.

4. Discovering Voting Groups in the United Nations*

BRUCE M. RUSSETT

1. An Inductive Approach to Voting Patterns

THE discussion of voting groups or blocs within the United Nations General Assembly has long been a popular pastime. It is, of course, merely a special case of a wider concern with groups and coalitions in all aspects of international politics. With the apparent loosening of the early postwar bipolarity it is increasingly important to discern the number, composition, and relative strength of whatever coalitions of nations may emerge from the present seemingly transitional period.

Voting groups in the General Assembly provide a relevant datum, though hardly the only one, for an effort to identify these groups. The United Nations gives no perfect image of broader international politics; due to the one-nation one-vote principle and to the fact that it is not a world government with authority to enforce its decisions, power relationships within the Assembly are not the same as in other arenas, such as functional or geographic ones. It might well be argued that because of the majority-rule principle the smaller and poorer states have an incentive to band together in the UN that they do not have elsewhere. Thus the discovery of a "bloc" of underdeveloped countries in the UN proves nothing about the cohesion of that "bloc" in other contexts. Yet votes in the General Assembly do provide a unique set of data where many national governments commit themselves simul-

taneously and publicly on a wide variety of major issues. The range of issues includes almost everything of major worldwide concern; even policy positions on parochial or regional questions (the intra-bloc relations of Communist states, for instance) can often be inferred from the nations' votes on other issues. However warped or distorted an image of general world politics the General Assembly may convey, it remains one of our best sources of replicable information policy positions for its 100-plus members.

An interest in voting groups may have a number of payoffs. From a frankly manipulative point of view, it may give information which can assist American policy-makers to increase their gains in the UN political process. Of more scientific interest, it can tell us about blocs and coalitions in ways that can be related to broader theories about parliamentary behavior. And finally it can indeed give some, admittedly imperfect, information about the nature—such as bipolar or multipolar, etc.—of the emerging international system.

The last concern must proceed from an inductive approach to the identification of voting groups, and so, for most purposes, should the second. That is, if one is asking how many such groups there are, the advance specification of certain aggregates, such as caucusing groups (Commonwealth, Communist, Afro-Asian) is a very roundabout way to get the answer. True, there is a tendency for caucusing groups to be more cohesive than any set of states picked purely at random, but the association between caucusing group membership

* From *The American Political Science Review*, Vol. LX, No. 2, 327–339. Reprinted by permission.

and voting identity is very rough, as Thomas Hovet has so compellingly demonstrated.[1] Furthermore, by dealing only with pre-selected groups one could easily conclude, for example, that disagreement and conflict within the Afro-Asian group is extremely high, but not even notice some subgroups, including some which do not formally caucus together, that nevertheless show very high agreement. Or one might ignore the cohesion of an aggregate of states (such as those of the North Atlantic area) which includes both one or more caucusing groups and a number of countries that are not in any caucusing group.

Most of the published studies to date have been directed to measuring the cohesion of caucusing, geographic, or other pre-selected groups.[2] One major exception is Leroy Rieselbach's article, which introduces an inductive method of bloc analysis.[3] He constructs a table showing the percentage of votes on which each of a large number of pairs of countries agree, and arranges the table in such a way as to indicate cohesion, with lines drawn around any group of countries achieving a given level of agreement. In the article he illustrates this method for selected countries, those in Latin America, but it becomes extremely awkward for a body as large as the entire Assembly in recent years (over 110 members). In such a large table (each of 110 countries' scores with every other nation) it is very difficult to be sure one has found all the "blocs" that meet one's criterion.[4] Rieselbach also illustrates an approach using Guttman scaling, but it can only find groups who vote together on a particular set of issues (cold war, colonial self-determination, etc.). We shall discuss this aspect below. In many ways it is a major improvement over studies which attempt to find groups when lumping all issues together, for coalitions on cold war issues are *not* identical with those on self-determination. Yet the inability to employ it simultaneously, when one wishes, to more than one issue is a limitation.

Arend Lijphart has with great force pointed out the overwhelming concentration of interest in the previous literature on analyzing pre-selected groups, and to counter it offers an ingenious inductive method which he illustrates for states in the 11th through 13th Sessions.[5] It again depends upon a version of an index of the percentage of times two states' voting positions agree, modified to account for the abstentions which are rather common in the General Assembly. He employs a graphic method of presentation (vaguely reminiscent of spider webs) that is superior to the tabular one but nevertheless becomes quite difficult to interpret for a body the size of the current Assembly. Furthermore, it can only identify those pairs or groups of states which achieve or exceed a particular *level* of agreement (in his illustration, 87.5 per cent), and is not an economical method for showing the *degrees* of agreement which may exist among all states.

[1] *Bloc Politics in the United Nations* (Cambridge: Harvard University Press, 1960).

[2] *Ibid.*, and Thomas Hovet, *Africa in the United Nations* (Evanston, Illinois: Northwestern University Press, 1963). See also M. Margaret Ball, "Bloc Voting in the General Assembly," *International Organization,* 5 (1951), 3–31; Robert E. Riggs, *Politics in the United Nations* (Champaign: University of Illinois Press, 1958); and Hayward R. Alker, Jr., and Bruce M. Russett, *World Politics in the General Assembly* (New Haven, Conn.: Yale University Press, 1965), ch. 12.

[3] "Quantitative Techniques for Studying Voting Behavior in the UN General Assembly," *International Organization,* 14 (1960), 291–306.

[4] Even in Rieselbach's Table 2 of Latin American countries there would seem to be one other group (Uruguay, Costa Rica, Paraguay, Honduras, Peru) that meets his criteria (five countries, 80 per cent agreement) for a bloc.

[5] "The Analysis of Bloc Voting in the General Assembly," this REVIEW, 57 (1963), 902–917.

Thus no fully satisfactory method for the identification of voting groups has yet appeared in the international organization literature. What is required is a technique which is *inductive,* given to a means of presentation which is readily *interpretable,* which shows *gradations* in agreement among nations (not just whether or not they exceed a particular level of agreement), which reliably *identifies all the groupings,* and which can be applied either to a *selected* set of issues or to *all* roll-call votes of a Session.

I believe that factor analysis, and more specifically a particular application of factor analysis, the so-called "Q-technique," is such a method. Originally developed by psychologists, during the past several years factor analysis has been employed sufficiently widely by political scientists that it probably requires no detailed introduction or justification to most readers, though its application to the United Nations has so far been limited.[6] In the most common employment of factor analysis every variable is correlated with every other variable, using the product-moment correlation coefficient. Factor analysis is then a data-reduction technique, as those variables which show high correlations among themselves and very low correlation with other variables are interpreted as pointing to a single underlying dimension, or *factor.* The factors themselves are uncorrelated with each other. Thus in Alker's initial application of the technique to UN voting patterns it was found that certain roll-calls (e.g. in 1961 on South Africa, Angola, Rho-

desia, Ruanda-Urundi, trade, and economic aid) had similar voting alignments that pointed to an underlying "self-determination" issue. These voting alignments were unrelated to those on such issues as Cuba, Hungary, Tibet, and disarmament, which were like each other and pointed to a different underlying issue (the cold war).[7] In this application each roll-call vote was a variable, with each "actor" (country) serving as an item or observation.

The versatility of factor analysis, however, suggests an alternative use. It can just as readily be used to find similar *actors* (test takers, legislators, nations) as similar *variables* (questions on a psychological test, roll-call votes). If, for example, one began with a table (matrix) where each country was a row and each column a roll-call, one could simply turn the table 90 degrees so that, in effect, the countries became variables and the roll-calls became observations. When the matrix is then factor-analyzed in this fashion the correlations identify *countries* with similar voting patterns and the factors point to voting groups or blocs. This procedure is usually designted "Q-analysis" to distinguish it from the somewhat more common technique mentioned first (R-analysis).[8] To repeat, the pro-

[6] Hayward R. Alker, Jr., "Dimensions of Conflict in the General Assembly," this REVIEW, 58 (1964), 642–657 and Alker and Russett, *op. cit.* A much more detailed discussion of how factor analysis is employed can be found in chapter 2 of the latter. As yet unpublished analyses of UN votes have been performed by George Chacko, Rudolph Rummel, Raymond Tanter, Charles Wrigley, and others.

[7] Alker, *op. cit.*

[8] Although it has been used rather frequently in other disciplines, to my knowledge the only application in comparative or international politics is a paper by Arthur S. Banks and Phillip Gregg, "Grouping Political Systems: Q-Factor Analysis of *A Cross-Polity Survey,*" *American Behavioral Scientist,* 9, 3 (November, 1965), 3–6. An application to the Kansas state legislature can be found in John Grumm, "A Factor Analysis of Legislative Behavior," *Midwest Journal of Political Science,* 7 (1963), 336–356. It is worth noting that in his pioneer study of voting blocs in the United States Congress David Truman discusses the difficulty of finding blocs in a large matrix and suggests factor analysis as a method possibly superior to his own; *The Congressional Party* (New York: John Wiley and Sons, 1959), p. 329.

cedure is inductive in that it involves no prior specification of the groups to be looked for, nor is even the number of such groups specified in advance.

II. Cohesive Voting Groups: A Q-Analysis of the 18th Session

We shall illustrate the technique with an analysis of roll-call votes in the 18th Session, beginning in the autumn of 1963, and in the process be able to make some useful substantive points about the nature of politics in the Assembly. Because of the United States vs. Russia and France controversy over dues there was only a single recorded vote in the 19th (1964) Session, so these are the most recent data available or likely to become so until the *Official Records* of the 20th (1965) Session are published sometime in 1967.

Our data consist of all 66 roll-call votes, both plenary and committee, except those which are virtually unanimous (defined here as more than 90 per cent of those voting taking one side—usually in favor).[9] This restriction is necessary because the product-moment correlation coefficient is seriously distorted by a distribution more lopsided than 90–10. The omission might result in the hiding of any very small group that was consistently in the minority, but is not likely to be important because typically such very lopsided votes account for less than 10 per cent of all those in a session. In practice the only real possibility of a group whose cohesion and isolation might be understated is the handful of states (Portugal, Spain, South Africa, France, Belgium, sometimes the United Kingdom) which are so out of step with the Assembly majority on African colonial

issues. As we shall see below Portugal and Spain do actually cluster together anyway, and South Africa is not even included in the analysis because of high absenteeism. This example, however, constitutes a warning against processing the data too mechanically without a careful inspection of the *Records*.

On every vote each state was coded either 2 (affirmative) 1 (abstain) or 0 (negative). Absenteeism is rather frequent in the Assembly, however, and posed something of a problem. In a few cases a country, though absent, later officially recorded its position. I listed it as if it had so voted. Also, in some cases an absence is clearly intended to demonstrate opposition to the resolution, or a conviction that the Assembly is overstepping the bounds of its authority in considering the issue. The United Kingdom found itself in such a position over several votes on Southern Rhodesia in the 18th Session. In those cases I recorded the absence as a negative vote. Both of these procedures are in conformity with the practice of earlier researches.[10]

The remaining absences are in general concentrated on a few countries, often those with small delegations. While it would sometimes be possible to estimate an absent nation's voting position from the votes of other states in its geographical area or caucusing group, in our inductive search for voting groups such a procedure would prejudice the results and would not be admissible. Instead I chose to equate an absence with abstention. In many instances an absence does in fact mean abstention, but by no means always, and when it does not the result is to incorporate a degree of imprecision in the analysis. The average absenteeism for the Assembly is about 12 per cent, and for the vast majority of states less than 25 per cent. Since the equation of absence with abstention actually assigns

---

[9] Committee votes often preview later plenary ones, but more frequently there is no plenary rollcall vote repeating one in committee. Even when the same paragraph or resolution does come up again the alignments usually shift somewhat; there are no duplicates in the following analysis.

[10] Lijphart, *op. cit.*, and Alker and Russett, *op. cit.*

a state to a middle position on our three-point scale, and since it is sometimes the correct interpretation anyway, this treatment of absences will not seriously distort the voting position of all countries with 25 per cent or fewer absences—their scores on the factors below are not affected by more than about 8 per cent. For those countries (11 in the 18th Session) with greater absenteeism the distortion is potentially more serious, and they are marked with a † symbol to indicate that their positions should be treated with some caution. Four other states (Dominican Republic, Honduras, Luxembourg, and South Africa) were absent more than 40 per cent of the time and so were excluded entirely from the analysis. Kenya and Zanzibar, admitted well after the Session was under way, were also omitted.

Table 1 presents the factor "loadings" of every country on each of the six meaningful factors which emerge from the analysis. Each factor identifies a group of countries whose voting patterns are very similar, and the loadings are product-moment correlation coefficients of a country's voting pattern with the underlying factor. The highest loadings or correlations identify those countries with the "purest" pattern, those whose voting is most fully described by the factor. Labelling the factors is always somewhat arbitrary, but in most cases the descriptive label should be appropriate. The percentages at the head of each column indicate the percentage of the total variation (variance) among all 107 countries that is explained (accounted for) by the factor. All loadings of .50 or greater have been underlined for emphasis, as loadings in the .40's are underscored with dashed lines. Squaring the correlation coefficient provides a means of discovering the amount of the country's total variance which is accounted for by the underlying factor. Thus it is reasonable largely to ignore correlations below .40 since the factor in question accounts

for less than a sixth of the variance. The countries are listed in descending order of their loadings on the factor which best "explains" their voting pattern. Countries with no loading above .49 (and thus for whom no one factor "explains" as much as one-fourth of their voting variance) seemed best left "unclassifiable." In factor analytic terms the table presents the orthogonal solution, which means that the factors are uncorrelated with each other.[11]

I have labelled the first factor "Western Community" in an attempt to indicate the predominance of European and European-settled states among those with high loadings. "Western Community" in this context must be interpreted as a cultural and not just a geographical phenomenon, including the white Commonwealth. This relationship is indicated by the fact that of 35 UN members either physically located in Europe or whose population is predominantly of European origin (Argentina, Australia, Canada, Costa Rica, Cyprus, New Zealand, Uruguay, and United States), 22 have loadings of .50 or greater on the second factor. This works out to a fairly low correlation coefficient of .35. Each of the top 15 loadings, however, is held by such a country.

Note also the high loadings of Japan and (nationalist) China on this factor. Japan's basic foreign policy has become

---

[11] In Tables 1 and 2 I present the factors as rotated according to the varimax technique. Unities were inserted in the principal diagonal of the correlation matrix. "Rotating" the original factors to "simple structure" maximizes the number of both very high and very low loadings, thus making interpretation easier. Each factor has an "eigen value" which expresses the amount of variance in the entire table that it accounts for. The eigen value, when divided by the total number of variables (countries), gives the *percentage* of variance accounted for by the factor. All 15 factors with eigen values greater than one were rotated. Nine factors which had no more than one loading as high as .50 are omitted from the table.

TABLE 1

UNITED NATIONS GROUPINGS IN 1963

Nation	Factor 1 "Western Community" 23%	Factor 2 "Brazzaville Africans" 17%	Factor 3 "Afro-Asians" 16%	Factor 4 "Communist Bloc" 11%	Factor 5 "Conservative Arabs" 4%	Factor 6 "Iberia" 2%
	"Western Community"					
Denmark	.90	.12	−.02	−.27	−.01	−.17
Norway	.89	.10	−.03	−.23	−.11	−.04
Sweden	.89	.09	−.03	−.25	−.12	−.09
Finland	.88	.06	.03	−.22	−.04	−.10
Austria	.87	.20	.00	−.17	−.10	−.01
Ireland	.86	.15	−.08	−.25	.16	−.03
Turkey	.83	.18	−.10	−.33	−.04	.23
Australia	.82	.10	−.15	−.38	.01	.10
Belgium	.82	.13	−.15	−.44	−.07	.15
New Zealand	.82	.17	−.14	−.27	.07	.05
Iceland	.82	.14	−.05	−.22	.14	−.20
United States	.81	.07	.23	−.27	.09	.23
Italy	.81	.12	−.12	−.37	.14	.11
Canada	.80	.09	−.15	−.44	−.02	.17
Netherlands	.80	.05	−.11	−.40	.03	.09
Japan	.76	.23	−.11	−.33	.31	.06
China	.75	.40	−.01	−.11	.07	.09
United Kingdom	.72	−.16	−.22	−.46	.07	.09
Greece	.71	.23	−.21	−.29	−.03	.15
*Venezuela	.70	.52	−.01	−.07	.13	−.02
*Argentina	.70	.49	−.04	−.10	.12	.09
*Guatemala	.65	.52	.07	−.17	.09	−.05
*Panama	.63	.51	.05	.08	.09	.05
*Colombia	.62	.52	.15	.08	.16	.09
*Ecuador	.62	.50	−.05	−.06	.32	.05
Iran	.61	.38	−.01	−.04	.33	−.04
*Costa Rica	.61	.61	.09	.11	.11	.05
*Mexico	.61	.52	.11	.01	.39	−.07
*Thailand	.60	.52	.05	−.02	.15	.14
*Jamaica	.59	.51	.03	.06	.32	−.19
†El Salvador	.59	.36	.00	−.29	.29	.34
France	.59	.01	−.48	−.02	−.23	.27
*Chile	.58	.59	.28	−.08	.18	.05
*Brazil	.56	.43	.01	−.04	.10	.05
*Peru	.56	.49	.03	.02	.17	.34
*Malaysia	.55	.55	.21	.06	.43	.03
†Nicaragua	.55	.38	.09	−.32	.02	.17
*Paraguay	.53	.47	.00	−.20	.19	.18
	"Brazzaville Africans"					
Chad	.12	.87	.17	.01	−.03	.06

* Moderately high loadings on Factors 1 and 2.
† More than 25% absenteeism (but less than 40%); absent equated with abstain.

TABLE 1 (*Continued*)

Nation	Factor 1 "Western Community" 23%	Factor 2 "Brazzaville Africans" 17%	Factor 3 "Afro-Asians" 16%	Factor 4 "Communist Bloc" 11%	Factor 5 "Conservative Arabs" 4%	Factor 6 "Iberia" 2%
Cameroun	.20	.79	.29	−.08	−.08	−.06
†Gabon	.20	.79	.23	.08	.06	.04
Central African Rep.	.17	.78	.03	.01	−.09	.10
Niger	.02	.78	.34	−.03	.04	.14
Congo (B)	.07	.77	.28	.08	−.09	−.00
Rwanda	.23	.76	.16	−.09	.05	−.20
†Haiti	.16	.74	−.06	.00	.01	.10
Ivory Coast	.08	.73	.35	−.04	.27	−.04
Upper Volta	−.09	.73	.37	.05	−.12	−.06
Congo (L)	.22	.72	.22	.01	.01	−.17
*Cyprus	.52	.71	.04	−.06	.08	.01
Dahomey	.07	.70	.32	−.03	.05	−.11
†Bolivia	.37	.68	.10	−.15	.14	.01
Senegal	.12	.68	.26	.19	.19	.15
Uruguay	.35	.68	.11	.08	.23	.04
*Philippines	.49	.63	.09	−.05	.26	.03
Madagascar	.39	.62	.05	−.14	.32	−.09
Sierra Leone	.05	.62	.41	−.01	−.02	−.09
Liberia	.41	.62	.09	−.14	.32	−.17
Togo	.09	.62	.49	−.02	.23	−.01
*Israel	.43	.53	−.04	−.18	.04	−.31
Mauretania	.08	.53	.38	.18	.49	.00
*Pakistan	.50	.51	.21	.01	.09	−.09
"Afro-Asians"						
Ghana	−.09	.14	.88	.17	−.11	−.04
Afghanistan	−.15	.15	.84	.23	−.00	.06
Indonesia	−.17	.08	.82	.13	−.19	.12
Egypt	−.09	.07	.82	.30	.06	.06
Syria	−.05	.09	.82	.30	.04	.07
Ethiopia	−.02	.11	.82	.18	.00	−.14
Yugoslavia	−.18	.15	.80	.29	−.03	.02
India	.12	.19	.75	.02	.31	−.07
Algeria	−.22	.16	.74	.40	.09	.02
Nigeria	.01	.26	.74	−.13	.04	.25
Iraq	−.24	.15	.73	.30	.25	−.04
Tunisia	−.02	.25	.73	.13	−.01	−.07
†Burma	.05	.13	.72	.24	−.06	.08
Cambodia	−.13	.13	.72	.31	.03	−.03
Tanganyika	−.18	.33	.67	.22	.10	−.16
Guinea	−.13	.29	.67	.32	.09	.05
Mali	−.25	.09	.65	.42	.27	−.11
Ceylon	.02	.19	.65	.21	.05	−.02

TABLE 1 (*Continued*)

Nation	Factor 1 "Western Community" 23%	Factor 2 "Brazzaville Africans" 17%	Factor 3 "Afro-Asians" 16%	Factor 4 "Communist Bloc" 11%	Factor 5 "Conservative Arabs" 4%	Factor 6 "Iberia" 2%
Sudan	.00	.24	.60	.24	.05	−.09
Kuwait	.14	.29	.58	.24	.47	−.06
Morocco	−.15	.13	.58	.35	.40	−.06
†Somalia	−.04	.22	.55	.11	.08	−.27
†Uganda	−.02	.32	.55	.27	.06	.03
†Yemen	−.02	.24	.53	.32	.04	−.13
"Communist Bloc"						
Czechoslovakia	−.42	−.04	.28	.85	−.02	−.02
U.S.S.R.	−.42	−.04	.28	.85	−.02	−.02
Bulgaria	−.41	−.05	.29	.85	−.03	−.02
Byelorussia	−.42	−.05	.29	.85	.07	−.06
Poland	−.42	−.05	.29	.85	.07	−.06
Cuba	−.36	.00	.28	.85	−.07	−.02
Romania	−.39	−.05	.32	.84	−.02	.02
Ukraine	−.45	−.02	.28	.83	−.04	−.03
Hungary	−.40	−.07	.27	.83	.16	−.08
Mongolia	−.42	−.06	.29	.82	.16	−.10
Albania	−.27	.01	.49	.59	−.05	−.07
"Conservative Arabs"						
Lebanon	.09	.16	.46	.08	.66	.10
Jordan	.17	.34	.46	.25	.58	−.03
Libya	.21	.44	.45	.01	.54	−.05
"Iberia"						
Portugal	.23	−.25	−.06	−.44	−.08	.68
Spain	.52	.13	−.11	−.26	.09	.66
Unclassifiable						
Burundi	.14	.30	.48	.19	−.09	−.17
†Laos	.26	.19	.40	.07	.27	.04
Nepal	.14	.36	.47	−.06	.04	−.01
†Saudi Arabia	.22	.14	.39	.32	.18	.15
Trinidad & Tobago	.42	.41	.18	.06	.07	−.03

quite well integrated with those of her North Atlantic associates in recent years, and is so perceived by Afro-Asian observers.[12] Nationalist China is of course heavily dependent upon United States military and diplomatic

[12] Cf. Saburo Okita, "Japan and the Developing Nations," *Contemporary Japan*, 28, 2 (1965), 1–14.

support. This leads to another observation about the factor: among those with .50 or higher loadings are 33 of the 38 UN members who have a formal military alliance with the United States (including the United States itself and counting Iran). Such a close association produces a correlation of .79. France is by far the lowest of all

NATO allies on this factor, with also a strong *negative* loading on the Afro-Asian factor (number three).

The second factor is named "Brazzaville Africans," though the name is far from perfect and a number of non-African states also correlate with it. The six highest loadings, and 14 above .50 in all, are possessed by countries which were members of the former Brazzaville caucusing group, of whom all but the Congo (Leopoldville) were ex-French colonies. Both the Brazzaville and Casablanca groupings had been formally dissolved by the 18th (1963) Session, ostensibly in the interest of promoting African unity, but the essential differences in voting patterns seem still to persist. Note also the high loadings of Haiti (Negro, very underdeveloped) and of several Asian and Latin American states. Previous studies have noted that the Brazzaville states tend to be less anti-Western on cold war issues than the Afro-Asian "neutralists," but more so, and especially on colonial questions, than the typical Latin American state. This second factor then picks out, in addition to the Brazzaville Africans, both several of the more pro-Western Asians (Philippines and Pakistan, plus Israel) and a number of Latin Americans who are rather to the "east" of their caucusing group (Uruguay and Bolivia, for example). The first two factors together account for 40 per cent of the total roll-call variance, and indicate most of the states which can generally be expected to take the Western position on most cold war issues.

The third factor quite clearly picks out those Asians and Africans sometimes identified by the term Afro-Asian neutralists. More often than not they vote with the Soviet Union on both cold war and colonial questions. They include such long-time leaders of this group as Egypt, India, and Indonesia, most of the Arab countries, Yugoslavia, and a number of African states, especially (but not only) those

with rather leftist governments which belonged to the former "Casablanca" caucusing group. And while these are (except for Yugoslavia) non-Communist governments, of 24 UN members outside of the Sino-Soviet bloc known to have received economic and/or military aid from China, the U.S.S.R., or Eastern Europe by mid-1962, 19 have loadings of at least .50 with this third factor. Using all 96 non-Soviet bloc governments in this table, and simple receipt or non-receipt of Sino-Soviet aid as the variable, this produces a correlation (r) of .72. All of the top nine countries on this factor received such aid.

Not surprisingly, the Soviet bloc accounts for the other major factor. Only Communist states load heavily on this factor—though Yugoslavia emphatically does not and belongs with Factor 3. Cuba and Mongolia are virtually indistinguishable from the European members of the bloc. But one important evidence of the crack in what had in previous years been a solid voting alignment is the behavior of Albania. Since the defection of Yugoslavia in 1948 this is the first time that any study of the United Nations has shown a noticeable deviation by a Communist nation. Albania's loading on the factor is a mere .59, and if we return to the original votes from which the factor analysis is derived, Albania's voting pattern correlates but .75 with those of other Soviet "bloc" states. That is, voting by the U.S.S.R. "accounts for" little more than half the variance in Albania's behavior in the Assembly.

Finally, there are two minor factors, each accounting for but four and two per cent of the total variance. Factor five has three countries loading highly on it: Lebanon, Jordan, and Libya. The name "Conservative Arabs" seems appropriate, for all are non-revolutionary regimes, in cold-war politics these states vote relatively often with the Western powers, and each has received substantial foreign aid from the United

States. Factor six picks out Portugal and Spain only; the label "Iberia" is obvious.

Most commonly in a factor analysis of this sort the factors can with relative ease be used to identify "groups" of variables (in this case nations). This is true for four of our six factors, but not for two other. Many of the countries loading either on Factors 1 or 2 (called "Western Community" and "Brazzaville Africans") actually show fairly high loadings on *both* factors, so that they cannot unequivocally be identified with either. The majority of states with loadings between .50 and .70 on either factor share this property. In such circumstances it is often useful to make a scattergram and plot the positions of the countries in question on the two competing factors. Figure 1 is a graph where the vertical axis repre-

sents the percentage of variance (simply 100 times the factor loading squared) accounted for by Factor 2, and the horizontal axis the percentage explained by Factor 1. All countries with loadings of .40 or higher on *both* factors are represented, as well as a couple of others for reference.

In some instances one factor accounts for three or more times as much of a country's variance as does the other, and when this happens there is little question as to where the nation should be grouped. This applies, for example, to Uruguay and Bolivia, for whom Factor 2 accounts for almost 50 per cent of the variance and Factor 1 less than 15 per cent. Any country which occupies a position either between the vertical axis and the sloping solid line to its right, or between the horizontal axis and the sloping solid line above

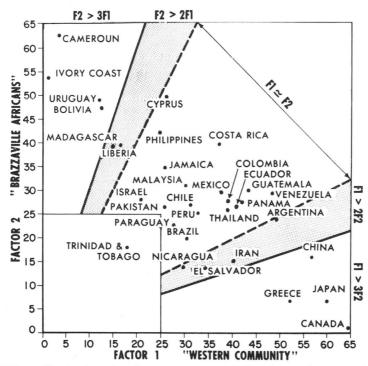

FIGURE 1: "Latin American" grouping as identified by moderate loadings on Factors 1 and 2.

it, has this variance ratio of more than three to one. The sloping dashed lines to the right and above the solid ones respectively mark the gray area where the variance ratio is over two to one. Although the countries occupying this space are distinctly more marginal than one lying closer to the axes, it is probably not unreasonable still to assign them as weak members of the group whose factor accounts for more than twice as much variance as any other. Most clearly it seems appropriate to think of Liberia and Madagascar with the "Brazzaville" countries. And for any state which has less than 25 per cent of its variance accounted for by any factor (e.g. Trinidad & Tobago) we have little choice but to term it "unclassifiable." The square in the lower left marks out this area of the diagram.

But for the countries where the percentage of variance explained by the most powerful factor is less than twice that of the next most important factor, it may be misleading to label them as belonging with either of the groups for which the factor is named. This is especially so in the situation illustrated in the above figure, where no less than 18 states occupy the area between the two dashed lines. Here we must speak of yet a sixth voting group, which we can label "Latin America." Twelve of these nations are physically located in the Western Hemisphere. With Honduras and the Dominican Republic excluded from our analysis for excessive absenteeism, only Haiti, Bolivia, Uruguay, Cuba, Trinidad & Tobago (in the lower left box) El Salvador, Argentina, and Nicaragua do not fall into this area. And the latter two are extremely marginal. Those 20 countries (including Argentina and Nicaragua) have been marked with an asterisk in Table 1 and should be considered as comprising a separate group. A number of pro-Western Asian states—Malaysia, Thailand, Pakistan, Philippines and Israel have quite similar voting patterns.

III. Groups and Super-Issues

The influences affecting these groupings are not unique or substantially peculiar to the 18th Session. By and large the issues voted upon in the Assembly during the Session closely resemble those that prevailed earlier. It has been shown through factor analyses with *issues as variables* (R-analysis) that three major issue dimensions or "super-issues" can be identified in each of four different Sessions spread over virtually the entire history of the United Nations.[13] They have been characterized as "cold war," "colonial self-determination," and "supranationalism" issues, and among them they regularly accounted for more than half the total variance in all roll-call voting. Two other super-issues, concerned with problems of intervention in southern Africa and of Palestine, were found in three of the four Sessions. The four or five factors appearing in any Session always accounted for between 59 and 70 per cent of the total variance in that Session.

A similar analysis of the 18th (1963) Session (using the roll-call data described earlier in this paper) showed these same five factors appearing and accounting for two-thirds of all the roll-call variance. Most prominent was the cold war issue, accounting for 21 per cent of the variance and characterized by votes on such specific matters as the seating of Communist China and the role of the United Nations in Korea—both topics which have long exemplified the cold war issue in the Assembly. A new matter, in form at least, concerned a resolution about extended participation in general multilateral treaties concluded under the League of Nations. Disagreement arose over whether all nations should be eligible, or merely those which were members of the United Nations and its specialized agencies. Since the latter formula would exclude mainland

[13] Alker and Russett, *op. cit.*

China and East Germany but include West Germany (which is a member of several specialized agencies), it is not surprising that the issue was perceived and voted upon in much the same way as the more familiar cold war issues. Another set of roll-calls loading highly on this super-issue came from discussing item A/5671, a resolution on "Consideration of Principles of International Law Concerning Friendly Relations and Cooperation Among States." One section which called for the establishment of an international center of inquiry and fact-finding for the peaceful settlement of disputes was opposed by the Soviet Union and its allies.[14]

A second super-issue, accounting for 19 per cent of the variance, concerned such familiar problems as Southern Rhodesia, South West Africa, and "territories under Portuguese administration." These issues formerly turned up on the self-determination factor or on the southern Africa one; here the super-issue can quite clearly be identified as southern Africa. With the dismemberment of the great overseas empires there are hardly any other concrete colonialism questions. A similar though less thorough convergence occurred in 1961.[15] What remains of any separate self-determination issue may perhaps be found in a small factor identified in only two roll-calls and accounting for but four per cent of the variance. A section on granting independence to colonial peoples and coun-

tries was inserted in the "Draft Declaration on the Elimination of All Forms of Racial Discrimination." The United Kingdom and some Western Europeans tried to have the section deleted, with the argument that it was irrelevant to the Declaration.

The other major super-issue, accounting for 18 per cent of the variance, is related to what has for previous years been called "supranationalism," composed of votes affecting the retention or expansion of the Organization's powers, especially its peacekeeping forces. As in earlier years votes on the United Nations' role in the Congo and UNEF in the Middle East loaded highly on it, as did a number of roll-calls about the proposed expansion and new composition of ECOSOC and the Security Council. While nations' votes on this dimension surely are not solely the product of their preference for or opposition to a stronger and more effective UN, this question is nevertheless a common thread through all these roll-calls. Finally, there was a factor composed primarily of two votes on the status of Palestine refugees and accounting for four per cent of the variance.

Thus the basic issues and alignments underlying the groupings in the 18th Session are familiar ones. But in the process of identifying them we are reminded of the distinct and uncorrelated nature of these super-issues; knowing a nation's position on one dimension provides no information by which we can predict its position on another. Because no two of these issue-dimensions or issue-areas[16] together account for more than 40 per cent of all members' voting variance we must reject one- or two-dimensional representations as *general* interpretations of group voting, for which we used the Q-analysis approach instead. Neverthe-

[14] In all there were nine factors with eigen values greater than one, accounting for 75 per cent of the total variance. I list here only those roll-calls which correlated at least .71 with the underlying factor, and thus more than half of whose variance can be accounted for by the factor. More detailed information on the resolutions can be found in the "Summary of Activities" of the General Assembly in *International Organization*, 18, 2 (1964), 313–467 and of course in the *Official Records* themselves. *International Conciliation*, No. 544 (September 1963) discusses the issues before their consideration by the Assembly.

[15] See Table 2 in Alker, *op. cit.*

[16] Cf. James Rosenau, "The Functioning of International Systems," *Background*, 7, 3 (1963), 111–117, for an illuminating discussion of issue-areas in national politics.

TABLE 2

CORRELATION OF GROUPING LOADINGS WITH SUPER-ISSUE FACTOR SCORES

National Groupings	"Cold War"	"Intervention in Africa"	"Supra-nationalism"
"Western Community"	.79	−.33	.38
"Brazzaville Africans"	.47	.45	.36
"Afro-Asians"	−.82	.43	.17
"Communists"	−.56	.45	−.64
"Conservative Arabs"	.11	.26	.16
"Iberia"	.10	−.74	−.06

less we return to the point raised by Lijphart and Rieselbach: for many purposes we want to distinguish behavior on one super-issue from that on another, and to see how voting on a particular issue-dimension is related to other behavioral or environmental influences.

One procedure has been to compute countries' factor scores on each of the major factors or super-issues from the R-analysis, and then to correlate those factor scores with caucusing or other group memberships and with ecological variables such as national per capita income, foreign aid receipts, or racial composition.[17] The factor score summarizes a nation's voting behavior, especially on those roll-calls which load heavily on the factor in question. It is computed according to an equation which weights each roll-call roughly according to its correlation with the factor, so that the roll-calls which are best accounted for by the factor make the greatest contribution to the factor score. Thus a country which voted affirmatively (coded as two) on virtually all successful roll-calls that loaded heavily on, say, the cold war factor would have a high factor score and a state regularly voting negatively (coded

zero) would have a very low one. Because the original factors are uncorrelated with each other the consequent factor scores will also be uncorrelated. These factor scores, serving as summary indices of national behavior on the major super-issues before the Assembly, can then be correlated with national factor loadings from the Q-analysis. Thus we can discover the basic issue-dimensions which distinguish our inductively identified "groupings" of countries. Table 2 gives the correlation of nations' factor scores on each of the three important super-issues (cold war, southern Africa, and supranationalism) with their factor loadings on each of the six factors from the Q-analysis.

From this we can quickly obtain a thumbnail sketch to characterize the behavior of each inductively derived "group" of countries. The Afro-Asians, for example, are pro-Soviet on cold war issues, or at least they share with the Soviets an opposition to Western use of the UN for cold-war purposes, and are quite anti-colonial about the problems of southern Africa.[18] But

[17] As was done in Alker, *op. cit.*, and Alker and Russett, *op. cit.*

[18] The fact that the Afro-Asians correlate more highly than do the Communists with the "cold war" factor indicates that the latter is a slightly misleading label. There are some roll-call votes, such as those about the role of the UN in reunifying and reha-

they generally favor initiatives, such as those concerning the role of ONUC in the Congo and expanding the Security Council and ECOSOC, which comprise the "supranationalism" dimension and which the Soviet Union vigorously opposed in 1963. It is on these issues that they oppose the Communists and on which Yugoslavia (rather favorable to strengthening the UN in these contexts) is distinguishable from the other Communists states of Eastern Europe. Similarly, the Brazzaville countries more or less share the Afro-Asians' position on southern Africa and supranationalism but are fairly pro-Western on cold-war questions. The Western Community countries generally vote in favor of those supranationalist initiatives that actually come to a roll call, and while moderately unsympathetic with the Assembly's basic position on intervention in Africa are nowhere nearly as isolated as are the lonely Iberians.

It is tempting to refer to some of our groups by more explicitly political labels. The "Brazzaville Africans," for instance, are not well named since they include Latin Americans, Asians, and other Africans as well. Possibly one might want to call them simply "pro-Western underdeveloped states." But we must ascetically refrain from plucking that apple. A word like "pro-Western" demands a unidimensional set of issues which does not exist. Each group's substantive position can be spotted only with reference to all *three* of the major issue dimensions. Imagine a cube defined by three axes—left to right: cold war, with the "West" at

bilitating Korea, or establishing a fact-finding commission for the peaceful settlement of disputes, which have substantial "supranational" loadings and overtones. On these votes the Afro-Asians and Communists often part company, at least to the degree of an abstention. Putting a descriptive label on a factor is always a somewhat tentative exercise, which is why I have here enclosed the labels in quotation marks.

the left and the Communists on the right; vertical: intervention in Africa, with the colonial powers at the top and the ex-colonies at the bottom; depth: supranationalism, with those favoring a stronger UN at the front and their opponents behind. These three axes can be thought of as dividing the whole cube into eight subcubes, and each of the major groups falls into a different subcube. The Western Community states belong in the upper left front cube, and the Communists are more or less polar opposites in the lower right rear segment. But the other two groups do *not* fall between the two poles; rather they are off to one side or the other of the shortest-distance-between-two-points lines. The Afro-Asians are lower right but front, and the Brazzaville nations lower front but left. Such a picture implies a multipolar pattern of cross-pressures and shifting coalitions that can mitigate international conflict.

In describing the correlations of the issue factor scores with the "grouping" loadings we of course are only ascertaining the typical voting positions of a group, especially those countries loading heavily on the R-factor. Any individual member may differ from the group pattern, as for example the United States is more "supranationalist" than are most states with equally high loadings on the Western Community factor. Except for establishing very general limits from the group, the behavior of a particular country can be determined only by a check of its own factor scores.

IV. Voting Groups and General Assembly Politics

In the Q-analysis we found that an inductive procedure identified six factors, and through them seven voting groups, in the Assembly. The six factors together accounted for 73 per cent of all the countries' variance. Thus the political process is relatively structured and subject to description by a small number of alignments. Yet the groups resembled only to a limited degree those which would be discovered from a list of geographical or caucusing groups alone. While geographical labels have sometimes been used they are very approximate and neither inclusive nor exclusive (e.g., "Brazzaville Africans"). Of our inductively-derived groups only the "Communists" closely resembled a caucusing group in terms both of who was included and who excluded.

In contrast to the mere evidence of caucusing groups the Q-analysis reveals other politically based groupings as follows:

1. The members of the Scandinavian caucusing group do indeed agree almost entirely among themselves in this Session, but Ireland and Austria differ from them in no significant way.

2. Analysis of the Latin American caucusing group would find a moderate element of cohesion, but entirely miss the very high similarity of Israel and several pro-Western Asians to the Latin voting pattern.

3. If the examination were based on caucusing groups extant in 1963 it would also not uncover the great consensus remaining within the officially disbanded Brazzaville and Casablanca groups.

4. The convergence of interest among the North Atlantic countries would not be found by examining any formal caucusing group.

The use of an inductive procedure also permits us to make some more general statements about politics in the Assembly. A simplified East-West-Neutral categorization which has characterized so much journalistic and even scholarly analysis of the world organization is utterly misleading. In terms of the states' behavior, five major groups (on four factors) emerge, in addition to two small groups and a few marginal countries. It should be emphasized that the identification of these groups depends upon their final behavior in the vote, not upon tacit or explicit bargaining among diverse logrolling coalitions which may exchange promises of support before the vote. It might be supposed, for instance, that one set of countries might offer its support to another set on cold war issues, in response to the other's votes on a self-determination roll-call. While this kind of bargaining undoubtedly does occur, an analysis of voting patterns alone would not find it since both sets of countries would *vote* identically, whatever their reasons for doing so. But a number of groups in the General Assembly retain their distinctiveness in the actual balloting. Two or more groups must combine to make a majority, and majorities on each of the different super-issues are composed differently. Comparisons with politics within national parliamentary assemblies may provide many fruitful insights and hypotheses, but the multi-party pattern of shifting coalitions that was approximated in the French Third and Fourth Republic may provide a closer analogy than will the aggregation of multiple interests within two stable parties as in Britain or even the United States.

Finally, there is reason to believe that this multi-group phenomenon is not especially new. It existed both before the well-known conflicts within NATO and the communist countries became evident, and largely before the admission of most of the new states. I conducted a similar Q-analysis of voters in the 1952 and 1957 sessions, to be reported upon more fully elsewhere.[19] By the same criteria employed here the 1952 analysis found four groups, and the 1957 analysis uncovered eight, though four were quite small. Therefore the discovery of but five large groups and two small ones in 1963 comes as something of a surprise, espe-

[19] Bruce M. Russett, *International Regions and International Integration* (Chicago: Rand McNally, forthcoming.).

cially since the 1952 and 1957 analyses were performed on only 57 and 81 countries respectively. The expansion of Assembly membership (to 107 for purposes of this analysis) has in fact outpaced the differentiation of new voting groups. Nor has their composition altered radically. Except for the emergence of the "Brazzaville" group and a certain greater differentiation between most other Afro-Asians and a somewhat pro-Western minority, the changes over the three sessions have not been great. Recent discoveries of a complex pattern of relationships in the General Assembly not only identify new reality but also show some lag between reality and our perception of it.

5. Beyond the Nation-State: Programming and Organizational Ideology*

ERNST B. HAAS

Programming, Self-Preservation, External Support, and Growth

WHAT budgeting is to public administration, programming is to the international organization dedicated to systemic transformation: without a growth-oriented program there will be no impact on the sluggish and unfriendly environment. But even if such a program is the very soul of the organization, it can flourish only within the confines of decisions made by judgment and compromise. In other words, it must evolve within the jaws of the ideological vise that is provided by the heterogeneous environment. Organizational objectives can be initially stated only as the minimum common denominator of these ideologies; they can evolve only within their permissive apathy or tolerance.

This feature imposes several unique needs on programming by international organizations. They cannot simply proceed to feed the world's poor, educate its illiterate, or cure its crip-

ples. The objective of plenty contains, by definition, subgoals involving coffee and wheat, land tenure and tax rates. The objective of education contains subgoals regarding literacy, school construction, teacher placement, and taxes. The subgoals of collective security defy simple enumeration. In order to meet overall objectives, appropriate sections of the bureaucracy must address themselves to programs directed at these subgoals. Subgoals beget specialists with primary interests in subgoals. They also beget alliances between these specialists on the one hand, and groups and governments on the other, these latter being concerned more with the narrow aim than with the broad organizational objective. Can bureaucratic leadership overcome this drag on dynamic programming? Can it subordinate the specialist with his ideological commitment to subgoals? The answer involves the knotty question of consensus, and the danger that programming will become part of a tacit general objective of mere survival.

Even if international organizations, in the sense of relationships among their member governments, are broadly "democratic," their bureaucracies should *not* be. No matter how demo-

* Reprinted from *Beyond the Nation-State* by Ernst B. Haas with the permission of the publishers, Stanford University Press. © 1964 by the Board of Trustees of the Leland Stanford Junior University.

cratic the organization, its programming must remain hierarchically dominated, or at least manipulated. Consensus must be maintained between leadership and member governments, leadership and expert groups, but not between every official and the Director-General.[1] But if the autonomy of the staff specialist is fully recognized, democracy will destroy the overall objective of the organization.

The possibility that subgoal-dominated programming will degenerate into survival policies calls for some comment on the nature of planning. According to Banfield, planning is to be distinguished from "opportunistic" decision-making by the fact that it subordinates all separate organizational acts to one overarching common purpose; the separate acts, in effect, are to be viewed as means, as instrumental intervening steps toward the achievement of the common purpose. Opportunistic decision-making, however, attaches other than instrumental value to the separate acts. They become ends in their own right and lose touch with what was once a common purpose.[2] It is to be feared that a specialist-dominated organization would lose sight of the common purpose. In order to prevent this, the leadership is called upon to analyze the situation, including the environmental constraints, in which it plans to choose specific intermediate ends, devise means of action to attain them, and then evaluate the consequences. . . .

Most international organizations originate in an environment of vague and imperfectly shared objectives. Hence the founders and bureaucratic

leaders at first often feel obliged to advance elaborate justification for the appropriateness of the new structure and the importance of its goals. This tends to stress the immediate survival of the organization at the possible expense of later adaptation to new objectives requiring different procedures. Further, the multiplicity of organizations creates a certain pressure on the leaders to emphasize, at first, the uniqueness and autonomy of their organization, again contributing to difficulties in adaptation at a later point. Imperfectly shared objectives, at the outset, result in the leadership's desperate attempts to find a core of allies and clients in the environment to assure a precarious survival in the short run. At the same time, vagueness of initial objectives, if bolstered by a core of supporters, gives the organization a better chance for long-run survival on the basis of adaptation, *provided* it can vary its procedures, adapt its goals, and find new supporters.[3] It follows that while the initial program should be broad enough to attract that initial core of clients, it should not be so exclusive as to sacrifice a change in objectives later on. On the other hand, bureaucracies that ignore the precariousness of their initial position, that hold out for a dynamic program immediately although they have few reliable clients, run a desperate survival risk.

Expansion in programming, then, can be achieved only on the basis of coalitions of interests sufficiently stable to enable the leadership to count on the persistence of identical or converging subgoals among certain of the associated governments and voluntary groups. The coalition need not be composed of the same members for each subgoal or issue: distinct coalitions can operate in each realm, provided only they last long enough to assure financial support and produce some impact

[1] This argument is well developed by Peter M. Blau, *Bureaucracy in Modern Society* (New York: Random House, 1956), pp. 106–7, with reference to bureaucratic discipline in a democratic national society.

[2] In Sidney Mailick and Edward H. VanNess, eds., *Concepts and Issues in Administrative Behavior* (Englewood Cliffs, N.J.: Prentice-Hall, 1962), pp. 71–73.

[3] William R. Dill, "The Impact of the Environment," in Mailick and VanNess, p. 104.

on the environment. Perhaps no single coalition is attached fully to all of the organization's formal objectives. But this does not matter so long as the operational subgoals remain tied to these objectives in the organizational ideology. There is no way of giving stability to the coalitions other than to "pay them off," to play the game of interest politics to the hilt. Creative innovations, similarly, must be born from some environmental impulse, some body of demands. The inclusion of the innovation in the program is then interpreted as a reward by certain members of the supporting coalition.

Now the demands on the perceptiveness of a sensitive leadership become tremendous. Innovation in the program is subject to certain imbalances between organization and environment, and these must be guarded against. At first, of course, objectives, because they are institutionalized to a degree, will remain acceptable to the initial body of supporters whether actual achievements are scored or not. The earliest bargains will remain confirmed for some time. If for some unforeseen environmental reason (e.g., a war or a depression) achievement suddenly slumps, the "good will" acquired by the bargain will not be immediately dissipated. Conversely, the organization will be able to make new bargains if some sharp improvement occurs in the environment, and if this is credited to the organization as an achievement, even though any connection between it and the program may be tenuous (e.g., the success of the European Common Market and unprecedented business prosperity). These slacks and imbalances involve dangers and opportunities for programming to which the leadership must be very attentive.[4]

If growth can take place only on the basis of programmatic innovation, the

[4] R. M. Cyert and J. G. March, "Organizational Objectives," in Mason Haire, ed., *Modern Organization Theory* (New York: Wiley, 1959), pp. 78–79, 85–88.

innovation can transform the international system only through its impact on the environment, through its "feedback." If we postulate the possibility of an expansion of international responsibilities along functional lines, and link such a process to the attraction and satisfaction of coalitions of clients, we nevertheless cannot automatically assume that new clients will be found, that old clients will readily adapt to new and more ambitious objectives, that there will be a feedback of sufficient power to generate new demands for organizational action. . . .

. . . If the leader of an international bureaucracy has true insight, he will manipulate the subgoals in such a way as to make the organizational influence as extensive as possible: he will spread his web of clients as widely as his interpretation of organizational objectives permits. The very fact that he can rely on no homogeneous and stable body of supporters gives him the chance to move and maneuver as the logic of functionalism suggests.

But relatively few heads of international bureaucracies succeed in doing so. Gunnar Myrdal, in line with his restrictive, though wholly realistic, view of the governmental environment, summed up his sobering impressions. Voting resolves no conflicts of a substantive nature, only procedural issues. It may be useful to put occasional pressure on a sensitive government identified with a minority. Since the main purpose of governmental participation in international organization is propaganda, the research function of the bureaucracy acquires real importance, for it enables a government trapped by its own propaganda to see itself as others see it. Governments will accept occasional collective censure, so long as they feel that the damage they suffer will be suffered by others on some later occasion. Institutional autonomy will develop only if and when the organization is used for regular review of national policy; such review must be based on dispassionate research, which can be soberly discussed by high national officials anxious to reach limited agreements among themselves. Then and only then will stable role patterns develop, etiquettes and mutual expectations that no one dares violate because everyone would be expected to suffer. Such an atmosphere can be created by the organizational leadership in technical bodies; in others, a "club" atmosphere of privilege among the participating delegates may do the same. Hence, even on so minimal a basis, organizations do survive. "Even in the absence of any very substantial results in terms of international agreements, it is apparent that practically no government has ever voiced doubt about the general usefulness of the United Nations as a regular means for national diplomacy," and new states invariably regard admission as the crowning symbol of their independence.[5] This minimal prescription provides a frail basis for growth according to the functional logic; yet a more ambitious choice of programs might render inapplicable some of Myrdal's more extreme constraints.

Organizational Ideology and Programming: Five Cases of Inspirational Leadership

If an organizatioin is to grow within these constraints, the head of an international bureaucracy must develop the organizational ideology in three distinct but equally necessary ways. First, the ideology must be based on a minimum common denominator of shared goals among the member units;

[5] Gunnar Myrdal, *Realities and Illusions in Regard to Inter-Governmental Organizations,* (London: Oxford University Press, 1955), pp. 13; also pp. 6–7. Myrdal is quite right in arguing that for purposes of maintaining a minimal attachment to certain common objectives during the Cold War, the veto provision in the United Nations Charter was— and is—essential.

it must then be so construed as to point to the selection of a program that is inherently expansive, but acceptable to some viable coalition among the members. Second, the ideology must be specific enough to act as a reliable guide for the organization's staff in making discrete programmatic proposals to the top policy-making organs, and remain true to the basic objectives. Third, it must point to needs, expectations, and demands in the environment that can be transformed systemically as the program is implemented to meet explicit subgoals.[6] Any or-

[6] In order to comprehend our criteria of success under more general rubrics, it would be tempting to have recourse to typologies of organizations developed by sociologists. Such typologies are offered in two recent studies, neither of which, however, concerns itself with public administrative agencies at the national or international levels. Hence the types were found to elucidate and classify very little of what appears to us as crucial in the life of international organizations.

Etzioni classifies all organizations in terms of their power-compliance patterns, a choice that would appear highly relevant to the international setting. Organizations exercise power on the basis of coercion, economic assets, or normative values. Each form of control has its own proper form of compliance, yielding organizations that are primarily coercive, utilitarian, or normative in their impact on the environment. *A Comparative Analysis of Complex Organizations* (New York, 1961). Now international organizations, at best, would be of the normative type. But are they? In view of our discussion of the heterogeneity and intractability of the environment, a normaive appeal to the clients and members would have to be a very selective process, summed up better in the descriptive terms of a functional, partial, and constantly changing consensus than in normative appeals and compliances.

Blau and Scott establish a typology based on the principle of *cui bono:* who benefits from the activities of the organization. They distinguish four types of beneficiaries: members and participants (mutual-benefit associations), owners and managers (business concerns), clients (service organizations), and the public at large (commonweal organizational ideology that does not satisfy *all* these desiderata will fail to overcome the obstacles experienced by Myrdal. To illustrate this, I shall examine briefly five examples of ideological dynamism as practiced by the heads of international bureaucracies.[7]

GUNNAR MYRDAL AND EAST-WEST ECONOMIC RAPPROCHEMENT

Myrdal's commitment in the UN Economic Commission for Europe (ECE) today appears almost quixotic: to maintain the economic unity of Europe by the rational use and planning of common resources in the face of ideological and political bloc formation, and thus to triumph over the logic of political division. The ECE's first effort, in 1947, was to obtain a mandate for the cooperative planning

ganizations). International organizations would be of the mutual-benefit variety; but they do not behave in terms of the canons for such organizations established by the authors! On the other hand, it is significant that the canons of behavior and the recurrent problems associated with service organizations seem to apply to international agencies. Blau and Scott, *Formal Organizaztions* (San Francisco: Chandler, 1962), pp. 42–81. This finding encourages me to retain my more limited scheme of classification, rather than seek to subsume international organizations under more general typologies that do not "fit" very well.

[7] The five examples used obviously do not exhaust the richness of this theme. It has been argued persuasively, in relation to Eugene Black's leadership in the International Bank for Reconstruction and Development, in Sewell, "An Evaluation of the Functional Approach." Similar cases could be made for Raúl Prebisch and the UN Economic Commission for Latin America, Fiorello La Guardia and UNRRA, Paul Hoffman and the Special Fund, Jean Monnet and the European Coal and Steel Community, Walter Hallstein and the European Economic Community, and, of course, Albert Thomas and the ILO. Of these, Monnet, Hallstein, and Prebisch probably come closest to having acted consistently on the basis of all three ideological canons.

of the reconstruction of devastated areas. Its second attempt, in 1948, was to request responsibility for planning the details for implementing the Marshall Plan—on the assumption of Soviet participation. With the failure of both attempts, the ECE seemed condemned to a fact-finding role, unlikely to meet Myrdal's central objective. He then sought to "revalue" these objectives by making it the main business of the ECE to restore East-West trade, despite the confirmation of two hostile blocs. He could draw on the desire of Western European countries to rely on East European rather than on dollar imports, and on the wishes of the satellites to retain trade outlets in the West. Converging national objectives were further reinforced by the Soviet Union's search for a formula to weaken American-sponsored export controls against the East. This sufficed for the creation of a trade committee in 1949, which, prodded by the ECE Secretariat, was to serve as the forum for East-West trade negotiations. By 1953, a significant revival in East-West trade had occurred, for which the energetic intervention of the ECE, the availability of specific negotiating facilities, and the good offices of the Executive Secretary could claim some credit. From then on, it became possible for the ECE Secretariat to mediate actively in easing payments arrangements, making long-term trade agreements, and improving commercial arbitration procedures.[8]

Yet despite Myrdal's partial success in meeting his objective, his efforts essentially failed: the economic integration of Europe has since become fixed in the very two camps he sought to bring together. Was the organizational ideology at fault? Myrdal was careful to base his program on shared and operational goals among the member

[8] My treatment relies on David Wightman, *Economic Cooperation in Europe* (London: Stevens, 1956), esp. Chapters 1, 2, 14, 15, 17, 18.

states. He was mindful of viable coalitions, and sought to choose subgoals with inherent integrative potential—when circumstances permitted. (It was, after all, not the ECE's fault that Washington and Moscow made a truly viable series of coalitions impossible because of their conflicting European policies.) Certainly Myrdal's ideology allowed him to organize a dedicated and energetic staff. Moreover, his policy of associating interest group representatives and a wide variety of unofficial and semi-official experts with the ECE's program could, under other circumstances, have gone a long way toward meeting the ideological canon requiring the transformation of demands in the environment. In short, ideology and program were properly meshed; but the very heterogeneity of the environment Myrdal tried to transform compelled the ECE to operate, eventually, at the level of the lowest common denominator—which found its lasting and visible symbol in the European convention on uniform road-signs!

JULIAN HUXLEY AND WORLD CULTURE

A simpler case is that of the first Director-General of UNESCO, Julian Huxley. Determined that his organization should meet the ringing phrases of its constitutional objectives by developing a generalized intellectual doctrine under which all cultures could find a niche, Huxley advanced his personal philosophy of "scientific humanism" as a proper guide for a specific organizational program.[9] He was also

[9] Julian Huxley, UNESCO: Its Purposes and Its Philosophy, UNESCO doc., C/6, Sept. 15, 1946. See also Charles S. Ascher, "The Development of UNESCO's Program," International Organization, Vol. IV, No. 1 (February 1950), for a vivid analysis of this phase in the organization's history. For a leadership doctrine friendly to subgoal domination, see the statement by the former Director-General of UNESCO Luther H. Evans in "Some Man-

motivated by the urgent need to find some kind of formula for screening and ordering the myriad specific needs and subgoals that were urged by UNESCO's members. Scientific humanism was chosen because it seemed to offer a possibility of uniting the West's belief in human dignity with the Marxist belief in economic welfare —but both under the roof of a materialism that Huxley developed as an analogue of Darwinian evolutionary theory. The proposal was, of course, rejected by UNESCO's General Conference. Huxley resigned soon afterward, and UNESCO quietly forgot about constructing a world culture as a guide to its program.

Which canons of organizational ideology-building did Huxley violate? If his program had been implemented, it would undoubtedly have satisfied the requirement of meeting needs that would lead to new demands transforming the environment. But that is the only canon it satisfied. The ideology was not based on the shared expectations of the member states—indeed one of UNESCO's initial problems was the absence of any shared operational goals—and the program selected was acceptable to no conceivable coalition. Finally, Huxley's own staff was not sufficiently committed to his philosophy to be capable of enthusiastic participation. It is doubtful whether scientific humanism, for all its ingenuity and dynamism, could have carried the day, even if it had not specifically proposed a world birth-control policy and shown a clear anti-religious bias.

JOHN BOYD ORR AND WORLD COMMODITY MARKETS

The ideological defeat of the first Director-General of the Food and Agriculture Organization (FAO) is more complex. Lord Orr had been identified

agement Problems of UNESCO," ibid., XVII (1963), 76–90.

with a group of Australian agricultural specialists before and during World War II, most prominently Lord Stanley Bruce and F. L. McDougall. These men were eager to bring about "the marriage of health and agriculture" by creating an international structure that would not only dispose of agricultural surpluses, but combat malnutrition at the same time. The same idea was pressed by Orr after he became head of the new FAO: he proposed the creation of a World Food Board that would stabilize prices by buying up surpluses in time of glut, and would dispose of them, subject to health and nutritional standards, in time of famine. Far from being merely an opportunistic plan developed to assure the survival of the FAO in 1945, this approach was part and parcel of a standing agricultural welfare doctrine actually practiced, as national policy, by many states. Yet the FAO turned down the Orr Plan, and the Director-General resigned. Why?

Again, the implementation of the plan would certainly have satisfied the third criterion of ideological need. Possibly it also satisfied the need of engaging the enthusiasm of the organization's staff. It failed with respect to the first criterion. Orr had had plenty of warning at the meeting at which the FAO was set up that the major agricultural exporting nations were not ready to consider an international commodity policy; but he did not heed it. In short, his timing was wrong: a marked decline in world demand and a drop in prices should have been the point at which to propose his plan, not a period of high demand and rising prices. Fortunately for the FAO, the members shared a sufficient number of explicit subgoals to give the organization a very respectable set of objectives despite the defeat of the Orr Plan.[10]

[10] Food and Agriculture Organization, *So Bold an Aim* (Rome, 1955), pp. 26–42. Gove Hambidge, *The Story of FAO* (Princeton: Van Nostrand, 1955), pp. 50–60. The Bruce-Orr-

BROCK CHISHOLM AND WORLD HEALTH

Huxley's Functionalism led him to believe that the inspired expert could overcome the ideological superstitions of governments. Orr's Functionalism made him feel that a commodity policy tied to a commitment to welfare could overcome the sloth of immediate price calculations. Dr. Brock Chisholm, first Director-General of the World Health Organization (WHO), is also a Functionalist; he holds that the expert in mental health can save the world from the obsolete politician. Chisholm differs from his colleagues in that he also had an operational ideology that enabled him to stress shared subgoals at the expense of the central argument; and he did not have to resign. The reason was his prudent separation of his private ideology from his public programming duties.

The private ideology is easily summarized. Man's scientific evolution now makes possible the total destruction of the race. In the past, the limited potential of destruction made reasonable the accepted attitudes toward war and exclusiveness. This is no longer so; political attitudes of anything less than complete world-mindedness are obsolete, and the politicians, educators, lawyers, and clergymen who adhere to them must be shorn of their power to mislead the generation that is now growing up. Good health demands that man "must take in his ability to function wholly, to function wholly in all circumstances—physical, mental, social." [11] Good mental health demands

McDougall ideology was eloquently expressed in the preamble of the FAO Constitution, but the delegates were not in sufficient agreement to include it in the operative portions of that document. The British government, for its part, saw fit to include Orr only as a technical adviser to its delegation.

[11] Brock Chisholm, *Prescription for Survival* (New York: Columbia University Press, 1957), p. 3. Note also that the Constitution of WHO defines health as a "state of complete physical, mental and social well-being."

that nations change their educational policies to make this evolution of world-mindedness inevitable. No other means to survival is apparent, because the politicians' inability to understand the contemporary world merely produces anxieties that tend to be cathartically resolved by violence and verbal aggressiveness. Moreover, ideologies and political systems unmindful of mental health are equally regressive.

But Chisholm apparently recognized that this stricture comprised the bulk of his clients and supporters. He admitted the limitations of international organizations much as did Myrdal— the answer he advances is to change the climate of opinion *at home,* so that it may fall into line with the ringing words of international constitutions and charters. But so far as carrying over the ideology into programming for WHO is concerned, there is almost no trace: more technical assistance, more understanding for underdeveloped societies, and more generous long-term financing for UN agencies —demands bearing little relevance to the fundamental reformism of the ideology.[12] The program of WHO remained geared to subgoals firmly accepted by a stable coalition of members; it concentrated on malaria, maternal and child health, and venereal

disease. Mental health remained a stepchild, and when it was discussed, there was no suggestion that Chisholm's ideology had made an impact. He remained firmly mindful of the first ideological canon and did well in meeting the second. But in so doing, he lost sight of the third, and committed WHO to a professionalized and routinized program.[13]

DAG HAMMARSKJÖLD AND
WORLD PEACE

The scholarly Swedish economist-civil servant who, in the last two years of his tenure, sought to infuse the UN with a dynamic and expansive ideology arrived at his doctrine gradually and perhaps even reluctantly. Following in the footsteps of a Secretary-General whose efforts at dynamic leadership were marked by failure, Hammarskjöld at first considered himself the neutral and dispassionate servant of the governments making up the UN.

My treatment of Chisholm is based on the work cited, his lectures delivered at the University of North Carolina, March 1959, and the Asilomar Conference of the Mental Health Society of Northern California, September 10, 1954.

[12] Chisholm said: "I think *the next appropriate step* is a good phrase to keep in mind. We try to do this in the WHO because everywhere there are visionaries and a visionary is fine—if he sees the bridge to his vision. But if he tries to jump to his vision without a bridge, he is in trouble. So we always try to think about what is the next appropriate step . . . what we do today and tomorrow, in order to be able to implement this in ten, twenty, or fifty years from now." Lecture at the University of North Carolina, p. 36, italics in original.

[13] Chisholm, however, would argue that this restrained approach is consistent with the third canon because it lays the necessary foundation for the systemic-attitudinal changes he wants. In order to agree, I would have to accept his ideology as an accurate prognosis for systemic change, which I do not. For my judgment concerning the WHO mental health program, see World Health Organization, *The First Ten Years of the World Health Organization* (Geneva, 1958); pp. 324–33. Chisholm's programmatic skill, however, is also evident in his ability to abide by certain crucial environmental constraints (e.g., appeasing the United States medical profession when the U.S. contributed 40 per cent of the WHO budget) and to ignore others as irrelevant to the subgoals that he selected (e.g., the early U.S. demand that WHO control the international trade in new and untried pharmaceuticals, which was opposed by most underdeveloped countries; and his neglect to persuade the Soviet bloc nations to remain in WHO when Moscow decided that it wanted medical supplies, not advice on treatment). For details, see Charles E. Allen, "World Health and World Politics," *International Organization,* IV (1950), 37, 38, 40–42.

Conscious of the negotiated political compromise on which his election had been based, he practiced his now famous "quiet" and "preventive" diplomacy only when encouraged to do so by significant groupings in UN organs. Only when specific military crises arose, crises that were characterized by the absence of any immediate consensus among and within important coalitions of governments, did he intervene on his own initiative and in the name of the United Nations. Only then did he elaborate his organizational ideology. The process began in the Suez Crisis of 1956, and found its practical and doctrinal culmination in the Congo episode of 1960–61. What was this ideology? [14]

The historical purpose of the UN is to encourage the evolution of a world community beyond the minimal level of cooperation represented by a permanent conference of governments; to reach a stage at which the organization can act autonomously for constructive and universal ends—in short, in

[14] The following treatment of Hammarskjöld's thoughts rests on three major statements by him: the Copenhagen speech of May 1, 1959, the Oxford University speech of May 30, 1961, and the Introduction to the Annual Report of the Secretary-General to the General Assembly, June 15, 1961—considered by himself to be his political testament. The last item is reprinted as "Two Differing Concepts of United Nations Assayed," in *International Organization*, XV (1961), 549–63. For a treatment of the ideology in the practical setting of the Congo Crisis, see Stanley Hoffmann, "In Search of a Thread: The UN in the Congo Labyrinth," *ibid.*, XVI (1962), 331–61. See also Richard I. Miller, *Dag Hammarskjöld and Crisis Diplomacy* (New York: Oceana Publications, 1962). For more general discussions of "strong" secretaries-general, with ample references to Hammarskjöld, see A. L. Burns and N. Heathcote, *Peace-Keeping by U.N. Forces from Suez to the Congo* (New York: Praeger, 1963); Jean Siotis, *Essai sur le Secrétariat International* (Geneva: Librairie Droz, 1963); Sidney D. Bailey, *The Secretariat of the United Nations* (New York: Carnegie Endowment for International Peace, 1962).

a more supranational manner than the bare words of the UN Charter suggest. But, true to the first canon of a wise organizational ideology, this can be done only on the basis of what is said or implied by that Charter—as interpreted by the organs of the UN—because the Charter represents the minimal convergence of common interests in the environment. Specifically, Hammarskjöld argued that the evolution he wished to encourage must be based on giving increasing reality to the Charter provisions regarding the equality of political rights, equal economic opportunity, and the rule of law. For this purpose it was essential to separate the legitimate from the unlawful use of force, and to encourage all techniques for the peaceful settlement of disputes. Normally, any discrepancy between these minimal "agreed" principles and actual state conduct would be resolved by action of the Security Council or the General Assembly: but, and this is the essence of Hammarskjöld's dynamic ideology, if there is insufficient consensus for meeting the aims of the Charter in a specific instance, it is the clear constitutional duty of the Secretariat and its head to overcome the discrepancy. Thus, the ideology postulates increasing functional scope for the organization on the basis of initial common objectives that have been insufficiently realized in fact. It postulates, further, a doctrine uniting the staff behind its chief in advancing interpretations and programs designed to realize these objectives in fact. And it certainly makes possible the realization of the third ideological canon, the meeting of demands and expectations in the environment that are designed to transform the system. The very scope of the Charter objectives could make this possible, *provided* that general objectives can be transformed into specific operational subgoals on the basis of reliable support by shifting coalitions.[15]

[15] My argument is deliberately confined to those aspects of Hammarskjöld's ideology

Despite the superficial success of Hammarskjöld's ideology, it is my contention that he ignored this proviso. He abided by the first canon in part only, and thereby deprived himself of reliable support and subgoal specificity in terms of the third canon. The Congo crisis exemplifies my argument. Hammarskjöld sought to exploit to the hilt the many and mutually contradictory UN Congo tasks, which had been so laboriously extracted from the process of parliamentary diplomacy, by placing his own interpretation of priorities upon them. He also sought to increase the UN's autonomy, with respect to its environment, by exercising the power to make his own proposals and take his own steps when parliamentary diplomacy produced no consensus and no clear guides for action. But since he invoked the Charter as his ideological scripture, he committed himself to mutually irreconcilable subgoals, which made the growth of a stable supporting coalition an impossibility. He sought at various times to (1) maintain order in the Congo, (2)

that were publicly advanced and defended by him. It is not yet possible to put the public argument within the full context into which it surely belongs, the private mystical world of the Secretary-General revealed posthumously in his *Vägmärken*.

expel the Belgians, (3) keep other "interested" foreign forces out, (4) unify the Congo, and (5) respect the right of *all* Congo factions to some degree of self-determination, *all without violation of the Charter injunction against intervention.*

The result was, of course, that no stable supporting coalition could be found for any one of these aims, since many conflicted with the national attitudes and purposes of the members. I suggest that if Hammarskjöld had opted for the expulsion of the Belgians, the exclusion of others, and the unification of the Congo, without going out of his way to make an issue over nonintervention, he would have had a stable coalition supporting him, including the bulk of the Afro-Asian states, the Soviet bloc, some Europeans, and the United States. He would have had to sacrifice the support of Britain, France, and Belgium—and this he was unwilling to do. Without a stable coalition there can be no continuity in attachment to subgoals and hence no feedback. Since the overall UN objective was not operational in the first place, though it may have been "shared" at a meaningless level of generality, such an ideology is likely to remain a heroic exercise in futility.

Chapter II

COMMUNICATIONS

II. COMMUNICATIONS

II. Communications

THE political import of messages, at least in the narrowest sense, has never been ignored. The legendary status of the Ems dispatch, the Zimmerman telegram, and the Khrushchev letters in the missile crisis all attest to this. Since von Ranke, the fine points of diplomatic history have hinged on the paper torrent from official archives. But this by no means exhausts the subject of political communications. First, the media of communications themselves have become more complex, less confined to the written word. Political scientists now lay equal, perhaps greater, weight on informal face-to-face communications of a kind never later embodied in official records. United Nations studies have profited from the lesson of Congressional research, that the cloakroom conference often outweighs in significance all of the exchanges of papers. The semi-parliamentary character of the UN allows the interviewing and observational techniques developed in legislatures to be applied to an international milieu.

Second, the purposes for which communications are studied have themselves altered. Initially, historians looked to the exchange of messages among heads of state and diplomats for what their content could disclose about events: to establish chronology, determine motivations, and compare competing accounts of the same circumstances. That this information was contained, let us say, in diplomatic dispatches was incidental, important only as a warrant of authenticity (save for the relatively few souls interested in the development of diplomacy itself). For many purposes, content is still more important than form, but increasingly behavioral scientists accept the validity of Marshall McLuhan's dictum that "the medium is the message." [1]

Increasingly, the search is for the functions communications provide for a political system. This unquestionably reflects the enormous repercussions of cybernectic theory on fields of inquiry far removed from engineering. As the eighteenth century was given to seeing reality as a series of clockworks, contemporary science represents reality through the metaphor of the computer, its main constituent being "informa-

[1] Marshall McLuhan, *Understanding Media* (New York: McGraw-Hill, 1965).

tion."[2] What then is "information"? It is "a name for the content of what is exchanged with the outer world as we adjust to it, and make our adjustment felt upon it."[3] "We" can be the editorial "we" of the individual, or it can be an organization or state. The important common thread here is that information provides the link between actor and environment. Note also that Wiener's definition suggests reciprocity: adjustment to the world and the impact that adjustment has on the world. This suggests the key concept of "feedback," or the effect incoming information has on future decisions. For example, a weekend sailing enthusiast wishes to steer his craft around a headland and in light of this objective and what his visual inspection of the situation relays in the way of information, he sets a course. Midway through the maneuver, however, he finds that were he to continue on his planned course, he would fail to clear the rocky obstruction. On the basis of this new information, he revises his course and goes merrily on his way. In other words, his original decision when implemented provided additional information that permitted mid-course correction; information kept flowing or "feeding back" from steersman to environment to steersman.

Insofar as the United Nations system is concerned, we can discern three salient ways in which information enters in. First, the UN has become a new factor in international diplomacy, and diplomacy itself is the exchange of messages. Diplomats, as some not among their admirers have been heard to remark, are glorified messenger boys. They are more, of course, but their function as bearers of the ruler's messages came first. In ancient times and among primitive peoples today, the envoy has this as almost his sole duty. The world diplomatic community serves as the nerves along which much of important interstate contact is maintained. Interestingly, modern means of direct electronic communications have not displaced diplomatic contacts. The Washington-Moscow "hotline" is an exception, arising out of exceptional circumstances. As the UN's own International Law Commission found, norms of diplomatic practice are more widely accepted than almost any other body of international rules.

The United Nations has a kind of clearinghouse function in the world of diplomacy. It is the difference between bilateral and multilateral contact. One unfortunate characteristic of traditional diplomacy was its leisurely pace. Even the prelude to World War I, usually portrayed in terms of a world hellbent on destruction, dragged on over

[2] Abraham Kaplan, *The Conduct of Inquiry* (San Francisco: Chandler, 1964), p. 384.
[3] Norbert Wiener, *The Human Use of Human Beings* (New York: Anchor, 1954), p. 17.

weeks. The General Assembly and informal corridor conversations permit many diplomatic contacts to be simultaneously maintained, an essential task at a time when decisions bearing on war and peace must for technological reasons be made much faster than the traditional diplomatic procedures that might hold them back. The United Nations has also contributed to the development of multilateral treaties, such as the outer space treaty, which would have been exceedingly difficult to negotiate and secure signatures for in the absence of a permanent collectivity of the world's diplomats.

This communications function portrays the United Nations as a passive participant, opening its facilities to as many nations as care to use them. The UN is also a complete communications system in its own right, and that is the second major function. Like any large organization, the UN has its hierarchical side, embodied in the departments and bureaus of the Secretariat. The situation is complicated by the problematic relationship between the Secretary-General and the General Assembly and Security Council, the ambiguous relationship between the latter two organs, and the essentially autonomous character of affiliated agencies like UNESCO. Most often attention has been focused on the Secretary-General's position in this bewildering sea of countervailing forces. As the section on recruitment and socialization indicates, the Secretary-General presides over a bureaucracy staffed multinationally and hence prey to the conflicting loyalties that may exist under such circumstances.

Third, the United Nations forms a communications system with its environment, and this is perhaps the most important communications function of all. The UN, though formed by its member-states, yet seeks an identity greater than the sum of the parts. In this it shares a characteristic in common with organizations of all kinds, a desire to perpetuate itself. Further, the substantive areas of its concern make mandatory interaction with the larger environment. An international organization preoccupied with its own internecine conflicts ceases to be of any value to the political stability of the world. In a sense, all the United Nations does outside its own chambers and offices is a kind of message.

Some activities, like technical assistance, are manifestly attempts to communicate new ideas. But other, non-verbal acts have a latent communications function, whether or not it was foreseen. We are only now beginning to see the extent to which actions convey messages. UN peacekeeping activities, wherein the organization is most assertive, cannot help but convey messages concerning the role of the organization. If the UN limits its activities to discussion, it communicates by omission to those who believe it is "just a debating society" (although as we shall see the true functions of debate have been obscured and misunderstood). In sum, then, every interaction in which the UN participates is a potential communication with its larger environment; even what it does not do, relative to commonly held expectations, communicates something. The second aspect of communications—the UN as a self-contained system—often merges with organization-environment communications. To the extent that media of communications, from diplomatic to newspaper dispatches, pick up and amplify what in their absence would be purely intraorganizational messages, they perform a conversion function, turning everything the organization does at every level into unintentional messages to the environment.

One advantage a communications approach has is that of emphasizing patterns of behavior we have long been aware of but never endowed with much significance. Like much of contemporary political science, this research penetrates the veil of appearances to examine the political purposes of the most mundane activities, tending in the process to deemphasize the formerly prominent study of documentary material. A case in point is the Alger article, drawn primarily from interviews with national delegates. The proximity in which delegates find themselves serves as a school in multilateral diplomacy, from which the delegates graduate to high positions in their national governments. Here communications and socialization intertwine. By the very attempt to inculcate its own norms and procedures in new members, the UN, largely unintentionally, communicates new diplomatic norms on a global basis. The socialization experiences of delegates become messages to the environment, not only in their dispatches home but in their actions when they leave the UN to return to more conventional policy-making posts.

Alger's data also suggest that the organization tends to be less structured than the diplomatic communities in national capitals. Contact extends across ranks and, even more important, between most countries whose traditional relationship with one another has been hostile (Israel and the Arab states constitute the major exception). The parliament-like milieu and the exceptional range of contacts provide an information flow to the outside vastly greater than the more ritualistic and insular contacts in national capitals.

Much attention has been paid to the content of resolutions, but Petersen suggests that the content generally reflects as broad a consensus as possible and in any case that the resolution is subordinate in importance to the "legislative" battle which preceded its adoption. This points up the hitherto ignored significance of debate: as a means of embarrassing the opponent, as a vehicle for addressing publics outside, as a psychological mechanism through which a delegate can symbolically express feelings of tension to a captive audience. Visitors to Washington are frequently perplexed by the sight of a Senator declaiming before a few dozing colleagues and a gallery of tourists. The prevalence of this behavior pattern in the American Congress and in the UN leaves the implication that the very act of speaking performs functions quite unrelated to the content of the speech.

On its face, the UN's Office of Public Information is more deeply concerned with communications than any other segment of the organization. Gordenker chronicles its largely successful struggle to maintain its autonomy and present scope. The opposition has been largely motivated by concern for organizational economies, save for the ideological antipathy of the Soviet Union. In contrast, the OPI has been able to put together a formidable coalition of its own, made up of underdeveloped states (particularly Latin American); the Secretary-General, defending his area of jurisdiction; press correspondents; and delegates whose speeches the OPI publicizes. Against this broad-based defense, counsels of economy could not prevail. Most interesting of all, one of OPI's most useful weapons has proved to be its assertion that the processing of information depended upon expertise, and only fellow experts could judge performance. This impressive survival record implies that important segments of the UN community felt that they could not tolerate a curtailed information program and that the manipulation of information was not an area with which the untrained outsider should tamper. The entrenched position of OPI follows logically from what we have been saying concerning the importance of information on both an organizational and international level. Far from being a peripheral activity, easily dispensed with, it is the cement that keeps the UN system and a semblance of world community in being.

6. Personal Contact in Intergovernmental Organizations*

CHADWICK F. ALGER

"THE best instrument of a Government wishing to persuade another Government will always remain the spoken words of a decent man." In the nuclear age this observation appears to be even more true than when it was written by Cambon over thirty years ago.[1] If this is a valid judgment there is some cause for rejoicing, since the number of participants in the dialogue between national governments has increased astronomically since Cambon's words were written. Heads of state, foreign ministers, and other cabinet officials as well, no longer consider personal consultation to be extraordinary. The diplomatic generalist has been joined by the economist, physicist, public relations specialist, and experts in virtually every other field of knowledge in the conduct of intergovernmental conversation. Growth in the number of independent nations has brought an increase in the size of the older diplomatic communities and the establishment of new ones. New international organizations have brought a further expansion of the number of sites of diplomatic activity, and old organizations have had increases in membership.

It should not be surprising that this population growth at the sites of face-to-face contact between different nations is not welcomed by all. Men's images of how intergovernmental relations have been organized in the past serve as restraints on change they are willing to accept. This is particularly true of many who have inhabited the diplomatic "villages" of a passing era. They do not find it easy to accept new inhabitants and transients who bring unfamiliar skills and often violate established customs for the carrying out of intergovernmental relationships. Resistance to this change has brought delays both in the integration of new inhabitants at diplomatic sites and in the integration of "new diplomats" into national foreign services.

Out of personal experience in Lend-Lease and the European Recovery Program, as well as study of the European Communities, Cardozo has written of the difficulty that diplomatic communities and national foreign services are having in integrating specialists in international economic programs and representatives to international organizations.[2] For example, he describes the difficulty that representatives to the European Communities encountered in their effort to get diplomatic status in Brussels. His account includes the rather humorous eventual disposition of their attempts to get diplomatic license plates.

[After some difficulty,] the permanent representatives to international organizations received diplomatic license plates, but their numbers started from the top of the list, whereas the diplomats accredited to the Belgian government got theirs from the more prestigious lower end.[3]

[1] J. Cambon, *The Diplomatist* (London: Philip Allan, 1931), p. 112.

[2] M. H. Cardozo, *Diplomats in International Cooperation: Stepchildren of the Foreign Service* (Ithaca: Cornell University Press, 1962).
[3] *Ibid.,* p. 121.

Cardozo deems it necessary to make a plea for broader vision on the part of diplomats, asserting:

They may profit by recalling that reluctant generals ultimately had to accept the tank and the airplane. How much better it would be if the careerists in all fields were the leaders rather than the laggards in developing and accepting the new techniques and training methods that progress demands.[4]

Senator Jackson of the United States delivered a widely noted address on the United Nations in early 1962 which revealed antagonism to the developing role of the United Nations, because it was not consistent with Jackson's image of how international relations should be conducted. He asserted that the United States Mission to the United Nations should be staffed "more as other embassies," dissented from the view that the United States Mission has a "unique role," and objected to the role the Mission is playing by arguing: "The Ambassador to the United Nations is not a second Secretary of State, but the present arrangement suggests a certain imbalance in the role assigned to the UN in the policy-making process."[5] He also objected to the press, radio, and television coverage of the United Nations, observing that "the space and time devoted to our UN delegation does not correctly reflect the relative importance of what is said in New York against what is said in Washington."[6] A similar dissent in Washington from developments in Paris NATO Headquarters was revealed by Sulzberger's explanation of the removal of General Norstad as Supreme Commander Allied Powers Europe. He explained that one of the reasons for removal was Norstad's "belief in the theory that the SHAPE commander was not only an American general but wore fifteen hats as an international Allied servant—a theory discounted by contemporary Washington."[7]

An outburst of negativism toward developments at diplomatic sites of international organizations, particularly the United Nations, has come from some diplomats who have been schooled at more traditional sites. For example, Nicolson, who says he was "born and nurtured in the old diplomacy,"[8] emits an emotional barrage when discussing the United Nations that is quite out of character with the restrained discourses to be found elsewhere in his works on diplomacy. He sees "lobbies being formed among the smaller countries (as for instance between the Asians and the Latin Americans), the sole unifying principle of which is to offer opposition even to the reasonable suggestions of the Great Powers." And he notes that public debate has led to "all rational discussion being abandoned in favour of interminable propaganda speeches."[9] Another diplomat with similar experience, Thayer, writes approvingly of an Italian diplomat's assertion that lobbying at the United Nations brings "hypocrisy" and "blackmail," and asserts that "the UN's parliamentary

---

[4] *Ibid.*, p. 136; see also the report of the Carnegie Endowment for International Peace, Committee on Foreign Affairs Personnel, *Personnel for the New Diplomacy*, especially pp. 54–55, for the most recent commentary on prejudice in the United States Foreign Service against "specialists."

[5] H. M. Jackson, "Do We Rely Too Much on the U.N.?" *New York Times Magazine*, April 1, 1962 (12), p. 110.

[6] *Ibid.*

[7] C. L. Sulzberger, "When and Why the Rug Was Pulled," *New York Times Magazine*, August 13, 1962, p. 24.

[8] H. Nicolson, *The Evolution of Diplomacy* (New York: Collier Books, 1962; first published London: Constable & Co., 1954 and New York: Macmillan, 1955), p. 1.

[9] *Ibid.*, p. 120.

diplomacy somehow lacks the quality of reality." [10] There is no doubt some truth in the comments of Nicolson and Thayer, although their extreme form of statement and almost totally negative appraisal does not engender confidence in their judgments. But one problem with commentators such as Nicolson and Thayer is that they have not dug deeply enough into the social fabric of international organizations. It seems that they are so distracted by their image of what ought to happen at diplomatic sites that they never reach an examination of much that is to be found at a site such as the United Nations.

Some Distinguishing Characteristics of International Organizations

One of the reasons why we have been slow to develop a broad sensitivity to the activity in international organizations has been the tendency to perceive this activity selectively, in the light of certain descriptive terms that highlight differences between more traditional diplomacy and international organizations. Activity in international organizations has usually been characterized as "multilateral" diplomacy in contrast to more traditional "bilateral" diplomacy. It is also described as "public" diplomacy in contrast to the more "private" traditional diplomacy. But the customary usage of these terms suggests only some aspects of the diplomatic revolution that is taking place. Diplomacy at the sites of international organizations is "multilateral" in the sense that meetings take place in which a number of nations participate. But it is important to note that much bilateral diplomacy also takes place at these diplomatic sites. Likewise, "public" meetings of councils and assemblies are important activities at international organizations.

But much of the work done on items on the agenda of these bodies is done in private. And private diplomacy is conducted on many problems that never get on the agenda of councils and assemblies.

Nevertheless, the regular public meetings of multilateral assemblies and councils are a distinguishing characteristic of international organization diplomacy. For this reason Rusk has described the activity of these sites as parliamentary diplomacy. [11] This diplomacy is parliamentary not only in the sense that it involves public debates followed by votes on resolutions, but it also requires the diplomat to perform supporting parliamentary tasks, such as lobbying for resolutions and keeping in touch with a wide range of delegates in order to know both how his resolution will be received and what resolutions others are planning to introduce. Attending meetings and discharging these functions require that the diplomat spend much time moving around the "parliamentary" chambers, extending and maintaining contacts with other diplomats.

A second distinguishing characteristic of international organization diplomatic sites is that each national mission has the responsibility of representing its nation to *all* other nations represented at the site. This is quite a different assignment than that of national capital missions, which represent their nation to the host government and protect the interests of their own citizens in the country in which they are located. It is helpful to view the development of missions to international organizations in historical perspective. From one viewpoint the history of diplomacy reveals a gradual evolution toward the establishment and extension of permanent face-to-face links between national governments. The first

[10] C. Thayer, *Diplomat* (New York: Harper, 1959), p. 112.

[11] D. Rusk, "Parliamentary Diplomacy," *World Affairs Interpreter,* 1955 (26), pp. 121–138.

step took place in the fifteenth century when permanent diplomatic missions in foreign countries began to develop out of temporary missions that had been dispatched for special tasks.[12] The development of permanent missions to international organizations can be regarded as a second important step toward this permanency. This step saw the development of permanent international conferences, or international organizations, out of *ad hoc* international conferences. The new sites joined the old ones to provide more extensive permanent social links between national governments. Dag Hammarskjöld gave the following assessment of the importance of the creation of permanent national missions to the United Nations:

A development of special significance is the establishment of permanent delegations at United Nations Headquarters with standing senior representation there for all members of the Organization. While in one sense reducing the practical importance of the public sessions of the various organs, this development has, basically, tended to give these organs greater real weight in present-day diplomacy. The public debate, and the decisions reached, gain added significance when the attitudes presented in public result from practically uninterrupted informal contacts and negotiations.[13]

A third distinguishing characteristic is that international organization diplomatic sites also have nonnational features not present at other sites. Secretariat officials are likely to be more numerous than national officials. Much has been written about the "quiet dip-

[12] R. Numelin, *The Beginnings of Diplomacy* (New York: Oxford University Press, 1950).
[13] Dag Hammarskjöld, "The Developing Role of the United Nations," *United Nations Review*, 1959 (6), p. 10.

lomacy" of the Secretary-General of the United Nations. But the work of the Secretary-General provides only one dramatic example of the opportunities afforded thousands of other members of the United Nations Secretariat and secretariats of other international organizations in the day-to-day activity of these organizations. Furthermore, the international organization not only introduces nonnational people, but also nonnational corridors, chairs, tables, and buildings. In a national capital contact takes place either on the territory of the host government or in the embassy of the visiting diplomat. But the international organization headquarters is neutral ground. Since there is common membership in the organization and frequent visits to the "clubhouse," the occasions for contact that is unscheduled (although not necessarily unplanned by one or both parties) are greatly increased.

Description of some easily observable characteristics of international organizations whets the appetite for information that might be gathered from deeper probes into their social fabric. For example: (a) Are communication patterns between nations and the kinds of information that are communicated different in international organizations than they are in more traditional diplomatic settings? And, if they are different, do they have any impact on aspects of international relations that we might call significant? (b) What functions do nonnational roles perform? (c) Do participants in international organizations have learning experiences that are significantly different from those acquired in more traditional diplomacy? The remainder of this chapter will be devoted to throwing some light on these three questions. These have been chosen because observational and interview data are available. Though the data are of modest dimensions, they will provide a sounder basis for hypothesis development than a wider-ranging discussion based wholly on conjecture. The three questions also illustrate three ways in which international organizations affect international systems: through reshaping the patterns of inter-governmental contact, through creating new roles that intervene in these relationships, and through changing the experiences of national officials.

Intergovernmental Communications in International Organizations

Superficial knowledge of international organizations reveals that participation in them brings extensive changes in intergovernmental communications. In international organizations some nations have continual access to each other that have very slight opportunity for contact elsewhere.[14] The opportunity for interaction between Paraguay and Nepal in the United Nations would offer a striking example. The consideration of a common agenda by virtually all nations in an international system encourages the creation of new coalitions around certain issues. An example would be cooperation in the United Nations between Latin Americans and Afro-Asians on economic development questions. When new coalitions are created around certain issues, they establish new communication networks. The analysis that follows reveals that the creation of international organizations transforms intergovernmental communications in terms of the amount of contact between diplomats, the mode of contact, who communicates with whom, and what is communicated. Discussion will be based on the writer's personal observations at the United Nations over a number of years and responses to a question-

naire administered by Best in 1960 in an effort to assess more systematically hypotheses that developed out of these observations. In these interviews a randomly selected member of each national permanent mission to the United Nations was asked to make comparisons between the United Nations and national capital diplomatic sites.

First, respondents were asked about the amount of contact they had with diplomats from other nations. Responses to the question, "As compared with a post in a national capital, here at the UN do you personally have more contact or less contact with diplomats from countries other than your own?" were distributed as follows:[15]

	Number	Percent
Much more	27	35
More	40	51
Same	6	7
Less	4	5
Much less	1	1
TOTAL	78	99

Clearly, diplomats at the United Nations have more (or feel they have more) contact with diplomats from other nations, in part because they have fewer responsibilities for citizens of their own nations. Best found the following comment by an Eastern European delegate to be "typical of the majority of all delegates" interviewed:

The contact that you have here with other diplomats is ten or twenty times more than that which you would have in a national capital. This is especially true during the Assembly sessions. You have contacts every day and not with just one person, but rather with many per-

[14] See C. F. Alger, "Decision-making Theory and Human Conflict," in E. B. McNeil, Ed., *The Nature of Human Conflict* (Englewood Cliffs, N.J.: Prentice-Hall, 1965), pp. 274–294, for fuller discussion.

[15] The following table, and all subsequent tables in this chapter, are reprinted from the unpublished doctoral dissertation of the late Gary Best, by permission of the author's parents, Mr. and Mrs. Donald Best.

sons. Between sessions, there is still more contact here with diplomats from other countries than there would be in a national capital.[16]

The mode of contact was also investigated by asking: "As compared with a post in a national capital, here at the United Nations would you personally be more likely or less likely to communicate orally with representatives of other countries?" The following responses were obtained:

	Number	Percent
Much more	7	9
More	55	73
Same	13	17
Less	0	0
Much less	0	0
	—	—
TOTAL	75	99

It is not only the sharing of UN headquarters that encourages increased oral contact, but also the fact that UN diplomats perform a different kind of role. One diplomat replied:

In Washington you have few opportunities to meet diplomats from any other country than the U.S. You even meet those from the U.S. infrequently and by appointment. When you do meet someone from another country, such as India, you have nothing in particular to talk about. In Washington, if I were to ask an Indian about some aspect of Indian relations with the State Department, this might be considered improper. Here you can ask an Indian his position on any problem.[17]

It is likely that contact between diplomats at the United Nations is predominantly face-to-face, although interview data are not available to docu-

ment this observation. This contact is at its highest peak during the three months in which the General Assembly is in session. The Assembly's seven committees, which are all committees of the whole with 114 nations represented in each, meet simultaneously throughout the September to December period. Some delegates sit next to each other for three months and engage in long discussions while public debate is in progress. Almost all delegates participate in the public debate in these committees and many participate in the concurrent lobbying, drafting of resolutions, and exchange of ideas that take place in pairs and small groups in the committee rooms, in the corridors, and in missions. Many continue these conversations at the bar in the delegates' lounge and in the delegates' dining room, and at cocktail parties and smaller gatherings. The public debate of the Assembly provides the impetus for much of this activity, but it is only a part of the total dialogue. Though not at such a frenzied pace, the network of conversations continues at United Nations headquarters throughout the year as subcommittees of the Assembly, the Councils and their subcommittees, and sometimes additional sessions of the Assembly itself meet. Even when the Assembly is not in session 51 percent of the members of permanent missions go to United Nations headquarters three or more times a week and 82 percent go twice a week.[18]

Respondents not only judged that they had more personal contact with diplomats from other nations at the United Nations, but also indicated that communication patterns are different in some interesting respects. Because of the considerable attention that the literature on diplomacy has given to diplomatic rank, delegates were asked: "As compared with a post in a national capital, here at the UN would you

---

[16] *Ibid.*, p. 121.
[17] *Ibid.*, p. 132.

[18] *Ibid.*, p. 98.

110   COMMUNICATIONS

to communicate with another delegate
without regard for diplomatic rank?"
The distribution of responses was:

	Number	Percent
Much more	10	13
More	53	70
Same	11	14
Less	2	3
Much less	0	0
TOTAL	76	100

Delegates indicated that the most important reason for increased contact across ranks is the fact that people of differing ranks sit on the same bodies of the United Nations, making contact across ranks a practical necessity. For example, a diplomat who had previously served in London remarked:

> Such contacts are much easier here. If an attaché and a minister are both concerned with the same program here, they will communicate with each other frequently. They will talk almost as equals. This would be unheard of in London. In fact, here very few people even know the ranks of other people with whom they are working. In London, you would definitely know the rank of someone before you communicated with him.[19]

Best also learned that diplomats find it easier to make contact with representatives of unfriendly countries at the United Nations than is the case in national capitals. The respondents were asked: "As compared with a post in a national capital, here at the UN would you personally be more likely or less likely to have contacts with delegates from an unfriendly country?" Their replies were:

	Number	Percent
Much more	10	14
More	54	77
Same	6	9
Less	0	0
Much less	0	0
TOTAL	70	100

Quotations from two respondents indicate that both the meetings of United Nations bodies and more informal occasions provide the opportunity for increased contact between diplomats from unfriendly countries:

> Sometimes we vote for a Soviet resolution and sometimes the Soviets vote for one of ours. The negotiations leading to these votes bring about contacts between the two delegations.

> I would be far more likely to talk to Hungarians here than I would in a national capital. Many times this actually happens quite accidentally. You'll be talking with a group of delegates and one will just happen to be a Hungarian.[20]

It was found that contact between unfriendly countries did not extend to all unfriendly dyads; one exception mentioned was contact between Arabs and Israelis. However, some governments actually instruct their delegates to have contact with diplomats from unfriendly countries in the United Nations while at the same time instructing their diplomats in national capitals to the contrary.

Contact across ranks and between unfriendly countries are only two ways in which an international organization such as the United Nations alters patterns of communications that exist outside the organization. While serving on subcommittees, cooperating on a resolution, and sitting next to each

[19] *Ibid.*, p. 125.

[20] *Ibid.*, p. 129.

other in meetings, delegates often initiate contacts that would never be established except for these events. For example, seatmates in General Assembly committees have been observed in conversations that go on for an hour or more and that add up to many days of dialogue during a General Assembly. Such extensive conversations have been observed between diplomats from Hungary and Honduras, from Netherlands and Nepal, and from Afghanistan and Yugoslavia. Perhaps the most intriguing were the conversations of a facile Irish diplomat who alternated between his seatmates on either side— the representatives from Iraq and Israel. It is quite likely that much of this talk is not about business. But it is also most certain that some of it is.

Observers and participants often use the term "informal" to describe United Nations diplomacy. Accordingly, respondents were asked: "In general, as compared with a post in a national capital, here at the UN are your relations with other representatives more formal or less formal?" The responses were distributed as follows:

	Number	Percent
Much more formal	I	I
More formal	2	3
Same	II	14
Less formal	59	77
Much less formal	4	5
	—	—
TOTAL	77	100

Two comments illustrate contrasting attitudes toward the more informal UN society:

There is none of this silly stuff that there is in capitals. . . . Delegates at the United Nations become colleagues.

Protocol is not stiff here. In fact there is no protocol at all. . . . The situation is one of anarchy.[21]

[21] Ibid., p. 135.

Although there was probably no common definition of "informal" on the part of respondents, the 82 percent who believe the United Nations to be more informal tend to corroborate responses obtained on the unfriendly-nations and across-ranks communication questions. There is clearly a feeling of much less restraint on the establishment of contact with other diplomats than is the case at national capital sites.

The interview also investigated the diplomat's perception of the exchange of information at the United Nations. Each diplomat was asked: "As compared with a post in a national capital, here at the UN is it more difficult or less difficult to exchange 'off the record' information with another nation?" The following replies were obtained:

	Number	Percent
Much more difficult	0	0
More difficult	3	4
Same	21	28
Less difficult	41	55
Much less difficult	9	12
	—	—
TOTAL	74	99

The two comments below were made by respondents who thought it less difficult to exchange "off the record" information at the United Nations:

In a national capital when one ambassador goes to visit another ambassador, each knows that the one has come for some specific reason. It's not just a social visit. Here two ambassadors can just begin chatting, and one can find out something from the other without the other person knowing that this was the specific purpose of the meeting.

There is a daily exchange of views that goes on at the UN that would be impossible in a national capital. . . . There was just no such common meeting place in Washington as there is in New York. You couldn't just go down to the State Department and sit around chatting with diplomats from other countries.[22]

Another dimension of the usefulness of the United Nations as an arena for the exchange of information was also explored by asking: "Is your UN mission more important as a source of information than a post in a national capital?" These were the replies:

	Number	Percent
Most important	9	20
More important	25	57
Same	3	7
Less important	7	16
TOTAL	44	100

It is notable that 34 respondents did not reply to this question, with a number feeling unable to compare the two kinds of diplomatic sites on this basis because they considered them to be so different that they found comparison impossible. As one delegate expressed it:

The UN is our best over-all observation post. This is the best place to find out how the general international winds are blowing. However, if our government wanted to know specifically about something that was going on in Paris, it would contact the ambassador in Paris.[23]

One of the qualities of the United Nations as a source of information is the ability of diplomats to contact quickly a large number of countries. As one delegate explained it:

When a piece of news like this takes place it is most useful to just wander through the corridors of the

UN or to stroll aimlessly through the Delegates' Lounge. You can talk with a great number of people from a large number of countries to find out how they are reacting. You can't do something like this in a national capital. There is no building, no meeting place, where all these people would just happen to be. And in very few capitals would there be this many people even present.[24]

In drawing conclusions from these interview data, it is important to bear in mind that they are based on participant perceptions rather than on direct measures of the phenomena under examination. Furthermore, the comparisons between the United Nations and national capitals were all made by diplomats who were at the time active in United Nations roles. A replication of the study with interviews of national capital diplomats would provide additional data that would permit more reliable comparison. While recognizing these limitations, it seems prudent to probe the potential significance of the characteristics of United Nations communications as perceived by participants. The data presented suggest that, when an issue is inscribed on the agenda of a United Nations body, its consideration is not only affected by the rules of procedure and norms for public debate and decision-making, but it is also introduced into a diplomatic community where the norms for intergovernmental contact and intergovernmental information exchange are different than in national capitals.

There are grounds for speculating that intergovernmental communication systems in international organizations bear an important relationship to their capacity for managing conflict. For example, the communication system at the United Nations brings to mind March and Simon's discussion

[22] Ibid., p. 191.
[23] Ibid., p. 188.
[24] Ibid., p. 192.

of "channelling of information" in their summary of the propositions to be found in the literature on *Organizations*.[25] By channelling of information, they mean "limiting the number of organization members to whom any given bit of information is transmitted."[26] The available data on intergovernmental communications at the United Nations suggest that there is less channelling of information at the United Nations than in national capitals. March and Simon assert that: "The greater the channelling of information processing, the greater the differentiation of perceptions within the organization."[27] Fanelli reports a strikingly similar finding:

. . . to the extent that the individual is cut off from significant interaction with others he is likely to develop "private" (as opposed to "shared") frames of reference which effectively limit his grasp of social reality.

Extending this idea to the community situation under consideration here, we suggest that high communicators . . . are likely to perceive the community in a different way than do low communicators.[28]

March and Simon find that differing perceptions of reality are one of the causes of conflict. This suggests that the United Nations communication system would tend to diminish conflict that is based on differing perceptions of reality.

The greater amount of face-to-face interaction at the United Nations permits the communication of additional information through gesture, facial expression, and tone of voice. It also permits a variety of opportunities for feedback in parliamentary debate, small negotiation sessions, and impromptu encounters in corridors and lounges. Leavitt and Mueller offer experimental evidence that both face-to-face contact and feedback resulting from opportunity to ask questions provide a receiver with a better understanding of what a sender is trying to communicate.[29] They also report that when there is opportunity for feedback both "the sender and the receiver can feel, correctly, more confident that they have respectively sent and received accurately."[30] This suggests that conflict generated by inaccurate communications and also by lack of confidence in communication systems would tend to be diminished at the United Nations.

Related also are Kelley's findings in the study of communication in hierarchies.[31] He found that "communication serves as a substitute for real upward locomotion in the case of low status persons who have little or no possibility of real locomotion."[32] Hermann has proposed the application of this proposition to international organizations, suggesting that providing a place "for smaller and developing countries to become high communicators, makes them better able to endure a status position which otherwise can be modified by peaceful means only by a rather long process."[33]

---

[25] J. March and H. Simon, with H. Guetzkow, *Organizations* (New York: Wiley, 1963).

[26] *Ibid.*, p. 128.

[27] *Ibid.*

[28] A. Fanelli, "Extensiveness of Communications Contacts and Perceptions of the Community," *American Sociological Review,* 1956 (21), p. 443.

[29] H. J. Leavitt and R. A. H. Mueller, "Some Effects of Feedback on Communications," in A. P. Hare, E. F. Borgatta, & R. F. Bales, Eds., *Small Groups* (New York: Knopf, 1955), pp. 414–423.

[30] *Ibid.,* p. 414.

[31] H. Kelley, "Communications in Experimentally Created Hierarchies," *Human Relations,* 1951 (4:1), 39–56.

[32] *Ibid.,* p. 55.

[33] C. Hermann, "Some Findings on the Nature of Communication Relevant to International Organization," Unpublished paper, Northwestern University, 1961, p. 17.

Nonnational Roles

Though there is much truth in the often repeated assertion that an international organization is nothing more than a composite picture of member nations, this is not entirely true. International organizations have nonnational roles that are performed both by members of secretariats and by national officials. These nonnational roles have limited capacity for affecting international relations, because they operate under the scrutiny of bodies made up of national representatives. Nevertheless, they comprise a social structure that intervenes in relations between national roles from different nations. Discussion will first focus on national diplomats who perform nonnational roles, followed by consideration of the more widely publicized nonnational roles of members of secretariats. Information has largely been obtained through personal observation and discussion with United Nations diplomats.

NATIONAL OFFICIALS

The parliamentary framework of intergovernmental relations in the United Nations, and in other international organizations as well, requires that national officials assume a variety of nonnational roles. Efforts to make collective decisions in committees with as many as 114 members stimulate the aggregation of national interests, division of labor, and the assignment of leadership roles. Some of the roles that are created to serve those purposes, such as those of officials in committees of the General Assembly, are filled by election or formal appointment. In other cases more informal selection takes place, such as the selection of those who serve as intellectual leaders of the diplomatic community, as facilitators of agreement, and as representatives of a number of nations in negotiations. All of these nonnational roles

help to make the social structure found at the United Nations more elaborate than that found in national capitals. They make the United Nations and other international organizations more than a society of national officials and secretariats.

The three kinds of more informal roles that were mentioned above will be discussed first: facilitators of agreement, representatives of a group of nations, and intellectual leaders.

A United Nations diplomat may facilitate the reaching of agreement by mediating between two conflicting points of view or by helping to find common ground in a body that has such diverse tendencies that it may be unable to take any action at all. Mediation efforts range from casual individual initiatives in lounge and corridor to more formal sessions in which certain representatives are asked by representatives from other nations to meet singly or jointly with conflicting parties. An example of how national and nonnational roles can be played by the same person was provided in the Special Session of the General Assembly on peace-keeping finance in 1963. The major issue was the apportionment of expenses for the Congo and Suez peace-keeping forces among the members. The Soviet bloc and the French objected to any apportionment at all, saying that the expenditures had been incurred in operations that violated the Charter. Most of the remainder of the membership acknowledged their responsibility but split into two groups with differing views on how the expenses should be apportioned. On one side was a small number of developed nations who would be asked to provide most of the money required and on the other side were the less-developed nations who controlled well over a majority of the votes. Each group preferred methods of apportionment more favorable to the kind of nation in its group. In order to get the necessary money and also the required number of votes, a compromise between the two groups was necessary. An agreement was negotiated in a ten-nation group made up of two teams, five representatives from the developed nations and five from the less-developed nations. A Canadian representative served as chairman of the negotiation sessions and is given much credit by both sides for helping to mediate points of difference between them. However, he also served as a forceful Canadian spokesman and would at these times tell the group that he was stepping out of his role as chairman. In addition, he was chairman of the developed nation negotiating team.

Delegates may also attempt to facilitate agreement through refusing to take a stand in the early stages of debate, in the belief that it is necessary for some to hold aloof so that they are available for mediation. At the same time they may be working hard privately, encouraging others to introduce resolutions and perhaps even writing resolutions for them to introduce. Willingness to accept public anonymity, and even anonymity so far as some of their colleagues are concerned, may permit delegates to exert considerable influence by selecting the one who will take the public initiative on a given item and perhaps even by writing his speech and resolution. Such strategies may, of course, be used as more effective means of advancing national policy than public debate. For example, the United States may decide that certain proposals it wishes to make will be more likely to get a sympathetic hearing if introduced by a small nation rather than by the United States. On the other hand, delegates at times deprive themselves of the opportunity to advance the preferred policy of their own nation in the interest of advancing what seems to be the most feasible basis for general agreement.

Diplomats may also represent a number of nations in negotiations with other diplomats. In one instance in a General Assembly committee in 1962, two diplomats from Western nations met with representatives of Afro-Asian nations in an attempt to arrange a compromise between a resolution favored by the Afro-Asians and Western amendments. The Western diplomats undertook these negotiations not as representatives of their *own* nations but as representatives of a *group* of nations, having the power to commit other Western nations to a compromise within certain specified limits. This successful effort was the conclusion to an intriguing parliamentary drama in which one of the Western negotiators had actually participated in the writing of the Afro-Asian resolution. This was done with the desire to get a moderate Afro-Asian resolution introduced early in the debate that would have sufficient backing to head off possibly more extreme drafts. When other Western nations would not support the resolution, this diplomat then attempted to salvage as much of it as possible through representing the West in negotiations that produced a compromise. In this case the Western diplomat, who played so important a role, was never associated publicly with either the Afro-Asian resolution, the proposed Western amendments, or with the eventual compromise. He played a very minor role in the public debate, and, therefore, he left no public record of his efforts. In fact, only some of the committee members were aware of his significant part in the eventual compromise solution.

Some diplomats become intellectual leaders in certain problem areas because of the information they possess and are able to bring to bear on problems at hand. This superior knowledge may be explained by a variety of factors: long tenure, the importance of a problem area to the diplomat's government, his personal interest, or perhaps his experience on a UN subcommittee or special mission that studied the problem in detail. The possession and effective use of information enables some diplomats to exert greater influence than others in United Nations bodies.

Examples of this kind of role are provided by some of the members of the twelve-man Advisory Committee on Administrative and Budgetary Questions, who review the Secretary-General's annual budget before it is presented to the Administrative and Budgetary Committee (Fifth Committee) of the General Assembly each fall. With rare exceptions, the recommendations of this committee are accepted by the General Assembly. Members of the twelve-man Advisory Committee, who serve on it as individual experts, subsequently play prominent roles in the General Assembly committee on matters that have been examined in the Advisory Committee. In the General Assembly committee they speak more than other members, and their advice is often sought. In a study of the Advisory Committee, Singer describes the "Two-Hat Problem" that results from persons serving both as experts on the Advisory Committee and as national representatives on the larger body.[34] He quotes Trygve Lie's assertion, when he was Secretary-General, that "membership in the Advisory Committee should disqualify a person from service as a member or alternate in the Fifth Committee." Lie saw danger in a situation where Advisory Committee members "also represent their Governments, as representatives or as advisers, in the [General Assembly] . . . where they act as advocates for the Advisory Committee, or may argue or vote against its recommendations."[35] On the other hand, the participation of Advisory Committee members in the Fifth Committee gives

[34] J. D. Singer, "The United Nations Advisory Committee on Administrative and Budgetary Questions," *Public Administration,* 1957 (35), 395–410.
[35] *Ibid.,* p. 402.

them opportunities for injecting their more thorough knowledge of many committee issues into private and public General Assembly debate. They would not have such opportunities if they did not wear two hats.

Thus far the discussion has been about what might be called *ad hoc* roles that are exercised in connection with specific agenda items or problem areas. In addition, there are roles to which diplomats are elected by their colleagues, such as that of chairman, vice-chairman, and rapporteur of committees, and President of the General Assembly. These roles are generally exercised with considerable detachment from national roles by diplomats from all regions of the world. The chairman of a committee, for example, normally satisfies even those from countries unfriendly to his own that he has tried to give a fair hearing to all and has not steered debate in ways advantageous to his own nation. One reason a chairman finds it necessary to do this is that retaliation for unfair treatment could be quickly applied in other bodies where diplomats from other nations have the chair. But it is also the case that unfairness might wreck the proceedings of his own committee by encouraging unnecessary argument and wrangling. This route is avoided, it seems, because there is a desire on the part of chairmen and other elected officials to be recognized as good performers. As a result, chairmen are concerned with such things as getting through the agenda on time, having a full list of speakers for each meeting, and getting resolutions in on time. Thus, the institutional norms for a "good" chairman cause diplomats to behave much differently than they would if sitting at their country's seat in the body concerned.

Diplomats are also called upon to fill other nonnational roles when small groups are asked to draw up recommendations or reports for the consideration of larger bodies. Examples of such tasks are visiting missions to colonial territories and the Committee on Contributions of the General Assembly which recommends how the expenses of the United Nations should be apportioned. Involvement in such tasks seems to have an effect on the behavior of national delegations when reports are submitted to the parent body. Participation provides a delegate's government with new information that may affect policy. Furthermore, there is a tendency for national delegations to support reports and recommendations for which their own diplomats share some responsibility. For example, possibly because of preoccupation with the India-China border dispute, the Indian delegation was most inactive in the Administrative and Budgetary Committee of the General Assembly in 1962. However, when the Committee on Contributions made its report, suggesting a formula for making budgetary assessments on members, the Indian delegation became quite active in efforts to obtain support for the report. This appeared to be related to the fact that the Committee on Contributions' report was presented by its Indian chairman, a former Indian Ambassador to the United Nations.

Though there is evidence to indicate that United Nations diplomats handling both national and nonnational roles are adept at wearing more than one hat, there is also indication of stress between different roles that are being handled by one person. For example, during recent private negotiations in the United Nations General Assembly, in which a few delegates were trying to find a solution acceptable to the entire Assembly, a delegate said to me: "If some of our governments knew in detail what we are doing here, we would be fired." William J. Goode draws attention to the fact that "conflicting [role] strains fre-

quently result in changes in the social structure." [36] It is clear that the nonnational roles that national diplomats perform at the United Nations are bringing change in the intergovernmental social structure, though as Goode concludes, "whether the resulting societal pattern is 'harmonious' or integrated, or whether it is even effective in maintaining the society, are separate empirical questions." [37]

The nonnational roles held by national officials at the United Nations would appear to integrate the membership through developing capacity for making common decisions. It has been described how occupants of these roles help to aggregate diverse interests around a common policy and how they sometimes provide information and standards of judgment that are independent of any particular national interest. In addition, the exercise of these roles by national officials permits them to inject new information and perspectives into their own national systems. Sometimes their involvement in an international enterprise brings their government to support an activity that they might not otherwise have supported. Thus, there is some indication that the exercise of nonnational roles has an effect on national policies.

SECRETARIAT

Secretariat roles at international organization diplomatic sites have received more attention than nonnational roles occupied by national diplomats. Interest is usually focused, however, on certain dramatic activities on the part of high secretariat officials, such as mediation efforts of the Secretary-General of the United Nations in the Cuban crisis of 1962 and the Suez crisis

[36] W. J. Goode, "A Theory of Role Strain," *American Sociologial Review*, 1960 (25), 483–496.
[37] *Ibid.*, p. 494.

of 1956. But the functioning of secretariats, like that of national missions, also includes the continuous participation in an intergovernmental society by hundreds and sometimes thousands of international civil servants engaged in a multitude of activities. It is this aspect of the performance of secretariats that will be considered here.

As members of a secretariat take part in the daily life of an international organization, they provide a continuous flow of messages into its society. They (a) inform others of past practice and accepted norms of the organization, (b) provide background information through documents and the spoken word, and (c) serve as nonnational monitors of relations among national representatives and of the health of the organization. Like some of the nonnational role activity of national diplomats, much secretariat activity is more effective if few know about it.

Secretariat officials, along with national diplomats having long terms of service in an international organization, serve as reservoirs of knowledge on past practice and accepted norms in a variety of ways. One example that can be publicly observed in the case of the United Nations is the support provided by the secretariat during public meetings. On the dais of a General Assembly committee the chairman, a national diplomat, has on one side of him the undersecretary responsible for secretariat activities on the problems being debated and on the other side a committee-secretary provided by the secretariat. Committee chairmen change each year, but there is considerable continuity in the undersecretary and committee-secretary posts. There is also continuity in the staffs that assist these officials and sit behind them on the dais. Even if a chairman has served in the committee on previous occasions, he has not had experience in guiding the work of the committee and must rely a great deal on experienced members of the secretariat when the intricacies of both substance and procedure are faced.

The chairing of a General Assembly committee thus becomes a cooperative project between secretariat and chairman. Particularly crucial is the function of the committee-secretary, who helps the chairman keep an eye on the pace at which the committee is handling its work; maintains a list of delegates having indicated a desire to speak; prods those who have not yet signed up to do so, if they intend to speak; and encourages those intending to propose resolutions to submit them. During meetings the conversations between chairman and committee-secretary are frequent. Their cooperative judgments about committee pace can be important to final outcomes on issues. To push an item to a vote too soon may stop the private negotiation that takes place alongside public debate in any parliamentary body before it achieves a fruitful consensus. To fail to close debate at the appropriate time may permit an existing consensus to disintegrate during subsequent public argument. Committee-secretaries play a role in these decisions. In the rapid interaction that takes place as a committee reaches the point of decision on an agenda item, the committee chairman sometimes neglects to turn off his microphone before consulting his secretary. On one occasion the meeting room of a General Assembly committee echoed the hurried advice of a committee-secretary to his chairman: "Have them vote now!"

An important part of the role of any secretariat is the gathering of information on substantive issues for the use of the councils and assemblies that it services. This pool of information may be considerable. In the case of the United Nations, the documentary product is often more than participating diplomats can consume. Secretariats thus are common information agencies for participating nations, thereby tending to increase agreement on what the facts are and what the significant problems are. H. G. Nicholas, in *The United Nations as a Political Institution,* asserts:

> The collection, ordering and providing of information at the points where it is most needed and can produce its greatest effect is one of the most important services that U.N. officials discharge. It is much more than an archivist's or statistician's function; it is political in the highest degree, calling for qualities of political judgment and forethought no less than of accuracy and integrity.[38]

The documentary product of the secretariat is particularly important for the small national missions which cannot afford research staffs. Information is not only provided in documents, but also in a continual round of discussion between secretariat and national diplomats, in lounges and corridors, in secretariat offices, and during public meetings. Two United Nations diplomats have written:

> Many international civil servants have better technical qualifications for discussing some of the subjects within the jurisdiction of ECOSOC than do the government representatives attending particular meetings. It is sometimes difficult to avoid feelings of inferiority on the part of delegates, and of superiority on the part of the Secretariat caused by a misunderstanding of the nature of their functions.[39]

On occasions the secretariat provides nonnational pools of information that erode away some of the more extreme information products of national governments. An example has been the information supplied by secretariat and national diplomats who have gone to colonial territories on visiting missions. Information provided both by nations administering territories and by nations attacking their colonial administrations has received effective challenge by information collected under United Nations auspices.

There are a variety of ways in which secretariat personnel can act as nonnational monitors of an international system represented in an organization. This may simply mean correcting a message garbled in transit between two nations, or making certain that antagonists stay in contact through the good offices of the secretariat. Secretariats cannot always help, do not always seize all opportunities, nor do they act with desired effect in all situations. But the nonnational element they provide in the continuing conversation in an international organization is different than the contribution of any nation. From their nonnational posture they sometimes see undesirable consequences of certain projected actions that more partisan diplomats do not see in the heat of battle. They are a continuing source of suggestions on how things might be done. Not infrequently there is an available national diplomat willing to take credit for advancing their ideas. On occasion the "suggestions" of the secretariat may consist of texts of resolutions and have even included speeches introducing resolutions.

This brief discussion of secretariats has highlighted some of their less publicized, though not necessarily less significant, contributions. In particular, it has demonstrated that secretariat participation in the political process in international organizations is not confined to the dramatic mediation or "quiet diplomacy" of a few high-ranking officials. Many members of secretariats are also vital participants in the

[38] H. G. Nicholas, *The United Nations as a Political Institution* (New York: Oxford, 1959).

[39] J. G. Hadwen and J. Kaufmann, *How United Nations Decisions Are Made* (New York: Oceana; Leyden: A. W. Sythoff, 1962), p. 21.

continuous debate and discussion in which national officials are engaged. Because of their tenure, expertise, and detachment (from national roles), they are able to exert influence on decisions. In this respect they have an impact on policy in much the same way as members of national bureaucracies.

Like national officials who also occupy nonnational roles, members of secretariats can also occasionally inject information and perspectives gained in their roles into the foreign affairs apparatuses of their own nations. While from one viewpoint it may be regretted that the national origins of members of secretariats may inhibit loyalty to an international organization, national affiliations permit secretariats to have lines of communication to resident national diplomats that are at times quite useful. On some occasions contact between secretariat officials and national diplomats is looked upon with suspicion. One occasion received much note in the press when the United Nations Undersecretary for Political Affairs, a Soviet citizen, passed several notes to the Soviet representative during a Security Council meeting. The assumption by the press that the Undersecretary was engaging in improper conduct was never supported by information about the content of his messages. There could be alternative explanations of his behavior. For example, he could have been communicating information consistent with his UN obligations but which the Soviet delegate would not have deemed reliable had it come from a secretariat official of any other nationality. This is a kind of role not peculiar to international politics. Executives in the U.S. government sometimes serve as useful links to officials in their native states. For example, it might be recalled that Assistant Attorney General Louis F. Oberdorfer, an Alabaman, helped to mediate the Birmingham racial dispute in May 1963.

There has been much discussion of the importance of developing loyalty to international organizations on the part of secretariats and of national officials who assume such posts as President of the United Nations General Assembly. In addition, there is naturally concern that they have necessary *expertise* on substantive questions. It is, indeed, crucial that occupants of these roles not receive instructions from governments and that they have a high degree of substantive *expertise*. But the preceding discussion reveals that these are not the only necessary attributes of effective performance of nonnational roles. Particular attitude and skill requirements must be appraised in the context of social processes in which nonnational roles are involved. Technically competent and loyal secretariats can achieve little without the development of a high degree of consensus, on specific issues, among member nations. This requires the continual redefinition of the interests of particular nations in the context of the developing interests of other nations. Observation indicates that nonnational roles encourage the development of consensus through the part they play in linking nations in a common political process. Though it may in some ways seem paradoxical, the nationalism of the occupants of some nonnational roles may provide indispensable links between this political process and national governments.

It is sometimes forgotten that bureaucrats in many settings are, to some degree, representatives as well as experts. The performance of the United States Foreign Service, to use a national bureaucracy example, has been appraised with suspicion and severely criticized by legislators and citizens from other areas of the United States because it recruits a disproportionate number of its officers from a few Northeastern schools. In response, the Foreign Service is intensifying recruitment in other areas and is also encouraging officers to spend their leaves among the people in their native states. It is hoped that this program will extend the links between the implementation of United States foreign policy in the field and the population throughout the nation. Is it reasonable to expect that links between secretariats and their constituent national governments are any less important?

Learning Experiences of Participants

The flow of information, patterns of contact, and exercise of and contact with new roles provide new kinds of experiences for participants in international organizations. The members of national missions are, like members of all diplomatic missions, extensions of national bureaucracies. However, broader geographic scope of contact, more numerous discussions with diplomats from other nations, and perhaps exercise of nonnational roles require them to see a broader panorama of the world than before. Members of secretariats have similar experiences, usually with more intense effect, because of their greater independence from the governments of their own nations. The learning experiences of individual participants in an international organization are a factor that contributes to the quality of its society. The images that participants acquire of the organization itself and of the international system that is represented in it affect the communication patterns that these individuals establish and the kind of social environment that they help provide for other participants. In addition, when these individuals move on to other roles, probably elsewhere in their national governments, they may apply their learning at other sites.

Addressing themselves to the effects of participation in the United Nations, two career diplomats wrote as follows, after serving for several years in the missions of Canada and the Netherlands to the United Nations:

In the U.N. . . . the word "diplomat" is rapidly losing its old connotation of elegance and wealth. As the U.N. security services have noted, "It is difficult to tell the delegates from the visitors." Thus the U.N. has had an effect even on the appearance of U.N. delegates, and by its methods of operation possibly on their characters. There is no doubt that the personal and parliamentary experience which delegates get at the U.N. may have long run consequences of value to the international community.[40]

B. F. Matecki offers a supporting observation when he mentions "the profound changes that the personal contact of members of United States delegations to international institutions has wrought in their thinking and outlook."[41] He also cites examples in which United States delegates have, as a result of changed attitudes, been able to get United States policy changed.[42] Alexander Dallin writes the following about Soviet officials:

While there are wide variations, one gains the impression that Soviet personnel stationed at the U.N.—be it with the U.S.S.R. mission or on the United Nations staff—tend to be more practical and pragmatic in outlook than those in the "home office"; at times, they seem less concerned with doctrine than with success. And while it is easy to exaggerate such nuances, there are occasional suggestions of different perceptions of reality.[43]

The writer has investigated the dimensions of learning experiences acquired through participation in the United Nations by means of inter-

[40] *Ibid.*, p. 54.

[41] B. F. Matecki, *Establishment of the International Finance Corporation* (New York: Praeger, 1957), p. 143.

[42] *Ibid.*, pp. 92, 142–143, 159–160.

[43] A. Dallin, *The Soviet Union at the United Nations* (New York: Praeger, 1962), p. 96.

views, discussions with delegates, and by observation. The interviews were conducted in 1959 with twenty-five General Assembly delegates both during the first two weeks of their service in the General Assembly and two months later.[44] The sample includes nine delegates from the Far East, three from the Middle East, six from Europe, three from Africa, and four from the Americas. These delegates all had their first experience in the United Nations during the period between the before-and-after-experience interviews. Thirteen came to the General Assembly from other foreign affairs posts (eight from their respective foreign offices and five from overseas posts). Of the remaining twelve, three came from other government posts, four were parliamentarians, and five were private citizens.

The interviews revealed that, after only two months at the United Nations, the participants were aware of an expanded number of issues and nations. Of the twenty-three who were asked to select an agenda item for discussion, only seven felt able to do so on the pretest. At least eleven of the twenty-three, and probably more, did not feel informed enough to discuss an agenda item. However, all delegates but one were willing to discuss an agenda item with the interviewer in the posttest, providing evidence of change from very little information on certain issues to greatly extended knowledge. A dramatic example of expanded awareness was the delegate from a Middle East foreign office who indicated that he had never even heard of some of the African countries that his committee discussed. As an example, he cited the North and South Cameroons, still dependent territories at the time. He indicated that he now knew "how they emerged, what factors

concerning them have political significance, and what the role of various blocs is in relation to such countries as these."

Scattered throughout the interviews are occasional comments by delegates in which they indicated surprise at positions taken by other nations on certain issues. An Eastern European delegate was surprised to find that the Scandinavian nations sometimes "lined up with the colonial powers" on colonial questions. An African delegate from one of the newer countries was extremely surprised to find that the United States voted with his nation on the South West Africa issue. A Far Eastern delegate who had served in his foreign office for twelve years was surprised to find that the white dominated nations of the Commonwealth did not vote as a bloc in his committee.

Several commented on the value of learning about the problems of other nations and the effect of the policies of their own nation on these problems. A number of delegates volunteered comments on how informative it was to hear delegates from other nations explain their policies and viewpoints. Two United States congressmen who have served in the General Assembly have written of their estimate of the effect of the exchange of such information on individual viewpoints:

One reason for the importance of these contacts was that many delegates coming from distant countries, relying on their own press and on diplomatic channels for their background information, frequently did not understand why the United States took the position it did on many issues. In a surprising number of instances, delegates altered their views on matters under discussion after acquiring additional background as a result of talks with representatives of the United States and of other nations.[45]

[44] For a full report on these interviews, see C. F. Alger, "United Nations Participation as a Learning Experience," *Public Opinion Quarterly,* 1963 (27), 411–426.

[45] A. S. J. Carnahan and W. H. Judd, Re-

Although the interview did not have a question on the point, four delegates emphasized the importance of opportunities to establish face-to-face contact with officials of other nations. At the end of his interview a Western European delegate volunteered this statement:

On my committee men come year after year, and friendly relations continue despite disagreement over policy. It is very important that people in international conferences know each other well. It permits the reaching of compromises. One has choices of many kinds of words for stating the same thing in either very polite or very rash words. With friends, you are more likely to use friendly words. Therefore, it is useful to have friends negotiating in international conferences.

Some delegates had seen some nations as negative stereotypes whose policies were grossly simplified and exaggerated. Under these conditions face-to-face contact in the United Nations is much like other intercultural exchange in which "contact will provide richer and more accurate information about other people and will show them to be much like members of one's own group." [46] Not all stated the effects of face-to-face experience as dramatically as an African delegate who said of the delegations of some nations: "It has helped me to realize that they are, after all, human beings." Although the interviews were not designed to test the proposition, evidence gathered in the interviews and

other information available leave little doubt that participation in the United Nations expands the number of nations as well as the number of issues of which the delegate is aware. Interview material suggests that this awareness extends the number of nations and number of issues in which the delegate feels involved and sometimes for which he even feels some responsibility. There is also evidence to indicate that there is sometimes a change in the delegate's affective map of the world, that is, in whom he designates as the "good guys" and the "bad guys." As the positions of nations become known on a wider range of issues, it becomes more difficult to evaluate these nations as being either all good or all bad.

Thus it appears that participation in an international organization tends to give the participant a more extensive and more realistic image of the system of nations represented and perhaps a feeling of more extended involvement.[47] The intergovernmental society in the organization provides a microcosm of this system that enables the delegate to see the total system in operation, look into the faces of officials from all its units, and direct words to those faces and see and hear their response. In the United Nations he may feel that 113 other nations are too many to contend with at one time and might wish not to try, but he is nevertheless continually reminded of their presence. Delegates from all countries have votes, and delegates from countries he might consider insignificant may have influence by virtue of talent or elected post. The "good guys" are not always voting with him and the "bad guys" sometimes are. Thus the pointed walls of

port on the Twelfth Session of the General Assembly of the United Nations. U.S. House of Representatives, Committee on Foreign Affairs, 85th Congress, 2nd Session, House Report No. 1611. (Washington: U.S. Government Printing Office, 1958), p. 3.

[46] D. Katz, "The Functional Approach to the Study of Attitudes," *Public Opinion Quarterly*, 1960 (24), p. 193.

[47] Cardozo concludes that experiences of national officials serving as permanent representatives to the European Communities "have made them likely to be more devoted to international cooperation than many of the officials with whom they deal in their own government departments." Cardozo, *op. cit.*, p. 108.

certitude that isolate the "good" and "bad" may be eroded round. In the interviews, a Norwegian parliamentarian stated: "I will go back with a clearer view of the fact that my nation belongs to the whole world."

Interviews with General Assembly delegates, before experience in the body, also revealed considerable ignorance of how the General Assembly operates. One revelation of this was the posttest question that asked how experiences in the General Assembly were different than had been expected. Three delegates indicated that they had had no clear expectations at all; two of these were from foreign offices. Of the twelve who experienced differences from what they had expected, three delegates from smaller nations were surprised at the prominent roles small nations play in the Assembly. A parliamentarian had thought that the General Assembly "would be a forum for speeches." But during his Assembly experience, he found that "draft resolutions involve a good deal of lobbying and negotiation." He had "had no idea of this." A delegate from a foreign office found that "things that go on in the corridor seem more important" than he had anticipated. Ten of the twenty-five responded that their experiences were no different than expected. It was remarkable to find, however, that one of these had said in the pretest that his duties would not differ much from his obligations in the foreign office, while in the posttest he said that his duties in the General Assembly were much different from those in the foreign office.

In responses to other questions, there was some indication that participation in the General Assembly would permit more effective use of the United Nations by governmental posts at home. A delegate whose permanent post was in a foreign office said that he would now be able to suggest policy for his nation's General Assembly delegation "that can really be carried out." A del-egate from another department of the government said that "before I came I knew that there were committees and I knew the general organization, but I didn't know precisely what they were doing and how things were done. Now I know procedure better, and this will enable me to make better recommendations to the Foreign Office." The interviews revealed initial lack of information, vagueness, and even erroneous information about how the United Nations actually operates on the part of General Assembly delegates, some of whom were in positions in which they could directly affect their nation's United Nations policies.

Finally, material in these interviews and more general discussion with United Nations diplomats suggest that participation permits diplomats to learn social skills that they did not have before. For example, a career foreign service officer said: "It made me more tolerant of long speeches." Some adaptation is required to develop the patience and perspective necessary for handling a problem in the context of 113 other nations instead of just one. Pursuing national objectives and collecting information as a mobile "parliamentarian" requires a quite different pattern of behavior than most diplomats have engaged in before. It may be significant both that these new skills are learned and that they are learned in a society whose norms are the product of the combined participation of representatives from most national governments of the world.

Conclusion

In the introduction to this chapter, it was pointed out that some of the terms used to describe activity in international organizations, such as "multilateral" and "public," offer only partial images of these institutions. Material drawn from interviews and personal observations at the United Nations has been presented as evidence supporting this assertion. After explicating how international organizations affect intergovernmental communications, we suggested some potential consequences of these effects for international conflict. Following description of nonnational roles in international organizations, it was indicated how these roles provide a social structure that helps to link nations in a common political process and how these roles have subtle effects on national policies. While reporting on the broadened perspective of the international system and the new social skills that are acquired by participants in international organizations, it was indicated that these learning experiences contribute to the distinctive milieu of international organizations. Since most officials who participate in international organizations eventually move on to other posts in their national governments, these learning experiences are later fed directly into governments.

On the basis of these three probes into the social fabric of one international organization, more general conclusions will now be drawn as a contribution to the development of international organization theory. An international organization is a microcosm of an international system that is created through involving representatives from national governments in parliamentary-like activity. These microcosms differ from the international systems they represent, however, in that they are in some respects more like small societies and parliaments than international systems. Participants in the organization learn about the other units in the system primarily through direct contact with human beings rather than through indirect means. Communications are less like those usually found between large organizations and more like those within decentralized organizations or in parliaments. This not only permits the development of new contacts and an increase in quantity of communications, but also extends the kinds of informa-

tion that can be exchanged, permitting greater "off the record" exchanges.

International organizations are also more than microcosms of international systems in that they become new units in these systems. Not only do they develop norms for intergovernmental communications and for the development of consensus that are different from the rest of the system, but they also have an array of nonnational roles that become involved in intergovernmental relations. There is a body of permanent officials who participate in the definition of norms and in monitoring intergovernmental relations. National officials are also co-opted into nonnational roles. One important way in which international organizations are different from nation units is the fact that they overlap these units. The exercise by national officials of international organization roles is one manifestation of this overlap. It is important that what Guetzkow calls an "exclusiveness norm" does not inhibit national officials from performing nonnational roles in the way an exclusiveness norm inhibits an individual from serving two national governments at the same time.[48] Since the existence of a relatively small quantity of overlapping memberships is one of the distinguishing characteristics of international systems, this feature of international organizations attracts our attention. Overlapping group memberships have been cited by a number of writers as restraints on intergroup conflict.[49]

[48] H. Guetzkow, *Multiple Loyalties: Theoretical Approach to a Problem in International Organization* (Princeton: Center for Research on World Political Institutions, 1955), p. 61.

[49] For example, see M. Gluckman, *Custom and Conflict in Africa* (New York: Free Press, 1955), pp. 4, 68, 74; M. Fortes and E. E. Evans-Pritchard, *African Political Systems* (New York: Oxford, 1940, reprinted 1961), p. 14; and R. Williams, *American Society* (New York: Knopf, 1951), p. 531. For fuller discussion of the relevance of overlapping group memberships to international relations see C. F. Alger, "Non-Resolution Consequences

Participation in international organizations tends to produce national policies that are responsive to total systems represented in organizations rather than policies responsive to individual units. Effective response to the parliamentary decision-making milieu of an international organization creates pressure for greater decision latitude on the part of representatives in international organizations. This suggests that there are pressures on nations that participate in international organizations for responsiveness to the external environment that are in some respects greater than those in more traditional diplomatic relations. Max Beloff supports this line of speculation when he concludes, after examining recent developments in British participation in foreign affairs:

In bilateral negotiations national objectives are pre-determined; the object of negotiation is to reconcile those of one party with those of the other, by compromising, where necessary, on their respective demands. In multilateral negotiations, the national interest cannot be settled in advance, but is worked out co-operatively in a "seminar" atmosphere, more like that of an interdepartmental committee. One of the features of the new type of multilateral negotiation is that one can never be certain what is going to come up next. This makes detailed instructions on tactics impossible.[50]

of the United Nations and Their Effect on International Conflict," *Journal of Conflict Resolution*, 1961 (5), pp. 139–140; "Comparison of Intranational and International Politics," *American Political Science Review*, 1963 (57), pp. 417–418; and "Hypotheses on Relationships Between the Organization of International Society and International Order," *Proceedings of the American Society of International Society and International Order*

[50] M. Beloff, *New Dimensions in Foreign Policy: A Study in Administrative Experience, 1947–1959* (New York: Macmillan, 1961), p. 176.

Senators Hickenlooper and Mansfield also offer supporting evidence in a report to the Senate after serving in the United States delegation to the United Nations General Assembly in 1959. They complained that the links between Washington and New York cause United States participation to be "cumbersome and slow to respond to changing situations." They concluded:

If policy is to be pursued effectively in a General Assembly which includes over 80 other nations—nations whose differing views as well as the idiosyncrasies of their representatives must be reckoned with—the Ambassador and the members of the permanent mission must have a measure of freedom for parliamentary maneuver.[51]

The foregoing suggests that the character of the intergovernmental society in an international organization may have important bearing on the capacity that the organization has for handling international problems. The addition of such a society to an international system greatly increases the number of intergovernmental linkages and provides a different kind of milieu for contact. The occasions for exerting influence on other governments and for responding to other governments are greatly increased. International organizations, such as the United Nations, therefore, increase the size of the "influence pie." This is similar to Likert's finding, in the study of business organizations, that more productive departments were characterized by "greater amounts of reciprocal influence" between managers and subordinates.[52] This is made possible because

[51] B. B. Hickenlooper and M. Mansfield, Observations on the United Nations. U.S. Senate. 86th Congress, 1st Session, Senate Document No. 26. (Washington: U.S. Government Printing Office, 1959), pp. 6–7.

[52] R. Likert, *Influence and National Sovereignty* (Ann Arbor: Institute for Social Re-

both leaders and members *"learn more complex and different forms of social interaction."* [53] Likert indicates that his findings may have relevance for international relations, suggesting that the "sovereignty pie" (a synonym for "influence pie") may be increased in the same way.

In handling problems, the United Nations not only offers decision-making bodies, such as the Assembly and councils, but builds an intergovernmental society around a problem. When a problem arises, such as the Congo or

search, University of Michigan, 1960) (Mimeographed).

[53] *Ibid.*, p. 11.

the financing of peace-keeping operations, this society is continually active on the problem, whether more formal bodies are in session or not. It facilitates continual adjustments in national policies, tending to substitute a host of small adjustments for extraordinary confrontations that require adjustments of great magnitude. Thus, relations are conducted more through a host of capillaries and less through a few main arteries. When a problem eventually reaches the public arena in the Assembly or one of the councils, the outcome will be importantly shaped by the nature of the intergovernmental society that has developed around the issue.

7. The Uses of the United Nations*

KEITH S. PETERSEN

THE uses of the United Nations are closely related to its processes. What the United Nations does, after a decade and a half of experience, is heavily influenced by the way it does it, and vice versa. Furthermore, there is increasingly a general UN "way," rather than a series of related but separate powers, procedures, and jurisdictions of the main organs as indicated by the Charter. The processes, and the purposes, of the General Assembly and the Security Council, for example, have become more like each other's in the 1960's than the framers of the Charter apparently intended. If these purposes, and the areas of UN activity in which they are primarily sought, are to be better understood or predicted, the related processes must be looked into. If these processes are increasingly similar among the various main organs of the UN, an analysis of the processes of

any one should suffice. By common agreement the role of the General Assembly has become the most critical. It is the behavior of that body that will be emphasized here.[1]

The following analysis will describe the nature and tactics of the Assembly's general process in recent years. It is based on the two assumptions indicated above: that this process is now basically similar to that of almost any other UN political organ and that the uses to which it is put, and with what success, are in part determined by the mechanics of the process itself. A few examples of Security Council activity will be cited along with those from General Assembly experience, and the

* *The Southwestern Social Science Quarterly,* Vol. 44, No. 1, 51–61. Reprinted by permission.

[1] Many of the examples of General Assembly action to be cited below are drawn from direct observation of them during my tenure, 1958–1959, as the Rockefeller Fellow for the Study of International Organizations at the World Affairs Center for the United States (now the Foreign Policy Association-World Affairs Center) in New York City.

relationship between procedure and purpose will be touched upon and then discussed more extensively. It is hoped that the analysis will show the relationship not only between what the operating UN mechanism is and what it is used for, but also between both of these and the types of issues to which they are most frequently applied. The overall argument may be briefly stated in advance. The United Nations process is most conducive to parliamentary debate and public appeal; the rewards of these types of endeavor are therefore most commonly and fruitfully pursued; they have been best and most easily achieved in the general area of what may be called "colonial" issues, to which UN attention has been increasingly directed.

The Points of the Product

There are numerous points and purposes to the UN process. One of them is obviously the resolution itself, with the passage of which the consideration of any given agenda item almost always terminates. It is the final point, of course: the official product that is aimed at. Hardly ever is it the most important or meaningful point. The content of a resolution, furthermore, may frequently embody either one of two misrepresentations. It may seem, or pretend, to do what it cannot do, or it may simply record an agreement which the UN itself did not achieve.

Resolutions which pretend beyond their capacity are always among the most bitterly debated and generally controversial of an Assembly session. They are frequently statements of disapproval (as, for example, of the government of Hungary in 1958 for suppression of the 1956 revolt) or, less commonly, of approval (as, again in 1958, of the alleged "willingness of the Provisional Algerian Government to negotiate" with France). Either way, pass or fail, they have practically no effect. The resolution on Hungary was adopted in 1958; the one on Algeria was not. The situation in either location was not immediately affected by either result. A similar verdict may perhaps be reached on the Security Council's more recent condemnation of the "disturbances" in the spring of 1960 in the Union of South Africa.[2]

Ineffectiveness does not deter these resolutions from being passed, or from being justified. The record is a long one, and may be sampled at random. On 3 December 1953 the Assembly adopted a resolution, over Soviet dissent and neutralist abstention, expressing its "grave concern at reports . . . that North Korean and Chinese Communist forces have, in a large number of instances, employed inhuman practices against the heroic soldiers of forces under the United Nations Command in Korea . . ." and condemning the commission of such acts "as a violation of the rules of international law and basic standards of conduct and morality."[3] In a press conference statement the same day, chief United States delegate Henry Cabot Lodge argued the usefulness of the resolution by asserting that it "has accomplished these things: It has proved that our charges of Communist atrocities in Korea are true . . . [It] has reaffirmed that civilized standards of conduct cannot and

[2] This was in reference to the so-called Sharpeville Massacre of 23 March 1960. The Council resolution "called upon" the government of South Africa "to initiate measures aimed at bringing about racial harmony based on equality." United Nations Document (hereafter: UN Doc.) S/4300, Security Council, Official Records (hereafter SCOR), 15th Yr., Supp. for April, May and June 1960, pp. 1–2. The resolution was adopted by vote of 9–0 with two abstentions (UK and France), SCOR, 15th Yr., 856th Mtg., p. 13.
[3] General Assembly Resolution (hereafter: GA Res) 804 (VIII), General Assembly, Official Records (hereafter, GAOR), 8th Sess., Supp. No. 17, p. 54. The resolution was adopted by vote of 42–5, with 10 abstentions, GAOR, 8th Sess., Plenary Mtgs., 467th Mtg., pp. 417–418.

must not be impaired even in the face of a movement of world reaction called communism which seeks to destroy these standards." [4]

Mr. Lodge may be pardoned for this vehemence in advocacy of his own case. Whatever this resolution may have achieved, it manifestly did not demonstrate that "civilized standards of conduct *cannot* . . . be impaired." One may question equally the conclusion that they must not. Even the assertion that U.S. charges are hereby somehow "proved" to be "true" is not above serious doubt. Nevertheless, the condemnation of certain national actions has nearly always been one of the uses of the UN. As long as there are majorities to vote them, there will be moralistic indictments of alleged or actual misbehavior, indictments with little noticeable effect.

Resolutions, secondly, which record pre-existing agreement or achievement are a different matter. They are themselves perhaps of two sorts. The first expresses a sentiment already widely held, even before a resolution is drafted, or one about which there may have been no disagreement from the very beginning. This type is illustrated by a 1958 resolution on the second UN Conference on the Peaceful Uses of Atomic Energy, which was adopted by a vote of 77–0, with no abstentions.[5] It had seven sponsors: Brazil, Canada, France, India, the Soviet Union, the United Kingdom and the United States. Whatever these seven could agree upon would doubtless get done in world affairs whether embodied in the language of a UN resolution or not. In this first type, in other words, neither the content of the resolution nor even the making of it is very relevant to the result achieved.

In the second method of registering

agreement, the process, or the pressure, of making a resolution is of considerable significance, whether the language finally employed is of any particular consequence or not. The 1958 resolution on Cyprus, for example, simply expressed the Assembly's "confidence" that "continued efforts" would be made to settle the problem.[6] Those efforts were made and the problem was settled. It must be admitted that the Assembly resolution neither accomplished that result nor even described it. But the Assembly session provided at least the convenient stage setting for the serious private negotiations upon which the final settlement was based, and the resolution may have brought some pressure of time and events on the holding of them.

A similar instance apparently occurred in the 1960 Assembly. One of the items on this session's agenda was "the problem of the Austrian minority in Italy." On 27 October the Special Committee unanimously adopted a draft resolution on the wording of which the Italians and Austrians had just previously agreed. It pledged both parties to resume bilateral talks to try to resolve "all differences" between them, but added that if such talks did not produce satisfactory results within a "reasonable period" then the parties should consider recourse to the International Court of Justice or "any other peaceful means of their own choice." The problem, of course, was not hereby resolved nor could it be guaranteed under these procedures that it would be. But both parties got something that they wanted (the resumption of talks for Austria, reference to the Court for Italy) that UN endorsement could give and each was prevailed upon to accept the equal gain of the other. Although the outcome remained to be seen, the arrangements as described in the res-

---

[4] *New York Times,* 4 December 1953.

[5] GA Res. 1344 (XIII), GAOR, 13th Sess., Supp. No. 18, Vol. I, p. 60. For the official record of Assembly action see GAOR, 13th Sess., Plenary Mtgs., 791st Mtg., p. 605.

[6] GA Res. 1287 (XIII), GAOR, 13th Sess., Supp. No. 18, Vol. I, p. 5. The resolution was adopted without objection. GAOR, 13th Sess., Plenary Mtgs., 782nd Mtg., p. 458.

olution were immediately afterwards "praised privately by some delegates as a concrete success in United Nations diplomacy." [7] The United Nations always provides an opportunity for, and sometimes it adds a little public pressure to, the conduct of private conversations and the achievement of negotiated settlements. When good results are achieved, resolutions can easily be composed with which either to describe or to record them.

The vast majority of UN resolutions, however, at least on matters at all controversial, neither pronounce vigorous indictments nor register a final settlement. They try, rather, to express as wide a consensus as may be possible in as vague or watered-down terminology as may be necessary. The essence of the UN mechanic is not that one faction's position is accepted and the other's rejected. No outright victory is usually gained. In reaching agreement on the final language of a draft resolution, division of the difference is much more typical.

There are innumerable examples of this. The Assembly's Fourth, or Trusteeship, Committee was considering at one point in its 1958 session a resolution which would "invite" UN members who administer "non-self-governing territories" to work toward the abolition of racial discrimination in those territories. One of its paragraphs *"noted"* the *"inadequate* nature of information transmitted [by administering powers] on human rights." [8] A British amendment would have changed the provision to read: "Noting the *desirability* of providing more *complete* information on human rights." An Indian counterproposal suggested the substitution of "necessity" for "desirability" and "adequate" for "complete." After about seven hours of argument over a two-day period on this and numerous other dis-

puted provisions in the same resolution, the committee at last adopted a complete compromise text. Its "preambular paragraph #2" finally read: "Noting the *need* for providing more *adequate* information on human rights." [9]

This version was of course much closer to the Indian counterproposal than to the first British revision; India was, after all, speaking for the committee majority. But British objections had shifted the emphasis of the provision from negative (as it was in the original draft) to positive: it was the difference between admitting having transmitted *in*adequate information and being asked to transmit *more* adequate information. The substantive point involved is, admittedly, as insignificant as any that concerned the 13th General Assembly. But the tactics of semantic compromise by mutual erosion are sharply revealed. They pervade the UN process.

What would seem to have been an example of the same kind of thing emerged from Security Council meetings in May of 1960. On the 18th of May the Soviet Union requested an urgent meeting of the Council "to examine the question of aggressive acts by the Air Force of the United States of America." This was in consequence of the incident of the U-2 "spy plane," downed over Soviet territory on the 1st of May. The Council first met to consider this complaint on the 23rd. On the 26th a Russian draft resolution "condemning" the alleged "incursion" was defeated and the Council went on to consider a relatively innocuous 4-Power resolution recommending, in-

[7] *New York Times,* 28 October 1960.

[8] UN Doc. A/C.4/L.565. Italics have been added throughout the account of this incident.

[9] The final decision was taken, indicatively, without vote and without objection, i.e., unanimously; this was done in the afternoon meeting of 4 December 1958. For the official summary record of these arguments, which agrees in substance but not in all details with the eyewitness account offered here, see: GAOR, 13th Sess., 4th Cmtte., Summ. Records, 828th to 830th Mtgs.

stead, that "the governments concerned . . . seek solutions of existing international problems by negotiation or other peaceful means."

This resolution was finally adopted by the Council on the 27th, but only after the rejection of Soviet-proposed amendments and the addition of certain revisions by the sponsors themselves. One of these last inserted the words "general and complete" before the word "disarmament" in the original draft, thus giving recognition to the recent Russian slogan on the subject, while counterpacifying the West with the addition of the word "effective" to the words "international control." According to a newspaper report "the revision was designed to avoid a Soviet veto that might have been applied to the original text." [10]

The veto was avoided. The resolution was adopted with nine votes in favor and two abstentions (Russia and Poland).[11] Once again, conflicting demands for different versions had evolved into a compromise of somewhat balanced concessions. It is not especially significant that the resolution finally adopted was essentially irrelevant to the U-2 incident which apparently occasioned it and to which it made no specific reference at all. The point is that this was the wording

of a policy position, no matter how remotely related to the original issue, upon which agreement could be reached. The UN usually struggles mightily to achieve consent and consensus. It will ordinarily do this at the sacrifice of precision, forthrightness, and even relevance. UN resolutions are less defeated than debilitated.

It is for this reason that the resolution itself is hardly ever the crucial point of the UN process. It is the getting there that counts. The "parliamentary" battle and its tactics are generally of much greater consequence than the "legislative" victory and its results. This, it has been argued, is largely because the victory is usually a compromise, or even a standoff, and its results are substantially nil. The battle itself and the way it goes are the real achievements of the UN process and are the purposes for which that process is really used. The following such uses of the UN process—these are essentially procedural purposes—may be isolated and noted.

The Points of the Process

One of the most important objects of this character is to score what may be called "debating points." These may very well have no effect whatever on the substance of the issue at stake, but are satisfying to their maker and embarrassing to the opposition. These achievements are their own reward. An example of this may be seen in the First, or Political, Committee's argument in 1958 over the establishment and composition of a new special committee on the "peaceful uses of outer space." There were two draft resolutions presented—one Soviet and one American—which contained conflicting lists of prospective members for this committee. Just before the final vote was taken, however, the Soviet draft was withdrawn. The reason given for withdrawal was a sly and masterful understatement: because,

[10] *New York Times,* 28 May 1960. For complete, official record of Security Council debates and votes, see SCOR, 15th Yr., 857th through 863rd Mtgs. The Russian draft resolution, UN Doc. S/4321, is quoted in SCOR, 15th Yr., 857th Mtg., pp. 18–19. It was defeated by 2 votes in favor (Poland, USSR), 7 against, and 2 abstentions (Ceylon, Tunisia). *Ibid.,* 860th Mtg., pp. 16–17. The original 4-Power draft is contained in UN Doc. S/4323; Soviet sponsored amendments to this are UN Doc. S/4326; the revisions made by the sponsors in their own draft can be determined by comparison of UN Doc. S/4323 with UN Doc. S/4328, which is the text of the resolution as finally adopted. See SCOR, 15th Yr., Suppl. for April, May and June 1960, pp. 13–14, 18–19, and 22–23.

[11] SCOR, 15th Yr., 863rd Mtg., pp. 7–8.

Russian delegate Valerian Zorin explained, "it could not be adopted unanimously." The point is that the United States draft could not be adopted unanimously either. When the vote on it was finally taken the committee adopted it by 51–9, with an impressive total of 21 abstentions.[12] By pushing its eventually winning membership slate to a vote the United States had clearly incurred the disgust and displeasure of a substantial minority in the committee who were dissatisfied with this outcome. This would have happened anyway. The Soviet representative's carefully invidious statement of withdrawal had merely underlined the point a little more heavily.

It was a point worth underlining. Neutralist sentiment in this debate, most sharply expressed by Indian delegate Krishna Menon, had been that of "a plague on both your houses." Neutralists were irritated that neither side would give in sufficiently to establish a compromise-membership committee on which both would serve. The Soviet gesture represented the preference of the neutralists that if such an agreement could not be made it would be better to have no new committee at all. The Russians had nothing to lose; their own slate could not have been adopted in any event. But they had increased the psychological loss to the United States by emphasizing American callousness and futility in voting what Zorin called its "mechanical majority" in the Assembly and not getting an effective committee on "the peaceful uses of outer space" anyway, since neither Soviet bloc representatives nor

neutralists would serve on it. The Soviet bloc had clearly lost the vote. But it had won an important debating point. In this particular issue, such points were practically all there was to win.

Another common purpose of debate for its own sake is to talk not to the assembled delegates but purely for the record—really to address, as it were, the gallery, "world public opinion," or, more likely, public opinion at home. This is a good part of what the Assembly's opening "general debate" is all about. Two fairly obviously points about the operation of the General Assembly may be made in this connection in order that they may be given special emphasis. There is a difference between the work of an Assembly plenary and that of its several main committees. It is in the plenary that "general debate" takes place at the beginning of any given session, and where resolutions are finally adopted, usually at the end. The detailed work of debate on particular issues and drafting of resolutions, on the other hand, commonly transpires in one or another of the seven main standing committees. The first point to be noted about this distinction is that the plenary meetings of the Assembly are generally much better reported—and when available to them, much better attended by the public—than committee meetings. The plenary is inherently a better sounding board than the committee.

Secondly, the location in which the plenary is held is physically more conducive to declamation than it is to discussion, or even debate. This is simply an architectural condition. In the Assembly hall all delegates sit on the main floor facing the same direction. Behind them, and in the balcony above, sits the press and the public. In front of all of these, on a raised dais, is the speaker's lectern. Any delegates addressing the plenary must walk from his seat up onto the dais and turn around

[12] In the afternoon meeting of 24 November 1958. The vote cited here was technically on the critically important "operative paragraph #1" of the US (or 20-Power) draft (UN Doc. A/C.1/L.220/Rev. 1), and was taken by roll call. The draft resolution as a whole was adopted immediately afterwards, by show of hands, 54–9–18. GAOR, 13th Sess., 1st Cmtte., Summ. Records, 995th Mtg., pp. 245–246.

to face not only his fellow delegates but also the representatives of the press and all members of the immediate public audience. The standing committee, by comparison, ordinarily meets in a "conference room." Here seating is arranged in a double horseshoe with the committee officers located at the open end of it—so that delegates, for the most part, are always facing *each other,* as well as the presiding officer, rather than the press and the public. Furthermore, delegates speak from their seats and remain sitting while they do so.

For both of these reasons—the degree of public attention and the nature of the architectural environment—whatever real public discussion there is in an Assembly session tends to take place in committee rather than plenary meetings. Conversely, the most flamboyant appeals and theatrical posturings emanate from the plenary. An understanding of this state of affairs will place in better perspective the Khrushchev shoe-waving incident of the 1960 Assembly. Not only did it take place in a plenary meeting, but the specific issue involved in the attendant debate was whether or not the consideration of the question of "colonialism" would be assigned to one of the standing committees, as is the usual UN practice, or be continued and completed in the plenary itself. The decision taken next day,[13] was to keep it in the plenary. This was a procedural victory for the Soviet Union, of course. One of its favorite propaganda points—that it is emphatically opposed to (Western European) imperialism—could simply be made much more loudly in the plenary than it could in committee. It was of no consequence, if, indeed, it was not a further propaganda advantage, that the Assembly eventually adopted a declaration on colonialism which pointedly

did not include Soviet-proposed amendments of more extreme language that were voted down one by one.[14] The laying down of these propaganda barrages, whatever the outcome of voting on resolutions may be, has become increasingly a purpose of resort to the General Assembly, and perhaps prospectively, the Security Council. The General Assembly, in particular, and the Security Council have already seen much of this sort of thing in the past. It is reasonable to expect that they both will see more in the future. In either setting, the apparent irrelevance or intransigence of much UN debate should not be misjudged. The prospective audience is always wider than the meeting room.

Still another objective of pure debate may be finally noted: a delegate may be talking, literally, to himself. In doing this he may be seeking only to unburden his personal or national psyche, and he may well succeed. Part of the burden lies in the essentially captive audience. Other representatives may read their newspapers, chat with their neighbors, or even doze in their chairs, but they do not usually walk out. On one occasion in the Fifth (Administrative and Budgetary) Committee in 1958 one delegate was polite enough to warn his colleagues in advance that he would "expatiate at quite some length on the item before us." He did —for one hour and ten minutes.[15]

[13] This was on the 12th of October, 1960. The shoe-waving had taken place on the 12th. *New York Times,* 13 and 14 October 1960.

[14] The Assembly voted for "immediate steps" to be taken toward the complete independence of all remaining trust, non-self-governing, and other colonial territories, and in general, for "the necessity of bringing to a speedy and unconditional end colonialism in all its forms and manifestations." GA Res. 1514 (XV), GAOR, 15th Sess., Supp. No. 16, Vol. I, pp. 66–67. It rejected Soviet proposals for (1) a one-year deadline on this process, (2) automatic inscription of the same item on the 1961 (16th) Assembly agenda, and (3) incorporation of a 14-page Russian declaration on colonialism. *New York Times,* 15 December 1960.

[15] In the afternoon meeting of 18 November

Furthermore, it was extremely tedious talk: full of the self-importance of the speaker and the righteous indignation of his country at having been allegedly insulted by a UN group whose report the committee was then considering. It was a deadly performance. But the man himself felt better personally when it was over and his government's injured pride had doubtless been soothed. How much of a tension-releasing element there is in any formal UN presentation can only be guessed at. The opportunity is certainly open to all. This one illustration of its use may be somewhat extreme in degree. But it does not represent an isolated phenomenon. Either the pacifying or the vaunting of egos, more commonly national or cultural than personal, is clearly one of the functions that the UN performs. It is an important function. It is performed almost continuously.

All of these procedural purposes are self-contained. Their achievement is usually without relationship not only to the particular end product of the resolution but even to the substance of the issue in question at all. A delegation may "score points," or talk to its public, or unburden itself without having the least effect on the outcome of the problem or without even wanting to. Nothing in the real world of actual disputes and practical solutions necessarily happens thereby, any more than it does when some UN organ adopts a resolution of thundering judgment or of weakly worded hopes. Such achievements are not therefore to be denied. They easily may be, and typically are, sufficient unto themselves.

1958. The speaker was Mr. Rueda Vargas of the Colombian delegation. The introductory remark quoted here is not reproduced in the official record, in which the summary of the speech itself covers over five columns of print. GAOR, 13th Sess., 5th Cmtt., Summ. Records, 687th Mtg., pp. 204–207. By comparison, no other speech in this meeting is summarized in more than two columns.

The Outside Effects of the Process

It is perhaps not unusual to concede that the United Nations process may have its own self-contained fascination and possibly even its specific, if mainly incidental, rewards. The further and final contention is advanced, however, that the UN process probably does affect the outcome of particular, concrete problems on which it is brought to bear. It does this in the same way that it arrives at the product of its own resolutions, by incessant erosion, by a perpetual pushing and badgering, especially if one of the parties to the dispute must face an almost permanently and even increasingly hostile UN majority.

The process is especially effective in the area of UN concern with what were earlier labeled colonial issues. Administering powers of trust and non-self-governing territories are called upon in effect to explain every year why they have not yet granted independence to their remaining colonies, or when they will. Wealthy countries are pressed every year to supply larger amounts of development capital on easier and easier terms. Segregationist policies, especially in still colonial areas, are exposed, and must be explained and defended all over again, in every succeeding Assembly session. Defenders, delayers, and explainers grow weary—especially if their case is not particularly a good one, not even by their own lights.

What is more or less inevitable is doubtless therefore hastened by the anxiety of these badgered parties to escape from the relentless pressure of the process itself. The wholesale conversion to independence of the new states of the former French Community in Africa is probably testimony to this. Where the overwhelming anti-colonial majority encounters determined intransigence—as it does, for example, in South Africa—the process is certainly not directly effective, or at least not immediately so. There is indeed always the risk that the majority may delay or defeat its own policy purposes by pushing an extremely reluctant party too hard, pushing it beyond compromise or even contact. The record of the outcome in South Africa remains to be written, and judged.

Some things the UN can scarcely affect at all, even if it should try. This is generally the case with the major issues in the Soviet bloc-Western rivalry, or the Cold War. It can exhibit petulance, or anxiety, or unconcern. It can urge, and hope for, concessions or settlements. It cannot make them. When Mr. Zorin, in a 1958 debate referred to earlier, was presenting the Soviet view on the "peaceful uses of outer space," he dared the United States to set up officially its new Western-majority committee, on which the Soviet Union would refuse to serve, but ominously urged it to remember that it had "no majority of votes in outer space." [16] The UN, as such and by comparison, has no vote at all in outer space. This is a symbol of its helplessness in the impasse between the giants among its own members. It has had virtually no effect whatever on the concrete issues of this nature. It is not very frequently asked even to express its opinion on them. Cold War contestants, of course, use the UN for the same procedural purposes as do parties to any other dispute: to make as many debating or propaganda points as they can, or achieve any of the other incidental results of the

process already described. The UN does not otherwise concern itself with the Cold War, on which it does not expect to have much effect.

It does concern itself with what it thinks it will be able to affect and these are, again, the so-called colonial issues. The argument is no doubt circular, but the evidence of activity is perhaps in part the evidence of effectiveness. Possibly, also, even the incidental rewards of using the UN process may simply be more attractive to the newer, smaller, recently independent States than they are to the established Powers. Since the new States are presumably vitally concerned with "colonial" issues, they might bring these to the attention of the UN whether any directly practical results could be expected or not. There are doubtless many other factors contributing to these inter-related patterns of process and purpose, and of application and success. The argument advanced in these conclusions does not pretend to be all-inclusive. It is intended only to be suggestive of possible relationships which have not been sufficiently investigated or emphasized heretofore.

These, in any event, are uses of the United Nations: to strive conscientiously to adopt resolutions having, usually, no direct consequence; to achieve individual, mostly incidental purposes in this process; and thereby also to affect, over a long period of incessant concern, the actual outcome of some of the disputes considered. These are what, with greatest effectiveness, it is used on: the colonial issues in their political, economic, and social contexts. At least in the short run, they will almost certainly continue to be its major concern.

[16] This was in the Assembly's First Committee debate, 24 November 1958. The official summary record (cited above, note 12) does not contain the quoted remark.

8. Policy Making and Secretariat Influence in the UN General Assembly: The Case of Public Information*

LEON GORDENKER

DURING the annual sessions of the General Assembly of the United Nations the policy and budget of the Office of Public Information (OPI) of the organization have been the perennial center of a complex debate. Instructions first given the Secretariat in 1946 [1] provide some elements of this debate, while others depend on the professional expertise of the international civil service and on its influence and support in a General Assembly divided several ways. As a whole, the outcome demonstrates once more both the durable force of an attractive idea and the truth of the maxim that secretariats have great weight in the policy processes of international, as of other, organizations. For despite repeated debate and attack OPI has proved enduring and resilient.

During the last 15 years the many-faceted program of the agency [2] has shrunk somewhat, to be sure, under the economizer's knife. In particular, it was under unusually severe criticism in 1957, when the General Assembly established an expert committee to investigate UN public information activities, and also in 1958, when the results of the inquiry were discussed. This committee, appointed with the unenthusiastic concurrence of the Secretary-General,[3] and made up of six governmental nominees not all of whom had experience with public information, directly challenged some of the working assumptions of OPI and called attention to difficulties with others. Their report struck a blow, too, at the internal balance of OPI, accused it of substantive failures and urged it to design new programs. OPI's first reaction was defensive; its second, embodied in a paper the Secretary-General placed before the General Assembly, disclosed some organizational changes made in concession to the ex-

* The American Political Science Review, Vol. LIV, No. 2, 359–373. Reprinted by permission.

[1] UN General Assembly Resolution 13 (I).

[2] For a comment on the development of the program, see Robert H. Cory, Jr., "Forging a Public Information Policy for the United Nations," International Organization, Vol. VII, No. 2 (May 1953), pp. 229–242. Each of the Annual Reports of the Secretary-General, published as Supplement No. 1 to the Official Records of each session of the General Assembly, includes a descriptive and analytical section on public information and public opinion.

[3] United Nations, Official Records, General Assembly: Twelfth Session, Annexes, Agenda Item 41, p. 34 (hereafter cited as GA: 12th sess., etc.). The committee was established under General Assembly Resolution 1177 (XII). Its report, dated Sept. 20, 1958, is UN Document A/3928, "Report of the Expert Committee on United Nations Public Information." The committee members were: Robert A. O. Bevan, a British advertising man; Ahmed M. El-Messiri, an Egyptian lawyer and representative at UN meetings since 1948; Enrique Rodriguez-Fabregat, head of the Uruguayan mission to the UN since 1947; P. N. Haksar, director of the External Publicity Division of the Indian foreign office and a lawyer; Louis P. Lochner, veteran American foreign correspondent; and Alexey F. Sokirkin, a Soviet diplomat. UN Press Release ORG/364, March 13, 1958.

perts' report.[4] These responses notwithstanding, the General Assembly probably has not eliminated fundamental contradictions in the UN concept which have troubled OPI since 1946, nor has it overcome the advantages which enable OPI to maintain its organizational identity and stability. The outcome instead illuminates both the problems and the strength of an administrative agency charged with conflicting goals, but shielded by strong leadership at the top and benefited by divisions among its critics.

My purpose here is to show the influence of OPI on the policy-making process of the United Nations and how its policies and organization are maintained uninjured despite repeated onslaughts in the General Assembly. I shall argue that its acknowledged status as an expert body and a program strongly supported by one group of states in a divided General Assembly produced decisions which prevent radical changes in OPI.

I. Contradictory Instructions

The work of OPI has echoed a contradiction written into the UN Charter, the contradiction inherent in confederations. The Charter begins strikingly with a preamble recounting the determination of the *peoples* of the United Nations to seek a peaceful world. It then drops these admirable sentiments in favor of a set of legal obligations and limitations on *states* whose governments may or may not be responsive to these postulated wishes of their peoples.

OPI has always aimed its program at the peoples of the world, not just at their governments. In its first declaration of principles for public information, the General Assembly told the Secretariat that "the United Nations cannot achieve the purposes for which it has been created unless the peoples

[4] UN Document A/4122.

of the world are fully informed of its aims and activities."[5] On this premise the information department was instructed to "... promote to the greatest possible extent an informed understanding of the work and purposes of the United Nations among the peoples of the world." The premise is only as good as the success of the effort called for in the instruction. Less than fully informed peoples of the world must logically lead to a failure of the United Nations.

But after crediting the peoples of the world with holding the life of the United Nations in their hands, the General Assembly delivered a further instruction. OPI was primarily to assist and rely "... upon the co-operation of the established government and non-governmental agencies of information to provide the public with information. . . ." Thus, the Secretariat had to depend on organizations outside of its control to pass along communications. Nevertheless, OPI could "... on its own initiative, engage in positive information activities that will supplement the services of existing agencies . . . to the extent that these are insufficient to realize the purpose

[5] These and subsequent quotations of public information principles are from General Assembly Resolution 13 (I). The resolution itself is brief, containing only the cited material and the remark that the recommendations of the Technical Advisory Committee on Information, which reported to the Preparatory Commission, constitute a sound foundation for the UN public information program. These recommendations were attached to Resolution 13 (I) as an annex and thus adopted by the General Assembly. Establishment of the Technical Advisory Committee had been favored by the Executive Committee of the Preparatory Commission. It was established and its report was adopted by the Preparatory Commission and submitted textually to the General Assembly. Thus, information policy was a concern of the United Nations from its early days. See *Report of the Preparatory Commission of the United Nations* (London, 1945), pp. 89, 102–103.

set forth. . . ." Here OPI again faced a contradiction, for it was clearly to have a marginal role in informing the peoples of the world. But if necessary, it might act on its own initiative. Because it is unlikely that the peoples of any part of the world approach the "fully informed" state on UN affairs, the functions of OPI soon might become as comprehensive as the world was ill-informed.

This was only the beginning of contradiction. OPI also was told not to engage in "propaganda." Distinguishing between public information and propaganda is at best difficult and frequently quite impossible, if propaganda be understood to consist of information fed to a public with the intention of having it adopt given views. The department enjoined from putting out propaganda had already been instructed to promote an informed understanding of the United Nations, whose members had authorized writing into the Charter a determination to "reaffirm faith in fundamental human rights . . . in the equal rights of men and women and of the nations large and small. . . ." Could it then introduce this statement into the Union of South Africa, the State of Mississippi and Soviet Uzbekistan, under the heading of public information? But if not, how could the Charter be understood; and without an understanding of the Charter, how could the UN be understood? Similar questions could be asked about many of the most publicized UN activities, ranging from studies of full employment (controversial in the United States), to self-determination (presumably of high interest in Hungary) and human rights (not uninteresting in the Dominican Republic); from the despairing reiteration by the General Assembly of the need for disarmament (a matter under negotiation between the United States and the Soviet Union) to its condemnation of all propaganda against the peace (an idea with as many meanings as there are definers). If the Secretariat attempted to promote understanding of such activities *without* careful selection of material and location, it would surely be accused by some governments of engaging in "propaganda." If publicity subjects were drawn from among other resolutions of the General Assembly, or *were* carefully adapted to particular areas or audiences, other governments would surely hold that the Secretariat had failed to maintain objectivity.

An attempt by the General Assembly to redefine its injunction against propaganda resulted in renewed insistence on vagueness, for an expert committee declared that the prohibition was not intended to limit OPI in promoting public understanding of the UN. Rather the Office was to avoid ". . . a bias in contradistinction to a policy of strict impartiality and objectivity in the presentation of news and information." [6]

Other instructions vested the main responsibility for formulating information policy in the Secretary-General and the head of OPI, where it has remained. Establishment of branch offices was to be considered. The functions of OPI, it was decided, fell into media categories—press, publications, radio, films, graphics and exhibitions, public liaison and reference. Services to the press were to be provided and pamphlets and other publications prepared. The work of other media was to be encouraged and material provided them when necessary. Also to be considered was the use of an advisory committee.

In carrying out these instructions, OPI strives to put an attractive face on UN activities but usually does not spend much effort in deliberately obscuring disagreeable aspects. The substance of the information disseminated

[6] *GA: 6th sess., Annexes, Agenda Item 41,* p. 53.

appears to fall into two overlapping categories. In the first are reports and announcements of decisions by United Nations organs and the processes by which decisions are taken. For example, OPI spreads information on meetings of the General Assembly and the Security Council. The second category includes the explanation and application of policies determined by the various organs. This covers the work of the Secretariat and other field organizations and the compliance of governments with the policies of the organization. For example, OPI publicizes the character and work of the United Nations Emergency Force and, at the same time, indicates how governments contributing to it have responded to the recommendations of the General Assembly.

OPI employs both facilitative and direct means to spread its message. The "hot" news media benefit mainly from the facilitative part of the program. Working space, documents, television and radio booths, press releases, press conferences and other conveniences, furnished by OPI, help them get the story of United Nations work. Press relations and radio officers guide them through the procedural maze, arrange interviews and offer briefings. Members of the general public, too, receive direct services on visits to major UN establishments. Scholars and "opinion makers" may also receive certain services. Thus, the facilitative functions have a largely indirect effect on the peoples of the world. Only part of the material channeled through the facilitative operations of OPI originates with it; most of it represents the actual work of the United Nations. And, in addition, members of national delegations frequently feed into these channels copies of their speeches, supporting information, other materials and personal appearances. For them, and especially for the smaller delegations, these OPI operations offer important, easily available access to the public.

Direct means by which OPI reaches the public include pamphlets and other publications, prepared radio broadcasts and television shows, pictures and posters and cinema. Much of this material originates in OPI and, while based on UN activities, is produced mainly by permanent officials. The direct means used by OPI represent the major part of its effort to supplement existing means of communication.

The UN Information Centers, manned by OPI personnel in more than 25 locations on every continent, mirror the headquarters activities on a local scale. Their production resembles that of headquarters but in local languages and adaptations; they also distribute quantities of materials from New York. Because they have restricted geographical scope and personnel presumed expert in local practices, they respond more quickly and flexibly to local needs but within instructions received from headquarters. They report to New York on local problems and observations.

II. Criticism in the General Assembly

Fixing OPI in a field between opposed instructions was both the cause and the result of difficulty in the General Assembly. Contradictory instructions provide no rational basis for judging the work of the office. No one could estimate with any accuracy how closely the peoples of the world approach full information on the United Nations, how much supplementary effort would be needed, what was propaganda and where or in what situations more rather than less effort might be needed—and above all how much money should be devoted to such efforts. The OPI nevertheless had to prepare a program and a budget. The General Assembly had to examine it.

Without a clear standard, the examination inevitably fell into confusion.

From the beginning, discussion in the Fifth Committee of the General Assembly, where detailed readings of the budget presented by the Secretary-General take place, tended both to develop general support for the OPI program and also to arouse opposition on the ground that OPI required an excessive proportion of the planned expenditure. By 1948, an enduring pattern of debate had formed. Those governments which stood primarily for economy joined others, which objected to the content of the OPI program, to demand lower information appropriations. They were opposed by a majority, including all the Latin American states and many underdeveloped countries, which supported both the substance of the information program and the budget. Generally, the economy bloc was led by the United Kingdom, which was anxious to preserve its dollar reserves, and had heavy Commonwealth support. The Soviet Union and its allies promptly joined in criticizing the costs and sometimes added specific denunciations of the program. The United States opposed inefficiency and waste but supported OPI. Because OPI had the positive approval of a large number of members, it suffered only slight budgetary cuts.

What reductions were made followed suggestions by the Advisory Committee on Administrative and Budgetary Questions.[7] This body, elected by the General Assembly, at first viewed the OPI proposals with only mild scepticism, pointing out that it was difficult to rationalize the budget of a growing organization. But it soon complained of ". . . the difficulties of proceeding into this field without spe-

cific guidance from the General Assembly concerning the limits of the activities undertaken . . . and the proportion of expenditure for public information to the total budget for the United Nations."[8] The Committee also made clear in 1949 its regret that a serious effort by the economy group to set the maximum expenditure on public information at 10 per cent of the total UN outlay had been defeated.[9] Therefore the Advisory Committee, again declaring that ". . . the proportion of public information expenditures remains too high . . . ," reviewed and shaved individual budget items.[10] OPI lost a post here and a voyage there, a pamphlet here and an edition there, but on the whole succeeded in preserving its original program.

The constant effort to limit the growth of OPI and to shape its form nevertheless bore fruit during 1950, when the Fifth Committee asked the Advisory Committee to look for economies. OPI responded with the declaration that ". . . no further reductions can be made in its expenditures without impairing the efficiency of its services." This meant that the Advisory Committee would have to take responsibility for suppressing or contracting existing services, a move sure to be unpopular with many governments. To an Advisory Committee request for a list of activities together with their priorities, OPI failed, in the opinion of the Committee, to reply in accordance with the spirit and purpose of the Assembly resolution. Although the Advisory Committee insisted that a priority scheme was essential, it nevertheless suggested specific budget reductions but admitted that it had less than

---

[7] For a comment on this body, see J. David Singer, "The United Nations Advisory Committee on Administrative and Budgetary Questions," *Public Administration*, Vol. XXXV (Winter 1957), pp. 395–410.

[8] *GA: 4th sess., Suppl. No. 7, Advisory Committee on Administrative and Budgetary Questions, Second Report of 1949 to the GA,* p. 22.

[9] See *GA: 3d sess., Part I, Fifth Committee, Summary Records,* pp. 300 ff.

[10] *Loc. cit.,* note 8 above, p. 22.

the full factual picture. This it had been unable to obtain from OPI.[11]

OPI shrank from any attempt to lay out formal priorities, a fact which was noticed in the Fifth Committee. A number of representatives endorsed the view of Pun Changprasoet of Thailand that ". . . it was not possible on the one hand arbitrarily to fix the amount of the appropriations . . . and on the other to apply the fundamental principles which had guided the Department during the previous five years." [12] The delegations attacking OPI then joined in establishing a new committee to review OPI activities. The new examining body was an 11-member subcommittee of the Fifth Committee, proposed by Syria to review the guiding principles of OPI and make recommendations to guide the Secretary-General in working out the 1953 budget.[13] Its membership included such critics of OPI as Australia, Czechoslovakia and Syria and such proponents as Chile, Pakistan and the Philippines. Its work during a busy Assembly session resulted in a shorter and clearer statement of principles, which nevertheless contained little of new substance and only two important changes.[14]

The first of these added to the old idea of the need for an informed understanding among the peoples of the

[11] *GA: 6th sess., Suppl. No. 7, Advisory Committee on Administrative and Budgetary Questions, Second Report of 1951 to the GA*, pp. 28–37.

[12] *GA: 6th sess., Fifth Committee, Summary Records*, p. 86.

[13] Subcommittee 8 of the Fifth Committee was established under a resolution contained in United Nations Document A/C.5/L.117, Rev. 1.

[14] *GA: 6th sess., Annexes, Agenda Item 41*, pp. 52–56. This *Annex* reprints United Nations Document A/C.5/L.172 and includes the complete text of the revised "Basic Principles Underlying the Public Information Activities of the United Nations." Subsequent discussion of Subcommittee 8 in this article is based on it.

world the qualification that OPI must operate "within its budgetary limitations" to promote understanding to the greatest possible extent. On this point, the Pakistani and Philippine representatives entered the logical reservation that such a limitation was superfluous since any UN department must work within its appropriation.

The second change instructed OPI to give special attention to places where information media were less fully developed. Thus, the underdeveloped countries had written into the principles the idea that they should be favored. But the injunction to give greater importance to the very areas where information media were least developed or active implied a greater assignment for OPI. The supplementary role given OPI would inevitably have to be enlarged to fill great *lacunae* in existing information media, and new programs of different varieties in new languages would have to be designed to meet new needs.

As for priorities, the subcommittee received from the head of OPI a three-paragraph statement which in effect rejected the request. It argued that since there was not enough money to go around, and many demands on it, the OPI had to look for the "greatest possible results . . . in the light of prevailing regional and language requirements," and that all factors set forth in the general principles were taken into account. "These budget estimates," the OPI said, "represent the sum-total of hundreds of individual priority judgments both within and between the various sections of the budget." This was the voice of the expert, speaking to the layman.

The subcommittee rather weakly retorted that it should not be "unduly difficult" for OPI to appraise the main categories of services in the light of needs and effectiveness. But it did not demand a table of priorities in the guiding principles nor did it insist that such a document was a prerequisite for any budgetary decisions.

The new principles quickly won acceptance in the Fifth Committee. Only the Soviet bloc—Czechoslovakia, a member of the subcommittee, had objected to the principles on the ground that OPI remained unrestricted—opposed the report, which was adopted by 35 favorable votes with five against and eight abstentions. This action, later approved by the General Assembly, had a double significance. In the first place, the economy bloc had won no victory; it had not been able during six years to limit absolutely or relatively the amount which OPI might propose to spend. Second, it had not forced OPI to work up a list of priorities. Above all, the revision of the OPI principles had resulted in no fundamental changes and had not eliminated contradictions. The chairman of the Fifth Committee remarked that a world information program raised problems which seemed to defy all definition and possibility of solution.[15]

III. Toward a Budgetary Ceiling

Despite the failure of the OPI critics to win a firm decision on priorities, the view that it would not be unduly difficult to work out a table of needs and an assessment of effectiveness gave them the basis of a renewed attack in 1955. The Advisory Committee on Administrative and Budgetary Questions then complained that it had been assured that priorities would be brought into effect but that ". . . the 1956 budget estimates do not visibly reflect any system of priorities. The Committee has, however, received a preliminary and tentative indication of the major areas of activity that are expected to claim special attention during 1956. These include the peaceful uses of atomic energy, disarmament problems,

and economic development with special reference to technical assistance." [16] These subjects represented the main themes selected by OPI in accordance with suggestions made by an advisory group it had meanwhile appointed. This body recommended reorganizing the work of OPI around a thematic approach,[17] a phrase to be heard later in discussions of the information program. Urging flexibility and imaginative planning (thus implying that these were absent), the Advisory Committee announced that ". . . the appropriate level of expenditure is largely a matter of judgment." It then judged that more than $5,117,000, planned for expenditure in 1956, was ". . . definitely on the high side, when viewed in relation to the aggregate cost of other activities." It thought that $4 million would be more appropriate and suggested this as a target to be attained during the next three years.[18]

The Fifth Committee, which rejected a move by the Soviet Union to reduce the budget to the target immediately, then accepted another Soviet resolution to adopt the Advisory Committee's report. The vote was 35 to three with one abstention.[19] This action indicated that the economy group had renewed strength, but the low vote also reflected the absence of many representatives of smaller states, which usually would oppose such a move. It also meant that for the first time a standing limit on expenditures faced OPI. Thus, priorities and an absolute limit on expenditure had been combined by the Advisory Committee as a means of reducing the scope of

[15] GA: 6th sess., Fifth Committee, Summary Records, p. 330.

[16] GA: 10th sess., Suppl. No. 7, Advisory Committee on Administrative and Budgetary Questions, First Report to the Tenth Session of the GA, p. 21.

[17] Ibid., and GA: 10th sess., Suppl. No. 1, Annual Report of the Secretary-General on the Work of the Organization, p. 115.

[18] Loc. cit., note 16 above, p. 21.

[19] GA: 10th sess., Fifth Committee, Summary Records, p. 147.

OPI's work. OPI could no longer look to the principles adopted four years earlier as a perfect means of protection. Moreover, the supporters of OPI would have to make up lost ground if the suggested limit was not to become a permanent ceiling.

While the General Assembly moved toward a fixed OPI budget, it also foresaw an increase in services as the result of the increase in UN membership. During 1954, the Secretary-General had put a survey group to work on the headquarters information establishment. Its report, made known to the General Assembly,[20] set off a demand for a similar survey outside of headquarters. Such a survey was undertaken, reported to the Fifth Committee, commented upon by the Advisory Committee, and discussed during the 1955 Assembly session.[21] The report, which urged reapportioning expenses between the field and headquarters, called attention to the frequent demand for more information centers and increased services to individual countries.

The general approval of the Advisory Committee's approach became specific the following year. The Advisory Committee firmly recommended a $4.5 million ceiling on OPI activities.[22] This proposal and the information program as a whole underwent a rather full discussion during which the Soviet Union proposed immediate adoption of the ceiling. But a British amendment postponed its application until 1959, the intervening years to be used for readjusting activities. This resolution was adopted by 27 votes to 15 with 19 abstentions. At the same time, the Fifth Committee unani-

mously commended the Secretary-General for proposing to extend the network of Information Centers and recommended that preferential attention be given the new Member States, especially the underdeveloped ones. The funds were to come from savings elsewhere in the OPI. The interest in the Information Centers also impelled the Fifth Committee to request the Advisory Committee to study field activities, but consideration of its report was deferred until the next session of the General Assembly.[23]

The great number of abstentions on the resolution establishing a $4.5 million ceiling indicated less than enthusiastic support. Yet the abstainers were unwilling to bear responsibility for a higher level of expenditure. At the same time, the Secretary-General clearly believed that such a ceiling was unrealistic because of the needs of new members, the general demands for information, probable price increases and the normal increase in salaries as the staff gained seniority.[24] The final complicating element was the resolution on Information Centers which found the Fifth Committee ready to sponsor what appeared to be a popular move.

IV. An Expert Committee Established

Considering the Secretary-General's views and the instructions given him to cut costs in order to take on more activities, his reply to the General Assembly in 1957 followed logically. In effect, he said that he could not help surpassing the $4.5 million target and would even find it difficult to avoid exceeding the previous year's budget— unless, of course, activities were reduced. To meet the request for more

[20] GA: 9th sess., Annexes, Agenda Item 53, pp. 1–3, 16, 28.
[21] GA: 10th sess., Annexes, Agenda Items 38 and 47, p. 7.
[22] GA: 11th sess., Suppl. No. 7, Advisory Committee on Administrative and Budgetary Questions, Second Report to the Eleventh Session of the General Assembly, p. 24.

[23] A fuller account of these incidents may be found in GA: 11th sess., Annexes, Agenda Item 43, pp. 89–92.
[24] GA: 11th sess., Fifth Committee, Summary Records, p. 117.

Information Centers, he proposed curtailing some activities in order to provide personnel and services for the new offices in Beirut, Madrid, Rangoon, Rome, and Tokyo. Radio operations would be reduced and the *United Nations Review* would appear quarterly instead of monthly.[25]

The real significance of this position lay not in its technical features but in its general political implications. If accepted, it would continue the standoff in the General Assembly which had permitted OPI to come through years of criticism without important damage. OPI supporters, pointing to the estimates of OPI experts, could again claim that lowering the information budget would reduce activity. This would affect many states, which then could be called upon to defeat the economy forces. The principles on which OPI was expected to operate need never be invoked. Rather the garnering of a majority would depend on simple horse-trading and even a cohesive economy bloc could be defeated, as on a rivers-and-harbors bill in Congress. In effect, the Secretariat proposal harked back to the situation before the Advisory Committee suggestion that the budget for information be limited by an absolute ceiling.

The Advisory Committee offered stiff resistance and new suggestions which eventually led during 1958 to a searching but controversial examination and a severe crisis for OPI. The Advisory Committee insisted that every effort be made to determine the appropriate level of public information expenditures and noted that the Secretary-General had not alluded to an overall reduction of activities. Calling attention to the ". . . fact that the details of the work programmes and priorities in the public information

field are left to the discretion of the Secretary-General, subject only to the broad policy directives of the General Assembly and to the limitations of the budget provision," it proposed a thorough investigation of the responsibilities and work of OPI. An earlier suggestion by the Advisory Committee that the Information Centers be surveyed was to be revived and the scope of the study expanded ". . . to include the entire range of the public information activities of the Organization." Meanwhile, reductions in the proposed program were suggested in order to approach a $4.5 million ceiling. But the Advisory Committee doubted the wisdom of turning the *United Nations Review* into a quarterly.[26]

These recommendations by the Advisory Committee put the entire question of public information with new clarity. To reject the Secretary-General's position decisively and to go behind his claims and programs would make possible a telling attempt at economy and give the Fifth Committee its own technical lever to use against the commanding prestige of the expert which OPI had hitherto had.

Because the heart of the proposal was an investigation of OPI, it was to it that Dag Hammarskjöld addressed himself. He fell back on his position as chief administrative officer to protect his prerogatives in the public information field and then made known that he had no objection to the idea of a small committee. He even suggested that the Advisory Committee on the Peaceful Uses of Atomic Energy and a similar body advising on the United Nations Emergency Force might serve as examples and welcomed the advice and observations of member states. He asked for a larger membership than three, for better geographical distribution, and also suggested that governments, rather than the General Assembly, appoint

[25] *GA: 12th sess., Suppl. No. 7, Advisory Committee on Administrative and Budgetary Questions, Fifth Report to the General Assembly,* p. 5.

[26] *Ibid.,* pp. 5–6, 24.

experts as members of the committee.[27] Chairman Aghnides of the Advisory Committee stuck by his original proposal and then reiterated the real point of the inquiry: ". . . we should bear in mind the fact that the Department of Public Information does not directly derive specific programme directives from any legislative organs."[28]

The economy bloc in the Fifth Committee promptly supported the proposal for an inquiring committee and now that the Secretary-General had accepted it in principle, the OPI backers had little choice but to go along. Max Aitken, the British delegate and floor leader of the economy proponents, added some bait for underdeveloped countries. He remarked that Information Centers in such places as London, Paris and Washington perhaps duplicated governmental activities but that they would be useful in many other locales, especially in new Member States. Thus, he implied that if the underdeveloped countries, new members and Latin American states would support the inquiry, they could get more Information Centers. The bait was snapped up by Ecuador, India, Ceylon, Indonesia, Haiti and Cambodia. Only the Egyptian delegate, El-Messiri, who was later to serve as a member of the committee of enquiry, opposed this idea, arguing that the Centers ensured impartial information in case of disputes.[29]

The Soviet Union and its satellites attacked the budget because it exceeded the recommended ceiling and supported the enquiry as a means to further economy. Such support, if nothing else, guaranteed representation for the Soviet bloc on the committee. Other representatives repeated earlier arguments that the proportion spent on public information remained too high and that a study would develop reductions. The United States cautiously supported the study but warned that it was difficult to determine an optimum level of expenditure. Perhaps the two strongest speeches in support of a virtually unchanged information program were made by the representatives of Iraq and Italy, both of whom pointed to the importance of such activities as a source of impartial information where it was needed.

The discussion developed two important points. The first was that the scope of the inquiry would, in Aitken's words, "be of a technical nature; a reappraisal of the underlying principles and policy was perhaps overdue, but it would first be necessary to inquire into the efficiency of the information services within the existing terms of reference."[30] Thus, it was not principles but practices which were to be examined: efficiency was the watchword. The second point grew out of the nature of the expert committee. Its size became the object of discussion and then compromise, which set it at six. The compromise was necessary because of the desire of several delegations to include all geographical regions in the body. In other words, they attempted to protect their own interests from possible damage. With the question of size resolved, largely because of American insistence, a resolution to establish the Expert Committee was sponsored by 13 powers, most of them identified with the economy proponents, and passed the Fifth Committee by a unanimous 66 votes with one abstention.[31]

V. The Report of the Experts

The Expert Committee labored some five months to turn out a detailed re-

[27] GA: 12th sess., Annexes, Agenda Item 41, p. 38.
[28] Ibid., p. 38.
[29] This and the subsequent account is based on GA: 12th sess., Fifth Committee, Summary Records, pp. 31–65, 69–72.
[30] Ibid., p. 59.
[31] Ibid., p. 72.

port based on 44 interviews at New York and visits to and interviews in 16 field offices. Whatever else may be said of the report, it touched off an impassioned debate and again called attention to the great difficulty of designing a public information program that would satisfy the Secretariat and the various groups in the General Assembly. The very existence of the Expert Committee, as well as its seriousness, challenged the stance adopted by OPI, which thought itself at least as expert as its examiners.

From the beginning, the Expert Committee went beyond a purely technical examination. It assumed that it had to look into the basic principles under which OPI operated and to make recommendations for their reform.[32] In doing so, it followed a rather ambiguous lead in a memorandum that Under-Secretary Ahmed Bokhari had presented at the outset of its work.[33] But the experts did not in fact try to revise the principles. Rather they suggested reinterpretations and implied that a reappraisal of the nature and scope of UN responsibilities in public information might lead to further economies.[34] Once again, therefore, the principles which had permitted the formation of a stable Secretariat unit to deal with public information escaped fundamental examination.

Nevertheless, the Expert Committee touched many sensitive places in OPI. It rejected what it claimed was the Secretariat's interpretation of the principles to the effect that OPI had to operate in all media. It pointed out that budgetary limitations as such had little meaning and that by failing to define its targets OPI had worsened a tendency in the General Assembly to make *ad hoc* reductions. The lack of definition of targets was a third major

difficulty. Thereupon, the experts suggested a target consisting of four classes of peoples and organizations. These were governmental agencies and public institutions which influence opinion; people working in mass communications; people and organizations demonstrating a real interest in the United Nations and willing to commit themselves; and persons and institutions concerned with education. These target groups, said the Committee, would fit into the principle enjoining the OPI to rely primarily on existing agencies.[35] The experts argued that much more could be done by OPI to use existing channels and stated

that no other target is possible or directly attainable. The best way, in the opinion of the Committee, for reaching the peoples of the world at this time is that of working through the Governments of Member States and through a select group of individuals and organizations. As for the OPI's work becoming stultified, the Committee has already shown the ineffectiveness of the present approach and the weaknesses which underlie it. The acceptance of the Committee's definition of the target will make it possible to impart a new sense of direction and purpose to the information activities of the United Nations.[36]

A main source of expense and difficulty had been a mass approach through mass communications. This was ineffective and should be replaced, the committee urged, with "the selective approach of public relations" in the best sense, with a person-to-person approach to influential people, groups and institutions. When OPI embarked on programs of its own, it should use selected themes but still should rely

[32] United Nations Document A/3928, p. 18.
[33] *Ibid.*, Annex I, *passim*.
[34] *Ibid.*, p. 104.

[35] *Ibid.*, pp. 82–83.
[36] *Ibid.*, p. 83.

primarily on existing information channels.[37]

At the same time, services to redisseminators at New York were not to be fundamentally altered. Rather, duplication and some of the perhaps overelaborate services, such as running summaries of meetings, might be eliminated. Basic facilities for correspondents would be available. While OPI products must be objective and impartial,

> particular care should be taken to present the information in a manner and form which leads to identification of people with the United Nations and not estrangement. The importance of the United Nations as a machinery for promoting international co-operation and peacefully resolving international disputes should be emphasized.[38]

Special importance was given Information Centers and their personnel, who should be rotated from headquarters, study their areas, cultivate personal contacts and pay special attention to the discovery of new persons and institutions willing to make commitments leading to the dissemination of information.[39]

The Expert Committee proposed reorganizing OPI in order to strengthen coordination and planning at headquarters, especially with regard to the Information Centers. A new Bureau of Planning and Coordination, with a superior status, would accomplish this job, while a Press and Publications Division and a Radio and Visual Services Division would provide materials and services. The existing Public Liaison Division was to disappear. For the Press and Publications Division, a specific reorganization plan was drawn up. The *United Nations Review* was

to be replaced by a quarterly and its contents altered sharply. Many leaflets and posters would disappear in favor of local production of information materials. The radio service would abandon many of its broadcasts and make available during the General Assembly a 15-minute news show only when there was a firm demand from a member state and when it would be rebroadcast at a satisfactory listening hour. This daily program would become weekly when the Assembly was adjourned. Where "adequate information use" of broadcasts was not made, they would be abandoned. A projected television studio should be deferred and production of feature programs for television abandoned because they had so few outlets. Film strips and exhibition photos should be produced locally with OPI supplying negatives, except in the case of underdeveloped areas where visual materials have special importance. A matrice service should be jettisoned. As for motion pictures the emphasis should be on a film library, with films produced outside the organization. As a means of helping the General Assembly formulate policy, the Expert Committee suggested that the Secretary-General submit an annual assessment of the public information program and a statement of coming operations. In addition, the experts thought that the Secretary-General might refer plans to an advisory group appointed by him from a list of nominees drawn up by the General Assembly. The advisory group would consider in some detail the plans projected by OPI.[40]

The adoption of the target suggested by the experts was intended sharply to reduce important features of the programs of the Press and Publications Bureau and the Radio and Visual Services Division, although all parts of the office would have been affected. The significance of the target, however,

---

[37] *Ibid.*, p. 87.
[38] *Ibid.*, p. 88.
[39] *Ibid.*, pp. 90–91.

[40] *Ibid.*, pp. 92–105.

was not merely technical. Rather, it meant that for the first time OPI faced a concrete suggestion of budget reductions expressed in expert terms. Earlier suggestions had been turned aside with the comment that valuable work would suffer. Now, by proposing a target, the experts had tried to define what was valuable and what was superfluous.

Furthermore, the specific reorganizations would upset the relative balance between press and radio services that had been maintained since 1946. Reduction of the number of posts would hit especially hard in the Radio and Visual Services Division. The elimination of an existing division would destroy one factor in making the OPI budget. Moreover, the establishment of a new Bureau of Planning and Coordination would downgrade the existing divisions and install hitherto unknown supervision over them and over the Information Centers. Indeed, the new bureau apparently would be at least as large as either the press or radio services. Its coordinating task and its influence over the use of personnel would soon give it controlling strength in determining the programs of the two service divisions. And because it would direct public information work toward the new targets, it would carry out the virtual amputation of services to the undifferentiated general public. Finally, an advisory committee nominated by the General Assembly would put OPI under continuing outside scrutiny and might well add another independent critical voice to that of the Advisory Committee on Administrative and Budgetary Questions. Given OPI's relatively immune position, such a suggestion might well have seemed revolutionary, although the Secretary-General himself had indicated that he might find an advisory body of governmental representatives useful.[41]

While some in OPI viewed the experts' report as a long step toward a needed reorganization, almost all of its higher officials shared the opinion that their organization was under direct and dangerous attack. The press corps at United Nations Headquarters got possession of parts of the report and blistering stories of a conspiracy to deprive the peoples of the world of objective information began to appear. *The Times*[42] of London spoke of the experts' report as advocating "militant proselytizing" and containing connotations amounting almost to brainwashing. It reported a wave of resentment among correspondents who knew themselves what was important. *The New York Times*[43] stated that the recommendation would "emasculate U.N.'s messages to the world." The United Nations Correspondents Association denounced the report and urged delegations to dissociate themselves from it; their resolution was circulated as an official document at the request of Cuba,[44] a veteran supporter of OPI.

In this controversial atmosphere, the Secretariat sharply retorted to the report with the argument that the Expert Committee had acted *ultra vires* in dealing with policy rather than operations. In a paper prepared by the OPI, the Secretary-General asserted that the new approach urged by the experts would turn national governments and organizations into "filters and transformers between the OPI and the peoples of the world."[45] This would destroy OPI's international character and minimize its important role as an initiator of information. Regarding unrelayed broadcasts, little money could be saved, but Russians, Chinese, Hungarian and Arabic shows would be suspended. As for the content of publications, OPI argued that the experts' dislike of feature treatment

[41] See above, note 27.

[42] Oct. 17, 1958.
[43] Oct. 20, 1958.
[44] UN Document A/C.5/757.
[45] This account is based on UN Document A/3945.

seemed unrelated to their advice to project ideas. It defended the *United Nations Review* and claimed to have served the press at headquarters well. In effect, the suggestions on Information Centers already were operative. As for reorganization, the Secretary-General agreed to three divisions but insisted that his directors, not a bureau of planning, be responsible for policy. The new division would consolidate other functions and strengthen relations with Information Centers. The suggestion of periodic reports to the General Assembly and of an advisory committee was rejected with the comment that the Secretary-General would seek advice when it would be useful, and that reports would be superfluous. In addition, he argued that little further savings could be made by carrying out the details of the report. Finally, his comment pointed up the Expert Committee's remark that it had a high opinion of the devotion to duty and professional skill of the personnel of OPI. In his oral presentation of this sharp report,[46] Hammarskjöld somewhat softened his language and accepted general recommendations but added the important thought that the General Assembly should remain satisfied with the principles guiding the department, leaving it to practice to work out details.

VI. *Action by the General Assembly*

Although some representatives in the Fifth Committee complained of the press campaign and presumed public reaction, and one charged it had been artificially created,[47] the publicity, together with the broader implications

of the Secretary-General's remarks on unrelayed broadcasts, gave a strongly political flavor to the question of public information. Recommendations by the Expert Committee that OPI shift to a public relations approach and a defined target provided a controversial focus for the debate. Supporters of the report argued that only a shift in emphasis was required both to safeguard conformity to the principles and to produce greater efficiency. Opponents insisted that public information was different from public relations, that working through governments and institutions could never ensure objectivity, and that a "thematic approach" led to propaganda. Other opponents agreed with the Secretariat's contention that the experts had exceeded their mandate. General accord greeted the idea of strengthening Information Centers.[48] Strenuous efforts by United Arab Republic representative El-Messiri, a member of the Expert Committee, to explain what he thought were the moderate suggestions of the report, were lost amidst professions of faith in free information and the need to inform the peoples of the world. The economy group, led by the United Kingdom, backed the report strongly but now found themselves in the position of urging reduced information to such countries as Hungary and the Soviet Union. And the latter's representatives added more confusion by attacking the Press and Publications Division as led and dominated by Americans,[49] thus casting discredit on the international civil service and violating the usual practice of commenting only on the work of responsible officials.

The supporters of OPI again were armed. With the political weapon, they could discredit the experts' report generally. The Secretary-General's statement gave them ammunition of a technical sort to reply to the arguments of

---

[46] UN Document A/C.5/764.

[47] Japan, Sweden and the Netherlands. *GA: 13th sess., Fifth Committee, Summary Records*, pp. 183, 188, 193. There is no reason to think that some OPI officials might not have encouraged correspondents to see a threat to services and facilities in the suggestions made by the experts.

[48] For a fuller summary of the debate, see UN Document A/4062, pp. 9–14.

[49] *Loc. cit.* above, note 47, p. 195.

the experts. One of the latter, Professor Rodriguez-Fabregat of Uruguay, aided the Latin American supporters of OPI by weakening the unanimity of the Expert Committee. He made much of his reservation on the recommendation to give up unrelayed broadcasts. Following Hammarskjöld's lead, several delegates reaffirmed their faith in the existing principles on public information. As Raul Quijano of Argentina said, the principles need not be modified, for they were approved by all members and it was universally recognized that the information provided should be objective and given world-wide distribution.

The United States threw its prestige behind the supporters of OPI. In doing so, it repudiated the work of Louis Lochner, the veteran correspondent it had placed on the Expert Committee. The American view, as explained by Senator Hickenlooper, who introduced a United States draft resolution, supported the principles adopted for OPI and wanted to avoid too rigid a definition of targets and close restrictions on the Secretary-General. Hickenlooper opposed spoon-feeding of information and refused to accept the veto of any government on transmission of objective broadcast information to its people. In short, the United States backed the Secretary-General and its resolution in fact would have given him a free hand to apply such parts of the report as he saw fit.[50]

Besides the American resolution, additional drafts were introduced by the United Kingdom, France, and Guatemala, while Bulgaria and Rumania submitted amendments.[51] As the discussion narrowed differences and opened up opportunities for compromise, the main points at issue were the $4.5 million budget ceiling on OPI

and the general recommendations made by the Expert Committee. These included injunctions to avoid propaganda, seek identification of peoples with the United Nations, serve correspondents and develop the Information Centers and other field distribution points. The principal differences between the British and American drafts were compromised. Their sponsors rejected the Soviet bloc's demands for an explicit statement of the $4.5 million limit and not even an implicit reference to it appeared. An effort by Honduras to give OPI the fullest possible backing by cutting out any reference to maximum effectiveness at lowest possible cost also was lost. The Fifth Committee finally adopted the compromise draft submitted by the United States and the United Kingdom, by 57 votes to none with 11 abstentions.[52] Most of the abstainers belonged to the Soviet bloc.

This resolution incorporated some recommendations of the Expert Committee. It considered that the Secretary-General should give priority to use of media which ensure maximum effectiveness at the lowest possible cost, that more cooperation should be enlisted from governments and other institutions and influential persons, and that more emphasis should be put on the Information Centers. The Secretary-General was requested to give what effect was practical to the Expert Committee recommendations, to consult the Advisory Committee on Administrative and Budgetary Questions and to report back on his progress.

In effect, this resolution asked the Secretary-General to do what he said he would do, leaving it up to him to decide how to do so. This meant the OPI still had command of its own policy and had weathered serious criticism without much damage. It also appeared to signal momentary defeat

[50] Ibid., pp. 177–178, and UN Document A/C.5/L.527.
[51] UN Documents A/C.5/L.529; A/C.5/ L.530; A/C.5/L.533; A/C.5/L.540; and A/ C.5/L.541.

[52] UN Document A/AC.5/L.539; GA: 13th sess., Fifth Committee, Summary Records, pp. 328–329.

for economy proponents. The technical considerations developed by the Expert Committee had failed to penetrate the OPI position, because they were turned into political questions linked to the hostility between the United States and the Soviet Union on such matters as Hungary and the Middle East, and because the bloc supporting OPI had members enough to balance the economy group. Further, the Soviet Union made a tactical error in attacking the Press and Publications Bureau; the attack boomeranged and strengthened arguments of OPI supporters who saw in the Expert Committee's recommendations on radio broadcasting and on targets a possible advantage to the Soviet bloc. As for such technical recommendations as the replacement of the *United Nations Review* by a quarterly or deferment of a new television studio, these were successfully challenged by OPI and by national representatives.

By the time the discussion in the Fifth Committee was ending, the issues were precisely what they had been before the Expert Committee did its work. They involved budgetary limitation and the further development of Information Centers, all without destroying existing services. The resolution drafted by the Fifth Committee did not resolve these issues. In essence, the discussion was superficial, because it never really posed the underlying questions of the purpose of OPI and the appropriate level of its activity. Its superficiality was finally demonstrated with the reaffirmation of the contradictory principles governing UN public information activities. The principles were not discussed as such in the Fifth Committee and the lead given by the Expert Committee in opening them for review never was followed. Instead, delegates attempted to prove that the recommendations of the Expert Committee conformed or did not conform with the principles.

That the work of OPI would re-main much as it had been, with some shifts in emphasis, was disclosed by the Secretary-General's report on public information for the General Assembly in 1958.[53] The steps already taken by OPI were viewed as part of a long term effort. A reorganization created a division to exercise tighter control of Information Centers; and new field offices were to open. But the effectiveness of the program was to be judged in terms of reaching the widest possible audience, and the report noted the absence of a measure for determining the level of activity. Staff and operational funds were to be stabilized. The Secretary-General intended to hold to a line of stabilization unless a marked change dictated a departure from that policy.

Over a period of several years, the development and strengthening of Information Centers and the new facilities for supervising them might well produce a marked shift in content and location of activities. But the rapid and radical change sought by the economy bloc and the Advisory Committee was not in sight. What limits had been set upon OPI expansion were not made formal and were not direct products of General Assembly supervision and control. Rather they were adopted as Secretariat policy but with reservations. Whether the General Assembly will soon reopen its discussion of the principles guiding public information is doubtful in view of the outcome of the 1958 consideration and the Secretary-General's rather conciliatory report. But even if it does, the result once more would probably be less than satisfactory for the reformers.[54]

[53] UN Document A/4122.

[54] Since this article was written, the General Assembly has again wrestled with the subject. As anticipated here, its debates did not deal with the principles of public information but rather took up details of the Secretary-General's proposals and his effort to apply as much as possible of the report of the Expert Committee. Views virtually identical

VII. Conclusions

The durability of the principles on public information corresponds to the essential stability which OPI has achieved. Repeated attacks have left OPI almost unaltered, either in form or function. The Secretary-General continues to state the test of effectiveness in terms of people reached, rather than, say, influence over elites or penetration to the depths of large but significant groups. OPI continues to balance its right to go directly to the peoples of the world against its instruction to concentrate on existing institutions. Its personnel and budget have remained virtually fixed, whether viewed as a proportion of UN expenditure or as an absolute number.[55]

with those of the past appeared again. The General Assembly this time, however, adopted a resolution [A/RES/1405 (XIV)] on public information by 79 favorable votes and no dissent. The size of the majority indicates that no radical changes were attempted. The resolution does contain three new features. One of them, based on an offer by the Secretary-General to try to stabilize the expenditure for OPI, requests him to plan a budget of about $5 million for 1960; thus, the General Assembly placed no ceiling on future expenditure, despite the usual move to do so. The second asks him to appoint a consultative panel of experts from the main cultures and geographical areas of the world; he had accepted a similar idea at the outset of the 1957 discussion and such panels had been employed on the initiative of the Secretariat before then. The third asks him to submit an outline of the policy and programs of OPI in a report to the General Assembly; in effect, OPI has always provided some information of this nature but not in such a formal manner. For the rest, the resolution echoes the wishes of both the underdeveloped countries and the economy bloc by urging him to continue with efforts to apply the ideas of the Expert Committee, to consider the importance of "adequate regional representation" in policy-making and field posts, and to establish new Information Centers, preferably by decentralizing headquarters staff.

[55] My calculations, based on actual expenditures as computed from the annual General

Whenever OPI has been challenged in the General Assembly, it relied on its expertise to support its program. That program is so complex and varied that it is difficult to grasp as a whole. The result is that OPI's expertise must be used by the Fifth Committee before it can make any apparently reasonable criticisms of the public information work.

When outside agencies have been called in, they failed to get at the fundamental policy questions either because of their bias toward administration rather than general policy, or because they lacked sufficient expertness. The Advisory Committee on Administrative and Budgetary Questions falls into the first of these categories. Primarily interested in economy and tight administration, the Advisory Committee constantly complained of the lack

Assembly resolution which includes supplementary appropriations, indicate that OPI from 1949 through 1957 never spent less than approximately six percent nor more than approximately eight percent of the total UN appropriation. The budgets, but not the actual amounts spent, indicated that in 1957 and 1958, OPI would spend about nine percent of the total, but unforeseen items elsewhere have lowered this proportion in the past. Delegates frequently have spoken of a 10 percent portion of the UN budget going to public information. This is true only of the estimate: the actual proportion has always been less. See General Assembly Resolutions 252 (III); 356 (IV); 471 (V); 583 (VI); 674 (VII); 786 (VIII); 890 (IX); 979 (X); 1083 (XI); and Documents A/3600, p. 83, and A/3825, p. 83. Personnel statistics are somewhat more difficult to obtain and compare. But relying on the annual budget submitted by the Secretary-General (always published as Supplement No. 5 to the *Official Records* of the General Assembly), a reasonably accurate comparison can be made for the years 1948 to 1956. Taking the Radio and Press and Publications Divisions, the structures of which remained fairly stable, as an index and adding to their personnel numbers those of the Information Centers, the following appears: in 1948, the two divisions and the centers employed 254 persons; in 1956, they included 226 persons.

of standards to apply to public information. But it could not or did not develop its own. The second category includes the Expert Committee, which asserted that it would touch on the principles guiding the public information department but failed to make good its claim in its report and provided grounds for the charge that it had acted *ultra vires*. Such a charge implies that the very body which established and instructed the Expert Committee may not have been perfectly clear—or more realistically, was divided—as to the results it anticipated or on the rules for developing a report. Earlier, Subcommittee 8 of the Fifth Committee, which revised the principles in 1951, was made up of governmental representatives who were hurried in their work and not sufficiently qualified as experts to challenge OPI positions. Their work, therefore, resulted simply in a restatement of principles, not a thorough examination of them.

Very early in its history, OPI began to benefit from a body of supporters in the General Assembly. The core of this bloc was made up of representatives from Latin America, perhaps because the personality and popularity of Benjamin A. Cohen, the Chilean diplomat who headed OPI, knitted it together. Underdeveloped countries from other parts of the world tended to join the Latin American states in backing OPI budgets. Plans for expansion received equal favor from this group.

The principal area of expansion was the network of Information Centers. After 1951, OPI was instructed to open new centers in less developed parts of the world. The existing centers gave most of the receiving states a definite interest in backing the OPI program. The new centers added more clients to this group. The fact that even during the 1958 debate nine states asked that new centers be located in their territory or regions[56] lends credence to the idea that the information offices in the field not only disseminated information but also tended to build support for OPI. Furthermore, at headquarters, the very existence of an information section brought Secretariat services to the favorable attention of delegations, for important speeches and statements could easily be publicized through the good offices of OPI. When the Information Centers also were brought into play, national delegations had a rather formidable distribution service at their disposal.

If the functions of OPI, whatever its intentions, tended to create a client group among UN members, they did the same thing among the media representatives. This was clearly indicated by the speed and forcefulness with which the United Nations Correspondents Association denounced the report of the Expert Committee. Moreover, some press accounts of the report implied that OPI had secured a strong commitment from correspondents working at Headquarters. Pressure from this source entered directly into the debate on the Expert Committee's report when the resolution of the Correspondents Association was circulated as an official document.

Generally speaking, the Secretary-General cannot be distinguished from OPI in public information matters. The head of OPI usually represented the Secretary-General before the Fifth Committee and OPI usually recommended and drafted Secretariat papers on matters affecting itself. In the 1958 debate, however, the Secretary-General personally spoke before the Fifth Committee. When he did so, his own prestige added strength to the OPI position. So when he opposed the heart of the report of the Expert Committee, double pressure was put on the Fifth Com-

---

[56] The territories or regions: North Africa, Central Africa, Central America, Afghanistan, Austria, Burma, Ceylon. Offices in them were urged by Afghanistan, Austria, Burma, El Salvador, Ethiopia, India, Indonesia, Iraq and Tunisia. *GA: 13th sess., Fifth Committee Summary Records*, pp. 175 ff.

mittee. His prestige supported his own experts and in turn he received the backing of their friends. Moreover, he also indicated what sort of recommendation he would welcome, and with this lead encouraged his supporters to attempt to gain from the General Assembly approval for a stated Secretariat policy.

Secretary-General, OPI, a bloc of national representatives and client groups made a formidable combination to oppose the economy bloc. To have gained the day, the economy bloc would have had to put together a consensus which has so far eluded it. Its great hope for victory lay in a technical discussion of the OPI program, based on the experts' report. But the OPI bloc, developing points made by the Secretary-General, quickly put the discussion onto a political path and once again the questions to which answers had never before been found were under examination. Thus, the real substance of the experts' report—the proposed target and the beginning of reinterpretation of the principles guiding public information—was lost.

In a more general way, it can be said that distinct groups have formed around the alternatives presented to the General Assembly for public information policy. The strongest of these groups include, on the one hand, the economizers and, on the other, the convinced partisans of OPI. An ideological group, led by the Soviet Union, unwaveringly joins the economizers. Least cohesive and most wavering are the states which have taken no firm advance position on public information; among this group one usually finds the United States.

None of these groups has quite the strength to carry the day by itself and a balance among them is reflected in the principles governing public information, for these can be variously interpreted to support almost any view. The Secretary-General makes the effective proposals on public information and around these, OPI supporters, plus some of the not-yet-committed, form a majority. Thus, the General Assembly has so far left the OPI program and organization basically unchanged. At the same time, the Secretariat has kept its grip on public information policy.

The ability of the Secretariat to return from the General Assembly time after time with a renewed mandate to carry out its own public information program reflects real influence. The views of the Secretariat act as a catalyst which encourages formation of alliances among the loosely related states in the General Assembly to form a majority. Through the Information Centers and headquarters services to assist governments, OPI cannot but nurture a constituency which is enlarged and deepened by another constituency in the press lobby. And using its expert knowledge and the ability to carry out a program that must be justified by reasoning deductively from contradictory precepts, OPI offers much that is desired by a broad spectrum of UN members. Its ability to do so does not necessarily answer criticism of the contents of its public information program, but it does demonstrate how effective a secretariat can be in forming policy in the divided assembly of an international organization.

Chapter III

SOCIALIZATION AND
RECRUITMENT

III. SOCIALIZATION AND RECRUITMENT

III. Socialization and Recruitment

IT is easy and natural to identify an organization with its head, whether it be the "Kennedy Administration" or the "Hammarskjöld UN." Despite the stamp individuals can place on an organization, the organization, by definition, will outlive them.[1] This ability to survive normal factors of attrition depends upon securing replacements and inculcating them with accepted values. It is only through the interchangeability of its parts and an instructional process productive of loyalty that a corporation, a governmental department, or an international organization renders itself less mortal than an individual. The process by which vacancies are filled (the *recruitment* function) must be complemented by a *socialization* function, by which the new recruit is taught to value what the organization values and to accept and learn its working procedures. If this sounds on the surface a bit unfeeling and dehumanized, it is nonetheless true that all organizations, including both those that we may cherish and those we may despise, must somehow meet these needs.

The United Nations, too, can be analyzed in this fashion. Its Secretariat, not to mention those of the specialized agencies, must be staffed, yet the staffing problem in an international setting acquires new and unfamiliar dimensions. International organizations are not free to pick and choose from an unrestricted labor market, for whatever they do has the potential of international visibility and the potential for acquiring symbolic significance. The prestige of states frequently is deemed to be expressed through shorthand means: a "great power" for instance is today a state possessing nuclear weapons, as in the nineteenth century it was a state with colonial possessions. There is the constant danger that staffing of international organizations will become another symbolic means by which international prestige is communicated.

There is a qualitative difference between staffing such an organization and staffing a traditional diplomatic conference. In the latter, each participant in essence brings along his own staff. Controversy may con-

---

[1] For a comprehensive definition of "organization," see Bernard Berelson and Gary A. Steiner, *Human Behavior* (New York: Harcourt, Brace and World, 1964), p. 364.

tinue to swirl about Colonel House's influence at Versailles, but not on the grounds that he failed in his obligations to an international community, for his obligations ran rather to the United States, even as those of other conference staff members were owed to their respective governments. There was no reason for it to be otherwise, for such conferences were brief affairs and placed no enduring burdens on subordinates. But precisely because the components of the United Nations system are ongoing organizations transcending particular crises, they must, at the staff level, maintain an organizational loyalty. There is a grain of truth in Khrushchev's dictum that "There are neutral nations but not neutral men." Yet the history of bureaucracy yields a different answer. Every bureaucratic organization is filled with individuals, who, *as individuals,* differ radically in their opinions. It has been one of the enduring contributions of that much-damned social entity, the bureaucracy, that it can subordinate these divisive tendencies. The homogenizing effects of bureaucracy come about through a strict definition of responsibilities, hierarchical command structures, and a common set of values.[2]

It is the last consideration that brings us to the process known as "socialization." In its broadest sense, socialization is the means whereby an individual is brought into membership in a given social system, which means that he must learn and accept a set of values, traditions, and skills. From the day of birth each of us is subject to the shaping influence of our own culture, through the family, schools, churches, peers, and communications media. Were it not for this internalization of values, no society could last more than a single generation and even within that generation divisive tendencies might well pull it apart.

It is easy to pinpoint the source of divisiveness in an international organization: national loyalties. Now as a matter of course in everyday life we accept and adjust to multiple loyalties and there seems to be a good deal of evidence that multiple loyalties can survive on the international level.[3] The ever-present threat in the UN system, however, is the possibility that national loyalties will dominate, creating a staff ostensibly dedicated to a transnational organization but in reality pursuing as many courses as there are member states.

How might this danger be met? Harold Guetzkow suggests that when the international civil servant is endowed with a sense of profes-

[2] For an introduction to classic thinking on bureaucracy, see Reinhard Bendix, *Max Weber* (Garden City, New York: Anchor, 1962).
[3] Harold Guetzkow, *Multiple Loyalties: Theoretical Approach to a Problem in International Organization* (Princeton, New Jersey: Center for Research on World Political Institutions, 1955).

sional identity he will resolve conflicts of loyalty in favor of what he perceives to be the demands of his professional role.[4] The development of a professional identity which places organizational survival above national policy would act as a brake on centrifugal tendencies.

While the socialization problem bulks larger in regard to secretariats, it enters also into the functions and activities of the delegates themselves—for the delegates must function day in and day out in a milieu quite different from classical diplomacy, and often closer in operation to parliamentary politics. Demands and tactics that may seem reasonable and rational to the foreign ministry in the home capital may look bizarre and ill-advised to a UN ambassador. This is attributable in part to the confusing mesh of diplomatic and parliamentary forms, but more generally it derives from conflicting role demands—for the UN representative may find his long-range effectiveness enhanced by tactics and attitudes his superiors regard as undesirable. The UN has, after all, endured long enough to generate its own norms and customs. Further, it provides opportunities for interaction far more than do the ordinary paths of diplomacy. In such a setting, compromise and respect for professional peers often seem the road to success and little premium may be put on intransigence or aloofness. Thus the UN delegate at first finds himself in a novel situation, where the confrontation between states is tempered by the give-and-take clubbiness of legislatures. He, almost as much as Secretariat employees, must be socialized, taught new norms and techniques, and gradually taught also to harbor an institutional loyalty.

The Secretariat worker can accommodate himself rather more easily, for he is expected to give loyalty only to his organizational employer. The delegate is rather less fortunate—for to the extent that he is socialized to the UN, he finds himself enmeshed in role conflicts. The demands of national representation potentially run afoul of accepted organization ways of doing things. In much the same way that a United States Senator often finds himself caught between the conflicting demands of constituent opinion and Senate folkways, so the UN representative must resolve an analogous set of antithetical allegiances.

Haas poses the special problem created by revolutionary states, who begin with a belief in the radical evil of the international status quo and the necessity of destroying it. Our century has unfortunately been rich in such states. The League of Nations never was able to cope with them. Subsequent experience, however, allows us to retain some measure of

[4] *Ibid.*, pp. 52–53.

optimism. The Soviet Union, spanning both the League era and the UN, now adheres to an astonishingly high degree to the procedural norms of international diplomatic practice. The mellowing of Soviet attitudes toward both international law and organizations may indicate that even revolutionary nations with a thoroughgoing Manichean outlook mellow in time and accept the necessity of dealing with adversaries. This form of the international socialization of a state sees the experiences of both diplomatic representatives and policy-makers as learning experiences through which they are brought up against the gap between their intentions to change the world and their capabilities.

We are accustomed to think of "due process" within the rich and varied framework of American constitutional law. But the provision of procedural rights lies at the heart of all normative systems, even at the most rudimentary state of their development. As Jenks demonstrates, the continued effective functioning of the United Nations depends upon consensus on the desirability of procedural rights—for if this consensus does not exist, the organization will ultimately end as a club to which only friends are admitted. The utility of it as a means for amicable dispute settlement depends upon objective values of fairness—objective in the sense that the membership perceives that all states are equally bound by them. The existence of such a value consensus is in itself a powerful socializing tool, for new members find quite early that they must join the consensus or suffer diminished diplomatic effectiveness.

The precarious position procedural rules occupy is demonstrated in Bailey's account of the exploitation of those rules in connection with issues of African colonialism. Non-Western nations, newly independent, easily accept one procedural rule—the principle of majority rule—for their numbers make that advantageous. Other rules, whose function traditional interpretations make that of protection of dissent, are apt to be slighted. It is perhaps significant that Bailey at the end invokes de Tocqueville, who saw so clearly the dangers tyranny of the majority held in an egalitarian society.

Dag Hammarskjöld's Oxford speech poses an interesting problem by no means limited to international organizations: Is there a difference between political and administrative decisions, and, if so, how operationally is the distinction to be made? As Hammarskjöld points out, one's answer is in part attributable to one's own immediate political environment—for British and American attitudes are in large part conditioned by differences in respective conceptions of the civil servant. It is demonstrable that "non-political" acts often have "political" consequences. The assertion that there is a realm of technical decision-making beyond the ken of politicians neglects the frequent and real disagreements among experts. What we are left with is a decisional world, fraught with political consequences even for the international civil servant. The crucial question then becomes not "How can we keep international civil servants from making political decisions?" but "How can we insure that international civil servants will owe their primary allegiance to the international community?"

Finally, Kay argues for the increased use of "secondment," the utilization of short-term staff positions filled with personnel recruited from member states. Secondment is at odds with the concept of an international civil service, in that seconded employees are only expected to remain a short time and then rejoin the civil services of their own governments. While one obvious advantage lies in the ease with which secondment can solve pressing personnel shortages, a less obvious but more important advantage lies in the patterns of interaction it sets up. The socialization experience of even a few years' service takes on additional significance if the individual involved later assumes an important policymaking position in his own government. Thus a latent function of secondment is to create a body of national officialdom schooled in the values of international organizations. The effectiveness of this circulation of elites can only be felt over a period of years, of course. Then, too, secondment in no sense does away with the necessity of a permanent core secretariat of career employees. Indeed, the feasibility of secondment depends upon the existence of a civil service which can assure smooth organizational functioning and to whom organizational loyalties are all-important.

In sum, the problems the UN system and its component parts face are part and parcel of organizational life. The UN is not unique in facing crises of loyalty and clashes of values. Every corporation and government has dealt with them. The UN, however, suffers an additional disadvantage: There is no clear structure of international roles into which individuals and, to a lesser extent, states can easily fit. Roles tell us what is expected of us in specific situations and ambiguity can enter in either of two ways: (1) either we are not sure what is expected of us or (2) we are sure and consequently reject the demands. The former, as Hammarskjöld tells us in recounting League and UN history, afflicts international organizational staffing; the latter, only too clear in Haas and Bailey, is the legacy of the anticolonial revolution.

9. Dynamic Environment and Static System: Revolutionary Regimes in the United Nations*

ERNST B. HAAS

I

REVOLUTIONARY regimes, for our purposes, possess two central attributes. They are committed to the complete reordering of their own societies, to the creation of a new order or the restoration of an old order radically different from the present. Dogmatic modernism and fanatical nativism are equally acceptable as criteria. Furthermore, a revolutionary regime typically sees itself as struggling against some kind of international "conspiracy" or fighting a global "historic force"; this implies an external dimension in the revolution, since the regime must cooperate with kindred movements in other countries. A few examples will illustrate this combination.

In the words of two students of modern Africa, revolutionary leadership "being exclusivist . . . lives in a world of friends and enemies. Moreover it finds itself uneasy in negotiating on other than on its own terms." It seeks to "combine the skills and talents of a community and mobilize them for a wholesale assault on the problems that lie ahead." While this state of mind suggests a rigid ideological commitment, ideology is no more than the servant of task-oriented expediency.

The immediate tasks of the day, whether to build a dam, change the tax structure or modify the political arrangements in government, will be put in the context of ideological slogans as a form of communication, but opportunism is more compelling than ideology.[1]

At the same time, a peculiar variety of charismatic leadership is often associated with this type of regime. While its local cultural attributes may differ and while the institutionalization of revolutionary progress may attenuate its features, the Latin American admiration for a personalist *jefe* who is also a *macho* (male) is widely repeated, a leader who

. . . is expected to show sexual prowess, zest for action, including verbal 'action,' daring, and, above all, absolute self-confidence. . . . In politics, a man is not commonly elected or acclaimed to office because he represents the social, economic and political position of his followers, but because he embodies in his own personality those inner qualities that they feel in themselves and they would like to manifest, had they but the talent to do so, in their own actions.[2]

---

* Morton A Kaplan, ed., *The Revolution in World Politics* (New York and London: John Wiley and Sons, Inc., 1962), pp. 267–309. Reprinted by permission.

[1] David E. Apter and Carl G. Rosberg, "Nationalism and Models of Political Change in Africa," The National Institute of Social and Behavioral Science, Symposia Studies Series No. 1 (Washington, D.C.: December 1959), pp. 8–9.

[2] John P. Gillin, "Some Aspects for Policy," in *Social Change in Latin America Today* (New York: Harper, 1960), p. 31.

If Fidel Castro fits this bill, so do Kwame Nkrumah, Sukarno, Sékou Touré, and Gamal Abdul Nasser.

Perhaps the most direct way to spell out the external aspect of revolutionary leadership is to furnish an example of post-colonial statecraft which self-consciously eschews pan-Africanism. As Félix Houphouet-Boigny put it just one year before the Ivory Coast became independent:

Why do we not demand independence? To answer this question I can only ask another: What is independence? Industrial and technical revolutions are making peoples more and more dependent on one another. . . . Indeed, the countries of Europe . . . are prepared to relinquish a part of their sovereignty. . . . Why, if not to bring about, by association and mutual aid, a more fully elaborated form of civilization which is more advantageous for their peoples and which transcends a nationalism that is too cramped, too dogmatic and by now out of date?[3]

Note in contrast, Kwame Nkrumah's thoughts on revolutionary statecraft:

My first advice to you who are struggling to be free is to aim for the attainment of the Political Kingdom—that is to say, the complete independence and self-determination of your territories. When you have achieved the Political Kingdom all else will follow. Only with the acquisition of political power—real power through the attainment of sovereign independence—will you be in a position to reshape your lives and destiny, only then will you be able to resolve the vexatious problems which harass our Continent.[4]

To what use should the Political Kingdom be put? It should consolidate freedom, create unity and community among African states, and finally, achieve the economic and social "reconstruction" of Africa by undoing the damage wrought by colonialism and tribalism. Pan-Africanism is an integral part of the program because only through African unity can the "African Personality" be called to life. Political boundaries and tribal divisions are the hallmarks of reaction; and African Personality able to demonstrate the black man's cultural equality with other races will arise only with their suppression. Cultural renaissance, economic progress, territorial revisionism, strong political leadership, and the Political Kingdom are one and inseparable.[5]

So much for the syndrome of factors making up the substance of the doctrine. They necessarily presuppose totalitarian national institutions, in embryo or in full bloom. In the Soviet case and in Cuba such institutions are clearly flowering; in Ghana and Guinea the buds are shooting out. If Egypt, Indonesia, and Bolivia appear merely as one-party or no-party states, it is because their authoritarian way has not advanced to full totalitarianism for

[3] Félix Houphouet-Boigny, "Black Africa and the French Union," *Foreign Affairs* (July 1957), p. 594.
[4] Speech by the Prime Minister of Ghana at the Opening Session, December 8, 1958, All-African People's Conference, Accra. The same point was made by the Tunisian delegate to the first Conference of Independent African States, Accra, April 22, 1958.
[5] *Ibid.*, for this train of thought. See also the similar remarks of Sékou Touré as reported in *Afro-Asian Bulletin*, Monthly Journal of the Permanent Secretariat of Afro-Asian Solidarity (Cairo: October–November, 1959), p. 6. The argument that "national" independence of single ex-colonial territories whose boundaries were fixed by Europeans is meaningless as long as any colonial situations survive is common to pan-African thought in English-speaking West Africa and the Cameroons. See George Padmore, *A Guide to Pan-African Socialism*. The same doctrine is expressed unblushingly in the Constitution of the Convention People's Party. See K. Nkrumah, *Ghana* (New York: Thomas Nelson and Sons, 1957), pp. 289–90.

reasons associated with underdevelopment rather than from lack of intent. But it is important *not* to equate revolutionary regimes with a number of closely related categories. Not every totalitarian state is also a revolutionary state, as shown by modern Spain, Portugal, and Yugoslavia. Policies of imperialism may well be pursued in the modern world without being linked to an intention to transform society. Thus, Egypt followed a pan-Arab course, often interpreted as simple Egyptian imperialism, under Farouk as well as under Nasser.[6] But this does not make the pre-1952 oligarchical regime a revolutionary one. Nor is every nationalist regime specifically revolutionary. Indian or Burmese nationalism is not revolutionary because it has no articulate external referents. But Ghana's nationalism is identifiable as revolutionary because of the pan-African strain; Indonesia's is equally so because it holds

. . . that God Almighty created the map of the world in such a fashion that even a child can tell that the British Isles are one entity . . . and that a child can see that the Indonesian Archipelago is a single entity, stretching between the Pacific and Indian oceans and the Asian and Australian continents, from the north tip of Sumatra to Papua.[7]

A further refinement in the application of this definition of revolutionary status is imperative. Having linked contemporary revolutionary pressures with totalitarian political institutions,

we automatically exclude from our purview such international revisionist dogmas as may be associated with oriental despotisms, mercantilist imperialisms, and early capitalist assertions. This is *not* to argue, as some contemporary commentators do, that revolutionary conduct in our era is purely a non-Western and anti-Western phenomenon which ought to be linked to cultural differences between the Western creators of international law and its Asian challengers. After all, the impetus underlying such attacks on the international status quo as were hurled from Moscow and Berlin during the thirties can hardly be shrugged off as "non-Western." The international politics and legal doctrines of sixteenth-century Spain, the seventeenth-century Dutch Republic, and the fledgling American Republic showed definite evidence of a "new" state's impatience with certain aspects of the status quo and resulted in the advocacy of international legal norms which were regarded as "revolutionary" in the context of their times. However, they are not "revolutionary" for our purposes because the element of drastic *internal* revolutionary zeal was lacking in the case of three examples adduced: There was no overwhelming commitment to remake Spanish, Dutch, or American society, and the refinements of totalitarian control remained to be invented.

Soviet behavior offers a still finer point. While the Soviet Union is clearly a revolutionary state whose foreign policy fits the requirements of our purpose, it does not follow that every Soviet move is part of a "necessary" and "planned" revolutionary behavior pattern. One careful study, for instance, casts doubt on the "inevitable" character of the communist *coup* in Czechoslovakia.[8] We are, therefore, con-

[6] See Farouk's use of the Arab League and of the caliphate in Elie Kedourie "Pan-Arabism and British Policy," in W. Laqueur (ed.), *The Middle East in Transition* (New York: Praeger, 1958), pp. 102–103. On Nasser's pan-Arab nationalism see Jean Vigneau, "The Ideology of the Egyptian Revolution," in *ibid.*, pp. 136–38.

[7] Quoted in R. Emerson, "Paradoxes of Asian Nationalism," *Far Eastern Quarterly*, Vol. 13, No. 2 (February 1954), p. 132.

[8] Morton A. Kaplan, *The Communist Coup in Czechoslovakia* (Princeton: Center of International Studies, January 1960).

cerned with the attitudes and poses, the demands and expectations, the style and doctrines, of totally revolutionary regimes rather than with every detail of their foreign policy moves.

Our concern can be pinpointed in another way. If we ask what type of political *system* constrains and limits a policy of self-assertion abroad, because the enunciation of such a course encounters well-entrenched domestic opposition or runs afoul of domestic weakness and disorganization, we come across a number of types which cannot be revolutionary in our sense. To use the typology of Edward Shils, political democracies, traditional and traditionalistic oligarchies do not fit;[9] modernizing oligarchies may, and totalitarian oligarchies, as well as tutelary democracies, most certainly do. The picture becomes clearer if we ask what type of domestic policy requires a foreign policy of self-assertion; or, under what circumstances a domestic policy aiming at the creation of a new society becomes revolutionary in the outside world as well? Put in these terms, we arrive at two varieties of revolutionary regimes, without having to commit ourselves to a specific typology of systems.

A revolutionary elite which is committed to a doctrine of historical struggle represents the first variety. It includes, of course, the major countries of the Communist bloc. The foreign policies of China and the Soviet Union may be interpreted merely as the international application of the inevitable rise to power of the proletariat through the establishment of Socialism and eventually Communism, first in certain countries and finally everywhere. While this implies neither commitment to the notion that war is inevitable, nor to the proposition that

all Soviet-bloc moves are part of a "Communist conspiracy," it does locate the Communist bloc within a revolutionary syndrome based on class struggle. In it, the security and survival of Communist states is the minimal, but only the minimal, motive of a foreign policy organizationally and doctrinally linked to drastic domestic change. In the mind of Fidel Castro, this class struggle is "nationalized" in the sense that underdeveloped countries living at the mercy of monopoly imperialism become the equivalent of the proletariat. The international class struggle now is identical with the struggle for freedom and progress on the part of all underdeveloped countries.[10] Agrarian reform in Cuba, for example, is held out as an internationally valid example of inevitable revolutionary transformation. It is hardly surprising, therefore, that Cuba had identified herself publicly with Egypt, Guinea, and Ghana.

Africa, however, offers a different example of thinking along lines of an international revolutionary struggle. As our examples of pan-African doctrines have shown, the creation of the African Personality ranks high among the goals of the revolutionary leaders. Class is here replaced by race. The fight against the racism of the imperialists includes the new self-assertion of "the African," suspicious, if not impatient, of all white institutions and practices. The salvation of Africa becomes the redemption of the black man, with the practical international consequence of giving a reverse racist

[9] As cited in G. A. Almond and J. S. Coleman (eds.), *The Politics of the Developing Areas* (Princeton: Princeton University Press, 1960), pp. 52–55.

[10] For Castro's views see the revealing marathon speech delivered to the United Nations General Assembly, September 26, 1960. A similar doctrine was developed as early as 1918 by Sultan Galiev. See A. Bennigsen, "Sultan Galiev," in Laqueur, *op. cit.*, pp. 398 ff. Peronista nationalism and policy often used the same arguments and conformed to similar social pressures. See John J. Johnson, *Political Change in Latin America* (Stanford: Stanford University Press, 1958), Chap. 6.

character to the foreign policy of Ghana and Guinea. To sum up: the Soviet Union, Cuba, Ghana, and Guinea represent a variety of revolutionary leadership in which international policy follows from a "historical struggle" doctrine which is initially and predominantly applied to the domestic plans of these nations.

No similar central theme is present in the variety of revolutionary leadership displayed by contemporary Indonesia, Egypt, Bolivia, and perhaps Iraq or Morocco. To be sure, the internal reformist emphasis is present here too, but it is by no means simply or dialectically translated into foreign policy. Instead, the linkage occurs through the strains and tensions set up by the dissociation between modernizing and traditional political structures and policies, by the vagaries of the so-called non-Western political process. At the simplest level of explanation, self-assertion and even aggressive attitudes on foreign policy are related to the familiar scapegoat, or displacement, device.

When the raison d'être of nationalism—the attainment of political independence—has no longer existed, leaders have endeavored in various ways to perpetuate nationalism as an active and unifying force: by demanding a positive role for their new state in world affairs, by creating new external enemies or threats, and by dramatizing the vision of a new society through monumental public works and other such symbols.[11]

[11] James S. Coleman, in Almond and Coleman, op. cit., p. 554. See the similar points made by Lucian W. Pye, "The Non-Western Political Process," The Journal of Politics, Vol. 29 (1958), pp. 473, 480. For the identification of such tensions in an African setting involving the danger of disintegration on the part of a pyramidal social structure, merging notions of legitimacy, kinship, religion, land ownership, and chieftaincy (Ashanti), see

Opposition groups have found it easiest to challenge authoritarian-reformist governments by merging their specific grievances with a global appeal for drastic external and internal change, a challenge the government leaders then tend to take up by making equally sweeping demands. . . .

To sum up again: Certain revolutionary regimes are compelled by the tension and crisis-ridden nature of their internal reform programs, suffering from the hiatus between modernizing and traditional political processes, to turn to foreign poses of self-assertion. The changes they thus come to demand in the international scene are every bit as revolutionary as their domestic aims, and often dovetail neatly with those advanced by revolutionary regimes impelled by doctrines of class and race.

So far we have concerned ourselves only with the substance of policy pursued by revolutionary regimes. But shoe-thumping, name-calling, unbearably long harangues by bearded heroes dressed in green fatigues, uncompromising language, appeals to some universal brotherhood—whether of the black, the downtrodden, or the victims of various conspiracies, are aspects of style rather than of policy. Because of the danger of confusing substance with style, and the possibility that unconventionality of style is not necessarily and always perfectly correlated with an inherently aggressive policy, an effort will now be made to isolate certain recurring stylistic aspects in the international behavior of revolutionary regimes.

It is a commonplace that the more rationally oriented among revolutionary regimes, that is, Communist regimes, rigorously subordinate means to the achievement of postulated ends.

David E. Apter, "The Role of Traditionalism in the Political Modernization of Ghana and Uganda," World Politics, Vol. 13, No. 1 (October 1960).

Hence, conventional and perverse styles of behavior alternate freely, depending on the immediate definition of ends. In the case of Fascist regimes the case is otherwise. Here the means themselves reflect certain end values, such as the glorification of violence. Hence, their international style is less flexible than the Communists' and more consistently at odds with the canons of "bourgeois" diplomacy. All revolutionary regimes share an affinity for "dual" diplomacy: the simultaneous conduct of their foreign policy through the medium of conventional channels, with their rules and decorum, and through various non-official channels. The search for allies among "the people," "the peace partisans," or "the freedom fighters" among the citizens of enemy states leads to the widespread use of revolutionary political parties and movements, front organizations, and other "progressive" elements as carriers of the revolutionary regime's policy. Since these non-official allies can be mobilized and disbanded at will, can be made to dovetail with conventional gambits, or can be deemphasized completely, they are aspects of revolutionary style rather than inherent attributes of doctrine or policy.[12]

Revolutionary style thrives on apocalyptic language, immoderate threats, and manufactured international crises. But it would be a mistake to dismiss these manifestations as evidences of infantilism or of irresponsibility. Like the practice of scapegoating, such techniques may well possess a functional role in the political processes of non-Western countries. The scarcity of stable, representative, and functionally specific interest groups and of well-organized political parties aggregating their demands, results in national policies being divorced from any sort of structured upward flow of communication. National leaders tend to act in isolation from popular concerns simply because they do not always know what important segments of the public may wish, and consequently feel compelled to appeal in vague and total terms to an undifferentiated public. At the same time, the very absence of specific policy impulses from below enables the leadership to take more clearly defined positions in the international than in the domestic field. To the extent that such positions, couched in the most undiplomatic terms of a Nasser, a Sukarno, and a Castro, reflect an apocalyptic vision, they may be aimed at unifying their own divided societies while staking out a claim for it in the United Nations.[13]

Immoderate style tends to carry with it an impatience for traditional, legal, as well as diplomatic, techniques. Modes of dealing with international conflict by peaceful means frequently imply the open or tacit acceptance of certain principles of law. Revolutionary leaders are always impelled, at least initially, to deny the legitimacy of aspects of international law, in the evolution of which they had no part but which hinder their aims. The practical reasons for this attitude are obvious. It may be suggested, however, that the very qualities of charismatic leadership which are a recurring feature in revolutionary regimes are connected with this impatience. In many non-Western countries the advent of the urban-industrial society implies the

---

[12] This judgment is not accepted by all observers. Michael Lindsay, for example, found that the Chinese Communists see no contradiction in professed allegiance to the *Panch Shila* and the simultaneous commitment to intervention in other countries through the medium of national liberation movements. If Lindsay is correct, the dualistic commitment is not a matter of style, but of doctrine. See his "China and Her Neighbors," in *The Challenge of Communist China* (Proceedings of a Conference held at the University of Minnesota, April 4 and 5, 1960), pp. 21-22.

[13] This point is developed in detail in Pye, *op. cit.,* pp. 480, 482, 484, and in Almond and Coleman, *op. cit.,* pp. 150 ff.

erosion of the uprooted villager's reliance on the rural *patrón,* or the tribal chief. In the unfamiliar urban environment he turns to a demagogic national leader as a substitute, identifies with him, relies on him, supports him unthinkingly.[14] The leader, thus supported, feels free to indulge his freedom of maneuver so as to make claims upon and embarrass foreign countries, and to indulge his charismatic role by denying the validity of international law and diplomatic protocol.

. . . Having thus pinpointed the characteristics of revolutionary regimes, in domestic politics, in substantive foreign policy, and in international style, we must put this force into the context of institutionalized world politics—the United Nations. And we must ask ourselves whether the success and multiplication of such regimes makes doubtful the survival of the kind of international system represented by it.

II

In assessing the responsiveness of revolutionary leaders to influences emanating from the international scene, we must posit the characteristics of the central international institution, the United Nations. In doing this, care must be taken to avoid the analytical extremes of assuming a completely structured and fully deterministic UN "system" or of complete freedom of the will for national actors to fashion a cooperative international commonwealth. Abstraction from reality is certainly a necessity, but the system we abstract must remain faithful to what we know to be true in the conduct of the actors. Hence, the recurring patterns and the structured relationships of UN life must be thrown into relief

[14] In the case of Brazil, this relationship is developed with respect to Vargas by Charles Wagley, in *Social Change in Latin America Today, op. cit.,* pp. 220 ff. A similar point is made by David Apter in his *The Gold Coast in Transition.*

without reification, without sinning on the side of determinism to the extent of not being able to accommodate the organizational evolution, which is not "instability," we know to have taken place. The "system" must permit the "free will" of the national actors to impinge on the totality of relations while retaining the necessarily deterministic properties of any system.

Hence, the category called the "loose bipolar system," made popular by Morton Kaplan, cannot be used as our point of reference. We sacrifice aesthetic neatness by not using this type of system and no claim for an equally cleanly structured approach can be advanced.[15] The desire to remain close to the data saddles us with a more ragged scheme which does not assume as regularly applicable to the UN the systemic rules abstracted by Kaplan. Furthermore, the kind of "systems" approach, here used deliberately, avoids the unnecessary and misleading "balance" and "structure" hypotheses offered by some social psychologists.[16]

But it is equally easy to sin on the side of free will. Some of the ablest commentators on the UN interpret the world organization as an attempt at international institutionalization of Western parliamentary deliberation based "upon the conviction of the reality of freedom of man in the social universe."[17] International organizations are held to fall squarely into the

[15] Morton A. Kaplan, *System and Process in International Politics* (New York: John Wiley and Sons, 1957), pp. 36–43, 56–64, 83–85, 117–20.

[16] For an example of a nonsensical systems approach to international relations, derived in simplistic fashion from Freudian theory, see Frank Harary, "A Structural Analysis of the Situation in the Middle East in 1956," *Journal of Conflict Resolution,* Vol. 5, No. 2 (June 1961).

[17] Inis L. Claude, *Swords Into Plowshares,* 2nd ed. (New York: Random House, 1959), p. 15. This work is the most incisive in treating the United Nations from this vantage point, as well as the most judicious.

liberal-thought pattern, in the sense that they presuppose sufficient freedom of the will for statesmen to alter the international environment by means of rational discussion, negotiation, and voting. Since the institutions of most of the founding states are held to conform to this view of things, the UN could be expected to reflect these influences and thereby gradually "civilize" international politics, if not reform the national political processes of new states. Gradually, a concept of "universal public interest" will come to inform UN deliberations.[18] It is unfortunate for this approach that we already possess convincing evidence from the mouths of Western statesmen that the UN has come under the antiparliamentary influences of the non-Western world, as the membership has grown more universal; the changing environment has influenced the system more than the liberal school is able to concede and it makes little sense to speak of the UN as a "Western system."[19] A universal public interest could be demonstrated only if members of the UN consistently practiced the kind of "wise statesmanship" which

[18] This idea is developed in some detail by Arthur N. Holcombe, "The United Nations and American Foreign Policy," University of Illinois *Bulletin* (October 1957). See also the reports of the Commission to Study the Organization of Peace for specific proposals for strengthening the UN in line with this conceptual commitment.

[19] See the blunt statement on this score by P. H. Spaak, "The Experiment of Collective Security," Carnegie Endowment for International Peace, *Perspectives on Peace, 1910–1960* (New York: Praeger, 1960), p. 85. Further evidence for increasing disappointment with the liberal-parliamentary aspect of the UN can be found in the Carnegie Endowment's series *National Studies on International Organization,* notably the volumes on Belgium, Australia, Canada, Sweden, and Britain. George Modelski treats the UN as a "western universal system" in *The Communist International System* (Princeton: Center of International Studies, December 1, 1960).

Arnold Wolfers advocated in his reconciliation between determinism and free will, his prescription for following the minimal national interest of self-preservation in such a way as to retain a maximum fidelity to universal values.[20] In the absence of such a demonstration, recourse to the liberal yardstick would saddle us with an approach too hortatory and too effervescent to yield more than disappointment.

Comparative historical-sociological analysis, as in Stanley Hoffmann's study of the Concert of Europe, the League of Nations, and the United Nations comes close to an appropriate system. Assessments are made on the basis of typologies of conflict situations correlated with the characteristics of the states which were prominent participants. And the conclusion:

> With respect to relations among the big powers, the record of the three organizations is this: when solidarity existed the organizations were unnecessary. When it did not exist, they were powerless. The remedy cannot be found in the formal association of these states, whose nature makes a real association impossible. In relations among the great powers, decisive for the maintenance of world peace, international organizations stand exposed to perpetual defeat.[21]

Although Hoffmann grants that in disputes among a minor power not allied with a great power, the methods of collective security have worked and, although he credits the League with advancing a concept of international legitimacy in compelling discussion of national aggressive designs, no funda-

[20] Arnold Wolfers and Laurence Martin (eds.), *The Anglo-American Tradition in Foreign Affairs* (New Haven: Yale University Press, 1956), pp. xxvi–xxvii.
[21] Stanley Hoffman, *Organisations Internationales et Pouvoirs Politiques des Etats* (Paris: Armand Colin, 1954), p. 412.

mental change in international relations should be attributed to these trends. My own interpretation of history differs in that it does not assume the category of "great power" to possess the same implications at all times. Put another way, the application of trend analysis to international *systems* requires equal, if not more, attention to the various *environments* in which they operate. Patterned relationships between demands and policies in international systems compel attention to the source of the demands. These remain rooted in the national aims of member states, but, as the advent of revolutionary regimes makes plain, these aims constantly change to produce a variety of environments. Hence, historical conclusions making no allowance for shifting environmental influences are not convincing.

Therefore, the United Nations must be described as a multi-phase system, whose characteristics and evolutionary potential must be specified in terms of the changing environment in which it operates. Environments, in turn, are made up of the totality of policies, aims, expectations, fears, hopes, and hatreds funneled into the institutional structure and its political processes, the "system" proper. If the policies of the United Nations can be demonstrated to change the environment, including the part contributed by the revolutionary regimes, perhaps systemic growth at the expense of the member units can be established. It is important here to distinguish between a "static" system and a "dynamic" one. In a static system the actors channel policies and demands through it and use it as a medium of communication as well as a forum for resolving some conflicts, but they do not necessarily increase the powers and functions of the system in so doing. No growth then takes place. In a dynamic setting, however, some of these efforts carry with them an accretion of new functions and powers for the system, im-

plying the kind of growth we wish to examine in connection with the demands provided by revolutionary regimes.[22]

The variety of demands contributed by member states can be easily grouped along the recurrent lines of discussion which prevail in the UN. They entail (1) collective security, including both enforcement and pacific settlement functions; (2) peaceful change, including the substantive aspects of such areas as the dissolution of colonial empires and disarmament, and the procedural concern with perfecting mediatory and arbitral methods; (3) economic development, technical assistance, and world economic policy; (4) the definition and implementation of human rights. General, as well as highly specific, issues arise in each meeting of UN bodies under each of these headings. But the manner of resolving the issues differs in each phase of the UN system and no issue has so far ever been settled in principle and in perpetuity.

Why is this the case? Formal as well as informal resolutions of issues always take place on the basis of bloc politics; member states never yield a position in its entirety and usually compromise their differences—at various levels of meaningfulness—by a mixture of negotiation and voting. But issues are rarely discussed with sole reference to the category in which a functionally specific analysis would place them. Foreign policy being a web of interlocking aims, the totality of state objectives is fed into the UN system, resulting in a pattern of decisions featuring inter-functional as well as inter-bloc compromise. The character of the environment seems to determine the nature of this compromise, and the environment is unstable with reference to the predominance of this or that

[22] For the distinction between static and dynamic systems see Kenneth E. Boulding, "Organization and Conflict," *Journal of Conflict Resolution*, Vol. 1 (1957), pp. 122–23.

aim. A further environmental instability is introduced by the enlargement of the membership and the resultant quantitative change in the relations among the blocs.

During the first phase of the UN system (1945–47), the honeymoon period among the great powers prevented these strains from impinging on one another. Collective security was the dominant concern and it hinged around skirmishing in the Security Council, and at times it looked as if the Churchillian notion of the postwar status quo might achieve institutionalization by virtue of the UN. But the real onset of the Cold War proved this suspicion wrong, and by 1948 the second phase of the system got under way, characterized by the dominance of the United States and its successful enlisting of the UN on its behalf.

During the second phase, the dominant *motif* was the identification of collective security with the military-political aims of the Western bloc, successfully asserted in Korea and in the Uniting for Peace Resolution. Demands for a world economic policy and far more ambitious economic-aid measures than actively championed by the West were put forward by Afro-Asian and Latin American states but were not implemented in full. Discussion of human rights was initiated and championed by the West so long as it fitted in with Cold-War policy, though non-Western blocs advanced demands in this area for quite different reasons. Peaceful change was demanded in a variety of anti-colonial claims but found implementation only in the case of the former Italian colonies. While the Soviet bloc placed itself in a non-bargaining position by completely disputing the legitimacy of all UN discussion and steps not in line with Soviet policy, the Western bloc dominated the system by successfully obtaining the support of the Latin American and part of the Afro-Asian blocs on collective security issues and "paying" for

this by occasional concessions in the economic and colonial fields.

By 1954 the second phase came to its end with important changes in the environment. The number of Afro-Asian members increased, especially after 1955. The European members of the Western bloc grew disenchanted with a policy of collective security which seemed too close to general warfare. The colonial and human-rights issues were linked ever more closely in the demands of the Latin American and Afro-Asian blocs, and the crescendo of economic demands rose as the American security policy grew more and more dependent on general support. And most importantly, Joseph Stalin died. With his demise the role of the Soviet Union in international organizations underwent such an important—if tactical—change as to destroy the environment of the second phase.

Since that time, the third phase has prevailed, involving institutionalized inter-regional and inter-functional bargaining in a setting in which the colonial and human-rights issues have furnished the dominant *motif,* and the practice of collective security has been increasingly subordinated to it in terms of the kind of support forthcoming for Western-bloc demands. Peaceful change, of sorts, has prevailed along with intensified international economic development efforts, in the relatively amicable way in which colonial empires have dissolved under UN prodding. Neutralism has come into its own, quantitatively, and the "balancing" pattern of collective security holds sway, featuring conciliation rather than enforcement.

Shortly, however, a fourth phase will arise. Functionally, it will be marked by the end of the colonial issue as a dominant theme. The human-rights issue well may be eliminated from the demands of the very Afro-Asian and Latin American states which have featured it in connection with their anti-colonial campaign and may reacquire value for Western nations freed from a variety of skeletons in their closets. Economic demands will increase, and collective security aims by the West will have to be paid for exclusively in this area now. Further, if the alliance between the Soviet and certain under-developed nations continues, the Soviet bloc may funnel its particular variety of collective security into the UN, and may be expected to pay for it in economic aid. Whatever the precise outline of the pattern of inter-functional and inter-bloc politics may be, a behavior pattern discerned for the revolutionary regimes during the second and third phases cannot *a priori* be expected to continue with the sharp change in the environment introduced by the end of colonialism.

The UN system is hyperdependent on its environment. Precedents set in one phase, therefore, do not necessarily predetermine action in the next. Unless a great deal of "internalization" of "rules" can be demonstrated, the very multiphase character of the system militates against substantial growth. All issues are resolved *ad hoc,* stable alliances among interests cannot develop, compromises and related communication patterns among participants can generate no fixed institutional characteristics. Even the "non-resolution consequences" of UN activity display no cumulative pattern.[23] Substituting debate and voting for fighting, in the sense of using the UN as a litmus paper for determining the strength of the opponent, wanes with the change in functional preoccupation. While communication among members may narrow differences in the perception of reality, in one phase, the process may have to start all over in the next. There is evidence that the United States has "learned" the lesson of Korea in no longer expecting the kind

of collective-security operation which it mounted in 1950 and is now seeking security through balancing; but there is less evidence that Nasser and Nkrumah have learned the same thing. . . .[24]

In fact, it must be stressed that in a different focus the UN is a successful, if phase-ridden and politics-dominated, international institution. It has served to channel aspects of national foreign policy never before submitted to any collective scrutiny. It has tamed and civilized national policies by serving as an approximation to an institutionalized process of interest politics, and thereby containing the interests. If the Western political process be conceived, not as dispassionate debate, capped by voting and subject to judicial review, but as the articulate defense of rival group interests in permanent confrontation and subject to cumulative compromises, the UN process is not so very different. The study of policies during the various phases of the system could thus become a study of the methods used to achieve various types of compromises. Systemic development or growth could be evaluated by the role of the organization itself, as distinguished from components contributed by the environment, in advancing compromises.

We already possess a good deal of evidence permitting such evaluations for the period 1945–55.[25] It permits the conclusion that the system did *not* increase the *legitimacy* it enjoys in the eyes of its members. Demands for UN action and invocation of its Charter were *not* accompanied by cumulative claims for a greater autonomous insti-

[23] Chadwick F. Alger, "Non-Resolution Consequences of the United Nations and Their Effect on International Conflict," *ibid.,* Vol. 5, No. 2 (June 1961).

[24] For such evidence see Arnold Wolfers (ed.), *Alliance Policy in the Cold War* (Baltimore: Johns Hopkins Press, 1959).

[25] See the seven volume study of the Brookings Institution, published between 1956 and 1958, as well as the twenty-odd volumes which make up the study of the Carnegie Endowment for International Peace, previously cited.

tutional role for the system. This was true for revolutionary as well as non-revolutionary states. However, the *authority* of the system *did* increase for all types of member states, in the sense that many of them increasingly heeded resolutions and decisions addressed to them.[26] In fact, authority tended to increase as many of the member states grew more and more dissatisfied with the style of debate and the quality of the decisions. Growing dissatisfaction, then, did not engender loss of authority. Whether a similar picture obtains more in recent years and whether it will be true in the next phase of the UN's life remains to be investigated.

Clearly, then, an effort must be made to assess changes produced on the environment, as reflected in the policies and attitudes of member states. But an effort must also be made to specify possible systemic changes after 1955; and the attitudes of revolutionary states with reference to accretions of autonomous UN powers is here a particularly sensitive yardstick.

Relationships developed in resolving conflicts peacefully also furnish a useful index at the level of the system itself. They may hinge around the degree to which member states have internalized the purposes and procedures used to resolve one conflict, and are then prepared to apply them to new ones. Since this would vary with the importance attached to the conflict, with the satisfaction derived from the solution, the adequacy of the attendant communications network and the number of roles served by the relationship, different patterns most likely can be found during various phases. An overall increase in involvement, irrespective of phase and type of state involved would provide excellent evidence of systemic growth.[27] But Robert North,

the author of this approach, also cautions that the extent to which a member state relies on the notion of the external and internal "enemy" to resolve or channel domestic conflict, is likely to determine his responsiveness to the international modes of resolving conflicts. Dependence on "enemies" is a typical feature of revolutionary regimes; but would this imply declining responsiveness to the peaceful solution of conflicts in the next phase of the UN's life? It should be remembered that the history of the League of Nations and of the nineteenth-century Concert of Europe indicates that revolutionary regimes are insensitive to the pressures of the international environment in their preoccupation with domestic change. In contrast to conservative and status-quo oriented regimes, external regulative mechanisms were not accepted in the value systems of revolutionary elites and therefore had to be imposed by the use or the threat of force.

Dag Hammarskjöld once described the UN as an "institutional system of coexistence" which might evolve toward a federative social system with its own public law if it is entrusted with new tasks which it alone can carry out, and if new environmental challenges are met by growing autonomy and delegated power, including the revitalization of portions of the Charter which have not yet been used.[28] One way of testing the evolutionary strength of the UN is to apply these yardsticks of development to the portion of the environment contributed by revolutionary regimes. If they prove responsive to the system's stimulus, growth is likely. The alternatives might be stated thus:

[26] This argument is developed in detail in E. B. Haas, "The Comparative Study of the United Nations," *World Politics*, Vol. 12, No. 2 (January 1960).

[27] Robert G. North, Howard E. Koch, Jr.,

and Dina A. Zinnes, "The Integrative Functions of Conflict," *Journal of Conflict Resolution*, Vol. 4, No. 3 (September 1960), p. 366.

[28] Dag Hammarskjöld, "Towards a Constitutional Order," in *Perspectives on Peace, op. cit.*, pp. 66–75.

1. Successful institutionalization of interest politics will enhance the authority of the UN system and transform the environment by toning down the international aspects of the revolutionary behavior of certain member states. A growth in legitimacy would also follow.

2. The growing number and extreme demands of revolutionary member states will substantially change the system during its next phase and perhaps destroy it.

3. New functional relationships will have the result of transforming the environment in toning down aspects of revolutionary behavior without concurrently contributing to the authority and legitimacy of the system itself.

III

Revolutionary states were exposed to the influence of international organization since 1919. If the revolutionary state simply withdraws from the system when national aims are in danger of being blunted by its rule, the problem of the system's transforming the environment can be simply dismissed. This, indeed, is what occurred in the League of Nations in relation to Japan, Italy, and Germany. Each pursued aims inconsistent with the rules of the system, and upon being stigmatized—however ineffectually—simply pursued the same aims outside the system. Withdrawal barely caused any soul-searching; the ideology and style of the revolutionary leadership in question was inconsistent with "international cooperation" in any case because of its insistence on national strength and self-sufficiency. The League's impact on the revolutionary environment was nil.

The same is true of the Soviet Union even though its role in the League was far more complex. Dallin interprets the Soviet role in Geneva as a species of popular front diplomacy designed to dovetail with the concomitant anti-Fascist work of the Comintern and aimed at maximizing Soviet security. While it certainly involved no doctrinal commitment to the rules of the Covenant, Soviet participation had the incidental consequence of seeking to strengthen the universal system. Not only did Moscow carry out the sanctions voted against Italy and Paraguay, but it actually sought to strengthen the legal powers of the League in the field of enforcement.[29] When contrasted with the earlier sweeping Russian denunciations of the League as "an alliance of world bandits against the proletariat," the Soviets then, as now, seemed to demonstrate a fine appreciation of systemic possibilities in *one* set of environmental circumstances. But the events of 1939 demonstrate that no internalization of rules was involved.

Since 1945 the international environment has undergone such drastic changes that a more functionally complex analysis is required to do it justice. The field of collective security will be examined first as a source of revolutionary initiatives, including the enforcement as well as the pacific settlement aspects.

Neutralism, not a specific revolutionary content, is responsible for the policy expectations regarding collective security put forth by Indonesia, Egypt, and Ghana. The monarchist regime in Egypt entertained great expectations of UN mediatory and armed help in its struggles with Britain and Israel, until it realized that the great-power balance in the Security Council would give its policy little solace. At that point it turned to neutralism even before the advent of the Nasser regime and denounced UN collective security

[29] Alexander Dallin, *The Soviet View of the United Nations* (Cambridge: MIT Center for International Studies, August 1959), pp. 10–12, 18–19. Elliott Goodman, *The Soviet Design for a World State* (New York: Columbia University Press, 1960), pp. 383–85. Kathryn Davis, *The Soviets at Geneva* (Geneva: Librairie Kundig, 1934), p. 21.

as "unjust power politics."[30] Whenever the East-West conflict dominates, these regimes seek to conciliate Moscow and Washington, and failing in this, abstain from endorsing any kind of collective action. Indonesia and Egypt gave no assistance to UN forces in Korea, opposed the crossing of the 38th parallel, and abstained on votes concerned with alleged atrocities by UN forces in Korea. Both abstained in the vote on the Assembly's critical report on Hungary, even though Indonesia had supported the creation of the Special Commission on Hungary. "The problem we have to solve here now," said the Indonesian delegate, "is how to diminish and if possible how to dissipate the distrust that exists among the opposing parties." But Indonesia was active in persuading Syria and Turkey not to press their differences to a vote in the Assembly in 1957. In Cold-War disputes, collective security implies exclusive dedication to conciliation by uncommitted powers and abstinence from any enforcement or investigatory action which would favor one side or the other. In disputes involving the colonial issue, however,

energetic action is advocated, provided it can be carried out in such a way as to exclude the East-West conflict. The full panoply of UN techniques is then to be thrown into the fray, including troops and neutralization agreements negotiated under the auspices of the General Assembly, as indicated by Ghana's role in the settlement of the Lebanese-Jordanian crisis of 1958. The prejudice against armed action or energetic peaceful settlement, in short, does not apply to the type of dispute which concerns revolutionary nations most intimately.[31]

Soviet policy in the UN conforms more closely to specifically revolutionary expectations. In the early years of the UN the Soviet regime still regarded the Charter and its rules as legitimating the postwar status quo of big-power dominance, institutionalized through a concert in which each major power wielded a veto and collective security was to be practiced at the expense of smaller powers. Even though the Soviet Union took a very conservative position with respect to the powers of the UN and the absolute sway of the principle of national sovereignty, it relaxed these opinions in practice to permit the peaceful solution of the Corfu Channel and Iranian disputes in such a manner as to strengthen the authority of UN organs. The system seemed to assert itself even over revolutionary members.

This trend was reversed with the announcement in 1948 of the "two camps" doctrine. No concessions to systemic authority were permitted in the Greek, Korean, Berlin, and satel-

[30] *Egypt and the United Nations*, Report of a Study Group Set up by the Egyptian Society of International Law (New York: Manhattan Publishing Company, 1957). However, the passage to "active" or "positive" neutralism was an innovation of the military regime. While no doubt produced by the internal needs for status and prestige of Nasser, both in Egypt and in the Arab world, this concept implies an enhanced role for the UN in collective security and in disarmament negotiations as a means to prevent superpower summitry and to institutionalize the balancing role of uncommitted nations. For an explicit argument along these lines see Clovis Maqsud, *The Meaning of Positive Neutrality* (in Arabic) (Beirut: 1960), pp. 128, 135, 137, as quoted in Binder, *op. cit.* Possible relationships between African neutralism and anomic conceptions of authority in new nations are explored by Francis X. Sutton, "Authority and Authoritarianism in the New Africa," *Journal of International Affairs,* Vol. 15, No. 1 (1961).

[31] Jan F. Triska and Howard E. Koch, "The Asian-African Nations and International Organization," *The Review of Politics,* Vol. 21, No. 2 (April 1959), pp. 450–51. Sydney D. Bailey, *The General Assembly* (New York: Praeger, 1960), p. 155. Consulate of Indonesia (San Francisco), *Indonesia's Voting Record in the United Nations.* Kwame Nkrumah, "African Prospect," *Foreign Affairs,* Vol. 37, No. 1 (October 1958), pp. 49–50.

lite peace-treaty cases. The UN became a holding operation in which the Soviets sought merely to protect the position of the "Socialist camp" by blocking American action and by propaganda attacks, buttressed with constitutional arguments opposing majority decision-making, functional expansion, and neutrality in administration. But the exceptions are vital: Whenever the interests of the Soviet Union happened to converge with those of the West (as in Palestine, Kashmir, Indonesia), the *ad hoc* concert produced by the international environment resulted in UN mediatory and enforcement action in which the Soviets ignored their own opposition to third-party intercession, commissions of investigation, Secretariat participation, and teams of military observers. But the outbreak of the Korean War proves that this pragmatic attitude of the Soviet Union involved no acceptance of the intrinsic legitimacy of the norms of the Charter.[32]

There are those who insist that the more recent active participation of the post-Stalinist Soviet leadership in the UN marks merely a tactical shift and no change in ultimate objectives: Weakness forced Stalin into an isolationist position toward the universal system, while strength and self-confidence propel Khrushchev into using the UN as a vehicle for actively advancing revolutionary aims.[33] While this may be true, it is not of direct importance to the problem of assessing a systemic impact on the environment; an upgrading of the UN in Soviet policy may bring with it unexpected consequences which must be accepted even by a revolutionary leadership if more basic Soviet aims are to be advanced. In any case, the settlement of the Korean crisis demonstrated for the first time Soviet responsiveness to the balancing efforts of the uncommitted Afro-Asian bloc, to be followed soon by the scrapping of the "two camps" theory. By granting the existence of an uncommitted bloc, a "zone of peace" was now interposed between East and West which had to be wooed in non-aggressive ways in order to assure the demise of capitalism without setting off nuclear war. In the process the UN was found useful for the propagation of the doctrine of competitive peaceful coexistence. In instances of outright challenge to the Soviet bloc, as in Hungary, the Stalinist tactics are revived; but in all other situations the new assessment has produced a thoroughly expediential attitude with respect to collective security in which balancing operations, involving conciliation, armed forces recruited from neutrals, and the intercession of the Secretary-General, are tolerated, even if not lauded. Korovin aptly summed up the current attitude with its invocation of the Charter on behalf of the new Soviet world view:

> . . . the constant growth of Soviet economic and defensive might, of the moral authority of the USSR, of the merger of the entire socialist camp on the basis of proletarian internationalism and its growing strength, the support of its international policy by the partisans of peace throughout the world vividly testify to the fact that the realization of the democratic principles of the UN Charter becomes increasingly the unanimous demand of all peace-loving humanity.[34]

[32] On this period see Alexander W. Rudzinski, "The Influence of the United Nations on Soviet Policy," *International Organization,* Vol. 5, No. 2 (May 1951), and Rupert Emerson and Inis L. Claude, "The Soviet Union and the United Nations," *ibid.,* Vol. 6, No. 1 (February 1952). Subsequent events have done nothing to change the validity of these interpretations.

[33] Especially, Goodman, *op. cit.,* pp. 128-52.

[34] Quoted in Dallin, *op. cit.,* p. 43. My interpretations owes much to Dallin's analysis

It is in this vein that the invocation of UN principles by the revolutionary government of Cuba must be understood. Its appeals to the Security Council and the General Assembly are devices of the Cold War, to equate the policies of the United States with colonialism, and to rally the "democratic principles of the UN Charter" to the side of Socialist and anti-colonial revolt. Although the revolutionary government of Bolivia has supported the Western conception of collective security, the growing link between Havana and Moscow has been accompanied by a Cuban attitude toward collective security which is identical with the Soviet position. The change in the international environment, which was ratified by the package deal on admission to UN membership in 1955, has been a source of self-confidence to the Communist bloc, inducing it to use UN institutions as a means for exacting recognition from the West of the legitimacy of the new status quo. In disputes not immediately invested with the aura of the Cold War, at least this change in the environment has facilitated continuation of balancing as a mode of maintaining collective security, at the expense of concerted big-power action and of permissive enforcement by one of them.

Policy aims in the context of collective security test the capacity of the UN system to deal with violent challenges to its norms. More commonly, however, demands for a change in international relations correspond to national policies falling short of recourse to war. Another test of the system's capacity, then, lies in its ability to facilitate peaceful change, especially the drastic demands put forward by

revolutionary member states. Peaceful change, as distinguished from collective security, is any successful adjustment in the international status quo brought about before a specific "dispute" involving force or the threat of it arises; this adjustment is always made at the expense of certain reluctant member states and is due to pressure organized through the medium of parliamentary diplomacy.[35] Peaceful change so defined does not imply the complete absence of violence; it merely covers situations in which no formal interstate hostilities take place, but in which the bone of contention does arouse competing state postures.

The contrast between Suez and the Congo provides an example. In the Suez case, previously unsuccessful efforts to change the status quo nonviolently (Nasser's unwillingness to satisfy France on Algeria and Britain on the continued neutrality of the Canal) resulted in an act of war, followed by pacific settlement and threatened enforcement measures voted and implemented by the General Assembly, thus restoring the *status quo ante bellum* by means of a balancing operation. The Congo, on the other hand, is an example of "preventive diplomacy," in which the UN, acting through the Secretary-General, sought to anticipate interstate rivalry by insulating the troublespot, and in so doing, "peacefully changing" the bubbling cauldron into a gently seething potion.[36]

This definition of peaceful change corresponds to the actual experience of

[35] I follow the definition of parliamentary diplomacy invented by Dean Rusk and applied by Philip C. Jessup in "Parliamentary Diplomacy: An Examination of the Legal Quality of the Rules of Procedure of Organs of the United Nations," *Recueil des Cours,* Vol. 89 (Leyden: Académie de Droit International, 1956).

[36] The difference is well developed by Inis L. Claude, "The United Nations and the Use of Force," *International Conciliation,* No. 532 (March 1961), p. 383.

of the post-1955 period. Dallin offers convincing evidence that the Soviet leadership made a reasoned decision in 1955 to profit from the tripolarization of power in the UN to upgrade the organization as a vehicle of national policy.

international organizations and thus conflicts with generally held legal conceptions. It takes for granted that there is no international judicial order which can induce major political change by legal techniques. As Brierly put it:

> When a state claims . . . something which is not its legal right, something even which it knows it can have only by an alteration of the legal position, it is useless to suggest that it should submit the determination of its claim to legal decision. It knows beforehand that the answer of the law will be adverse; and that answer is precisely what it claims to have altered.[37]

Nor does it assume the existence of an international legislative order which might give substance to Article 14 of the UN Charter. Legislating territorial change would imply the willingness of the drafters of the Charter to forego the very status quo they wished to institutionalize in writing the norms. Only when the territorial change corresponds to a new generally held consensus, or when it follows from a previous decision by the large powers to wash their hands of an unresolvable issue not vital to them, can the UN successfully perform a legislative task. This happened only in the case of the Italian colonies.[38]

So defined, the most conspicuously successful area of peaceful change has been the disengagement of the western powers from colonial responsibilities. The shrinking number of trust territories, the ever more intense examination by the General Assembly of colonial policy in other dependent areas, and the instituting of colonial reform by Britain, France, Holland, the United States, and New Zealand in anticipation of UN criticism are a matter of record. Belgium and Portugal, less responsive in the past to parliamentary diplomacy, are now being subjected to its possibilities. In general, all Afro-Asian, Soviet-bloc and most Latin American countries have made up the UN majorities providing the necessary pressure, whether the regimes were revolutionary or not. Yet it is instructive to single out certain countries and the Congo crisis in order to discover whether anti-colonial demands emanating from revolutionary regimes were exceptionally extreme.

The Soviets have taken the most extreme position in consistently putting forward measures aiming at immediate independence for all dependent territories and blaming the Western powers for failing to cooperate. They have used the debates of the Trusteeship Council for this purpose alone; they justify their acceptance of the principle of trusteeship only because it "contributes to the struggle of the colonial peoples for freedom," and continue to stand "for the revolutionary method of solving the national-colonial question."[39] The African and Asian revolutionary regimes sympathize, as do Cuba and Mexico, but they are willing to tone down specific resolutions

[37] As quoted in Lincoln Bloomfield, "Law, Politics and International Disputes," *ibid.,* No. 516 (January 1958), p. 284.

[38] For interesting information concerning the lack of success of attempted UN legislative change in the peaceful reunification of Korea prior to 1950, see Leon Gordenker, *The United Nations and the Peaceful Unification of Korea* (The Hague: Martinus Nijhoff, 1959). The same conclusion could be drawn from efforts "legislatively" to solve the Palestine issue prior to the outbreak of hostilities since the resolution recommending partition was never implemented in its official form. But it should be noted that unwillingness to agree to peaceful change is not the exclusive privilege of revolutionary regimes.

The Egyptian monarchy initiated the policy of closing the Suez Canal to Israel-bound ships. See Leo Gross, "Passage through the Suez Canal of Israel-Bound Cargo and Israel Ships," *American Journal of International Law,* Vol. 51, No. 3 (July 1957).

[39] B. M. Shrushalov, as quoted in Dallin, *op. cit.,* p. 60.

on concrete issues to permit gradualist compromises. Nkrumah is candid about his disregard for the legitimacy of the boundaries of UN trust territories when these stand in the way of pan-African aims. He and other revolutionary African leaders only invoke the principles of the Charter in support of specific demands for ejecting European influence but play them down when it comes to future programs. For the coming years they stress sealing off the African continent and creating a regional system of pacific settlement, non-intervention and economic development.[40] In the meantime they argue in favor of strengthening all conceivable agencies of the UN system which might bring closer the day when colonies will cease to exist: the constant use of UN-supervised plebiscites, UN inspections of progress toward independence, more UN follow-up on petitions, strengthening the Committee on Non-Self-Governing Territories, and requiring more and more detailed reports from the colonial powers under Article 73e of the Charter. Interestingly enough, this integrative aspect of the anti-colonial demands is supported by the Soviet Union, which otherwise opposes the creation of new UN institutions. It also has more support from Bolivia, Mexico, and Cuba than from traditional Latin American regimes.

The history of the Congo imbroglio, however, demonstrates the selectivity observed by revolutionary regimes in seeking to obtain satisfaction for na-

tional policy through UN action. The extreme of unilateralism is represented by the Soviet bloc. The Communist nations supported UN intervention, as long as such action unambiguously opposed Belgium and seemed to aid Lumumba. Soviet opposition to UN operations, which culminated in the attacks on the person and the institution of the Secretary-General, did not formally arise until the balance had shifted to Kasavubu. But approval of the early UN action had never precluded unilateral Soviet assistance to Congo factions. After the death of Lumumba, Moscow considered the Stanleyville regime of Antoine Gizenga as the only legitimate Congo government, even though the Leopoldville delegation had been seated in New York; drastic action against Belgium, the autonomous Katanga regime, and the Mobutu "mercenaires" were demanded. The failure of the UN to adopt sufficiently stringent resolutions was met by a Soviet refusal to participate in the financing of the Congo Operation. At the end of the fifteenth Session of the General Assembly, the Soviet bloc, alone among the revolutionary regimes, opposed the creation of the second Conciliation Commission, which, unlike the first, was to include European and American representatives; the Soviets also opposed the prompt convening of the Congo Parliament under UN protection and the UN-aided interfactional negotiations leading to a shoring up of the Kasavubu government.

Of the other revolutionary regimes, only Cuba and Guinea supported the Soviet extreme at all times. But up to March 1961, Ghana, Mali, Indonesia, Morocco, and the United Arab Republic had taken the same qualified position in favor of UN intervention: They went along with it as long at it seemed to serve the pan-African end of creating a united Congo under Lumumbist rule and opposed it when the balance swung to the Kasavubu forces. At that point these leaders withdrew their con-

[40] K. Nkrumah, *Ghana* (New York: Thomas Nelson, 1957), pp. 258 and 261. See also Nkrumah's speech and the final *Declaration* of the Conference of Independent African States, Accra, April 22, 1958, especially Resolutions 1 and 5. All revolutionary regimes sought to influence the plebiscite in British Cameroons so as to result in union with a radical independent Cameroons rather than with a moderate Nigeria. They also favored the attainment of independence by French Cameroons under such conditions as to strengthen the outlawed opposition groups.

tingents from the Congo or resigned from the first Conciliation Commission, thus demonstrating their displeasure with the policy of the Secretary-General. The United Arab Republic gave unilateral support to Gizenga, and Ghana openly intrigued against Mobutu.

Second thoughts seemed to arise among these governments when Hammerskjöld continued to take an uncompromising position in favor of following a patient policy of supporting whatever regime in the Congo seemed to offer the greatest promise of unifying the country in such a manner as to exclude Cold-War rivalries. Despite its threats, Ghana never withdrew its sizeable forces and the United Arab Republic sought to act as a conciliator (together with Ceylon) in the Security Council debate between the United States and the Soviet Union. As the fifteenth Session drew to its close, all the non-Communist revolutionary regimes went along with the creation of the second Conciliation Commission—which they no longer control—and thus separated themselves publicly from Soviet Congo policy.[41] The peculiar international role played by Guinea, Mali, Ghana, and the United Arab Republic in the deliberations of the UN concerning the Congo and the three Cameroons suggests that the utilization of these potentially integrative techniques remained, at first, rigidly subordinated to the achievement of pan-African goals.[42] But when the dan-

gers of such a course became apparent, they supported the continuation of the UN effort even when hopes for achieving the maximal program had to be abandoned.

Disarmament negotiations exemplify attempts at peacefully changing a serious international irritant which have so far been unsuccessful. Most of the recent substantive negotiations have been carried on outside the UN framework, with General Assembly debate merely creating a "moral climate" and concentrating on procedural aspects. The superpowers themselves have sharply narrowed the areas of difference between them, but this must be attributed to the nature and perception of warfare, rather than to any specific systemic impulse which can be credited to the UN.[43] On the procedural question of whether the Soviet or the Western proposals for various disarmament commissions should be followed, the

---

[41] This summary is based on the debates concerning the following resolutions: S/4369, S/4383, S/4386, S/4404, S/4426, S/4425, S/4453, S/4494, S/4519, S/4523, S/4525, A/L.292/rev 1, A/L.294, A/L.293, A/L.319 Rev 2, A/L.322 Rev 1, S/4578, S/4579, A/L.331 Rev 1, A/L.332, S/4625, S/4741, S/4733 Rev 1, S/4740. I have also drawn heavily on the Secretary-General's statement of December 7, 1960, embodying his comments on docs. S/4573 and S/4571.

[42] See Immanuel Wallerstein, "Pan-Africanism as Protest," in Morton A. Kaplan, ed., *The Revolution in World Politics* (New

York and London: John Wiley and Sons, Inc., 1962), pp. 137–151, for the explanation of how territorial pan-African goals fit into the revolutionary ideology of negritude and independent national modernization. However, the "conservative" new states of the Brazzaville grouping, though not uniformly in sympathy with pan-African principles, followed a course in the UN's handli ; of the Congo which was every bit as ex ediential in motivation as was the attitude of the "revolutionary" Casablanca groupin . When UN intervention seemed to protect a confederal solution to the Congo crisis they praised the organization; when, however, the intent of the intervention seemed to be the shoring up of Lumumba, the Brazzaville nations denounced UN action as interference with national sovereignty. See the excellent analysis by Robert C. Good, "Congo Crisis: The Role of the New States," *Neutralism* (Washington, D.C.: Washington Center of Foreign Policy Research, 1961), pp. 1–46.

[43] For a thoughtful analysis of the growth of agreement, see Philip E. Jacob, "The Disarmament Consensus," *International Organization*, Vol. 14, No. 2 (Spring 1960). My summary of UN discussions is based on General Assembly disarmament debates since 1955.

bulk of the revolutionary states has sided with the Soviet Union or abstained. Bolivia, however, regularly supports the United States; Mexico seeks to mediate, and the Cuban position shifted in 1960 from unswerving support for the West to equally fervid alignment with Moscow. All revolutionary states greeted Khrushchev's general disarmament plan with favor, whereas in previous years they had studiously avoided taking sides on the merits of rival proposals and had merely prodded the superpowers to continue negotiating, though Ghana, Morocco, Mali, and the United Arab Republic moderated their stance by stressing the mediation of uncommitted nations. Again, on the matter of suspending nuclear tests, in general, and preventing the French from going ahead with their plans, in particular, most revolutionary states espoused the extreme disarmament position also taken by the Soviet Union. To the extent that disarmament negotiations are at all influenced by the process of parliamentary diplomacy, the pressure of the revolutionary countries bolsters any proposal which looks promising even if the inspection provisions do not meet with Washington's approval. An eventual softening of the Western position on this point is likely, without implying an accretion of new powers of inspection and supervision to the UN. . . .

Multilateral action for technical assistance and economic development comes closest to meeting rigorous criteria for a general UN "consensus," as constituting a recognized "universal interest." It has not always been so. Prior to the period of Afro-Asian ascendancy in the UN, the economic development issue had split the membership into three blocs; but by 1955 a cumulative train of events had been unleashed which resulted in ever growing accretions of institutional and financial authority in UN hands. Expansion of the system's task was due to the

fact that the Western-developed nations gave in, up to a point, to the demands of the underdeveloped nations and that the Soviet bloc dropped its absolute condemnation of UN assistance.

Yet, with the exception of changing Soviet policy, little can be demonstrated about specific concerns of revolutionary regimes in policy aims relating to economic development. All underdeveloped member states stood for a maximum of multilateral aid, free from strings, and dispensed by international agencies which would be dominated by their votes. Revolutionary, as well as traditional, oligarchies, socialist and conservative regimes, called for the Expanded Program of Technical Assistance, SUNFED, the International Finance Corporation, and the Special Fund. Indeed, the striking feature is the willingness of revolutionary regimes to give up certain cherished aims in the process of finding compromises acceptable to the developed nations.[44]

Mexico, despite its intense nationalist suspicion of foreign capital, strongly supported IFC. The same is true of Egypt, Indonesia, and Bolivia. These revolutionary nations took the initiative in proposing the creation of the Special Fund and expressed their willingness to subordinate themselves to a strong managing director and a qualified majority voting formula in the Governing Council.[45]

[44] Benjamin Higgins and Guy Pauker, "Economic Aspects of the Asian-African Conference and its Aftermath," *Ekonomi dan Keuanqan Indonesia* (Nos. 5–6, 1955), pp. 16–17. Oscar Lewis, "Mexico Since Cardenas," in *Social Change in Latin America Today, op. cit.,* pp. 306–307. B. E. Matecki, "Establishment of the International Finance Corporation: A Case Study," *International Organization,* Vol. 10, No. 2 (May 1956). Robert E. Elder and Forrest D. Murden, "Economic Co-Operation: Special United Nations Fund for Economic Development" (New York: Woodrow Wilson Foundation, 1954).
[45] See the revealing case study on SUNFED

Soviet conduct is more complex. Until 1954 the policy of the Soviet Union in UN economic agencies was entirely negative: It blamed underdevelopment on imperialism and opposed multilateral aid as a camouflaged device for perpetuating colonial dependence, insisting instead on the wholesale application of socialist techniques; Soviet speeches and resolutions were confined to attacking Western economic moves, especially the strategic embargo, and to make propaganda charges. Stalin's death changed all this. With the offer of Soviet contributions to EPTA came the recognition of the propriety of multilateral aid. Suggestions for the creation of a new universal trade organization were made while some of the satellites offered to join GATT. Soviet participation in the work of the economic commissions for Europe and for Asia and the Far East grew cooperative, so much so that the Soviet Union offered to contribute to the Mekong River Project. Consistent with this change, Moscow then proceeded to support the creation of SUNFED, IFC, and the Special Fund. In procedural and administrative disputes with the Technical Assistance Board and the Secretariat over the degree of bilateralism to be permitted in the distribution of the Soviet contributions to these agencies, the Soviet position was invariably overruled—and yet the Soviet Union continued to participate on a modest scale. Bilateral aid is also offered by the Soviets within the confines of UN discussions and some commentators suspect that it is the long-range policy of Moscow to maneuver the UN aid effort into a universal bilateralist scheme. But in failing to achieve this, the Soviets as well as other revolutionary regimes have so far ac-

commodated themselves to the evolving rules of the UN system.[46]

Aspirations concerning economic development are common to all types of regimes and even revolutionary governments will swallow aspects of international control in this realm which would otherwise be an anathema. Hence, it is instructive to contrast the policy aims of revolutionary regimes in the field of the international protection of human rights with economic development. The Soviet Union, prior to 1953, strongly supported all general declarations and specific legal texts affirming and defining human rights, especially the rights to national self-determination and protection of natural resources against alien control. But it equally strongly opposed all efforts to provide even a minimal UN machinery for enforcing these rights or reporting on their implementation. A subtle change crept into this position after 1953: Soviet delegates proved quite willing to approve the creation of commissions of inquiry to probe into situations damaging to the West but continued to oppose these when they were to deal with allegations relating to the Soviet bloc. The mellowing of opposition to UN institutional competence in the human-rights field went hand in hand with some disagreement among Soviet jurists as to the degree of jurisdiction international judicial bodies might enjoy over national sovereignty. At the same time the Soviet Union consented to participation in several efforts by

[46] Dallin, op. cit., p. 63. Alvin Z. Rubinstein, "Soviet Policy Toward Underdeveloped Areas in the Economic and Social Council," International Organization, Vol. 9, No. 2 (May 1955); "Soviet Policy in ECAFE: A Case Study of Soviet Behavior in International Economic Organizations," ibid., Vol. 12, No. 4 (Autumn 1958). R. L. Allen, "United Nations Technical Assistance: Soviet and East European Participation," ibid., Vol. 11, No. 4 (Autumn 1957). Harold K. Jacobson, "The Soviet Union, the UN and World Trade," Western Political Quarterly, Vol. 11, No. 3 (September 1958).

and the Special Fund in John G. Hadwen and Johan Kaufmann, How United Nations Decisions Are Made (Leyden: A. W. Sythoff, 1960), pp. 85–122.

the International Labor Organization to probe the existence of trade-union rights in Russia.[47]

Other revolutionary nations show little evidence of an increasing willingness to submit to UN jurisdiction. To be sure, they all espouse the Universal Declaration of Human Rights and have supported the drafting of some of the two most far-reaching clauses of the two Covenants. Yet the emphasis is uniformly not on civil and political rights of individuals, but on the collective right of national self-determination, in its political and economic aspects. The African states use the Declaration to legitimize *national* freedom but ignore its provisions when it comes to the rights of *tribal* groups. Universal rights are invoked against present colonialism but untrammeled national sovereignty or regional cohesion is held out for future developments. UN commissions are created to inquire into the colonial aspect, but the revolutionary states vote against the establishment of commissions to define terms carefully, to investigate conditions of national development, or to protect tribal populations living within metropolitan territories. The very intensification of the attachment to non-intervention implies a hardening of opposition among revolutionary nations to international supervision of private and group rights, while the economic and social programs of these regimes make respect for such rights a matter of considerable doubt. When, in 1959, the General Assembly voted to condemn the Peking regime

for a violation of the Universal Declaration of Human Rights in Tibet, the bulk of the revolutionary states abstained; the Soviet Union voted "no"; Indonesia opposed the inclusion of the item on the agenda; but Bolivia, Mexico, and Cuba voted in the affirmative.[48] While policy expectations of the UN system correspond to permanent national aims in the field of economic development, they merely mirror a temporary concern in the area of human rights, thus being only an aspect of the current phase in the history of the system.

This survey of the policy aims of revolutionary states has demonstrated only that their demands are neither rigid nor uniform, that they respond to the give-and-take of parliamentary diplomacy, and that many of their aspirations do not differ from those of conservative regimes. Therefore, the emergence of new common interests in the realms of outer space and in the prevention of limited wars among uncommitted states may yet give the UN new tasks in the next phase of its life, which may facilitate a balancing process involving different functions and different balancers than in the current phase.

IV

The present phase in the life of the UN system, which began in 1955, is

---

[47] E. R. Goodman, "The Cry of National Liberation: Recent Soviet Attitudes Toward National Self-Determination," *International Organization*, Vol. 14, No. 1 (Winter 1960). J. A. Armstrong, "The Soviet Attitude Toward UNESCO," *ibid.*, Vol. 8, No. 2 (May 1954). Dallin, *op. cit.*, pp. 45–47. Dallin and Armstrong suggest that the post-1953 Soviet interest in human rights and international intellectual contacts is connected with the Soviet hope of turning all UN agencies into a pro-Communist front organization.

[48] See the resolutions of the All-African People's Conference, Accra, *op. cit.*, for the contrast between domestic exclusiveness and UN legitimacy for anti-colonialism alone. A similar case for Latin America is made by Martin Travis, "The Political and Social Basis for the Latin American Doctrine of Non-Intervention," *Proceedings of the American Society of International Law*, Vol. 53 (1959). The Tibetan case is discussed in Bailey, *op. cit.*, p. 248 ff. The fact that a number of western democracies and Latin American oligarchical regimes with minority and human rights problems also abstained suggests that many members were unwilling to set a precedent.

earmarked by an inter-regional and inter-functional balancing process. The policies of the system were produced as a result of continuous compromises among regional blocs which differ in internal cohesion with respect to specific UN functions. Functional differentiation, in turn, explains how the mediating role can be assumed by varying balancers and how stalemates can be avoided by shifting majorities. In some situations the mediating role is played so well and national aims are so interrelated that significant policy measures can be produced by almost unanimous votes. Compromises involve not only concessions by one bloc to another, but also feature bargaining on the basis of concessions among functions: increasing economic assistance and support for decolonization efforts are demanded in return for support on questions relating to collective security and peaceful change. Typical policies of the current phase, then, have included the cumulative creation of new UN economic aid institutions and procedures, a growing commitment to peaceful decolonization, and the protection of human rights in Africa and Asia, as well as institutionalized balancing through conciliation, police forces, and Secretariat intercession in crises involving an immediate threat to peace.

Policy aims contributed by revolutionary regimes in this pattern were examined above. While the imperatives of symmetry would be neatly satisfied if all the non-Communist revolutionary regimes were to be grouped as "balancing" states, this is obviously not the situation. If the Western bloc represents the "thesis" of the status quo and the Soviets the "antithesis" of change, revolutionary regimes may be found on both dialectical extremes as well as in the neutralist "synthesizing" force. We must now assess the impact of the system's policies on the revolutionary environment but we must let the chips fall where they belong. Our question is simply: Has the balancing

process resulted in a change in the demands and expectations of revolutionary states so as to demonstrate responsiveness to the system? If so, a revolutionary environment clearly need not destroy an institutionally static system based on imperfectly internalized norms.

Soviet conduct in relation to the collective-security issue illustrates this conclusion. It is impossible to demonstrate that the basic Soviet policy of advancing a gradual world revolution toward an international Socialist and Communist society has been abandoned; therefore, the UN has not influenced the substance of Moscow's policy aims. On the contrary, a careful study of Soviet attitudes toward international relations and systems makes clear that a policy of peaceful but competitive coexistence, conceived as a means of combat, has always been favored at least by some of Russia's leaders. Soviet participation in a variety of international systems, some of them hostile to Soviet aims, was always considered feasible in an international environment felt to be transitional on the road to Socialist internationalism.[49]

Membership in the UN system, however, has definitely influenced the tactical manner in which the Soviet Union participates in world affairs. All the early pronouncements concerning the sacrosanct nature of national sovereignty, big power unanimity and the dominance of the Security Council have been downgraded during the current phase of UN life. Despite Soviet hostility to international police and enforcement measures, the Soviet delegate merely abstained on votes creating such forces for Suez and the Congo; even though the veto is still cherished, little

[49] Julian Towster, "The Dogma of Communist Victory," *Current History* (November 1959). For a collection of statements supporting this conclusion see also *Khrushchev on the Shifting Balance of World Forces*, U.S. Senate, 86th Congress, 1st Session, Doc. No. 57 (September 1959).

effort was made to protest the Security Council's brushing aside of the double veto cast in the Laotian crisis of 1959; when it suited the Soviet purpose, the delegation was quite willing to make use of the General Assembly and the Secretariat; finally, whenever the immediate military security of the Soviet bloc itself was not at stake, the Soviet Union seemed eager to mobilize the UN for collective security operations.[50]

There has been no internalization of norms. The quality of Soviet UN diplomacy has become more sophisticated and self-reliant; its style of participation far from being defensive, is now self-confident. To that extent, the rigid rejection of institutional evolution has been abandoned and a tactical responsiveness to systemic forces is evident now. But this has been true of a period when the peaceful coexistence phase of Soviet thought happens to coincide with the decolonization phase of the UN. Certainly, a responsiveness to systemic influences is suggested by the continued membership of the Soviet Union in the UN even during the height of the phase of American dominance, though Zhdanov and his supporters seem to have advocated withdrawal.[51] Reciprocal converging interests with the West and with the uncommitted nations have clearly been experienced, thus explaining the continued stability of the system during the current phase. But the evaporation of the convergences may also imply a passing of the phase. As long as systemic rules have not been internalized, but merely "learned" for short-range tactical purposes, the revolutionary environment remains as volatile as before.

Ghana, Indonesia, and Morocco have shown themselves to be far more responsive to systemic influences on matters connected with peace and security. Even Egypt has complied with the bulk of the UN decisions connected with the liquidation of the Suez crisis, though not without hard bargaining and at little cost to itself. They have appreciated that collective security operations conducted by balancing states can stop local wars and confine the East-West conflict. Again, we cannot claim that long-range objectives have been abandoned, but short-range responsiveness to systemic pressure is pronounced enough to promise its outliving the current phase.

The difference in responsiveness between Communist and non-Communist revolutionary regimes is equally patent in activities relating to peaceful change. Soviet policy has been unflinching in opposing all formal procedural steps for strengthening the executive, legislative or judicial competence of the UN in providing centralized, third-party dominated solutions. Verbal demands for UN measures in South Africa or Spain have not been accompanied with institutional suggestions. Operations in the Congo were denounced as soon as they turned against the Soviet-sponsored regime. UN activities in the realms of disarmament, outer space, and other "frontier" areas of possibly converging interests were never supported unless the Soviet substantive position was also accepted. In short, there has been no increasing responsiveness to the possibilities of peaceful change offered by the UN system.

Other revolutionary regimes have been perfectly willing to respond to and initiate measures of peaceful change in problem areas in which they

[50] On Laos see Leo Gross in *American Journal of International Law*, Vol. 53, No. 1 (January 1960), pp. 118–30. The other examples are discussed in Dallin, *op. cit.*, pp. 49–51, 84, 90–94, 99–100. But it should be noted that the Soviet Union refused to contribute to the maintenance of these forces. Other revolutionary regimes declining to support UNEF include Bolivia, Cuba, Iraq, Mexico, and Egypt. All the other African and Asian revolutionary regimes have faithfully paid their contributions. Details in Bailey, *op. cit.*, p. 216 ff.

[51] Dallin, *op. cit.*, pp. 33–38.

had as yet no direct interest. With respect to disarmament and UN controls in space roadblocks, international agreement came from the nations with an established interest or policy, but not from Asia, Africa, or Latin America. But it should be noted that much less responsiveness was in evidence in the efforts of the International Atomic Energy Agency to establish rules for inspecting the utilization by revolutionary regimes of fissile materials. Here, after all, is an area in which even underdeveloped nations have already acquired a rudimentary vested interest. If systemic expansion through peaceful change is to take place in these frontier fields the current phase must be exploited before a changed international environment will make task expansion impossible here too.

Decolonization, it would appear at first blush, is the prime field of peaceful change commanding the responsiveness of revolutionary regimes. This is an accurate impression insofar as they invoke the phrases of the Charter and of the Universal Declaration of Human Rights to dislodge the colonial powers and to make use of international debate and supervision to implement the provisions of the trusteeship system. But the manipulative inspiration of this attitude stands revealed in the limelight of the Congo crisis, leading to the conclusion that the dominance of instrumental motives has led to no internalization of systemic rules. Ghana, for example, joined the other African revolutionary regimes in threatening, at the Casablanca Conference, to take "appropriate action" unilaterally unless the UN supported the Lumumbist forces. Nkrumah softened this position later to the extent of seeking to channel the same demands through the UN Operation, provided the Congo were made an all-African responsibility, with the independent African states acting as the "agent" of the UN, much as the United States did in Korea.[52]

[52] On the Casablanca Conference see Con-

This still implied a reduction in the powers of the Secretary-General and an indirect endorsement of the Soviet position with respect to supporting the Gizenga regime. Far from acting as neutral balancers, the Casablanca powers made themselves the mouthpiece, under "African" auspices, of the Soviet extreme position; Liberia, Tunisia, and Ceylon—none of them revolutionary nations—acted as the classical balancers. If the search for an African Personality persuaded Guinea, Ghana, Mali, and Morocco to subordinate the processes of the world organization to their specific aims, Ghana at least did not carry its regional focus to the extreme of withdrawing its forces from the Congo. Nasser's United Arab Republic, however, did precisely that, while undertaking unilateral assistance to Gizenga. Egyptian support for UN operations aiming at peaceful change was strictly calculated on the basis of its convergence with Cairo's policy of penetrating Africa. Nasser was far less inclined to assume a balancing role in the Congo, as compared to Nkrumah, and has shown no interest in maximizing the peaceful-change capacity of the UN. The policy of revolutionary Egypt in relation to international institutions is as inconsistently imperialistic as its general foreign policy.[53] . . .

If we are to believe speeches and conference declarations, the devotion to the universal protection of human

ference of Heads of African States, Casablanca, January 3–7, 1961, "Declaration Concerning the Situation in the Congo." Also Kwame Nkrumah, speech at General Assembly session, March 7, 1961. When the Osagyefo took the oath of office as President of Ghana, he swore "that the union of Africa should be striven for by every lawful means and, when attained, should be faithfully preserved . . ." *External Affairs* (September 1960), p. 221.

[53] My assessment of UAR foreign policy objectives and their "inconsistent imperialism," is based on Keith Wheelock, *Nasser's New Egypt* (New York: Praeger, 1960), esp. pp. 223–57, 270–82.

rights felt by revolutionary regimes is much greater than such devotion elsewhere. The context in which such sentiments are expressed was explored above; here responsiveness and internalization of the procedures and values involved are under scrutiny. The Soviet Union has flatly asserted that the rights envisaged in the Covenants exist already on its territory so that no special enforcement machinery is necessary. Guinea's Constitution endorses the Universal Declaration by name and enumerates, as binding on herself, the rights there defined. Apparently, this example is followed only by those African territories which owe their status to UN action, but not by Ghana, Mali, or Morocco.[54] Dedication to the UN as the instrument for effectively enforcing human rights cannot be assumed any more than devotion to institutionalized processes of peaceful change controlled by third parties. Mere repetition of verbal sincerity has had no discernible impact on the environment.

As far as the international style of revolutionary regimes is concerned, the balancing politics of the UN's third phase can hardly be credited with having toned down manifestations of truculence and impatience. The fifteenth session of the General Assembly would seem to represent a high point in overt instances of revolutionary style. But to view the systemic impact on style purely in terms of parliamentary behavior is to miss another possible pattern of responsiveness to institutionalized diplomacy, the attitude toward international law as a means of peaceful change.[55] Assuming, at least

for the sake of argument, that the Western powers—as the representatives of the international status quo—took the provisions of the Charter with respect to legal means of peacefully changing the norms of the international system literally in 1945, it is easy to demonstrate that certain key revolutionary regimes did not. Communist unwillingness to submit to any kind of UN judicial process is well known, an attitude shared quite obviously by Nasser.[56]

But just as the Western powers, in their inability to mobilize the law consistently in support of the old status quo, have displayed a more and more instrumental attitude toward UN judicial institutions, the doctrinal opposition of revolutionary regimes to this aspect of the system has weakened.[57] This is especially true of the Soviets. The sharp contrast between Communist and Western attitudes toward international law, which is so often pointed out, applies only if we

rather than as a rubric of peaceful change because of the predominantly verbal role of UN legal discussion. Thus far, at any rate, judicial considerations have figured more as an aspect of propaganda inputs than as a constituent of an institutionalized pattern of outputs.

[56] Nasser, when asked why he did not wait until 1956 for the natural expiration of the 1936 treaty on the Suez Canal, maintained: "We are quite aware that this treaty wouldn't just expire. The British would take it before some international tribunal and obtain permission for prolonging it. We smaller nations haven't much confidence in these tribunals, which we know full well to be nothing more than courts run by and for the big nations." J. and S. Lacouture, *Egypt in Transition* (London: Methuen, 1958), p. 459.

[57] The limited role of the International Court of Justice is reviewed and explained by Shabtai Rosenne, *The International Court of Justice* (New York: Central Book Company, 1957) and Max Sørensen, "The International Court of Justice: Its Role in Contemporary International Relations," *International Organization,* Vol. 14, No. 2 (Spring 1960).

[54] For details see Egon Schwelb, "The Influence of the Universal Declaration of Human Rights on International and National Law," *Proceedings . . . , op. cit.,* pp. 223–28. Court decisions citing the Declaration were handed down in West Germany, Belgium, Italy, United States, and the Philippines.

[55] Attitudes toward international law are deliberately treated as aspects of "style"

compare *Soviet practice* with *Western doctrine,* a facile and meaningless juxtaposition. If Soviet practice is compared with that of the West, the differences are much less pronounced. The "law habit" of the West—in international relations—is not much better developed than the Soviets': Both sides observe and violate their treaty and customary obligations when it suits their policy purposes. More striking, still, when we examine lower-level legal habits with reference to very specific fields, rather than focus on central points of legal doctrine, the Soviet practice has increasingly approached that of most states in the last decade.[58]

Differences are narrowed further if we compare *Soviet doctrine* with *Western practice.* The early Soviet insistence on the role of treaties as the sole source of international obligations has given way to an instrumentally motivated recognition of custom and general principles of law as sometimes useful, just as the West has increasingly turned to treaties: By now both postures have met somewhere between these extremes. Western legal doctrine is increasingly moving in the direction of a less absolute and more instrumentally oriented view of the origin and purpose of norms.[59] And as William

Welch has shown in an admirable survey of Soviet legal doctrine concerning the position of regional arrangements, these are viewed essentially as the West interprets its military pacts: Both postures are explicable easily on the basis of the search for immediate military security and the desire to manipulate the rules of the UN Charter so as to sanctify one's own treaties and castigate the opponent's. In the process, the arguments have become very much alike.[60] To the extent, then, that revolutionary and status-quo powers have turned to the UN to legitimate their national policies, they have responded to the systemic forces they invoke by relaxing their earlier legal styles.

Observations of the impact of the system on the revolutionary environment and assessments of changes in revolutionary style do not exhaust the analytic means at our disposal for determining whether the universal system is mastering its impatient members or whether they are destroying the system. The evidence is uneven with respect to the moderation of revolutionary demands, and it may be doubted that the rapprochement of legal styles is of permanent significance. But if we can establish that the system itself has grown in the legitimacy it enjoys in the eyes of its members and in the authority it exercises over them then the inconsistent impact of UN decisions on member state expectations is not a fatal blow to the survival of the organization.

We may conclude that the system proper has increased in importance, at the expense of the states which make up the environment, if cumulative institutional decisions continue to be regarded as "legitimate" even by revolutionary regimes. The criterion of legitimacy is the regular invocation of UN Charter principles in advocacy and

---

[58] On this point see the articles by Oliver J. Lissitzyn and John N. Hazard, in *Proceedings . . . , op. cit.*

[59] On the evolution of Soviet thought on the sources of international law, see Jan F. Triska and Robert M. Slusser, "Treaties and Other Sources of Order in International Relations: The Soviet View," *American Journal of International Law,* Vol. 52, No. 4 (October 1958), especially pp. 724–26. An Egyptian lawyer has argued that the revolutionary regime in Cairo has abandoned the doctrine of the two *dars* in Islamic legal thought, including the concept of the *jihad,* and thus reapproached a universal law which recognizes an identity of norms governing the relations among Muslims and non-Muslims. Saba Habachy, in *Proceedings, op. cit.,* p. 61. The Western position on the reorientation of international law is prominently represented by Myres McDougal and his associates.

[60] William Welch, "Soviet Commitments to Collective Action," in A. Wolfers (ed.), *Alliance Policy in the Cold War* (Baltimore: Johns Hopkins, 1959).

debate by those holding out for more UN action as well as by those who seek to block such action (the balancer and the aggressor both invoke the Charter regularly), *plus* the demonstrated willingness to expand the UN's task in order to implement the Charter principles put forward. What is especially significant here, of course, is the willingness of states to support eventually new organizational tasks which they had initially opposed. "Authority," by contrast, implies no acceptance of the rightness of specific organizational action. The "authority" of the system might be said to increase if member states carry out decisions even if they did not advocate them, if they continue to oppose them in principle, and if they do not link the continued exercise of the task to the invocation of Charter principles.

The growth in legitimacy enjoyed by the UN should be observable in the utterances of prominent statesmen associated with the Afro-Asian Solidarity Conference, a grouping particularly useful for the study of revolutionary leadership since it tends to serve as an international front organization for the United Arab Republic as well as for the Communist bloc. Indeed there seems to have been a considerable amount of tugging between Cairo and Moscow as to who should manipulate the Conference.[61] Typical causes which the Conference espouses, apart from a general condemnation of "imperialism" and "colonialism" in terms which conform to the Communist line, include the banning of nuclear weapons testing in Africa, complete disarmament, the Stockholm World Peace Council, the Japanese drive against the United States Security Treaty, the return of Okinawa to Japan, the elimination of all foreign military bases everywhere, Castro's Cuba, and the complete rejection of any Western influence whatsoever in recently "liberated" countries, including economic and military ties

voluntarily accepted by the new governments. Indeed, the Conference shows a marked consistency in serving as the mouthpiece of the most extreme anti-Western strands of opinions to be found in Africa and Asia: the UPC in the Cameroons as opposed to the Ahidjo government, the FIN in Algeria, the opposition parties in Somalia against the Somali Youth League government, Lumumba against Kasavubu, etc.[62]

Legitimacy appears to receive a strong prop when the demands of states and of independence movements invoke the phrascology of the Charter in connection with the drive against colonialism. To be sure, such invocations are heard *ad nauseam* when they are useful in supporting the argument for independence. But the Charter principles are held to be violated unless "freedom" conforms to the international revolutionary *mystique:*

A nation cannot attain real independence if there are foreign troops stationed in its independent territory and if it is a member of an organization controlled by an imperialist State if it joins military pacts within impcrialist power. [sic] [63]

Therefore, the legitimacy of the UN operation in the Congo was vehemently denied when it appeared that the "unlawful activity of Mr. Hammerskjold" [sic] proved unsuccessful in bolstering Lumumba.[64] On the occasion of the fifteenth anniversary of the UN, the Conference Secretariat again "hails all the efforts aiming at the application of the principles of the Charter, such as for example, those of the neutralist and Afro-Asian countries," but also noted that "the enchantment vanished. The cases are in fact very rare when the UN served the

---

[61] Wheelock, *op. cit.,* pp. 266–68.

[62] For a complete survey of such causes see *Afro-Asian Bulletin,* Vol. 2, Nos. 11–12 (September–October, 1960).

[63] *Ibid.,* p. 32.

[64] *Ibid.,* p. 60.

cause of peace and the liberty of peoples." [65] One African spokesman flatly asserted that whenever the pan-African variety of nationalism fails to win endorsement in New York, the American imperialists succeed in subverting the organization and its Secretary-General. He also argued that multilateral economic aid under UN auspices is to be resisted in such circumstances because "this would only help perpetuating economical neo-colonialism [sic]." [66] Yet it should be noted that the Conference Secretary-General, Youssef El Sebai, urged that:

. . . because of the pressing need for the United Nations in the present circumstances, Afro-Asian peoples are determined to see that the World Organization does not collapse. It is our duty to consolidate it by every possible means, and to endeavour to enable it to play its great role in World affairs, uninfluenced by pressure or intimidation, for the sole benefit of all peoples of the world, for Justice and for Peace.[67]

Clearly, the failure to achieve full endorsement for revolutionary objectives in New York is reflected in a continued overt denial of legitimacy. But the ambivalence of El Sebai's statement and the support Ghana still gives the UN in the Congo warrant the conclusion that eventual legitimacy may still develop either because the UN is a useful Soviet front in some future crisis, or because it still offers the safest way out of a dangerous situation. But it should be noted that the second part of the criterion of legitimacy, consent to an expanded UN task, has been lacking as far as the Soviet bloc and several African revolutionary regimes are concerned.

[65] *Ibid.*, p. 61.
[66] Osende Afana, "Consolidating Afro-Asian Solidarity," *ibid.*, p. 7.
[67] Youssef El Sebai, "Afro-Asian Solidarity Marches On," *ibid.*, pp. 4–5.

Some precision is needed at this point. The two criteria of legitimacy have clearly been satisfied in the case of the expanded UN task in economic development. Charter invocation, equally clearly, has not been accompanied by task expansion with respect to collective security, human rights, and most aspects of peaceful change. Decolonization, however, has conferred increasing legitimacy on the UN even if the reservations explicit in the activities of the Afro-Asian Solidarity Conference are borne in mind. Plebiscites have been held and their results implemented; Trusteeship Council and General Assembly injunctions concerning steps for achieving self-government and independence have been carried out; groups and individuals persecuted by the colonial administrations have achieved respectability and even power as a result of UN intervention. While the Soviet Union, Cuba, Guinea, and Mali have denied the UN full legitimacy over the Congo, they have acquiesced in it with respect to other colonial episodes, thus altering an earlier, more intransigent position. But even if decolonization has conferred increasing legitimacy on the world organization, the passing of the colonial phase makes it doubtful that this acquisition will be readily transferred to new tasks.

Growth in authority, rather than in legitimacy, is the most striking aspect of UN history in its current phase—even at the expense of certain revolutionary regimes. This growth is demonstrable by observing the accretions of power of certain UN institutions and the implementation of their decisions by revolutionary member nations in the face of declared indifference or opposition, following the adoption of appropriate resolutions in the Security Council or the General Assembly. Even though a general consensus embracing almost the entire membership has developed with respect to the increased institutional role of the UN system in economic development, the revolutionary states had been among those who were most anxious to retain a maximum of national freedom of action in the preparation and execution of development projects. The Soviet Union, in fact, had made a fetish of the need for absolute national autonomy in economic planning. Notwithstanding these commitments of principle, the evolution of UN techniques shows a growth of power on the part of international officials and a willingness of revolutionary regimes to carry out their proposals. The Special Fund exercises much more detailed supervision over national development projects enjoying UN support than did the Technical Assistance Board in earlier years, and the TAB is now adopting more stringent measures. The recommendations of survey teams and inspectors dispatched by the International Bank for Reconstruction and Development are readily implemented by borrowing nations, despite the "Wall Street connections" of that institution. Bolivia has agreed to comply with the drastic deflationary "recommendations" of the International Monetary Fund as a price for receiving further loans in the face of strong domestic resentment. The mediating role of the Bank, when sweetened with appropriate financial sugar, has been a significant one in resolving such crises as restitution to the Universal Suez Canal Company and development of the Indus River Basin. The most capitalistic of aid-giving institutions receives cooperation from revolutionary (but non-Communist) nations when systematic economic development is at stake.[68]

[68] On Egypt's relations with the TAB and specialized agency programs see Walter R. Sharp, "The United Nations System in Egypt," *International Organization,* Vol. 10, No. 2 (May 1956). On the Special Fund see Hadwen and Kaufmann, *op. cit.,* and UN Special Fund, Doc. SF 1 (January 1, 1959). On the Bank see Eugene Black, "The Indus: Moral for Nations," *New York Times Mag-*

A similar conclusion is made possible by the experience of the rapidly growing system of UN Resident Representatives in aid-receiving countries, an institution not initially proposed by the underdeveloped nations. Almost fifty such officials now reside in member states receiving technical assistance, proposing and channelling projects, coordinating and supervising their execution. On their impact, one UN official writes:

> It is an administrative maxim that power should equal responsibility. The role of resident representative violates the precept; its responsibilities are endless, its powers nil. The resident representative knows that in whatever direction he looks—at the [Technical Assistance] Board, the participating organizations, the governments, or the experts —he can order no one. For the essence of the post is that the person holding it achieves results not by commanding and ordering, but by persuasion and giving good counsel.[69]

Obviously, the actual influence of these officials varies from country to country. But since, increasingly, the

azine, December 11, 1960, p. 51. Wheelock, *op. cit.,* pp. 190–97. Conditions imposed by the IMF in Bolivia were widely disregarded in 1957–58, but a new IMF effort in 1960 was apparently accompanied by firm assurances on the part of the Bolivian regime. The Left-Wing of the MNR continued to oppose cooperation with the IMF and equated UN "imperialism" with that of the International Cooperation Administration. For details see, Robert J. Alexander, *The Bolivian National Revolution* (New Brunswick: Rutgers University Press, 1958), Chap. 13. Richard W. Patch, "Bolivia: Decision or Debacle," *American Universities Field Staff,* Latin America (Bolivia) RWP-3-'59 (April 18, 1959).

[69] C. Hart Schaaf, "The Role of Resident Representatives of the UN Technical Assistance Board," *International Organization,* Vol. 14, No. 4 (Autumn 1960), p. 556.

flow of new grants, loans, experts, and fellowships depends in no small measure on the confidential reports submitted by the resident representatives to authorities at UN headquarters and to specialized agencies, their counsel on the spot is unlikely to be disregarded. Guinea was anxious to receive assistance in this form and turned to the Soviet bloc only when the UN was unprepared to meet hurried requests; Bolivia accommodated itself to it despite a nationalist revolution.[70]

Undoubtedly the most convincing item in an argument stressing the growth of UN authority is the development of the office of the Secretary-General. Compared to the ineffectual groping for autonomous influence displayed by Trygve Lie, Dag Hammarskjöld had some right to claim that his stand on actual or emerging conflicts

---

[70] See Alexander, op. cit., pp. 245–46. Carter Goodrich, The Economic Transformation of Bolivia (Ithaca: Cornell University Press, 1955). Albert Lepawsky, "The Bolivian Operation," International Conciliation, No. 479 (March 1952). This, of course, is not to deny that many governments—though not necessarily revolutionary ones—disregard the advice tendered by technical assistance personnel and that resident representatives vary a good deal in the measure of their influence in proportion to their own personalities. While some, in effect, act as key advisers on economic development plans to governments, others are content to play a modest "clearing house" role. For a wealth of information on the degree of control exercised on behalf of the UN system by field personnel and headquarters review procedure, see Walter R. Sharp, Field Administration in the United Nations System (New York: Praeger, 1961), especially pp. 376–401, 406–17, 449–63, 494–503. On the discreet controls exercised by international financial institutions see Henry Bloch, "The Fiscal Advisory Functions of United Nations Technical Assistance," International Organization (Spring 1957). International Bank for Reconstruction and Development, The World Bank: Policies and Operations (Washington, D.C., 1957). R. G. A. Jackson, The Case for an International Development Authority (Syracuse: Syracuse University Press, 1959).

"to the extent that such stands can be firmly based on the Charter and its principles . . . thus express what may be called the *independent judgment of the Organization*."[71] The Secretary-General, thus, can speak and act as if he, rather than the member states, represents the system *if* he is able to practice "quiet diplomacy" and enjoy the support of governments as a truly independent agent. If these conditions are not met, admitted Hammarskjöld, "he must be prepared to see his future value as a negotiator endangered or even lost. In the latter case, he ought, naturally, to resign from his post."[72] To what extent, then, has this claim to a new autonomous status withstood the test of international politics? . . .

Quiet diplomacy, far from being separable from parliamentary diplomacy, functions best as an arm of some consensus, however limited temporally or functionally among the member governments. This consensus must include the major revolutionary regimes, if only because most of the tensions have arisen in their areas of the world.[73] In the Arab-Israeli and Laotian crises this condition was not met, since mediation was not preceded by unambiguous Security Council and General Assembly resolutions and *ad hoc* meetings of the mind. But in the Suez Canal crisis, the General Assembly did furnish the Secretary-General with explicit authorization born from the process of parliamentary diplomacy, and in the resolution of the Lebanese-Jordanian civil war of 1958 the governments again welcomed a balancing operation which would free the area from the danger of American, Soviet,

---

[71] Address in Copenhagen, UN Doc. SG/812 (May 1, 1959), p. 9. (Italics mine.)
[72] Ibid.
[73] The success of the Beck-Friis Mission in mediating the border dispute between Thailand and Cambodia is an exception. It was a very minor affair which remained outside the policy aims of all other member states.

and Egyptian armed action. In all these situations the Soviet Union and the UAR, as the major revolutionary regimes concerned, deferred to UN authority even though they did not welcome or advocate it. Whether the same principle is established by the example of the Congo Operation is still uncertain. To be sure, a consensus produced by parliamentary diplomacy accompanied the actions of the Secretary-General in recruiting and deploying armed forces and in running the Congo economy; but the consensus proved to be ephemeral and had to be bolstered by repeated threats on the part of Hammarskjöld to tender his resignation. While the endorsement given to the Secretary-General's authority in the Congo in the resolution of April 15, 1961 was a sweeping one, the revolutionary regimes did not join in it.[74] In the Suez Crisis, the General Assembly created an Advisory Committee on the UN Emergency Force which functioned peacefully, without voting, in backing up the Secretary General.[75] In the Congo Crisis, the

[74] Conclusions were drawn from the debate and vote on the 17-power resolution A/L.340 and Adds. 1–4, Add. 3–Corr. 1, as well as draft amendments A/L.348 and A/L.342. The overall tenor of the resolution was to "balance" various Congo factions while strengthening the authority of the Secretary-General and of UN conciliation in stabilizing the broadened Leopoldville regime. It was sponsored by non-revolutionary Afro-Asian states. The unsuccessful amendments seeking to limit the UN role were introduced by Guinea. On the final vote, the Soviet bloc and some of the French Community African states voted in opposition; all the other revolutionary regimes (except Bolivia) abstained. *United Nations Review,* Vol. 8, No. 5 (May 1961), pp. 35–37.
[75] Details on the Committee in Bailey, *op. cit.,* p. 25. A judicious evaluation of the independent role of the Secretary-General and of ways of reducing the impact of some kind of "troika" system on the Secretariat can be found in Michel Virally, "Vers Une Réforme du Secrétariat des Nations Unies?," *International Organization,* Vol. 15, No. 2 (Spring 1961).

Advisory Committee created for similar purposes led to a less harmonious existence. The success of the Secretary-General in asserting the authority of the system depends on the mobilization of a majority of member states—including the revolutionary governments—in favor of a balancing operation for the maintenance of peace. It remains linked to the environment and has not yet attained the force of an autonomous agency superimposed over it. . . .

Systemic growth at the expense of a fluid environment demands concurrent growth of authority and legitimacy. With one but without the other the survival of a stable system into the next phase of its life is all that can be expected.

This, as yet non-existent, unity of authority and legitimacy can also be regarded as the global *consensus* which must inhere in any system which is supreme over its environment. It is at this level that those who speak of an international public interest can make a conceptually meaningful contribution. The objective existence of such an "interest," some basic values, and associated policies experienced in common by the membership, could be demonstrated if there were a reliable substantive consensus in the organization. To be sure, each phase in the system's history exhibited substantive areas of agreement among and within many of the blocs: But a shift in environment caused this substantive agreement to be dissipated. A pervasive substantive consensus, an agreement on an interest of mankind transcending short periods of almost accidental convergences of national demands, has emerged neither with respect to the imperative of preserving peace, nor with reference to peaceful and orderly changes in troublesome conditions, nor yet on the issue of exalting and protecting the individual as a subject of international law. But substantive consensus, so defined, has come about with reference to meeting the revolution of rising expectations. Furthermore, it is extremely unlikely that this would have happened without the political pressures and avenues of accommodation opened up by the UN system. And so the Marxist, as well as the Liberal, who fashions policy on the basis of some kind of economic determination has come into his own in the machinery of international organizations. His efforts, not those of the direct advocate of peace, order, and human rights, have carried the day in fashioning a genuine international interest.[76]

But there is also a procedural dimension to consensus, the dimension held basic to the life of democratic systems. If procedural uniformities transcending the phases of the UN's history can be isolated, systemic growth could again be demonstrated to have occurred. The role of majoritarian as against unanimous voting, provided whatever trend exists outlives a given phase, would furnish an indicator here. Thus we find that voting in the Security Council has in effect been gradually emancipated from dependence on an absolute unanimity rule on substantive matters, and that this development has not been obliterated by changes in national policy. The admission that abstention by a permanent member does not constitute a veto originated in the early "honeymoon" phase of the system; but it has survived. More striking still, the "consensus" procedure of issuing directives or recommendations without formal vote and the liberalization of the rules regarding the participation of the Secretary-General in Council meetings evolved during the Western-dominated second phase; not only did the Soviet Union acquiesce, but the procedure has been carried over into the third phase in situations not requiring a new basic decision of the Security Council.

Yet no such conclusion can be stated for the General Assembly. The rules of procedure are notoriously permissive and presiding officers are very inconsistent in holding member governments to them. Permanent agreement has not emerged as to whether votes on certain questions involving decolonization demand a simple or a two-thirds majority; the First Committee makes all its decisions on a two-thirds vote even though some of the issues before it could be considered as "unimportant" under the Charter and the Rules of Procedure. No discernible evolution seems to have occurred.[77] And so consensus remains as changeable as the environment which it might stabilize.

V

Let us assume that within the next two or three years the current phase

---

[76] Francis Canavan, S.J., in "The Levels of Consensus," unpublished paper read at the American Political Science Association Convention, September 8–10, 1960, argued that "consensus" in a democratic society can never mean more than pragmatic, mundane, task-oriented agreement that certain governmental functions of a non-controversial character should be carried out. While he also suggests that this kind of consensus is probably inadequate to legitimate the activities of a strong welfare state, his formulation goes a long way toward accurately identifying the international consensus.

[77] I do not mean to suggest, in my analysis of voting rules, that "voting" should be considered as *the* supreme integrative device which explains consensus in the sense of telling us why minorities submit to majorities. Demonstrably, consensus comes about in certain situations without voting and may fare better if voting is avoided. But the history of decision-making on certain issues in the UN also suggests that cumulative votes do create a new consensus, though this consensus does *not* carry over to other functional contexts. I would argue as a general proposition, however, that voting is an integral constituent of the process of parliamentary diplomacy —which is basic to UN decision-making— and that an evolution of voting rules is a meaningful indicator of systemic development.

of inter-regional and inter-functional balancing will come to an end—at least in its present form. This will occur because the policy aims uniting the Afro-Asians will begin to diverge as the colonial issue ceases to be relevant. Even now the internal cohesion of the Afro-Asian caucusing groups, like that of the Latin American caucus, is among the weakest of any of the Assembly groups.[78] The elimination of the colonial issues will probably imply the further splitting of both groups, who will remain united only on questions of economic development. As concerns human rights, the revolutionary states in all regions will factor themselves out from status-quo powers in opposing an expansion of the systemic task. Hence, it will become much more difficult for the Western and Soviet blocs to attract uncommitted and underdeveloped nations to their respective positions on collective security because the fields in which concessions can be offered will shrink in scope. Under these circumstances it is difficult to predict whether the Latin American and Afro-Asian nations will unite on the issue of mediating in the Cold War, or will begin to choose sides in that conflict to a greater extent than heretofore.

In any case if the current phase, with its great opportunities for bargaining, has been unable to transform the UN system into an organization in which institutionalized-interest politics brings about increasing consensus, authority, and legitimacy, a future phase which reduces the scope for bargaining is unlikely to succeed. Hence, we cannot predict that the system will increasingly control that portion of the environment which is due to the aims of revolutionary regimes. But the opposite conclusion, that the revolutionary environment will destroy the system, is equally unlikely. Legitimate authority, if we argue on the analogy

of administrative behavior in democratic states, *follows* the successful co-ordination of separate group and institutional efforts achieved by means of continuous bargaining, which results in a revolution of attitudes—a "breakthrough." In the UN we have merely had compromises based on quantitative bargaining and rigid insistence on concessions of equal value, with a failure to yield "integration" in the sense of the visualization by the parties of new alternatives for common action in which no state "gives up" anything.[79] But we have had continuous bargaining in which the revolutionary states have fully participated. There is no reason for thinking that even an environment offering fewer opportunities for the exchange of concessions will eliminate the incentives for retaining such stability as the system now possesses. And if the UN task does expand to the "new frontier" of space and science, the level of negotiation which results in integration may yet be achieved during the next phase.

We thus arrive at the conclusion that revolutionary regimes may be deterred into truculent inactivity by their participation in the United Nations, but not thereby be socialized into the gentle arts of accommodation, leading to ever higher planes of universal progress under the benevolent aegis of the hundred-odd flags displayed at the East River. "We tend to identify peace, stability, and the quiescence of conflict with notions like trust, good faith, and mutual respect," wrote T. C. Schelling.

To the extent that this point of view actually encourages trust and respect it is good. But where trust and good faith do not exist and

---

[78] See Table 1.

[79] The distinction between accommodation based on "compromise" and "integration" is elaborated in North, Koch, and Zinnes, *op. cit.*, pp. 370–73. They, in turn, draw heavily on the definitions of Lasswell, Mary Follett, and Chester Barnard.

TABLE 1

COHESION OF REGIONAL CAUCUS GROUP IN THE UNITED NATIONS GENERAL
ASSEMBLY 1945–1958

	Cohesion of Member State								
Caucus	Before Creation of Caucus %			After Creation of Caucus %			During the Whole Period %*		
	Iden-tical	Soli-darity	Di-vided	Iden-tical	Soli-darity	Di-vided	Iden-tical	Soli-darity	Di-vided
African**	—	—	—	46.7	33.3	20.0			
Western European	65.0	23.8	11.2	82.4	11.0	6.6			
Asian-African	11.4	36.4	53.9	34.4	42.2	23.4			
Benelux							77.5	17.0	5.5
Scandinavian							68.3	23.9	7.8
Commonwealth							13.0	27.7	59.3
Arab							63.4	27.2	9.4
Latin American							28.8	33.2	38.0
Soviet							96.0	3.9	0.1

Source: Thomas Hovet, Jr., *Bloc Politics in the United Nations* (Cambridge: MIT, Center for International Studies, 1958), pp. 64–65, 86, 98, 111, 121–122, 131, 155, 172, 187.
* The Caucusing groups listed for "the whole period" were formed before or at the time of the first meeting of the General Assembly.
** The African Caucus had functioned for only two sessions at the time these computations were made, thus precluding firm conclusions. Prior to the formation of the Caucus there were not enough African member states to create a meaningful pattern.

Hovet's study is based on the counting of an "adjusted gross" number of roll-call votes. For the meaning of this device, see Hovet, pp. 239 ff. On an "identical" vote the frequency of members voting the same way, not considering abstentions, is counted; on a "solidarity" vote, the frequency of members of a caucusing group abstaining rather than voting against their colleagues is determined; a "divided" vote covers the situations of direct opposition among members of a group.

cannot be made to by our acting as though they did, we may wish to solicit advice from the underworld, or from ancient despotisms, on how to make agreements work when trust and good faith are lacking and there is no legal recourse for breach of contract. The ancients exchanged hostages, drank wine from the same glass to demonstrate the absence of poison, met in public places to inhibit the massacre of one by the other, and even deliberately exchanged spies to facilitate transmittal of authentic information.[80]

[80] T. C. Schelling, *The Strategy of Conflict* (Cambridge: Harvard University Press, 1961), p. 20.

If we add that participation in the politics of the UN acts as a channel for the transmission of blackmail threats, even if it be multilateral and multifunctional blackmail, the civilizing impact of the United Nations system on the revolutionary component of its environment will have been established. The environment is changed even if the system itself sustains no growth in task and receives no shining new mantle of legitimate authority.

This relationship bears a marked— if grim—resemblance to the notion of "mutual recognition" of the limit on violence in the theory of limited war. The Yalu River was so perceived by the belligerents, but

. . . not as something that we and the Chinese recognized unilaterally and simultaneously. . . . . We recognized that they recognized it, they recognized that we recognized it, we recognized that they recognized that we recognized it, and so on. . . . In that sense, limits and precedents and traditions of this kind have an authority that is not exactly granted to them voluntarily by the participants in a conflict; they ac-

quire a magnetism or focal power of their own.[81]

Likewise, in United Nations bodies, debates and votes, without directly and self-consciously motivating those who debate and vote to behave differently than they rationally wish to do, deter them just the same.

[81] T. C. Schelling, "Toward a General Theory of Conflict Applicable to International Relations," *Midwest Journal of Political Science*, Vol. 4, No. 2, pp. 136–37.

10. Due Process of Law in International Organizations*

C. WILFRED JENKS

I

THOSE of us who have lived through the growth of international organizations during the last 45 years have witnessed a remarkable series of transformations in their membership, their procedures, their authority, their effectiveness, and even in their fundamental conception, purposes, and function.

Designed to supplement the inherited and traditional political structure of the world, the League of Nations was to consist primarily of new arrangements for avoiding any repetition of the breakdown in the conduct of international relations represented by the outbreak of war in 1914. The United Nations, as originally conceived, was designed to be a central element in a political structure of a world which was recognized to be changing. But there was little appre-

* *International Organization*, Vol. XIX, 163–176. Reprinted by permission. This article is adapted from an address delivered before the Faculty of Law of Haile Selassie I University, Addis Ababa, on December 4, 1964.

ciation, when the Charter was drafted, of how sudden, far-reaching, and decisive the changes would prove to be.

The United Nations has now become the basis, and the only possible basis, of a wholly new political structure of the world. It has become so with an institutional framework originally fashioned for more modest purposes. These changes in basic conception and function are not matters of controversial opinion; they are facts reflected in authoritative statements.

The League of Nations was intended "to promote international co-operation and to achieve international peace and security." The words come from the preamble to the Covenant of the League of Nations, but the measures envisaged for this purpose in the preamble did not go beyond the fields of political morality and international law. They consisted of "the acceptance of obligations not to resort to war," "the prescription of open, just and honorable relations between nations," "the firm establishment of the understandings of international law as the actual rule of conduct among Governments," and "the maintenance of justice and a scrupulous respect for all treaty obligations in the dealings of organized peoples with one another." Only in the Constitution of the International Labor Organization (ILO) do we find, in the typical international thinking of 1919, a wider and richer vision with a constructive and forward-looking economic and social content still accepted as valid today.

The United Nations was given from the outset a broader mandate, set out in the preamble to the UN Charter: not only "to save succeeding generations from the scourge of war" and "to establish conditions under which justice and respect for" international obligations could be maintained but also "to reaffirm faith in fundamental human rights" and "in the dignity and worth of the human person" and to promote "better standards of life in larger freedom." With these ends in view the peoples of the United Nations were not only to unite their strength "to maintain international peace and security" and to ensure that "armed force shall not be used, save in the common interest," but also "to practice tolerance and live together in peace with one another as good neighbors" and "to employ international machinery for the promotion of the economic and social advancement of all peoples." The Charter itself embodies a pledge by all Members of the United Nations to take joint and separate action in cooperation with the Organization to promote higher standards of living, full employment, conditions of economic and social progress and development, and universal respect for and observance of human rights and fundamental freedoms for all, without distinction as to race, sex, language, or religion. Whereas the primary purpose of the League was to prevent great-power conflicts and rivalries from escaping the control of diplomacy and degenerating into war, the United Nations was to accomplish the more ambitious purpose of bridging what we

have since come to call the East-West and North-South conflicts. It was, however, so constructed upon the assumption that the UN would operate within the traditional framework of international society as it existed in 1945, that is, it was based upon the continuing ascendancy of the Great Powers which were granted permanent seats on the Security Council.

The United Nations today has a much more far-reaching role than was or could have been foreseen by the most gifted of its begetters: to fill the vacuum in world affairs resulting from the collapse of the old order everywhere and to provide a framework within which the new political forces of our time can come to terms with each other. Although this role has grown out of ineluctable facts, there has been no opportunity to formulate this expanded concept of its role in an instrument with an authority comparable with the preamble to the Charter. Dag Hammarskjöld gave apt expression to the general concept when, in his last two *Annual Reports of the Secretary-General,* he spoke of the United Nations as an instrument for the overriding common interest of the world community and emphasized the increasing importance of the international executive functions resulting from the process and pace of decolonization.

In the context of this greatly widened range of responsibility the problem of due process of law in international organizations has assumed an importance of the first order for the whole future of mankind. The peace and stability of the world, the rule of law in world affairs, the protection of the dignity and worth of the human person, the promotion of better standards of life, the practice of tolerance and good neighborship as vital elements in the common peace, freedom, and welfare: the attainment of these primary objectives of international and every rational national policy now depends on the effectiveness of the United Nations and the specialized and regional organizations operating within its framework as instruments for achieving these purposes. Man's stake in peace, his stake in justice, his stake in freedom, his stake in welfare all depend in large measure on the effectiveness of the United Nations system, and the United Nations system cannot be effective for these purposes without the rule of law and due process of law.

It is not surprising that the problem should arise most acutely when the world community is confronted with its most intractable problems. Questions relating to South Africa, Portugal, and Southern Rhodesia, essentially different in nature but nevertheless interrelated, have become some of the most emotionally charged issues of contemporary international politics, and the frustration arising from the difficulty of resolving these problems has produced a widespread impatience of due process of law as a method of seeking their solution. This impatience has found expression in the proceedings of a wide range of world organizations, notably the United Nations, the International Labor Organization, the Food and Agriculture Organization (FAO), the United Nations Educational, Scientific and Cultural Organization (UNESCO), the World Health Organization (WHO), the International Telecommunications Union (ITU), and the Universal Postal Union (UPU), in all of which the obligation to abide by due process of law has been questioned in varying degrees in the name of natural justice and the overriding claims of morality. It would be tedious, it is unnecessary, and it would not be appropriate to attempt to recapitulate the precise course of events in these various organizations. In all of them the question raised in varying forms has been that of how far a state which defies or is regarded by certain other states as defying the conscience of mankind is entitled to continue to exercise its rights as such in the proceedings of world organizations. The question has become acute in respect of South Africa, but it is clearly a wider question which may arise at any time in relation to any state the ideology, policy, and interests of which conflict sharply with those of its neighbors or of its rivals on the world stage.

There have been as regards this matter wide divergences of policy between different states and significant differences of practice between different international organizations. It would be neither proper nor helpful for me as an international civil servant to criticize the policy or practice followed by any state or organization in the course of the exceptionally difficult period of groping and readjustment during which the questions at issue have been coming into focus, but it is entirely proper and may perhaps be helpful to attempt to analyze objectively some of the issues of long-range policy affecting the whole future of world organization which have now been brought into focus and call for long-term answers. Some of the questions which have arisen raise the broadest issues of policy and clearly call for intensive study, reflection, and debate.

II

Among these questions two are of an essentially preliminary character. The first is that of universality versus community of outlook and interest as the basis of international organization; the second is that of the distribution of responsibility for political matters between the central political organs of the United Nations system and bodies with more specialized responsibilities. The answers given to these questions will determine much of the setting within which the further questions at issue arise.

It is not surprising that intense disapproval of the policy of a particular state should, when deep emotional currents are in full spate and the state concerned shows itself unresponsive to international criticism and unwilling to enter into international negotiation, find expression in proposals to expel the state in question from the world community. By violating the ethics of the community, by challenging and persistently challenging its fundamental values, that state almost invites the reprisal of rejection from its membership. But any such proposal raises the fundamental policy question of whether the basis of membership is community of outlook and interest or the need for universality, irrespective of differences of outlook or interest, in the wider interest of the world as a whole.

In this respect there may well be an essential difference between world and regional organizations. No regional organization has any obligation to admit to its membership a state which does not share its sense of common purpose. It can determine how inclusive or exclusive it should be by weighing the extent to which the participation of particular states is necessary for the effective discharge of its functions against the possibility or probability that their participation may dilute the sense of common purpose and reduce the effectiveness of common action. That the Council of Europe, the Organization of American States (OAS), or the Organization of African Unity (OAU) should determine, and if need be contract, their membership on the basis of such an approach is entirely natural. World organizations are differently placed by reason of their having been established as world organizations aspiring to universality of membership, influence, and function. For them any proposal for expulsion, however provoking the circumstances, inevitably raises the question of its compatibility with their universal nature and function. Germs, for example, know no frontiers and the vocation to universality which this implies for the World Health Organization is paralleled in varying degrees over wide areas of international policy.

Let us therefore consider some of the issues involved. I personally have had occasion to express a view on the problem at three different times, in 1935, 1942, and 1945, the first of these 30 years ago, the last fifteen years before the question became an issue in respect of South Africa. In order to detach these views from the context of current problems they are restated by quoting the manner in which I formulated them years ago during the aftermath of the proposal to expel Japan from the League of Nations and the subsequent expulsion of the Soviet Union from the League.

My view in 1935 was that expulsion, while in the last resort conceivably necessary in an organization based on the principle of unanimity if a state in breach of covenant sought to systematically block all League business, was at best a crude device. Quoting Maitland's dictum that "a ready recourse to outlawry is, we are told, one of the tests by which the relative barbarousness of various bodies of ancient law may be measured,"[1] I took the view that

a weapon which was at best clumsy, even in societies the units of which were individuals, is quite incapable of achieving any lasting result in a community the units of which are States and one of the characteristics of which is therefore a very low rate of mortality.[2]

[1] Frederick Pollock and Frederic William Maitland, *The History of English Law Before the Time of Edward I* (2nd ed.; Boston: Little, Brown and Company, 1899), Vol. 2, p. 450.
[2] "Expulsion from the League of Nations," *British Year Book of International Law, 1935* (London: Oxford University Press, 1936), Vol. 16, p. 157.

While particular political regimes have of course a higher rate of mortality than states, that basically remains true today.

In 1942 I was dealing primarily with the suggestion that expulsion might be an appropriate remedy for financial default, but in rejecting this suggestion I commented briefly on the wider issues involved in the following terms:

International institutions are not clubs from which unpleasant and disagreeable members can be black-balled to the general advantage; they are an attempt to create machinery of government in a world where the unpleasant and the disagreeable cannot be assumed not to exist.[3]

That remains wholly true today.

In 1945, when the present United Nations system was in the process of creation, I reexamined the whole question in a broader perspective and ventured to restate the position as follows:

The effect of expulsion is to release a State from its obligations towards other States under the constitution of the organization from which it is expelled; such action affords no real remedy for breaches of international law or of international public morality; at best it is merely an *alibi* for the failure of other States to devise effective means of enforcing the provisions which have been flouted; a decision to expel is liable to be taken in a discriminatory manner on the basis of transient political considerations rather than on the basis of the relative gravity of the breach of law and order which has occurred; and it is likely to make vastly more difficult the reintegra-

tion of the State concerned into an organized international community when circumstances have changed. Where the continued membership in an organization of a State violating the obligations of membership would prevent the organization from fulfilling its functions effectively, expulsion may be a necessary evil; but it should normally be possible to provide for such cases by empowering the organization to suspend defaulting members from all or any of the rights and privileges of membership without thereby releasing them from any of their obligations towards the organization or producing the long-term political effects of an irrevocable act of expulsion.[4]

That also remains wholly true today.

These old quotations have been disinterred in order to emphasize that the principles involved transcend the details and accidents of time, place, and case; they have a permanent importance for the whole future of world organization. These principles are not stale stuff, no longer applicable to the brave new world of today; they go to the heart of the effectiveness of world organization on which all our hopes for future years depend.

The second question, that of the distribution of responsibility for political matters between the central political organs of the United Nations system and bodies with more specialized responsibilities, is likewise fundamental for the future of world organization. The scheme of world organization provided for in the Charter of the United Nations is one of functional decentralization within a broader framework of concerted action. The underlying thought is that the world is much too large and complex to be

---

[3] "Some Legal Aspects of the Financing of International Institutions," *Transactions of the Grotius Society, 1942* (London: Sweet and Maxwell, 1943), Vol. 28, p. 111.

[4] "Some Constitutional Problems of International Organizations," *British Year Book of International Law, 1945* (London: Oxford University Press, 1946), Vol. 22, pp. 25–26.

governed by a world executive and world legislature responsible for the full spectrum of public policy. The basic policy of functional decentralization within a broader framework of concerted action, far from being the outcome of a series of historical accidents or representing the dead hand of the past, is the result of deliberate decisions of high policy, maturely weighed, which are an accurate reflection of the political realities and technical factors which condition the present-day development of world organization. The functional decentralization of authority in the United Nations family is an aspect of one of the most characteristic and irresistible tendencies inherent in the complexity of contemporary civilization. No human mind, no tidy scheme of centralized world organization, and no network of communications centralized through essentially diplomatic channels can encompass on the world scale the ever increasing complexity of the interests, preoccupations, and problems which transcend frontiers in the modern world. In such circumstances the functional decentralization within a broader framework represented by the United Nations system is not a synonym for chaos but the only workable compromise between breadth of vision and depth of insight, between comprehensiveness of approach and effectiveness of impact, between full responsiveness to centrally focused considerations of overall policy and the close and continuous interlocking of international and national action in particular fields.

Upon the success of this wholly new venture in the art of government depends the possibility of developing an adequate institutional framework for the future conduct of world affairs. There are, however, certain conditions which must be fulfilled in order to create any real prospect of such success. As I ventured to put it some years ago:

There are, of course, responsibilities fundamental for the maintenance of world peace which must be centralized; there must also be effective means of evolving by discussion and consent general policies to guide the whole international effort; and, if the limited resources available are to be widely used, there must be appropriate provision for functions more effectively discharged by united than by divided effort.[5]

III

It is in this perspective that we must consider the problem of how political questions and, in particular, questions with an important and direct bearing on peace and security should be dealt with in this decentralized international system.

The original concept was that the United Nations would deal with political questions, the progressive development of international law, the general coordination of economic and social policy, and matters not otherwise provided for. The International Labor Organization would promote social justice and deal with labor policy, industrial relations, social security, and suchlike matters. The Food and Agriculture Organization, UNESCO, and the World Health Organization would deal with their respective spheres. The Universal Postal Union would be responsible for posts, the International Telecommunications Union for telecommunications, the International Civil Aviation Organization (ICAO) for aviation, the Intergovernmental Maritime Consultative Organization (IMCO) for merchant shipping, and the World Meteorological Organization (WMO) for meteorology. The International Monetary Fund (IMF) and the International Bank for Reconstruction and Development

[5] C. Wilfred Jenks, *Law, Freedom and Welfare* (London: Stevens and Sons, 1963), p. 31.

(IBRD) would maintain monetary stability and promote investment. Provision was also being made, but is only now taking a generally acceptable form, for appropriate machinery to deal with problems of trade and development. This was and is a rational and reasonable scheme of world organization. But its workability presupposes that the World Health Organization will concern itself with the ills of the body rather than those of the body politic, that UNESCO will educate people for self-government rather than attempt to decide how and when they should become self-governing, that the Food and Agriculture Organization will devote itself to bridging the gap between food production and population increase rather than attempting to determine what political readjustments and changes the increase in world population may involve, and so forth. The eminent meteorologists of the World Meteorological Organization know more of the weather than of the political weather; postal officials and telecommunication experts are neither qualified nor authorized to deal in the Universal Postal Union and the International Telecommunications Union with race relations and the consequences of colonialism.

If we once depart from the general principle that the responsibility for political matters rests primarily with the United Nations, the whole scheme of functional decentralization on the basis of which so much progress in world organization has been made during the last generation becomes unworkable. The political organs of the United Nations lose control of political issues; the technical work of technical agencies is disrupted; within individual governments as well as in international organizations technical departments become involved in political matters for which they have no continuing responsibility and which they are ill-equipped to handle; chief

inspectors of factories find themselves wrestling with riddles for prime ministers and registrars of copyright with the dilemmas of foreign secretaries. The prospect of widespread agreement on dynamic solutions for major problems at the highest levels of political responsibility is prejudiced rather than improved by such a dispersion and dilution of responsibility. The effect is to weaken and discredit the whole structure of world organization on the further development of which the political, economic, and social progress of mankind depends. The purpose of the functional decentralization of the United Nations system was to take politics out of the widest possible area of international cooperation; a decentralization which operates in practice to multiply the occasions for political conflict defeats its own purpose and frustrates both the political and the technical effectiveness of the system as a whole.

This does not imply that the specialized agencies of the United Nations are or can ever be political eunuchs unmoved by the passions of the world. The political difficulties and preoccupations of the time will inevitably be reflected in their proceedings. ILO, for instance, dedicated by its Constitution and the Declaration of Philadelphia to human freedom and dignity, economic security, and equal opportunity, can never come to terms with *apartheid* or forced labor. Some of these agencies, notably ILO and the World Bank, may have important contributions to make within their own fields of competence to the solution of major political problems. None of them is entitled to claim that its field of action is so technical that it should be immune from the political consequences of decisions taken in a proper manner by the political organs of the United Nations. What it does imply is a general recognition that the responsibility for primarily political decisions should rest with the political organs; restraint in raising in technical bodies political matters beyond their competence which have not yet been raised in or are still pending before the political organs; a vigorous use of the proper political machinery for the solution of political problems; and full cooperation in the implementation of the political decisions of the central political organs by the other agencies of the United Nations system. Each of these elements in such an approach is a necessary complement to the others.

The objective in the handling of acute political problems should therefore be to compel rather than to expel and to seek to resolve such problems in the appropriate forum, dealing with their political aspects in their generality through the central political organs of the United Nations, seeking the cooperation of each specialized agency in its own field of competence (which may sometimes represent a vital part of the political problem), and securing the cooperation of the specialized agencies generally in making the political decisions of the central political organs effective.

IV

What are the further requirements of due process? Four are of special importance.

Firstly, each member of an international organization is entitled to participate in its proceedings through its own chosen spokesman. His person and policies, his past record, present associates, and future plans do not determine or destroy his representative quality. They may destroy his reputation and influence and forfeit the respect and confidence of his colleagues, but, assuming that a recognized government exists, whether he is representative is a matter for the country appointing him to determine for itself. It is as much a denial of due process to unseat or refuse to sit with a

duly accredited representative in an international organization as for the majority of a parliamentary body to unseat a minority. Any such denial of due process creates a precedent which can be invoked at any time to undermine the political independence of any member of the international community.

Secondly, freedom of speech is an inherent right of all duly accredited representatives participating in a meeting of an international organization. It is implied in the UN Charter and by the rules of procedure of virtually all international organizations, and it would indeed be a startling paradox if one of the fundamental freedoms proclaimed by the Universal Declaration of Human Rights were to be denied by the international organizations themselves in respect of their own proceedings. Without freedom of speech international organizations relapse into the ways of tyranny against which those denying such freedom seek to protest. Freedom has nothing to fear from itself; to allow the evil and the foolish to exhibit the evil and foolishness of their ways is the price of free institutions in a free society. Any arbitrary restraint of arrogance and imbecility also throttles freedom. This has been the experience of all mature political societies, and it has a vital bearing on the future of world organization. There are, of course, no captive audiences in international organizations; freedom of speech is qualified by the freedom to refuse to listen. But when the freedom to refuse to listen encroaches upon the freedom of those who wish or are prepared to hear, the principle of freedom of speech is at issue and freedom itself is in jeopardy.

Thirdly, no state or government should be condemned unheard. The principle is common to all reputable legal systems. Let me quote my old friend Dr. Olawale Elias, the Attorney General of Nigeria:

Aude alteram partem is as much a principle of African, as it is of English, legal procedure; a popular Yoruba saying is: "Wicked and iniquitous is he who decides a case upon the testimony of only one party to it." [6]

Respect for this principle is vital to the authority of international organizations. However reprehensible the policy of a state may be thought to be or may in fact be, it is entitled to have the facts judicially established if it so desires before its policy is condemned on the basis of the allegations of its opponents. That state is not empowered to defer political discussion and action indefinitely by a simulacrum of judicial proceedings, but it is entitled to a prompt, full, and fair hearing. It is, of course, essential that the body conducting any such hearing should be wholly independent, completely impartial, thorough in its investigation, and expeditious in its procedure. Although these are conditions which it may not be easy to fulfill, where there is a reasonable assurance that they will be fulfilled, to refuse a fair hearing is a denial of due process.

Fourthly, due process requires regularity of procedure. A proper forum, freedom of speech, and a fair hearing are important elements in, but they do not exhaust the requirements of, regularity of procedure. The inclusion in the agenda in accordance with recognized rules of questions which it is desired to raise, respect for time limits designed to secure due notice of such questions, the dispatch of business in an orderly manner, and respect by international bodies for their own terms of reference and the limits of their constitutional powers are not tedious technicalities which it is legitimate to sweep aside in the name of a higher

[6] Taflim Olawale Elias, *The Nature of African Customary Law* (Manchester, England: Manchester University Press, 1956), p. 243.

morality. They are essential ingredients of substantial justice on which all members, whether directly involved in the matter or not, are entitled to rely as guarantees that, before being called upon to participate in a decision which may have far-reaching implications, they will be able to ascertain and give responsible expression to the considered views of their governments or other constituents. There is no place for guerrilla warfare in the proceedings of international organizations; its inevitable result is to disrupt and discredit the organization in which it occurs to the prejudice of its potentialities as an instrument of effective action.

V

There remains the question whether these are realistic counsels or counsels of perfection which can lead to no practical result but frustration and despair. Let me put the question in its simplest form. Can due process bring results? It can. And due process alone can bring results which will endure.

We must, of course, recognize that there are certain well-defined limits to the possible effectiveness of any form of international action. International action can influence and in certain circumstances determine, but it cannot replace, national policy and action. What a state does within its own territory is in the last resort determined by itself unless concerted and overwhelming political, economic, and, if need be, military pressure is brought against it by the international community. In practice this means pressure by the most powerful members of the international community acting in agreement with each other. To change a national policy we must either persuade the state concerned to change its policy or persuade other states to compel it to change its policy; only by due process of law can we hope to do either of these without plunging the world into chaos. Only a program of change promulgated by due process of law can hope to have any impact on the national policies which one desires to change; only such a program can provide the political and moral basis for the concerted and overwhelming pressure necessary to compel changes.

As an illustration of such a program we may take the Declaration Concerning the Policy of *Apartheid* of the Republic of South Africa and the ILO Program for the Elimination of *Apartheid* in Labor Matters in the Republic of South Africa which were adopted by the International Labor Conference on July 8, 1964.

The Declaration is no exercise in idle rhetoric. It is an important step forward for five reasons: 1) It is unanimous; 2) it is objective; 3) it is based on the unequivocal international obligations of South Africa; 4) it is specific; and 5) it is conceived as the beginning, not the end, of effective and practical ILO action for the elimination of *apartheid*.

Backed by the governments, the employers, and the workers of the whole world, the Declaration is a unanimous expression of the social conscience of mankind, not a partisan manifesto but the voice of reason raised above the tumult and promulgated by due process of law. The Declaration is a unanimous determination by the International Labor Conference that South Africa has been found, by objective and dispassionate inquiry, to be persistently and flagrantly violating principles in respect of which it has undertaken solemn international obligations which continue to remain binding upon it.

The Declaration sets forth a specific program of reform indicating precisely the changes in labor policy necessary to eliminate *apartheid* and elaborated in further detail by the ILO Program for the Elimination of *Apartheid*. This Program concentrates on three broad areas, namely, equality of opportunity in respect of admission to employment and training; freedom from forced labor (including practices which involve or may involve an element of coercion to labor); and freedom of association and the right to organize.

The Program focuses on these matters for four reasons: 1) They are the fundamentals of freedom and dignity in the field of employment; 2) well-established standards approved by the International Labor Conference with near unanimity exist in respect of all of them; 3) the widespread acceptance of these standards in Africa generally and in substantial measure by South Africa's immediate neighbors in southern Africa refutes any suggestion that "the present stage of social and economic development" of South Africa, which is generally conceded to be technically the most advanced of all African countries, precludes their immediate application; and 4) they have all been the subject of an exhaustive inquiry by authoritative ILO bodies which affords an objective basis for the formulation of recommendations relating to them.

In respect of each of these matters the Program sets out the present situation, primarily in the form of an analysis of the applicable laws and regulations; summarizes the findings concerning this situation which have been made by authoritative ILO bodies; contains a proposed recommendation for the amendment of the laws of South Africa to eliminate *apartheid;* and indicates specifically the changes in the laws of South Africa necessary to make the recommendation effective.

The recommendations for action are concrete. They call upon South Africa to *promote* equality of opportunity and treatment in employment and occupation irrespective of race; to *repeal* the statutory provisions which provide for compulsory job reservation or institute discrimination on the basis of race as regards access to vocational training and employment; to *repeal* all legislation providing for penal sanctions for contracts of employment, for the hiring of prison labor for work in agriculture or industry, and for any other form of direct or indirect compulsion to labor, including discrimination on grounds of race in respect of travel and residence, which involves racial discrimination or operates in practice as the basis for such discrimination; and to *repeal* the statutory discrimination on grounds of race in respect of the right to organize and to bargain collectively and the statutory prohibition and restrictions upon mixed trade unions which include persons of more than one race, and so to *amend* the Industrial Conciliation Acts that all workers, without discrimination of race, enjoy the right to organize and may participate in collective bargaining.

The Declaration provides for a continuing review of the position by the International Labor Conference year by year. It concludes with a pressing appeal to the governments, employers, and workers of all states members of ILO to combine their efforts and put into application all appropriate measures to lead the Republic of South Africa to heed the call of humanity and renounce its shameful policy of *apartheid,* together with a reaffirmation of the resolve of ILO to cooperate with the United Nations in seeking and guaranteeing freedom and dignity, economic security, and equal opportunity for all the people of South Africa. South Africa no longer considers itself a member of ILO, but the International Labor Conference has unanimously made it clear that it does not consider South Africa to have been released from any of its obligations.

Although the cooperation of South Africa has not been secured, the work of ILO to secure the freedom and welfare of the people of South Africa has only just begun. When all the peoples of South Africa sit down together on a footing of equality to work out their common destiny by mutual agreement, they will find in the ILO Program for the Elimination of *Apartheid* in Labor Matters a starting point for one of the most crucial parts of their work.

The most critical test lies at some point in the near future. Ethiopia and Liberia have instituted proceedings against South Africa in the International Court of Justice (ICJ) claiming that South Africa continues to be bound in respect of South West Africa by the terms of the mandate and has the duty to cease the practice of *apartheid* in the territory. The Court, by 8 votes to 7, has held that it has jurisdiction to adjudicate upon the merits of the dispute.[7] When the Court does rule upon the merits,* it will be for the Security Council to decide whether to take measures which would give effect to the judgment. The ILO Program for the Elimination of *Apartheid* may well play an important part at that stage.

VI

Let me in conclusion attempt to recapitulate the broad principles by which international organizations must be guided in attempting to resolve these vital and complex problems.

[7] *South West Africa Cases (Ethiopia v. South Africa; Liberia v. South Africa), Preliminary Objections, Judgment of 21 December 1962: I.C.J. Reports 1962,* p. 319.

* Editor's note. In a controversial judgment delivered on July 18, 1966, the ICJ decided that Ethiopia and Liberia had not established any legal right or interest in their claims. The judgment, reached by the President's casting vote, had the effect of dashing the hopes of many UN members for a strong legal case with which to proceed against South Africa. Subsequently, on October 27, the General Assembly adopted, by a vote of 114 to 2, with 3 abstentions, a resolution terminating South Africa's mandate and declaring Southwest Africa to be "the direct responsibility of the United Nations."

The first principle is the rule of law with all that it implies—freedom of speech, fair hearing, and due process. Without the rule of law no international organization can protect the weak nor restrain the strong. Without the rule of law arbitrary action will engender further arbitrary action and injustice breed injustice. Without the rule of law there can be no international society at all.

The second principle is that the moral basis of the rule of law is the protection which it affords to human freedom and the equality of man. No legal system has ever survived the strains of revolutionary changes in society without adapting itself to what Justice Oliver Wendell Holmes so aptly described as "the felt necessities of the time." Only by commanding general acceptance as the symbol and safeguard of freedom and welfare can the law hold the allegiance of society and avert political and social disintegration. This is even more true of the world of international organization than it is of national societies with longer and stabler traditions.

The third principle is that freedom under law is not a negative but a positive and dynamic concept. The freedom we cherish is freedom in dignity. It embraces equality of opportunity. It includes economic security. It cannot thrive amid hunger and poverty or in a climate of frustration and despair. It is the birthright of all men everywhere, irrespective of race, color, or creed. Any lesser concept of law or freedom will be overwhelmed by the turbulent indignation born of festering injustice and bred by all the forces of evil which batten upon injustice.

These three principles represent the only basis on which an effective and lasting world order can be established; they are the only basis on which South Africa can play its full part as an equal partner in a world community founded upon and dedicated to peace and justice, freedom and welfare; they are the principles upon which the United Nations system must, and I believe will, always stand.

Our problem today, the problem of the whole United Nations family, the problem of the whole world, is to find ways of applying these three essentially complementary principles simultaneously and with equal vigor. The problem is not one of reconciling inconsistent principles. It is one of so harmonizing these three component elements of justice in effective forms of action as to make a reality of the mutual pledges of brotherhood whereby we are bound to each other by the terms of the Charter.

11. UN Voting: Tyranny of the Majority?*

SYDNEY D. BAILEY

A MAJORITY in any assembly is tempted to use its power not only to get its way but also to bend the rules to its own advantage. Soviet spokes-

*This article originally appeared in the June 1966 issue of *The World Today*, the monthly journal published by the Royal Institute of International Affairs, London.

men have often referred to the "automatic majority" which the United States is said to have enjoyed in the UN General Assembly, and they have asserted that this majority was sometimes used to short-circuit the Charter or the Rules of Procedure so as to make things easier for the West. An example of this, in the Soviet view, was the Uniting for Peace resolution of 1950, which conferred responsibilities on the General Assembly should the Security Council be deadlocked by the veto. The Soviet Union maintains that this purported to amend the Charter without going through the regular amending process.

Whatever may have been true in the past, however, the situation now is that the West is more usually the victim rather than the initiator of procedural manœuvres. This was true, for example, in April when the President of the Security Council, Mr. Keita of Mali, delayed for forty-eight hours convening a meeting to consider a British proposal for action under Chapter VII in connection with Rhodesia. These tactics were contrary to the tradition of the Council which, according to the Charter, Article 28(1), "shall be so organized as to be able to function continuously." The Council's Rules of Procedure state that the President "shall" (not "may") call a meeting at the request of any member of the Council. The President normally consults the members about the timing of a meeting and sets the time to meet the wishes of the majority. There has, moreover, been a disposition, as the President of the Council (Poland) once put it, "to give the benefit of the doubt . . . to the member who considers the matter as urgent, rather than to the member, or members, who consider it not urgent." [1]

The difficulty concerning the calling of a meeting on Rhodesia had been foreshadowed by three particular problems which had arisen during the last session of the General Assembly and which had rightly caused disquiet. The first problem concerned proposals to delete unpopular speeches from the official UN records. The matter arose initially early in November when the Fifth Committee was discussing the budget estimates. During the course of the debate, the South African representative referred to the work of the UN Office of Public Information and suggested that it should engage in "positive informational activities" but not in "propaganda." The representative of Nigeria intervened on a point of order to the effect that the remarks of the South African representative were not relevant to the matter under discussion, and the chairman of the Committee, rather surprisingly, ruled to that effect.

That was not the end of the incident, however. When the Committee met the next morning, the Indian representative proposed that the South African statement should be expunged from the record, and this proposal was supported by Tanzania and Nigeria. The South African delegate objected strenuously, and Ireland held that it was contrary to established practice and would constitute an unfortunate precedent. There was no further debate, and the Committee approved the Indian proposal by 39 votes to 16 (with 16 abstentions and 46 delegations absent or not participating in the vote).[2]

Later in the session, another attempt was made to have remarks expunged from the record. The plenary Assembly was considering a draft resolution on Cyprus recommended by the First Committee. The representative of Saudi Arabia went to the rostrum to place on record his view that the First Committee had not followed the rules in dealing with the Cyprus item; what had occurred was, in his view (and, indeed, in the view of other delegates), "illegal, unconstitutional, unparliamentary and a rejection of fair play and the sense of equity." The representative of Cameroun formally proposed that the Saudi Arabian

[1] Security Council Official Records, 1st year, 2nd series, 57th meeting (29 August 1946), p. 149.

[2] UN Doc. A/C.5/SR.1086, p. 2.

speech be deleted from the records, though he was later persuaded to withdraw the proposal.[3] The Assembly then proceeded to adopt the resolution on Cyprus by 47 votes to 5, with 54 abstentions and 11 members absent or not participating in the vote. This was the notorious resolution which was adopted by the Assembly with substantial African backing but without the support of Turkey, or any of the five permanent members of the Security Council, or any of the States supplying military or police contingents to the UN Force in Cyprus.

It is, of course, possible to dissent vehemently from the views of the South African, the Saudi Arabian, or any other Government, and yet hold that the official records of the United Nations should reflect accurately what has been said. In 1961, a similar attempt had been made to remove from the records a South African speech, but after a disagreeable debate the Assembly decided by an overwhelming majority to leave the speech in the official records but to "censure" the South African representative for making a statement which was "offensive, fictitious and erroneous." [4]

The second example of the misuse of procedure comprised attempts to prevent free debate by the arbitrary use of the closure. Various forms of closure are permitted by the Rules of Procedure, but there has been a general reluctance to stifle debate except in the case of deliberate filibustering.

The worst instance of the use of the closure during the last session of the Assembly occurred in December when the Special Political Committee was discussing a British-sponsored item concerned with the peaceful settlement of disputes. On the morning of 16 December, the Assembly met in plenary meeting to hear the British Prime Minister and for a number of other items of business. The Assembly's Committees were due to convene immediately thereafter. The Special Political Committee duly met and heard four speeches; then, without warning, Ghana proposed that the "peaceful settlement" item be deferred for a year. This proposal was supported by a number of African and Communist delegates, and adopted by 48 votes to 27 (8 abstentions, 34 delegations absent or not participating in the vote).[5] At the time the vote was taken, more than twenty delegates were still awaiting their turn to speak.

While it is unfortunate that this British initiative should have foundered, at any rate temporarily, the long-term consequences are less serious than those arising from attempts to ignore that Article of the Charter which stipulates that certain matters require a two-thirds majority for decision and other matters only a simple majority.

There has often been confusion about this because of a difference between the procedures of the Security Council and of the General Assembly. In the Security Council, a distinction is made between "procedural" and "all other" matters, and decisions on the former cannot be vetoed (Article 27(2) and (3) of the Charter). The distinction in the General Assembly is not between procedural and other matters, but between "important questions," of which examples are given in the Charter, and "other" questions (Article 18(2) and (3)). Important questions in plenary meetings of the Assembly are decided by a two-thirds majority of the members present and voting, other questions by a simple majority. In Committees of the Assem-

[3] UN Doc. A/PV.1402, pp. 12–25.

[4] GAOR, 16th Session, 1033rd plenary meeting (11 Oct. 1961), paras. 151–186: 1034th plenary meeting (11 Oct. 1961), paras. 1–90.

[5] UN Docs. A/SPC/SR.491, pp. 7–11; A/SPC/SR.492, pp. 2–15.

bly, a simple majority is sufficient for a decision.

A simple majority in the plenary Assembly can also determine "additional categories of questions to be decided by a two-thirds majority." The Assembly has not yet made a specific determination regarding such additional categories, though Special Rule F provides that decisions relating to reports and petitions on South West Africa are regarded as "important questions" within the meaning of Article 18(2).

The Charter does not specify which decisions of the Security Council are to be regarded as procedural and which are not, with the result that there have been difficulties over whether the veto can properly be used in connection with the preliminary question whether a particular draft resolution is or is not a matter of procedure (the so-called "double veto"). Until recently the equivalent question had rarely arisen in the Assembly, partly at least because the Charter specifies a number of questions which are "important" and which therefore require a two-thirds vote for decision in plenary meeting: recommendations with respect to the maintenance of international peace and security; elections to the Security Council, the Economic and Social Council, and the Trusteeship Council; decisions regarding UN membership; questions relating to the operation of the trusteeship system; and budgetary questions.

The situation in the plenary Assembly is therefore as follows. All decisions on matters referred to in the previous paragraph require a two-thirds majority. A two-thirds majority would also be needed for decisions relating to any "additional categories of questions" which the Assembly can decide require such a majority, though any decision to apply the "two-thirds rule" would be taken by only a simple majority. In addition, three Rules of Procedure (Rules 15, 19, and 83) specifically provide that a two-thirds majority is needed for certain decisions. In all other cases, the issue is straightforward: is the question "important" or not? If it is, the "two-thirds rule" applies; if it is not, a simple majority is sufficient. In practice, the Assembly has regarded a simple majority as sufficient for decisions relating to the organization and conduct of its own business, except in those three cases where the Rules of Procedure specify a two-thirds majority.

This is complicated enough, but a further difficulty arises from the fact that whether an issue is "important" or not may depend, or may appear to depend, on how it is formulated and presented. The approval or rejection of the credentials of representatives might be regarded as nothing more than an internal matter relating to the organization and conduct of the work of the Assembly, and therefore to be decided by a simple majority. On the other hand, a specific proposal to reject the credentials of the Chinese Nationalists and to recognize the credentials issued by the People's Republic of China might be regarded as an "important" matter within the meaning of the Charter, and therefore requiring a two-thirds majority.

During the period 1956–60, when the United States opposed any UN discussion of Chinese representation, the Assembly did in fact decide by only a simple majority "not to consider" proposals to exclude representatives of Nationalist China or to seat representatives of the People's Republic of China.[6] In 1961 and 1965, however, when the question of Chinese representation had been inscribed on the agenda, the Assembly decided, also by a simple majority, that any proposal to *change* the representation of China was an "important" question and

[6] GA resolutions 1108(xi), 1135(xii), 1239(xiii), 1351(xiv), and 1493(xv).

would therefore require a two-thirds majority.[7] The United Kingdom was the only UN member in 1965 to vote both that the question was "important" *and* in favour of the representation of the People's Republic of China.

One's mind boggles at the prospect that the Assembly might eventually, by a simple majority, decide that any proposal to leave the representation of China unchanged would be "important," therefore requiring a two-thirds majority!

The "simple majority" decisions regarding Chinese representation in the period 1956–60 were, however, exceptional. Prior to the twentieth session of the General Assembly, over 2,000 resolutions had been adopted by the Assembly, of which only twenty were by a simple majority.[8] All the others

[7] GA resolutions 1668(xvi) and 2025(xx).

[8] General Assembly resolutions adopted by a simple majority vote, 1946–65 (1st to 19th regular Sessions, 1st to 4th Special Sessions, 1st to 4th Emergency Special Sessions).

Session	Res. No.	Subject
1	17	Amendments to the Provisional Rules of Procedure.
1	49B	Request of the World Federation of Trade Unions for a closer connection with the Economic and Social Council.
2	184	Place of meeting of the third regular session of the General Assembly.
3	247	Proposal for the adoption of Spanish as one of the working languages of the General Assembly.
5	497	Place of meeting of the sixth regular session of the General Assembly.
5	499	Place of meeting of the sixth regular session of the General Assembly.
6	520A	Financing of economic development of under-developed countries.
6	543	Preparation of two Draft International Covenants on Human Rights.
6	598	Reservations to multilateral conventions.
7	630	Convention on the International Right of Correction.
8	742	Factors which should be taken into account in deciding whether a Territory is or is not a Territory whose people have not yet attained a full measure of self-government.
8	748	Cessation of the transmission of information under Article 73 (e) of the Charter in respect of Puerto Rico.
10	957	Procedure for review of United Nations Administrative Tribunal judgements: amendments to the Statute of the Administrative Tribunal.
11	1108	Representation of China in the United Nations.
12	1135	Representation of China in the United Nations.
12	1181	Question of defining aggression.
13	1239	Representation of China in the United Nations.
13	1333	Verbatim record of the debate on the report of the Good Offices Committee on South West Africa.
14	1351	Representation of China in the United Nations.
15	1493	Representation of China in the United Nations.

General Assembly resolutions regarding which amendments or parts were adopted by a simple majority vote, 1946–65 (1st to 19th regular Sessions, 1st to 4th Special Sessions, 1st to 4th Emergency Special Sessions).

Session	Res. No.	Subject
11	1040	Convention on the Nationality of Married Women.
13	1240	Establishment of the Special Fund.
13	1323	Questions relating to the promotion of international trade and to assistance in the development of the less developed countries.
13	1330	Effects of the European Economic Community on the development of certain Non-Self-Governing Territories.
15	1573	Question of Algeria.
17	1763	Draft Convention on Consent to Marriage, Minimum Age for Marriage, and Registration of Marriages.

were adopted either unanimously or by at least a two-thirds majority. Last December, however, there were several blatant attempts to ignore the requirements of Article 18 of the Charter.

On 16 December, the same day as the British item on peaceful settlement had been smothered, the plenary Assembly was considering a draft resolution on colonial territories; two paragraphs of the draft, referring to military bases of colonial Powers, had been previously approved in the Fourth Committee. Paragraph-by-paragraph votes were requested in the plenary, and the first of the two paragraphs received 48 votes in favour and 33 against. The President declared that, as it had failed to secure a two-thirds majority, it had not been adopted. The U.S.S.R. challenged this statement, but the President insisted that the paragraph related to the maintenance of peace and was, therefore, an "important" matter. Following a number of unsuccessful attempts to have the meeting suspended or adjourned, the Soviet challenge to the President's ruling was put to the vote and defeated. The Assembly then failed to give a two-thirds majority to the second of the paragraphs dealing with military bases.[9]

The next morning, the Assembly met to consider reports and draft resolutions relating to South West Africa and Oman. Assembly procedures regarding South West Africa are governed by six Special Rules, which are themselves based on Advisory Opinions of the World Court. As noted above, one of the Special Rules provides that decisions on "questions relating to reports and petitions" concerning South West Africa shall be regarded as "important."

After the report of the Fourth Committee had been presented, the Liberian representative intervened on a point of order to ask that the draft resolutions

on South West Africa be adopted by simple majorities "since the Assembly is the master of its own procedure." This led to a debate about the applicability of the Special Rule, and in the end it was decided to defer the item on South West Africa and take up the draft resolution on Oman.[10] Iraq had already proposed that this draft resolution should be adopted by a simple majority and, after further debate, this was approved by 63 votes to 37 (12 abstentions, 5 absent or not participating in the vote).[11] The draft resolution on Oman was then approved. At the next meeting, the Liberian representative withdrew her proposal regarding the majority required for the draft resolutions on South West Africa,[12] but this was only a lull before the storm. Before the meeting was over, a group of Afro-Asian States plus Yugoslavia had introduced an anti-colonial resolution which included the following operative paragraph: *"Requests* the colonial Powers to dismantle the military bases installed in colonial Territories and to refrain from establishing new ones." The representative of Mali, on behalf of the sponsors, proposed that the resolution be adopted by a simple majority.[13]

Ambassador Goldberg at once intervened to submit a procedural motion to the effect that the Afro-Asian-Yugoslav draft "makes recommendations with respect to the maintenance of international peace and security" and accordingly a two-thirds majority would be needed.[14] That was on the Friday evening.

The Assembly met again later that night, twice on the Saturday, and on the Monday morning, but it was not until the Monday afternoon (the penultimate day of the session) that a

[9] UN Doc. A/PV.1398, pp. 51–65.

[10] UN Doc. A/PV.1399, pp. 6–36.
[11] *Ibid.,* p. 61.
[12] UN Doc. A/PV.1400, pp. 7–10.
[13] *ibid.,* p. 66.
[14] UN Doc. A/L.478.

weary Assembly returned to Ambassador Goldberg's procedural proposal. After a lengthy debate, the proposal of Mali was put to the vote and approved by 59 votes to 45 (4 abstentions, 9 absent or not participating in the vote).[15] The main resolution was then put to the vote and, although the paragraph referring to military bases did not receive a two-thirds majority, the resolution as a whole was adopted.[16]

The remarkable thing about the debates on whether to dispense with the two-thirds rule was that little serious attempt was made to state any legal arguments for doing so. In the case of the South West African resolutions, where a Special Rule of Procedure adopted in 1954 had specifically provided for decisions by a two-thirds majority, the Liberian representative supported her case for a simple majority merely by claiming that the Assembly is master of its own procedure. This is at best a half-truth, though it has acquired a certain sanctity by constant repetition, and the idea has regrettably found its way into an Annex to the Assembly's Rules of Procedure (Annex I, para. 39). The fact is that the Assembly is bound by the Charter, and can dispense with its own Rules of Procedure only by amending them in the proper way or by unanimous consent, and even then the Charter must be honoured.[17]

In his book on American democracy, Alexis de Tocqueville deals at some length with what he calls "the tyranny of the majority." The danger of arbitrary and unlimited majority rule, he argues, is that minorities feel they have no alternative but to resort to violence, and anarchy results. The United Nations is a tentative step away from anarchy in international relations and towards a system of law and justice, and it is the States which lack the traditional means of power which have much to gain from a United Nations which can ask States to respect what international law there is because it abides by the rules itself. It is not in the true interests of States to dispense with the rules simply because they sometimes, and in the short term, seem to be inconvenient.

Recent developments regarding Assembly procedure have added to the importance of choosing presiding officers of skill, impartiality, and integrity. The Rules require a system of equitable geographical distribution, but this is only one criterion; experience and personal competence are also mandatory. It is also essential that members of delegations should be familiar with the procedure and practice of the Assembly, so that they can deal promptly and confidently with all proposals (whether deliberate or unwitting) to subvert the Rules. Moreover, every Committee of the Assembly should at all times have the services of an expert adviser from the Secretariat, as urged by the Assembly's Special Committee on Methods and Procedures seventeen years ago.[18]

None of these devices, however, can of themselves ensure compliance with the Rules. The Charter requirement of a two-thirds majority in the Assembly for "important" questions is intended to encourage moderation in the drafting of resolutions, and moderation is an important element in securing compliance. Most of the Assembly's resolutions are only recommendations or expressions of opinion. If the tendencies of the last session of the Assembly were to continue or increase, the certain result would be that recommendations would be ignored, the Assembly devalued, and the authority of the United Nations undermined. This is a consummation devoutly to be resisted.

[15] UN Doc. A/PV.1405, pp. 73–5.

[16] GA resolution 2105(xx).

[17] See my *The General Assembly of the United Nations,* 2nd ed., 1964, pp. 112, 117–18, 322.

[18] GAOR, 4th Session, Supplement No. 12A(A/937), para. 39.

12. The International Civil Servant in Law and in Fact*

DAG HAMMARSKJÖLD

I

IN A RECENT article Mr. Walter Lippmann tells about an interview in Moscow with Mr. Krushchev. According to the article, Chairman Krushchev stated that "while there are neutral countries, there are no neutral men," and the author draws the conclusion that it is now the view of the Soviet Government "that there can be no such thing as an impartial civil servant in this deeply divided world, and that the kind of political celibacy which the British theory of the civil servant calls for, is in international affairs a fiction."

Whether this accurately sums up the views held by the Soviet Government, as reflected in the interview, or not, one thing is certain: The attitude which the article reflects is one which we find nowadays in many political quarters, communist and non-communist alike, and it raises a problem which cannot be treated lightly. In fact, it challenges basic tenets in the philosophy of both the League of Nations and the United Nations, as one of the essential points on which these experiments in international cooperation represent an advance beyond traditional "conference diplomacy" is the introduction on the international arena of joint permanent organs, employing a neutral civil service, and the use of such organs for executive purposes on behalf of all the members of the organizations. Were it to be considered that the experience shows that this

radical innovation in international life rests on a false assumption, because "no man can be neutral," then we would be thrown back to 1919, and a searching re-appraisal would become necessary.

II

The international civil service had its genesis in the League of Nations but it did not spring full-blown in the Treaty of Versailles and the Covenant. The Covenant was in fact silent on the international character of the Secretariat. It contained no provisions comparable to those of Article 100 of the Charter and simply stated:

> "The permanent Secretariat shall be established at the Seat of the League. The Secretariat shall comprise a Secretary-General and such secretaries and staff as may be required."

In the earliest proposals for the Secretariat of the League, it was apparently taken for granted that there could not be a truly international secretariat but that there would have to be nine national secretaries, each assisted by a national staff and performing, in turn, the duties of Secretary to the Council, under the supervision of the Secretary-General. This plan, which had been drawn up by Sir Maurice Hankey, who had been offered the post of Secretary-General of the League by the Allied Powers, was in keeping with the precedents set by the various international bureaux established before the war which were staffed by officials

* Lecture delivered to Congregation at Oxford University, 30 May 1961. Reprinted by permission of the Clarendon Press, Oxford.

seconded by Member countries on a temporary basis.

It was Sir Eric Drummond, first Secretary-General of the League, who is generally regarded as mainly responsible for building upon the vague language of the Covenant a truly international secretariat. The classic statement of the principles he first espoused is found in the report submitted to the Council of the League by its British member, Arthur Balfour:

> "By the terms of the Treaty, the duty of selecting the staff falls upon the Secretary-General, just as the duty of approving it falls upon the Council. In making his appointments, he had primarily to secure the best available men and women for the particular duties which had to be performed; but in doing so, it was necessary to have regard to the great importance of selecting the officials from various nations. Evidently, no one nation or group of nations ought to have a monopoly in providing the material for this international institution. I emphasize the word 'international,' because the members of the Secretariat once appointed are no longer the servants of the country of which they are citizens, but become for the time being the servants only of the League of Nations. Their duties are not national but international."

Thus, in this statement, we have two of the essential principles of an international civil service: (1) its international composition and (2) its international responsibilities. The latter principle found its legal expression in the Regulations subsequently adopted which enjoined all officials "to discharge their functions and to regulate their conduct with the interests of the League alone in view" and prohibited them from seeking or receiving "instructions from any Government or other authority external to the Secretariat of the League of Nations."

Along with the conception of an independent, internationally responsible staff, another major idea was to be found: the international Secretariat was to be solely an administrative organ, eschewing political judgments and actions. It is not at all surprising that this third principle should have originated with a British Secretary-General. In the United Kingdom, as in certain other European countries, a system of patronage, political or personal, had been gradually replaced in the course of the nineteenth century by the principle of a permanent civil service based on efficiency and competence and owing allegiance only to the State which it served. It followed that a civil service so organized and dedicated would be non-political. The civil servant could not be expected to serve two masters and consequently he could not, in his official duties, display any political allegiance to a political party or ideology. Those decisions which involved a political choice were left to the Government and to Parliament; the civil servant was the nonpartisan administrator of those decisions. His discretion was a limited one, bound by the framework of national law and authority and by rules and instructions issued by his political superiors. True, there were choices for him, since neither legal rules nor policy decisions can wholly eliminate the discretion of the administrative official, but the choices to be made were confined to relatively narrow limits by legislative enactment, Government decision and the great body of precedent and tradition. The necessary condition was that there should exist at all times a higher political authority with the capacity to take the political decisions. With that condition it seemed almost axiomatic that the civil service had to be "politically celibate" (though not perhaps politically virgin). It could not take sides in any political controversy and, accordingly, it could not be given tasks which required it to do so. This was reflected in the basic statements laying down the policy to govern the international Secretariat. I may quote two of them:

"We recommend with special urgency that, in the interests of the League, as well as in its own interests, the Secretariat should not extend the sphere of its activities, that in the preparation of the work and the decisions of the various organizations of the League, it should regard it as its first duty to collate the relevant documents, and to prepare the ground for these decisions without suggesting what these decisions should be; finally, that once these decisions have been taken by the bodies solely responsible for them, it should confine itself to executing them in the letter and in the spirit." [1]

"Une fois les décisions prises, le rôle du Secrétariat est de les appliquer. Ici encore, il y a un lieu de faire une distinction entre application et interprétation, non pas, à coup sûr, que je demande au Secrétariat de ne jamais interpréter; c'est son métier! Mais je lui demande, et vous lui demanderez certainement tous, d'interpréter le moins loin possible, le plus fidèlement possible, et surtout de ne jamais substituer son interprétation à la vôtre." [2]

Historians of the League have noted the self-restraining role played by the Secretary-General. He never addressed the Assembly of the League and in the Council "he tended to speak . . . as a Secretary of a committee and not more than that." [3] For him to have entered into political tasks which involved in any substantial degree the taking of a position was regarded as compromising the very basis of the impartiality essential for the Secretariat.

True, this does not mean that political matters as such were entirely excluded from the area of the Secretariat's interests. It has been reported by Sir Eric Drummond and others that he played a role behind the scenes, acting as a confidential channel of communication to Governments engaged in controversy or dispute, but this behind-the-scenes role was never extended to taking action in a politically controversial case that was deemed objectionable by one of the sides concerned.

III

The legacy of the international Secretariat of the League is marked in the Charter of the United Nations. Article 100 follows almost verbatim the League regulations on independence and international responsibility—barring the seeking or receiving of instructions from States or other external authority. This was originally proposed at San Francisco by the four sponsoring powers—China, the USSR, the United Kingdom and the United States—and unanimously accepted. The League experience had shown that an international civil service, responsible only to the Organization, was workable and efficient. It had also revealed as manifested in the behaviour of German and Italian Fascists, that there was a danger of national pressures corroding the concept of international loyalty. That experience underlined the desirability of including in the Charter itself an explicit obligation on officials and governments alike to respect fully the independence and the exclusively international character of the responsibilities of the Secretariat. It was also recognized that an in-

[1] Report of Committee Four, records of the Second Assembly.

[2] Statement by M. Noblemaire, Second Assembly, 1 October 1921.

[3] Proceedings of Conference on Experience in International Administration, Washington, D.C., Carnegie Endowment, 1943.

ternational civil service of this kind could not be made up of persons indirectly responsible to their national governments. The weight attached to this by the majority of Members was demonstrated in the Preparatory Commission, London, when it was proposed that appointments of officials should be subject to the consent of the government of the Member State of which the candidate was a national. Even in making this proposal, its sponsor explained that it was only intended to build up a staff adequately representative of the governments and acceptable to them. He maintained that prior approval of officials was necessary, in order to obtain the confidence of their governments which was essential to the Secretariat, but once the officials were appointed, the exclusively international character of their responsibilities would be respected. However, the great majority of Member States rejected this proposal, for they believed that it would be extremely undesirable to write into the regulations anything that would give national governments particular rights in respect of appointments and thus indirectly permit political pressures on the Secretary-General.

Similarly in line with Article 100, the Preparatory Commission laid emphasis on the fact that the Secretary-General "alone is responsible to the other principal organs for the Secretariat's work," and that all officials in the Organization must recognize the exclusive authority of the Secretary-General and submit themselves to rules of discipline laid down by him.

The principle of the independence of the Secretariat from national pressures was also reinforced in the Charter by Article 105, which provides for granting officials of the Organization "such privileges and immunities as are necessary for the independent exercise of their functions in connection with the Organization." It was in fact foreseen at San Francisco that in excep-

tional circumstances there might be a clash between the independent position of a member of the Secretariat and the position of his country, and consequently that an immunity in respect of official acts would be necessary for the protection of the officials from pressure by individual governments and to permit them to carry out their international responsibilities without interference.

In all of these legal provisions, the Charter built essentially on the experience of the League and affirmed the principles already accepted there. However, when it came to the functions and authority of the Secretary-General, the Charter broke new ground.

In Article 97 the Secretary-General is described as the "chief administrative officer of the Organization," a phrase not found in the Covenant, though probably implicit in the position of the Secretary-General of the League. Its explicit inclusion in the Charter made it a constitutional requirement—not simply a matter left to the discretion of the organs—that the administration of the Organization shall be left to the Secretary-General. The Preparatory Commission observed that the administrative responsibility under Article 97 involves the essential tasks of preparing the ground for the decisions of the organs and of "executing" them in cooperation with the Members.

Article 97 is of fundamental importance for the status of the international Secretariat of the United Nations, and thus for the international civil servant employed by the Organization, as together with Articles 100 and 101 it creates for the Secretariat a position, administratively, of full political independence. However, it does not, or at least it need not represent an element in the picture which raises the question of the "neutrality" of the international civil servant. This is so because the decisions and actions of the Secretary-General as chief administrative officer naturally can be envisaged as limited to administrative problems outside the sphere of political conflicts of interest or ideology, and thus as maintaining the concept of the international civil servant as first developed in the League of Nations.

However, Article 97 is followed by Article 98, and Article 98 is followed by Article 99. And these two Articles together open the door to the problem of neutrality in a sense unknown in the history of the League of Nations.

In Article 98 it is, thus, provided not only that the Secretary-General "shall act in that capacity" in meetings of the organs, but that he "shall perform such other functions as are entrusted to him by these organs." This latter provision was not in the Covenant of the League. It has substantial significance in the Charter, for it entitles the General Assembly and the Security Council to entrust the Secretary-General with tasks involving the execution of political decisions, even when this would bring him—and with him the Secretariat and its members—into the arena of possible political conflict. The organs are, of course, not required to delegate such tasks to the Secretary-General but it is clear that they *may* do so. Moreover, it may be said that in doing so the General Assembly and the Security Council are in no way in conflict with the spirit of the Charter—even if some might like to give the word "chief administrative officer" in Article 97 a normative and limitative significance —since the Charter itself gives to the Secretary-General an explicit political role.

It is Article 99 more than any other which was considered by the drafters of the Charter to have transformed the Secretary-General of the United Nations from a purely administrative official to one with an explicit political responsibility. Considering its importance, it is perhaps surprising that Article 99 was hardly debated: most delegates appeared to share Smuts' opinion that the position of the Secre-tary-General "should be of the highest importance and for this reason a large measure of initiative was expressly conferred." Legal scholars have observed that Article 99 not only confers upon the Secretary-General a right to bring matters to the attention of the Security Council but that this right carries with it, by necessary implication, a broad discretion to conduct inquiries and to engage in informal diplomatic activity in regard to matters which "may threaten the maintenance of international peace and security."

It is not without some significance that this new conception of a Secretary-General originated principally with the United States rather than the United Kingdom. It has been reported that at an early stage in the preparation of the papers that later became the Dumbarton Oaks proposals, the United States gave serious consideration to the idea that the Organization should have a President as well as a Secretary-General. Subsequently, it was decided to propose only a single officer, but one in whom there would be combined both the political and executive functions of a President with the internal administrative functions that were previously accorded to a Secretary-General. Obviously, this is a reflection, in some measure, of the American political system, which places authority in a chief executive officer who is not simply subordinated to the legislative organs but who is constitutionally responsible alone for the execution of legislation and in some respects for carrying out the authority derived from the constitutional instrument directly.

The fact that the Secretary-General is an official with political power as well as administrative functions had direct implications for the method of his selection. Proposals at San Francisco to eliminate the participation of the Security Council in the election process were rejected precisely because it was recognized that the role of the Secretary-General in the field of political and security matters properly involved the Security Council and made it logical that the unanimity rule of the permanent Members should apply. At the same time, it was recognized that the necessity of such unanimous agreement would have to be limited only to the selection of the Secretary-General and that it was equally essential that he be protected against the pressure of a Member during his term in office. Thus a proposal for a three-year term was rejected on the ground that so short a term might impair his independent role.

The concern with the independence of the Secretary-General from national pressures was also reflected at San Francisco in the decision of the Conference to reject proposals for Deputies Secretary-General appointed in the same manner as the Secretary-General. The opponents of this provision maintained that a proposal of this kind would result in a group of high officials who would not be responsible to the Secretary-General but to the bodies which elected them. This would inevitably mean a dilution of the responsibility of the Secretary-General for the conduct of the Organization and would be conducive neither to the efficient functioning of the Secretariat nor to its independent position. In this action and other related decisions, the drafters of the Charter laid emphasis on the personal responsibility of the Secretary-General; it is he who is solely responsible for performing the functions entrusted to him for the appointment of all members of the Secretariat and for assuring the organ that the Secretariat will carry out their tasks under his exclusive authority. The idea of a "Cabinet system" in which responsibility for administration and political functions would be distributed among several individuals was squarely rejected.

It is also relevant in this connection that the provision for "due regard to geographical representation" in the recruitment of the Secretariat was never treated as calling for political or ideological representation. It was rather an affirmation of the idea accepted since the beginning of the League Secretariat that the staff of the Organization was to have an international composition and that its basis would be as "geographically" broad as possible. Moreover, as clearly indicated in the language of Article 101, the "paramount consideration in the employment of the staff" should be the necessity of securing the highest standards of efficiency, competence and integrity. This terminology is evidence of the intention of the drafters to accord priority to considerations of efficiency and competence over those of geographical representation, important though the latter be.

To sum up, the Charter laid down these essential legal principles for an international civil service:

It was to be an international body, recruited primarily for efficiency, competence and integrity, but on as wide a geographical basis as possible;

It was to be headed by a Secretary-General who carried constitutionally the responsibility to the other principal organs for the Secretariat's work;

And finally, Article 98 entitled the General Assembly and the Security Council to entrust the Secretary-General with tasks going beyond the *verba formalia* of Article 97—with its emphasis on the administrative function —thus opening the door to a measure of political responsibility which is distinct from the authority explicitly accorded to the Secretary-General under Article 99 but in keeping with the spirit of that article.

This last-mentioned development concerning the Secretary-General, with its obvious consequences for the Secretariat as such, takes us beyond the concept of a non-political civil service into an area where the official, in the exercise of his functions, may be forced to take stands of a politically controversial nature. It does this, however, on an international basis and, thus, without departing from the basic concept of "neutrality"; in fact, Article 98, as well as Article 99, would be unthinkable without the complement of Article 100 strictly observed both in letter and spirit.

Reverting for a moment to our initial question, I have tried to emphasize the distinction just made. If a demand for neutrality is made, by present critics of the international civil service, with the intent that the international civil servant should not be permitted to take a stand on political issues, in response to requests of the General Assembly or the Security Council, then the demand is in conflict with the Charter itself. If, however, "neutrality" means that the international civil servant, also in executive tasks with political implications, must remain wholly uninfluenced by national or group interests or ideologics, then the obligation to observe such neutrality is just as basic to the Charter concept of the international civil service as it was to the concept once found in the Covenant of the League. Due to the circumstances then prevailing the distinction to which I have just drawn attention probably never was clearly made in the League, but it has become fundamental for the interpretation of the actions of the Secretariat as established by the Charter.

The criticism to which I referred at the beginning of this lecture can be directed against the very Charter concept of the Secretariat and imply a demand for a reduction of the functions of the Secretariat to the role assigned to it in the League and explicitly mentioned in Article 97 of the Charter; this would be a retrograde development in sharp conflict with the way in which the functions of the international Secretariat over the years have been extended by the main organs of the United Nations, in response to arising needs. Another possibility would be that the actual developments under

Articles 98 and 99 are accepted but that a lack of confidence in the possibility of personal "neutrality" is considered to render necessary administrative arrangements putting the persons in question under special constitutional controls, either built into the structure of the Secretariat or established through organs outside the Secretariat.

IV

The conception of an independent international civil service, although reasonably clear in the Charter provisions, was almost continuously subjected to stress in the history of the Organization. International tensions, changes in governments, concern with national security, all had their inevitable repercussions on the still fragile institution dedicated to the international community. Governments not only strove for the acceptance of their views in the organs of the Organization, but they concerned themselves in varying degrees with the attitude of their nationals in the Secretariat. Some governments sought in one way or another to revive the substance of the proposal defeated at London for the clearance of their nationals prior to employment in the Secretariat; other governments on occasion demanded the dismissal of staff members who were said to be inappropriately representative of the country of their nationality for political, racial or even cultural reasons.

In consequence, the Charter Articles underwent a continual process of interpretation and clarification in the face of pressures brought to bear on the Secretary-General. On the whole the results tended to affirm and strengthen the independence of the international civil service. These developments involved two complementary aspects: first, the relation between the Organization and the Member States in regard to the selection and employment of nationals of those States; and second, the relation between the international official, his own State and the international responsibilities of the Organization. It is apparent that these relationships involved a complex set of obligations and rights applying to the several interested parties.

One of the most difficult of the problems was presented as a result of the interest of several national governments in passing upon the recruitment of their nationals by the Secretariat. It was of course a matter of fundamental principle that the selection of the staff should be made by the Secretary-General on his own responsibility and not on the responsibility of the national governments. The interest of the governments in placing certain nationals and in barring the employment of others had to be subordinated, as a matter of principle and law, to the independent determination of the Organization. Otherwise there would have been an abandonment of the position adopted at San Francisco and affirmed by the Preparatory Commission in London.

On the other hand, there were practical considerations which required the Organization to utilize the services of governments for the purpose of obtaining applicants for positions and, as a corollary of this, for information as to the competence, integrity and general suitability of such nationals for employment. The United Nations could not have an investigating agency comparable to those available to national governments, and the Organization had therefore to accept assistance from governments in obtaining information and records concerning possible applicants. However, the Secretary-General consistently reserved the right to make the final determination on the basis of all the facts and his own independent appreciation of these facts.

It may be recalled that this problem assumed critical proportions in 1952 and 1953 when various authorities of the United States Government, host to the United Nations Headquarters, conducted a series of highly publicized investigations of the loyalty of its nationals in the Secretariat. Charges were made which, although relating to a small number of individuals and largely founded upon inference rather than on direct evidence or admissions, led to proposals which implicitly challenged the international character of the responsibilities of the Secretary-General and his staff. In certain other countries similar proposals were made and in some cases adopted in legislation or by administrative action.

In response, the Secretary-General and the Organization as a whole affirmed the necessity of independent action by the United Nations in regard to selection and recruitment of staff. The Organization was only prepared to accept information from governments concerning suitability for employment, including information that might be relevant to political considerations such as activity which would be regarded as inconsistent with the obligation of international civil servants. It was recognized that there should be a relationship of mutual confidence and trust between international officials and the governments of Member States. At the same time, the Secretary-General took a strong position that the dismissal of a staff member on the basis of the mere suspicion of a government of a Member State or a bare conclusion arrived at by that government on evidence which is denied the Secretary-General would amount to receiving instructions in violation of his obligation under Article 100, paragraph 1, of the Charter "not to receive in the performance of his duties instructions from any government." It should be said that, as a result of the stand taken by the Organization, this principle was recognized by the United States Government in the procedures it established for hearings and submission of information to the Secretary-General regarding U.S. citizens.

A risk of national pressure on the international official may also be introduced, in a somewhat more subtle way, by the terms and duration of his appointment. A national official, seconded by his government for a year or two with an international organization, is evidently in a different position psychologically—and one might say, politically—from the permanent international civil servant who does not contemplate a subsequent career with his national government. This was recognized by the Preparatory Commission in London in 1945 when it concluded that members of the Secretariat staff could not be expected "fully to subordinate the special interests of their countries to the international interest if they are merely detached temporarily from national administrations and dependent upon them for their future." Recently, however, assertions have been made that it is necessary to switch from the present system, which makes permanent appointments and career service the rule, to a predominant system of fixed-term appointments to be granted mainly to officials seconded by their governments. This line is prompted by governments which show little enthusiasm for making officials available on a long-term basis, and, moreover, seem to regard—as a matter of principle or, at least, of "realistic" psychology—the international civil servant primarily as a national official representing his country and its ideology. On this view, the international civil service should be recognized and developed as being an "intergovernmental" secretariat composed principally of national officials assigned by their governments, rather than as an "international" secretariat as conceived from the days of the League of Nations and until now. In the light of what I have already said regarding the provisions of the Charter, I need not demonstrate that this conception runs squarely against the principles of Articles 100 and 101.

This is not to say that there is not room for a reasonable number of "seconded" officials in the Secretariat. It has in fact been accepted that it is highly desirable to have a number of officials available from governments for short periods, especially to perform particular tasks calling for diplomatic or technical backgrounds. Experience has shown that such seconded officials, true to their obligations under the Charter, perform valuable service but as a matter of good policy it should, of course, be avoided as much as possible to put them on assignments in which their status and nationality might be embarrassing to themselves or the parties concerned. However, this is quite different from having a large portion of the Secretariat—say, in excess of one-third—composed of short-term officials. To have so large a proportion of the Secretariat staff in the seconded category would be likely to impose serious strains on its ability to function as a body dedicated exclusively to international responsibilities. Especially if there were any doubts as to the principles ruling their work in the minds of the governments on which their future might depend, this might result in a radical departure from the basic concepts of the Charter and the destruction of the international civil service as it has been developed in the League and up to now in the United Nations.

It can fairly be said that the United Nations has increasingly succeeded in affirming the original idea of a dedicated professional service responsible only to the Organization in the performance of its duties and protected insofar as possible from the inevitable pressures of national governments. And this has been done in spite of strong pressures which are easily explained in terms of historic tradition and national interests. Obviously, however, the problem is ultimately one of the spirit of service shown by the international civil servant and respected by Member governments. The International Secretariat is not what it is meant to be until the day when it can be recruited on a wide geographical basis without the risk that then some will be under—or consider themselves to be under—two masters in respect of their official functions.

V

The independence and international character of the Secretariat required not only resistance to national pressures in matters of personnel, but also —and this was more complex—the independent implementation of controversial political decisions in a manner fully consistent with the exclusively international responsibility of the Secretary-General. True, in some cases implementation was largely administrative; the political organs stated their objectives and the measures to be taken in reasonably specific terms, leaving only a narrow area for executive discretion. But in other cases—and these generally involved the most controversial situations—the Secretary-General was confronted with mandates of a highly general character, expressing the bare minimum of agreement attainable in the organs. That the execution of these tasks involved the exercise of political judgment by the Secretary-General was, of course, evident to the Member States themselves.

It could perhaps be surmised that virtually no one at San Francisco envisaged the extent to which the Members of the Organization would assign to the Secretary-General functions which necessarily required him to take positions in highly controversial political matters. A few examples of these mandates in recent years will demonstrate how wide has been the scope of authority delegated to the Secretary-General by the Security Council and the General Assembly in matters of peace and security.

One might begin in 1956 with the Palestine armistice problem when the Security Council instructed the Secretary-General "to arrange with the parties for adoption of any measures" which he would consider "would reduce existing tensions along the armistice demarcation lines." A few months later, after the outbreak of hostilities in Egypt, the General Assembly authorized the Secretary-General immediately to "obtain compliance of the withdrawal of foreign forces." At the same session he was requested to submit a plan for a United Nations Force to "secure and supervise the cessation of hostilities," and subsequently he was instructed "to take all . . . necessary administrative and executive action to organize this Force and dispatch it to Egypt."

In 1958 the Secretary-General was requested "to dispatch urgently an Observation Group . . . to Lebanon so as to insure that there is no illegal infiltration of personnel or supply of arms or other matériel across the Lebanese borders." Two months later he was asked to make forthwith "such practical arrangements as would adequately help in upholding the purposes and principles of the Charter in relation to Lebanon and Jordan."

Most recently, in July 1960, the Secretary-General was requested to provide military assistance to the Central Government of the Republic of the Congo. The basic mandate is contained in a single paragraph of a resolution adopted by the Security Council on 13 July 1960, which reads as follows:

The Security Council
. . . .

2. *Decides* to authorize the Secretary-General to take the necessary steps, in consultation with the Government of the Republic of the

Congo, to provide the Government with such military assistance, as may be necessary, until, through the efforts of the Congolese Government with the technical assistance of the United Nations, the national security forces may be able, in the opinion of the Government, to meet fully their tasks.

The only additional guidance was provided by a set of principles concerning the use of United Nations Forces which had been evolved during the experience of the United Nations Emergency Force. I had informed the Security Council before the adoption of the resolution that I would base any action that I might be required to take on these principles, drawing attention specifically to some of the most significant of the rules applied in the UNEF operation. At the request of the Security Council I later submitted an elaboration of the same principles to the extent they appeared to me to be applicable to the Congo operation. A report on the matter was explicitly approved by the Council, but naturally it proved to leave wide gaps; unforeseen and unforeseeable problems, which we quickly came to face, made it necessary for me repeatedly to invite the Council to express themselves on the interpretation given by the Secretary-General to the mandate. The needs for added interpretation referred especially to the politically extremely charged situation which arose because of the secession of Katanga and because of the disintegration of the Central Government, which, according to the basic resolution of the Security Council, was to be the party in consultation with which the United Nations activities had to be developed.

These recent examples demonstrate the extent to which the Member States have entrusted the Secretary-General with tasks that have required him to take action which unavoidably may have to run counter to the views of at least some of these Member States. The agreement reached in the general terms of a resolution, as we have seen, no longer need obtain when more specific issues are presented. Even when the original resolution is fairly precise, subsequent developments, previously unforeseen, may render highly controversial the action called for under the resolution. Thus, for example, the unanimous resolution authorizing assistance to the Central Government of the Congo offered little guidance to the Secretary-General when that Government split into competing centers of authority, each claiming to be the Central Government and each supported by different groups of Member States within and outside the Security Council.

A simple solution for the dilemmas thus posed for the Secretary-General might seem to be for him to refer the problem to the political organ for it to resolve the question. Under a national parliamentary regime, this would often be the obvious course of action for the executive to take. Indeed, this is what the Secretary-General must also do whenever it is feasible. But the serious problems arise precisely because it is so often not possible for the organs themselves to resolve the controversial issue faced by the Secretary-General. When brought down to specific cases involving a clash of interests and positions, the required majority in the Security Council or General Assembly may not be available for any particular solution. This will frequently be evident in advance of a meeting and the Member States will conclude that it would be futile for the organs to attempt to reach a decision and consequently that the problem has to be left to the Secretary-General to solve on one basis or another, on his own risk but with as faithful an interpretation of the instructions, rights and obligations of the Organization as possible in view of international law and the decisions already taken.

It might be said that in this situation the Secretary-General should refuse to implement the resolution, since implementation would offend one or another group of Member States and open him to the charge that he has abandoned the political neutrality and impartiality essential to his office. The only way to avoid such criticism, it is said, is for the Secretary-General to refrain from execution of the original resolution until the organs have decided the issue by the required majority (and, in the case of the Security Council, with the unanimous concurrence of the permanent members) or he, maybe, has found another way to pass responsibility over on to governments.

For the Secretary-General this course of action—or more precisely, non-action—may be tempting; it enables him to avoid criticism by refusing to act until other political organs resolve the dilemma. An easy refuge may thus appear to be available. But would such refuge be compatible with the responsibility placed upon the Secretary-General by the Charter? Is he entitled to refuse to carry out the decision properly reached by the organs, on the ground that the specific implementation would be opposed to positions some Member States might wish to take, as indicated, perhaps, by an earlier minority vote? Of course the political organs may always instruct him to discontinue the implementation of a resolution, but when they do not so instruct him and the resolution remains in effect, is the Secretary-General legally and morally free to take no action, particularly in a matter considered to affect international peace and security? Should he, for example, have abandoned the operation in the Congo because almost any decision he made as to the composition of the Force or its role would have been contrary to the attitudes of some Members as reflected in debates, and maybe even in votes, although not in decisions?

The answers seem clear enough in law; the responsibilities of the Secretary-General under the Charter cannot be laid aside merely because the execution of decisions by him is likely to be politically controversial. The Secretary-General remains under the obligation to carry out the policies as adopted by the organs; the essential requirement is that he does this on the basis of his exclusively international responsibility and not in the interest of any particular State or groups of States.

This presents us with the crucial issue; is it possible for the Secretary-General to resolve controversial questions on a truly international basis without obtaining the formal decision of the organs? In my opinion and on the basis of my experience, the answer is in the affirmative; it is possible for the Secretary-General to carry out his tasks in controversial political situations with full regard to his exclusively international obligation under the Charter and without subservience to a particular national or ideological attitude. This is not to say that the Secretary-General is a kind of delphic oracle who alone speaks for the international community. He has available for his task varied means and resources.

Of primary importance in this respect are the principles and purposes of the Charter which are the fundamental law accepted by and binding on all States. Necessarily general and comprehensive, these principles and purposes still are specific enough to have practical significance in concrete cases.

The principles of the Charter are, moreover, supplemented by the body of legal doctrine and precepts that have been accepted by States generally, and particularly as manifested in the resolutions of United Nations organs. In this body of law there are rules and precedents that appropriately furnish guidance to the Secretary-General when he is faced with the duty of applying a general mandate in circumstances that had not been envisaged by the resolution.

Considerations of principle and law, important as they are, do not of course suffice to settle all the questions posed by the political tasks entrusted to the Secretary-General. Problems of political judgment still remain. In regard to these problems, the Secretary-General must find constitutional means and techniques to assist him, insofar as possible, in reducing the element of purely personal judgment. In my experience I have found several arrangements of value to enable the Secretary-General to obtain what might be regarded as the representative opinion of the Organization in respect of the political issues faced by him.

One such arrangement might be described as the institution of the permanent missions to the United Nations, through which the Member States have enabled the Secretary-General to carry on frequent consultations safeguarded by diplomatic privacy.

Another arrangement, which represents a further development of the first, has been the advisory committees of the Secretary-General, such as those on UNEF and the Congo, composed of representatives of governments most directly concerned with the activity involved, and also representing diverse political positions and interests. These advisory committees have furnished a large measure of the guidance required by the Secretary-General in carrying out his mandates relating to UNEF and the Congo operations. They have provided an essential link between the judgment of the executive and the consensus of the political bodies.

VI

Experience has thus indicated that the international civil servant may take steps to reduce the sphere within which he has to take stands on politically controversial issues. In summary, it may be said that he will carefully seek guidance in the decisions of the main organs, in statements relevant for the interpretation of those decisions, in the Charter and in generally recognized principles of law, remembering that by his actions he may set important precedents. Further, he will submit as complete reporting to the main organs as circumstances permit, seeking their guidance whenever such guidance seems to be possible to obtain. Even if all of these steps are taken, it will still remain, as has been amply demonstrated in practice, that the reduced area of discretion will be large enough to expose the international Secretariat to heated political controversy and to accusations of a lack of neutrality.

I have already drawn attention to the ambiguity of the word "neutrality" in such a context. It is obvious from what I have said that the international civil servant cannot be accused of lack of neutrality simply for taking a stand on a controversial issue when this is his duty and cannot be avoided. But there remains a serious intellectual and moral problem as we move within an area inside which personal judgment must come into play. Finally, we have to deal here with a question of integrity or with, if you please, a question of conscience.

The international civil servant must keep himself under the strictest observation. He is not requested to be a neuter in the sense that he has to have no sympathies or antipathies, that there are to be no interests which are close to him in his personal capacity or that he is to have no ideas or ideals that matter for him. However, he is requested to be fully aware of those human reactions and meticulously check himself so that they are not permitted to influence his actions. This is nothing unique. Is not every judge professionally under the same obligation?

If the international civil servant knows himself to be free from such personal influences in his actions and guided solely by the common aims and rules laid down for, and by the Organization he serves and by recognized legal principles, then he has done his duty, and then he can face the criticism which, even so, will be unavoidable. As I said, at the final last, this is a question of integrity, and if integrity in the sense of respect for law and respect for truth were to drive him into positions of conflict with this or that interest, then that conflict is a sign of his neutrality and not of his failure to observe neutrality—then it is in line, not in conflict, with his duties as an international civil servant.

Recently, it has been said, this time in Western circles, that as the international Secretariat is going forward on the road of international thought and action, while Member States depart from it, a gap develops between them and they are growing into being mutually hostile elements; and this is said to increase the tension in the world which it was the purpose of the United Nations to diminish. From this view the conclusion has been drawn that we may have to switch from an international Secretariat, ruled by the principles described in this lecture, to an intergovernmental Secretariat, the members of which obviously would not be supposed to work in the direction of an internationalism considered unpalatable to their governments. Such a passive acceptance of a nationalism rendering it necessary to abandon present efforts in the direction of internationalism symbolized by the international civil service—somewhat surprisingly regarded as a cause of tension—might, if accepted by the Member nations, well prove to be the Munich of international cooperation as conceived after the first World War and further developed under the impression of the tragedy of the second World War. To abandon or to compromise with principles on which such cooperation is built may be no less dangerous than to compromise with principles regarding the rights of a nation. In both cases the price to be paid may be peace.

13. Secondment in the United Nations Secretariat: An Alternative View*

DAVID A. KAY

WITH the increased concern in the post-1960 period over the problem of achieving an equitable geographical distribution in the United Nations Secretariat, renewed attention has been focused on the role of short-term appointments in the recruitment of Secretariat personnel.[1] What in the pre-

* *International Organization*, Vol. XX, No. 1, 63–75. Reprinted by permission.

[1] In the United Nations Secretariat, staff appointed for periods of less than five years

vious fifteen years of the Organization's history had been viewed largely as a technical facet of personnel policy suddenly became an issue of political

are referred to as "fixed-term" staff. The United Nations practice has been to recruit these short-term personnel to a considerable extent from universities, research organizations, and private industrial firms and to a lesser extent from national civil services. This article is particularly concerned with that small group of short-term appointees who

contention in both the Fifth (Administrative and Budgetary) Committee and in the General Assembly itself. This article will first briefly detail the various positions in the debate over the role of short-term appointments. Its main focus, however, will be on the institutional dynamics to which secondment relates and on an attempt to gain insight into its operation through the experience of the European Communities with this type of appointment.

Divergent Views on Secondment

What has become the traditional United Nations view on the relation between permanent and temporary appointments to the Secretariat was first concisely stated by the Preparatory Commission of the United Nations in 1945.

> Unless members of the staff can be offered some assurance of being able to make their careers in the Secretariat, many of the best candidates from all countries will inevitably be kept away. Nor can members of the staff be expected fully to subordinate the special interests of their countries to the international interest if they are merely detached temporarily from national administrations and remain dependent upon them for their future. Finally, it is important that the advantages of experience should be secured and sound administrative traditions established within the Secretariat.
>
> For these reasons, it is essential that the bulk of the staff should consist of persons who will make their career in the Secretariat.[2]

The Committee of Experts on the Review of the Activities and Organization of the Secretariat reporting in 1961 said in the same vein that

> it is convinced that the bulk of the staff should consist of persons who intend to make service in the Secretariat a career and that the efficiency of the Secretariat is dependent on the existence of a substantial core of career officials. . . .[3]

In the post-1960 period of increased debate over the composition of the Secretariat, the Western and Latin American states have most strongly supported the concept of an international civil service staffed by personnel serving on a permanent basis. As the representative of New Zealand on the Fifth Committee stated in 1963:

> It was not simply a matter of geographical representation: it concerned the very nature of the Secretariat. The presence of career officials in an international Secretariat was a guarantee of impartiality and international loyalty. . . . Ideally in-

---

have been seconded from their national civil services to the United Nations but who expect to return within three to five years to their national services.

[2] *Report of the Preparatory Commission of the United Nations* (UN Document PC/20), p. 92. The Preparatory Commission was fol-

lowing in the footsteps of the League of Nations where permanency of tenure existed in principle, though not always in practice, at the Member of Section level (this level corresponds roughly to the P-1 and above rank of the United Nations Secretariat). In actual League practice there was a decided shift away from permanent contracts to short-term contracts after 1930. This shift, which resulted primarily as a consequence of the economic and political crisis of the 1930's, was so marked that by 1938 only about 50 percent of the persons of Member of Section and equivalent rank in the League Secretariat held permanent contracts. (Egon F. Ranshofen-Wertheimer, *The International Secretariat: A Great Experiment in International Administration* [Washington, D.C.: Carnegie Endowment for International Peace, 1945], p. 302.)

[3] General Assembly *Official Records . . . Annexes* (16th session), Agenda item 61, p. 13.

deed the whole staff should be permanent.[4]

Or as the United States representative on the same committee put it:

The proportion of fixed-term contracts was not a matter of percentages only: it was a vitally serious matter, as it could eventually destroy the career international staff, which must be the backbone of an effective United Nations.[5]

Although many more examples could be presented of what is called here the traditional United Nations view, these are sufficient to adduce the main elements of the argument. This position is most concerned with the efficiency, integrity, and loyalty of the Secretariat to the United Nations, and it views noncareer personnel as very real threats to each of these. Indeed, the major reason that it has gone along with any significant deviation from the ideal of a complete career service has been to accommodate the desires of the new nations for representation in the Secretariat. The hope is repeatedly expressed, however, that as these nations achieve a higher level of economic development the necessity to accept large numbers of short-term appointees will disappear.

The new developing nations view secondment as an opportunity rather than a threat. As the Tunisian representative on the Fifth Committee observed in 1963:

His delegation did not consider the present proportion of fixed-term staff in any way alarming and would not object to the figure of 29.7 per cent being exceeded, if that was necessary in order to achieve a more satisfactory geographical distribution.[6]

[4] General Assembly *Official Records . . . Fifth Committee* (18th session), p. 178.
[5] *Ibid.*, p. 162.
[6] *Ibid.*, p. 186.

The key element in the value system of the new nations that justifies their viewing short-term appointments as an opportunity is their ranking of an equitable geographical distribution ahead of a career Secretariat. But their position should not be misunderstood as opposition per se to the concept of a career Secretariat. They have taken great pains to emphasize the point that only the present inequitable geographical distribution of the Secretariat coupled with the inability of the less developed nations to lose permanently their small cadre of trained personnel justifies a temporary abandonment of the concept of a completely career civil service. E. O. Sanu, the Nigerian delegate on the Fifth Committee in 1963, expressed this point quite clearly:

At the present stage of their development, when a major effort to improve economic and social conditions required the harnessing of all available human resources, the African countries could hardly afford to release their officials to take up permanent careers in the United Nations Secretariat. However, his delegation believed that a reasonable proportion of the staff must continue to be recruited on a permanent basis if efficiency was to be maintained, and hoped that the time was not too far distant when the African countries would be able to permit their nationals to seek international employment of that kind.[7]

The principal elements in the position of the new nations are that: 1) in the interest of better geographical distribution in the Secretariat an increased use of short-term appointments is justified; 2) at the same time, however, the concept of a career staff is valid and important to the functioning of the United Nations; and 3) in the future, when larger trained cadres exist in the

[7] *Ibid.*, p. 189.

new nations, the use of short-term appointments can be decreased. Thus, there is little, if any, difference between the position of the new nations and that of the Western nations with regard to the long-range goal of a career Secretariat. The major area of divergence between these two groups lines in their short-term evaluation of the importance of a wide geographical distribution which can only be achieved at the expense of a certain lessening of the career element of the Secretariat.

The position of the Eastern bloc is marked not only by a short-run divergence with the Western position but also by a long-run divergence as to the most desirable composition of the United Nations Secretariat. As P. M. Chernyshev of the Soviet Union stated in 1962, "His delegation was against the whole principle of permanent contracts." [8] In 1963 the Soviet representative on the Fifth Committee, A. A. Roschin, proposed that 25 per cent of the Secretariat should be permanent and 75 per cent fixed-term.[9] The Eastern bloc rejects the comparison of the Secretariat with a national civil service.

To regard the career service as the backbone of the Secretariat was to make the mistake of comparing the work and the legal status of the United Nations Secretariat staff with the status of the civil servants of a State. The Secretariat of the United Nations had an entirely different character. It was not a government service; it was, or soon would be, an organ created by all Member States, on the basis of certain criteria, to serve rapidly growing needs. The world and the Organization itself had changed considerably since the foundation of the United Nations. . . . But the United Nations was a political organization, and all its organs, including the Secretariat, shared that political character.[10]

Emphasis is placed upon the fact that "the composition and structure of its Secretariat must be adapted to the changed conditions created at each successive stage of its existence." [11] It contends that this adaptability to the changing world can only be obtained if the concept of a career Secretariat is renounced in favor of one largely, if not entirely, composed of personnel seconded from national civil services for short periods. Coupled with its argument that the Secretariat can be a viable structure only if it more closely reflects the balance of forces in the world, the Eastern bloc argues that the present Secretariat is dominated by nationals of the Western bloc and that it has favored this group in its operations.[12]

The European Experience

While the idea of an international secretariat can be traced back to an essay by William Penn in 1693,[13] the creation and operation on a large scale of such a secretariat is of much more recent vintage. Sir Eric Drummond's pioneering creation of the League Secretariat as a career international civil service marked the birth of a new concept which the United Nations followed with little deviation and probably even less conscious thought of alternatives. But, in addition to the civil service of the United Nations, the post-World War II period has seen the creation of the European Communities with their own distinctive "European" civil service. However, in spite

[8] General Assembly *Official Records* . . . *Fifth Committee* (17th session), p. 216.
[9] General Assembly *Official Records* . . . *Fifth Committee* (18th session), p. 168.
[10] General Assembly *Official Records* . . . *Fifth Committee* (17th session), p. 235.
[11] *Ibid.*, p. 220.
[12] *Ibid.*, pp. 215–216.
[13] Sydney D. Bailey, *The Secretariat of the United Nations* (Rev. ed.; New York: Frederick A. Praeger, 1964), p. 16.

of the more or less simultaneous growth of the civil services of the United Nations and the European Communities, almost no attention has been devoted to a comparative analysis of their functioning. This article undertakes such a comparative analysis in the limited area of seconded personnel.[14]

The civil service of the European Economic Community (EEC) is primarily the staff of the Commission.[15] The Commission, the chief administrative authority of the EEC, is responsible for both the formulation of proposals for decision by the Council of Ministers and also for follow-through on such decisions. While the Treaty of Rome setting up the EEC contains a provision with respect to the independence and impartiality of the nine members of the Commission,[16] it contains no article comparable to Article 100 of the United Nations Charter concerning the independence of its staff. However, the understanding at the time of the drafting of the Common Market Treaty was that the staff of the Commission was to be the nucleus of a European civil service and was to represent the interests of the Community as a whole.[17]

The staff of the Commission was initially in 1958 and still is today to a considerable extent recruited from the national civil services of the EEC members. This staff has grown from 1,443 in 1960 to 2,340 posts in 1964.[18] Of this staff approximately 50 per cent has been drawn from the civil services of the member states.[19] However, this figure greatly understates the dependence of the EEC on the national civil services. If the 1961 staff is taken as an example, it is found that 75 per cent of the major administrative posts (Category A) are drawn from the national civil services. Even more striking is the fact that if only the major policy-making posts (Categories A-1 and A-2) of which there were 57 in 1961 are examined, it is found that 100 per cent are drawn from the national civil services of the member states. Of the 926 officials in Categories A and B in 1961 (the major administrative posts and the specialized technicians) approximately 685 were on temporary leave from their national civil services

---

[14] Primary emphasis will be placed on the experience of the European Economic Community (EEC) as it is by far the largest, both in size and scope of activities, of the Communities.

[15] The following chart gives the number of staff positions authorized for the various Community institutions in the EEC budgets for 1961 and 1962:

	1961	1962
Commission	1,846	1,933
European Parliament	415	415
Council Secretariat	296	315
Court of Justice	87	92
Economic and Social Committee	59	64
Common services (legal, statistical, etc.)	328	344

(Leon N. Lindberg, *The Political Dynamics of European Economic Integration* [Stanford, Calif: Stanford University Press, 1963], p. 54.)

[16] Article 157(2), *Treaty Establishing the European Economic Community* (Brussels: Secretariat of the Interim Committee for the Common Market and Euratom, n.d.).

[17] Lindberg, p. 55.

[18] The composition of the Commission's staff is as follows:

Category	1960	1961	1963
A (administrators and policy makers)	423	537	653
B (specialized technicians)	284	389	483
C (secretariat, etc.)	648	780	1,006
Translators	88	140	204
Total	1,443	1,846	2,340

(*Ibid.*, p. 325. See also, European Economic Community, Commission, *Seventh General Report on the Activities of the Community* [*1 April 1963—31 March 1964*] [Brussels: Publishing Service of the European Communities, June 1964], p. 364.)

[19] Lindberg, p. 55.

to which they expected to return.[20]

The French administration in par-in the Commission staff as a way of ticular has accepted short-term service life. They have adopted the principle that all civil servants with significant responsibilities must become competent in European affairs. Toward this goal the French have advocated a system of four- or five-year appointments of national civil servants to the Commission staff. Oddly enough in view of the actual practice of Commission staffing set out above, the French position has been a source of conflict in the EEC. The "Europeans" in the EEC have regarded the French position as a threat to the concept of an independent Commission. With considerable logic and the record of past EEC practice, the French have argued that regularized secondment would result in copenetration of national bureaucracies which would accelerate European integration to an extent that competing national and international bureaucracies could never achieve. All observers agree that at least to the present the French civil servants working on the Commission staff have been extremely competent and enthusiastic "Europeans." [21] The French position at its most malevolent is no worse than an argument that the current practice be continued.

[20] Ibid.

[21] Ibid., p. 85. According to the new personnel statute which took effect in 1962, agents temporaires can occupy Commission posts only for a maximum of two years plus one renewal of one year. After this period, such agents temporaires must either resign or go through the process of becoming permanent EEC civil servants. There has been insufficient time since the entry into force of this statute to assess any possible effect on the Commission staff. See Règlement No. 31 (CEE) et No. 11 (CEEA), fixant le statut des fonctionnaires et le régime applicable aux autres agents de la CEE et de la CEEA, reprinted in European Communities, Journal Officiel, June 14, 1962, and cited in Lindberg, p. 327.

The extent to which the national administrations and the staff of the European Communities are interwoven is well illustrated by Eric Stein.

On the national level officials of national administrations form the staff of the Permanent Representatives in Brussels and national official experts are called in to work with the staff of the "executive." These same officials advise their respective Ministers on the Councils as well as their own governments generally. The staffs of the Commission and of other "executives" as well as the staff of the Councils' Secretariat have been recruited to a large measure from national administrations. Some former Ministers have become members of one of the "executives" and former representatives in the Assembly have become Ministers or members of an "executive." [22]

The above analysis indicates that secondment of personnel from the national civil services to the Commission staff has been carried to an extent undreamed of in the United Nations by anyone except possibly the Soviet bloc. What has been the result of this wholesale renunciation of what has usually been taken as the keystone to the creation of an international civil service? One of the most discerning observers of the inner workings of the EEC has noted that the restructuring of activities and aspirations is most noticeable

at the level of high policy-makers and civil servants, for the EEC policy-making process, by its very nature, engages an ever-expanding circle of national officials. There is strong evidence that this sort of in-

[22] Eric Stein and Thomas L. Nicholson (ed.), American Enterprise in the European Common Market: A Legal Profile (Ann Arbor: University of Michigan Press, 1960), Vol. 2, pp. 94–95.

teraction contributes to a "Community-mindedness," by broadening perspectives, developing personal friendships, and fostering a camaraderie of expertise, all of which come from being involved in a joint problem-solving operation. Such developments can be expected to occur in a rough correlation to the frequency of contact.[23]

Indeed, it appears that its extensive use of secondment has given the EEC a most valuable tool for increasing its impact by allowing it to penetrate into national administrations to a previously unheard-of extent. Secondment has proved to be a prime instrument for the political socialization and recruitment of national decision makers to a "European" service. Leon N. Lindberg has noted that this has been carried to such an extent in the case of agriculture as to create "a *community of functional specialists* with a distinct interest in maintaining the system." [24]

The Organizational Dynamics

It is the contention of this article that the acceptance of the concept of a career international secretariat for the United Nations by both the Western and the new nations is based on an inadequate analysis of the organizational dynamics involved. On the basis of the European experience and several theoretical constructs an attempt will be made to show that a career international civil service is not the most effective design in terms of achieving its stated purposes for an international secretariat.

It is clear that the position of the Western powers and to a considerable

extent that of the new nations on the desirable composition of the Secretariat is based on a construction at an international level of the Weberian bureaucratic model of national and subnational bureaucracies.[25] Max Weber's construct involved a rigid hierarchical ordering of the staff designed to optimize its technical efficiency in the accomplishment of regularized tasks. In Weber's model such values as precision, speed, unambiguity, expert control, continuity, and strict subordination are maximized.[26] The very reason that the Weberian construct has exercised such decisive influence on organizational theory is its great technical superiority over any other form of organization. However, it should be remembered that Weber was only concerned with national and subnational structures and that the international environment may contain certain factors which necessitate the modification of the pure Weberian model. Certainly the change is a sufficient quantitative jump (perhaps enough to be considered a qualitative jump) to warrant an examination as to how these new conditions affect Weber's construct.

Weber's bureaucratic model is based on a rigid hierarchical ordering, heavily laden with discipline, with each individual occupying a sphere of clearly defined competence.[27] The bureaucratic model is denoted by its rationalized

---

[23] Lindberg, pp. 286–287.

[24] Leon N. Lindberg, "Decision Making and Integration in the European Community," *International Organization,* Winter 1965 (Vol. 19, No. 1), p. 71. Italics in original.

[25] Dag Hammarskjöld recognized the origin of the international civil service to be the domestic traditions of the British civil service. See Dag Hammarskjöld, "The International Civil Servant in Law and in Fact," in *Dag Hammarskjöld: Servant of Peace,* ed. Wilder Foote (New York: Harper & Row, 1963), p. 331.

[26] Robert K. Merton, *Social Theory and Social Structure* (Glencoe, Ill: The Free Press, 1957), p. 196; and H. H. Gerth and C. Wright Mills (ed. and trans.), *From Max Weber: Essays in Sociology* (New York: Oxford University Press, 1958), p. 214.

[27] Talcott Parsons, *The Structure of Social Action* (Glencoe, Ill: The Free Press, 1949), p. 507; and Gerth and Mills, p. 196.

job structure and high degree of formalization. Of even greater importance is that Weber staffs his bureaucratic model with individuals of clearly superior training and competence based on a matrix of values that is common most especially to the bureaucracy but indeed in some degree to all of the society it serves. The bureaucracy is called upon to regularize decision making to such an extent that every action to be taken can be found in a clearly formulated rule. It is the essence of the Weberian bureaucracy that it must adjust to the forces that constitute its environment in order to ensure its own preservation. Indeed, the various hallmarks of this bureaucratic model, such as its high degree of formalization, hierarchical ranking, and emphasis on tradition transmitted through trained cadres, ensure that it attempts to adjust to its environment rather than attempts to overcome it.

With these characteristics of the Weberian bureaucratic model one should contrast the current international environment and the role of international organizations. The first obvious difference from Weber's model is that the international civil servant does not even closely approach Weber's administrative class with its high level of training and common matrix of values. The United Nations Secretariat is staffed with a heterogeneity of ideologies and of prior administrative experience that Weber certainly could not have conceived as being represented in one bureaucracy. Even within the European Communities with their greater "common-ness" of values and cultural backgrounds, there is markedly more heterogeneity of values and traditions than in Weber's model.

Though this is an important deviation from Weber's model, it is not the most important one presented by the United Nations. The most fundamental difference relates to the differing relationship between the United Nations

Secretariat and its environment and the relationship between Weber's bureaucratic construct and its environment. If the United Nations is to achieve in any degree the purposes set out in Article 1 of the Charter, it must change the environment within which it operates. The difficulty of this task is apparent when one realizes that the major forces in the environment also happen to be the principal Members of the United Nations. However, it is for just this task of restructuring its environment that the Weberian model was not designed. Indeed, as was seen above, there is considerable internal organizational pressure working in the Weberian model against any tampering with environmental givens.

As Ernst B. Haas has pointed out, unless the international organization is able to change its environment by making alliances with sources of external support, the organization will be confined to the realm of the technical and the routine.[28] The Weberian bureaucratic construct is an excellent model when one is concerned with questions dealing with the internal efficiency of the bureaucracy[29] and with the operation of a bureaucracy within a stable environment. But when one is dealing with an international organization that aspires to be more than a technical body, questions of internal efficiency lose the primacy that they hold in national bureaucracy.[30] With such international organizations what is needed

[28] Ernst B. Haas, *Beyond the Nation-State: Functionalism and International Organization* (Stanford, Calif: Stanford University Press, 1964), p. 101.

[29] The great attention that the delegates of Western countries in the Fifth Committee have paid to the effects of temporary appointments on the internal efficiency of the Secretariat is a reflection of the paramount importance that internal efficiency has in the Weberian model.

[30] This is also true of national bureaucracies in times of rapid and important change. See Thorstein Veblen in Merton, p. 198.

is "an effectiveness model in which the criterion of success is the *transformation* of the international system . . . instead of the survival of the existing system." [31] Efficiency, which is the focus of Weber, concerns the commitment and happiness of the staff of an organization in seeking to realize purposes within a given environmental context. Efficiency is maximized through the use of a trained, career bureaucracy possessing a homogeneous background such that internal communication and decision making can be highly regularized and contained within the bounds of environmental givens. On the other hand, effectiveness, which should be the focus of international organizations, concerns the relation between the organization and its environment. [32] The criterion of success of the "effectiveness model" is its ability to achieve a transformation of the existing international system or subsystem within which it operates. [33]

In seeking an "effectiveness model" the experience of the European Communities should provide some useful guidelines. Even if one discounts the hopes of the "Europeans" such as Jean Monnet, it is apparent that the accomplishment of just the stated purposes of the Treaty of Rome would require a fundamental restructuring of the international subsystem existing in Europe in 1958. The achievement of the stated aims of the EEC requires a vast readjustment in national perspectives, not only of the various national leadership elites but also of the per-

spectives of individual farmers, miners, and industrial workers. [34] The EEC in order to work requires the eventual harmonization of national social policies which directly affect every citizen. Although it certainly has not yet accomplished all that Monnet had hoped it would, few would deny that the EEC has caused a fundamental alteration in the internal subsystem existing in Europe at the time of its adoption.

Is there anything that can be gleaned from this success of the EEC that might prove useful in the search for an "effectiveness model" of international organizations and their bureaucracies? Leon Lindberg, as well as Ernst Haas and Allen Whiting, agrees that one of the main obstacles to the successful transformation of an international system by an international organization is its lack of direct access to individuals and groups in the national communities composing the existing international system. [35] But it is just this access to individuals and groups that the EEC has gained from its extensive reliance on national civil servants serving as *agents temporaires* on the Commission staff. In fact, Lindberg has suggested as a rough index of the extent to which high national civil servants participate in the decision-making process of the EEC the fact that the Commission through the national civil servants on its own staff and the use

[31] Haas, p. 92. Italics in original.

[32] *Ibid.,* p. 91.

[33] In positing an "effectiveness model" in contrast to the Weberian "efficiency model" it is certainly not intended to convey the impression that these are mutually exclusive models and that, for example, all considerations of efficiency are to be exorcised from the "effectiveness model." What is different between the two models is the criterion of success that is used in each model.

[34] And while it is true that the national elites of the EEC countries do have a substantially similar matrix of values and cultural backgrounds (although one suspects that this similarity of background is not substantially greater than that of the educated elite of the rest of the world who in most cases were either educated in the West or under the influence of the West), there is a vast divergence in this matrix when one moves below the level of the national elites.

[35] Lindberg, *The Political Dynamics of European Economic Integration,* p. 9; and Ernst B. Haas and Allen S. Whiting, *Dynamics of International Relations* (New York: McGraw-Hill, 1956), p. 443.

of expert groups composed of national civil servants annually consults with approximately 17,500 national civil servants.[36] As noted earlier, observers of the EEC have stressed the importance to the success of the EEC of the development of a "Community-mindedness" by the Commission staff which is carried back to their national governments upon their return to their national civil services. It is this ability to "engage" important national civil servants in a Community solution achieved through a process of joint problem solving that has been an important technique in the Commission's repertory of techniques designed to transform the European system.

On the basis of the European experience one important element in any "effectiveness model" would seem to be the ability to penetrate the national civil services and to bring these national officials into contact with each other in a joint problem-solving context.[37] An important technique of achieving this penetration is the extensive use of seconded national servants in the international secretariat. To the criticism that such a large-scale use of seconded personnel will adversely affect the efficiency and morale of an international organization, the model

[36] Lindberg, *The Political Dynamics of European Economic Integration*, p. 58.

[37] "Functionalists pin their hopes for rational organizational action on the technical and non-controversial character of international welfare activity. I have argued that the process by which a given activity becomes non-controversial is itself a political matter, derived not from initial consensus but from initial conflict, which may shake down to a consensus as a result of national redefinition of 'need.' If this is true, it follows that a purely rational decision-making model is as inappropriate for a public international organization as it is for any public administrative agency that performs more than routine tasks, such as selling postage stamps or regulating the diameter of telegraph wires." Haas, p. 93.

presented in this article yields but one answer: If an international organization is to have aspirations of achieving a transformation of the international system, concern for internal efficiency must yield priority to concern for the effectiveness with which the organization deals with environmental forces. Weber could properly concern himself with maximizing the internal efficiency of his bureaucratic model because he accepted as an environmental given the political system within which the model was to operate. But no one can logically believe it important and desirable to achieve the purposes of an international organization such as the United Nations and at the same time believe that these purposes can be achieved without a transformation of the existing international system. Hence the paramount role properly assumed by standards of internal efficiency in Weber's model of national administration must be assumed by standards of the effectiveness with which the organization relates to its environment in the "effectiveness model" of international organization. To the third major objection to a large-scale use of seconded personnel, that of a lack of sufficient international loyalty in a staff having a large element of seconded personnel, a twofold answer is available. First, one should remember that the major activities of the United Nations in the foreseeable future are most likely to lie in the area of nation building, not bomb building, and to a very significant extent the scope for disloyalty varies directly with the nature of the activity engaged in. Secondly, the "effectiveness model" calling as it does for a large-scale use of secondment contains a built-in safety check on disloyalty. The model in its decision-making process is designed to elicit conflict between national officials serving in the international secretariat as a means of achieving a redefinition and broadening of the international "need." Thus, conflict between national officials within the Secretariat, far from being counter-productive, would actually facilitate the working of the decision-making process in the "effectiveness model."

In terms of the application of this analysis to the United Nations several points are relevant. First, the European Communities have had the important advantage of being able to draw on a pool of trained personnel possessing a broadly similar matrix of values and this has aided both the efficiency and effectiveness of the staff. The United Nations certainly does not have this same advantage in using personnel from its 117 Members. However, this difference is somewhat lessened, thanks to the ubiquity of Western education, when one restricts the comparison to educated elites. Secondly, to a much greater extent than the EEC, the United Nations is a multipurpose structure. This multipurpose nature along with its heterogeneity increases the difficulty of new staff in gaining competency in handling their newly assumed roles. It is not felt that this vitiates the analysis as much as it argues for longer secondments (from three to five years) and better planning in the orientation and use of seconded staff. Also, the analysis suggested by the "effectiveness model" would call for a definite shift in the sources of United Nations fixed-term personnel. Rather than recruiting a considerable portion of fixed-term staff from universities, research organizations, and private industrial firms as is now done, conscious preference should be given to securing individuals involved in the public service of national governments. To do other than this would be to weaken the degree of penetration sought in the "effectiveness model."

The United Nations is to a much greater extent than the EEC a multipurpose organization served by a secretariat performing a wide range of tasks. This multipurpose nature ensures that the institutional dynamics to which secondment relates will not be uniform throughout the Secretariat. To take the obvious case, there is no reason to assume either on the basis of the EEC experience or the theoretical constructs used above that a seconded typist is likely to add to the effectiveness of the Organization. Similarly, there seems little to recommend itself in a policy of replacing with seconded personnel the highly trained group of statisticians that the United Nations has with great difficulty built up. Such a policy would seem to offer little potential gain in effectiveness and an almost certain loss in efficiency. As a rule of thumb, secondment would seem most suitable for those positions whose occupants as a matter of career expectations would eventually move into policy-making positions.[38] This would mean that an opening for an economist in the Economic Commission for Africa (ECA) would seem a more profitable use for a seconded official than seconding a demographer to the United Nations Statistical Office.

What is suggested here is that greater analysis should be devoted to determining the nature of the relation between international bureaucracies and the aims of the international organizations that they serve. It is further suggested that the national civil services and models based on such services do not provide the most fitting guides for the operation of international bureaucracies because of fundamental differences in aims and environments. It is argued that in the United Nations

[38] The difficulty in drawing a more distinct line between positions suitable and unsuitable for secondment will become readily apparent if one considers the role played by the staff in the Bureau of the Budget in the United States government. What must be optimized is the contact within a problem-solving context of officials who will eventually be called upon to occupy policy-making positions in national governments.

specifically the large-scale purposeful use of secondment is an important, but currently underutilized, instrument for achieving the aims of the Organization. In summary, this article suggests that additional analysis of this significant area of international organization should not be constrained by either the hallowed traditions of such organizations or by the position taken by the Soviet bloc on this topic.[39]

[39] In this connection is should be noted that the measures suggested here in no way resemble the Soviet troika proposal which provided for a collective executive body to replace the Secretary-General. Each member of the troika would have been able to halt the implementation of decisions of the policy-making bodies of the United Nations through the exercise of a veto.

Chapter IV

CONFLICT MANAGEMENT

IV. CONFLICT MANAGEMENT

IV. Conflict Management

WE are prone to make two assumptions about conflict, neither of which is necessarily correct: (1) that conflict is inherently evil and destructive of the social fabric, and (2) that the goal of society in general and the legal system in particular is to eliminate it. In fact, the American political system bestows a high degree of legitimacy on conflict, both through the adversary process in the courts and the clash of viewpoints in Congress.[1] There is also persuasive evidence that conflict, properly distributed, can unite rather than polarize, for actors hostile in one set of circumstances find themselves allies in another.[2] The result is to maintain only that level of conflict consistent with the ability to contract future alliances. Finally, so far as history records, no legal system has ever done away with conflict. As long as the tangibles and intangibles men value remain scarce, there will be disagreements about their distribution. Even the most affluent societies seem to find it necessary to maldistribute something, be it only intangible patterns of deference.

Conflict of course *can* deliver severe, even mortal, blows to any group. But long-term damage does not follow from conflict *per se* but from (a) its intensity; and (b) its distribution. We know from the history of warfare that even physical conflict has not always been pursued to the limits of human capability—a consideration at no point more germane than in our own time. We know also that conflict does not always result in the division of a community into two hostile camps, that even the most apparently implacable adversaries are in fact tied together by unstated considerations of mutual interest,[3] an observation amply born out by recent American-Soviet relations.

It is, consequently, more significant to ask how conflict is managed rather than how it is eliminated. American society, for example, does not eliminate conflict but rather channels it into acceptable forms. The United Nations system, motivated as it is by strong considerations of peace and security, has an overriding conflict management function.

[1] S. M. Lipset, *Political Man* (Garden City, New York: Anchor, 1963).
[2] Lewis Coser, *The Functions of Social Conflict* (New York: Free Press of Glencoe, 1956).
[3] Thomas Schelling, *The Strategy of Conflict* (New York: Oxford, 1963).

This function, however, is a complex one, for the loci of conflict are numerous and the international environment has in the past not been very congenial to institutional forms of conflict management on the court and parliamentary model.

One source of conflict is what we can call *intrasystemic* conflict among or within parts of the UN system: between the General Assembly and the Security Council, for example. Other conflicts are *intersystemic,* between the UN system and other political systems; the Congo affair is an example. But this perhaps too neat division fails to take account of the numerous instances of international conflict which are reflected in UN conflicts. The occasionally acrimonious relations in the UN between the United States and the Soviet Union stem far less from parochial organizational quarrels than from larger political rivalries. Indeed, it is precisely to the extent that larger conflicts are expressed symbolically in the UN that it has a chance to perform an important conflict management function. The insulation of the UN from pressing international problems might produce a certain degree of intraorganizational harmony but at the price of making the UN a literally useless organization. We may say, then, that the UN frequently functions as a microcosm of global conflicts, in which they are played out in symbolic form. Few who watched the Security Council debate during the Cuban missile crisis can doubt the value symbolic conflict expression holds.

Thus the UN is both a generator of conflict and in itself a manager of conflict. Intraorganizational disputes must be handled, while the organizational system itself must provide means for "defusing" conflicts in its larger international environment. What is the significance of international law for these problems? As to the first, it can have only a peripheral role, since these intramural concerns are analogous to the problems of all parliamentary bodies and formal organizations, both of which are incorporated into the UN system. In such situations, a new set of norms, situationally generated, must develop. We are likely to see the growth of norms and a concept of organizational due process in this area, just as we have seen it in diverse bodies ranging from the United States Senate to large universities.

But the second problem—broadly conceived as the war-peace problem —is one which has traditionally occupied the energies of international law. The United Nations, at one and the same time, offers a challenge to international law and a new arena in which it can operate. The international law familiar to us in texts and casebooks is an evolving, largely customary system, growing from case to case, much as the English Common Law grew. It evolved in an era of states, not of international organizations, and hence must expand to assimilate these new organizational units. There is, consequently, a certain amount of law revision made necessary by the UN, and the speed with which international law has moved is remarkable. In part, this is probably due to the recognition by the community of international lawyers that the success of international order is intimately tied to the success of international organization.

The UN in a sense inherited one major legal institution from its predecessor, the League: this was the World Court. The General Assembly moreover engaged in one major legal innovation, the International Law Commission. Its massive efforts at codification have laid bare the considerable degree of consensus upon which international law has always ultimately depended. While the mere production of draft treaties will not of itself guarantee compliance, the UN as a major locus of legal activity provides a promising way out of the current dilemma of international law: namely, that it is at base a customary system, geared to incremental change and functioning best in a slow-changing society. It now bears the burdens of rapid social, economic, and political change, and its already strained capacity for revision can only be augmented by some new and superior means of international communication. That, at least in potential, now seems to exist—for the UN as a meeting ground for the exchange of international messages allows the shifting wishes and aims of a state to be rapidly diffused and incorporated into the interlocking policy decisions of its peers.

Finally, the UN has, more by accident than design, engaged in much *ad hoc* mediation and armed intervention. Often this was without precedent in international law simply because opportunities for international organizational initiative did not exist previously. It is at this point that the UN finds itself at the leading edge of international legal growth, building new norms of procedure through its own activity and experimentation forced upon it by events. The pragmatic development of the Secretary General's role and the equally task-oriented development of peacekeeping forces in Cyprus, the Middle East, the Congo and elsewhere quite unknowingly have set patterns for legitimate third-party conflict management that may eventually be formally incorporated into legal rules. Indeed, the superior effectiveness of these *ad hoc* measures, as opposed to more structured devices such as international arbitration conventions, gives weight to the intuitive judgment that conflict management must be tailored to the special requirements of the international system rather than be imposed upon it.

Compliance is generally discussed in a narrowly legal context but, as Manno demonstrates, is of considerable relevance in the framework of General Assembly voting patterns. In a state system, noncompliance by a legislative minority is rare and rarer still is it successful—a point amply demonstrated by North-South relations in nineteenth century America. The General Assembly turns out to be a body favoring rather lopsided majorities. While this indicates a surprisingly high degree of consensus, it also forces minorities into extreme tactical positions. Since many General Assembly actions can be directly implemented by UN agencies, simple noncompliance is more often than not in no sense an alternative. Similarly, formation of a new coalition to reverse an unwanted decision becomes harder and harder as majorities become larger and larger. The minority, consequently, becomes increasingly alienated and increasingly oriented towards tactics that subvert the organization, such as withholding assessments.

Claude suggests that we may harbor some mistaken notions of the kinds of extramural conflicts the UN was set up to handle. The rhetoric of collective security proponents implies that the organization's primary function lies in this direction, an idea doubtless stimulated by a desire to retrieve collective security from the abyss of history, whence it plunged in the late thirties. But a close inspection of the early history of the UN demonstrates that the founders did not anticipate or desire the complete abolition of balance of power; that such collective security ventures as were intended to fall under the UN's aegis were supposed to be limited to non-Great Power conflicts. In other words, the balance of power was to be accepted as the principal means for averting conflicts among the Great Powers. And, as Claude's analysis bears out, the sanctioning of both balance of power and collective security is reflected in the history of the United Nations, rhetoric to the contrary notwithstanding.

When most of us think of the role of the United Nations in conflict management, we think naturally of the spectrum of activities we call peacekeeping, those ventures in which the Organization physically intervenes between adversaries. Citrin examines four notable instances of this: Lebanon, the Congo, West Irian, and Cyprus, in all of which the UN found itself involved at least in part in intrastate as well as interstate conflict. The detailed analysis of these cases in a sense bears out Claude's contention that UN conflict management is a dichotomized affair—relying upon physical intervention when Great Powers are not directly involved; dependent upon the self-regulation of the balance of power when they are. Citrin's discussion also indicates that the task expansion that ensues from peacekeeping may extend to further peacekeeping duties in the future, but should not be depended upon to generate wider integrative capacity.

With Coplin we turn, finally, to the World Court itself, in both its League and UN manifestations. The analysis of case characteristics suggests that perhaps we have been asking the wrong questions regarding international tribunals. The query, How can a powerless Court ensure compliance?, turns out to be the least pressing concern, for the compliance record is excellent. The points raised are rather more disturbing: Is the World Court suited only to a residue of trivial disputes? Is it truly a "world" court or simply a mechanism for the difficulties of Western nations, masquerading as a universal institution? What are the effects on conflict management when the process is deliberately prolonged over a period of years? The answers, by no means comforting to advocates of international legal institutions, suggest that we have been insufficiently aware of the environment in which legal institutions are set down: whether there are pre-existing perceptions of self-interest and consensus on substance and/or procedure. This is the more important in a largely customary system, where, apart from the rudimentary mechanism of self-help through reprisals, norms must be supported non-coercively.

14. Majority Decisions and Minority Responses in the UN General Assembly*

CATHERINE SENF MANNO

I. Introduction

TWENTY years ago, when the representatives of 50 countries met in San Francisco to found the United Na-

tions, they decided to adopt a new rule of international decision-making—the rule of the majority. The defunct League of Nations had gradually reduced the severity of the principle of unanimity which it took over from the practice of centuries of international conferences and applied to decisions of both its principal organs, the League Assembly and Council.[1] But those who drafted the UN Charter in

* The Journal of Conflict Resolution, Vol. 10, 1–20. Reprinted by permission. This article is adapted from a chapter of an unpublished doctoral dissertation, "Weighted Voting in the UN General Assembly: A Study of Feasibility and Methods" (American University, 1964). The author is a statistician in the U.S. Census Bureau, Washington; the research reported here has no relation to official duties.

[1] Cromwell A. Riches, The Unanimity Rule and the League of Nations (Baltimore, 1933).

1945 completely abandoned the unanimity principle in favor of majority or qualified majority voting, by equal voting states, for the representative political organ—the General Assembly. Some two thousand resolutions later, the Nineteenth Session of the General Assembly returned once more to unanimity as the basis for decision-making. In that crisis-ridden session, decisions were limited to those few matters that all could agree upon.

The crisis had its origin in the refusal of two permanent Security Council members (France and the USSR) to accept assessments imposed by a General Assembly majority decision, even though the binding nature of those budgetary obligations was upheld by the International Court of Justice. The Charter provides a sanction against this particular form of noncompliance in Article 19, but no member state was willing to risk the consequences of invoking that sanction by taking away the Assembly voting rights of those in excessive arrears. In the absence of agreement on a compromise between the principal parties to the conflict—the United States and the Soviet Union—the Assembly decided to hold the problem in abeyance. This course was more attractive than solving the problem either by sacrificing part of the Assembly's authority or by risking defections of important Members.

The result was a tacit recognition that the framework of rights, obligations, and sanctions contained in the Charter could not only prove ineffective (as when recommendations are ignored), but could also lead to actions destructive of the legal and institutional foundation for world order as agreed upon in San Francisco. The reluctance of the majority to assert its authority and take away the voting rights of certain Members was probably due in part to a realization of the ethical weakness (whatever the legal soundness) of the majority's case

against the nonpaying Members who were vulnerable to Article 19. To enforce the sanction would have required the votes of many Members who were themselves in arrears on one or both of the peacekeeping operations in question (UNEF or ONUC). Many of the small, new countries who held the balance of voting power on this decision, and who had earlier voted with the overwhelming majority that accepted the World Court's opinion affirming the compulsory nature of peacekeeping assessments, had paid nothing on either peacekeeping force.[2] Yet they escaped the penalty of Article 19 because they had in recent years (by virtue of the same favorable balance of power) voted themselves rebates and reductions in peacekeeping assessments. The sanctioning article specifies loss of voting rights when "the amount of . . . arrears . . . exceeds the amount of contributions due . . . for the preceding two full years." Thus, by continuing to pay only their *regular budget* assessments, those with reduced peacekeeping dues could hold their arrears below the critical point without even paying the reduced peacekeeping assessments. The countries heavily assessed for peacekeeping, on the other hand, found that a few years of nonpayment of peacekeeping assessments put them in the excessive arrears category.

This dilemma of the Nineteenth Session was a symptom of a more general malaise. Instead of growing in authority, resources, and universality to meet the challenges posed by nuclear weapons, the UN entered the third decade of the nuclear age a bystander to escalating war, fearful of exercising its authority, unable to adopt a budget, and helpless witness to its first defection in membership. Many UN-related activities—fortu-

[2] Cf. individual vote records on Res. 1854A (XVII) with data on status of payments in UN Doc. St/Adm./Ser. B/168 (December 31, 1962).

nately sheltered by the roofs of the specialized agencies—continued without interruption, but functionalism in the less political areas seemed to have little of the hoped-for spillover into the political arena.

In seeking the reasons why the nations have failed to establish conditions for the "take-off" to a stronger UN, or even to assure the survival and minimum functioning of the existing body, it is helpful to refer to some general principles of organization. The survival and successful functioning of any organization depend on two things: (1) its ability to satisfy the common group needs which are its reason for being ("effectiveness"); (2) its ability to provide individual members with a satisfactory balance between the costs and the benefits of participation ("efficiency").[3]

The writer assumes that to be *effective* the UN must be more than a voluntary center for harmonizing the relations between states. It must have some powers to act despite dissenting minorities. For *efficiency,* there must be equilibrating factors that keep essential actors participating despite the costs to them of decisions taken against their wishes. In political decision-making *accommodation* is sometimes inherently impossible, or the costs of achieving the necessary consensus are too great. Group interests may then be frustrated unless the members are willing and able to avail themselves of the other balancing principle of *alternation.*[4]

The present study attempts a systematic analysis of the composition of

majorities and minorities in the UN General Assembly, the degree of alternation of majority–minority roles by individual states, and the responses of those in losing minorities in relation to the content and implementation of decisions. There is no pretense of employing the full panoply of scientific method—with hypotheses, observation, and the testing and recasting of hypotheses. The relevant variables are not yet well identified; the conceptual framework is still too poorly defined, and it may indeed be too little quantifiable to bear that burden. But the searchlight of systematic observation and classification can be brought to focus, revealing some facts which may already be familiar to close observers of the United Nations, but whose implications have not received due attention.

The study is based on 363 resolutions of the General Assembly—all those adopted by the Ninth, Fourteenth, and Seventeenth regular sessions (1954, 1959, and 1962). We present the principal conclusions, followed by a discussion of evidence. Finally some policy implications are considered.

II. Summary of Conclusions

1. Along with the doubling of membership in the United Nations since 1954, there has been an increasing trend toward overwhelming majority decisions or unanimity in the General Assembly.

2. For those decisions which are contested, there is an imbalance in decision power in the General Assembly, even after allowance for informal sources of influence; it favors the emerging countries as against the older, developed countries of both East and West.

3. Over half of all General Assembly resolutions which require implementation are *internal decisions,* carried out by UN organs and not directly de-

[3] That distinction is made by Chester I. Barnard, *The Functions of the Executive* (Cambridge, 1945), 56.
[4] For a well-reasoned analysis of the effects of constitutional decision-making rules and the rationale for departures from unanimity, see James M. Buchanan and Gordon Tullock, *The Calculus of Consent: Logical Foundations of Constitutional Democracy* (Ann Arbor, 1962).

pendent on individual states for compliance.

4. While there are conspicuous exceptions, the Assembly's *recommendatory decisions* achieve a greater measure of compliance than is generally recognized.

5. Outvoted minority members have responded with a variety of equilibrium-seeking actions depending on the content of resolutions. The most damaging to the authority and resources of the Organization are the responses evoked by internal decisions and assessment decisions. Imbalance in decision power is therefore most serious with respect to decisions in these categories.

III. Evidence and Interpretation

CONCLUSION I: OVERWHELMING
MAJORITIES AND UNANIMITY

Figure 1 shows the trend toward increasing unanimity in General Assembly voting since 1954, in terms of *resolutions*. The percentage of unanimous resolutions more than doubled while the percentage of contested resolutions (those with one or more "No" votes) was halved. The middle segment of each bar shows the percentage of "abstained" resolutions (those having one

or more abstentions but no "No" votes).

Classifications based on the subject matter of resolutions give some clues to the significance of unanimity, as do the records of debate and accommodation. Figure 2 shows the percentage of unanimous, abstained, and contested resolutions adopted in each subject category for the Ninth, Fourteenth, and Seventeenth General Assembly Sessions combined (1954, 1959, and 1962). The subject matter classification is based on the main committee having preliminary jurisdiction, although the results are for *plenary* votes. As might be expected, Assembly resolutions are most often contested on Political Committee and Trusteeship Committee matters. The Administrative and Budgetary category includes a high percentage of unanimous resolutions because this committee handles a large number of routine administrative resolutions (e.g., confirming appointments to administrative boards). Some minor appropriation items were also adopted unanimously.

When resolutions in individual subject categories are examined for trend, results are generally parallel to the trend shown in Figure 1, except in the political category, where the percentage of unanimous resolutions de-

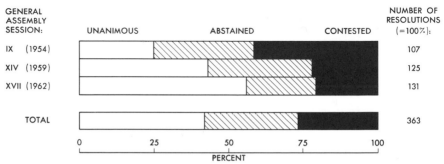

FIGURE 1: Percentage of unanimous, abstained, and contested resolutions adopted in the 9th, 14th, and 17th General Assembly Sessions. "Abstained" resolutions are those adopted with abstentions but no "No" votes; "contested" resolutions are those adopted with one or more "No" votes.

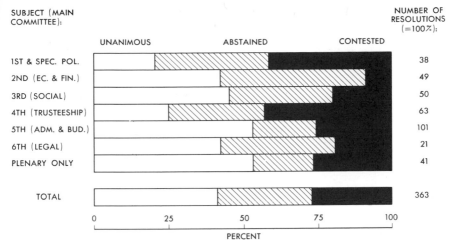

SUBJECT (MAIN COMMITTEE):

NUMBER OF RESOLUTIONS (=100%):

FIGURE 2: Percentage of unanimous, abstained, and contested resolutions adopted in the 9th, 14th, and 17th General Assembly Sessions (combined), by subject. For definitions see Figure 1. "Plenary only" means those resolutions not handled by a main committee before plenary action.

creased from 1954 to 1962. The greatest increase in unanimity occurred for economic and social matters—a reflection of the increased output of recommendations related to the Development Decade, and of increasingly numerous hortatory resolutions on human rights. The widely recognized value of UN technical assistance programs is attested by unanimity on some decisions extending the scope of such aid. Legal Committee matters showed a sharp increase in unanimity, which may be due to structural changes bringing a better balance of representation in the International Law Commission, the subsidiary organ partly responsible for the Legal Committee's agenda. However, the number of Legal Committee items is too small to attribute much significance to the trend.

Another aspect of the trend toward unanimity is the increasingly lopsided majorities by which resolutions were adopted in the later sessions. For the contested resolutions adopted, the average ratio of majority to minority members was 7 to 1 in 1954, 8 to 1

in 1959, and 9 to 1 in 1962. The combined effect of the two trends appears in the distribution of states' voting choices. Figure 3 shows this distribution for each of the three sessions studied (top of chart). The 363 adopted resolutions which were analyzed represent over 31,000 "vote choices" (states eligible times issues on which they could vote). The tiny black segments at the extreme right represent the proportion of "No" votes out of all these choices. This proportion was only 4.3 per cent in 1954, and it dropped to 2.1 per cent in 1959 and to 1.5 per cent in 1962. These figures make the unanimity-bound Nineteenth Session (1964–65) seem like the natural projection of a trend.

The shaded segments on the left in Figure 3 represent the choice of "non-objection" on resolutions adopted "without objection" [5] or unanimously. The trend parallels that for the percentage of unanimous resolutions in

[5] Since there is no count of Members present at such votes, we have imputed a "non-objection" vote to all states having UN membership when the action was taken.

VOTE CHOICES

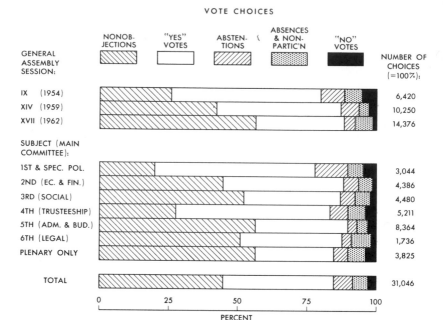

FIGURE 3: Percentage distribution of vote choices on 363 resolutions in the 9th, 14th, and 17th General Assembly Sessions, by session and subject. "Non-objections" refer to resolutions without counted votes, and all states eligible to vote are attributed this choice in these cases. For other definitions see Figures 1 and 2.

Figure 1. The remaining sections of each bar show "Yes" votes, abstentions, and absences and "nonparticipations."[6] Abstentions and absences each account for about 6 per cent of all vote choices, compared with 2 per cent for "No" votes.

Figure 3 also shows the distribution of vote choices by the subject matter of resolutions. The profile of "No" votes is similar to that for contested resolutions in Figure 2, but the rarity of dissent is clearly revealed only in the vote choice data.

[6] "Nonparticipation" is a choice often be-speaking strong dissent or a rejection of the Assembly's claim to competence in the question acted upon. Cases are rare and we have somewhat crudely lumped them with absences.

More significant than the trends discussed above is the overwhelming size of majorities throughout the entire period and for all subjects.[7] Only four of the 363 resolutions were adopted by close votes—by majorities of 75 per cent or less of those voting.[8] In-

[7] Most issues require a two-thirds majority. The Assembly very rarely makes an explicit determination of the kind of majority required, and in view of the overwhelming majorities, the question is seldom important. *Repertory of Practice of U.N. Organs*, Vol. 1, Suppl. 1, 1958, p. 195.

[8] These cases were: Res. 902 (IX), postponing the Assembly's closing date; Res. 904 (IX), asking the International Court for an advisory opinion on the Assembly's voting procedures concerning South West Africa; Res. 1351 (XIV), keeping the Chinese representation question off the agenda; and Res.

dividual countries' votes are documented only for the 79 resolutions (of the total of 363) which were adopted by roll-call vote. Thirty-eight countries never cast a single "No" vote on these roll calls, although they were, on the average, eligible to vote on 46 roll calls (depending on when admitted to membership).

Winning majorities far exceed the "minimal winning coalitions" which political theory would predict if decisions have zero-sum (i.e., redistributive) elements. A prolonged departure from minimal winning coalitions suggests that decisions are either innocuous or genuinely cooperative, i.e., zero stakes or positive-sum.[9] We did not attempt a systematic analysis of the factors of commitment or cooperation in this study, and can offer only a few impressions on these important matters. Undoubtedly unanimity was often obtained at the price of innocuousness or of watering down the level of commitment sought in resolutions. Cases where complete unanimity reflected major accommodation without weakening the basis for action were rare, but there was one outstanding example in each of the sessions studied: Res. 810 (IX), presaging establishment of the International Atomic Energy Agency; Res. 1472 (XIV), reconstituting the Committee on Peaceful Uses of Outer Space; and Res. 1771 (XVII), appointing U Thant to the full title of Secretary-General.

CONCLUSION 2: IMBALANCE IN
DECISION POWER

It is a commonplace that, under the one-state, one-vote procedure, the emerging nations have voting strength out of all proportion to their populations, contributions, and responsibili-

ties in the UN. Cartoonists use the wildly tipping seesaw or the little man on enormous stilts to tell the story. Here we describe more definitely the nature and extent of imbalance in actual vote results, in order to document the conclusion that the "great powers" of East and West have not succeeded —in terms of voting victories—in offsetting their small share of formal voting strength by informal sources of influence.[10]

Evidence of the imbalance in decision power is based on the analysis of the 79 roll-call votes on whole resolutions among the 363 resolutions adopted in the three years studied. Table 1 lists Member states in order from those most often outvoted to those most often in successful majorities, in proportion to the times eligible to vote, depending on when states became Members of the United Nations.[11] Those listed first may safely be regarded as low in decision power. The position of others may be due to conformity, coincidence of viewpoint, or effective exertion of influence. (Since data relate to adopted resolutions, all dissenting votes were unsuccessful.)

The table shows that decision power in the General Assembly is inversely related to power in an economic or military sense. The Big Four—France, USSR, UK, and US—are among the lowest 25 per cent, in that ascending

[10] The situation regarding formal voting strength is illustrated by the fact that in 1964, 76 member countries, accounting for about five per cent of regular budget assessments and 16 per cent of the population of all Members, could form a two-thirds majority.

[11] See appendix on methods for a discussion of other possible methods of measuring decision power. [We have not included this appendix. We have, however, retained Mrs. Manno's footnote, as it may have pertinence for those readers who may be interested in exploring the subject in the original article. —EDS.]

1784 (XVII), asking contributions for Chinese refugees in Hong Kong.

[9] William H. Riker, The Theory of Political Coalitions (New Haven, 1962).

TABLE 1

UN MEMBERS RANKED FROM LEAST TO MOST CONFORMING WITH ASSEMBLY MAJORITIES ON WHOLE RESOLUTIONS ADOPTED BY ROLL-CALL VOTES: 9TH, 14TH, AND 17TH GENERAL ASSEMBLY SESSIONS COMBINED

Country	Number of times eligible to vote[a]	Percentage of times			Country	Number of times eligible to vote[a]	Percentage of times		
		Voting "No"[b]	Voting "Yes"	Not voting[c]			Voting "No"[b]	Voting "Yes"	vo
South Africa	79	32	33	35	Syria[d]	45	4	71	
France	79	28	42	30	Dominican Republic	79	4	52	
Mongolia	22	27	50	23	Morocco	56	4	64	
Portugal	56	27	30	43	Nepal	56	4	68	
USSR, Byelo SSR, Czech., Pol., and Ukr. SSR	79	25	58	17	Austria	56	4	76	
Belgium	79	24	48	28	Cambodia	56	4	76	
Albania	56	23	57	20	Ghana	56	4	80	
Bulg., Hung., and Rom.	56	23	63	14	Honduras	79	3	67	
United Kingdom	79	22	52	26	China	79	3	72	
Australia	79	15	47	38	Burma	79	3	77	
United States	79	15	71	14	Colombia	79	3	77	
Netherlands	79	13	63	24	Egypt—UAR[e]	79	3	78	
New Zealand	79	13	67	20	Israel	79	3	79	
Italy	56	12	66	22	Uruguay	79	3	83	
Luxembourg	79	11	38	51	India	79	3	84	
Spain	56	11	52	37	Liberia	79	3	84	
Sweden	79	10	73	17	Argentina	79	3	86	
Canada	79	9	67	24	Jordan	56	2	71	
Denmark	79	9	73	18	Sudan	56	2	73	
Norway	79	8	75	17	Tunisia	56	2	73	
Cuba	79	8	76	16	Ceylon	56	2	87	
Yugoslavia	79	8	78	14	Japan	56	2	91	
Ireland	56	7	86	7	Nicaragua	79	1	43	
Peru	79	6	69	25	Yemen	79	1	57	
Finland	56	5	61	34	Afghanistan	79	1	70	
Guinea	56	5	68	27	Saudi Arabia	79	1	71	
Turkey	79	5	66	29	Haiti	79	1	75	
Algeria	21	5	71	24	Indonesia	79	1	75	
Rwanda	22	5	45	50	Lebanon	79	1	77	
Somalia	22	5	50	45	Brazil	79	1	81	
Malagasy Republic	22	5	59	36	Greece	79	1	81	
Mali	22	5	68	27	Iraq	79	1	82	
					Chile	79	1	88	
					Philippines	79	1	96	
					Iceland	79	0	59	

(37 additional states—all Asian, African, Latin American—had no "No" votes.)

[a] Countries admitted to the UN before 1954 were eligible to vote on all 79 issues, those admitted from 1955 to 1958 were eligible on 56, those admitted from 1960 to 1962 on 22 issues (except Algeria, which was eligible on 21 issues).

[b] Ranking is based on this column, before rounding.

[c] Includes times abstaining, absent, or nonparticipating.

[d] Included in UAR in 14th Session.

[e] Includes Egypt's votes in 9th Session, UAR other Sessions.

order. This lowest fourth includes all Warsaw Treaty countries, most of the NATO countries, and four Commonwealth countries. Over three-fourths of the UN's regular budget assessments are paid by this lowest fourth in decision power. Members of the Asian-African group and Latin American states are entirely absent, except for Cuba. New and underdeveloped countries are conspicuously missing.

It is often said that the equal voting formula understates the actual capacity of great powers to influence United Nations decisions. These data show that, on the contrary, judged by their ability to bring about General Assembly decisions in which they are able and willing to concur, the great powers are at the losing end of the scale. The median or middle-ranking country in this array (Argentina) was outvoted on only three per cent of the issues on which it was eligible to vote. France was outvoted on 28 per cent of the issues, being exceeded only by South Africa. The USSR bloc was outvoted on 25 per cent of the issues, the UK on 22 per cent, and the US on 15 per cent. These figures are based on all 79 roll-call votes, of which only 52 were contested—i.e., included any "No" votes. Using only the contested issues, and comparing the Big Four with Argentina, the results of Table 2 are obtained. To the extent that voting victories in the Assembly are meaningful, it is clear that Argentina is better off than any of the Big Four. Among the latter, the United States was in closest agreement with Assembly majorities on final votes. But besides the remaining Big Three and the Soviet bloc countries, the only countries in *less* agreement with majorities than the United States were South Africa, Portugal, Belgium, and Australia.

This picture suggests the nature of the parliamentary diplomacy being transacted at the General Assembly. As between the underdeveloped and

TABLE 2

DISTRIBUTION OF VOTES ON 52 CONTESTED ROLL CALLS FOR SELECTED STATES: 9TH, 14TH, AND 17TH GENERAL ASSEMBLY SESSIONS COMBINED.

Country	Number of times eligible to vote	Percentage of times		
		Voting "No"	Voting "Yes"	Not voting[a]
France	52	42	40	18
USSR	52	38	50	12
UK	52	32	50	18
US	52	23	63	14
Argentina	52	4	78	18

[a] Absent, abstaining, or nonparticipating.

the advanced countries, the newly independent countries and those still administering or recently divested of colonial possessions, there is not a balance of winnings and losses, but rather a constant pressure through massive majorities of the former for redistribution in their favor. Redistribution attempts take many forms: statements of principles that seek to reduce the legal rights of the "haves" and enhance those of the "have-nots"; decisions asserting the Assembly's competence to supervise the decolonization process; requests for voluntary contributions to the UN's widely varied activities in furtherance of economic development; and the fixing of assessment scales based on capacity to pay.

Western dissents occurred chiefly on decolonization issues, broadly interpreted, while the dissenting votes of the USSR were cast chiefly on East-West issues and on a few constitutional questions. The dissenters in all these actions rather infrequently called attention to the obvious imbalance in voting strength. Instead they emphasized Charter limits to Assembly competence. The Soviet Union has often urged the claims of domestic jurisdiction or exclusive Security Council competence when threatened by the domination of Western-sympathizing majorities. In the period studied, the sure allies of the Soviet Union remained a minority of about 10 per cent, as was true in the pre-1954 United Nations. But the USSR could sometimes rally—or conform to majorities with—the new and nonaligned countries on certain political and economic issues. Soviet efforts in recent years to obtain a "balanced" three-way power distribution in various organs (East, West, and nonaligned) may indicate a greater confidence in the ability to influence positive decision-making, rather than merely prevent it.

The present sample of 52 contested roll calls does not show (nor definitely disprove) the existence of a significant trend of change in the relative decision power of the United States and the USSR from 1954 to 1962. However, when this group of 52 issues is compared with pre-1954 roll calls, it is found that the very great advantage the United States had in achieving voting victories over the USSR in the earlier period has been substantially reduced.[12] A reflection of these facts appears in the changing strategy of US government spokesmen in defending the United Nations against its critics. Not long ago it was emphasized that the United States has never lost out on a vital issue, but more recently it has been stated that the United States cannot expect to win *all* the time. This is a salutary recognition of the need for alternation in a decision-making system that is to retain the loyalty of all members, and to induce compliance by those who are outvoted at any given time. Actu-

ally, the situation of the United States is not quite so favorable as is often claimed, nor is the prospect for the development of a world political community as unfavorable as it would be if those claims were true.

The empirical data presented above show that the well-known imbalance in *formal* vote strength in the General Assembly is reflected in an imbalance in *actual* ability to form or join winning majorities. The most striking characteristic is the preponderant vote strength and decision power of the new and emerging countries compared with the older, developed countries of both East and West. Among the economically advanced countries, a lesser aspect of imbalance (which complicates the problem of dealing with the major imbalance) is the fact that the United States enjoys a somewhat more favorable position than the Soviet Union.

CONCLUSION 3: LARGE NUMBER
OF INTERNAL DECISIONS

The evidence of the large incidence of *internal decisions* comes from a classification of the 363 resolutions under study into four content classes, depending on the nature of the obligation to comply: *internal decisions* (legally binding on UN organs): resolutions addressed to the General Assembly itself or UN organs acting under its authority; *recommendations:* resolutions asking action by agencies whose compliance is optional; *scale of assessment decisions* (legally binding on Members): resolutions on scales of assessment, and those on the Working Capital Fund which were keyed in to the scale of assessments; *statements:* resolutions requiring no substantive action (perfunctory and procedural resolutions "taking note," commending, postponing action—except those regarding credentials, which were classed as internal decisions; also res-

---

[12] For this comparison use was made of 24 roll calls from the Third to the Eighth Sessions, analyzed by the present author. Catherine Senf, "A Proposal for Weighting Votes in the UN General Assembly," in *Ninth Report of the Commission to Study the Organization of Peace* (New York, 1955), 107–29.

TABLE 3

NUMBER AND PERCENTAGE OF ADOPTED RESOLUTIONS IN EACH CONTENT CLASS:
9TH, 14TH, AND 17TH GENERAL ASSEMBLY SESSIONS COMBINED

Content class	Number of resolutions	Percentage of total	Percentage of those requiring implementation
Internal decisions	163	44.8	54.9
Recommendations	124	34.2	41.8
Scale of assessment decisions	10	2.8	3.3
Subtotal requiring implementation	297	81.8	100.0
Statements (not requiring implementation)	66	18.2	
Total	363	100.0	

olutions deciding not to act on an item).

In sorting the 363 adopted resolutions into these groups, mixed resolutions were classed according to the addressee whose compliance would substantially fulfill the immediate purposes of the resolution.[13] Table 3 shows the number and per cent of resolutions of each kind. The largest category is "internal decisions," which make up more than half of all resolutions requiring implementation (i.e., of the total excluding "statements"). The implementation of internal decisions is almost automatic since it depends, not on actions by individual states, but on actions of organs subject to the Assembly's jurisdiction.

[13] For an example of the variety of groups sometimes addressed, see Res. 1764 (XVII) on the effects of atomic radiation. The 12 operating paragraphs of this resolution include orders or requests addressed to the Scientific Committee on the Effects of Atomic Radiation, the International Atomic Energy Agency, the World Meteorological Organization, the other specialized agencies, international non-governmental and national scientific organizations, individual scientists, Member states, and "all concerned."

Internal decisions are the means by which the Assembly organizes itself and guides and budgets the activities of its own subsidiary organs, the Secretariat, and other organs and agencies insofar as they come under its jurisdiction. With the exception of the Security Council, all parts of the system are subject in some degree to the General Assembly, either directly or indirectly. The degree of the Assembly's authority over the specialized agencies varies, and this study treats its direct requests for action by those agencies as "recommendations" rather than as "internal decisions."

Until they were recently curtailed by austerity budgets, the extensive activities carried out under internal decisions belied the description of the United Nations as a "debating society." These activities have included many fact-finding studies regarding the practices and attitudes of Member states on various subjects, often reported with a degree of objectivity not found in studies by individual nations or researchers. The normal progress of economic and social projects on the Assembly's agenda is through internal

TABLE 4

NUMBER AND PERCENTAGE OF INTERNAL DECISIONS BY ORGAN PRIMARILY
RESPONSIBLE FOR IMPLEMENTATION: 9TH, 14TH, AND 17TH
GENERAL ASSEMBLY SESSIONS COMBINED

Organ primarily responsible for implementation of internal decisions	Internal decisions	
	Number	Percent of total
Secretary-General	76	46.6
General Assembly and subsidiary organs	64	39.3
ECOSOC and subsidiary organs	17	10.4
Trusteeship Council	5	3.1
International Court of Justice	1	0.6
Total	163	100.0

decisions—studies of facts, studies of attitudes, and policy formulation—to recommendations for action by Members, or recommendations for action by specialized agencies and contributions by Members. Some few projects, such as OPEX,[14] start and end as internal decisions; after policy formulation they move into an experimental stage, and finally find a modest place in the regular budget, where compliance is almost certain.

The further breakdown of internal decisions in Table 4 shows that the great majority were primarily directed either to the Secretary-General or to the General Assembly and its own subsidiaries. The remaining categories in the table show the rarity with which the Assembly directly addresses the other principal organs of the United Nations.

CONCLUSION 4: MODERATELY GOOD
COMPLIANCE WITH RECOMMENDATIONS

While there is no problem of getting internal decisions implemented, the situation is quite different with recommendatory decisions. In opening

[14] The program to provide operational and executive personnel to serve in the civil service of requesting countries. See Res. 1385 (XIV).

the general debate at the Eighteenth Session of the General Assembly, João de Araujo Castro of Brazil commented on the emergence at the United Nations of a

parliamentary grouping of small and medium powers, which unite . . . to conduct a continuous struggle around three fundamental themes: disarmament, development, and decolonization. [He added:] And yet . . . we must admit that the recommendations of this majority with regard to each one of these . . . themes are left, with noticeable frequency, unimplemented [*General Assembly Official Records,* Eighteenth Session Plenary Meetings, September 19, 1963].

Is it true that the Assembly's recommendations are often ignored, and if so, who is responsible? The 124 recommendatory resolutions adopted (in the three years studied) were divided according to the agency primarily responsible for implementation, with results shown on the extreme right of Figure 4. The bars in the figure show the relative number of unanimous, abstained, and contested resolutions directed to each type of responsible agency. The following discussion of

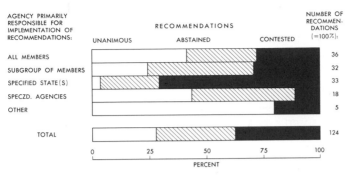

FIGURE 4: Percentage of unanimous, abstained, and contested recommendations adopted by the 9th, 14th, and 17th General Assembly Sessions (combined), by agency primarily responsible for implementation. For definitions see Figure 1.

compliance focuses chiefly on the divided resolutions (those having one or more abstentions or "No" votes). Without attempting an exact quantitative analysis of compliance, enough evidence is presented to suggest that pessimistic evaluations of the record need serious qualification.

Resolutions addressed to the Members for action were more controversial in proportion as the group addressed became more selective (see Figure 4). They were also less satisfactorily implemented in like proportion. Those addressed to all Members included many that could be and were substantially implemented even though some Members withheld approval and compliance. These included requests for aid to refugees and contributions to other voluntary budgets or aid programs. Other divided resolutions addressed to all Members defy neat generalization. In the legal area such recommendations were successful in producing conventions on the reduction of statelessness and on diplomatic immunities, and in bringing the Assembly majority's case for trusteeship for South West Africa before the International Court of Justice. An important divided resolution in the political area, calling for sanctions against South Africa, met with partial imple-

mentation (Res. 1761 [XVII]).[15] Still others dealing with economically sensitive subjects (international trade patterns) or culturally sensitive subjects (women's rights in marriage), together with a few propagandistic resolutions, had little or no effect (see Resolutions 836, 840, 842, and 843 [IX]; 1421 [XIV], 1763A and 1820 [XVII]).

Even though directed to all Members, Assembly recommendations seldom have an equal impact on all. However small the scale, a redistributive process is usually involved. This differential nature of decisions is more marked in the next category of Figure 4: recommendations mainly dependent for compliance on a particular subgroup of Members. Over half the recommendations in this category were addressed to the administering authorities of Trust Territories or of Non-Self-Governing Territories. These au-

[15] The attempted embargo against South Africa illustrates the difficulties of partial implementation in some situations. This effort proved largely ineffective because of noncompliance by a number of states including non-members of the United Nations. Some of those who did comply suffered serious economic losses, giving rise to suggestions that they should be compensated for the costs to them of compliance (See *UN Chronicle*, 2, 4 [1965], pp. 23–27).

thorities were importuned in increasingly imperative terms to fix target dates for independence; with regard to the Fifteenth Assembly's much publicized Declaration on Colonialism, they were entreated to disseminate information widely in their territories, to establish representative legislative bodies, to train indigenous cadres for administrative work, and to furnish "voluntary" information on these subjects to the UN. Occasionally the Assembly expressed qualified satisfaction with steps taken in compliance, but more often it reiterated earlier appeals which had not been satisfactorily implemented. Other examples of resolutions requiring action by a particular subgroup are the largely ineffective resolutions seeking cooperation of prospective donors to the Capital Development Fund (successor to the long-sought SUNFED). In general, recommendations directly seeking redistributive changes of a political or economic nature met with limited compliance at best.

The 33 recommendations addressed to a specific state or states showed almost no unanimity and very little compliance. What were these recommendations and what was done about them? Twenty concerned decolonization and related matters, with the Union of South Africa the most frequent and least compliant target. Eight resolutions were directed to the United Kingdom as administering authority. Two of these (Resolutions 1352 and 1473 [XIV]) dealt with arrangements for plebiscites in the Trust Territory of the Cameroons, and were fully implemented.[16] The other

[16] The result of the plebiscite in the northern part of the territory—resulting in that area becoming a province of Nigeria—was disputed by the Republic of Cameroon which sought unsuccessfully to have the International Court of Justice adjudicate its claim (*United Nations Review*, 11, 1 [1964], p. 3).

six resolutions, addressed to the UK by the Seventeenth Assembly, asked various reforms and early implementation of the Declaration on Colonialism in a number of British dependencies in Africa. They have been partially implemented. Two recommendations addressed to Portugal as administering authority have not met with satisfactory compliance, although Portugal has undertaken some steps in response to them.

Of six recommendations on disarmament and nuclear tests, five were directed to all the nuclear powers and one to France alone (on French Sahara tests). Whereas the tone of anticolonial resolutions by 1962 had become suggestive of an angry younger generation rebelling against the parents, disarmament resolutions continued to remind one of respectful children watching anxiously as the parents threatened to incinerate the family under the guise of "deterrence." The Assembly's resolutions have not produced disarmament, but its constant pressure probably helped to bring about the partial test ban treaty and the resumption of negotiations after deadlocks.

Most of the remaining recommendations to specific states were directed to nonmembers: the three annual reiterations of the United Nations goal of a unified Korea, implicitly addressed to North Korea; a resolution on Tibet, aimed at the People's Republic of China; and one condemning the detention of 11 American airmen captured by Chinese forces in Korea. The last-named action (Res. 906 [IX]) also authorized the Secretary-General to take initiatives "by the means most appropriate in his judgment" for the airmen's release. It is the only one of the five successfully implemented. Dag Hammarskjöld, through private negotiations in Peking, set the stage for the men's release on the basis of a tacit trade involving the release of 76

Chinese students held in the United States.[17]

The last category in Figure 4, except for the small "Other" group, is recommendations to the specialized agencies. These were less controversial and better implemented than recommendations directed to the Members as such. The agencies' excellent record of effective response to the Assembly's requests for action is attested by many expressions of appreciation for their help in answer to earlier resolutions. Some examples from the years studied may be cited here. The Food and Agriculture Organization held an international conference on the conservation of resources of the sea in answer to the resolution of the Ninth Assembly, it also took a large measure of responsibility for the World Food Program (Res. 1825 [XVII]). Both UNESCO and the World Bank responded to a call to help meet the educational needs of Africa (Res. 1832 [XVII]). The World Meteorological Organization and the International Atomic Energy Agency aided the Assembly's Committee on the Effects of Atomic Radiation (Res. 1764 [XVII]). The WMO and the International Telecommunications Union have important technical roles in the work of the Assembly's Committee on the Peaceful Uses of Outer Space (Res. 1472 [XIV] and 1802 [XVII]).

This review of the compliance record suggests that, besides the conspicuous cases of defiance of Assembly recommendations, there are also important cases of substantial compliance. In any event, noncompliance with recommendations is a permissible response which does not threaten the constitutional foundation of the United Nations Organization. The recommendations most often and most completely ignored are those directed at one or a

[17] *International Conciliation*, No. 504 (1955), 48–50.

few states and they deal chiefly with a shrinking field of problems—those of colonies seeking independence.

CONCLUSION 5: HARMFUL MINORITY RESPONSES TO BINDING DECISIONS

The very fact that internal decisions *are* implemented, regardless of dissenters, gives rise to a serious disequilibrium for chronic minorities. They are forced to accept the results of such decisions and, where there are financial implications, to help pay for carrying them out. Not having recourse to simple noncompliance—as with unwanted recommendations—they have resorted to one or more of the following responses:

(1) Attempts to limit the area of the Assembly's competence by rigid interpretation of Charter restrictions.

(2) Strong expressions of disapproval including boycotting of organs, nonparticipation in voting, and temporary "walk-outs."

(3) Withdrawal from UN membership.

(4) Delaying or refusing to pay assessments.

(5) Trying harder to win voting allies—more politicking and accommodation.

(6) Seeking more influence in the *execution* of decisions (e.g., the troika proposal as applied to the Secretary-General and Secretariat staff).

(7) Seeking better representation of one's likely coalition partners in organs of preliminary consideration of agenda items.

The method of invoking Charter limitations on Assembly competence is often voiced for the record but rarely pressed to a judicial test. The Assembly majority still distrusts the UN's principal legal organ, whose composition it has only slowly been able to modify through triennial elections of judges. The request for an advisory opinion on the status of peacekeeping expenses (Res. 1731 [XVI]) was an important exception.

The next three responses, like the first, are essentially negative, being based on threatened or actual noncompliance. The method of conspicuously not taking part in deliberations and voting has occasionally brought modification of decisions, as when the Assembly changed its stance on the Algerian question in response to a French walk-out.[18] There was by mid-1965 only one instance of withdrawal of membership (Indonesia's, which took effect in early 1965). It was precipitated by an internal decision without financial implications: the seating of Malaysia in the Security Council for the year 1965.[19] The fourth response, financial noncompliance, is both the most effective and the most dangerous. It has brought about the crisis that threatens to split the Organization or to reduce drastically the authority of the General Assembly. That crisis reflects the failure of important contributors to find an equilibrium— a balance between the costs and the benefits of participation—through the other responses.

The remaining reactions are essentially positive, seeking to influence decision-making rather than to prevent or defy it. The fifth response is the preeminent political method and its scope of operation indicates the extent to which a political community exists. This method—more politicking—is the principal method used by the United States to hold her losses to a minimum as the enlarged membership and increasing nonalignment shifts the balance of votes away from her. It is a method used by the Soviet Union with still modest success, somewhat en-

hanced by the same trend. As to the sixth category, the Soviet proposal to substitute a three-man body for the Secretary-General was rejected but the pressure has brought some changes in the Secretariat staff.

The seventh method is shown in those shifts in the composition of suborgans which are the major structural changes affecting the equilibrium of the Organization, apart from changes in the size and composition of the Assembly itself.[20] These changes touch every field of Assembly concern, and they result in a variety of patterns of influence in different organs. For example, the 18-member Disarmament Committee and the 28-member Committee on the Peaceful Uses of Outer Space have come close to "three-way parity" between East, West, and nonaligned. In other cases, the constant pressure for "equitable geographical distribution" has converted suborgans into smaller replicas of the whole Assembly, reflecting the imbalances found in the parent body.

To summarize: both positive and negative reactions are possible and have occurred in response to unwanted decisions which the UN Assembly has the legal or actual power to impose. The very imbalance in Assembly voting power often prevents the achievement of equilibrium via the positive methods, all of which depend on successful coalition formation. The negative methods of withdrawing participation and withholding assessments can be exercised by individual states, and they are the most damaging to the Organization.

IV. Policy Implications

This study deliberately avoided a major focusing on the area of decision-

---

[18] See Res. 909 (X) and *International Conciliation*, No. 510 (1956), 143–44.

[19] This resulted from a bargain struck in the 1963 Security Council elections, splitting the two-year term between Czechoslovakia and Malaysia.

[20] Catherine Senf Manno, "Problems and Trends in the Composition of Nonplenary UN Organs," *International Organization*, 19, 1 (1965), 37–55.

making which precipitated the UN crisis of 1964–65 (the execution and financing of peacekeeping operations). Instead we have been concerned with General Assembly activities as seen in fuller scope and context. Not only in the disposal of collectively organized force and the allocation of its costs among Members, but also in the allocation of other resources of the Organization and in the allocation of power within the Organization, the imbalance of decision power has serious consequences. The "internal decisions" which were also found to present great danger include budgetary decisions on the expenditure side of the regular budget, substantive decisions with financial implications for that budget, and decisions on matters affecting the institutional distribution of power. Among the latter are questions of credentials and admission of new Members, as well as questions about the composition of the many less-than-whole subsidiary organs which have assumed increasing importance in the preliminary stages of decision-making, as the parent body has grown in size.

The judgment that there is an "imbalance" in the General Assembly rests in part on the internal analysis of winning and losing coalitions. But it is also a comment on the discrepancy between institutional and real power of certain international actors whose participation is essential to the successful functioning of the United Nations.[21] A State Department spokesman has characterized the problem as the "international apportionment issue."[22]

Our analysis suggests that the majority's response to this problem has not notably been that of taking advantage of the imbalance by exercising its own formal voting strength to the maximum. While the Assembly majority theoretically has the legal power to vote large compulsory budgets for economic development or other purposes,[23] it has wisely refrained from asserting such authority. In fact the Assembly has often responded to the situation by watering down resolutions far below the level that could have commanded the necessary two-thirds majorities. Thus, instead of the contests that might have been expected for actions which impose costs on some and confer benefits on others, the level of both costs and benefits has been kept low enough to permit unanimous decisions in increasingly numerous cases.

Where decisions are not unanimous, the responses of those in dissenting minorities have sometimes been more negative: nonpayment and withdrawal of participation or membership. There is an obvious need for other equilibrating factors compatible with a growing level of commitment to the United Nations. There is a place for *accommodation* and a place for *alternation* as equilibrating factors. These two approaches differ in their areas of relevance and in their impact on the two aspects of the costs of group decision-making.[24] Insistence on accommodation costs more in terms of the effort of bargaining, watering down of content, and postponement of action, but risks less in terms of unwanted decisions. Acceptance of alternation risks some unwanted decisions in order to get on

---

[21] Another aspect of imbalance which increases the irrelevance of the UN to its major purpose of preventing war is the continued absence of representatives of the People's Republic of China. This study deals only with the imbalance among present Members.

[22] Harlan Cleveland, "The Evolution of Rising Responsibility," address to UN Association of the USA. *UNA News*, 36, 10 (1964–65), 3–6. See also the address of

Richard N. Gardner on "UN Procedures and Power Realities: the International Apportionment Problem," given before the American Society of International Law, April 23, 1965.

[23] Leo Gross, "Expenses of the United Nations for Peace-keeping Operations," *International Organization*, 17, 1 (1963), 1–35.

[24] Buchanan and Tullock.

with action and to increase the area susceptible to group decision.

It is of interest to compare various proposed reforms of the UN system with respect to these two kinds of decision costs. Gardner[25] lists six proposed answers to the problem of "international apportionment":

(1) Weighted voting in the General Assembly.

(2) Dual voting (requiring "double majorities," e.g., a two-thirds General Assembly majority that includes also the votes of two-thirds of the Security Council members).

(3) Bicameralism (e.g., requiring that some matters must be approved by both the General Assembly and the Security Council).

(4) Committees with selective representation (combined perhaps with a "self-denying ordinance" by which the Assembly would agree not to adopt proposals opposed by these selective bodies).

(5) Informal relations with international secretariats (by which major contributors would inform heads of the specialized agencies of their preferences before programs are formulated by the latter).

(6) Conciliation (formal or informal agreements to make full use of this procedure before making decisions opposed by countries with important interests at stake).

The first alternative, weighted voting, would change the composition of majorities and minorities, presumably giving essential actors a means of finding equilibrium through direct influence on the content of decisions by their votes, rather than through withholding compliance. This reform encounters opposition from small states, which wish to retain their equal votes. It is opposed by the State Department because, while it would give both the US and the USSR more positive decision power vis-à-vis the new and de-

veloping countries, it risks more frequent alternation between the US and the USSR.[26]

Both dual voting and bicameralism would provide safeguards against unwanted decisions at the expense of making any decision harder to get. They would increase the power of minorities to block action.

Committees with selective representation are theoretically very promising, since a variety of criteria of representation could be applied to adapt to various subject areas. In return for their long-run benefits (presumably better compliance with decisions), they require more immediate acts of abnegation by the majority—both when the committees are set up and when their decisions are presented for plenary action. Some recent changes in committee composition are moves in this direction, but many are in the opposite direction: toward "equitable geographical distribution."

Earlier consultation with the heads of the functional agencies is an unexceptionable method of improving communications and presumably thus reducing the costs of decision-making in terms of the time and effort needed for bargaining and negotiation. Emphasis on conciliation to maximize the possibilities of accommodation reflects a willingness to spend more effort on this phase at the expense of deferring or preventing decision.

Except for weighted voting, most of these methods are essentially defensive: they risk reducing the area or immediacy of group decisions rather than risking the imposition of unwanted decisions. They show little disposition on the part of those proposing them to settle for occasional defeats in order that collective action can be taken. This

[26] Some proposed formulas for weighting votes in the General Assembly are presented in Catherine Senf Manno, "Selective Weighted Voting in the UN General Assembly: Rationale and Methods," *International Organization*, 20, 1 (1966).

[25] *Op. cit.*

reluctance is a measure of the present very rudimentary state of world political community, especially as perceived by national representatives. Perhaps the stubborn resistance of the UN's crisis to a solution is a reflection of its entanglement in deep-rooted attitudes and opinions that are incompatible with the stronger United Nations that is so often proclaimed as a goal.

15. The Management of Power in the Changing United Nations*

INIS L. CLAUDE, JR.

I

THE central problem of our time is to achieve the effective management of the power relations of states. The world is constituted as a system of independent but interdependent states—independent in authority but interdependent in destiny. States are units of power. While power is a complex conception, for present purposes it may be construed in the narrow sense of force. Physical ability to kill, to damage, or to coerce, is the particular aspect of power which serves as the focus of this article. States are characterized by the possession, in varying degrees, of this capacity to damage or destroy each other. This power may be used in competitive struggle, producing destruction on a massive scale. It may be used unilaterally, producing enslavement and degradation of its victims. In short, both survival and freedom, both sheer existence and the higher values that enrich existence, are implicated in the problem of power. The national interest of every state, and the common interest of all men, in the preservation and development of civilization are threatened by the paroxysms of violence which states are capable of unleashing. Hence, the primacy of the task of controlling the use of force by states,

of managing the power relations of states, cannot seriously be questioned.

I use the term, *management,* to convey the conviction that the problem of power is here to stay; it is, realistically, not a problem to be eliminated, but one to be managed. At all levels of society, human beings inherently possess and inexorably retain the capacity to do physical violence to each other. The task of socialization is not to abolish power, but to control its exercise. At the level of collectivities, I take it as a basic postulate that there will always be human groups—if no longer national states, then other social sub-divisions—which will be capable of damaging each other. They cannot ultimately be deprived of this capacity. Given brains and brawn, men can contrive instruments of lethal warfare, be they clubs or hydrogen bombs; given human social instincts and skills, men can contrive to organize their violence as the clash of collectivities. The issue will never be whether power exists; it will always be whether power is subjected to effective management.

My emphasis upon the concept of management of power carries with it the specific implication that disarmament is not the key to the problem of international violence. In the literal sense, the notion of disarmament would seem to suggest reliance upon the unattainable ideal of eliminating the po-

* *International Organization,* Vol. XV, pp. 219–235. Reprinted by permission.

tential of states for violence. Most actual disarmament efforts are, of course, more modestly conceived; they aim at checking the arms race and securing the adoption of systematic programs of arms limitation or reduction. The value of such achievements, if they should prove possible, might be considerable. They might, by restricting the distribution of certain types of weapons and limiting the quantitative levels of power accumulation, prevent the power situation from becoming inherently unmanageable. Thus, that brand of disarmament which is more accurately characterized as arms control may be an essential prologue to, or accompaniment of, any effective scheme for the management of power in the contemporary world. Whether or not disarmament can be attained, however, the basic problem will remain that of establishing and maintaining reliable control over the exercise of power. Even if all existing weapons were destroyed and production of armaments totally suspended, the capacity to devise instruments of terrible power would remain a permanent potentiality; man cannot unlearn what he knows about the means of creating power. My basic criticism of the disarmament motif is that it tends to foster an emphasis upon abolition of power as the key to peace and security, whereas it seems to me that the problem is more realistically defined in terms of the necessity of bringing the exercise of power by states under effective and reliable control.

The theory of international relations, if one may apply that term to a literature which is more a thing of shreds and patches than a seamless garment covering our understanding of the processes of international relations, contains three basic concepts which may be regarded as relevant to the problem of the management of power: balance of power, collective security, and world government. These concepts have not been defined with care, used with precision, or made to serve as bases for systematically elaborated theoretical structures; at best, they stand as rudimentary snippets of theory which have been used more for polemical than for analytical purposes. Each of them has attracted its quota of advocates and detractors, who have tended to treat the concepts competitively rather than comparatively. In short, balance of power, collective security, and world government are not terms which designate well-developed and generally understood bodies of doctrine. Nevertheless, they do represent the leading ideas regarding the problem of the management of power in international relations, and they figure as the focal points of contemporary discussion and controversy concerning this problem.

It is, of course, hazardous to try to establish definite meanings for terms which have customarily been used so loosely and inconsistently as these. Recognizing that others may exercise the right to invest them with meanings different from mine, I nevertheless venture to suggest that these three concepts can, with considerable justification derived from the literature of the international relations field, be taken as characterizing disparate systems of relationship among states—systems related to each other as successive points along a continuum and differing most fundamentally in the degree of centralization of power and authority which they imply. In this view, balance of power represents the extreme of decentralization, a kind of *laissez-faire* arrangement in the sphere of power politics. It suggests a scheme within which individual states, separate units of power and policy, operate autonomously, without subordination to a central agency for the management of power relations. Singly or in combinations reflecting the coincidence of interests, states seek to influence the pattern of power distribution and to determine their own places within that pattern. In such a balancing system, the constituent states function as coordinate managers of the power situation.

Collective security falls next in line along the scale of centralization, representing an effort to deal with the power problem by superimposing a scheme of partially centralized management upon a situation in which power remains diffused among national units. It involves a centralization of authority over the use of force, to the extent that states are deprived of the legal right to use violence at their own discretion. In its ideal form, it calls for an international organization with authority to determine when a resort to force is illegitimate and to require states to collaborate under its direction in suppressing such use of force.

Finally, world government takes its place at the opposite end of the scale from balance of power, suggesting the creation of an institutional system involving a monopoly of power, comparable to that alleged to exist in a well-ordered national state. In this scheme, both the possession of the instruments of force and the control of policy concerning their use are presumably centralized in an institution superior to the state.

Unfortunately, the differences among these concepts have more often than not been exaggerated and mis-stated. The case for adoption of one or another has often been argued as if a choice had to be made between totally dissimilar systems, one offering hopeful prospects for order and security, and the other leaving the world mired in hopelessness. In fact, the differences among them are far from absolute and are perhaps less interesting and significant than the similarities—to the analyst, if not to the propagandist. Having plotted them along a common scale, I would suggest that they tend to slide into each other, developing points of approximation or overlap, rather than to maintain fixed distances of separation. Both balance of power and collective security are deterrent schemes in that they rely upon countervailing

power to frustrate the ambitions of powerful aggressors; moreover, the two systems are heavily dependent upon sets of prerequisite conditions which are similar in important respects. One can argue, for instance, that the balance system requires the diffusion of power among a number of major states so that no single state will control such a large fraction of the world's power resources as to make the task of counterbalancing it inordinately difficult; the same requirement can be cited for a collective security system, to avoid the possibility that any state will be invulnerable to the pressure of collective sanctions. Thus, a global power configuration marked by bipolarity is equally unfavorable to the operation of a balance system or of a collective security system. One can demonstrate that a successful balance system requires that national policies be adaptable to contingencies that may arise rather than rigidly fixed, so that old friends can be resisted when they endanger the stability of the system and former enemies can be supported when the exigencies of the power situation so require. A similar flexibility of policy, involving the capacity to switch the foci of friendship and enmity, is essential to collective security.

On the other hand, the ideal scheme of collective security is not wholly unlike that of world government. It involves a concentration of authority in a central organ giving that organ a government-like quality that can be ignored only if one dogmatically denies, as many proponents of world government do, that there are many shadings of gray between the "black" of essential anarchy and the "white" of actual government. Moreover, a scheme of world government which undertook to maintain order on a global scale by methods comparable to those used within limited boundaries by national governments would, in fact, involve reliance upon intricate and delicate processes of balancing the power of constituent units of the society. The proposition that government is a matter of exercising a literal or virtual monopoly of power over a society, rather than of presiding over a balancing process, is largely a myth, even though totalitarian dictators have sometimes gained considerable success in translating it into reality. The point is that the typical enthusiast for world government wants a system which has more in common with the balance of power system than he customarily realizes or admits.

Despite these and other points of similarity which might be cited, there are characteristic differences among the implications of the concepts of balance of power, collective security, and world government, sufficiently important to justify the proposition that they designate alternative patterns for the ordering of power relations among states. The balance of power concept allows states to maneuver freely in a competitive world. Its typical institutional expression is a set of flexible alliances within which recurrent shifts of alignment take place; its promise of order lies in the expectation that competing power urges will somehow balance and thereby cancel each other, producing deterrence through equilibration. Collective security looks to a general international organization, presiding over a collaborative, rather than a competitive, arrangement. It purports to inhibit any aggressor by making virtually all the other states the *ad hoc* allies of any state that suffer attack; thus, it promises deterrence through the mobilization of a preponderance of power against any member of the system which threatens its peace and order. World government relies upon neither the interplay of competitive states nor the collaboration of states organized to uphold the principle of order; it promises to deprive states of their standing as centers of power and policy, where issues of war and peace are concerned, and to superimpose upon them an institution possessed of the authority and capability to maintain, by unchallengeable force so far as may be necessary, the order and stability of a global community.

These are not necessarily the only conceivable patterns for the management of power in international relations. They are, however, the patterns which have become the common currency of intellectual transactions concerning world affairs in the twentieth century. Whether any of these patterns has been, or can be, or should be, fully realized in actuality is not at issue here. They constitute the standard list of theoretical alternatives; they are the intellectual pigeon-holes in constant use.

With this introductory statement of the categories which, however poorly defined, dominate contemporary thinking about the problem of ordering international relations, we can turn to the questions to be considered in parts II and III of this article: (1) what was the nature of the system for management of power in international relations envisaged by the founders of the United Nations; and (2) what is the nature of the system which has in fact taken shape during the period of operation—and alteration—of the United Nations, from 1946 to 1961?

II

It has been widely assumed and frequently asserted that the United Nations was originally intended and expected to function as the institutional manager of a full-fledged collective security system, capable of bringing collective force to bear against any aggressor. In most instances, this assertion is made in the context of a discussion of the failure of the United Nations to realize that ideal. Sometimes the founders of the Organization are convicted of idealism; they should have known better than to expect the United Nations to be effective as an instrument of collective security. Sometimes an objective analysis of the changes which have ocurred in the setting within which the Organization operates is presented as explaining the failure of the collective security scheme; thus:

> The great-power split, together with the admission of large numbers of African, Asian, and European neutralist states, has almost destroyed the collective security functions that were to be the organization's principal reason for existence.[1]

More often, the Soviet Union is pictured as the villain in the piece; by abusing the veto power and obstructing the creation of the enforcement mechanism envisaged in Article 43 of the Charter, it has frustrated the realization of the promise of collective security.[2] Whatever the explanatory argument, the essential point in such statements is that the United Nations was intended to be, but has failed to become, the directing mechanism of a universally effective collective security system.

Why has it been so generally assumed that the establishment of the United Nations represented an effort to institutionalize collective security in the postwar world? An attempt to answer this question must precede an assessment of the validity of the assumption itself.

In the first place, it may be suspected that this interpretation of the United Nations experiment was reached by the

processes of elimination and deduction from a preconceived definition of the purposes of general international organization. Was the new world order designed as a balance of power system? Certainly not. Participants in the creation of the United Nations were too emphatic in their criticism of reliance upon balance of power, and too insistent in their assertion that they were creating a system better than balance of power, to permit that interpretation. True, they did not whip the balance of power as vigorously and persistently as their Wilsonian ancestors had done a generation before, but that was presumably because they thought it uneconomical to spend their time in flogging a dead horse. In any case, the United Nations was essentially a new version of the League of Nations, and it was well understood that the latter organization had been conceived by men who repudiated the balance of power system and aspired to introduce an alternative system. If the projected scheme were not a balance of power system, was it then a world government? No, it was clearly much more modest than that. If proof were needed, one could refer to the Moscow Declaration of October 30, 1943, in which the major powers of the anti-Axis coalition had declared the purpose of "establishing . . . a general international organization, based on the principle of the sovereign equality of all peace-loving states,"[3] or to President Roosevelt's decisive assertion that:

> We are not thinking of a superstate with its own police forces and other paraphernalia of coercive power. We are seeking effective agreement and arrangements through which the nations would maintain, according to their capacities, adequate forces to

[1] Thomas J. Hamilton, "The Changing United Nations: Morale Lowered by Deadlocks," *New York Times,* December 30, 1960.

[2] See Eisenhower's letter to Bulganin, January 12, 1958, reproduced in Paul E. Zinner, ed., *Documents on American Foreign Relations, 1958* (New York: Harper, 1959), p. 89; see also, Sir Leslie Munro, "The Case for a Standing UN Army," *New York Times Magazine,* July 27, 1958, p. 27.

[3] *A Decade of American Foreign Policy, Basic Documents, 1941–49,* Senate Document No. 123, 81st Congress, 1st Session (Washington, 1950), p. 12.

meet the needs of preventing war and of making impossible deliberate preparation for war and to have such forces available for joint action when necessary.[4]

Only one of the standard categories remained. If the United Nations were not designed to implement the concepts of balance of power or world government, then who could doubt that it must be an experiment in collective security? This conclusion must have come easily to men who stressed the resemblance of the new Organization to the defunct League. The original general international organization had been dedicated to the effectuation of collective security. It was natural to assume that the second edition was dedicated to the same purpose.

Secondly, it must be noted that the entire process of planning and formulating the United Nations Charter was dominated by the theme: "We are going to create a collective security system, and this time we are going to make it work." The United States planners were preoccupied with the necessity of providing the new Organization with an enforcement mechanism which would enable it to effectuate the collective security principle by coercive means which had been denied to the League.[5] In the opening sessions of the San Francisco Conference, a long procession of speakers reiterated the proposition that statesmen had gathered to create a world organization which could and would maintain the peace, by force if necessary. A typical expression of the prevailing viewpoint was provided by Joseph Bech,

speaking for Luxembourg, who declared that the peoples of the world

would not forgive their leaders if they returned to a policy of balance of power, which would inevitably result in a race for armaments heading straight for another war. The protection of peace can only be insured on the basis of collective security.[6]

Moreover, the end of the conference was marked by exultant speeches proclaiming the initiation of a real collective security system. Joseph Paul-Boncour of France declared that "the international organization will no longer be unarmed against violence. . . . That is the great thing, the great historic act accomplished by the San Francisco Conference. . . ."[7] The venerable Jan C. Smuts said of the Charter:

It provides for a peace with teeth; for a united front of peace-loving peoples against future aggressors; for a united front among the great powers backed by the forces of the smaller powers as well. . . . And it provides for central organization and direction of the joint forces for peace.[8]

Thus, the assumption that the creation of the United Nations signaled a new effort to institute a universal collective security system was encouraged. In view of the circumstances, it is hardly surprising that this interpretation gained general acceptance. Nevertheless, it is fundamentally incorrect, as a careful analysis of what the world's statesmen did at San Francisco and a

[4] *Postwar Foreign Policy Preparation 1939–1945*, Department of State Publication 3580, General Foreign Policy Series 15 (Washington, 1949), p. 269.

[5] See Ruth B. Russell and Jeannette E. Muther, *A History of the United Nations Charter* (Washington: Brookings, 1958), pp. 3, 4, 206, 209, 227–228, 395, 557.

[6] UN Information Organizations and U.S. Library of Congress, *Documents of the United Nations Conference on International Organization* (New York, 1945), I, p. 502.

[7] *Ibid.*, p. 668.

[8] *Ibid.*, p. 678.

more extensive review of what they said about their handiwork, will indicate.

The crucial element in the analysis is an understanding of the import of the veto rule which enables any of the five permanent members of the Security Council to block decisions on substantive matters in that organ—including the determination that aggression has taken place, the designation of the guilty party, and the decision to resort to sanctions, military or otherwise, against the aggressor. Such decisions, be it noted, are fundamental to the operation of a collective security system. The veto rule clearly gives each of the great powers the capacity to prevent the operation of the United Nations enforcement system against itself, against any state which it chooses to support and protect, or in any other case in which it prefers not to participate or to have others participate in an enforcement venture under United Nations auspices. The veto provision, in short, renders collective security impossible in all the instances most vital to the preservation of world peace and order, and problematical in cases of lesser importance.

It will not do to say that the founding fathers of the United Nations went home from San Francisco with the blissful assurance that they had formulated a beautiful system of collective security, only to be rudely shaken later by the discovery that the system was spoiled by a devilish Soviet Union which insisted upon taking seriously its right to use the veto power. In the first place, logic denies the probability that the veto was regarded as an obstructive capability that would never be used and would therefore never interfere with the operation of collective security. It is difficult to believe that the major powers worked as hard as they did to secure acceptance of the veto provision, in the conviction that it would be superfluous; this grant of a special power to a dissenter reflects the assumption that there will be dissent, not that there will be unity. The veto provision was not inserted in the Charter in a fit of absent-mindedness. It was adopted with full awareness, and deliberate intent, that any of the major powers might use it to block collective action. Its insertion can only be interpreted as a declaration that the United Nations should not and could not be drawn into any attempt to implement the principle of collective security in opposition to a great power.[9]

We need not rely solely upon logical analysis of the provisions of the Charter for evidence that the original United Nations scheme involved a repudiation of the ambition to construct a collective security system which would be operative in the type of case most critically relevant to the issue of global war or peace. The records of the San Francisco Conference show that the participants were thoroughly aware of the fact that, in adopting the veto provision, they were renouncing that ambition. The United States declared that the veto rule "meant that if a major power became the aggressor the Council had no power to prevent war."[10] An Indian spokesman warned against the delusion "that the proposed Organization could prevent wars between the great nations or even between small nations, if the great powers were divided in their sympathies."[11] The general understanding of the import of the veto rule was expressed by a delegate from New Zealand, who said that it made collective security impossible.[12] This interpretation of the limits of the

[9] For an early and perceptive statement of this interpretation, see Wellington Koo, Jr., *Voting Procedures in International Political Organizations* (New York: Columbia, 1947), p. 117, 124, 134.

[10] UN Information Organizations and U.S. Library of Congress, *Documents of the United Nations Conference on International Organization* (New York, 1945), XI, p. 514.

[11] *Ibid., XII*, p. 307–308.

[12] *Ibid.*, p. 296.

system contemplated in the Charter was stated explicitly by Secretary of State Stettinius in the hearings on the Charter.[13]

As I have intimated, a case can be made for the proposition that the founding fathers of the United Nations engaged in some misrepresentation of their product; they did not *always* qualify their praise of the projected Organization with explicit acknowledgment of its deliberately contrived incapacity to function as a collective security agency in cases involving great-power aggression or great-power support of aggressors. Realistically, one should not have expected that they would stress this important limitation of the new Organization. We have, after all, a working understanding that statesmen are not expected or required, any more than advertisers of soap or cigarettes, to put their worst feet forward. However, the accusation that the United Nations was "oversold" by its creators and sponsors has often been made too loosely and without adequate consideration of all the evidence.[14]

The sober truth about the built-in restrictions on the capability of the United Nations as an organ of collective security was frequently and prominently stated. There is, indeed, ample evidence that this limitation was widely understood within the interested United States public. The National League of Women Voters was only one of many groups which revealed this understanding in public statements soon after the San Francisco Conference; in a memorandum inserted in the record of the hearings on the Charter, this organization stated the view that:

If a great power becomes an aggressor, the United Nations Organization will not be able to act, and the situation will have to be handled outside the Organization. This is because we are still in the experimental stage of collective security, and world opinion has not yet developed to the point where nations are willing to delegate sufficient authority to an international organization to make it capable of coercing a great power.[15]

The Senate Committee on Foreign Relations proved itself both cognizant of and eager to encourage public understanding of the inherent limitations of the United Nations when it took care to point out, in its report on the Charter, that:

neither this Charter nor any other document or formula that might be devised can prevent war, and the committee would be performing a disservice to the public if its action with respect to the Charter should indicate any such opinion on its part.

The committee held that the creation of the new Organization "will at best be a beginning toward the creation of those conditions of stability throughout the world which will foster peace and security." [16]

The evidence leads me to the conclusion that the formulators of the United Nations Charter deliberately refrained from attempting to create an organization which would under-

[13] *The Charter of the United Nations,* Hearings Before the Committee on Foreign Relations, U.S. Senate, 79th Congress, 1st Session (Washington, 1945), p. 215.

[14] See Robert E. Riggs, "Overselling the UN Charter—Fact and Myth," *International Organization,* Spring 1960 (Vol. 14, No. 2), p. 277–290.

[15] *The Charter of the United Nations,* Hearings . . . , p. 422. For other expressions of this viewpoint, see p. 396, 416, 531, 585, 608, 654, 661, 707.

[16] Report of the Senate Committee on Foreign Relations on the United Nations Charter, July 16, 1945, reproduced in *Review of the United Nations Charter: A Collection of Documents,* Senate Document No. 87, 83d Congress, 2d Session (Washington, 1954), p. 68.

take to control the use of force by great powers or states supported by them, through the operation of a collective security system. They acted on the assumption that such a venture could not succeed, and ought not to be attempted. In this fundamentally important sense, the establishment of the United Nations represented the repudiation of the idea of collective security, not an unsuccessful effort to institutionalize its application.

What then was the nature of the scheme for management of power in international relations which the Charter set forth? The answer can be found only if we emancipate ourselves from the rigidity of the categories of balance of power, collective security, and world government.

The influence of the collective security orientation is evident in many of the provisions of the Charter. Aggression is prohibited, though left undefined; in principle, states are deprived of the legal right to use force against each other at their own discretion, in pursuit of their unilaterally defined interests and purposes. The legitimacy of resort to international violence is made subject to the determination of an international body; an effort is made even to hold states accountable to an international body in their invocation and exercise of the right of defensive action. Moreover, the principle is asserted that any illegitimate use of force in international relations is properly a matter of concern to all Members of the United Nations. The Security Council is expected to be equipped, through agreements to be concluded with Member States, with military forces constantly ready for action at its decision; it bears the responsibility for taking action to uphold peace and security and has a general authority to command the assistance of all member states—except that their obligation to provide military units is limited to the commitments which may be stated in their agreements with the Security Council.[17]

In its restriction of the right of states to resort to force, its espousal of the principle of collective action to repress illegal violence, and its provision for an organ to preside over the arrangements pertaining to the use of force, the UN scheme exhibits some of the essential characteristics of a collective security system. It should be noted that it is incomplete, in that the acceptance by states of an operative obligation to put force at the disposal of the Security Council—and, consequently, the equipping of the Council to perform its enforcement role—is postponed; on this score, the Charter registers merely an agreement to agree. Nevertheless, the scheme clearly reflects the intention to create an international enforcement mechanism capable of functioning in cases which do not involve a conflict of interest and will among the great powers. It might be described as a design for a collective security system applicable only to situations of relatively minor importance as far as maintenance of the general peace is concerned. The framers of the Charter contemplated a system in which the great powers would bear the major responsibility for providing United Nations enforcement potential, with supplementary contributions by lesser states, for the purpose of dealing with aggressors acting without the support or sympathy of any of the major powers. The great powers, it should be recalled, persistently spoke at San Francisco of the "unanimity rule," not the "veto rule," thereby emphasizing the positive hope that the Security Council would be able to act decisively against aggression insofar as its permanent members could achieve unanimity in supporting such action. There was no middle ground in this arrangement. Either an act of

[17] This summary of the scheme is based upon Articles 2, 24–25, and 39–51 of the Charter.

aggression would be committed by a minor state with all the major powers ranged against it, in which case collective suppression of the misdeed would be a relatively simple matter, or it would be committed by a major power or its protégé, in which case the United Nations would be debarred from attempting collective suppression. Although the applicability of the United Nations enforcement scheme to the control of the defeated Axis powers of World War II was excluded, it was provided that this limitation might be removed at the request of the victorious allies.[18]

The key prescription of the Charter for dealing with the potential crises of greatest international importance—those involving antagonism among the great powers or aggressive action undertaken or sponsored by one or more of the great powers—is to be found in Article 51, with its recognition of "the inherent right of individual or collective self-defense" in response to armed attack. This provision may be interpreted as a declaration that it is incumbent upon states to take the necessary measures, outside the structure of the United Nations, for dealing with the most crucial threats to peace and security which might arise. The framers of the Charter were saying, in effect, that they saw no possibility of implementing collective security safely and effectively against major powers, and that some device other than collective security would have to be improvised if a major power should go on the warpath. They did not, as has often been suggested, assume that no such problem would arise; in this respect, they were hopeful but not smugly confident. Rather, they asserted the conviction that it was impossible to construct a collective security system adequate to deal with such a problem, if it should arise. The advice implicit in Article 51 is that states should es-

[18] See Articles 53 and 107 of the Charter.

tablish alliances—combinations for collective self-defense—for dealing with the actuality or threat of attack by powers exempted by the veto rule from the impact of the projected United Nations enforcement mechanism.

In this vitally important respect, the Charter contemplates what is in essence a balance of power system. This was no doubt an unhappy choice for the founding fathers. Their ideological bias clearly ran not toward the balance of power but toward collective security. Their sense of realism, however, impelled them to acknowledge that they could see no way to devise a workable alternative to the balance of power system for dealing with aggressive threats posed directly or indirectly by great powers. It should be noted that the balance of power system, involving the freedom and responsibility of states to look to their own position within the international configuration of power, does not have to be adopted; it exists, until and unless an alternative arrangement for managing the power relationships of states is put into effect. Failing even to formulate—much less to put into effect—a more centralized scheme for handling conflicts in which major powers might be competitively engaged, the creators of the United Nations left states to "do what comes naturally" in such situations: that is, to develop the power and policy, individually and in alignment with others, for coping with security threats presented by dangerously powerful antagonists.

The original scheme of the United Nations for the management of power on the international scene may thus be described as one which left the balance of power system intact for cases of major importance to global peace and order, and provided for a collective security system to be applicable in cases of relatively minor significance. The Charter endorsed the *ideal* of collective security in unqualified terms, but envisaged its application in severely limited terms. It limited the legal right of states, great or small, to engage in the unfettered maneuvering which has been traditionally associated with the operation of a balance of power system, and reflected the hope that the political processes of the United Nations would inhibit the tendency of states to abuse their strength under the pretext of protecting their relative power positions. In the final analysis, however, the Charter acknowledged that the new Organization could not relieve states of the necessity of attempting on their own to match power with power, as the means of attaining security within the context of great-power rivalry. The scheme of the Charter was a curious amalgam of collective security, dominant in ideological terms, and balance of power, dominant in terms of practical application. The concept of world government, insofar as it figured at all in the consideration of the San Francisco Conference, was viewed as a distant ideal.

III

The history of the actual operation of the United Nations in the realm of power politics is largely a story of vacillation concerning the degree to which the implementation of collective security should be attempted, and of efforts to find other means by which international organization can be used to modify the working of a balance of power system. The reluctance with which the framers of the Charter viewed the continued dependence of the world, by default, upon the balance of power system has been shared by many of the statesmen who have shaped the subsequent development of the United Nations.

One of the first tasks which confronted the new Organization was that of attempting to create the enforcement mechanism envisaged in Chapter VII—and particular in Articles 43 and 45—of the Charter. This project, essential to the fulfillment of the promise that the Security Council would function as an agent of collective security in cases not involving discord among the major powers, was fundamentally dependent upon the capacity of the Big Five to agree concerning their contributions to the military force the Council would have at its disposal. Those powers undertook, within the Military Staff Committee and the Security Council, to reach agreement; they failed in 1947, and, despite occasional expressions of interest in trying again, they have not seriously reopened the issue since that time.

These abortive negotiations were marked by a curious refusal on the part of the United States to recognize and adhere to the principle that the United Nations enforcement system was to be operative only against minor aggressors which neither possessed the veto power nor enjoyed the protection of a great power's capacity to block Security Council action. This deviation from the understanding reached at San Francisco was implicitly expressed in a United States position which insisted that a relatively large force should be assigned to the Security Council; the other powers, estimating the requirements of the Council more modestly,[19] evidently based their proposals on the assumption that the force was intended to be used, and therefore needed to be strong enough for effective use, only in coercing states of minor military importance. The United States' deviation was stated explicitly in the argument that the Council should be equipped "to bring to bear, against any breach of the peace anywhere in the world, balanced striking forces drawn from the most powerful and best equipped

[19] For the provisional estimates submitted by the five permanent members of the Security Council, see *Yearbook of the United Nations, 1947–1948*, p. 495.

forces that could be provided by the Members," so that the organization could "enforce peace in all parts of the world."[20] It appeared that the United States had either forgotten or repudiated the consensus, registered in the veto provision of the Charter, that the United Nations should not be constitutionally capable of functioning as an instrument of collective security against, or in opposition to the will of, any of the major powers.

If the United States confused the negotiations with the claim that the task was to create a universally applicable system of collective security, the real lesson of the negotiations was that neither the Soviet Union nor the West seemed sufficiently trustful of the other to contemplate joint action under United Nations auspices for implementing collective security even in a limited range of cases. The various items of disagreement which plagued the discussions all pointed to the same conclusion: each of the major contestants, the Soviet Union and the United States, feared that the other might attempt to dominate any collective action in which it participated, using the pretext of serving the United Nations as a means of exploiting troubled situations to its own ends.[21] One or the other of the great powers may, of course, have been actuated by ulterior motives. What appears from the record of negotiations, however, is that this mutual suspicion operated to force the discarding of the scheme for establishing a limited collective security system under the United Nations. Collective security operations pitting great powers against each other had been ex-

cluded in the original design; collective security operations involving collaboration among the great powers were now seen to be politically infeasible.

This initial decline to zero of the modest expectations of collective security entertained by the drafters of the Charter was sharply reversed by the events of 1950. The United Nations response to North Korean aggression against South Korea was attributable to a unique complex of circumstances, and it was not by any means a "pure" example of collective security in action. Nevertheless, the early phase of the collective military action in Korea under the banner of the United Nations produced among its participants and supporters an exhilarating sense of involvement in an unprecedented effort to give effect to the principle of collective security. Member States found themselves joined together to suppress an act of aggression which could plausibly be regarded as one sponsored or supported by two major powers, the Soviet Union and Communist China, and they seemed likely to carry off this bold enterprise both successfully and safely. They had, by improvising a reasonable facsimile of collective security action to meet North Korean aggression, cast aside what now seemed the excessive timidity of the framers of the Charter, who had believed it would be neither possible nor prudent for the United Nations to take action in such cases.

The sudden enthusiasm for collective security engendered by the Korean action was translated into support for the Uniting for Peace Resolution, a United States initiative adopted by the General Assembly in the fall of 1950.[22] This scheme involved an assertion by the General Assembly of competence to take over the consideration of threatening situations from a veto-bound Security Council, designate the aggressor,

[20] Security Council *Official Records*, 138th Meeting, June 4, 1947, p. 954–955, 956.

[21] See my analysis of this point in "The United Nations and the Use of Force," *International Conciliation*, March 1961. Cf. William Reitzel, Morton A. Kaplan, and Constance G. Coblenz, *United States Foreign Policy, 1945–1955* (Washington: Brookings Institution, 1956), p. 239–240.

[22] General Assembly Resolution 377 (V), November 3, 1950.

and recommend collective action by Member States. Among other things, it provided for the establishment of a Collective Measures Committee to study the problems of giving effect to the principle of collective security, and called upon states to designate special military units for possible participation in future United Nations enforcement actions. Concretely, this was a plan for enabling the United Nations to react in future situations as it had in Korea. While the Uniting for Peace plan fell short of a full-fledged collective security system, notably in its failure to provide for obligatory participation by states in sanctions, it was clearly put forward as a device for transforming the United Nations into an agency of universal collective security.[23]

Thus, the United Nations moved in 1950 from the expectation that no collective security action would be forthcoming in any case, to the hypothetical possibility of collective security action in every case of aggression. In adopting the Uniting for Peace plan, Members of the United Nations purported to express the determination to develop an international enforcement system applicable even to violations of the peace in which great powers might be directly or indirectly involved. In scope, if not in legal depth, this plan for collective security was far more ambitious than that stated in the Charter.

This was the high-water mark of enthusiasm for turning the United Nations into a collective security system. The flood receded rather quickly and, apparently, irreversibly. The later stages of the Korean conflict engendered second thoughts about the desirability of repeating that experiment. By the time Members of the United Nations had managed to disengage themselves from active fighting in Korea, they had de-veloped a renewed appreciation for the prudence of the founding fathers who had decreed that the Organization ought not to attempt collective action in the face of great-power opposition. Uncommitted states came gradually to recognize that they had a stake in preventing the United Nations from being invoked as an instrumentality of one side against the other in "cold war" conflicts; in these terms, the veto was not so much a special privilege of the great powers as a protection for the minor powers against being pulled, through their membership in the United Nations, into the maelstrom of great-power struggle. The United States, which had conceived the Uniting for Peace plan as a device primarily for legitimizing and mobilizing support for Western action in resistance to Soviet expansionism, gradually lost confidence that the General Assembly could be counted on to put the plan to that use, and began to doubt both the wisdom and the utility of the venture in enhancing the quasi-collective security possibilities of the United Nations which it had sponsored.

The earliest indication of the subsiding of collective security sentiment was provided by the hesitation of Member States to respond positively to the suggestion they had addressed to themselves in the Uniting for Peace Resolution, i.e., that they set aside definite military units for possible use in United Nations enforcement actions. This recommendation produced little more than vague affirmations that armed forces might under certain circumstances be supplied; in effect, this project for developing a military arm of the United Nations was soon relegated to the dead-letter office along with Article 43, which it had been intended to replace.

The Hungarian and Suez crises of 1956 produced further evidence that the aspirations for giving effect to collective security, so fervently expressed

[23] See General Assembly Official Records, Fifth Session, 295th Plenary Meeting, October 24, 1950, p. 246, and 299th Plenary Meeting, November 1, 1950, p. 291–292.

in 1950, had been dispelled by sober second thoughts. In these critical cases, both involving coercive action by great powers, the Uniting for Peace plan was invoked and was operative to the point of bringing about condemnation by the General Assembly of the Soviet Union in the one case, and of the United Kingdom, France, and Israel in the other. The latter three states, involved in attacks upon Egypt, were induced to withdraw and thus to spare the Assembly the necessity of deciding whether it should attempt to organize collective compulsion. The Soviet Union, having ruthlessly suppressed the Hungarian Revolution, stood in defiance of an Assembly which gave no evidence of even considering the possibility of attempting to impose military sanctions.

The position of the United States in these two cases reveals the extent to which the urge for collective security had declined since the adoption of the Uniting for Peace Resolution. In the Suez case, the United States exhibited a measure of devotion to the collective security ideology in supporting the condemnation of friends and allies for their attack upon a state whose behavior the United States patently disapproved. United States leaders, however, clearly had no stomach for the possibility of being called upon to participate in coercive measures to enforce the Assembly's demands against the United Kingdom, France, and Israel. Most notably, they were appalled at the thought that the Soviet Union might use "participation in collective security action under the United Nations" as a device for establishing a foothold in the Middle East. When President Eisenhower recoiled at the "unthinkable" suggestion of the Soviet Union that the two giant powers join to enforce the will of the United Nations in that region,[24] he was giving new

[24] *New York Times,* November 6, 1956, p. 10.

expression to the mistrust which had been apparent in the negotiations, in 1947, for creating a United Nations force to be placed at the disposal of the Security Council. The notion of a collective security action which would bring Soviet Union forces into the Middle East was profoundly unattractive to the United States.

In the Hungarian case, the United States demonstrated that it was equally unattracted by the idea of leading or participating in collective action against the Soviet Union, lest such a move precipitate a general war. In refraining from the initiation of a collective campaign to oust Soviet Union forces from Hungary, the Assembly was supporting, not frustrating, the policy of the United States. This was the sort of case for which the Uniting for Peace plan had ostensibly been designed; the fact that collective measures against the Soviet Union were not seriously contemplated was evidence that the ambition to overcome the veto barrier to the functioning of the United Nations as an agency of collective security had been abandoned.

We have seen that the history of the United Nations has been marked by the fluctuation of sentiment regarding the desirability and feasibility of making the Organization a mechanism to implement the principle of collective security. It seems likely that the ephemeral enthusiasm for collective security engendered by the early phase of the Korean experience and registered in the Uniting for Peace Resolution will prove the last flurry for some time to come. The creators of the United Nations envisaged an extremely modest version of collective security; in the present situation, there is no evidence that Members of the Organization entertain either the expectation or the intention of operating a collective security system, limited or universal in its impact, within the institutional framework of the United Nations. Force may be used for limited purposes under United Nations auspices in particular cases, as in the Congo, for instance. This, however, does not imply that there is a meaningful possibility of organizing a dependable system of collective military sanctions to repel international aggression. The repudiation of the urge to establish collective security as an operative system for the management of power in international relations appears, for the foreseeable future, definitive.

The Charter's implicit recognition of the necessity for a residual balance of power system to cope with great-power antagonisms has had substantially greater effect than its design for a collective security system to deal with situations of less critical importance. Once it became clear that a struggle between the Soviet Union and the West was to be the dominant motif of postwar international relations, the process of alliance-building and of competitive armament began. On the Western side, the formulation of the North Atlantic Treaty represented an acknowledgement that no alternative to the methods characteristic of the balance of power system could be envisaged for meeting the threat of Soviet Union aggressiveness. It is notable that the United States responded to the lesson of communist aggression in Korea, not simply by sponsoring the Uniting for Peace plan, but also by taking the lead in strengthening the Western alliance, both militarily and institutionally, giving it the form of the North Atlantic Treaty Organization. In the one case, the United States endorsed the ideology of collective security; in the other, it expressed the intent to seek security within the context of a balance of power system. There can be little doubt that the latter was the more significant move, the more reliable indicator of the emphasis which was to characterize United States foreign policy. While the doctrine of collective security has been alternately played up and played down

in the United Nations, statesmen have treated the problem of maneuvering successfully within the framework of a balance of power system as the serious business of contemporary diplomacy. This represents the confirmation, not the invalidation, of the assumption expressed in the Charter; if one considers the combination of Articles 27 and 51 of the Charter, one finds the statesmen of San Francisco implying that security problems stemming from discord among the giants call for the application of the concept of balance of power, not the concept of collective security. Great-power antagonisms have dominated the international scene, and they have evoked the type of response which the Charter indicated would be necessary.

In the final analysis, then, the effort to control the use of force in international relations since World War II has been expressed in the form of a balance of power system. What has emerged is a balance system modified by a number of factors including, most significantly for purposes of this analysis, the existence of a general international organization. It would be too much to say that the United Nations "presides over" the operation of the balance of power system, but its functioning does have considerable relevance to the working of that system.

The real question for our time is not whether the United Nations is likely to develop a collective security system —or, more remotely, to institute a scheme for the management of power which would deserve the name of world government—to replace the balance of power system. The real question relates to the manner in which, and the degree to which, the United Nations can and will modify the operation of the balance system and contribute to its success as a device for preventing war. In facilitating diplomatic confrontation, fostering serious and meaningful negotiation, and providing assistance in the pacific settlement of disputes, the Organization plays a role which may be useful in mitigating the dangers of failure. In putting moral and political pressure upon states to conform to the principles of international conduct which the Charter prescribes, the United Nations may help to limit the abusive aspects of state behavior which balance of power operations may otherwise entail. In carrying out its wide-ranging activities within the economic and social sectors, the Organization may contribute to a long-term transformation of the global situation which will create new possibilities for the effective management of the power problem.

Finally, it should be noted that a role for the United Nations, more immediately and directly related to the issue of military violence, has been for some time in the process of development. In a number of instances, the Organization has secured and provided military personnel for supervising truce arrangements, patrolling armistice lines, observing developments in zones of particular instability, and otherwise contributing to the maintenance of precariously peaceful relationships. Against this background, an act of creative political ingenuity occurred in 1956, when the Organization was given the mission of mobilizing a United Nations Emergency Force, composed exclusively of military elements from states other than great powers, to function as a stabilizer of the dangerously tense situation in the Middle East. When a somewhat analogous, albeit infinitely more complex, situation arose in the Congo in 1960, the machinery of the United Nations was again used to organize and carry out a military operation. There were basic differences in the tasks required of United Nations forces in these two situations, and it may be that those differences will produce different outcomes for the two ventures; at this

writing, there seems grave danger that the Congo operation will fail as clearly as the Middle Eastern operation succeeded.

What is important for this analysis, however, is the element of similarity in the two cases. In both instances, the United Nations was used as a device for bringing into a troubled situation military contingents contributed voluntarily by smaller states and placed under the direction of the Secretary-General, for the purpose of preventing the eruption of disorders that might result in the competitive intervention of the rival great-power blocs. This is a far cry from the original notion of a United Nations enforcement system which would depend upon the unanimous participation of the great powers; it expresses the notion of a United Nations stabilization system dependent upon the unanimous abstention of the great powers.[25] Such a system cannot be forced upon unwilling great powers. It can function successfully only with their acquiescence, derived from the recognition that they have a stake in the avoidance of conflicts that might precipitate war. Intervention by the United Nations in the Middle East and in the Congo represents the experimental development of a significant role for the Organization in the balance of power system, that of assisting in its orderly operation by undertaking to insulate particular trouble-spots from the impact of the rivalry which dominates the relationships of the major powers. This experimentation, whatever its outcome, is a hopeful sign, for it points to the general recognition of a basic truth: *i.e.,* that the potential contribution of the United Nations in our time to the management of international power relationships lies not in implementing collective security or

[25] Cf. Lincoln P. Bloomfield, *The United Nations and U.S. Foreign Policy* (Boston: Little, Brown, 1960), p. 44–45, 67.

instituting world government, but in helping to improve and stabilize the working of the balance of power system which is, for better or for worse, the operative mechanism of contemporary international politics.

16. United Nations Peacekeeping Activities: A Case Study in Organizational Task Expansion*

JACK CITRIN

I. Introduction: A Framework for the Analysis of Organizational Task Expansion

SINCE 1956, the United Nations has involved itself in a number of peacekeeping operations which have been characterized by the participation of military forces under UN command. This study presents a systematic analysis of four such peacekeeping operations—the Lebanon crisis of 1958, the lengthy United Nations military presence in the Congo beginning in July 1960, the UN's role in the transfer of West Irian from Dutch to Indonesian control, and the still continuing activity of the United Nations Force in Cyprus (UNFICYP). The analysis, however, is undertaken from a distinct perspective, for its primary assumption is that the role of the United Nations in these four cases should be considered an example of organizational task expansion.[1] By this I mean simply that these peacekeeping operations constitute a significant innovation in the activities of the United Nations with respect to the maintenance of international peace and security, an innovation in the context of both the Organization's formal objectives as stated in the Charter and the empirical realities of UN practices in this sphere before 1956.

It is beyond dispute that the Charter, in its Preamble, Purposes, and Principles, states unequivocally that the fundamental aim of the United Nations is to seek and maintain international peace and security. . . .

Furthermore, the Charter included specific provisions for undertaking military operations in the Organization's name and under its command. These procedures, elaborated in Chapter VII of the Charter, can be briefly summarized. The Security Council, having determined the existence of any threat to the peace, breach of the peace, or act of aggression, decides what measures should be taken to reestablish conditions of international peace. These decisions are binding on the member states and can, in the last resort, result in military operations against the aggressor state in the name of the United Nations. Chapter VII also called on all member states to make available to the Security Council, on its call, armed forces and other military facilities deemed necessary for the maintenance of international peace and security.

* Monograph Series in World Affairs, Vol. III, Monograph No. 1, 1965–66, The University of Denver. Reprinted by permission.
[1] The term organizational task expansion has been formulated and developed by E. Haas, Beyond the Nation-State, Palo Alto, 1964, Part I. I use it here in the same way. . . .

Member states were called on to hold immediately available national air force contingents, and a Military Staff Committee was to be established in order to furnish the Security Council with expert advice and assistance on all questions concerning its military requirements.

. . . The UN Charter, while it does elaborate a scheme for universal collective security,[2] also limits the intervention of the Organization to matters which are not essentially within the domestic jurisdiction of the member states. (Article 2, para. 7) While the principle of domestic jurisdiction was not to prejudice the application of enforcement measures under Chapter VII, it was clearly not intended that the UN involve itself in such internal security problems as riots and political demonstrations. And, although the relationship of the UN to civil wars was more ambiguous, it appears probable that this form of dispute was also not intended to be subject to military intervention under UN auspices.[3]

The special character of the examples of UN peacekeeping operations with which this paper is concerned now become easier to discern. In the Lebanon, Congo, and Cyprus crises, the United Nations intervened in what were at least in part civil war situations. In each of the four cases, although to varying degrees, the UN was responsible for the maintenance of law and order, undertaking, therefore, to perform the fundamental duty of any civil government. To some ex-

tent, in short, the United Nations forces in question intruded into areas of domestic jurisdiction. Yet in no case were the provisions of Chapter VII invoked. On the other hand, in every instance the UN presence was sanctioned by the host government of the countries in question. For these reasons, then, if for no others, it was assumed that we are dealing with an instance of organizational task expansion.

. . . It is appropriate to indicate what general questions will be put to the data. (1) One purpose of the study is the comparative description of the four cases with which we are concerned. In what sense did the four crises share common characteristics? To what extent were the disputes internal in character? To what extent was the UN's response to each crisis affected by its experience in the previous ones? Was the UN able to formulate and observe a set of norms relevant to military operations of this kind? What can we expect of future UN activity of this kind and what policies might the UN adopt to facilitate and strengthen its peacekeeping activities? (2) What were the conditions both within and without the United Nations Organization that permitted organizational task expansion in the sphere of military security to take place? (3) What is the relationship between this particular example of organizational task expansion and the larger process of international integration? Can we legitimately argue, from this example, that integration and task expansion are positively correlated?[4]

CONCEPTS, THEORY, AND HYPOTHESES

This paper is deliberately modeled on the conceptual framework Haas

---

[2] See I. Claude's discussion of the concept of collective security in his *Power and International Relations,* New York, 1962. Also E. Haas, "Some Operational Concepts of Collective Security," in *American Political Science Review,* vol. 49, 1955, pp. 40–43, and K. Thompson, "Collective Security Reexamined," *American Political Science Review,* vol. 47, 1953.

[3] I. Claude, "The United Nations and the Use of Force," *International Conciliation,* no. 532, 1961, p. 326.

[4] This question is pursued by Haas, *op. cit.;* see also his *The Uniting of Europe,* Palo Alto, 1958, and "International Integration," *International Organization,* vol. 15, 1961.

proposed for the study of international integration.[5] Haas focuses on the role played by international organizations in the process of international integration. The term integration refers to the process by which the international system moves from a condition of society, where conflicts between the units of the system are frequently settled by the resort to force, to a condition of community, which is characterized by the strong likelihood of "peaceful change in a setting of contending groups with mutually antagonistic claims." [6] The communal condition, therefore, closely resembles what Deutsch labels a security community.[7] Integration (in the contemporary context) involves the transfer of loyalties from national and subnational institutions to agencies supranational in character.

In what way do international organizations contribute to this process? It is, I believe, the fundamental hypothesis of Haas' model that organizational task expansion is positively correlated with international integration; that is, when international organizations, through the successful performance of certain organizational tasks, take on new responsibilities and widen their mandate, progress toward the terminal condition of political community is made. It should be stressed, however, that this relationship between task expansion and integration is formulated in hypothetical form; whether or not this proposition is valid, therefore, is a matter for empirical verification.

. . . At any given moment in time, international organizations are confronted with conflicting demands of its members, be they national governments or voluntary associations. These demands express the perceived interests of the constituent units of the organization. Typically, representatives of the organization's members negotiate their demands and attempt to formulate a common set of organizational goals. When a successful compromise is effected, the separate purposes of the various actors are transformed into an organizational task, formally expressed in a program of activities. The demands of its members represent inputs for the organization, and the specific administrative decisions which constitute task performance are regarded as outputs. These outputs, to continue, impinge on the organization's environment—the international system and the interests of its members; if the environment is transformed, we can speak of feedback from the organization's activities. There can, in turn, be both negative and positive feedback processes.

Both the environment and the organization itself can be transformed by a given set of outputs. The meaning of feedback, in this context, is that, faced with unanticipated consequences of the organization's actions, its members reformulate their purposes with respect to the organizational goals. These new demands, the result of social learning from the unanticipated consequences of task performance in previous time periods, are called "functions" if they result in new organizational tasks, "dysfunctions" if they result in a diminishing of organizational activities and a weakening of its structures.[8] The results of any organizational activity, therefore, are functional or dysfunctional with respect to organizational task expansion. If the former, they contribute to the strengthening of the structures of the international organization involved, to the broadening of its mandate and respon-

---

[5] This is outlined in detail in *Beyond the Nation-State*, pp. 1–136. Much of what follows is a summary of Haas' discussion.

[6] Haas, "International Integration," p. 366.

[7] K. Deutsch, *Political Community at the International Level*, Garden City, 1954, p. 33.

[8] This summary is taken from remarks made in seminar Jan. 7, 1965.

sibilities, and to the long-term process of international integration.

The concepts of organizational purposes, tasks, and activities are central to Haas' model, but it is sometimes difficult to distinguish them, both analytically and concretely, from each other. Perhaps the principal cause of this difficulty is that the words purpose and task, as commonly used, have several meanings. It is important, I believe, that these terms be defined in such a way that they are mutually exclusive; and to this end I now propose certain modifications to their definitions. . . .

The *purposes* of an international organization, in this context, are its formal objectives, as enumerated in its written constitution and official declarations. By this criterion, international organizations can, and most do, have several purposes; one of the United Nation's purposes is the maintenance of international peace and security. Organizational *tasks,* by contrast, are instrumental in character: they are action-oriented programs related to specific purposes. However, given this definition, it becomes necessary to distinguish a specific *instance of task performance* from the organizational task more generally conceived, for unless this is done one can quite easily make the mistake of treating every concrete organizational program as a *task* and every novel element in a program as evidence of task expansion. And, in order to develop a *theory* of organizational growth, we must transcend the level of historical accounts of unique cases to elaborate concepts which group cases that are comparable in terms of certain recurring relationships. Hence, to repeat, it is necessary to differentiate between the organizational task as general category, which I will call an organizational *task-type,* and specific instances of task performance.

Given this terminology, United Nations intervention in Korea is considered an instance of task performance; so is the sending of a team of

UN observers to Laos. These two cases, however, illustrate distinct *task-types,* the former being an example of the "permissive inforcement" variant of collective security,[9] the latter of preventive diplomacy. Although difficulties in defining its content and antecedents remain, what is meant by a task-type now becomes clearer. One approach to the definition of a set of organizational task-types related to a given *purpose* is to extract from the organization's constitution and resolutions the procedures specified as the instrumentalities for attaining that general objective. In this sense, Chapter VII of the Charter and the Uniting for Peace Resolution define a program of activities to be undertaken in response to a certain set of environmental stimuli and collective security becomes a task-type.

While perhaps a useful beginning to the enumeration of task-types, this approach is by itself insufficient, for it is both empirically true and a fundamental assumption of the model that well-designed formulae fall into disuse and new modes of organizational behavior develop to deal with both originally specified and previously unanticipated sets of situations. A more fruitful method of isolating task-types, therefore, is the detailed comparison of organizational activities in a series of broadly comparable situations. The history of an organization becomes, in this way, of fundamental relevance, for in this formulation task-types are empirically defined by the relative consistency over time of an organization's behavioral responses to comparable situations. This approach leaves open the question of whether task-types are institutionalized in formal resolutions and constitutional amendments.

Any given *instance of task performance,* to continue, consists of a set of specific *actions* or *activities* undertaken by the organization. In the context of

[9] Haas, "Some Operational Concepts of Collective Security," pp. 47 ff.

this study, the dismantling of Greek or Turkish Cypriot fortifications by UN personnel is considered one organizational activity, the expulsion of foreign mercenaries from the Congo another. Careful comparisons of the organization's activities in separate instances of task performance tell the observer whether organizational task expansion has taken place. This, of course, is the critical operation.

The introduction of the task-type as an additional concept makes it necessary to define two kinds of task expansion. One sort of expansion refers to the emergence of a new task-type, that is, of a novel system of responses to situations previously dealt with in another way. In the context of this study, as I have noted, the four instances of United Nations peacekeeping activities are considered instances of the same organizational task-type, which can be called preventive diplomacy. With reference to previous modes of UN behavior related to the maintenance of international peace, preventive diplomacy is considered a new task-type and its emergence as an example of one kind of task expansion, which might be called qualitative.

Within each task-type, however, there can also be task expansion. This takes place when the organization's activities in a given instance of task performance manifest or result in an increased scope for the organization's authoritative decisions, while the general character of the activities and the situation in question remains basically unchanged. This evaluation is always made, obviously, by reference to the organization's activities in previous instances of task performance. In the present context, two criteria for this kind of task expansion are suggested. These are: first, the lessening of restriction on the use of force by UN troops, and second, the increasing participation of the United Nations in the fulfillment of the administrative responsibilities of the government of the

territory in which the UN Force is deployed. Activities that reflect these changes can be initiated without a *formal* broadening of the Force's mandate by the Security Council or General Assembly, but this increased scope of organizational activity must be manifested in future instances of task performance to confirm the hypothesis that task expansion has taken place.

. . . Finally, a word about the relationship of an organization's *purposes* to its *tasks*. The former are both more general and more stable, but it is plausible that an instance of task expansion legitimized by time's passage may result in the translation of a task into a purpose.

The model I have outlined tends to focus on the determinants of organizational task expansion which stem primarily from within the organization itself, but it is also necessary to indicate the kinds of extra-organizational forces that affect the process. Whether or not organizational task expansion takes place, as well as the particular nature of the new tasks or activities, depends in part on the nature of the international system and environment. The international system is defined by the pattern of recurring relationships between its component units, the international actors, the international environment by the level of technology, culture, and modal values of a given historical epoch.[10] Together these factors set limits to the scope and direction of organizational task expansion. In studying UN peacekeeping operations, the prevalence of a bipolar distribution of ultimate military power, the existence of nuclear weapons, the ideological conflict between the Soviet and Western blocs, and the overweening

[10] This definition of the system and its environment is that of S. Hoffman, "International Systems and International Law," *World Politics*, vol. 14, 1961–62, especially pp. 205–210. I will use the term system in this concrete sense, referring in particular to the contemporary character of the world order.

priority given the value of decolonization by the uncommitted states of Africa and Asia are all considered important determinants of the organization's actions.

There are, too, as has been indicated, influences on organizational growth emanating at the level of the national actors. Thus, the interests of its member states and the way these interests are reflected in the distribution of support for alternative UN programs will affect the course of task expansion. Finally, to make a point emphasized by Haas, whether or not organizational task expansion takes place, or whether an organization's activities can be made to contribute positively to the strengthening of loyalty toward the supranational organization and to international integration, also depends on the quality of organizational leadership. . . .

Finally, one further proposition stated by Haas will be tested: that "functionally specific international programs, if organizationally separated from diffuse orientations, maximize . . . integration." [11] With reference to peacekeeping operations this hypothesis means that the more limited in scope and purely military in character the UN's activities, the more likely the contribution of the instance of task performance to task expansion in this sphere. For example, a program of activities which included UN observers patrolling national borders is considered functionally specific in relation to one which, in addition, provides for UN protection of agricultural workers and civilian traffic, or UN officials acting as customs agents to prevent arms smuggling. It must be noted, however, that the close connection between military power and political control means that the military operations of the United Nations can rarely, if ever, fail to evoke the "diffuse orientations" of member states. . . .

[11] *Beyond the Nation-State*, p. 47.

The results of such a study are often only tentative, for there is probably no definitive answer as to what constitutes sufficient evidence of this nature to confirm the propositions being tested. Whether or not the analysis is convincing depends in large part on the judiciousness, skill, and honesty of the observer. Even when these characteristics are maximized, "proof" of the validity of a proposition tested in this way will be less certain than in research in which experimental conditions can be approximated and the statistical manipulation of measurable variables is possible.

For this reason and in order to systematize the descriptive task, the four cases examined will be discussed in terms of a structured classification scheme. As it is commonplace to assert, the description of complex historical phenomena is invariably selective. It is, therefore, appropriate to specify the dimensions on which the comparisons will be made and necessary to develop a set of categories related to the theoretical formulation of the preceding section. Since a closed system of nar-

TABLE I

A TENTATIVE CHECKLIST FOR THE
ANALYSIS OF UN PEACEKEEPING FORCES

A. Nature of the Crisis.
  1. Characteristics of the domestic conflict: foreign policy, treatment of minorities, constitutional crisis, etc.
  2. International implications of internal disputes: relationship to cold war issues, relationship to problems of decolonization.
B. UN Intervention—the Initial Stage.
  1. Previous involvement of UN in affairs of host country.
  2. Manner in which UN consideration of dispute undertaken.
  3. The initial UN mandate—objectives of the force.

rowly defined categories may lead to the exclusion from consideration of theoretically damaging data, the following schema should be seen primarily as a checklist whose makeup is essentially flexible. It is open to large-scale amendments based on judgments of its utility in guiding specific analyses.

THE CONTEMPORARY WORLD ORDER AND THE POSSIBILITY OF COLLECTIVE SECURITY

UN intervention in the Lebanon, Congo, West Irian, and Cyprus crises has occurred within the same, unique historical context and it is important to specify those characteristics of the contemporary world order that set the limits for military activities of this kind.

1. The fact of nuclear bipolarity dominates the contemporary international system. Ultimate military power is shared by two mutually antagonistic major blocs, each of which has the capacity to destroy the other in a full-scale war. At the same time, however, neither bloc, or major actor within each bloc,[12] is able to destroy its antagonist and emerge victorious by launching a surprise or preventive attack; both sides are sufficiently powerful to withstand the initial assault and retain the degree of nuclear capability required to destroy the hypothetical attacker.[13]

2. The reality of a "balance of terror" has led the major powers, the Soviet Union and the United States, to agree that a state of relatively peaceful coexistence is preferable to an exercise in reciprocal annihilation. In short, there has emerged a minimal consensus that nuclear war should be

[12] For a more abstract discussion of bipolarity, see M. Kaplan, *System and Process in International Relations*, New York, 1957.

[13] H. Kissinger, *The Necessity for Choice*, New York, 1961, discusses various aspects of deterrence policy. See also G. Snyder, *Deterrence or Defence*, New York, 1962.

avoided. This has meant mutual restraint in the pursuit of objectives which impinge in a significant sense on the fundamental interests of the rival bloc. There is considerable empirical evidence for this assertion.[14] Briefly, we can mention the tacit agreement to limit the scope of the Korean War, the reluctance of the United States to intervene in Hungary in the face of Soviet "aggression," the Test Ban Treaty, and, most spectacularly, the withdrawal of Soviet missiles from Cuba in October, 1962.

3. The nuclear stalemate and the resulting consensus on the necessity to avoid a major war has had the following consequences. The ideological conflict between the Soviet and Western blocs has been muted, although by no means eliminated. Tacit agreement on non-intervention in spheres of primary influence and interest has emerged. Thus, the reality of Soviet predominance in Eastern Europe was merely confirmed by the Western powers' unwillingness to tear down Mr. Khrushchev's "infamous" Berlin Wall; similarly, the *military* hegemony of the United States in Western Europe and Latin America is, I believe, recognized by the Communist bloc. Interbloc competition, therefore, is conducted in these geographical regions solely by non-military techniques.

4. Nuclear bipolarity has not, however, resulted in absolute rigidity in the pattern of international interactions. In fact, this bipolarity, combined with the existence of a substantial number of international actors which do not belong to either major bloc, does not eliminate the possibility of minor conflicts in areas which are perceived by both major powers as marginal to their fundamental interests. Furthermore, technological developments and the scope of the ideological conflict between the major blocs have resulted in

the globalization of world politics; no region is so remote as to be impervious to the intrusion of cold war issues.

5. The uncommitted nations of the "tiers monde" are today the focus of interbloc rivalry. These states, despite or perhaps because of their lack of military and economic strength, have substantial flexibility in their foreign policies, often being able to secure economic and technical assistance from both blocs. This is because both seek to limit the rival's influence in these areas.[15] The more radical of the uncommitted states more strongly favor revising the world order than do either of the major actors—newly independent African and Asian states, ex-colonies of European powers, have provided the impetus for the drive toward immediate and universal decolonization. The result of this pressure has been a consensus, in which some of the Western powers have only grudgingly acquiesced, that self-determination for all colonies and non-self-governing territories should be a major objective of all states and that it should be affected in large part through UN participation and supervision. In competition with the "anti-imperialist" Soviet Union, the United States in particular has been led to change its position on this issue.

6. Bipolarity operates only with respect to nuclear power, however, and, ironically, rigidity at this level has facilitated the development of a multipolar system of interactions on other issues. Neither the Western bloc, nor the uncommitted nations, nor, it seems, the Soviet bloc are monolithic entities; its members differ widely in their interests and policies over a whole range of issues from tariff regulations, farm commodities agreements, and attitudes toward the United Nations to defense

---

[14] See J. Hertz, *International Politics in an Atomic Age,* New York, 1958, Chs. 7 and 8.

[15] R. Aron discusses the role of the new states in *On War,* London, 1958. See also L. Martin (ed.), *Neutralism and Non-Alignment,* New York, 1962.

policy and the proper response to "national liberation movements." What is more, the pattern of bloc alignments varies from issue to issue. There is considerable overlap, particularly among the members of the same bloc, but not complete symmetry in the makeup of the opposing coalitions.

The United Nations, therefore, is, in part, an arena in which these patterns of interactions between states are reflected. Its ability to serve as an agency for the creation of a genuine international community is limited by the realities of conflicting national demands. However, the nuclear stalemate and relatively strong support from the uncommitted states has enabled the UN to undertake the peacekeeping operations with which I am concerned.

These operations must, to repeat, always be considered in the context of the prevailing pattern of recurring interactions between the units of the international system. The nature of UN intervention in postwar military crises has, therefore, varied with changes in the international system. The Charter set up a plan for universal collective security, nominally providing for the alliance of all peaceloving states against any aggressor, but Claude has convincingly argued that this principle was included in the Charter only as an ideal for the future.[16] In fact, granting the veto power to the permanent members of the Security Council meant that the United Nations was to undertake enforcement measures only when there was big power agreement. This meant that the UN military operations would be relatively minor; it was definitely not intended to be an instrument for intervention in armed conflicts between the big powers.[17]

The dissolution of the wartime concert meant that the collective security principles of the UN Charter became almost inoperative. There was certainly no concert of great powers on a viable, continuing basis, but ad hoc concerts, limited instances in which the US and USSR could agree on a course for UN participation, did arise. Examples of this are the dispatch of a UN observer team to Kashmir in 1947 and the agreement on UNEF in 1956. At any rate, one precondition of any UN military operation is an initial agreement on the part of the Soviet Union and the United States to forswear direct intervention and rely on the UN.

The UN intervention in Korea could hardly be called the result of an ad hoc concert of the two major powers; instead it should be regarded as what Haas has called an example of permissive enforcement,[18] a case in which the UN was able to circumvent great power opposition to intervention by resorting to General Assembly recommendations as the basis for military operations, in the name of the United Nations. The UN force in Korea included contingents from only sixteen nations, all pro-Western, and the entire effort might best be described as a successful attempt by the United States to legitimize national policy involving military measures in terms of global symbols.[19] Events after Korea, however, proved that even this conception of collective security is inapplicable to crises involving great powers. The United States was able to obtain General Assembly passage of a resolution condemning Soviet intervention in Hungary, but itself discouraged any moves to recommend enforcement measures.[20] In short, the essential soundness of the proposals of the

---

[16] See I. Claude, "The Management of Power in International Relations," *International Organization*, vol. 15, 1961, pp. 223–229.

[17] *Ibid*. See also Haas, "Operational Concepts of Collective Security," pp. 40–47.

[18] Haas, "Some Operational Concepts of Collective Security," p. 47.

[19] *Ibid.*, p. 48.

[20] C. Cruise O'Brien, *Two Conflicting Views of the United Nations*, Leeds, 1964, pp. 7–8.

Charter's framers was recognized; the United Nations is not to be mobilized by one major bloc to take military action against its rival.

The international peacekeeping operations to which I now turn are an example of another species of collective action. Not the product of a concert of great powers except in a minimal sense, nor an example of permissive enforcement, they are best described as instances of preventive diplomacy.[21] This concept, first formulated explicitly by Dag Hammarskjöld, refers to actions taken by the United Nations in areas of conflict outside of, or marginal to, cold war struggles, actions designed to prevent the intrusion of rival power blocs into these areas.[22] Preventive diplomacy involves great flexibility in the choice of means of United Nations intervention, but central to the operation of this approach to peace is an innovative and resourceful Secretary General, whose guide is often only the principles of the Charter. In Hammarskjöld's case, he was guided by the belief that

. . . the Secretary General should use his office, and, indeed, the machinery of the Organization to its utmost capacity and to the full extent permitted at each stage by practical circumstance . . . [the Secretary General] should be expected to act without [specific] guidance, should this appear to him necessary in order to help in filling any vacuum that may appear in the systems

which the Charter and traditional diplomacy provide for the safeguarding of peace and security.[23]

This organizational ideology, in the context of an international system characterized by the bipolar conflict global in scope and, therefore, by the likelihood that crises initially remote from the central area of big power conflict will become infused by overtones of this conflict, clearly influenced the conduct of the United Nations peacekeeping missions in Lebanon, the Congo, West Irian, and Cyprus. This said, I turn to the analysis of the crises in question.

II. The United Nations Observer Group in Lebanon (UNOGIL)

NATURE OF THE CONFLICT

. . . The [Lebanese] internal conflict which reached the proportions of a civil war in May, 1958 must be seen in relation both to the requirement for stability in Lebanon of harmony in the political relations of its diverse religious communities and to developments with the larger Arab community following Nasser's rise to power in Egypt.

The fundamental cause of the 1958 civil war was the widespread and growing dissatisfaction of large elements of Lebanon's Moslem population with the government of President Chamoun, himself a Christian Maronite.[24] . . . In a period of increasing Soviet influence in the Middle East and the concomitant diminution of British and French power in the region, Lebanese foreign policy remained strongly pro-

[21] See the chapter, "Preventive Diplomacy as an Approach to Peace," in I. Claude, *Swords into Plowshares,* 3rd. ed., New York, 1964. Also S. Hoffman, "In Search of a Thread: the U.N. Experience in the Congo Labyrinth," *International Organization,* vol. 16, 1962, p. 357.

[22] Hammarskjöld elaborates the concept in his report to the General Assembly on the activity of the Organization in 1958–1959, General Assembly Official Records (GAOR) 15th Session, Supplement IA. (A/4390, Add. 1).

[23] *Statement of Secretary-General Dag Hammarskjöld before the General Assembly on his Reappointment to a Second Term,* United Nations Department of Public Information Press Release SG/616/, p. 2.

[24] See F. Qubain, *Lebanon in Crisis,* Washington, 1961, Ch. III, for a treatment of this.

Western. . . . The Lebanese government looked on the rapid rise of Nasser with less than enthusiasm—Cairo Radio reciprocated by encouraging the Opposition groups—and feared that the motive force of Arab nationalism would lead to a breakdown in the delicate balance between religious communities which underlay Lebanese political stability.[25] . . . Following the results of the 1957 elections, tension between government and opposition supporters grew. . . . On May 8, a prominent opposition newspaper editor was murdered in Beirut and on May 12 an armed insurrection broke out in Lebanon's major cities.

The Lebanese government, in calling on the United Nations for assistance, did not appeal for support to defeat its domestic opposition. It claimed, rather, that the armed conflict had been fomented by the interference in Lebanese affairs of the United Arab Republic. . . . On May 14, the United States announced that it was sending small arms and police equipment to the Chamoun government. The Sixth Fleet in the Mediterranean was reinforced and on May 16 the US announced that it was ready to send tanks and men, if requested, to assist in the restoration of normal conditions in Lebanon.[26] The Soviet Union, for its part, warned that it regarded the Lebanese crisis as an essentially domestic matter and warned the West against intervention. When the United Nations took up the Lebanese complaint, therefore, the big powers had already taken opposing sides on the issues. The possibilities of UN action were circumscribed by the necessity to work with this framework.

UN INTERVENTION—THE INITIAL STAGE

Beginning with its vote for the ending of the British mandate in Palestine and the creation of an independent Jewish state, the United Nations has played a substantial role in Middle Eastern affairs. . . . It is true that the UN's concerns and activities focused primarily on Egypt, Syria, and Jordan rather than on Lebanon, but there can be little doubt that previous experience in the Middle East and the availability of personnel in the area facilitated the creation of the United Nations Observer Group in Lebanon (UNOGIL).

. . . In the ensuing debate, the United States, United Kingdom, and France sided with Lebanon, the Soviet Union with the UAR. While some members of the Security Council, notably Sweden, expressed uncertainty as to the nature of the evidence of foreign interference in Lebanon, the United States was not so troubled. Mr. Lodge asserted that "the conclusion is clear that there has been outside interference in the internal affairs of the Republic of Lebanon, that this interference has been designed to promote civil strife . . ." [27]

. . . Finally, at the June 11 meeting of the Council, . . . a Swedish resolution was passed. This called for the urgent establishment of an observation group which would proceed to Lebanon "so as to insure that there is no illegal infiltration of personnel or supply of arms or other material across the Lebanese borders." [28] The Secretary-General was authorized to undertake the necessary arrangements and to inform the Security Council of the observation group's activities.

Lebanon and the United Arab Republic both accepted this plan and the Swedish resolution was supported by Colombia, China, France, Iraq, Japan, Panama, Sweden, Canada, the United Kingdom, and the United States. The Soviet Union abstained, noting that, since both the UAR and Lebanon had

---

[25] *Ibid.,* p. 42.
[26] *New York Times,* May 17, 1958, p. 1.

[27] Official Records of the Security Council (ORSC), 823rd Meeting, p. 47.
[28] The text of the resolution can be found in ORSC, 825th Meeting, p. 7.

agreed to the plan, it would not oppose the resolution. . . .

The wording of the Security Council resolution establishing UNOGIL was capable of both a broad and narrow interpretation. The former, which the Lebanese government and the United States would have preferred, stressed that the observation group was to *insure* that no illegal infiltration of arms or personnel took place.[29] This view held that it was possible for UNOGIL to act to prevent such infiltration, by arresting suspected infiltrators, confiscating arms, and so on. Such an interpretation would obviously have increased the likelihood of use of force by UN personnel. Mr. Hammarskjöld, however, took the narrower view. He made it clear that he envisaged UNOGIL as an observation group designed to gather information and not a police force.[30] Unlike the United States, the UN could not prejudge the validity of Lebanon's charges. In this view, UNOGIL's task was not to intervene in an internal dispute nor to take action against an alleged aggressor. It was rather to determine whether or not the dispute should properly be considered a domestic conflict. . . .

UNOGIL was headed by a three-man Executive Committee composed of Mr. Galo Plaza, Mr. Dayal (India) and General Bull (Norway), who supervised the observations operations. The force itself consisted of two levels: the observation group proper made up of experienced men from all over the globe and a servicing group recruited primarily from the staff of the UN Truce Supervision Organization

[29] See G. Curtis, "The United Nations Observation Group in Lebanon," *International Organization,* vol. 18, 1964, pp. 742–43, for a discussion of conflicting interpretations of the resolution.
[30] *Ibid.*

(UNTSO) in Palestine. Initially, the observers themselves were also drawn from UNTSO personnel. A Liaison Committee was established to handle negotiations on day to day matters between UNOGIL and the Lebanese government. Finally, somewhat later, on July 24, the Secretary-General announced the appointment of a seven-man Advisory Committee which would provide him with political advice and support. . . . The presence of UN observers in Lebanon was subject to the agreement of the host government which thus could exercise substantial practical control over the choice of national contingents for the international force and personnel of UNOGIL were recruited from countries that could be regarded as neutral on the Lebanese complaint. Permanent members of the Security Council were excluded from UNOGIL as they were from UNEF. . . .

Once in Lebanon, UNOGIL set out to establish a network of observation posts throughout the country, trying to obtain secure vantage points at probable supply routes. The principal techniques of observation were motorized patrols made up of two observation cars and a communications jeep. As the observation group acquired more men and equipment aerial reconaissance became increasingly important. In addition to continuous patrols, UNOGIL conducted investigations of alleged cases of infiltration reported to them by the Lebanese government. Whenever possible, rebel-held areas were inspected and suspicious traffic was stopped and searched. . . .

. . . Meanwhile, however, the situation had been transformed by the landing of US Marines in Lebanon on July 15. . . .

The US military intervention in Lebanon, triggered by the revolution in

Iraq and fears that this might be the spark which would ignite a similar course of events in pro-Western Lebanon and Jordan, completely transformed the nature of UNOGIL's position. As its own reports pointed out, the US intervention renewed rebel suspicions about the UN's role and caused UNOGIL to lose ground in its efforts to secure freedom of movement across rebel-held areas.[31] However, despite the insistence of the Secretary-General and UNOGIL personnel that the observer's role was in no way altered by the US landing, the United Nations had been unable to create conditions such that the big powers would not interfere in Lebanon.

Following the events of July 14–15, the Security Council met from July 15–22 to reevaluate the situation in Lebanon. The United States explained that its action had been taken at the request of the Lebanese government and that it was consonant with the provisions of Article 51 of the Charter.[32] The United Nations effort had been helpful, Mr. Lodge said, and should continue, but the means at UNOGIL's disposal were not sufficient to secure the objective of defending a legitimate and democratically elected government from indirect aggression. Infiltration was still continuing, he asserted, and the events in Iraq have led the United States to believe that there were "ruthless, unscrupulous, and lawless forces at work in the Middle East."[33] Nevertheless, the United States would withdraw its forces as soon as the UN strengthened its operations to the extent required by the situation.

Mr. Hammarskjöld spoke little during the debates of the week, but he did comment that UNOGIL was extending its operations and was fully equipped

to play the part envisaged for it. The implied disapproval of the US maneuver was clear.[34] The Soviet Union's disapproval was much more explicit. . . .

. . . Four resolutions were debated by the Security Council, but none secured passage. . . .

. . . The United States proposed a United Nations Command, similar to the Korean force, which would take over the US Marines' role as the effective military arm of the Chamoun regime. This resolution was vetoed by the Soviet Union, Japan and Sweden abstaining. Only Britain and France were enthusiastic supporters, and even Canada expressed misgivings.[35] The Marine landings were almost uniformly denounced by the Afro-Asian states.

The Soviet resolution called on the United States and United Kingdom to cease their illegal armed intervention in Lebanon and Jordan and to withdraw their troops immediately. It secured only its own vote, however, and the abstention of Sweden. The Swedish delegation then introduced a resolution calling for the withdrawal of UNOGIL, pointing out that "it is from a political point of view superfluous . . . and it is unsuitable that United Nations observers in Lebanon perform their functions in the presence of foreign troops."[36] This position received almost no support, although the Soviet Union ultimately voted for it. The meaning of the Swedish proposal, however, was incorporated into the UN resolutions during the Congo crisis which called on all aid to that nation to be channeled through ONUC.

Finally, on July 21–22 the Japanese draft resolution was discussed. This requested the Secretary-General to take

---

[31] UNOGIL 3rd Report, S/4085.

[32] Mr. Lodge explained the U.S. government's position at the Security Council meeting. See ORSC, 827th Meeting.

[33] *New York Times*, July 16, 1958, p. 1.

[34] The Secretary-General's remarks can be found in Doc. S/PV. 827, pp. 33–35.

[35] There seems little doubt that the Anglo-American action in sending troops to Lebanon and Jordan while a UN mission was on the job was resented by many states.

[36] Doc. S/PV. 829, p. 21.

additional measures which he may consider necessary to fulfill the general purposes of the June 11 resolution and to protect the territorial integrity and political independence of Lebanon, so as to enable the earliest possible withdrawal of the United States forces.[37] The Japanese delegate and the Secretary-General assured the Members that the resolution did not contemplate the establishment of a United Nations Police Force. It was stressed that the "additional measures" would consist of expanding and strengthening UNOGIL within the scope of its original mandate.[38] The Soviet Union, however, vetoed the resolution because it failed to condemn the US and UK for "aggressive acts" and to demand the "immediate withdrawal" of US forces from Lebanon.

At this juncture, Mr. Hammarskjöld invoked the doctrine that "the Secretary-General should act to fill a vacuum in the systems provided for the safeguarding of peace and security," [39] and stated that he would continue to develop UNOGIL in a manner consistent with the June 11 resolution unless instructed to the contrary by the Security Council. In fact, he was proposing to act as though the Japanese resolution had been adopted. Since the Soviet Union had not objected to the continuance of UNOGIL in its original form, it did not publicly call the Secretary-General to task.[40]

With the Security Council at an obvious impasse, the General Assembly took up the Lebanon issue from August 8–21, following almost three weeks of exchanges between the Soviet Union on the one hand, and the US, Britain, and France on the other, concerning

the possibility of a summit conference on Middle Eastern issues, perhaps within the framework of the UN. The various proposals for a summit meeting failed to win general acceptance, however, and the emergency session then began.

. . . The Soviet Union emphasized the primacy of the withdrawal of Western troops, while the United States stressed the need for a long-term policy to ensure political stability in the region. Notwithstanding these considerations, the ultimate outcome of the debates was primarily influenced by events in Lebanon. President Chamoun having reiterated his pledge to step down at the end of his term, General Chehab, the Army Chief of Staff and a man acceptable to the majority of both sides in the dispute, was elected President by the Chamber of Deputies on July 31. A number of Opposition deputies attended this meeting, traveling under promises of safe conduct from General Chehab. After this, the intensity of the conflict diminished and armed fighting became infrequent. UNOGIL confirmed this by reporting that after the election almost no instances of infiltration or alleged infiltration were discovered.[41] Chamoun's refusal to resign before the end of his term on September 23, however, hampered Chehab's attempts to effect a general reconciliation and the barricades in the cities remained intact.

The obvious prospects of a civil peace and considerable diplomatic activity among the Arab states produced a resolution which the General Assembly passed unanimously on August 21. This resolution called on Arab states to live together in mutual tolerance and a spirit of good neighborliness; it noted that the Charter of the Arab League called for the mutual respect of the political independence of its Members and asked them to observe this principle; it called for the Secretary-General

[37] The text of the Japanese resolution is in UN Doc. S/PV. 835, p. 6.

[38] *Ibid.*, pp. 7–10.

[39] His statement of Sept. 26, 1957 has already been cited.

[40] The difference between this attitude and Soviet actions during the Congo crisis is striking.

[41] UNOGIL 4th Report (S/4110).

to make such practical arrangements which would both uphold the principles of the Charter in Lebanon and Jordan and also facilitate the early withdrawal of foreign troops.[42] At the same time, Lebanon withdrew its original complaint about the UAR interference in its domestic affairs.

UNOGIL continued to expand its operations following the General Assembly emergency session. In Lebanon, sporadic violence continued until the end of October, sparked on this occasion by the dissatisfaction of Chamoun's extreme supporters with the appointment of Mr. Karami, the rebel leader from Tripoli, as Premier. Finally, a coalition government of four men was named to act as the government pending new elections. This agreement ended all fighting and on November 14 Mr. Hammarskjöld announced the withdrawal of UNOGIL from Lebanon. The American Marines had left about a month earlier.

TASK PERFORMANCE, TASK EXPANSION, AND INTEGRATION

How should UNOGIL be evaluated with reference to the principal concerns of this paper? Its objectives were, it appears, both to determine the extent of external intervention in Lebanon and, by its presence, to discourage any such intervention. It was hoped, following the doctrine of preventive diplomacy, that the intervention of the UN would prevent the direct intervention of the big powers in Lebanon, while providing the political atmosphere for a solution based on negotiations at the local and regional level. To this end, Hammarskjöld engaged in extensive diplomatic negotiations with the various Middle Eastern governments.

The intervention of the United States obviously meant that the UN had

failed in one of its most important aims. The principal spur to the US action, however, the coup d'etat in Iraq, was not subject to UN control; this is an excellent example of the thwarting of intra-organizational programs for organizational growth by historical occurrences and by environmental factors. Ironically, it is true that, given its initial purposes, UNOGIL was most efficient when its services were least needed.[43]

The Lebanese experience did, nevertheless, contribute to the growing importance of the Secretary-General. Mr. Hammarskjöld acted his role as "Foreign Minister of the UN"[44] to the hilt in this crisis and emerged with more personal prestige and power. His concept of "preventive diplomacy" and the principles he elaborated for the structure and activities of UNOGIL won some support from the great powers and enthusiastic advocacy by many of the uncommitted states. However, when the nature of the situation changed dramatically, the ideology of preventive diplomacy no longer fit the new conditions. UN impartiality was not a sufficient guarantee for the US when it felt its interests in the Middle East more directly threatened.

The UN presence probably did help to confine the conflict to a fairly low level of intensity. Given its public position and the presence of UNOGIL, the UAR could not very well have intervened in any large-scale sense. Most important, however, UNOGIL indicated that the Organization could be neutral even if this meant a conflict with American interests and policy. This, I believe, had to be understood by the uncommitted states and the Soviet Union if these states were to support future United Nations peacekeeping opera-

[42] The text of the Arab resolution is given by Qubain, Appendix IV B.

[43] Curtis, op. cit., p. 761.

[44] See the comparison of the Secretary-General's executive function to that of the American President in J. Lash, "Hammarskjöld's Conception of his Office," International Organization, vol. 16, 1962, p. 547.

tions with any enthusiasm. The limited scope, or functional specificity, of the UN operation in Lebanon was probably instrumental in restriction to an absolute minimum its involvement in Lebanon's *political* crisis. In this case, Hammarskjöld's hope of limited military intervention combined with political non-interference through maximal compliance with the domestic jurisdiction clause was realized. Finally, while UNOGIL did give rise to renewed discussion of a permanent UN force, no such new structure was created. The Lebanese experience, particularly at the staff level, could only have been helpful in altering UN personnel to the myriad technical problems involved in the running of such an international force.

III. The United Nations Operation in the Congo (ONUC)

NATURE OF THE CRISIS

On June 30, 1960, the Belgian Congo became an independent state, a full-fledged member of the international community. It is by now a mere commonplace to assert that the Belgians had not prepared their ex-subjects for this new role.[45] While the Congo is a vast and wealthy nation, its native human resources were clearly inadequate in 1960 for the management of a modern administrative and political framework. . . . In short, given what we know of the social, economic, and cultural requisites of democracy,[46] a dem-

ocratic and stable Congolese polity would have been a poor bet on Independence Day. And, within a week of its newly-won independence, the Congo quickly descended into chaos . . .

On July 5, Congolese troops mutinied against their Belgian officers in camps at Thysville and Leopoldville. In the months preceding Independence the Belgians had made no attempt to speed up Africanization of the Force Publique, which thus became an immediate source of demands for such "fruits of independence" as higher pay and promotions.[47] Over the next few days the disorders spread to other garrisons and anti-Belgian riots and violence spread. . . .

. . . On [July 11] Belgian paratroopers were dropped throughout the country and Moise Tshombe declared the secession of Katanga, the Congo's wealthiest province.[48] . . .

Faced with this chaotic and dangerous situation, the Congolese leaders, Lumumba and Kasavubu, together emitted a stream of cables calling for military assistance. Their appeal was directed first to the United States and then, with US encouragement, to the United Nations. . . . The purposes of the aid were, according to these telegrams, to put an end to Belgian aggression and to the Belgian-inspired secession of Katanga. The Congolese government, therefore, looked on the crisis as *primarily external*. . . .

In the Congo crisis, therefore, we

---

[45] The Belgian administration did, however, have certain salutary aspects. Consonant with the paternalism of its approach, it encouraged primary education and developed adequate health service. See K. Gordon, *The UN in the Congo*, New York, 1962, p. 8 for some brief remarks on this point.

[46] I do not imply that a fully developed empirical theory of democracy exists. Nevertheless, the findings of S. M. Lipset, reported in Ch. 2 and 3 of *Political Man*, New York, 1960 and of J. Coleman in G. Almond and J. Coleman, *The Politics of Developing Areas*,

Princeton, 1960 alone would lead to this conclusion.

[47] Gordon, *op. cit.*, p. 13.

[48] *Ibid.* A. Van Bilsen, "Some Aspects of the Congo Problem," *International Affairs*, vol. 38, 1962, notes that before Independence the Belgians always favored a centralized governmental structure for the Congo. How the fortunes of war lead one to change one's tunes! More seriously, the change in policy was not indicative of new Belgian interests; rather Katanga's secession now came to be seen as the best way of preserving Belgian economic interests.

find a similar complex of general forces which operated in Lebanon. A domestic conflict was enmeshed in the larger context of the global decolonization movement and the cold war. In July, 1960, however, the big powers were not directly involved, and prompt UN action to insulate the Congo from their intrusion was dictated by the precepts of "preventive diplomacy."

UN INTERVENTION—THE INITIAL STAGE

The United Nations had not participated in any way in the supervision of Belgian administration in the Congo. It was, however, prepared to help the Congo overcome its grievous need for technical assistance; to this end a small technical assistance team headed by Dr. Sture Linner accompanied Dr. Bunche to the Independence Day ceremonies. But when the UN intervened in the Congo it was starting from scratch; indeed, its only extended experience with military operations resembling what it now undertook had been in the Middle East, not Africa. It was natural, therefore, for the Secretary-General to draw on the experience of UNEF and UNOGIL in directing the Congo operation.

The Security Council first met to consider the Congo problem on July 13. . . . The Secretary-General [successfully sought] . . . to have the Council deliberate under the terms of Article 99, which he considered an important constitutional weapon and basis for his conception of an energetic, impartial, and independent Secretariat.[49] Article 99 enables the Secretary-General himself to bring to the attention of the Security Council "any matter which in his opinion may threaten the maintenance of international peace and security." This procedural gambit

made it easier to adopt measures other than those dictated in Chapter VII of the Charter.

The Secretary-General played the leading role in the formation of ONUC and the Ceylonese and Tunisian joint resolution which provided ONUC its initial mandate was tailored to Hammarskjöld's own conceptions. Before the Council even met he had consulted with a number of African delegates and had even secured promises of contingents for the yet unborn UN Force.[50] The resolution called on Belgium to withdraw its troops from the Congo and requested the Secretary-General, in consultation with the government of the Congo, to provide such military assistance as was necessary until the security forces were able to perform their normal duties.[51] The resolution was passed by 8 votes to 0, Britain, China, and France abstaining.

The United States and Soviet Union voted together to set up ONUC, although neither was absolutely satisfied with the resolution. . . . Nevertheless, at the outset, the "great powers, whatever their ultimate interests, were generally willing to allow the United Nations to assume responsibility and save them from involvement in what might turn out to be a situation endangering world peace." [52] For a time, then, the fundamental precondition of preventive diplomacy prevailed.[53] . . . Mr. Hammarskjöld relied heavily on the precedent of UNEF and UNOGIL— ONUC was to enter the Congo with the agreement of the host government, yet was to refrain from any intervention in internal political disputes. By the procedural device of avoiding recourse to Articles 41 and 42, Article 2 (para.

[49] A. Burns and N. Heathcote, *Peacekeeping by UN Forces*, Princeton, 1963, p. 24, see also J. Lash, *op. cit.*, p. 546.

[50] Miller, *op. cit.*, pp. 271–273.

[51] S/4387. The text of the resolution is included in Burns and Heathcote, p. 249.

[52] Gordon, p. 23.

[53] Claude cites big power unanimity in agreeing not to intervene directly as the fundamental precondition of preventive diplomacy.

7), would be observed.[54] . . . Neutral-ity in military operations was consid-ered to have no political bias.[55]

All this aside, it is imperative to underline the fact that the July 14 resolution established a UN Force which was to undertake security duties within a sovereign state. This cer-tainly represented an instance of task expansion; that is, of new responsi-bilities in the military security sphere. Furthermore, even the initial mandate of ONUC meant that its activities were to be functionally more diffuse than those of UNOGIL, which never under-took the wide ranging duties of polic-ing.

CHARACTERISTICS AND PERFORMANCE OF THE UN FORCE

The principles underlying the makeup of the ONUC forces were those which had informed the UN's Middle Eastern experiences. The sources of military assistance were to be African in the first place, the forces of the per-manent members of the Security Coun-cil being explicitly excluded. ONUC contingents from non-African states, nominally neutral on the issues in the Congo crisis, were also included.[56] The UN Force was, to repeat, not to be-come a party to internal political con-flicts; nor were its personnel to use force except in self-defense.

The organizational structure for ONUC, which developed over a period of months, was headed by the Secre-tary-General. . . . In New York, he was advised by members of his staff, by the Advisory Committee on the

Congo, on which each nation contrib-uting forces to ONUC had a repre-sentative, and from February, 1961, by a Conciliation Committee which was made up of the African members of the Force and whose energies were devoted to seeking a political solution to Congolese political disunity.[57] In the Congo, the heads of the operation were the Secretary-General's Special Representative, in his capacity as chief administrative officer, the Commander of the UN Force, and the Head of ONUC Civilian Operations. . . .

Political overtones pervaded even staffing phases of the UN operation. Thus, Hammarskjöld was criticized be-cause, at least in the beginning, his principal advisers happened to be Amer-icans.[58] Congolese government dissatis-faction with Mr. Bunche contributed to his replacement,[59] but his successor, Mr. Dayal, was himself transferred in the face of British and American pres-sure.[60] There were also instances which caused some doubt as to what course a national contingent would follow should its government's view and that of the UN differ. Ghana's General Alexander's desire to disarm the Force Publique is a case in point.[61] In late 1960, dissatisfied with the course of events which had seen Lumumba's in-fluence drastically reduced, a number of African and Asian states, among them, Guinea, Mali, UAR and Indo-nesia, began to withdraw their con-tingents. It seemed that other Afro-Asian states would follow suit, but, fortunately for the United Nations, India was willing to express its support

---

[54] Burns and Heathcote include a good dis-cussion of the legal basis for UN intervention, pp. 22–27.

[55] The point is made by Hoffman, "In Search of a Thread," pp. 352–355.

[56] The principles underlying ONUC's or-ganization were summarized by Hammar-skjöld in his 1st Interim Report to the Secu-rity Council, S/4389.

[57] This committee was set up following the passage of a General Assembly resolution (A/4510, Resolution 1474) on Sept. 20, 1960.

[58] These were Mr. Bunche, Mr. Cordier, and Mr. Wieschloff. Even a pro-American and pro-Hammarskjöld observer, Miller, suggests that UN officials were somewhat anti-Lu-mumba. Miller, *op. cit.,* p. 293.

[59] Miller, p. 285.

[60] Burns and Heathcote, pp. 92–93.

[61] *Ibid.,* p. 42.

by sending additional men.[62] This helped reverse the tide.

The UN Force in the Congo was much larger than either UNEF or UNOGIL—throughout its stay it numbered more than 10,000 men and the number rose in late 1961 to more than 20,000.[63] . . . The scope of ONUC military activities went far beyond those of the previous UN peacekeeping forces. In fact, one problem was that the UN Force, spread thin over a vast territory, was not always strong enough to be assured of military superiority. Briefly, the military and police duties which ONUC at some time performed included: disarming of Congolese security forces and irregular armed groups, guarding political leaders, control of airports and other major transportation and communications centers, interposition to prevent tribal warfare, action taken to halt ongoing tribal massacres, riot control, acts of self-defense when fired on, and military offensives against Katangese forces led by mercenaries. . . .

. . . The relationship between the United Nations Force and the host government was the fount of the most severe problems which the Secretary-General's policy encountered. The primary objective of the UN in the Congo was to prevent a direct confrontation of the Soviet Union and the United States, or of Belgium with some of the African states. More specific subgoals, however, were: expulsion of the Belgians, the maintenance of law and order, the unification of the Congo, and fair and equal treatment of all domestic political factions.[64] All this was to be achieved *without* intervention in the Congo's internal political

conflicts; in addition, at first the use of force was not contemplated as a means to these ends. To put the matter succinctly as does Hoffman, the means were simply not commensurate with the ends.[65]

The difficulty for Hammarskjöld was that UNOGIL and UNEF were not apt precedents for ONUC. UNEF did not have to deal with *internal* political divisions, and the latent conflict between UNOGIL and the Chamoun government was stifled by the US military intervention, which, in a sense, rendered Chamoun impervious to UNOGIL's reports. In the Congo, the broad functions of the UN with respect to internal security inevitably gave its activities a political dimension, for particular actions, say, the occupation of an airport, would favor certain Congolese factions but not others.

The UN was in the Congo at the request of the legitimate central government of that state. The Security Council resolution of July 14 called on the Secretary-General to provide this government with military assistance until the national security forces would be able to fully meet their tasks.[66] It was, however, immediately apparent that the Secretary-General and the Congolese government, or Lumumba at least, differed widely in their interpretation of this clause. This was disastrous since another precondition of UN preventive intervention seems to be the cooperation of the host government. . . .

. . . While Hammarskjöld insisted that the UN, once admitted into the Congo, could not serve in any way as the instrument of the central government and must remain neutral if it were to fulfill its purpose, Lumumba felt that the UN Force was, in a sense, the replacement for his non-functioning army. He resented not being more fully consulted on UN decisions and claimed that the UN's objective should

[62] *Ibid.*, p. 69.
[63] B. Urquhart, "Lessons of Suez and Congo, A UN Perspective," in L. Bloomfield, et al., *International Military Forces*, Boston, 1964, p. 139.
[64] For an illuminating discussion of the incompatibility of these objectives, see Haas, *Beyond the Nation-State*, p. 125.

[65] "In Search for a Thread," p. 338.
[66] S/4387, para. 2.

be to reunite the Congo, using force against Katanga if necessary. . . .

The split between the Congolese Premier and the Secretary-General had profound ramifications, for many of the Afro-Asian states participating in ONUC shared the Congolese leader's objectives. When the constitutional crisis of September, 1960 led to Lumumba losing most of his power, Mr. Hammarskjöld's carefully constructed coalition of supporters began to disintegrate. The UN's action in preventing Lumumba from making a radio speech at the height of the crisis was attacked as having pro-Kasavubu consequences.[67] . . . the UN's de facto policy of dealing with whichever figures appeared to hold a semblance of stable power resulted in the reinforcement of the status quo. The continuation of this policy did not resolve but merely froze at a pre-existing level the Congo's political chaos.[68]

In short, once internal divisions proliferated and governmental stagnation proved the rule, the partisan cleavage on the domestic front was quickly reflected in the opposing attitudes of UN members. Non-intervention ceased to be a viable organizational ideology, capable of securing variable coalitions of support for specific subgoals; it now helped lead to the repudiation of the Secretary-General by one of the great powers. Not only did this limit the possibility of similar UN operations in the future, but it also narrowed the possible base of his support. Hammarskjöld was forced from September, 1960 on to rely on a coalition made up of most of the Afro-Asian states and the United States and several smaller Western powers. When this group was divided, as in the period before Lumumba's death, ONUC reached its

lowest ebb; when the group agreed to support the Adoula government, new impetus was given ONUC. The principle of non-intervention in Congolese internal affairs, however, slipped into the background. . . .

. . . Resolutions passed by the Security Council on February 11,[69] and November 24, 1961,[70] . . . authorized ONUC, by the end of 1961, to resort to the use of force, if absolutely necessary, to avert civil war and to expel unauthorized foreign personnel from the Congo. Military encounters between the UN Force, which was not able to act, and Tshombe's mercenary-led army took place in September and December, 1961 and December, 1962. The first battle was a defeat for the UN; tragically, in flying to a meeting on ceasefire arrangements with Tshombe, the Secretary-General died in an air crash. By the time of the subsequent two military operations, the UN had secured superior air power, and ONUC won decisive victories. On each occasion, however, political agreements with Tshombe failed to be translated into concrete arrangements providing for substantial unity and stability in the Congo. It should be noted that the UN's military "sorties" were strongly criticized by Britain, France, and such pro-Katanga Americans as Senator Thomas Dodd. . . .

Following the creation of the Adoula government and the agreement between the UN and President Kasavubu of April 17, 1961, the UN political officers in the Congo worked very closely with the Leopoldville government in political negotiations with the Premier of Katanga. The best examples of this were the negotiations leading up to the Kitona Declaration, signed December 28, 1961. At this conference Mr. Adoula was being advised by four senior UN officials.[71] In the middle of 1961, the

[67] Gordon, pp. 55–57 discusses this point and describes the events of the chaotic constitutional crisis of September, 1960.

[68] See Hoffman's discussion of the first phases of ONUC, "In Search of a Thread," pp. 323 ff.

[69] S/4741.

[70] S/5002.

[71] Gordon, p. 146.

United States too came to regard the Adoula regime as the Congo's best hope for a non-Communist government which could provide national unity; US diplomats cooperated closely both with the new Secretary-General and with the UN officials in the Congo during the negotiations with Tshombe in late 1961 and 1962.[72]

TASK PERFORMANCE AND THE
ORIGINAL UN MANDATE

Following the establishment of ONUC on July 14, further considerations of the Congo crisis focused on the clarification or modification of the UN mandate. Events in the Congo, and the impact of these on the Member-States' formulations of their national interest with respect to ONUC strategy, influenced the outcome of the renewed UN debates. In these subsequent resolutions of the Security Council and General Assembly, the original restrictions on the use of force were modified and the postures of ONUC toward the Congolese government and the Katangese regime respectively were substantially altered. The changes in policy reflected shifts in the Secretary-General's "parliamentary situation" and the realization that the policy of non-intervention would likely result in a stable Katangese regime, opening the door for intervention by "anti-colonialist" powers. U Thant, it appears, was less legalistic in his approach than Hammarskjöld, whom he succeeded in November, 1961.

The change in the degree of support for Hammarskjöld is evident if the votes on UN resolutions from July to December, 1960, are compared. On July 22 and August 9, resolutions which essentially reaffirmed the Force's original mandate were passed by the Security Council, France and China abstaining on both, Britain on one. These

resolutions represented votes of confidence in Hammarskjöld's approach to the problem. . . . However, at a meeting it called on September 14, the Soviet Union publicly broke with the Secretary-General. . . .

The ensuing General Assembly session included Khrushchev's famous tirade against the Secretary-General and his call for a UN executive troika. More significantly, in December, with public attention focused on Lumumba's arrest, a resolution that expressed in effect a vote of confidence in the Secretary-General's policy failed by one vote to obtain the required 2/3 majority.[73] The Soviet bloc and some of the "radical" Afro-Asian states,[74] such as Indonesia, Mali, Ghana, and Guinea, voted against the pro-Hammarskjöld resolution.[75]

The first explicit recognition of domestic political strife in a UN resolution was the Security Council resolution of February 21, 1961. This most important decision followed Lumumba's assassination and represented a fairly successful attempt to recreate a broad coalition which would include the US and most Afro-Asian states. The Soviet Union did not veto the proposal, which anticipated more vigorous UN action and received the votes of Lumumba's Afro-Asian supporters. The UN was authorized to use force if necessary, in the last resort, to prevent civil war; all Belgian and other foreign military and paramilitary personnel, mercenaries and political advisers were called upon to leave the Congo. . . .

The Soviet Union abstained on this resolution, which was reaffirmed by the Assembly in April. This resolution did not refer specifically to the

---

[72] Burns and Heathcote, pp. 142–144, pp. 196–198.

[73] Miller, op. cit., p. 302.

[74] I use this description in the sense elaborated by R. Good, "Congo Crisis, A Study in Postcolonial Politics," in L. Martin ed., Neutralism and Non-Alignment, pp. 35–37.

[75] The vote took place with Lumumba under arrest and the UN cooperating, willy-nilly, with the Kasavubu-Mobutu regime.

secession of Katanga, but the emphasis on the undesirability of non-UN foreign advisers left no doubt that the reintegration of Katanga with the rest of the Congo was becoming an operational goal of ONUC.

In November, 1961, following the setback to UN forces in Katanga and the accession of U Thant, another resolution was passed. . . .

It went further than previous statements, however, in formally deprecating Katanga's secession and rejecting its claim to be a sovereign state. The use of force against foreign personnel, if necessary, was now authorized, and it was implied that such action could be used to bring Katanga to heel. . . .[76]

Britain and France expressed reservations concerning the grant of these military powers without Chapter VII being invoked. Their failure to veto the resolutions in question undermined their position, however, and contributed to the expansion of ONUC's military powers.[77] Whether or not the UN could convincingly rationalize its military offensives of December, 1961 and December, 1962, in terms of the above provisions is hard to determine; observers tend to agree,[78] however, that the resolution of November, 1961 implicitly suggested that force might have to be used to end Katanga's secession.

The UN, finally, dealt with the domestic political issue by the use of force, supporting the central government against both Tshombe and Gizenga.[79] Temporary peace and order

were thus imposed by the abandonment of the "non-political" approach developed by Hammarskjöld. But the political solution came when the great powers no longer could support, if they ever had been able to, the same central government. . . .

Finally, ONUC was unable to remain totally unaffected by the buffets of great power attempts to secure advantage for its local supporter. The Soviet Union did, in the early stages, send arms to Lumumba, but this was not continued. . . . For the most part, the Soviet Union was relatively isolated from direct participation in the Congo crisis; there is little evidence that it supported the Gizenga regime with arms. For its part, the United States was quite deeply involved in ONUC. A policy which it could support prevailed most of the time; in 1962 in particular US officials were active in attempting to induce the Congolese factions to agree on a political settlement. In terms of material, the US did provide ONUC with logistic support and equipment, but channeled this through the UN. Because, I would venture, its interests and policy preferences with respect to the Congo were compatible with the goals of most Afro-Asian states, the US had reason to be relatively satisfied with ONUC's military operation.

TASK PERFORMANCE, TASK EXPANSION, AND INTEGRATION

The scope of the military activities undertaken by ONUC without invoking the Charter's enforcement procedures certainly represented the assumption ad hoc of far greater responsibilities by the UN in the military sphere. The fundamental obstacles to the peace and political stability in the Congo were internal: the lack of trained ad-

---

[76] Burns and Heathcote, pp. 136–137. The resolution explicitly called for the end forthwith of Katanga's secession, although the use of force clauses referred to "ending civil war."

[77] Burns and Heathcote, pp. 81–82 note Sir Patrick Dean's remarks on the dubious legality of permitting the use of force without invoking Articles 41 and 42.

[78] See footnote 76 above.

[79] The action against the Gizengists is described in Burns and Heathcote, pp. 154–160. Apparently, since the Western powers were

united in their opposition to him, ONUC troops were more readily used in support of Congolese forces than they had been in the battles of the central government and Katanga.

ministrators and professionals capable of running the apparatus of a modern state, the regionalism of Congolese party politics, the absence of any experience in the management of democratic institutions, personal rivalries among the politicians. The UN undertook to intervene in this situation; first, to bring Belgian intervention to an end and then to go on with the task of building a modern Congo. This last required law and order throughout the territory. Finally, by the use of force, Congolese unity and the expulsion of foreign elements were at least temporarily attained. The case of ONUC, despite its failures, must therefore be considered as an instance of organizational growth, relative to previous UN operations.

While this is, I believe, true, it is also probable that the Congolese experience is proving dysfunctional for the longer-term process of task expansion in this field. Despite its partial success insofar as several of the operation's subgoals are concerned, ONUC saw its efforts repudiated by one of the major powers which is unlikely, therefore, to support future initiatives of this kind made by the Secretary-General. Further, the Congo operation engendered a financial crisis for the Organization which was not settled when the International Court's advisory opinion held that the regular system of assessments should apply to peacekeeping operations as well. Today, the UN is on the verge of bankruptcy; in 1962 and 1964 such operations as the United Nations Temporary Executive Authority (UNTEA) in West Irian and the United Nations Force in Cyprus (UNFICYP) were financed by voluntary contributions, certainly a disintegrative tendency. ONUC did not lead to the creation of stronger United Nations structures, quite the contrary. The very status and character of the Secretariat was challenged and in the Cyprus case, the Security Council's exercising stricter control of the UNFICYP activities.[80] Both great powers, it may be, are interested in limiting the power of the Afro-Asian majority in the Assembly.

An evaluation of organizational leadership with respect to ONUC is a complex issue. Hammarskjöld's policy, following the Middle Eastern precedents, has already been criticized. It is impossible to deny, however, his important achievements. He successfully used Article 99 to structure the agenda of a Security Council meeting so as to leave him considerable initiative of action. He received important grants of power from the Organization and used considerable imagination in interpreting the ambiguities of the mandate.[81] The negative side of the story should not be forgotten, however. Hammarskjöld's policy of non-intervention failed to secure his objectives. His specific subgoals would have been mutually irreconcilable, even had he not maintained his insistence on non-intervention.[82] His assumption that neutrality was the means to secure the broadest base of support from the Member States was a crucial mistake, for his ranking of ONUC's subgoals differed from the priorities favored by many states. In fact, only by opting for a vigorous policy directed at Congolese unification and the expulsion of Belgian and other foreign elements could a stable base of support for ONUC have possibly been maintained.[83] This coalition might have included the US, Soviet bloc, some Europeans, and the Afro-Asian states. . . . Britain, France, and Belgium would have been the only important powers opposed.

[80] This point will be discussed more fully in the section of the paper dealing with UNFICYP.
[81] Hoffman, "In Search of a Thread," p. 351.
[82] See Haas, *Beyond the Nation-State*, p. 125.
[83] *Ibid.*

Furthermore, in the Congolese situation, non-intervention and political neutrality were never truly observed, for ONUC did not refrain from taking action to preserve human life and public property. Why, then, should Hammarskjöld have insisted on a legalistic approach which confronted him with such severe contradictions?

One answer may be that he felt organizational growth could only take place within the context of legal norms and behavioral practices consistent with the Charter. In this view, non-intervention, the basis of UN impartiality, may well be the only principle capable of attracting, in the long run, the support of the UN's staff and clients.

Haas has suggested that the Secretary-General may have been trapped by his own ideology.[84] Noting that preventive diplomacy means that the Secretary-General will have to take the initiative with only the Charter's principles as a consistent guide, he points out that an organizational ideology which derives from the organization's formal principles usually can serve as a basis for programs capable of obtaining staff support.[85] There is no similar probability that subgoals so closely related to ultimate principles can obtain the requisite support of the less internationally-oriented Member-States.

Comparing the UNOGIL and ONUC cases, it is clear that the activities of the former were functionally more specific. It is at least arguable that UNOGIL was functional for task expansion; ONUC itself could be cited as evidence for this. The dysfunctional consequences of the UN Congo operation have already been pointed out, tending to confirm the specificity-diffuseness hypothesis.[86]

Finally, what was ONUC's impact

on the Congo, referring only to the political and military aspects of the operation? Barely a year after the withdrawal of the UN Force, fighting continued in that troubled state. Foreign mercenaries again serve Tshombe, now Premier of the central government, while Afro-Asian "radicals," particularly Egypt, are reportedly supplying and training the rebels. There has even been a Belgian paratroop drop with US cooperation in order to free white hostages held by the rebels. The wheel has come full circle. But no voice is raised to suggest another UN intervention. Apparently, the first effort was dysfunctional for task expansion.

IV. The West Irian Case: The United Nations Temporary Emergency Authority (UNTEA)

NATURE OF THE CRISIS

When Indonesia achieved full independence in 1949, West Irian remained under Dutch control. The Charter of Sovereignty, which formulized the terms of the end of Indonesia's colonial status, stipulated that the future status of West Irian would be settled in negotiations between the Netherlands and Indonesia. From 1949 to 1962 their failure to agree on this issue governed the nature of the relations between the two countries. Indonesia, the revisionist party in this instance, made the annexation of West Irian a point of national honor. Negotiations took place periodically, and the United Nations General Assembly discussed the crisis on four occasions between 1954 and 1961. Virtually no progress was made towards a settlement, however, while relations between the two countries steadily deteriorated.

. . . In December, 1961, . . . President Sukarno called for the general mobilization of the army and popula-

[84] *Ibid.*, p. 124.
[85] *Ibid.*
[86] *Ibid.*, p. 47.

tion in order to "free West Irian." [87] A seaborne landing and several paratroop raids were attempted early in 1962, but all were quickly repulsed by Dutch military forces.

Until the concluding set of negotiations, neither party budged significantly from its original position. Indonesia held that it had legal sovereignty over West Irian, basing this claim on "the centuries we have lived together" as parts first of the ancient Indonesian empire and then of the Dutch East Indies. . . .

The Dutch adamantly refused to accept this position and occasionally rejected proposals for negotiation on the grounds that Indonesia's insistence on the prior recognition of her sovereignty over West Irian made serious discussion impossible. . . .

In the final years of the dispute, the Dutch became increasingly receptive to the idea of a UN role in West Irian, suggesting first a UN mission and in September, 1961, UN trusteeship for the territory.[88] Indonesia, however, in an ironic reversal of the more customary Afro-Asian and Western European position, refused to consider any UN role which was not directly connected to her own ultimate annexation of West Irian. . . .

UN INTERVENTION—THE INITIAL STAGE

The United States was also actively encouraging a negotiated settlement at this time and, largely through its efforts, secret negotiations began on March 12 at the home of Ellsworth Bunker, an American diplomat who served as the "third party" and Secretary-General's representative during the talks.

An agreement reached on August 15, 1962, included the following terms:[89]

1. A temporary United Nations trusteeship over West Irian would be established beginning October 1, 1962. It would be headed by a mutually acceptable non-Indonesian administrator, and Dutch officials would be replaced by Administrators drawn from other Member-states.

2. The first phase of the UN administration would last until May 1, 1963. After this date, administration of the territory would be transferred as soon as possible to Indonesia.

3. Within seven years of the Indonesian takeover, in 1969, a plebiscite would be held to determine whether the population of West Irian desired independence or joining the Republic of Indonesia. During the period of Indonesian administration United Nations representatives could remain in West Irian; one year before the plebiscite a United Nations Special Representative would be appointed to help in the supervision of its conduct.

4. The residents of West Irian were guaranteed the rights of free speech and free assembly; the right to elect local officials was to be expanded.

5. The costs of UN Administration would be shared by the Netherlands and Indonesia.

6. It was hoped that diplomatic relations between the two countries would be resumed as soon as possible.

7. The agreement would take effect when ratified by the United Nations General Assembly and the constitutional authorities in Indonesia and the Netherlands.

When the General Assembly did unanimously ratify the agreement, it

---

[87] *Keesing's Contemporary Archives*, p. 18845. [88] *Ibid.*, p. 18848.

[89] The full text of the Agreement, from which these points were paraphrased, is given in *United Nations Review*, vol. 9, no. 9, September, 1962, pp. 37–43. See also *Keesing's Contemporary Archives*, pp. 18939 ff.

marked the first time that the United Nations undertook direct executive authority over any territory. In this sense, therefore, the creation of UNTEA was clearly an instance of organizational task expansion. Our present concern, however, is with the peacekeeping or security operations of the UN. UNTEA was responsible for the maintenance of law and order in West Irian, as well as its security from external attack. Formally, therefore, it was undertaking all the security functions of a national government or colonial administration; at least nominally, its military duties were functionally diffuse. In fact, however, UNTEA's security function was confined to policing activities; invasion of West Irian was no longer a real possibility and the only potential large-scale military opposition to the UN, a Papuan revolt, never materialized. I would argue, therefore, that, empirically, UNTEA's security duties were functionally highly specific.

CHARACTERISTICS AND PERFORMANCE OF THE UN FORCE

The bulk of the UN security forces on West Irian was constituted by 1000 Pakistani troops; it was felt that Pakistan, as a Moslem state, would be more satisfactory to Indonesia than other possible sources of troops.[90] UNTEA also relied on the native population for policemen, and the Indonesian armed forces remaining in West Irian (as a result of the earlier invasions) were to be placed under UN Command. The Commander of the security force, the chief Pakistani officer, was responsible to the United Nations Administrator and, through him, to the Secretary-General.

Very little has been written of the United Nations' brief trusteeship over West Irian[91] and there have been no reports of any military actions taken by the UN security force. So far as can be determined, then, no serious disturbances to law and order occurred and the UN force performed its police function efficiently and without incident. A police force which has very little to police, evidently, is a successful police force. In West Irian, therefore, the question of the UN's use of force never became an issue. Since the formal status of the UN security force was that of a national army, there were no formal restrictions on its right to resort to the use of force. It is safe to say, however, that a situation requiring vigorous action by the UN force in West Irian would have led to specific instructions from the Security Council or General Assembly.

. . . UNTEA was also supposed to educate the Papuan population on the meaning of the Dutch-Indonesian Agreement. The reports of the Administrator to the United Nations have, as is perhaps normal, tended to be self-congratulatory. UNTEA has been criticized for administering policy in a manner favorable to Indonesian rather than to local Papuan interests.[92] . . .

Regardless of the truth of these assertions, it is true that the Agreement was ambiguous regarding the powers of the UN during the period of Indonesian administration, which began on May 1, 1963. It seems doubtful that UN action against Indonesian infringements of the Agreement's stipulations was seriously anticipated. . . . In short, Van der Vear is probably correct in asserting that the United Nations and the United States had acted as brokers in a transaction which gave Indonesia what she wanted, while allowing the Dutch to withdraw gracefully.[93]

---

[90] United Nations Review, vol. 9, no. 10, October, 1962, p. 10.

[91] The one full-length article is P. Van der Vear, "The United Nations in West Irian: a Critique," International Organization, no. 1, vol. 18, 1964.

[92] Van der Vear, op. cit., pp. 56–59.

[93] Ibid., pp. 71–72.

TASK PERFORMANCE AND THE
ORIGINAL UN MANDATE

. . . Neither great power was involved in UNTEA itself. The Soviet Union, in fact, appeared only slightly interested in the entire affair, supporting Indonesia as a matter of course but doing little more. Great power intervention in this dispute, therefore, was never imminent; the only danger of this would have been a major war between Indonesia and the Netherlands. The intense American effort to achieve a peaceful settlement was probably motivated by the desire to avoid ever being faced with this situation.

TASK PERFORMANCE, TASK EXPANSION,
AND INTEGRATION

The objective of the United Nations in West Irian was to avoid armed conflict between the Netherlands and Indonesia. This objective was achieved. UNTEA was a structural innovation which helped the UN secure a settlement mutually acceptable to the parties to the conflict. Since cold war issues were not involved in the dispute, the great powers were not committed to opposing sides and were able to accept the final outcome. The UN, therefore, again pursued a policy of preventive diplomacy, acting as a buffer between Member-states on the verge of armed conflict.

Once the diplomatic agreement had been secured, however, the peacekeeping activities of the UN were merely routine. The specificity diffuseness hypothesis, as previously mentioned, was confirmed in West Irian. UNTEA is an example of organizational growth, but not in the area of military operations. It represented a technical innovation in the UN's activities in the decolonization area, for the West Irian dispute is best considered a postcolonial conflict.[94] From the point of view of Indonesia and her supporters, West

Irian was a Dutch Katanga. The technique of temporary UN administration of territories which are the focus of conflict between colonial states and ex-colonies could become relevant elsewhere. If it is resorted to again the UN's experience in West Irian will have strengthened the Organization's structures and represented long-term growth.

Finally, a word about organizational leadership. U Thant's activity in this crisis was consonant with Hammarskjöld's view that the Secretary-General does not need an explicit mandate from the General Assembly or Security Council to undertake diplomatic activities designed to end threats to international peace. The part played by the General Assembly was minimal and the Trusteeship Council was never consulted. The UN's role in West Irian represented a growing centralization of the executive functions in the Secretariat.

V. The United Nations Force
in Cyprus (UNFICYP)

NATURE OF THE CRISIS

Cyprus became an independent state in August, 1960, under the terms of the Zurich and London Agreements. These Agreements established the constitutional framework of Cyprus' government and consisted largely of a series of complex arrangements safeguarding the rights of the Turkish community. . . .

There were several incidents of inter-communal violence in 1962, but the possibility of large-scale conflict arose only in 1963, after the Court's decisions, based on the vote of the neutral judge, satisfied neither group.[95] Dis-

[94] This term is used by Good, *op. cit.*, to describe disputes developing soon after decolonization between the former mother country and the ex-colony. I use it in the same sense.

[95] *Keesing's Contemporary Archives*, pp. 20114-15.

cussions between Makarios and Kutchuk failed to reach a compromise and on November 30, 1963, Makarios announced a set of proposals for the amendment of the constitution. The Turkish government rejected the plan even before Kutchuk replied, and on December 21 large-scale fighting broke out in Nicosia and spread in the next few days to other parts of the island. . . .

There was little enthusiasm in Britain for its policeman's role in Cyprus and on January 24 its government suggested the creation of a NATO force. This force would enforce the ceasefire while negotiations were conducted on the political issues. Although Greece and Turkey accepted the plan, it was rejected by the Greek Cypriots, as was a later modified version. The grounds were that Cyprus would have no role in the "political guidance" of the force.[96] Makarios announced his willingness to accept the principle of an international force, but insisted that it be a United Nations force.

Greek and Turkish fleet and troop movements were renewed, meanwhile, and fighting, the abduction of hostages, and reprisal raids continued on Cyprus despite the British efforts. Large-scale and concerted fighting broke out in Limassol on February 11 and a temporary ceasefire was broken the next day. In this context, both Britain and Cyprus called for a Security Council meeting to consider the dispute and, after continuous meetings from February 18 to March 4, UNFICYP was created. . . .

UNITED NATIONS INTERVENTION—
THE INITIAL STAGE

The Cyprus question was taken up by the Security Council as a situation

which represented a threat to international peace and security. A United Nations presence had already been established on the island and definite proposals for a UN force had been made, both by Makarios and, at the time of the meeting, by Britain. On March 4, a resolution proposed by Bolivia, Brazil, the Ivory Coast, Morocco, and Norway was adopted.

This resolution referred to the threat to international peace and, taking note of the positions adopted by the parties concerned, called on Member-States to refrain from any action likely to worsen the situation. The parties involved in the dispute were reminded of their obligation under the Charter to refrain from the threat or use of force against the territorial integrity of any state (Article 2, para. 4). The Cypriot government, which was responsible for the preservation of law and order on the island, was asked to take steps to end the violence on the island. The resolution further recommended the creation of a peacekeeping force, to be established in consultation with the governments of Cyprus, Britain, Greece, and Turkey, the Commander of the Force to be appointed by and responsible to the Secretary-General. The Force was to serve for three months; its functions were to prevent armed conflict on Cyprus, to contribute to the restoration of law and order, and to help bring about normal social conditions. The costs of the Force were to be paid by voluntary contributions. Finally, the resolution recommended the appointment of a UN Mediator who would assist in efforts to negotiate a political settlement.[97]

The resolution was unanimously adopted, but the Soviet Union called for a separate vote on the paragraph calling for the establishment of the peacekeeping force. On this vote, the Soviet Union, Czechoslovakia, and France abstained. The Soviet delegate

---

[96] *United Nations Monthly Chronicle,* vol. 11, no. 4, April, 1964, summarizes the Security Council debate and includes the text of the resolution (p. 8).

[97] *Ibid.,* pp. 10–11.

noted his government's opposition to the principle of force but stated that its creation would not be vetoed.[98] (Presumably the Soviet Union preferred a UN Force to its probable alternative, one drawn from NATO.) France's abstention was a protest against the delegation of power to the Secretary-General.[99]

The impact of earlier UN peacekeeping activities on the resolution should be noted. The three-month limit to UNFICYP's operation was a built-in control of its activities by the Security Council, for its extension would require the unanimous consent of the permanent members. The appointment of a Mediator also indicated a recognition that the Force's success depended on a political solution to the crisis. As will be made clear, however, force was not to be used in the achievement of this solution. Finally, the experience of the Congo was reflected in the explicit reference to ad hoc financing of the Force.

CHARACTERISTICS AND PERFORMANCE OF THE UN FORCE

An exception to the principle that no permanent members should serve on a peacekeeping force was made in this instance. The British troops on Cyprus, for the obvious reason that they were there and doing a necessary job, became a part of UNFICYP. Canada, Finland, Denmark, Sweden, Ireland, and Austria contributed military and police contingents. General Gyani of India, who was already the United Nations Special Representative on Cyprus, was appointed Commander of the Force. . . .

The scope of UNFICYP's military activities were broader than those of UNOGIL but more limited than those of ONUC. UNFICYP's primary concern was arranging a ceasefire whenever fighting broke out. The procedure followed in such cases was to confer with the leaders of both Greek and Turkish Cypriot forces and attempt to persuade them to accept a ceasefire and the interposition of UN troops to create a neutral zone. If it seemed that the attempt to interpose themselves between the two sides while fighting was taking place would expose UN troops to heavy fire, it was usually not attempted. In such situations, it was not permitted for the UN to use force to create a buffer zone.[100]

The procedure was slightly different in cases when armed conflict seemed imminent but had not yet erupted. Again the local leaders would be approached and asked to create a neutral zone which UN mobile units would patrol. If persuasion failed, the UN troops would be deployed and would announce to both sides their intention to set up a neutral zone as described. If attacked or threatened while performing this act, force could be used.

Other important activities of UNFICYP were dismantling military fortifications and disarming irregulars. It attempted to open all roads to traffic and could search travelers for arms. UNFICYP's objective was to create an atmosphere of security which would permit at least partial resumption of normal economic and social activities. By manifesting its military presence, it was felt, UNFICYP made the risks of an armed attack greater and therefore reduced the frequency and intensity of inter-communal conflict. The success of its policy was perhaps greatest in Nicosia, where UN troops stationed themselves on the "green line" dividing the city into its Greek and Turkish quarters. The creation of this

---

[98] *Ibid.*, p. 14.
[99] *Keesing's Contemporary Archives*, pp. 20122–23.

[100] A description of UN activities on the "green line" was recently given (January 6, 1965) by a CBS television broadcaster in a report from Nicosia.

heavily guarded buffer zone has ended fighting in the city.[101]

. . . In his report to the Security Council on April 29, U Thant listed the resumption of public services, the resettlement of refugees, the release of hostages, the control of police abuses, and the mediation between the warring communities at all levels of government.[102] While the military force, particularly at the staff level, could contribute in some of these areas, it is clear that the direction of such efforts would be with the Secretary-General's Political Representative on Cyprus, a position created on May 11 at the request of General Gyani.[103]

There is little evidence concerning the degree to which these objectives have been attained. It seems, however, that the resumption of the essential public services, freedom of movement on the main roads, and the renewed agricultural activity have been substantially achieved.[104] There have also been several exchanges of hostages. Urban economic life, however, remains stagnant and political and administrative activities ethnically bifurcated.

The attempts at political mediation have so far failed to produce a solution. . . . Thus, as time passes, it appears that UNFICYP has managed to end the fighting, but only freeze the political crisis at its original level. This in itself, however, is no mean achievement.

As in the Congo and Lebanon, the status of UNFICYP personnel was spelled out in an agreement with the host government. . . . Conflicts with the government did occur, but they were relatively infrequent. . . .

The Turkish Cypriots, having

[101] *Keesing's Contemporary Archives*, p. 20124.

[102] *Ibid.*

[103] Again, my most recent information on this point is the CBS broadcast cited in footnote 10.

[104] The Acheson plan is summarized in *Keesing's Contemporary Archives*, p. 20265.

broken with President Makarios, refused to recognize publicly the Greek Cypriot authorities as the legitimate government. They could thus claim that any agreement signed between the official government and the UN was invalid. When this occurred and its activities were hindered, UNFICYP would attempt to obtain the approval of the Turkish Cypriot leader on the spot. The de facto authority of President Makarios and his subordinates was recognized, however, both on Cyprus and in diplomatic circles throughout the world. However, the general problem of how to act when the host government no longer maintains de facto authority is a difficult one. It will probably be handled ad hoc by future UN forces, as agreement on a general principle seems unlikely.

The Congo experience, combined with the reluctance of the states participating in the Force to take sides, resulted in the UN's use of force being subject to greater restrictions than ONUC in its later stages. In this respect UNFICYP resembled the early ONUC and a return to Hammarskjöld's non-intervention and "fire only in self-defense" policies. A different situation helped account for this change. The use of force in a manner which could be interpreted as affecting the political outcome of the dispute could not have obtained general support from the Security Council; it might also have led to Turkish or Greek intervention.[105]

UNFICYP personnel were instructed to express no public opinion on the dispute and to maintain strict neutrality in their actions. They were to fire only in self-defense and take no action which would result in direct conflict unless compelled to do so in self-defense. In every instance, UN objectives were to be sought with the minimum of force. The violation of UN premises

[105] *Keesing's Contemporary Archives*, p. 20122.

and interference with its personnel while performing their duties, of course, would be resisted.[106]

While there was undoubtedly considerable flexibility in the application of these principles, the UN used force rarely. The first major incident involving its application occurred in August, some five months after UNFICYP's arrival. Then, Canadian and Finnish troops charged and dismantled a Turkish Cypriot emplacement threatening their position, previous warnings having been ignored. It is important to note that at the September 20 meeting of the Security Council U Thant's request for a broader mandate, including the right of the UN to use force to create buffer zones, dismantle fortifications, and ensure its freedom of movement was turned down, despite his plea that UN troops were in many places in an untenable position.

TASK PERFORMANCE AND THE
ORIGINAL UN MANDATE

Consideration of UNFICYP's performance was confined to the Security Council. Since the Soviet Union did not deadlock the Council by using its veto, there was no cause for an emergency General Assembly session. . . .

Neither the Soviet Union nor the United States directly participated in UNFICYP. The Soviet Union's involvement in the dispute itself was limited to expressions of support for the Makarios regime and of willingness to respect his appeal for military aid. Since the conflict was in a sense an intra-NATO affair, the rules of the bipolar game restricted Soviet freedom of action. Precisely because Cyprus was partly an intra-bloc dispute, the United States was and is anxious to have it settled. Hence the Acheson mission, President Johnson's conferences with

---

[106] This debate is summarized in *United Nations Monthly Chronicle*, vol. 1, no. 5, October, 1964.

---

the Greek and Turkish prime ministers, and other diplomatic representation. For this reason too the Western powers had sought to establish a NATO peacekeeping force; this having failed, it was hoped that UNFICYP would succeed in preventing Greek and Turkish intervention.

TASK PERFORMANCE, TASK EXPANSION,
AND INTEGRATION

Since UNFICYP remains today an ongoing operation, any conclusions concerning its activity must be premature and therefore tentative at best. It is possible, however, to compare this peacekeeping mission with the others analyzed. As I have made clear, the experience of the Congo weighed heavily on UNFICYP. While a military solution to the political crisis was at least feasible in the former case, it is not in Cyprus. From the outset, therefore, UNFICYP's use of force was limited and non-intervention again became the operative rule. It is doubtful that any other policy would have secured general support from the Security Council, the Western powers being insistent on not choosing between the allies.

UNFICYP has been surprisingly effective in attaining its immediate objectives. Helped no doubt by Cypriot war fatigue, it has managed to maintain a general ceasefire since early November, 1964, and peaceful conditions have provided the foundation for a measure of normalcy in economic and social life. As long as the political stalemate continues, however, the danger of a new round of violence remains.

UNFICYP's structural characteristics closely resemble ONUC's military organization. As it is smaller, however, it is less elaborate. Also, there is no non-military UNFICYP staff to speak of and no Advisory Committee. General control over the operation has resided in the Secretary-General; this seems to be inevitable in any continuing UN effort of this kind. However, as noted previously, the Security Council took pains to preserve more power over the Force in Cyprus than it had over ONUC.

There is no real evidence on which to make an assessment of organizational leadership in this crisis. I have pointed out that U Thant might have handled the initial organization of UNFICYP with more dispatch. The failure to obtain a broader mandate, however, probably can not be laid at his door. Nor can the failure to reach a political settlement. The present Secretary-General seems to lack his predecessor's creativity, imagination, and diplomatic skill, but, ironically, Mr. Hammarskjöld's failure in the Congo may mean that future UN peacekeeping activities involving intervention in an internal dispute will be limited to the non-interventionist, "buffer-creating" type of operation.

VI. Conclusions

I

It has been argued in this study that United Nations military activities in Lebanon, the Congo, West Irian, and Cyprus should, when taken together, be considered an instance of organizational task expansion, defining a "task-type." In each of these cases, the enforcement procedures outlined by the Charter were bypassed in favor of the less institutionalized and more flexible techniques of preventive diplomacy. In each case also, the United Nations intervened in what was, to a considerable extent, an *internal* political dispute, although as has been noted, there were in every instance implications of the dispute which could realistically be perceived as threats to *international* peace and security. In other words, the United Nations intervened in internal conflicts in order to avoid being faced with large-scale armed conflict between several of its member states.

Very generally, the following appear to be preconditions of United Nations military involvement in disputes of this character: first, and most important, the willingness of the rival great powers, the U.S. and U.S.S.R., to refrain from independent intervention; the cooperation of the host government; and the initiative and ability of the Secretary-General to secure from member states the men, material, and money required to deploy an effective UN Force. It should be pointed out, however, that while minimal agreement between the United States and the Soviet Union is a necessary condition for the establishment of a UN Force, subsequent changes in the situation and activities of the UN are likely to result in a breakdown of this consensus and the development of conflicting attitudes toward the status and program of the UN Force in question. This was evident in both the Lebanese and Congo crises which are also instructive in another way. The experience of UNOGIL and ONUC suggest that whatever its own preference, neither great power can secure the dismantlement of a UN Force while its existence and activities are supported by a great majority of the lesser powers and uncommitted states. This is not to say, of course, that the great powers are precluded from acting unilaterally to influence the outcome of the dispute in question in their own favor.

The constitutional basis of United Nations military intervention in at least partially internal conflicts has been a "bilateral" agreement with the host government. Experience indicates that friction between the avowedly neutral UN Force and the host government, one of the belligerent parties, is very likely to occur. The probability that the host government and the UN differ in their conceptions of the role of the international organization was enhanced by Hammarskjöld's insistence that the UN Force remain strictly neutral in domestic political conflicts. Only in this way, it was argued, could the Organization observe the strictures imposed on it by the domestic jurisdiction clause of the Charter. His position was based on the implicit assumption that the military and political aspects of the relevant disputes could be separated, the United Nations acting as a policeman in its military role and a mediator or broker of interests in its political role. The success of this policy, as the Congo experience indicates, depends on the ability of both domestic and international parties to the dispute to reach a relatively speedy political settlement or on their willingness to accept a military ceasefire and a permanent political stalemate. It must also be noted that what would occur should the host government request the withdrawal of the UN Force is as yet untested.

II

The above remarks are relevant to our reconsideration of the specificity-diffuseness proposition elaborated earlier. In a general sense, analysis of four instances of task performance supports the hypothesis. The more limited the range of the Force's military activities, the greater the restrictions on the UN's right to use armed force, and the less its involvement in non-military administrative activities, the less controversial were its programs and the greater was the Organization's ability to satisfy its "clients." Although UNOGIL's activities and reports were not received without controversy, its overall performance was such that it generally increased the willingness of member states to support UN peacekeeping activities. ONUC's more ambitious program failed to obtain the political pacification and unification of the Congo,

exacerbated great power differences as to the "proper" role of a UN Force, and led to "task reduction" in UNFICYP's program.

A comparison of the UN's activities in Lebanon and Cyprus supports the contention that organizational task expansion *within* the "task-type" has taken place. UNOGIL observers at no time used armed force in the performance of their duties, while UNFICYP duties were more broadly defined and the use of force was necessary. UNFICYP's activities, which included, for example, ensuring the safety of civilian traffic on the Kyrenia Road, made greater inroads on the normal jurisdiction of the host government than was true in the case of UNOGIL. It must be reiterated, however, that the stability over time of this increased scope of international authority is the ultimate test of the above conclusion regarding organizational task expansion.

It is by no means certain, however, that repeated performances of functionally specific programs related to military security will lead to stronger organizational structures and broader responsibilities. While it does appear that the United Nations will, in the future, be called on to establish observer groups and "non-interventionist, buffer-creating" Forces, it is possible that these functionally specific sets of activities may become routinized. In Selznick's terms, they will fail to be "infused with value."[107] On the other hand, while functionally diffuse military activities and the use of force to attain the settlement of a dispute lead to controversy and conflict among member states, should the United Nations prove able to bring about a broadly acceptable political solution, the relevant task performance is likely to contribute to an increased willingness to expand the scope of UN au-

[107] See P. Selznick, *Leadership in Administration,* New York, 1956.

thority in the handling of future disputes. By the same token, of course, diffuse programs which fail thwart the process of organizational growth.

Since the possibility of strong support for functionally diffuse operations in the peacekeeping sphere depends on a relatively stable confluence of American and Soviet interests, international forces with broad military and political powers will continue to be the rare exception. The inability of ONUC to retain even the acquiescence of the Soviet Union in its policies was dysfunctional for organizational task expansion. The most striking evidence that the authority of the United Nations to undertake peacekeeping activities had been reduced was the necessity to finance UNFICYP by voluntary contributions. For the immediate present, it appears that all further UN emergency forces will be financed on an ad hoc basis. Functionally specific programs, therefore, are what can be expected, but at best it is doubtful that successful, that is, generally approved, performances of this kind will result in the legitimization of United Nations operations more diffuse and politicized in orientation.

III

United Nations activities in the four cases examined were characterized by the increasing centralization of administrative control in the person of the Secretary-General. These powers were at a maximum in the management of ONUC, but the Congo experience also served as a lesson that the very scope of his power can be a threat to the Secretary-General, making it simple for opposition to the United Nations policy to focus on him. The Congo crisis generated a severe threat to the very notion of an independent Secretariat and Mr. Hammarskjöld's death, callous though this may sound, probably

was instrumental in saving his own conception of the Secretary-General's role.

The influence of the General Assembly was also at its peak in the Congo case. As I have already indicated, both major powers emerged from the experience apparently more cautious of allowing a large role in the guidance of peacekeeping operations to the Afro-Asian dominated Assembly. The Cyprus question, to illustrate the point, was discussed only in the Security Council. And by making the existence of UNFICYP subject to periodic votes of extension, the Security Council also limited the Secretary-General's freedom of action. It must, however, be noted that in future disputes more relevant to the primary foreign policy goals of the Afro-Asians there is likely to be greater participation in policy making of the Assembly.

Several structural innovations which emerged from the peacekeeping experiences of the United Nations have become relatively well institutionalized. The principle that permanent members of the Security Council be excluded from active participation in UN Forces is firmly established, Great Britain's role in UNFICYP being due to a unique set of circumstances. Similarly, the importance of establishing a political arm of the military operation has been recognized. Thus, the Advisory Committee is a device to mobilize political support for the policies of the Secretary-General and the Special Political Representative an attempt to lessen the Force Commander's work load and facilitate the development of harmonious relations between the UN Force and the host government. However, no permanent military structure has been created.

The myriad technical and political problems encountered by the United Nations in the course of its peacekeeping activities can not be exhaustively investigated here, but some of the difficulties relating to the UN's status vis-a-vis the host government and to the organization and administration of international forces should be briefly discussed.

It has been stressed that a sense of mutual trust and confidence between the United Nations and the host government is a precondition of the smooth functioning of the international forces. The UN, therefore, faces a serious dilemma when, as was the case in the Congo, precisely what individual or group represents the legitimate government of the host country appears ambiguous. Unfortunately, no general principle can guide the UN in such a situation and probably the best course for the administrators of the Force to follow is consultation with the Security Council or General Assembly. This policy may on occasion reveal an overriding conflict between competing groups of member states and lead to paralysis of the UN operation, but the most probable alternative, the selection without general consultation of one of the competing local factions as the de facto regime with which the UN should deal, is likely to lead to the disintegration of any viable basis of political support for the further activities of the Force.

When the legitimate representatives of the host government are clearly identifiable, the problems of the Force are less complicated. In all instances, the United Nations must insist on securing certain important privileges. Most important of these are: complete freedom of movement for UN Forces within the host territory, freedom of entry for UN troops and equipment, and suitable accommodations for and complete jurisdiction over the conduct of its personnel. These principles were, in general, observed in the four cases studied. If task expansion is to take place, these should be expanded to include the right of the UN to disarm local belligerents when necessary, the

right to arrest and interrogate suspected terrorists and mercenaries, and the right to search traffic for hidden weapons.[108] In the ultimate case of complete political chaos in the host country, it may be necessary to set up a temporary United Nations trusteeship.

Despite a rebirth of academic interest in international military forces, which has led to the circulation of several interesting proposals for the creation of a permanent United Nations army,[109] both Mr. Hammarskjöld and U Thant have argued that, given the uniqueness of each situation in which the UN is called on to intervene, it is preferable to maximize flexibility by dealing with crises on an ad hoc basis. There is some merit to this view, particularly since controversy is likely to attend any plan for a stand-by force.[110] Nevertheless, the accounts of the logistical and technical difficulties which beset UN operations in the Congo and Cyprus suggest that some alternative to almost complete unpreparedness would be desirable.

A useful beginning would be to train a permanent body of middle and high-ranking staff officers, the procurement of relatively mobile logistical facilities, including transportation and communication equipment, and the establishment of a mobile training unit, that is, a group of qualified and experienced instructors who would train national security forces, in their own countries,

---

[108] Burns and Heathcote attempt to systematize a set of principles for the basis of the relations between a UN Force and the host government. These suggestions are taken in part from their list. See their Ch. IX.

[109] There has been a renascence of interest in international military forces since 1956 and suggestions for the creation of a permanent UN Force. Prominent examples are W. Frye, *A United Nations Peace Force,* New York, 1957, and L. Bloomfield, et al., *International Military Forces.*

[110] This is pointed out by Claude's discussion of the activities of the Military Staff Committee, "The UN and the Use of Force."

in such relevant procedures as riot control.

This approach seems more capable of securing general agreement than a plan based on the expectation of integrating large national contingents into a stand-by army of considerable size. The recruitment and training of staff officers and logistic experts, on the other hand, should not be difficult, particularly since they might well be employed conjointly by one of the Organization's Specialized Agencies. Given their record of solid support for UN peacekeeping activities, the Scandinavian countries are probably willing to provide the Organization with a skeleton transportation and procurement service. Finally, the training unit would be sent to those member states willing to be bound by a general and prior commitment to participate in a UN Force when asked. Both parties would benefit from such an arrangement: the Afro-Asian countries involved would gain well-trained local security contingents and the UN would secure a source of reliable personnel for an emergency Force. Care in the recruitment and training of staff officers would minimize the possibility of widespread communication breakdowns during the conduct of operations.

IV

Only the naive will deny the fragility of the international community in the contemporary world. International organizations are founded on the conviction that this tenuousness is not permanent and that a strong sense of international community can be created by national cooperation in common endeavors. This, in a sense, is the meaning of the hypothesis that organizational task expansion contributes to international integration.

It is fair, I think, to say that in a divided world permanently threatened by the possibility of a nuclear holocaust, United Nations peacekeeping operations have come to be regarded by most states as a technique that can limit and localize the scope of conflicts. A UN Force, in this sense, is an attempt to stabilize armed conflict at a low level while diplomatic negotiations attempt to secure a political settlement. The establishment of UNFICYP and UNTEA indicated that they have come to accept the utility of this technique, if only as a last resort. The strongest supporters of UN Forces have been the Afro-Asian states, Canada, and the Scandinavian countries. For the former group, United Nations involvement is attractive because it maximizes their own participation in the settlement of the dispute and because the alternative may be intervention in an African or Asian state by one or more of the "colonialist" powers. And, as President Makarios' role in the creation of UNFICYP showed, the very availability of the United Nations as a source of international police forces enables the host government to reject any other form of international intervention. Post-colonial conflicts of the type described in this paper are likely to recur, confronting Western, particularly American, policy-makers with a continuing dilemma. It is likely that intervention under United Nations auspices will be the only form of international involvement acceptable to the uncommitted states, but Western power to control the decisions of the United Nations is decreasing.

UN involvement in internal disputes contributes, if only slightly, to the process of international integration by adding to the store of techniques available to deal with threats to international peace and by increasing the arena in which the presence of the United Nations serves as at least a moral restraint on the conduct of international actors. I do not mean to imply that the United Nations was the only or even the most important influence in the prevention of large-scale war in the four crises discussed. Undoubtedly the influences of systematic factors and the interests of national actors, as well as the nature of the disputes themselves, were more important determinants. Nevertheless, the existence of the United Nations and its ability to resourcefully undertake peacekeeping activities involving military operations facilitated the maintenance of international peace. The Organization's activity served to lessen the intensity of conflict before great power involvement could threaten nuclear disaster.

For whatever reason, it is difficult for most parties to internal disputes to sanction armed attacks on the blue-helmeted UN soldiers separating it from its antagonists. The presence of a United Nations Force, therefore, is likely to result in the less vigorous pursuit of highly valued political objectives. To some degree, the reluctance to attack UN personnel stems from the recognition that a UN Force represents the international community, if only in the minimal sense of reflecting the lowest common denominator shared by (otherwise) many conflicting private interests. If this is true, willful attacks on soldiers serving with the UN are unlikely to win friends for one's cause and their very presence may serve to encourage parties to the dispute in question to negotiate rather than fight.

Unfortunately, I must close on a less optimistic note. The ability of the United Nations to undertake military operations in the pursuit of international peace depends, in the contemporary world order, on the convergence of widely conflicting private interests. Since such a convergence is unlikely to be more than partial and very temporary, organizational task expansion in this area is an uneven and tenuous process. The benefits which are dispensed by several moderately successful instances of task performance, such as the programs of UNEF and UNOGIL, can be wiped out by one partial failure, such as ONUC. Furthermore, changes in the international environment can make irrelevant the authority that an international organization has laboriously built up over a period of years. In short, it is a hard struggle simply to stay even. Finally, when, as in the Congo and Cyprus, the Organization's leadership is able or forced to choose between alternative policies it is unlikely that either choice will be wholly satisfactory.[111] Organizational task expansion in the military sphere, to repeat, continues to be largely attendant on changes in the international system.

[111] This point is made by Hoffman, "In Search of a Thread," pp. 359–61.

17. The World Court in the International Bargaining Process*

WILLIAM D. COPLIN

ALTHOUGH the World Court (Hudson's phrase for the Permanent Court

* Printed with the permission of William D. Coplin.

of International Justice and the International Court of Justice) has been operating in the international system for over forty years, the scholarly literature on its role in world affairs is, on the whole, unsystematic and polemical.[1] Like so many of the scholars analysing international law in general, those discussing the World Court have usually done so in the framework of "for" or "against." Consequently, the literature on the Court does not contain a common theoretical framework and often does not share the same factual basis.

On the one hand, there are those writers—probably in the majority— who maintain that the Court does not settle important, i.e., political, disputes. Among the arguments put forth by these writers, the following are typical:

1.1 The World Court does not treat the reason for conflict but only the symptoms of the conflict. The conflict results from different opinions of the existing *status quo,* and the Court cannot really deal with such conflict.[2]

1.2 In its history, the Court has dealt with no or almost no real political questions.[3]

1.3 Certain disputes are non-justiciable, and these are the most important in terms of questions of war or peace.[4]

1.4 Peaceful conditions exist prior to an effective judicial process. The judicial process cannot create peace in a hostile world.[5]

On the other hand, there are those writers who maintain that the World Court has handled political questions and, moreover, has been instrumental in preventing potentially disruptive disputes from maturing. These scholars usually argue in the following terms:

2.1 Judicial settlement is a functional replacement for war in relations among states.[6]

2.2 The justiciability/non-justiciability dichotomy is unwarranted since all disputes are potentially justiciable.[7]

2.3 The World Court has settled a number of political disputes.[8]

2.4 The World Court allows disputants time to "cool-off" and the leaders of states the chance to avoid the extremism of their nationalistic publics.[9]

[1] This is not to say that there are no thoughtful works on the World Court. Some of the better discussions of the Court are Manley O. Hudson, *International Tribunals: Past and Future* (Washington, 1944); Julius Stone, "The International Court and World Crisis," *International Conciliation* No. 536 (January, 1962); Shabtai Rosenne, *The International Court of Justice* (Leyden, 1957); and Leo Gross, "Some Observations on the International Court of Justice," *American Journal of International Law* 56: 33–63 (1962).

[2] E.g., Charles De Visscher, *Theory and Reality in Public International Law* (Trans. by P. E. Corbett) (Princeton, 1957), p. 327; Morton A. Kaplan and Nicholas DeB. Katzenbach, *The Political Foundations of International Law* (New York, 1961), p. 280; and Hans J. Morgenthau, *Politics Among Nations* (New York, 1961), p. 427.

[3] E.g., Morgenthau, *op. cit.,* p. 432 referring to the record of the PCIJ, and Lincoln P. Bloomfield, *Evolution or Revolution? The United Nations and the Problem of Peaceful Territorial Change* (Cambridge, 1957), pp. 151–52 since 1945.

[4] E.g., Julius Stone, *Local Controls of International Conflict* (New York, 1954), pp. 146–152; P. E. Corbett, *Law and Society in the Relations of States* (New York, 1951), p. 78; and E. H. Carr, *The Twenty Years' Crisis* (London, 1939), p. 205.

[5] E.g., De Visscher, *op. cit.,* p. 327.

[6] E.g., R. P. Anand, *Compulsory Jurisdiction of the International Court of Justice* (New York, 1961), p. 4; J. L. Brierly, *The Basis of Obligation in International Law* (Oxford, 1958), p. 94; and Hans Kelsen, *Peace Through Law* (Chapel Hill, 1944), p. 13.

[7] E.g., Brierly, *op. cit.,* p. 101; Kelsen, *op. cit.* (*Peace Through Law*), p. 27; and Manley O. Hudson, *op. cit.* (*International Tribunals* . . .), p. 239.

[8] E. g., Rosenne, *op. cit.,* p. 2; and Hersch Lauterpacht, *The Development of International Law by the International Court* (New York, 1958), p. 3.

[9] E.g., Manley O. Hudson. *By Pacific Means* (New Haven, 1935), p. 71; De Visscher, *op. cit.,* p. 330; and Lauterpacht, *op. cit.,* p. 4.

The scholarly literature on the World Court may also be surveyed in terms of suggestions for making the Court more effective. Generally, there have been three areas upon which these suggestions have focused.

First, many analysts of the Court assume that the success of the Court will be limited as long as men are not willing to invest the authority for certain decisions in centralized international institutions. While the analysts have pinned the responsibility for the lack of willingness on various factors —international tensions, sovereignty, habitual behavior, etc.—, they all agree that a central judicial process for settling disputes will not become more effective until a willingness to rely on such a process becomes widespread.[10]

Secondly, many writers have called for improvement of the World Court as a judicial instrument. Criticism has been leveled at the length and costs of the cases, the alleged biases of the Judges, and the procedures for developing the rules of law. These writers assume that the institution itself rather than, or in addition to, the conditions surrounding the institution must be improved.[11]

Finally, many writers argue that the nature of the post-adjudicative phase inhibits the effectiveness of the Court. Some maintain that a centralized system for enforcing decisions of the Court is a prerequisite for the successful operating of the Court. Although other writers have claimed that the relatively successful record of the execution of judicial decisions renders unnecessary a centralized institution for executing decisions at this time, explicit as well as implicit concern over the post-adjudication process is apparent in many discussions of the Court.[12]

From this brief discussion, it is apparent that the existing literature on the World Court lacks both theoretical clarity and, in some cases, a general body of agreed-upon data. The purpose of this paper is to make a start at supplying an explicit theoretical framework as well as a systematic collection of data on the role of the Court in international affairs. The paper will be focused at the level of macro-analysis—that is, at the level of looking at the entire record of the Court on contentious cases. Although this study will not suffice for a detailed analysis of each case and the intentions as well as actions of states in each case, it should supply a basis for further studies at the level of micro-analysis. We have collected data on all of the contentious cases which single litigants have submitted to the Court between 1922 and 1964 as well as on the relationship between the litigants and the characteristics of the states which use the Courts.[13] At the same time, we have

[12] E.g., for those arguing that the lack of execution powers is important, see R. P. Anand, "Execution of International Judicial Awards: Experience Since 1945," *University of Pittsburgh Law Review* 26: 671–703; Oscar Schachter, "The Enforcement of International Judicial and Arbitral Decisions," *American Journal of International Law* (1960), pp. 1–24; and Rosenne, *op. cit.*, pp. 3–4.

For a writer who has minimized the importance of the execution power, see Hans Kelsen, *Law and Peace in International Relations* (Cambridge, 1942), p. 145.

[13] The Appendix at the end of the paper presents tables of the data collected. This study does not include Advisory Opinions as well as the contentious cases which had multiple applicants. Although the former category includes a number of very important cases, the latter includes only four cases. To complete the study of the World Court in the International Bargaining Process, it would be

[10] E.g., Inis L. Claude, Jr., *Swords Into Plowshares* (New York, 1964), pp. 209–10; Brierly, *op. cit.,* p. 94; De Visscher, *op. cit.,* p. 330; and Lauterpacht, *op. cit.,* p. 5.

[11] E.g., Arthur Larson, *When Nations Disagree* (Baton Rouge, 1961), p. 86; Hans Wehberg, *The Problem of the International Court of Justice* (New York, 1918), pp. 7–8; Kaplan and Katzenbach, *op. cit.,* p. 281; and Stone, *op. cit. (International Court and World Crisis),* pp. 60–1.

tried to analyse the trends and data from an explicit theoretical framework.

I. The Nature of the International Bargaining Process

Bargaining relationships exist in every type of social system. Before examining the international bargaining process, we will look at the bargaining process in domestic social systems. A bargaining situation between two persons in the United States, for example, is the middle stage in a three-stage interaction relating to the distribution of objectives among the two persons. The first stage may be called the "pre-bargaining stage" where citizen A inquires into the willingness of citizen B to comply with citizen A's wish. If citizen B is willing, the bargaining stage of the interaction is never reached. However, if citizen B communicates a lack of willingness, the second stage of the interaction, or the "bargaining stage," begins. This involves a series of communications concerning the intentions of each side in regard to the objectives involved and can be set in terms of threats as well as promises. If two citizens are unable to reach an outcome, the "post-bargaining stage" in the interaction is reached. In the post-bargaining stage in domestic society, the Courts make a definitive and authoritative decision on the bargaining outcome.[14]

In domestic societies, the law and the courts shape all three stages of interaction. In the pre-bargaining stage, they operate covertly by telling citizen A what demands he can make of citizen B which citizen B might be willing to accept because he would not expect support from the law. In the bargaining stage, the law operates covertly by communicating what citizen A might expect citizen B's attitude to be on certain bargaining positions, and overtly by constraining the bargaining agents in their choice of strategies (e.g., not to employ force). Finally, the law operates explicitly in the post-bargaining stage because it gives authority and guidelines to the Courts so that they may make authoritative decisions on the bargaining outcomes.

Although the interaction among states can be viewed in terms of the pre-bargaining, bargaining and post-bargaining stages, it is substantially different from the interaction among people in the domestic setting, particularly in its relation to law and the World Court. The international system, as a social system, is characterized by the lack of centralized authority to regulate and administer the process of which states "get what, when and how" through their interactions. In pursuing their objectives, states find it neither feasible nor desirable to allow common international institutions to make final and authoritative decisions concerning the distribution of objectives. Rather, states have depended upon a process of interaction among themselves to determine the authorita-

---

necessary to analyze the Advisory Opinions. They have been excluded in this study because they should be treated in a different theoretical framework than contentious cases. The dates 1922 to 1964 represent the major portion of the Court's history. This assumes that the World Court is distinct from the Permanent Court of International Arbitration. [The Appendix has been omitted from this Reading—ED.]

[14] The model just outlined applies to private citizens. When groups are involved—e.g., labor, management, corporations or political parties—, there are other institutions for allocating payoffs. However, law and the courts still play an essential role in the bar-

gaining among groups since they outline specific procedural restraints on the bargaining process. We will raise the question at the end of the paper of whether or not it might be better to base the analysis on the model of groups bargaining in domestic society. The reason the model presented here is focused on citizens is because the World Court, rather than other international institutions, is the focus of analysis for the paper.

tive allocation of values. As a result, most international interactions are bargaining interactions. Both the pre-bargaining and the post-bargaining stages are not distinctly distinguishable from the bargaining stage. The lack of stable relationships and the varied nature of international demands limit the frequency of the pre-bargaining situation where compliance is a matter of course, and the unwillingness of states to give central institutions the authority to make decisions on bargaining outcomes create extended bargaining situations where the outcome depends on one party's "giving in." Interaction among states, then, remains primarily a set of bargaining relationships.

The relationship of international law and the world Court to the interaction among states is different from the relationship between Courts and individual interactions in the domestic setting. First, because international law is a decentralized system of law,[15] expressions of the law by states are often indistinguishable from expressions of policy. Hence, state B might have announced a "legal" position or a general principle of law which communicates to state A that its request will be accepted or, conversely, refused. Secondly, because the constraints which international law places on the ways in which states bargain are flexible to the point of ambiguity, the bargaining stage of interaction can range from negotiation, through tacit communications and explicit threats, to the use of force in a symbolic manner.[16] Fi-

nally, unlike the domestic social system where the authoritative decision on bargaining outcomes is reached through the Courts for citizens (although it might be reached through other centralized institutions for certain groups), the authoritative decision on bargaining outcomes in the international system can occur in a number of ways. The World Court is only one of many international institutions. Global as well as regional inter-governmental organizations, arbitration and mixed tribunals on the regional as well as inter-regional levels, intervention of a third state and war represent other "institutional processes" in which bargaining outcomes can be reached.[17]

The interaction between two states, then, takes place in a social and institutional setting different from the environment for interaction in domestic social systems. Because of the lack of explicitly operating constraints on the ways states bargain, the pre-bargaining stage is difficult to distinguish from the bargaining stage. Because the "institutions" for making authoritative decisions on bargaining outcomes are manifold and not located primarily in one centralized international institution, the post-bargaining stage is difficult to distinguish from the bargaining stage. Therefore, it is reasonable to maintain that international interactions still remain primarily a bargaining process and to investigate the World Court primarily in terms of its role in that bargaining process.[18]

---

[15] The concept of decentralized system of law is most highly developed by Hans Kelsen. See Hans Kelsen, *Principles of International Law* (New York, 1966 2nd Edition Edited by Robert W. Tucker).

[16] It is necessary to distinguish between the symbolic use of force which Morton Halperin, *Limited War in the Nuclear Age* (New York, 1963) calls the use of force for political effects and war as an institution or process for determining bargaining outcomes. In terms of

the framework developed in this paper, the former use of force is involved in the bargaining stage, while the latter is the post-bargaining stage in international interaction.

[17] It is hoped that studies of these other institutions can be made in frameworks somewhat similar to the one being employed in this paper.

[18] Much of the theoretical framework underlying the above discussion depends upon excellent discussions of bargaining and international relations appearing in Thomas C. Schelling, *The Strategy of Conflict* (New

II. The Role of the Court in the International Bargaining Process

We will examine the role of the Court in the international bargaining process. The study will be at the macro-level since it will look at the entire record of the Court and the general behavior of states in relation to the Court. This study has been undertaken in the belief that an analysis of this type should precede, but not preclude, a study on the micro-level—that is, in terms of the impact of the Court on particular national decisions.

A. THE EXTENT TO WHICH THE COURT AFFECTS THE PROCESS

One can get an idea of the limited extent the World Court operates in the international bargaining process merely by counting the number of contentious issues that have been submitted to the Court in the forty-one years from 1923 to 1964. Excluding the few cases where there were multiple litigants, fifty-five disputes (although a number of disputes have been submitted more than once) have reached the Court. If one subtracts the eight cases where the prospective respondent refused to acknowledge the jurisdiction of the Court unconditionally, it is apparent that only a small portion of the bargaining relationships that develop in the international system involved the World Court.[19]

Moreover, it is a special type of state which uses the World Court. To use the terms of the *Cross-Polity Survey*,[20] it is a state with a "constitutional government" (61%), a "polyarchic" pattern of representativeness (55%) and a developed or intermediately developed economy (82%).[21] The typical state is culturally and geographically Eastern or Western European (68%).[22] It is an extensive participant in global international organizations (79%) and has signed the "Optional Clause" (76%), although it may have made "Connally-type" reservations to the Clause.

The argument made by a number of analysts that the Court does not have universal appeal is substantiated by the types of states using the Court. Of the fifty-five cases, only three have not involved a European state as one or both of the litigants. Two of those were Latin American states and one Asian. Although these three cases have occurred since the Second World War and represent a modest trend toward more universal appeal, the absence of Eastern European participation in the Court since 1945 represents a countertrend in the use of the Court. A further indication of the predominant European use of the Court is the fact that out of eighteen non-European states which have been involved in cases with European states, only Israel, the United States and Cameroun have been ap-

York, 1961), and Harold Guetzkow and Jack Sawyer, "Bargaining and Negotiation in International Relations," in Herbert Kelman, *International Behavior* (New York, 1965). For a discussion of international law in a bargaining framework, see William D. Coplin, *The Functions of International Law* (Chicago, in press), Chapter Three. An excellent discussion of the World Court which employs partial reference to a bargaining framework can be found in Gross, *op. cit.*, pp. 40–42.

[19] The basis for selecting the cases per dispute as well as the data collected on the disputes appear in the Appendix [not included]. Although the term "cases" will be used in

the text, we are referring to "case-units," that is, the cluster of cases around one issue, as described in the Appendix.

[20] Arthur S. Banks and Robert B. Textor, *The Cross-Polity Survey* (Cambridge, 1963). To classify states using the Court prior to 1956, we applied the Banks-Textor categories.

[21] These percentages are weighted by the fact that the same state is counted each time it participates in five different periods over the forty-one year period. . . .

[22] The classification of socio-cultural regions was developed by Bruce M. Russett in a lecture given at the Mental Health Research Institute, University of Michigan, Fall, 1965.

plicants. Although the number of inter-regional cases (as opposed to intra-regional) [23] have grown from two of the twenty-four under the PCIJ to twenty-four of the thirty-one under the ICJ, which clearly indicates a more universal use of the Court, the Court continues to be of use to a small number of states and for a small number of issues. The reason for this shift lies in the fact that the number of non-European states in the Inter-War Period was very low.

B. RELATIONSHIPS OF THE BARGAINING STATE TO THE WORLD COURT

As we pointed out in the preceding pages, the World Court stands in a different relationship to the international bargaining process from the way in which the domestic courts are related to domestic bargaining among citizens. Instead of being clearly associated with the post-bargaining process as domestic courts are, the World Court is usually involved—if it is involved at all—in the actual bargaining process. In domestic societies, the Courts remove the two antagonists from the fluid context of bargaining to the rigorous applicant-respondent relationship, but in the international system the applicant-respondent relationship is clearly established only on few occasions.

Twelve out of fifty-five cases before the Court have involved one state's introducing a dispute and the prospective respondent's unconditionally accepting the jurisdiction of the Court.[24] Eight of these cases were introduced through compulsory jurisdiction with the respondent's accepting the Court's jurisdiction, and four were unilateral applications accepted by the respondent.[25] Of the remaining forty-three cases, twenty-two found the respondent making preliminary objections to the Court's jurisdiction, thirteen were by joint submission and eight were unilateral applications which the prospective respondent refused to accept as an invitation to the case.

From these figures, it is obvious that the World Court has not served in the majority of cases as an institution in the post-bargaining process. Most of the states that have used the Court have done so with the assumption that their relationship to the Court was something other than the applying or responding litigant. We can note a number of types of attitudes and/or relationships to the Court held by states which have had dealings with the Court.

The first and most common type is avoidance. We have already pointed out that the majority of states have avoided the Court completely on most issues. This type also includes the states which have declined to accept the Court's jurisdiction even though another state has called upon the state to accept the jurisdiction of the Court.

The second use of the Court is to communicate willingness to settle the dispute through the symbolic gesture of unilateral application. Whether the act of unilateral application can be viewed as a serious attempt to have the dispute settled by the Court and, therefore, a communication to only the major antagonist (as the Danish application in the "Legal Status of Greenland" seems to have been) or as

---

[23] It could be argued that the main business of the Court should be interregional since regional courts like the European Court of Justice have existed for some time and mixed tribunals and arbitral arrangements can be made easily at the intra-regional level.

[24] The coding is based on *ICJ Reports*.

[25] It is possible that the unilateral application accepted by the respondent does not represent a genuine applicant-respondent relationship either, since the respondent could have agreed prior to the application in which case it would be a joint submission. Without analysis into the specific interaction of the four cases, however, it was decided to consider the four cases as applicant-respondent relationships.

an attempt to communicate the willingness to settle the dispute to "world public opinion" (as one suspects the use of the Court by the United States under the Eisenhower Administration was) [26] or a combination of the two, it is obvious that the state making the unilateral declaration is using the Court to communicate a bargaining position or information that will affect its bargaining position.

The third use of the Court is the joint agreement to submit the dispute to the adjudication process. Resembling arbitration in domestic as well as international society where the antagonists seek the help of a disinterested third party to decide the final outcome, this use has occurred thirteen times in the Court's history. The strategy followed by both parties is to use the adjudication process as a plateau in the bargaining process where both sides agree that the settlement of the dispute is more important than the relative distribution of objectives resulting from the final decision. In this type, the applicant-respondent relationship is replaced by an arbitral-type relationship although the law rather than *ad hoc* principles are employed to reach the decision.

The fourth use of the Court lies somewhere between complete avoidance and the other two strategies. It is the policy of a number of states which have signed the "Optional Clause" but which try to avoid the jurisdiction of the Court by raising preliminary objections whenever put in the respondent position. It might be argued that the strategy of raising preliminary objections should not be considered distinct from the applicant-respondent relationship since the respondent is willing to

[26] Between 1954 and 1960, the United States made its only eight applications. All were against the Communist states for alleged failure to give air rights to American planes on certain occasions, and all were unilateral applications rejected by the prospective respondent.

let the final authority for the decision of jurisdiction rest with the Court, and the question of jurisdiction is legitimate to raise in any legal system. However, these arguments are countered by the extensive use made of preliminary objections. The preliminary objection was raised in twenty-two out of thirty cases where it was possible. Furthermore, three of the four instances where there was some difficulty with the execution of the judgment were cases in which preliminary objections had been overruled. Finally, a number of states which have signed the "Optional Clause" since 1945 have refused to accept the respondent relationship without preliminary objections.[27]

We have noted four uses of the Court which cannot be classified in the terms of the normal applicant-respondent relationship which exists in the post-bargaining stage in domestic societies. By comparing the PCIJ to the ICJ in terms of these uses, a number of significant developments (as illustrated in the graph below) in the relationship between the Court and the international bargaining process can be examined. First there has been a shift away from the use of joint submissions in the post-World War II period. While over 40% of the cases under the PCIJ were introduced through a joint application, less than 10% of the ICJ cases have been. An equally significant development has been the occurrence of unanswered unilateral applications to the Court. Under the PCIJ, there were four unilateral applications, but they were all accepted by prospective respondents. Under the ICJ, there have been eight unilateral applications, all rejected. Finally, the frequency of submissions involving compulsory jurisdiction have increased from ten in the

[27] E.g., the UK has twice made preliminary objections and has not accepted compulsory jurisdiction since 1945. Bulgaria and Albania have raised preliminary objections. The latter still has not complied with the merit decision of the Court in the Corfu Channel Case.

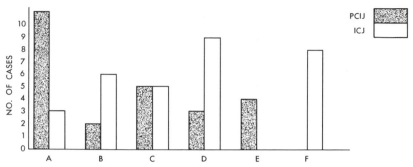

FIGURE 1. Manner in which the dispute was first introduced to the court.

MANNER OF INTRODUCTION

A. Mutual Agreement.
B. Compulsory Jurisdiction Accepted by the Respondent.
C. Compulsory Jurisdiction Challenged by Respondent but Overruled by Court.
D. Compulsory Jurisdiction Challenged by Respondent and Upheld by Court.
E. Application Accepted by Second Party.
F. Application Refused by Second Party.

PCIJ to twenty in the ICJ, but so have the number of preliminary objections (from eight to fourteen). In this latter aspect, the preliminary objections upheld by the Court have tripled, which is probably a result of the more frequent occurrence of Connally-type reservations to the "Optional Clause."

In surveying the uses made of the Court in the past, its relationship to bargaining among states contrasts sharply with the relationship of domestic courts to bargaining among people. First, the Court does not cover the universe of interactions among units in the international system as the law does in domestic social systems. Secondly, the relationship of the states to the World Court are only infrequently in the applicant-respondent framework. Although the historical trend away from the joint application to the Court and toward the applicant-respondent framework based on the compulsory jurisdiction clause might appear to indicate the transformation of the operation of the World Court into something more akin to domestic courts, the increase in preliminary ob-

jections, the instances of unanswered unilateral applications and the failure of the Court to increase its business relative to the increase in the number of states and frequency of contacts quite possibly indicates an opposite trend. At any rate, it indicates that the typical attitude of states toward the Court remains incompatible with the applicant-respondent relationship which exists in domestic societies.

C. DIMENSIONS OF THE INTERNATIONAL
BARGAINING PROCESS AFFECTED
BY THE COURT

In this section we will discuss a number of dimensions in the international bargaining process which the Court seems to affect. The discussion will include the types of disputes handled by the Court, the point of time at which the Court enters the bargaining relationship, the element of time introduced by the Court, and the question of the types of relationships existing between the states that get involved in international litigations.

1. *Types of Disputes.* One of the

more popular issues for debate among scholars of the Court is the question concerning types of disputes which the Court has handled. The juxtaposition of political, justiciable and important to non-political, non-justiciable and unimportant is made by both those defending and those attacking the Court. In the typology developed for this study, the following categories were used: (1) territorial; (2) jurisdiction and/or control over persons; (3) jurisdiction and/or control over property; (4) interpretation of treaties; and (5) responsibility for acts. Although there were a number of cases which overlapped, classification on all cases were made. The use of such a classification avoids the traditional set of juxtapositions since it makes no judgment on the "political quality" of the dispute. This is not to imply that an operational scheme for measuring the "political quality" of disputes would not have been valuable.[28]

The distribution of cases according to the typology discussed above indicates that the most frequent type of dispute is one involving jurisdiction and/or control over materials (twenty-four out of fifty-five cases). Of the remaining thirty-one cases, twelve were classified as jurisdiction and/or control over persons; eleven as territorial disputes; seven as treaty interpretation; and one under responsibility for acts. As far as the historical trend from the PCIJ to the ICJ, there are two noticeable developments. On the one hand, treaty interpretation has dropped from five under the PCIJ to two under the ICJ. On the other hand, the number of territorial disputes handled by the Court has risen from three under the PCIJ to eight under the ICJ.

[28] See the suggestions in the concluding sections. On a broader scale, an attempt to operationalize the distinction between international *politics* and international *relations* often made in the literature would be of great aid to the discipline.

Although it is difficult to draw inferences at this level of analysis concerning the degree to which each type of dispute has raised political overtones, it appears that as a whole disputes over material control over jurisdiction created the greatest amount of disagreement over the role of the Court between the two litigants. Evidence for this inference, which is by no means conclusive, appears when one correlates the types of disputes to the manner in which the case was brought to the Court. In seventeen out of twenty-four cases involving disputes over material control and jurisdiction, one party refused to accept unconditionally the jurisdiction of the Court (eleven preliminary objections and six rejections of unilateral applications). This compares with the thirteen out of thirty-one cases involving other types of disputes where one party refused to accept unconditionally the jurisdiction of the Court. In terms of relating the willingness of states to use the Court to the type of dispute, then, material disputes tended to occasion a more negative response than other types of disputes.[29]

2. *The Age of the Dispute and the Court.* Although the age of disputes (the date of the incident subtracted from the date of introduction to the Court) before they are brought to the Court has varied between less than a year and more than twenty years, only eight of the fifty-five disputes were less than a year old when first introduced. Over sixty-five percent of the cases involved disputes ranging from over a year to ten years old. The relative long length of time between the

[29] The percentage difference between the material disputes and the other types is only twenty-nine percent. Seventy-one percent of all cases involving material disputes resulted in one side refusing to accept unconditionally the jurisdiction of the Court, while forty-two percent of non-material disputes resulted in this phenomenon. Therefore, the validity of this inference should depend on further analysis at the micro-level.

initiation of the bargaining stage and its introduction to the Court indicates that states do not consider the Court to be among the first alternatives in their bargaining with another state.

As far as the historical trend between the PCIJ and the ICJ in regard to the age of disputes goes, the following graph illustrates an interesting shift.

tion of the Court generally freezes other interactions in the bargaining process. The length of time which the Court takes in dealing with the case varies in the following manner: twenty cases lasted less than a year; eighteen, between one and two years; fourteen, between two and four years; and three cases, over four years.

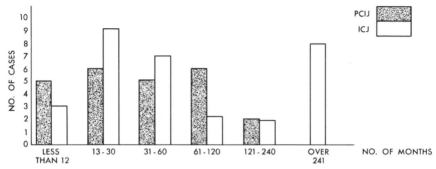

FIGURE 2. Number of months between beginning of dispute and first introduction to the court.

The graph illustrates that disputes less than one year were more often submitted under the PCIJ than under the ICJ and, conversely, disputes of more than twenty years (some over 100 years) were not submitted to the PCIJ but comprise an important segment (over 25%) of the business of the ICJ. This shift seems to indicate that states viewed the PCIJ as a policy alternative of higher priority than they have viewed the ICJ. The willingness of states to use the Court for old disputes in the ICJ period might also indicate a different shift in attitude toward the Court. However, it would be necessary to investigate these trends at the micro-level in order to assert their true significance.

3. *The Court and the Time Dimension in the Bargaining Process.* If the submission of a dispute to the Court does nothing else, it does take time in the bargaining process. Although extra-Court bargaining might continue while the case is in Court, the interven-

The length of the case is related closely to the type of submission to the Court. Eight of the twenty one-year cases were unilateral unanswered applications. Eighteen of the twenty-four cases submitted jointly, through unchallenged compulsory jurisdiction or acceptance of a unilateral application, were settled within two years. Eighteen out of twenty-two disputes which involved preliminary objections lasted from two to four years. From this pattern it appears that, excluding the eight unanswered unilateral declarations, the shorter the decision time of the Court, the more willing the litigants to have the Court settle the case.

4. *Effects of the Court on the International Bargaining Process.* In analysing the effect of the Court on bargaining relationships between states, it is necessary to remember that the authoritative decision on the distribution of objectives which we normally associate with the role of domestic courts has not been the sole role of the World Court.

Less than half (24) of the cases have involved merit decisions. The rest have resulted in procedural decisions or no decisions at all. Compliance with merit decisions of the Court, while not as automatic as some writers have implied, has been the general rule. There have been four cases in which compliance did not immediately follow the decision, but only one—The Corfu Channel Case—where there has not been eventual compliance.[30]

However, the effect of the Court on the bargaining process does not stop with merit decisions. A number of disputes have been settled outside the Court even while the Court was deliberating. In eight of the PCIJ and four of the ICJ cases, the parties decided to withdraw the case based on settlements or the prospect of settlement outside the Court. It would be a mistake to consider the Court unimportant in these extra-Court settlements, since the act of taking the case to Court by one state might have been instrumental in communicating to the other state its intentions (good faith or seriousness).

It would also be a mistake to consider as inconsequential the role of the Court in cases where only preliminary objections were decided or where the prospective respondent refused to accept the jurisdiction of the Court. In many cases, the introduction of the Court into the bargaining process may have been instrumental in communicating the perspective of the states on the particular dispute. However, without a micro-analysis of each case, it would be difficult to speculate on the extent to which the Court has influenced the bargaining process in this respect.

5. *How Litigants Have Been Re-lated to Each Other.* A final dimension which we have investigated is the relationship between each litigant set in each of the fifty-five cases. We have measured geographic, economic and military "distances" between litigants as well as the relative distribution of power (measured by GNP).

In terms of the three dimensions of "distances" between litigants, there is no overall pattern in terms of the entire history of the Court. In twenty-six cases, the litigants had no military ties, while in sixteen they had some military ties, and in twelve there were members of hostile alliances.[31] In terms of economic interdependence, twenty-seven litigant acts had little or no interdependence, while twenty-eight had moderate or heavy economic interdependence. Geographically, although most of the cases were intra-regional, the litigants in fourteen cases had common borders. A majority of cases were between litigants separated by more than eight hundred miles (air distance between capitals).

If one compares the three "distances" between litigants in terms of historical trends between the two Courts, a pattern emerges which is indicative of the universalization of the state system and the bi-polar alliance structure which has characterized international relations since 1946. It was found that while military proximity among litigants has increased, economic and geographical proximity has decreased in the ICJ period. There were fewer cases between allies and "indirect allies," and more cases of moderate and heavy economic interdependence, and common borders and closer capitals in the PCIJ period than in the ICJ period. These shifts in "distances" probably represent the changing nature of inter-

[30] According to the articles cited in footnote 12, the four cases are the Société Commerciale De Belgique, the Corfu Channel Case, the Asylum Case and the Temple of Preah Vihear.

[31] Data on military distance was taken from J. David Singer and Melvin Small, "Formal Alliances: A Quantitative Description," *Journal of Peace Research* (1966), pp. 1–32. Data on economic distance was taken from volumes of the *Statesman's Yearbook*.

national relations in the post-Second World War Period rather than a shift in the attitudes of states toward the Court.

Finally, we have attempted to find the relative strength between the litigants as measured by GNP.[32] Eighteen of the fifty-five disputes have been between states with relatively equal strength. However, the assumption that international law and the Court would benefit states of lesser strength in their relationships with stronger states is not indicated by the patterns in the use of the Court.[33] Twenty-three out of twenty-nine cases where there were unequal applications (as distinct from joint submissions) have been by states with the preponderant strength. The use of the Court by the stronger states perhaps indicates that in dealing with weaker states, the stronger ones wish to appear as law-abiding and fair as possible.

III. The Future Role of the Court in the International Bargaining Process

If one were to posit as a goal that the World Court should some day be related to interactions between states as the courts in domestic settings are

related to interaction between people, the data and trends presented are far from encouraging. Although the treatment of the Court in a manner similar to an arbitral tribunal has declined in the post-1945 world, there has not been a concomitant increase in the use of the Court as a post-bargaining process where the applicant-respondent relationship suffices and where an authoritative decision on the bargaining outcome is reached. Like the United Nations and many regional organizations —even those supposedly performing narrow functional tasks—states treat the World Court ambiguously. On the one hand, there is the aspiration, most often spoken but sometimes acted upon, of a Court which states have empowered to make authoritative decisions. On the other hand, there is the increasing use of the Court as a bargaining alternative, that is, as part of the setting for the interaction of bargaining strategies.

In one way, the pragmatic attitude of states toward the Court might be viewed as a healthy development in terms of developing non-violent means of international bargaining.[34] By accepting the Court as an instrument for dealing with other states, states are giving vitality to central international institutions which someday might provide a more substantial context for bargaining. If this position is accepted, what is most distressing about the use of the Court in the post-1946 world is not so much how it is being used but that, in relative terms, it is being used less frequently.[35]

It must be remembered, however,

[32] Although GNP or its equivalent leaves a great deal to be desired as an indicator of "power," the author has used it as a rough indicator for purposes of this study. It would be more appropriate to measure the perception of relative strength among litigants, but this would have involved a micro-level analysis. Only gross differences in GNP levels between litigants was coded as unequal. Data was taken from Bruce M. Russett, *Handbook of World Political Indicators* (New Haven: Yale University Press, 1965).

[33] The behavior of weak states in the past has been to emphasize international law in their policy. E.g., the United States in her early period or the small Eastern European states in the Inter-War Period. However, from the record of the Court, it does not appear that this general rule applies to the use of the Court by small states.

[34] For other discussions of the role of international organization in limiting violence and providing a substitute for violence in international bargaining see Coplin, *op. cit.*

[35] In the PCIJ period, the Court was used for contentious cases 1.41 times per year, and in the ICJ period it was used for contentious cases 1.77 cases per year. However, the increase is small compared to the increased membership of the Court.

that the failure of the Court to increase its business relative to the number of members in the international system is not necessarily indicative of the removal of all international institutions from the international bargaining process. Rather, the growth of regional international institutions—including regional courts, which in some areas (e.g., Western Europe) have grown simultaneously with the World Court —represents a more efficient forum for the international bargaining process in terms of cost, time and ameliorating hostility normally associated with the bargaining process. On the global level, the United Nations has become the central institutional forum for international bargaining for a number of reasons. One is the generally static quality of the law and the association of international law with the so-called failures of the Inter-War Period. Another and more important reason is that the UN as an institution with quasi-legislative, administrative and settlement functions represents a broader stage upon which the bargaining process may take place.

This raises a question in terms of the interaction model outlined at the beginning of the paper. While it is true that domestic courts from the post-bargaining stage in interactions among *people* in domestic society, it is also true that the courts in domestic societies represent only one institution in the post-bargaining process among *groups* in society. Generally speaking, the more important the issues at stake to the whole society, the more likely that the settlement will occur outside the courts. The processes of government, then, act as a central institution for inter-group bargaining in domestic society if the issues involved are "political" rather than "legal." In domestic society, the determination of political rather than legal is not as difficult as in international society because of the more highly developed set of criteria for making the distinction. Conversely, the domestic courts are so ef-

fective because there is a consensus within the society that certain issues should be settled by them rather than by the governmental institutions.

This line of reasoning suggests that the World Court should be viewed as part of a series of developing international institutions which have an impact on the international bargaining process. While none of the central international institutions have become effective enough to extensively regulate the international bargaining process and to make respected decisions on bargaining outcomes, they nonetheless have had an increasing impact on international interactions. However, the impact has been at the level of the bargaining rather than the post-bargaining stage of the interactions. In these terms, it might be argued that the Court— except in its capacity to make Advisory Opinions—is not adequately structured to operate effectively and extensively in the bargaining process. Like its domestic analogue, the Court is best designed to operate as a post-bargaining institution. Notwithstanding the arguments of those who are fond of maintaining that the judicial settlement of disputes is crucial to the initial development of a more orderly international system,[36] then, it is possible that the evolution of general international institutions with broad functions and powers must precede the development of a successful World Court.

IV. Suggestions for Further Study

Not only would it be valuable to investigate other international institutions (regional as well as global, multi-functional as well as uni-functional) in a macro-analysis similar to the one presented here for purposes of comparison,[37] but it would be useful to make

[36] Kelsen, *op. cit.* (*Law and Peace in International Relations*), p. 145.
[37] The author is planning to use the model outlined in this paper in an analysis of the

a micro-analysis of the Court. Throughout the paper, research tasks on a micro-level have been suggested. The reason for the emphasis on micro-analysis is that because the role of perception is so important in international relations, it is necessary to develop operational indicators of the way in which states have perceived their interaction with other states as well as with the Court. The following list presents some of the micro-level analyses which would increase understanding of the role of the Court in the international bargaining process:

1.1 The development and application of a method for scaling the degree of "political quality" or "importance" which states have attached to issues.

1.2 A typology of the attitudes of states toward the Court based on official public statements.

1.3 Operational categories for assessing the reaction of states to the decisions of the Court.

1.4 A study on history of disputes after the case has been dropped by preliminary objection or unanswered application.

1.5 A study of the contacts, negotiation and results of extra-Court bargaining while the case has been in Court.

1.6 A study of the perception of the other states' intentions and capabilities by litigants.

The above related projects are suggestive not only for studies of the role of the Court in international interactions but also for the role of international institutions in those interactions as well as the general study of international relations. The development of operational concepts to study international relations generally[38] would also facilitate the study of the Court.

[38] One of the conclusions concerning the proper approach to the study of international relations reached in writing this paper is that an effort is necessary to develop operational concepts to gather data on types of international policies followed by states as well as structural qualities of the international system. The classification of types of foreign policy could be developed along the lines of the Banks/Textor classification of internal variable and the system for studying structural qualities could be patterned on some of the studies already done by J. David Singer and Melvin Small on alliance activity and status. E.g., J. David Singer and Melvin Small, "The Composition and Status Ordering of the International System: 1815–1940," *World Politics* 18: 236–283 (January, 1966).

impact of other international institutions on the international bargaining process.

Chapter V

REDISTRIBUTION

V. Redistribution

ONE of the conspicuous facts about the international system is that virtually every commodity we can imagine, both tangible and intangible, is distributed unevenly among member states of the system, not to mention its uneven distribution among individuals within those states. Wealth is unevenly distributed—some would say maldistributed, as evidenced by a 1964 GNP in the United States of $628.7 billion and in Gabon and Mauritania of less than $100 million, or by a 1964 per capita GNP in Canada of almost $2,250 and in India of approximately $96.[1] Military capabilities are equally uneven in distribution, with the division of the world into nuclear powers and non-nuclear powers only the most obvious of indices of this uneven distribution. Add to wealth and military capability such other variables as population, natural resources, literacy, and national prestige (to name but a few), and the result is a series of distribution patterns which create or sustain pressure for redistribution. State A wants commodity C, which state B has, or A wants as much of commodity C as B has. Or perhaps, at the very least, A wants guarantees that the uneven distribution of commodity C will not adversely affect A in some crucial way. Uneven distribution of wealth, power, status, and influence is the very stuff of politics.

The demands which are made by states at the United Nations may be classified according to whether they are essentially status quo or revisionist, i.e., whether the state is satisfied with respect to every issue area, but enough states make revisionist demands with respect to enough issues to permit the observation that the UN is viewed by most of its members as a vehicle for the redistribution of *something*. The saliency of this observation is enhanced in the 1960s by the presence within the organization of pronounced majorities of underdeveloped and non-aligned states, with predominantly non-Caucasian populations. The perceived conditions of economic underdevelopment, military vulnerability, and racial discrimination, added to the ideological demands of other states, notably those of Communist persuasion, generate a redistributive thrust within the UN system.

[1] See *Bulletin of the Atomic Scientists* (September 1966), 46–47.

International organizations need not have redistribution as a primary or even as a conscious purpose. Insofar as their task is to keep the peace, they may in fact find themselves insisting upon the status quo. Thus the United Nations Charter's collective security mandate may be viewed as a prescription for preserving the status quo; even when the UN is engaged in peaceful settlement, in which case its role is more nearly that of mediator than policeman, its conflict management responsibilities do not necessarily call for a redistributive posture. However, the present configuration of forces within the UN encourages conflict management by means of activities which seek to bring about fundamental changes in patterns of interstate and intrastate relationships. Peace will be kept, not only by freezing existing relationships, but by effecting a redistribution of power and wealth and of responsibility and authority. Immediate threats to international stability, such as nuclear weapons and the cold war, may be regulated by UN-sponsored draft treaties and exhortative resolutions, which by inhibiting resort to violence may contribute to a redistribution of effective power among states. Intermediate range threats, such as European colonialism and racial tensions, may be regulated by UN-induced transfer of sovereignty from metropole to dependent territory and from white minority to black majority. Long-range problems of stability arising from conditions of economic under-development and the social upheaval which attends modernization may be regulated by UN system efforts to transfer technology, provide capital, restructure trade relationships, and otherwise bridge the gap between rich and poor states.

But the redistributive function is not only ancillary to the conflict management function of the UN system. The very existence of international bodies with large memberships and long agenda contributes to a change in the attention paid to certain issues and even to certain states, and this in turn may contribute to a reallocation of values or to what Inis Claude has termed "collective legitimization" of policies and actions.[2] Thus the UN may be said to have effected a redistribution of values with respect to such phenomena as colonialism (it is no longer defensible), forcible termination of colonialism (it is now, by transposition, the colonialism rather than its forcible liquidation which is aggression), and assistance for economic development (it is a right of the developing states to be given such aid and a duty of the developed states to provide it). It would be hyperbole to assert that all states subscribe to

[2] Inis L. Claude, Jr., "Collective Legitimization as a Political Function of the United Nations," *International Organization*, Vol. XX, Number 3 (Summer 1966), 367–379.

these values, but far more states publicly endorse them or are constrained to rationalize and defend contradictory values as a result of UN attention and pronouncements.

Similarly, relative status, prestige, and influence are affected by participation in international organizations, even if it is probably impossible to measure redistribution of these intangible commodities. Although the possession of a veto by certain states in the UN Security Council and the weighting of votes according to contributions in the World Bank are proximate reflections of the actual distribution of power in the world, the UN and its specialized agencies provide important opportunities for non-powers to play disproportionately large roles in international affairs. The "status gap" cannot be bridged by UN membership, but it can be closed to some extent. Not only is the UN perceived to be an equalitarian organization in which Ghana and Afghanistan may debate and vote on an equal footing with super-powers and compel the latter to discuss issues which the former deem important; it is also a body whose leadership posts are systematically allocated to smaller and less powerful states and their nationals, thereby increasing their relative capacity to exercise influence and perhaps enhancing their prestige.

But it is with respect to wealth and skills that the redistributive function is most conspicuously and consciously performed. The UN itself, having abjured the relatively narrow preoccupation with political and security matters which characterized the League of Nations Covenant, has been from its inception a multipurpose organization with an important mandate in the economic and social areas. In effect, the UN era has been distinguished by an ambitious if limited attempt to put the doctrine of functionalism into practice. The jury is still out, and may remain out for generations, on the thesis that enduring peace is more likely to be achieved by "doing things together in workshop and market place rather than by signing pacts in chancelleries." [3] Evidence of spillover from technical cooperation in such areas as malaria and locust control, mineral and soil surveys, improvement of fishing gear, and vocational training is not very conspicuous, and the contributions of the international lending agencies have made but a small impact on the pace of economic development. Nonetheless, the UN system has moved out of its offices and "gone operational," reallocating in the process some of the skills and some of the dollars which are so unevenly distributed. Measured by standards of need or of bilateral assistance, the UN system

[3] David Mitrany, *A Working Peace System* (London and New York: Royal Institute of International Affairs, 1946), 5.

effort is negligible; but given the fact that in 1964 the World Bank (IBRD) made original loan commitments of $810 million,[4] that the UN Special Fund allocated $92 million in pre-investment funds,[5] that more than 3,500 UN-recruited technical assistance experts were serving in the field under the Expanded Program of Technical Assistance,[6] and that within the UN itself the Department of Economics and Social Affairs was the largest unit of the Secretariat (to mention but a few indicators), it is not only possible but obligatory to speak of the UN system as performing a redistributive function.

UN system outputs in the area of economic development fall under at least four headings: (a) research; (b) technical assistance, which usually consists of experts or fellowships; (c) capital development loans and grants; and (d) the restructuring of trade relationships. Although developing states have sought all four, they have for obvious reasons wanted to move on from research to operational development programs with a visible and hopefully an early pay-off, from an emphasis on transfer of technology to an emphasis on capital development, from loans to outright grants (i.e., from World Bank type asssistance to a UN capital development fund), and to some extent from aid to trade. However, the IBRD remains the most important of the intergovernmental instrumentalities for promoting economic development. This major lending agency of the UN system is placed in political perspective by Baldwin, who reminds us that redistribution of the world's wealth by international organizations, and by the Bank preeminently, continues to be controlled by the "have" states and proceeds largely according to criteria common to their own domestic capital transfer practices. It is the author's contention that the Bank's activities are highly political in that political considerations affect lending decisions, in that the Bank seeks to influence governments' behavior, and in that its loans have political implications because they affect the distribution of power.

In 1964 the UN staged one of the most widely heralded conferences in its history, the United Nations Conference on Trade and Development (UNCTAD). Frustrated by their inability to launch a capital development fund and propelled by economic theories emanating from the UN's Economic Commission for Latin America, which identified

[4] See James Patrick Sewell, *Functionalism and World Politics* (Princeton: Princeton University Press, 1966), 133.
[5] *Ibid.*
[6] See Yonah Alexander, *International Technical Assistance Experts* (New York: Frederick A. Praeger, 1966), 197.

trade rather than aid as the key to sustained economic growth, the developing states promoted the Geneva Conference, made concerted demands upon the developed countries there, and established continuing machinery to assist in achieving their objectives. Horowitz not only chronicles the emergence at Geneva of a cohesive Third World force, the "77," but analyzed UNCTAD in terms of the confrontation between this revisionist majority and the United States. The "77" prevailed at Geneva, but changes in trade patterns and preferences have not followed, in part due to the subsequent decline in solidarity among the developing countries but more significantly due to the intransigence of the United States and other Western countries. As in the case of the World Bank, UNCTAD seems to demonstrate that significant redistribution of economic strength is unlikely to be effected by international organizations without the active support of the key industrial states, any more than the UN is likely to play a significant role in the regulation of threats to peace without the support or at least the toleration of the principal powers.

Manno identifies a totally different kind of redistributive activity within the UN's orbit. The United Nations is too large, its tasks too complicated, for it to deal effectively with many important issue areas exclusively in plenary, even if its members preferred to, which they apparently do not. The system of specialization of labor which has inevitably developed within the UN recurrently raises questions concerning the composition of its nonplenary organs. The UN's Councils are, of course, a special case. The Security Council, in particular, allocates seats according to a Charter-mandated formula which recognizes the primacy of power. But even with regard to the Security Council, not to mention numerous organs created by the UN General Assembly to develop programs and policies in various areas, decisions must be made by the General Assembly membership regarding criteria for election and appointment. The choice of these criteria is a highly political decision and it affects the distribution of power and influence within the UN. Theoretically, as Manno points out, two options are available: nonplenary organs may replicate the General Assembly or they may be selectively weighted. The UN employs both. But most of these organs, including some of the most important, such as the Committee of 24 on Colonialism, are microcosmic versions of the General Assembly. This arrangement reinforces the status and influence accorded to the smaller states by the equalitarian nature of the Assembly.

In the final essay in this chapter, Friedheim focuses on the question of the reallocation of values or, more specifically, on the modification of international law under the aegis of the United Nations. Case studies of many an issue would reveal a challenge to traditionally held values, norms, and practices by "new" actors on the international scene. The UN does not usually make new rules by repudiating old ones as much as it dramatically publicizes the decline in support for the old rules, thereby ratifying a redistribution of values or, as suggested earlier, legitimating the revisionist position. Friedheim's case study deals with two UN-sponsored Conferences on the Law of the Sea, and describes and analyzes a confrontation between two groups of states best characterized as "have" and "have-not" states. Although the dialogue turned on such matters as the width of territorial waters, the bargaining styles of the two groups and their respective views of the nature of the international system are representative of a much more pervasive cleavage which may be observed in the UN on almost any day on almost any issue. The author observes that the conference was viewed as a legal process by the one group and as a political process by the other. The dissatisfied states had obviously learned well the UN maxim: Always use good political arguments; if there are no good political arguments, use bad political arguments; if there are no political arguments, use legal arguments.

18. The International Bank in Political Perspective*

DAVID A. BALDWIN

I. Introduction

ALTHOUGH the International Bank for Reconstruction and Development has been in existence for nearly two decades, the political aspects of its activities have received scant attention. Most

* World Politics, Vol. XVIII, 68–81. Reprinted by permission. This article is based on research conducted by the author while a Research Fellow at The Brookings Institution. The findings and conclusions are those of the author and do not purport to represent the views of The Brookings Institution, its trustees, officers, or staff members.

of the literature on IBRD operations has been written by economists, who quite naturally emphasize the economic aspects. Political scientists, to the extent that they have discussed it at all, have described most of its operations as removed "from the sphere of international or domestic politics."[1] The purpose of the following analysis is to determine in what respects the activities of the International Bank may be described as "political." Such a deter-

[1] John D. Montgomery, The Politics of Foreign Aid (New York 1962), 184.

mination would be useful in three ways. First, it would, it is hoped, stimulate research on international organizations as actors in international politics; second, it would require revision of the standard explanations of the evolution of international development aid programs; and third, it would aid in evaluating the argument for more multilateral aid which assumes that such aid is "nonpolitical."

There is no universal agreement about just what it means to "be political." It is therefore useful to pause for a moment to examine the possible meanings of such a term as it might be applied to World Bank operations. The following pages will argue that these operations are "political" in three respects: (1) In carrying out their duties Bank officials cannot ignore political considerations, despite a formal ban on their doing so. (2) Activities of the IBRD affect the distribution of influence both within and among international actors, which is to say that such activities have political effects. (3) The IBRD performs as an international actor when it attempts to get governments to do things that they would not otherwise do. The discussion of these "political" aspects of IBRD operations will focus first on the relation between commercial banks and politics, next on some alleged limits on Bank lending, and finally, on some real limits on this lending.

II. Commercial Banks and Politics

One of the great myths of American political folklore is that the activities of private businessmen are "nonpolitical." Businessmen in general, and bankers in particular, do not like to be described as wielding power. They prefer to minimize the amount of choice ascribed to them and to exaggerate the degree to which they are slaves of impersonal market forces that are beyond their control. In the case of bankers, the "maintenance of sound banking standards" is usually the impersonal, uncontrollable standard that is invoked to justify an act. Bankers like to perpetuate this image for two reasons. First, it serves as a front line of defense against government regulation. Why regulate those who exercise no discretion? And second, the device promotes smoother interpersonal relations. It is one thing to refuse a loan application because the applicant has failed to meet the "objective standards of bankability"; but it is another to say "I don't trust you." It will be seen later that IBRD officials, like commercial bankers, have tended to describe their loan denials in terms of the potential borrower's failure to pass certain "objective" tests of economic "soundness."

In which of the three senses identified above can normal commercial banking activities be described as "political"? Private commercial banking is "political" in the sense that political considerations must be accounted for in making a loan decision. Since the commercial banker's primary object is to make money, he is interested in answering two questions as he evaluates a loan application. Will the borrower be able to repay on time? And can I trust him to do so? The first question always involves political judgments; and when the borrower is a foreign government, both questions require such judgments. Although it is often implied that one can evaluate the "intrinsic economic merit" of a project without reference to political factors, it is actually impossible to do so. In a world where governments can expropriate property, manipulate exchange rates, and control the currency supply, it is nonsense to speak of evaluating the economic soundness of a project without reference to government behavior. Skeptics are invited to perform a simple empirical test. Ask any banker whether or not he would lend to a firm in Ruritania if he believed that the Ruritanian government was about to expropriate that firm's assets. If he says no, that indicates that he makes implicit—or perhaps even explicit—assumptions about political behavior in evaluating a loan application.

Private commercial banking is "political" not only in the sense that political factors must be assessed but also in the sense that banking decisions have political implications. Although a banker may perceive a loan to Ruritania for building an atomic reactor as merely business, such a loan would probably affect the international distribution of influence. Besides this international effect, a loan to a foreign borrower tends to affect the domestic politics of the borrowing nation. Given the existence of several groups in a nation, each with different opinions about how social and economic life should be organized, the transfer of capital to one group (such as landlords, businessmen, peasants, or government) will probably tend to increase the influence of that group.

In sum, private banking is "political" in two of the three senses of the word specified above. Thus, even if it were true, as Montgomery argues, that IBRD loans "were granted on the conventional banker's criterion of creditworthiness," [2] it would not follow that Bank activities were removed "from the sphere of international or domestic politics." [3]

III. IBRD Lending: The Standard Explanations

The conventional explanation of Bank lending emphasizes the similarity between IBRD and commercial banking activities. The IBRD is usually described as asking the same questions about willingness and ability to repay that the private banker asks. The usual discussion goes on to point out that certain limits are imposed on IBRD lending by the Articles of Agreement upon which the Bank is based. The three requirements most often cited as limits on Bank lending are the ban on competition with private investors, the limitation of loans to specific projects, and the restriction of financing to foreign-exchange costs of projects.[4] Let us analyze the degree to which these formal prohibitions actually do place restrictions on Bank officials.

COMPETITION WITH PRIVATE CAPITAL

The Articles of Agreement specifically forbid Bank administrators to lend to anyone unless they are satisfied that the borrower could not obtain a loan elsewhere "under conditions which *in the opinion of the Bank* are reasonable for the borrower." [5] The fact that the phrase in italics was included indicates the framers' recognition of the ambiguity of "reasonable terms." Since the Articles leave it to Bank officials to define "reasonable terms" in each specific case, one can hardly accept the proposition that Bank officials are inhibited in this respect.

Furthermore, the Articles say nothing about the time factor. What does one do if private capital is unavailable this year but there is reason to believe that it might be available next year? Bank officials are free to base their calculations of the availability of private capital on any time factor they choose.

All this is not to say that the IBRD does not try to avoid competing with private investors; it does. The point is that this action cannot be explained in terms of the formal "requirements" of the Articles of Agreement but can

---

[2] *Ibid.*, 182.
[3] *Ibid.*, 184.

[4] For examples of standard explanations see the following: Alec Cairncross, *The International Bank for Reconstruction and Development*, Essays in International Finance, No. 33 (Princeton 1959); and Delbert A. Snider, *Introduction to International Economics* (Homewood, Ill., 1954), 426–37.
[5] IBRD, *Articles of Agreement*, Article III, Sec. 4 (ii). (Italics added.)

probably be more adequately explained in terms of the attitudes of Bank administrators. If one wants to account for the Bank's hesitancy to compete with private capital, he would do well to place less emphasis on the Articles of Agreement and more on the social and professional backgrounds of Bank officials. It is hardly a coincidence that the IBRD president, since 1947, has been drawn from the New York financial community.

SPECIFIC PROJECTS

A second alleged restriction on Bank administrators is the requirement that the IBRD lend only for "specific projects." [6] Few aspects of IBRD operations have been so misunderstood as the "specific project" provision. The project approach is supposed to limit total IBRD lending because of the small number of development projects that can be financed by hard loans.[7] By constant references to two types of projects, the "bankable" and "nonbankable," this line of thought implies that all projects are intrinsically of one type or the other. Not so. A nation, if it were earning foreign exchange from some other project in the economy, might be able to finance a totally worthless project—such as digging holes and filling them again—by means of a World Bank loan calling for repayment at commercial interest rates in foreign exchange. On the other hand, a government might default on a loan used to develop a "bankable" project, such as a petroleum field, because a corrupt government official stole all the foreign exchange from the

treasury before the loan payment could be made.

National economies do not present themselves to IBRD officials neatly carved into easily identifiable specific projects, each with a tag designating it either "bankable" or "nonbankable." The administrators can exercise judgment in deciding what constitutes a project. Is a project, for example, a railroad tie, a track, a switch engine, a train, a set of operators, a whole railroad, or a transportation system? The capacity of a nation to service foreign debt—the capacity that determines whether a project is "bankable" or not—depends on its overall foreign exchange earnings, not on foreign exchange generated by a particular project.

It has been argued thus far that project lending need not restrict World Bank activities both because the term "project" is ambiguous and because the "bankability" of a project is not determined by the nature of the project but by the overall foreign exchange position of the country. Yet among typical descriptions of the IBRD are the following: "The necessity for the IBRD to be guided predominantly by sound business standards means . . . that there is not now any international organization which could finance non-self-liquidating projects in the underdeveloped countries." [8] "It is impossible . . . to raise money for various forms of social investment which the Bank rules out as unproductive; housing, schools, health services, and so on." [9] Such propositions notwithstanding, it is quite possible for the IBRD to finance such "non-self-liquidating" projects as schools, health services, and housing. To illustrate this possibility, suppose that the Ruritanian government plans to improve its harbors.

---

[6] Ibid., Sec. 4 (vii).

[7] See, for example, the comments by Harlan Cleveland in his introduction to Robert G. A. Jackson, The Case for an International Development Authority (Syracuse 1959), 7; and Richard P. Stebbins, The United States in World Affairs, 1958 (New York 1959), 404.

[8] William Y. Elliott, and others, The Political Economy of American Foreign Policy (New York 1955), 343.

[9] Cairncross, 18.

Now harbor improvement is one of the World Bank's favorite "specific projects." If the Bank were to finance Ruritania's harbor improvement projects, the Ruritanian government would have available those resources which it had intended to spend on harbor improvement but which it could now transfer to finance health services and housing. The net effect of the IBRD loan in this case would be to permit building hospitals and housing; yet in the bookkeeping the loan was tied to a specific harbor improvement project. The only sensible way to measure the economic impact of an IBRD loan is to ask in what way the economy is different from what it would have been in the absence of the loan. If harbor improvements would have been undertaken even in the absence of an IBRD loan, but health services and housing would not, then the impact of the IBRD loan is on health services and housing. It is thus conceivable that the IBRD could finance health services and housing around the globe merely by tying its loans to "specific projects," such as harbor improvement, which would be financed even in the absence of IBRD loans. On paper, however, the Bank would have financed no housing or health services.[10] Thus, one must conclude that the "specific project" requirement need not limit IBRD loans, since the IBRD can always find some project to tie its loans to when it wants to make funds available to a nation.

Bank officials have been especially nettled by one criticism heard often in the first decade of Bank activities, but less frequently in the second. The criticism accuses IBRD administrators of evaluating particular projects in isolation, without reference to the overall development needs of the borrowing

country.[11] The Bank has flatly stated that it does precisely the opposite.[12] In fact, one of the early Annual Reports pointed out that Bank lending was being held back not so much by a dearth of projects as by the absence of overall development plans in terms of which the proposed projects could be evaluated.[13] In reacting against criticism of its "specific project" approach the Bank has gone on to argue that "the *only* requirement which it imposes is that, before a loan is granted, there shall be a clear agreement both on how the proceeds of the loan are to be expended and on what the loan is expected to achieve." [14] One hesitates to accept even this statement of the extent to which the specific project provision "imposes requirements" on Bank lending. Although the provision does require that each loan be administratively tied to a specific project, this tie neither requires nor ensures that the ultimate impact of the loan will be on the financing of the project for which the loan is earmarked. The Bank's insistence on advance agreement on the use of loan proceeds is not "required" by the specific projects provision at all, but arises from its interest in knowing what it is financing.

If the specific-project provision need not and does not limit total IBRD lending, why do Bank officials cling to it? First, the Articles of Agreement demand formal allegiance. Second, the specific-project approach provides a useful facade behind which the IBRD

---

[10] Few economists have discussed the economic insignificance of the project approach. The best discussion is in Thomas C. Schelling, *International Economics* (Boston 1958), 439–56.

[11] For an example of such criticism of the IBRD see Maxwell Graduate School of Citizenship and Public Affairs, Syracuse University, *The Operational Aspects of United States Foreign Policy*, U.S. Foreign Policy Study No. 6 (86th Cong., 1st Sess., 1959), 52.

[12] IBRD, *Policies and Operations of the World Bank, IFC, and IDA* (Washington 1962), 33.

[13] IBRD, *Third Annual Report, 1947–1948*, 16.

[14] IBRD, *Policies and Operations*, 32. (Italics added.)

can and does advise on governmental policies affecting all parts of the economy. If someone objects to IBRD advice on governmental fiscal policy, Bank officials can always justify it by citing the possible ramifications of fiscal policy affecting the project they are financing—no matter how remote such connections might be. And third, the specific-project approach provides a convenient mechanism for joint consultation with the government in the recipient country and for channeling a continuing flow of information from the country to the IBRD. Whereas governments might be sensitive about Bank demands for information on the state of the economy if the Bank loans were for general purposes, they are apparently less so when the demands are justified in terms of the Bank's interest in a specific project. The significance, in sum, of the specific-project provision is tactical, not economic.[15]

FOREIGN EXCHANGE COSTS

A third supposed constitutional limit on Bank operations is the provision that the Bank will normally finance only the direct foreign exchange costs of a project.[16] Actually, this provision should be considered in the light of the basic operating principles delineated by the Bank in the *Second Annual Report*. In this statement the Bank clearly indicates its reluctance to finance —or rather, to appear to be financing —the total cost of any single project.[17] This is a means of inducing self-help measures on the part of the recipient. Recent IBRD statements also describe the "foreign exchange costs" approach as "a practical way of assuring that they [the recipients] will mobilize their own resources to meet a substantial

part of the cost of the projects or programs concerned."[18] If IBRD administrators so desired, they could easily circumvent this provision, at least to the extent that imported goods and services could be substituted for domestic ones. They could also negate the provision's limiting effects by tying loans to projects which, first, would have especially high foreign exchange costs and, second, would be financed even without Bank assistance. Thus foreign exchange would be freed for use elsewhere.

If the above discussion of the ban on competition with private capital, the specific-projects provision, and the foreign-exchange-costs provision is accepted, one must conclude that the activities of IBRD officials are not restricted by these formal provisions of the Articles of Agreement. If these limits are ineffective, the standard explanation of IBRD operations leaves one without criteria for distinguishing between World Bank and commercial lending. The next question we shall take up, therefore, is whether or not the IBRD does differ from a private commercial bank.

IV. IBRD and Politics

The purpose of this study, to repeat, is to identify the "political" dimensions of IBRD operations. Having already established that private commercial banking is "political" in its effects on power distribution and its need to make political judgments, it follows that insofar as IBRD and commercial bank activities are similar, the IBRD activities are also "political." With regard to political factors in making loan decisions, the Bank has candidly admitted that "creditworthiness is not determined by economic forces alone."[19] The Bank has been less candid, however, in noting how greatly it has di-

[15] Cf. Schelling, 456–57.
[16] IBRD, *Articles of Agreement*, Article IV, Sec. 3.
[17] IBRD, *Second Annual Report, 1946–1947*, 15–18.
[18] IBRD, *Policies and Operations*, 38.
[19] *Ibid.*, 32.

verged from that provision in the Articles of Agreement which specifically forbids consideration of political factors.[20] The following passage implies that the Articles prohibit only the pursuit of political objectives and not the weighing of political factors: "Although the Bank is precluded by its Articles from making or declining to make loans to achieve political objectives, it cannot ignore conditions of obvious political instability or uncertainty which may directly affect the economic and financial prospects of the borrower, and the political situation, to the extent that it may bear upon the soundness of the proposed loan, must therefore be taken into account in the initial investigation." [21]

The operations of the IBRD are political not only in the same sense as are commercial bank activities, but in another sense as well. This additional political dimension stands out if one focuses on the differences between IBRD and commercial lending. In the first place, conventional commercial bankers pursue a goal different from that of the World Bank. Whereas the commercial banker is interested in making money, the administrators of the IBRD have viewed as its goal promoting economic reconstruction and development. Keynes had a dictum that the Bank would not have discharged its duty if it had not dissipated its assets within ten years; and although few at Bretton Woods accepted this dictum, all agreed that the Bank's primary purpose was not to earn profits. Any student of Adam Smith knows that concentration on maximizing profits may be an effective way of promoting economic growth and that the commercial banker may well be inadvertently promoting this goal. If Bank administrators saw this as the case, there might be little to distinguish the behavior of the IBRD, with a primary goal of promoting growth, from that of the private bank

[20] Article IV, Sec. 10.

[21] IBRD, *Policies and Operations*, 47.

in pursuit of profit. Those in charge of the IBRD, however, decided that they could best stimulate economic development by behaving in ways quite different from those of commercial lenders.

The private lender's goal of profit leads him to concentrate on answering two important questions in considering a loan application: Will the borrower be able to repay? And can he be trusted to repay? In answering these questions the private lender accepts as "given" the political and economic situation of the potential borrower, and together they work out the amount of debt which the potential borrower can safely incur. Although it is true that opinions may differ on this point, the borrower and lender presumably share a common interest in reaching a correct estimate. The IBRD, on the other hand, in considering a loan application, does not accept as "given" many of the things that a private lender does. It does not, for example, accept the political and economic situation of the potential borrower as given. In private lending terms, it is as if a boy were trying to borrow money to study law. The banker, despite his trust in the boy's ability and willingness to repay the loan, tells him that lawyers are bad people and that he should be a farmer. The banker then adds that he is going to "encourage" the boy to become a farmer instead of a lawyer by refusing to lend him the money to go to law school. In such a situation the banker would have refused to accept as "given" the boy's desire to study law and would have taken upon himself the task of changing the boy's desires. Similar examples are rare in private lending practice because bankers are usually more interested in making money than in reforming their potential borrowers. Examples of the strategic withholding of loans in IBRD practice, however, are numerous because the IBRD is more interested in promoting economic development than in earning money. To a potential borrower who estimates his debt-servicing capacity in terms of a given political and economic situation, the IBRD is likely to reply, "Change the situation." In reply to underdeveloped countries that complain of a "need" for capital on lenient terms because of their "inability" to attract private capital and to service orthodox loans, the Bank is likely to advise adopting new governmental policies that would enable them to attract private capital and service hard loans.

One important result of the International Bank's refusal to accept political and economic situations as "given" is that its lending situations involve a higher degree of conflict than those of private lenders. Moreover, since there are various ways of stimulating economic development, opinions differ about which are best. Because IBRD lending situations involve a high degree of conflict, it will be argued that certain concepts developed by the game theorists are helpful in understanding the political aspects of World Bank operations. Thomas C. Schelling has suggested that most conflict situations are essentially bargaining situations; that is, they are situations in which the ability of one participant to gain his ends is dependent to an important degree on the decisions that the other participant will make.[22] Officials of the IBRD do seem to believe that the amount of capital requested from the Bank by underdeveloped countries depends to a large extent on the amount the governments of those countries think is likely to be forthcoming.[23] One could plausibly argue that the behavior of potential recipient governments is affected by their expectations of IBRD

behavior. For example, if a government were convinced that neither the IBRD nor other public sources were likely to make capital available, it might decide to be especially hospitable to private foreign investors. On the other hand, if there were reason to believe that large-scale public capital probably would be available, the governments of potential recipient nations would have an incentive to treat private foreign investors especially harshly in order that they could later show a greater "need" for public capital.

Many of the Bank's actions in promoting economic development are clearly those of an actor in international politics; that is, the Bank often tries to induce governments to behave in ways in which they would not otherwise behave.[24] Early in its history the Bank decided to interest itself first in influencing the behavior of governments and only secondarily in making loans. The *Second Annual Report* refers to the goal of exerting a "helpful influence" on member governments in order to persuade them to remove trade barriers and adopt sound financial programs.[25] And the *Third Annual Report* clarifies further the objectives of the Bank as seen by its administrators: "It seems clear that the real measure of the Bank's effectiveness will be, not so much the number or amount of its loans and guarantees, significant as they may be, but rather its success in influencing attitudes—in promoting a realistic, constructive approach to development problems on the part of its members and in fostering a greater degree of confidence among investors."[26]

In its efforts to stimulate economic development by influencing governmental behavior, the International Bank has employed tactics similar to those discussed by students of game theory. The essence of these tactics,

[22] *The Strategy of Conflict* (Cambridge, Mass., 1960), 5.

[23] Professor Machlup has argued that this is a sensible way to conceive the borrower-lender situation. See Fritz Machlup, "Three Concepts of the Balance of Payments and the So-Called Dollar Shortage," *Economic Journal*, LX (March 1950), 56–58.

[24] On this point see Robert A. Dahl, *Modern Political Analysis* (Englewood Cliffs, N.J., 1963), 39–54.

[25] p. 8.   [26] p. 21

according to Schelling, is some "voluntary but irreversible sacrifice of freedom of choice."[27] They rest on the paradox that the power to constrain an adversary may depend on the power to bind oneself. Various IBRD statements and actions in the last twenty years have indicated clearly the Bank's desire to constrain potential borrowers by encouraging them to (1) pass legislation favorable to private foreign investors,[28] (2) control inflation,[29] (3) pay private external debts,[30] (4) avoid government-managed enterprises,[31] (5) improve the "climate of investment" in other ways,[32] and (6) plan development programs to provide a basis on which the IBRD could judge the net effect of a proposed loan.[33] In pursuing these goals the Bank has relied primarily on the technique of binding itself by declarations that it would withhold loans from governments following undesirable policies. Although this strategic nonlending is probably the most important technique by which the

[27] *Strategy of Conflict*, 22.

[28] IBRD, *Second Annual Report*, 14.

[29] IBRD, Eleventh Annual Meeting of the Board of Governors, *Summary Proceedings* (1956), 12–13; *Second Annual Report*, 13–14; *Third Annual Report*, 15–16; *Policies and Operations*, 40–41.

[30] IBRD, *Second Annual Report*, 13; IBRD, *The International Bank for Reconstruction and Development, 1946–1953* (Baltimore 1954), 54 (this is an early version of *Policies and Operations*, and is cited here to illustrate the continuity of bank thinking; contrary to widespread belief, there is very little difference between the 1954 and 1962 editions of this book); *Policies and Operations*, 41.

[31] James Morris, *The Road to Huddersfield* (New York 1963), 43; IBRD, *IBRD, 1946–1953*, 49, 54–55; *Policies and Operations*, 37, 41–42.

[32] IBRD, *Fourth Annual Report, 1948–1949*, 8; *Second Annual Report*, 13; *IBRD, 1946–1953*, 43–44, 54, 61; *Policies and Operations*, 31–32, 40–42, 47.

[33] IBRD, *Third Annual Report*, 16; IBRD, *1946–1953*, 44–45; *Policies and Operations*, 32–38.

IBRD has sought to achieve its goals, it has been overlooked by most critics of IBRD activities. One author, for example, lists the guaranteeing of private loans and the financing of "basic" projects as the means by which the IBRD has sought to stimulate private investment.[34] There is no mention of the most important device used by the Bank to stimulate private investment —the refusal to lend for projects which, in the judgment of the Bank officials, could be financed by private capital. Another writer describes the IBRD as "first and foremost a lender on long-term."[35] Such a description is understandable in view of the ease of counting loans actually made and the difficulty of counting loans withheld; but if one conceives of Bank operations in terms of a bargaining situation, he will realize that one could just as plausibly describe the IBRD as "first and foremost a nonlender." The full significance of the conventonal explanation of the Bank's failure to make more hard loans—the explanation based on the constitutional limitations discussed in Section III above—can be appreciated only after one understands the Bank's strategic nonlending policy. Not only is such an explanation wrong, but it also draws attention away from the real reasons for withholding certain loans, and thus it inhibits understanding of the most important technique used by the IBRD to influence the behavior of governments. Given the widespread acceptance of this standard explanation of IBRD lending, it is small wonder that the political dimension of Bank operations has been overlooked.

V. Conclusion
IBRD AND POLITICS

On the basis of the foregoing discussion one may conclude that the activities of the International Bank are

[34] Snider, 435.

[35] Cairncross, 6.

"political" in three respects: (1) Bank administrators must take political considerations into account in assessing the willingness and ability of a potential borrower to repay a loan, despite the fact that such action is specifically forbidden by the Articles of Agreement. (2) World Bank loans, like all capital transfers, have political implications insofar as they affect the distribution of power both among and within nations. (3) At times the IBRD behaves like other actors in international politics in that it tries to influence the behavior of governments.

The foregoing analysis suggests that students of foreign policy should be wary of the contention of Senator J. W. Fulbright and others that aid furnished via multilateral channels is "nonpolitical."

GAME THEORY

It has been argued that IBRD operations can be conceived of in terms of the "bargaining situations" which have been discussed by game theorists. Such conceptualization proves useful in ferreting out a neglected aspect of IBRD activities—the strategic withholding of loans. Failure to think of IBRD operations in bargaining terms largely accounts for the absence of discussion of the political aspects of such operations.

FOREIGN AID HISTORY

Since World War II, the form of public capital transfers for economic development has tended to change from hard loans to soft ones. Standard explanations of this tendency have depicted the situation as one in which the hard lenders, such as the IBRD, were trying to maximize the amount of capital they were moving abroad. In this effort they were limited only by considerations of "bankability" and, in the case of the IBRD, by certain constitutional limitations. There was a "need," so the story goes, for additional capital to finance projects which were innately "nonbankable" and which therefore "could not" be financed by the IBRD. As proof, the standard explanations often cite the absence of financing for schools or other "worthwhile" projects. There is rarely any indication that the IBRD might have withheld loans for "worthwhile" projects in order to induce changes in governmental policies. Instead, one finds great stress being placed on "limited debt-servicing capacities" and "non-self-liquidating projects" and on what the World Bank "could" and "could not" do. There is little mention of what the Bank "would" and "would not" do. It is implicitly assumed that the IBRD and the underdeveloped countries shared a desire to maximize the amount of IBRD lending. I submit that the history of the evolution of international development aid programs needs to be rewritten on the basis of an explicit recognition of the bargaining aspects of the lender-borrower relationship.

RESEARCH IMPLICATIONS

The foregoing discussion of the political aspects of an international economic organization suggests the usefulness of similar studies. Two relatively neglected topics need to be analyzed: (1) the political aspects of activities of economic organizations and (2) the role of international organizations as actors in international politics.

Research implications for IBRD activities also emerge. If Bank officials do indeed have considerable latitude for the exercise of judgment in administering Bank affairs, then it would be interesting to know what factors influence their decisions. Little research has so far been done on the political and social backgrounds of those in charge of the IBRD. Rejection of the view of

Bank officials as puppets following the dictates of "sound banking practice" and the Articles of Agreement would also pave the way for reconsideration of the relationship of the United States to the IBRD. Suggestions that the IBRD is subservient to the United States have been variously denounced as a "complete travesty,"[36] a "myth,"[37] or as "alleged."[38] It may be that the question of IBRD subservience to the United States is merely poorly framed. Perhaps one should ask instead: (1) What is the degree of subservience; (2) to which agencies or interest groups in the United States is the Bank subservient; and (3) on what types of issues? There are at least the following reasons for suspecting some degree

[36] Ibid., 31.
[37] B. E. Matecki, Establishment of the International Finance Corporation and United States Policy (New York 1957), 162.
[38] Robert E. Asher, and others, The United Nations and Economic and Social Cooperation (Washington 1957), 166.

of subservience, to some groups, on some issues: (1) The United States economy is so large, relative to the world economy, that the World Bank would have an incentive to coordinate its efforts with those of the United States even if the United States were not a Bank member. American aid programs, for example, could seriously undermine the effectiveness of any IBRD activity. (2) The United States is a member and is the biggest contributor; it wields one-third of the voting power, and its position as the biggest potential contributor affects Bank policies. (3) The Bank depends, although to a diminishing degree, on the American private capital market. (4) The United States has always selected the Bank president, who presumably has "internalized" American values which lead him to see things in the American frame of reference. Any proof that the IBRD is not subservient to American interests must account for these facts; none to date has done so.

19. The United Nations and the Third World: East-West Conflict in Focus*

IRVING LOUIS HOROWITZ

In the very process of a transformation in its size and character, the United Nations has become the locus for the emergence of the Third World as an organized, institutionalized bloc. Curiously, through the legitimizing functions of the United Nations, the Third World is no longer a loose confederation of ideological formulas, as was the case at the first Bandung Conference

* From Three Worlds of Development: The Theory and Practice of International Stratification by Irving L. Horowitz. Copyright © 1966 by Irving Louis Horowitz. Reprinted by permission of Oxford University Press, Inc.

in 1955. Indeed, so far has this process evolved that the need for the United Nations has itself become minimized. Sukarno has taken the big psychological step of removing Indonesia from United Nations membership, and thus demonstrated that the Third World is somehow more significant than it. Conflict in the Congo has also served to expose the racial nerve separating the old colonialist powers, such as Belgium and Portugal, from the rising tide of African and Asian nationalism. Lesser strains are revealed in France's call for a summit meeting to revise and update the United Nations charter, in the Soviet Union's demands for a reorganization of the Secretariat, and in the incapacity of United Nations agencies to finance their peace-keeping efforts.

Perhaps the most powerful gap of all was revealed in the various postures evident at a little summit meeting on Trade and Development held in 1964. At this Geneva conference the United States found itself in splendid isolation on matters concerning the economic and social lifeblood of the Third World. Few significant events in recent times have received so little journalistic attention. For what the conference reflected was not simply a mounting pressure for multilateral economic relations, but a deepening of American isolation from the world political economy.

The profound schism between the Third World and the United States is reflected in specific areas. While the issues raised may in time produce a general schism between the Third World and the fully developed world, there is no doubt that at present the central focus of the animosity is the United States. What follows is a catalogue of grievances which form the background and prelude to the public rift which took place at the United Nations Conference on Trade and Development.

(1) *Bilateralism versus Multilateralism:* Third World commentators, like Raúl Prebisch of Argentina and Edmundo Flores of Mexico, claim that the character of United States aid is strictly bilateral, and that this aid often deteriorates into idiosyncratic assistance based upon tests of political allegiance. In addition to driving political bargains, bilateralism helps the advanced nation drive economic bargains as well, by setting up favorable terms of credit, shipping surplus goods in place of fluid capital, demanding certain raw material advantages, and determining with whom and under what conditions trade with others is to take place. Finally, the bilateral approach often limits recipient countries from extending their trade lines with others.

(2) *Modernism versus Structuralism:* It is the contention of many Third World nations that the basic posture of the United States is to discourage self-sustaining economic units in favor of heavy consumer-oriented economies. Thus, the United States lends its weight and prestige to nations securing finished consumer products, with little or no emphasis on the costs, in independence and growth, of such an arrangement. The hub of the argument is that the United States, in advocating modernism, in effect supports the relatively small elite within the developing nations able to pay for the import of manufactured goods, while it ignores the needs of the large mass who would be aided much more substantially if the country emphasized industrial goods for public use rather than commodity goods for private use.

(3) *Agriculturalism versus Industrialism:* In general, Third World nations dislike the role they are being assigned as agricultural and raw materials areas. At the present time most of the Third World is forced to import expensive finished consumer goods and export relatively inexpensive farm and mineral raw materials. Such a trade pattern saddles a nation with a deepening inflationary spiral due to the imbalance between high-priced consumer goods and low-cost raw materials and with perpetual indebtedness, also because of the price differential. This trade pattern can only be broken if the United States gives meaningful across-the-board trade and tariff concessions. At the present time the United States appears reluctant to offer such assistance. Such a condition contributes greatly to social unrest in the Third World. It is ironic that the United States' very insistence on the present international division of production helps sustain social unrest which it feels compelled to treat as a military threat.

(4) *Private Sector versus Public Sector:* While the Third World recognizes that the United States, like every other dynamic economy in the world, is a mixed economy, it is still viewed as a predominantly private-sector economy. What is more, the United States does little to disabuse the Third World of this impression. Indeed, its official posture is private enterprise. This stands in profound contrast to the economy of most Third World nations, which are debating what type of public-sector economy they prefer rather than assessing the degree of public or private enterprise they should adopt. Third World nations are upset that the United States fails to understand their needs and demands an adhesion to an economic philosophy of private-sector pre-eminence which even the most highly industrialized nation can itself no longer pursue.

(5) *Economic versus Political Determinism:* The Third World views the United States as a parliamentary democracy. At the same time it considers the introduction of such a system into less developed regions an impossibility. The historical conditions which have given rise to the Third World, particularly the lack of a mature and self-sustaining polity as well as the demands for rapid economic acceleration, seem to imply the need for much more centralized authority than was present in the United States at the time of its take-off. The failure on the part of the United States to appreciate the need for political centralization is held to be a key abrasive in the situation.

(6) *Integration versus Fragmentation:* Third World nations tend to be racially homogeneous, have a high density of population, widespread illiteracy, and a relatively large rural population; and caste, class, and tribal sectors which make them fragmented and ascriptive societies. The United States does not sufficiently appreciate their lack of structural solidarity. The problems of the modern world presuppose participation in international relations; and this is hard to achieve in societies still bound by class, caste, and racial schisms. Yet it is true that Third World nations cannot obtain their legitimate role in the international arena while the United States hinders their efforts.

The basic premise of the "Prebisch thesis," [1] upon which the whole United Nations Conference on World Trade and Development was based, was that the gap between rich and poor nations is widening. The reasons for this, it was stated, had to do with the intense fluctuation in the world price of raw materials, a fluctuation often manipulated by fully developed industrial nations. The increased cost of purchasing finished commodities from the fully industrialized nations is a primary consequence, not a cause, of the gap. This gap led directly to the formation of a "77" nation bloc within the Third World. Thus Prebisch directly challenges the classical assumption that progress resulting from technological innovation will automatically benefit industrialized and non-industrialized nations alike through the mechanism of free trade. The United States seems directly opposed to this thesis with Bismark's motto: "Free trade is the weapon of the strongest."

The group of Third World nations known as the "77" have termed this period the "development decade." They recognize the need for concerted international action to create prosperous growth in presently underdeveloped and developing nations. Emergence of

[1] Raúl Prebisch, *Towards a New Trade Policy for Development.* New York: United Nations Publications, 1964 (E/Conf/46/3). For empirical confirmation of the widening gap between the economic growth of industrial countries in contrast to underdeveloped "primary producing areas," see Alfred Maizels, *Industrial Growth and World Trade.* Cambridge: Cambridge University Press, 1963.

the "77" indicates the extent to which the Third World countries have made their needs known to advanced industrialized nations, especially the United States and the Soviet Union. They have attempted to persuade the First and Second Worlds to treat them as a new international combination of powers, instead of as a loose network of easily manipulated subordinates, and to negotiate with them as legitimate nation-states. Much of the business of the United Nations is taken up with this bloc's quest for parity. In its efforts to meet the demands of the "77," in the form of proliferating conferences and studies, the major powers have left a pattern of votes and rhetoric reflecting their reception of the social and economic demands of the Third World.

In recognition of the "development decade" the United Nations General Assembly set a minimum target to be achieved by newly developing countries by 1970; a minimal annual economic growth rate of 5 per cent. The United Nations Conference on Trade and Development is designed to create an international trade environment which would offset the trade disadvantages to developing countries. It is first necessary to determine how developing countries hope to attain equality in trade. Though United Nations publications and numerous scholarly studies discuss this matter, it is still not clear what the Third World is demanding.

While underdeveloped countries have an increasing need to import industrial equipment, their exports do not earn enough to pay for basic capital imports. The result is a trade gap, which gold and foreign exchange reserves have not been able to bridge. The gap must be then filled by capital import. Neither foreign loans nor foreign investment provide a permanent solution. Eventually the richer nations will refuse to lend to or invest in nations with faltering economies. Even in the short run, the expenses incurred in servicing external debts diminish the stop-gap ef-

fect of capital import. Many developing countries are faced with declining prices for their exports of primary commodities at a time when the prices of their imports of manufactures, especially of equipment, have greatly increased. Their dependence on primary commodity exports has reduced their capacity to import. This trend represents a major obstacle to their efforts to diversify and industrialize their economies. Recognition of this trade pattern as a barrier to development led to the Conference on Trade and Development which convened at Geneva on March 23, 1964, and continued until June 16.

The 1964 conference was based on the following findings: (1) World export has more than doubled since 1950 through overall expansion of the "world economy" aided by socio-economic change and scientific and technological progress. (2) The countries of the world do not share proportionately in this expansion of international trade. Although exports of developing countries rose from nineteen billion dollars to twenty-nine billion dollars between 1950 and 1962, that is, by 50 per cent, the expansion of exports from these countries proceeded at an appreciably lower rate than that of developed countries. As a result, the share of developing countries in world exports declined from nearly one-third in 1950 to only slightly more than one-fifth in 1962. Concurrently, the developed market economies increased their share from three-fifths to two-thirds, and the centrally planned economies from 8 per cent to 13 per cent. (3) The rate of expansion of world exports declined from 8½ per cent per annum in the early 'fifties to rather less than 5 per cent in the early 'sixties. One reason for the decline is the inability of the developing countries to attain a higher rate of export expansion.[2] (4)

[2] *Final Act. United Nations Conference on Trade and Development,* E/Conf. 46/L.28, June 16, 1964, p. 8, Section III.

The demand for the export products of underdeveloped countries is relatively inelastic. And they have little chance of gaining ground, not only because they are faced with artificial tariff restrictions, but also because raw material substitutes are being created, for example, the replacement of rubber, leather, and fabrics by plastic goods. (5) The monopolistic elements in developed nations channel technological innovation into higher profits, shorter working hours, and higher wages for their own populations. Thus, technological progress does not automatically become an advantage for the developing regions. (6) Finally, because their exports are not expanding significantly, developing nations are unable to increase their purchases of capital goods from the developed countries. The "development decade" looks more like a "stagnation decade."

World trade was aggravated by deterioration in the terms of trade between 1950 and 1963. "The slower growth in the quantity of exports of the developing countries and the adverse movement of their terms of trade were largely the reflection of the present commodity composition of their trade, consisting, as it does, predominantly of the exchange of primary product exports for manufactured imports whose relative positions in world markets have undergone significant changes. World trade in manufactures has been increasing at an annual rate more than twice that of trade in primary products." [3] This imbalance has produced widespread use of substitutes and synthetics, increasing technological efficiency in primary products in advanced countries, increased productivity there, and the low consumer demand for food compared to increases in consumer income, in the advanced countries where incomes and food consumption are already high. The gap between import requirements of Third

World countries and their export earnings has been widening. "According to United Nations Secretariat estimates, this gap could be of the order of $20 billion a year in 1970, on the basis of a five percent per annum rate of growth set as the target for the United Nations Development Decade, assuming no change in the trends of the 'fifties upon which these estimates were based." [4]

Slowly, Third World countries have been turning to economic and social planning as a technique for accelerating growth, if only to keep pace with the developed economies. While planning carries with it a clear-cut responsibility to consider, impose, and carry out structural changes, they are hindered externally by the instability of the international market for primary commodities; and by restrictions on access to markets of the developed countries. If the developing countries are to succeed, there must be appropriate changes in the structure of international trade which will afford them an opportunity to earn adequate amounts of foreign exchange.

In spite of the risk of antagonizing the United States, Third World nations have turned to Communist bloc countries. At the present time, however, trade between Third World countries and centrally planned economies remains but a small part of the trade turnover of developing countries as a whole. "In 1962, $1,630 million, or 5.6% of the total exports of the developing countries went to the centrally planned economies, while imports from the latter into the former totalled $2,150 million and formed 7.3% of total imports. This trade has, however, shown a tendency to increase rapidly in recent years." [5]

There are obvious economic advantages in Third World countries trading with the centrally planned economies

[3] Ibid., pp. 8–9.

[4] Ibid., p. 9.
[5] Ibid., p. 11.

of the socialist bloc. The establishment of "normal relations" between these blocs becomes an important factor in the creation of an international push to improve the trade balance of developing countries with advanced countries in general. The General Principles of the United Nations Conference on Trade and Development underline this point: "There shall be no discrimination on the basis of differences in socioeconomic systems. Adaptation of trading methods shall be consistent with this principle." [6]

The most striking aspect of the resolutions presented at the conference is the voting patterns of the United States, tacitly supported by France and Britain (though they abstained from voting whenever possible and whenever they felt no direct economic stake), and of the Soviet Union. The United States consistently opposed the resolutions of the conference, even where it was the only nation at the conference to do so. The Soviet Union consistently supported the claims of the developing nations. It is therefore necessary to further explore the economics in back of these resolutions.

A 5 per cent minimum growth target is considered extremely good. But, even with such a growth rate, the real wealth of Third World nations will continue to lag behind the developed nations. Since the rate of increase of consumer imports continues at a 6 per cent rate, payments for these imports more than absorb any growth in the national economy. "One of the reasons for this is that any acceleration in the rate of growth requires additional investment; and the import content of this investment is normally higher than that of income as a whole. Consequently, it is not going too far to conclude that imports would have to rise at a rate somewhat higher than that of total income." [7]

It would also be necessary for exports of developing countries to increase by 6 per cent to pay for a volume of imports increasing each year at that rate. The income thus derived would help create the necessary capital formation for economic "take-off." Austerity policies, high taxation, and the creation of investment capital are fundamental for the realization of this goal. Trade is not considered a substitute for this responsibility.[8] Redressing the trade balance, however, is an important preliminary stage, one that cannot await the resolution of internal change.

The Third World has repeatedly emphasized, although judiciously and politely, that it opposes present trade associations and agreements such as the General Agreement on Tariffs and Trade and the Common Market. The first Trade and Development Conference, held in Havana nearly thirty years ago, took place in a context of a world economic crisis and impending involvement of advanced countries in World War Two. At that time the developing nations could not exert sufficient pressure to produce trade agreements designed to encourage their economic development. The code of rules and principles of that conference are still, with slight modifications, embodied in the General Agreement on Tariffs and Trade. The GATT agreement, as it is called, is based on an abstract notion of economic heterogeneity, just as were regional protectionist measures before it. GATT simply internationalizes protectionism.

The GATT agreement does not take into account the considerable structural differences which exist between big industrial centers and peripheral countries. In particular, it fallaciously assumes full employment, complete elasticity of supply and demand, and homogeneity of economic systems. Re-

[6] Ibid., Second Part, Section I, Principles, p. 17.
[7] Raúl Prebisch, op. cit.
[8] Raúl Prebisch, Towards a Dynamic Development Policy for Latin America. New York: United Nations Publication (E/Conf/12/680/1), 1963.

gional or international trade agreements have not benefited the Third World as they have developed nations. Structural economic change at the time of the GATT agreement was gaining momentum. The GATT negotiations were not designed to expand world trade but rather to develop the aggregate income of the Atlantic Community. It was reciprocal, based in the main on rationalizing trade between major centers. In the Common Market by contrast, the member countries grant each other, by means of industrial pooling, preferences which are expected to convert their reciprocal trade into higher industrial production. This preferential system therefore offers a powerful impetus to trade among member countries, whereas the GATT agreement does little to change the basic disequilibrium which obtains between "donor" and "recipient" nations. Third World countries have attempted to demonstrate that preferential trade systems need not conflict with one which encourages development in disadvantaged nations. But the developed sector's actual attitude toward the agricultural products of the Third World underscores the disparity between the interests of the two sectors. Western Europe's—especially France's—highly restrictive policy toward agricultural imports is one source of irritation.

Agriculture is a declining sector in the Six, as it is in most countries. The level of agricultural income has not kept pace with other sectors of the economy. Moreover, the share of agricultural income in total national income is markedly lower than the proportions of people working in agriculture would lead one to suspect. This lag in agricultural income is due to two sets of factors, first the relatively low productivity of agriculture resulting from such structural deficiencies as too many small holdings, the fragmentation of farms, the lack of available capital, and the

poor mobility of agricultural manpower; and, second, the inelasticity of demand for agricultural products and the unfavorable relationship between the prices received for agricultural products and those paid by the farmer for his means of production.[9]

This conflict of interests is further heightened by a high degree of political participation of French agricultural groups. The same holds true for German agriculture. Trade becomes based on a preferential system between industrialized nations, and is very difficult to change because of political as well as economic reasons. The declining importance of agriculture in these developed economies may bode well for future agreements which can support a principle of an "international division of labor." But this rationalization in the world economy depends on a rationalization of economic systems as such. Presently constituted preferential systems—the European Six, the United States, and the Atlantic Community— have not been able or willing to liberalize terms of trade to take account of other "preferential systems."

Until developing countries have sufficient capital formation for economic take-off, preferential systems established on regional grounds will have limited value for them. Such attempts as the Latin American Federation of Trade Associations have value mainly for articulating economic claims in political terms. At best, Third World regional systems tend to allocate resources more efficiently. But their supply and demand, shortages and abundance, are similar to each other. They cannot satisfy one another's needs for the materials offered . by developed countries. Hence regional organization cannot truly relieve economic pressure. As a result, aside from some minimal good

[9] Leon N. Lindberg, *The Political Dynamics of European Economic Integration.* London: Oxford University Press, 1963.

effects, such associations serve to organize Third World business interests for the purpose of articulating their claims. And conferences sponsored by the United Nations, which present these issues as a matter of world concern, serve as a platform where trade and financial policy of all the great blocs can be compared and perhaps adjudicated. It is a way for Third World nations to take fresh initiative in making their multilateral image of the economic world a reality.

Western objections to such multilateralism of Third World economic aims seek, at the very least, to purchase time for favored nations. Such aims, whatever the moral implications, are quite specious. Nor can the underdeveloped and developing nations be assuaged with token aid measures. Multilateralist trade arrangement is considered by Third World nations to be a virtual model for slow and modest change since their governments and business classes wish to avoid total renovation of their social structures. Hence, Western objections based on accusations of haste merely reveal the speciousness of such opposition. Such a position fails to take into account the precipitous haste with which colonial empires were forged to begin with. It has been pointed out that "in the ten years 1880–1890 five million square miles of African territory, containing a population of over 60 million, were seized by and subjected to European states." [10] Furthermore, what appeared to be a "scramble" for colonies was, in fact, a relatively well-integrated program of the advanced European powers to adjust their "spheres of influence" to their actual economic and political roles. Thus, by the beginning of the twentieth century, Asia and the Middle East were quickly absorbed in the colonial fold, along the classical lines evolved

in Africa.[11] If the processes of colonization were rapidly worked out, it is no wonder that demands for decolonization should now be insistently presented before the pivotal United Nations agencies.

Demands for preferential economic treatment and for multilateral decision-making in economic affairs have an obvious "anti-Western" political content. Yet, these demands also reveal a clear desire on the part of the Third World to avoid a policy of exaggerated economic self-determination which would make it too reliant upon the Soviet Union. This is done, particularly by the African nations, by extending invitations to major First World private enterprises to invest in their countries at favorable trade and exchange rates. Development may include an industrial base, but it is not defined by the presence of such a base. The satellite relation of Eastern Europe to the Soviet Union makes it clear that economic development without political sovereignty leads to structural reform without a resolution of basic social tensions.

Despite the highly liberal tone of the general principles recorded at the Conference on Tariffs and Trade, liberalization to Third World countries means new preferential systems based on the profitable sale of their goods in the advanced sector of the capitalist economy. Unless this "liberalization" occurs, developing countries will turn increasingly to trade arrangements and exchange with the centrally planned economies of Eastern Europe. This in turn would help relieve the economic pressures the East feels from the West.

After World War Two, the centralized economies of the Soviet type had twin aims: reconstruction and industrialization. They were obviously designed to change the character of these societies and to solve their basic problems—surplus population in agricul-

[10] Leonard Woolf, *Economic Imperialism,* pp. 33–4, as quoted in Maurice Dobb, *Political Economy and Capitalism.* New York: International Publishers, 1945, p. 243 f.

[11] On this subject, see Maurice Dobb, *Political Economy and Capitalism,* pp. 242–4.

ture, accelerated investment rate, and the need to curtail private consumption. Certain priorities were set which ultimately produced unintended strategic imbalances. Industry as a whole was emphasized as against agriculture, heavy industry over other industry, and heavy machinery within heavy industry. East European countries increased their investments in industry by 50 per cent and placed very low priorities on light industry and agriculture.[12]

The countries of Eastern Europe were greatly harmed by the Soviet Union's dogmatic insistence on a heavy industrial base. Despite attempts to coordinate labor, serious inefficiencies and imbalances in output and trade developed within the bloc itself and even led to alarming food shortages. After Stalin's death, those nations sought a new economic course.

> The allocation of investments was to be shifted, up to a point, in favor of light industry and agriculture, which were to receive a higher priority than before. However, no sooner had these shifts started to be implemented than it appeared such a reallocation implied the abandonment of many projects foreseen by the early plans. New pressures started to build up, then, in the opposite direction and finally, by mid-1954, many of the allocations of investment in favor of light industry were canceled. Cooperation in the sense of a broad division of labor still appears to be precluded by dogmatic adherence to the idea that each country "must develop its own heavy-industrial base." [13]

But from time to time, pressures to secure these "low priority" goods

through trade mount and it is clear that to head off these pressures from finding Western channels, it is to the advantage of the Soviet Union that the claims of the underdeveloped bloc be used economically.

Because there is no rift in Soviet policy then, between its economic and political aims with respect to the Third World, it can afford to carry out common assistance programs. The Soviet Union has assisted developing countries not just with consumer goods, but with industrial equipment and technical knowledge. Vast numbers of Third World technicians and workers are currently studying in Soviet universities and technological colleges and learning industrial skills in Soviet factories. As Deutscher notes,

> This is the cheapest and most effective assistance. It costs less than does American aid in consumer goods; and it helps the underdeveloped nations to help themselves. The effect of American assistance is largely ephemeral. This is why it earns so little gratitude. The results of Soviet assistance are lasting; and those who receive it have the sense of being raised up from backwardness and dependence. The Russians say: "We can do all this because we are not afraid of foreign competition; we do not tremble for our markets; and we are not afraid of sharing industrial know-how. Western capitalists cannot afford to do this." [14]

Quite aside from the obvious political advantages of such moves, the Soviet Union also has much to gain from expanded trade with underdeveloped countries. It is in a position to allocate long-term loans and monies on a more efficient basis than the United States, since it is not faced with the "problem

[12] Nicolas Spulber, "Planning and Development," in *Resources and Planning in Eastern Europe,* edited by N. J. G. Pounds and Nicolas Spulber. Bloomington: Indiana University Publications, 1957.

[13] N. Spulber, *op. cit.,* p. 93.

[14] See Isaac Deutscher, *The Great Contest: Russia and the West.* New York: Ballantine Books, 1961, pp. 117–18.

of perversity" from business or Congress as the United States is. But more important, the Soviet Union does not have a favorable trade balance with Eastern Europe. If Eastern Europe could import a large supply of foodstuffs, raw materials, and primary commodities from the underdeveloped countries instead of perpetuating its dependence on the Soviet Union, and if it could then ship its increasing surplus of "engineering products" to them instead of to the Soviet Union, Eastern Europe would obviously gain considerable economic maneuvering space. Such a policy would leave the Soviet Union economically freer, since it would reduce the present drain on its resources involved in directing the industrialization of Eastern Europe. Granick has pointed out that "The Eastern European countries would also gain, in the sense that they would have several eager trading partners instead of one reluctant one." [15]

Many development specialists of the United States have argued that American economic interests are compatible with the trade interests of the underdeveloped nations.[16] There is considerable misconception, among development specialists no less than among the general public, that aid to underdeveloped countries, whether given directly or in support of requested measures, represents generosity from the American taxpayer. But the funds made available are often smaller than generally believed. Aid figures often indicate commitments and authorizations rather than actual disbursements. Furthermore, amortization and interest payments must be deducted from gross aid figures. With respect to Latin America, disbursements are often in the form

of Eximbank loans, "Whose funds are derived from the sale of Treasury bills to investors." [17]

These loans have realized a profit for American investors. And with the aid of the Inter-American Bank potential investors are provided with new channels for development funds open to Latin American governments.[18]

Disbursement in part is made in the form of surplus commodities which would otherwise remain idle and be subject to storage costs or deterioration. Furthermore, United States taxpayer-consumers often benefit from a decline in prices paid for import products; this is particularly so when wholesale prices of United States exports rise. This decline in prices is linked to the purchase of U.S. goods produced or marketed abroad.

The final report of the conference contains what might be called "historical" background. In it the origins are traced to the Havana conference of the 'thirties. Its "preface" placed the United Nations Conference within a setting of economic problems which represent a continuation of the Havana Conference. The rest of the proceedings consist of the General and Special Principles together with recommendations which press further the multilateralist implications of Third World claims.

The table below shows the voting at the conference. It makes plain what the actual "gap" between the United States and the Third World has come to. And it also provides a graphic description of the blocs within the United Nations.

Let us examine the United States vot-

---

[15] David Granick, "Economic Relations with the USSR," in *Resources and Planning in Eastern Europe, op. cit.*

[16] Eugene Staley, *The Future of Underdeveloped Countries* (revised edition). New York: Frederick A. Praeger, 1961, esp. pp. 397–441.

[17] Irving L. Horowitz, *Revolution in Brazil: Politics and Society in a Developing Nation.* New York: E. P. Dutton & Co., 1964, esp. pp. 196–223.

[18] Tad Szulc, *Winds of Revolution.* New York: Frederick Praeger, 1963, esp. pp. 275–7.

TABLE I. GENERAL PROPOSITIONS OF THE UNITED NATIONS CONFERENCE ON TRADE AND DEVELOPMENT

Propositions*	Asian Bloc	Latin America	African Bloc	United Kingdom	United States	Soviet Union	Eastern Europe	Western Europe	Vote Explanation**	Composite Vote Yea +	Nay −	Abs. o
(G.P. *I*) Economic relations between countries shall be based on respect for the principle of sovereign equality of states, self-determination, and non-interference in internal affairs.	+	+	+	o	−	+	+	+	Australia, Ireland, & New Zealand voted Yea. Portugal abstained.	113	1	2
(G.P. *II*) There shall be no discrimination on the basis of differences in socio-economic systems. Adoption of trading methods shall be consistent with this principle.	+	+	+	o	−	+	+	+	Germany & Canada Against. S. Africa, Spain, Monaco, Sweden, Switzerland, Netherlands, Norway abstained.	96	3	16
(G.P. *III*) Every country has the right to trade with others, and freely to dispose of its natural resources in the interest of the economic development of its own people.	+	+	+	−	−	+	+	+	Germany abstained. Nicaragua, Peru, and Japan abstained.	94	4	18
(G.P. *IV*) All countries will pursue internal and external economic policies designed to accelerate economic growth throughout the world, at a rate which would narrow the gap between developed and developing nations.	+	+	+	−	−	+	+	+	Belgium, Finland, France, Italy, Holy See, Japan, Luxembourg, Monaco, Peru, Netherlands, Nicaragua, S. Africa, Switzerland abstained.	98	1	17
(G.P. *V*) Economic policies should be directed towards attaining an international division of labor in harmony with needs for diversification of developing economies.	+	+	+	o	o	+	+	+	As in vote explanation for G.P. *IV*, plus Canada and Spain abstained.	97	0	19
(G.P. *VI*) All countries should cooperate in creating conditions of international trade conducive to the achievement of the rapid increase in the export earnings of developing countries.	+	+	+	+	−	+	+	+	Taiwan (China) abstained.	114	1	1
(G.P. *VII*) Developed countries shall progressively eliminate barriers that hinder trade and consumption of products from developing countries, and take steps to create new export markets for developing countries.	+	+	+	−	−	+	+	+	Denmark and Switzerland Against.	87	8	19
(G.P. *VIII*) Developed countries should grant concessions to developing nations without extracting similar concessions in return. Special preferential arrangements presently in effect should be regarded as transitional.	+	+	+	−	−	+	+	o	Austria, Iceland, Sweden, Switzerland, Against. Brazil, Rwanda, Uganda, Venezuela abstained.	78	11	23
(G.P. *IX*) Developed countries participating in regional economic groupings should ensure that their economic integration does not cause injury to or adversely affect expansion of imports from developing countries.	+	+	+	+	+	+	+	o	Austria, Finland, Sweden, Switzerland did not abstain.	106	0	10

* (G.P.) stands for General Propositions; (S.P.) stands for Special Propositions.
** When a given nation does not vote with its given bloc, it will appear in the vote explanation column.

Table I *(Continued)*

Propositions*	Asian Bloc	Latin America	African Bloc	United Kingdom	United States	Soviet Union	Eastern Europe	Western Europe	Vote Explanation**	Composite Vote Yea +	Nay −	Abs. o
(G.P. X) All forms of economic cooperation should result in an expansion of intra-regional and extra-regional trade and encourage their growth and diversification with due regard to special features of each nation.	+	+	+	+	+	+	+	+	Japan abstained.	115	0	1
(G.P. XI) Developed countries should increase net flow of international financial, technical, economic assistance to aid export earnings of underdeveloped countries. No political or military conditions.	+	+	+	−	−	+	+	o	Australia, F.R. Germany, Against.	92	5	19
(G.P. XII) Resources released as outcome of agreement on disarmament should be allocated to economic developing by the fully developed countries.	+	+	+	o	−	o	o	o		83	1	30
(G.P. XIII) (land-locked countries)	+	+	+	+	+	+	+	+		108	0	0
(G.P. XIV) Complete decolonization as in U.N. Declaration of granting independence & liquidation of all forms of colonialism is necessary for economic development & exercise of sovereign rights over natural resources.	+	+	+	−	o	+	+	o	Australia Against	90	2	22
(G.P. XV) Different levels of development to be recognized in individual developing countries & special attention to least developed to insure equitable opportunity.	+	+	+	+	+	+	+	+	Albania, Brazil, Canada, Iceland, Jamaica, Syria, Liechtenstein, Japan, Spain abstained.	101	0	12
(S.P. 1) Developed countries should cooperate with developing countries in setting targets for expansion of trade of the latter & in periodically reviewing measures taken for their achievement.	+	+	+	o	−	+	+	+	Canada Against.	99	2	15
(S.P. 2) Developing countries should modernize agriculturally and industrially. Developed countries should supplement these efforts through financing, training programs & expanding imports of processed & manufactured goods from developing countries.	+	+	+	+	+	+	+	+		116	0	0
(S.P. 3) No action.												
(S.P. 4) Developing countries have the right to protect their infant industries.	+	+	+	+	o	+	+	+		115	0	1
(S.P. 5) Domestic support for primary commodities in developed countries shall not preclude a fair proportion of the domestic consumption being supplied by developing countries.	+	+	+	+	o	+	+	+	Australia, Austria, Belgium, F.R. Germany, Finland, France, San Marine, Greece, Holy See, Iceland abstained.	91	0	25
(S.P. 6) Developed countries should help developing countries promote new uses for products whose use has been reduced by synthetic innovations, by research, etc.	+	+	+	+	+	+	+	+		116	0	0

TABLE I (*Continued*)

Propositions*	Asian Bloc	Latin America	African Bloc	United Kingdom	United States	Soviet Union	Eastern Europe	Western Europe	Vote Explanation**	Composite Vote Yea +	Nay −	Abs. o
(S.P. 7) Whenever international measures taken are to stabilize primary product prices in relation to manufactured goods, equitable arrangements should be made in terms of facilitating the implementation of economic development plans.	+	+	+	−	−	o	o	o	Australia, Austria, Canada, Denmark, F.R. Germany, Iceland, Japan, Norway, S. Africa, Switzerland, Liechtenstein, Against	85	13	18
(S.P. 8) In the disposal of agricultural surpluses, developed countries should undertake to apply internationally agreed upon criteria of surplus disposal so as not to affect adversely export prospects of developing countries heavily dependent on the export narrow range of primary products. Criteria should also govern the disposal of all primary surpluses and stockpiles.	+	+	+	o	−	+	+	+	Denmark, France, Iceland, Monaco, Sweden, S. Africa abstained	106	1	9
(S.P. 9) Countries shall refrain from all forms of dumping.	+	+	+	o	o	+	+	+	Norway, S. Africa, Sweden abstained.	107	0	9
(S.P. 10) Scientific and technological achievements should be made accessible under favourable conditions to all developing countries and their application to the trade and development needs of those countries should be encouraged by an expansion of bilateral and multilateral programmes of technical assistance.	+	+	+	+	+	+	+	+		116	0	0
(S.P. 11) All countries should support an expansion of multilateral economic assistance to developing countries especially within the framework of the U.N. as well as bilateral assistance.	+	+	+	o	o	+	+	o	Japan, S. Africa abstained.	93	0	23
(S.P. 12) All countries should cooperate in devising measures to help developing countries build up transport for their economic development, to ensure the unhindered use of such facilities and to promote tourism in these countries in order to increase their earnings and reduce their expenditure on invisible trade.	+	+	+	−	−	+	+	o	Canada, Japan, Ireland abstained.	92	7	17
(S.P. 13) Mutually beneficial bilateral and multilateral trade and payments arrangements between developing countries constitute an essential element in the expansion and diversification of international trade.	+	+	+	o	+	+	+	+	Australia, Canada, Japan, Liechtenstein abstained.	111	0	5

ing response to the General and Special Principles of the Conference in more detail; particularly since the propositions as given in the chart have been condensed.

General Principle One states "Economic relations between countries, including trade relations, shall be based on respect for the principle of sovereign equality of states, self-determination of peoples, and non-interference in the internal affairs of other countries." The only vote against this proposition was cast by the United States.

General Principle Two: "There shall be no discrimination on the basis of differences in socio-economic systems. Adoption of trading methods shall be consistent with this principle." The United States voted against this.

General Principle Three: "Every country has the sovereign right freely to trade with other countries, and freely to dispose of its natural resources in the interest of the economic development and well-being of its own people." The United States voted against this.

General Principle Four calls for recognition of socio-economic development as the concern of the old community and co-operative policies among the nations of the world to enhance development. The only vote against it was cast by the United States. The United States, however, abstained on General Principle Five calling for measures to diversify and adjust underdeveloped countries to modern needs. This may well be because a portion of it, stating that "Developed countries should assist the developing countries in their efforts," is in keeping with unilateral and bilateral policies of the United States toward underdeveloped countries. Whenever independence, trade adjustment, expansion, sovereignty, economic diversification are called for, as for example in General Principle Six, the United States voted against acceptance. This is true for General Principles Seven, Eight, Eleven, Twelve. The United States

voted for General Principles Nine, Ten, Thirteen, Fifteen, since "regional groupings" of underdeveloped countries pose no immediate threat to United States interests. Principle Nine calls for regional groupings among developed countries not to inhibit or injure Third World economies. Here the language was sufficiently clear-cut. "To insure that their economic integration does not cause injury to . . ." It could not really have been opposed. Indeed, no country at the conference voted against Nine. General Principle Thirteen was a matter of arranging the parts of the conference to include Principles relating to the transit trade of landlocked countries. Since nothing was at stake, no country voted against it. The United States also voted for General Principle Fifteen calling for recognition of the different stages of developing economies and measures adopted to take cognizance of these stages to insure growth. Again the Principle did not call for sovereignty, diversification, independence, freedom, or autonomy, and hence did not represent a challenge to American hegemony.

The vote on Special Principles followed the same pattern. Where the propositions implied multilateralism, the United States voted against them. Where bilateralism was protected or unchallenged, reflecting current United States relations, there were abstentions. Where tariff curbs on developed countries were called for in strong or clearcut language, the United States either abstained or voted in favor of such a principle. Special Principles differed from General Principles in that the former covered more specific ground. They were more concrete and were concerned with suggestions for implementation.

The United States vote was preponderantly against most General and Special Principles because they called for the encouragement of independence, autonomy, free trade, and diversification of underdeveloped economies.

Measures strongly inhibiting developed countries from acting against the interests of developing countries were supported by the major blocs. Fair pricing of primary commodities and technical assistance were also widely supported by all blocs.

Special segments of development concerned with *international commodity arrangements and removal of obstacles to, and expansion of, trade* were adopted without dissent. These recommendations were primarily concerned with ending the great trade advantages developed countries held over the underdeveloped countries. For example, there should be equitable disposal of surplus goods and a fair price on primary commodities, so that fair sales competition could exist. Here too, positive independence, low tariffs, free trade, and sovereignty were not at stake.

The propositions calling for a review and proper administration of the World Food Aid Program found no dissent; nor was any opposition voiced to competition from synthetics and substitutes. Because of the advanced nature of the goods involved, these tenets held little relevance for developing countries and great relevance for advanced countries. So none of the advanced countries offered dissent. On special legislation, the United States voted consistently. Where its bilateral arrangements were either left intact or promoted, it abstained or supported the measures. Where sovereignty and free trade were involved, it voted negatively. It supported only measures recommending studies, surveys, information gathering, and technical assistance.

Each of the countries was invited to explain its votes in a section called Observations. The United States explained its general opposition on two grounds: (1) The measures called for were not really going to provide efficient assistance to underdeveloped countries; (2) the recommendations prejudged the results of the proposed study, for it re-

quested that a program of action be drawn up. United States objections sometimes reflected distaste for measures which encouraged trade with the "centrally planned" economies.

The following conclusions can be drawn from this welter of Propositions, Principles, and Observations. The Soviet vote was based on the union of its political and economic needs *vis à vis* the underdeveloped countries. The United States reflected the complications of its position. It would have been to its political advantage to support measures of the conference since they would be adopted anyway. But the internal political atmosphere of an election year affected political rationality. Economically, the United States has a policy of encouraging modernism at the expense of structural change for its own market needs. Thus far the United States is not prepared to consider its economic interests in a larger multilateral context. The latent mistrust of the capacity of Third World nations to guide their own destinies, or the implied competition involved, has led the United States to oppose measures which could enhance this process of development. This conference did shatter the myth that "development intellectuals" (who tend to favor measures such as those at the conference) are in charge of the nation's policy-making or diplomacy with respect to the underdeveloped world.

We tend to assume rationality in the decision-making process, particularly when it comes to questions of international relations. But this insistence on rationality has the defects of its virtue. In the case of the conference, for example, national explanations for the uniformly parochial and narrow reaction to Third World demands break down on the main point: that economists, political analysts, and scientific researchers from the United States were the *primum mobile* for the entire Prebisch position. Sociologically inclined economists such as Bert Hoselitz and

Albert O. Hirshman, have for some time supported these same sorts of demands.

Thus, we reach the conclusion that the voting pattern of the United States in the United Nations at the Geneva Conference was partially inspired by outside factors strong enough to occasion United States opposition to the best opinions voiced by its own policymakers. Chief of these "irrational" factors was the emergence of Goldwaterism as a political phenomenon during the early summer of 1964. The United Nations representatives were discouraged from any behavior which might be construed as precipitous, or as delivering ourselves into the hands of the socialist sector. Another is that the "hard line" with respect to Latin America had yielded major victories in Brazil with the April First *coup d'état,* with the collapse of guerrilla operations from Venezuela to Argentina, the election in Chile of Christian Democracy over the socialist opposition, etc. In short, the hard line was gaining points at the very time the developmental line was appealing for greater independence. And finally, American foreign policy in Southeast Asia became increasingly military and decreasingly political; so that it became less important to the United States to take the Third World voting bloc into account.

But these factors account only for low-order, immediately perceived irrationality. There exists, however, a higher irrationality. The United States, since entering international politics as a major force, has been confronted by a duality within its tradition. On one side, there is its revolutionary background, a belief in a democracy where each man counts as one, and no more nor less than one. On the other side, there is the United States of the manifest destiny, of the Monroe Doctrine, and of a general conviction that the fates of the world are determined by the march of American hegemony. But these political contradictions were no more a deterrence to American economic growth than was totalitarianism to Russia.

The confusions are well stated by Hans J. Morgenthau: "The traditional anti-imperialism of America was without a political objective either by virtue of its very nature or else because the radius of an active American foreign policy was limited to the Western Hemisphere." In contrast to this, "the new anti-imperialism can no longer afford to condemn the suppression of liberty from afar and limit its tribute to freedom to charitable deeds. Committed to the containment of communism, to the preservation of national freedom wherever it is threatened by Soviet imperialism, the United States can reconcile itself to this loss of national freedom only if it altogether ceases being anti-imperialistic." [19] In other words, anti-imperialism, by taking on anti-Communist pretensions, has become tough-minded instead of tender-hearted. But even Morgenthau shrinks away from the *Realpolitik* of this anti-Communist framework. He has to see United States interests as eternally linked to European allies in particular and to a "common civilization threatened by an alien and oppressive social system" in general. In other words, the classic stress between "interests" and "ethics" is seen as a uniquely American problem, and for that very reason, a certain jejune quality is manifested in United States international policies with respect to the Third World.

The United States of America, when faced with responsibilities and problems of world leadership, has shown that it is striving to be both powerful and ethical. It has not been, however, mature or wise in its attempts to reconcile power and morality, for it has

[19] See Hans J. Morgenthau, "The American Tradition in Foreign Policy," in *Foreign Policy in World Politics,* edited by R. C. Macridis. Englewood Cliffs, N.J.: Prentice-Hall, Inc., 1962, pp. 206, 211.

not yet awakened to the fact that in important ways the two aims are irreconcilable. It has striven for power to counterbalance totalitarian injustice, in addition to seeking self-enrichment. It has undertaken the "white man's burden" in order to extend the areas of what it conceived to be freedom. It undertook to build a counter-imperialism. The United States conceives the efforts of other nations to extend territorial influence as imperialistic; its own efforts to do so are often conceived as rescue operations. It is therefore blind to its own imperialism and considers the efforts to extend its own power as the height of justice.

With perfect moralistic consistency it can pursue policies which seek to extend its spheres of influence in the name of justice and deliverance from tyranny. The United States is an imperialistic democracy. But it cannot reconcile the nature of the terms. It could perhaps wield its power more ruthlessly in certain areas, but then it would not square with a democratic self-image. It could allow for the full autonomy of weaker nations, but then it would not be powerful. While it attempts both, it loses ground on both fronts. It cannot be frankly imperialistic as England and France were in earlier generations. Neither can it be truly just. It is ambivalent because it feels now the needs of one, now the needs of the other. Thus, it has never developed a satisfactory imperialistic style, nor a meaningful moral posture.

Every great nation has a sense of mission. It has often been noted that a great nation is both expansionist and imperialistic because it is in the nature of power that it be driven thus. The Soviet Union also has this divided self-image. It too is exporting democracy, economic if not political democracy. It also conceived the extension of its influence in the name of freedom from tyranny. It has sought to store immense power in its organs of government, and notions of its ethical mission have

guided its foreign policies. It too has undertaken to solve the "white man's burden." It acts in the name of moral justice, often sincerely. The Soviet Union amasses power to extend the areas of freedom, though its conception of this term is largely economic. Like the United States, it is sensitive to reactions to its policies from those whom it tries to influence. It perceives itself as anti-imperialist.

The United States defines justice in terms of political liberty. The Soviet Union defines justice in terms of economic welfare. The latter best suits the needs of the Third World. The United States defines imperialism as a form of injustice. According to its political libertarian definitions of justice the Soviet Union is unjust and imperialistic, the former because of the latter. The Soviet Union defines injustice as attempts to practice political libertarianism without solving economic dilemmas of poverty. Injustice of this kind can only be engaged in legitimately by an elite. Hence efforts to spread this false democracy are imperialistic and unjust, the former because of the latter. The First and Second Worlds are therefore mirror images of each other's shortcomings.

The underdeveloped countries conceive it to be their sovereign right to make their own choice between the First and Second Worlds. And the United Nations is in an important sense their instrument for limiting the imperialistic variations of both worlds, while holding both accountable for their ideal claims. Efforts on the part of the United States to obstruct United Nations conference decision-making are seen as unjust and imperialistic. For the Third World shares with the Soviet Union an economic conception of democracy and justice. The successes of the Soviet Union in the economic sphere seem to be confirmation of this belief. Hence the Soviet Union does not seem to be imperialistic. The Soviet Union, like the United States, is seen as powerful, but United States power is viewed as necessarily restrictive of the sovereignty of underdeveloped nations. This is defined as imperialist. American attempts to combat the imperialist image, by such programs as the Alliance for Progress and the Peace Corps, have aimed at paralleling its interests with altruistic actions, but have never made a significant sacrifice of the former. The Soviet Union is not in a similar bind at the present historical moment. The United States can attend a conference at which the underdeveloped countries present a number of proposals and resolutions for implementing programs to relieve their economic distress, and out of the simple fact that the Russians can support these proposals without serious sacrifice to its positions, the United States seems peculiarly colonialist and, hence, unjust. To counter this imperialism the United States has to surrender some part of its own immediate interest. When the United States does not give support to the Third World, it gives the classical argument of the rights of power. The United States balances these factors "pragmatically," issue by issue. It cannot surrender any part of its interest, nor will it recognize other legitimate definitions of justice. It cannot see the temporariness of these given issues, and tends to stand therefore for "eternal truths" when it votes as when it fights.

That this "self-interest" doctrine is gaining support is shown by the tendency of at least one wing of American policy-makers to consider foreign aid in militaristic rather than in developmental terms. One authority has summed up this position most candidly: "American policies regarding aid and trade may legitimately be employed as strategic weapons in the Cold War, and that in such employment, flexibility is both appropriate and necessary."[20] In short, all trade and aid

must be viewed in terms of enhancing the security of the United States, while any humanitarian concerns must be considered as a by-product of national objectives. The startling voting pattern of the United States, with respect to Third World trade demands, can be considered a response to the growing self-consciousness of America as a world power—something not in evidence during previous decades. The American dialogue between considerations of power in contrast to those of justice remains in evidence. It is also clear that the power factions within the political hierarchy now occupy command positions with respect to the issuance of foreign assistance.

The perverse voting pattern of the United States at the Conference on Trade and Development shows it to be combatting Soviet influence in the name of justice. It is, it believes, acting cautiously or out of principle. To the rest of the world, which does not share this dialectic of self-definition or self-interest with the Soviet Union, the United States is seen to be acting against its own interest. Hence, the United States is often looked upon as an imperialist which cannot extend the borders of democracy. The United States stands alone with irritating suspicions as to why, but with few explanations. This kind of political behavior, this incapacity to surrender anything but taxpayers' money for foreign aid, reveals it to be blind to the image cast. The United States cannot adopt colonialist positions as equivalent to justice. Modern imperialism is built into the American system of political democracy. This paradox cannot be easily removed by a new vocabulary or a new dedication to national purpose.

[20] James R. Schlesinger, "Strategic Leverage from Aid and Trade," in National Security: Political, Military, and Economic Strategies in the Decade Ahead, edited by David M. Abshire and Richard V. Allen. New York: Frederick A. Praeger (for the Hoover Institution on War, Revolution and Peace), 1963, pp. 688–9.

Perhaps the cruelest cut of all is that the political posture of the United States has itself become a unifying agency of Third World nations. What might easily deteriorate into national rivalries, regional jealousies and social distinctions are prevented from doing so, in some measure at least, by the fear of United States policy formulators that a positive line toward the Third World is tantamount to a betrayal of national interests. Thus the purposes of United States moral aims are contradicted not so much by the Communist challenge as by United States political decisions.

20. Problems and Trends in the Composition of Nonplenary UN Organs*

CATHERINE SENF MANNO

THOSE organs of the United Nations which do not include all Member States pose a challenging problem: How should such select bodies be constituted? There is no easy solution in view of the diversity of national policies, even between countries of a particular region, ideology, or stage of development. This paper presents a series of case studies illustrating some of the principles invoked and the nature of the accommodations arrived at by the General Assembly in dealing with the problem, especially in setting up its own subsidiary organs. On the basis of this evidence an assessment is made of the significance of recent changes in the structure of these nonplenary organs and the resulting impact on the balance of decision-making power in the Organization.

The admission of many new states and some old ones to the United Nations during the past ten years has nearly doubled the total membership. At the same time councils, commissions, and subcommittees made up of elected or selected members have become increasingly important in the formulation of UN programs and policies. Thus,

* International Organization, Vol. XIX, 37–55. Reprinted by permission.

some of the most controversial decisions made by the General Assembly have concerned the composition of and elections to these bodies. The competing claims to representation on these select organs have resulted in an uneasy accommodation between Soviet pressures for "troika" or "three-way parity" (East, West, and nonaligned), new countries' demands for a voice in decisions, the inertial force of preeminent Western influence, and other technical or functional elements. Although the final decisions on matters handled by the subsidiaries are made by a majority of the Assembly in which every state has an equal vote, a few countries, which may be in the minority, often have the power to determine whether the decisions will be implemented.

Some of these countries have come to regard the suborgans as the place to harmonize divergent interests: to redress the imbalance inherent in the rule of the majority. The United States, for example, apparently rests much of its hope for the financing of future peacekeeping operations upon the establishment of a standing special committee which would have a relatively high percentage of large contributors and which would apportion peacekeeping expenses by a qualified majority vote of the committee.[1] Such an approach would presumably be easier than the more explicit modification of "sovereign equality" by the direct weighting of votes. If this procedure could be effected, it would achieve a kind of weighting of influence without sacrificing cherished equalitarian values in the whole Assembly. This assumes, of course, that the whole Assembly would agree to constitute its subsidiary organs in a manner that adequately represents those countries with special interests and responsibilities, and that it would exercise restraint in not amending away during final plenary consideration the added element of responsibility.

The above remarks suggest two different approaches to the composition of suborgans. Under the first the aim is to set up a smaller replica of the whole Assembly, while the second attempts something quite different and as yet vaguely defined (reflecting "adequately" those with differing "capacities," "responsibilities," "interests," or "willingness to meet Charter obligations"). In addition to the dissimilarity of the numerous suborgans, the difficulty is compounded in the second approach by the vagueness of definitions and the lack of a consensus on the desirability of this kind of indirect weighting. Obviously we are far from having a theory to predict the effects that differently structured subcommittees have on the content and implementation of decisions. However, from the experience of the last nineteen years some trends are visible which offer clues to the effectiveness of a variety of kinds of committee composition in variety of contexts. They also reveal the attitude of the Assembly on the question of the proper balance of decision-making power in the smaller bodies that handle the important preliminary stage of its decision making.

[1] UN Document A/AC.113/30.

Background

Article 22 of the Charter authorizes the General Assembly to "establish such subsidiary organs as it deems necessary for the performance of its functions." In most cases, membership on subcommittees is specified in terms of the *countries* named and is of indefinite duration (unlike the rotational plan for members of the Security Council, the Economic and Social Council [ECOSOC], and various commissions). Often the authorizing resolution merely states the principles to be applied, and the President of the General Assembly names the countries to constitute a committee or those to be added in enlarging committees. For committees requiring technical competence it is usually left to the discretion of the appointed country to name a properly qualified individual. Occasionally the Secretary-General is asked to name an expert committee.

Especially relevant to this inquiry are the ways in which the subcommittees reflect opposing interests involved in the subjects with which each deals. How are they balanced between suppliers and consumers of international assistance? Between East and West or various regional groups? And, where they do indeed exhibit a different pattern of influence then the whole Assembly, how does that body finally dispose of their proposals? Since there are more than 40 fairly durable subsidiary organs of the Assembly, an attempt was made to choose for the exploration of these matters the more important committees in a variety of subject areas. Official records through mid-1964 were used, with emphasis on the period since 1954.

Case Studies in the Political Field

The experiences of the Disarmament Committee and the Committee on Peaceful Uses of Outer Space reveal the evolution and application of the "troika" concept of balance in the political field.

THE DISARMAMENT COMMITTEE [2]

The first resolution of the first session of the General Assembly dealt with the question of disarmament, and since that time the Assembly has never ceased in efforts to encourage the diplomacy of disarmament. In a world in which tribal and national loyalties have not yet abated the task has proved to be endlessly frustrating. By 1954 many procedural approaches had been tried: the subject matter had been sliced and recombined, the negotiating body contracted and enlarged. Meanwhile, the Soviet Union was catching up with the United States in technology. The Disarmament Commission's five-power subcommittee (Canada, France, the Soviet Union, the United Kingdom, and the United States), recommended by the eighth Assembly and approved by the major powers, began four years of private negotiations. With the Soviet demand for a more equitable balance between East and West, however, these talks ended in stalemate.

The Disarmament Commission itself consisted at that time of twelve members, of whom ten were allies of the United States. The twelfth session of the General Assembly sought to ameliorate the imbalance by enlarging the membership of the Commission to 25, of whom sixteen were United States allies. After boycotting the meetings, the Soviet Union induced the thirteenth Assembly in 1958 to enlarge the Commission to include all 82 Members of

the United Nations. Of course a body of this size could not negotiate anything. Finally, "hard parity" (a 50–50 division between East and West) was agreed upon in communications between President Eisenhower and Premier Khrushchev. The principle was applied in a ten-member conference dealing with surprise attack, then in an eight-member expert group dealing with cessation of nuclear tests, and finally in a ten-member general Disarmament Committee, all constituted outside the framework of the United Nations. The last-named group began its deliberations in 1960.

Shortly after the Disarmament Committee took up its work, the vexing issue of inspection was exacerbated by the dramatic revelation of United States aerial reconnaissance over the Soviet Union (the U-2 incident of May 1960). The Committee continued to meet for a while and important concessions brought the two sides somewhat closer together. However, the five Warsaw Treaty powers withdrew from the talks a few months later.

Pressed by the fifteenth Assembly to resume negotiations, the two superpowers produced a joint statement of agreed principles in the summer of 1961. They also agreed to the enlargement of the Disarmament Committee by the addition of eight nonnuclear, nonaligned countries, which gave the Committee the following total composition: [See table at top of p. 271.] This brought the Committee close to reflecting the three-way division of the world to which Soviet bloc spokesmen have so often alluded.[3] Despite overwhelming defeat of the "troika" idea

[2] See Joseph Nogee, "The Diplomacy of Disarmament," *International Conciliation,* January 1960 (No. 526), pp. 235–303; "Issues Before the Fifteenth General Assembly," *International Conciliation,* September 1960 (No. 529), pp. 9–35; and "Urgent Need for Progress on Vital Disarmament Issues," *United Nations Review,* December 1962 (Vol. 9, No. 12), pp. 9–11, 44–53.

[3] The categories in Soviet usage are "the Socialist countries, the non-aligned countries, and the members of Western military alliances." (*The New York Times,* June 16, 1961, p. 2.) The Latin American states do not fit well into this classification, and Soviet representatives have conceded that they should not be charged off entirely against the Western quota.

DISARMAMENT COMMITTEE, 1961 AND AFTER

East	Nonaligned and Latin America			West
Bulgaria	Burma	United Arab Republic		Canada
Czechoslovakia	Ethiopia	Brazil		France
Poland	India	Mexico		Italy
Rumania	Nigeria			United Kingdom
Soviet Union	Sweden			United States

as applied to the top Secretariat post, the Soviet Union thus won acceptance of three-way parity in this Committee. France, however, has refused to participate in the Committee's work, maintaining that disarmament negotiations should be limited to the nuclear club.

The Disarmament Committee, while not strictly a "subsidiary organ" of the General Assembly, has been endorsed and instructed by the Assembly. Eastern and Western spokesmen alike have paid tribute to the constructive role of the nonaligned members whose presence on the Committee gives more immediate expression to the interests of the rest of the world than do the annual resolutions of the General Assembly. The question of nations representing other nations presents no great problem as far as the nonaligned members are concerned. They represent a nearly unanimous interest and a broad consensus on how this interest can best be pursued, namely, through agreement between the opposing sides rather than excessive pressure on either.

The Committee thus reflects quite a different numerical balance than does the Assembly itself whose proportions break down to approximately 10 per cent East, 70 per cent nonaligned, and 20 per cent West (if Latin America is included in the nonaligned group). This Committee is really a symbol of the recognition of a rough equality in the division of real military power in the bipolar world and of the interest of the entire world in the decisions to

be bargained out. But the absence of representatives of General de Gaulle and Mao Tse-tung raises questions of whether the arrangement will suffice in a polycentric world. In other words, while it displays a workable balance *between* the two major coalitions and between them and the rest of the world, the Committee's structure takes no account of differences *within* the major coalitions and others they might develop within the rest of the world as disarmament approaches reality. Already the demand has been heard for another enlargement of the Committee since the nonaligned countries are "not sufficiently numerous to exercise the decisive influence that [is] to be desired." [4]

COMMITTEE ON THE PEACEFUL USES
OF OUTER SPACE [5]

On October 4, 1957, Sputnik I appeared in orbit around the earth. Launched during the International Geophysical Year, it seemed to augur well for international cooperation in the peaceful uses of outer space. Both the United States and the Soviet Union submitted items on the uses of

[4] *United Nations Review,* December 1962 (Vol. 9, No. 12), p. 50.

[5] See General Assembly Resolutions 1348 (XIII), December 13, 1958; 1472 (XIV), December 12, 1959; 1721 (XVI), December 20, 1961; 1802 (XVII), December 14, 1962; 1884 (XVIII), October 17, 1963; and 1962 and 1963 (XVIII), December 13, 1963.

outer space for the agenda of the thirteenth session of the General Assembly. In the First (Political and Security) adopted by 53 votes in favor, 9 against, with 19 abstentions.[6] This established the following committee: [*below*]

AD HOC COMMITTEE ON THE PEACEFUL USES OF OUTER SPACE, 1958

East	Nonaligned and Latin America		West and Allies	
Czechoslovakia	India	Argentina	Australia	Italy
Poland	Sweden	Brazil	Belgium	Japan
Soviet Union	United Arab Republic	Mexico	Canada	United Kingdom
			France	United States
			Iran	

Committee, substantive differences were resolved except for the question of the composition of an *ad hoc* committee on the peaceful uses of outer space. There was general agreement that the powers most advanced in space technology should be members, along with other states broadly reflecting the other UN Members. Concessions made in negotiations between Mr. Lodge (United States) and Mr. Sobolev (Soviet Union) did not succeed in bringing the two positions together. Failing acceptance of their proposal for an eleven-member committee, a roughly equal mixture of Soviet bloc, nonaligned, and Western-oriented states, the three Soviet bloc countries named as members in the United States draft resolution announced that they would not participate. These three Warsaw Pact countries saw themselves outnumbered by twelve countries allied with the United States with only three nonaligned countries as a buffer. A plea from the Assembly President for a last-minute break in the deadlock brought a bitter attack by Mr. Lodge on the "two-sides idea," followed by countercharges from Mr. Sobolev who withdrew the Soviet proposal, which had no chance of adoption. Thus in its last hours before adjournment the Assembly had only the Western-backed proposal, which was

Two of the three nonaligned countries named for membership on the *ad hoc* committee abstained in the vote and later joined the three Soviet bloc nominees in refusing to participate in the committee's work.

A year later, shortly after the Soviet Union had launched a rocket that took pictures of the far side of the moon, the fourteenth session of the General Assembly adopted a resolution enjoying sponsorship of both the United States and the Soviet Union. High hopes were held for international cooperation and a United Nations coordinating role in outer space activities. The 24-member Committee on the Peaceful Uses of Outer Space was established; it consisted of the original eighteen members of the *ad hoc* committee, plus two nonaligned countries and four additional Soviet bloc countries, and it thus represented a United States concession to Soviet demands for a better balance between East and West. Once more the mandate was to study the possibilities of United Nations action to promote peaceful cooperation in outer space activities and to study the legal problems related to space exploration; the Committee was

[6] General Assembly Resolution 1348 (XIII), December 13, 1958.

also asked to plan an international scientific conference on these subjects.

In the meantime the United States launched communications satellites, and the Soviet Union orbited several animals with safe return. But while science prospered a new deadlock developed over the composition of a subcommittee to plan the scientific conference. During the ensuing two-year stalemate, cosmic flights by astronauts Yuri Gagarin and Gherman Titov of the Soviet Union dramatized the need for some control over man's use of space. Also during this time 21 countries, mostly newly independent African nations, were admitted to the United Nations. To reflect the new membership the sixteenth Assembly enlarged the Committee to 28, distributed as follows: eight to represent the East; eleven for the nonaligned and Latin America; and nine for the West and its allies.

Thus, another important committee came to be constituted on a roughly three-way parity basis. In addition to balancing the East-West axis the Committee reflects, in more nearly even balance since the enlargements, both "producers" and "consumers" of space technology. It also embodies an assessment "loading" (a more than proportionate number of the highly assessed UN Members) since the 28 committee members account for over 80 per cent of the total assessments of all UN Members. Indeed, with three exceptions, every country assessed at more than one per cent of the total is on the Committee. Since it includes eight of the ten most populous countries in the United Nations, the Committee is also weighted in terms of population.

The Committee tried to conciliate the controversy in which it was born by agreeing informally to conduct its work in a manner which did not require voting. Under its guidance very gratifying progress is finally being made toward international cooperation

in this field. The Committee operates through two subcommittees of the whole, one of which works on scientific and technical matters while the other works on legal matters. Rapid progress in the former field is facilitated by the nature of many of its tasks which simply cannot be done without international cooperation (tracking orbits, gathering and collating meteorological data, allocating radio frequencies, etc.). Although the legal subcommittee has been understandably slower to report progress, in October 1963 the United States and the Soviet Union agreed not to station nuclear or other mass destructive weapons in outer space.

Case Studies in the Economic Field

While the question of decision-making power in the political area has revolved primarily around the balance of real power between East and West, that in the economic area reflects the less symmetrical relation between givers and receivers of assistance. In the former area subsidiary organs proved most effective in promoting voluntary East-West agreement when they recognized the near equality of real power (in weaponry and space technology) between East and West while providing a substantial voice for countries representing the common human interest of all. Disarmament would yield essentially the same kind of benefits to all: peace and security. Economic and technical assistance, on the other hand, involves different kinds of benefits for givers and receivers, and there are no countries unaligned with respect to economic development—all are either developed or want to be. Balancing the membership of subsidiary organs in the economic field thus presents a different problem.

Detailed below are two cases from the economic field, the organs concerned with a UN capital development fund and with the UN Trade and Development Conference (UNCTAD). Each was in turn the center of the continuing struggle evoked by the claims of the countries of the developing South upon the industrialized North.

THE PROPOSED UN CAPITAL DEVELOPMENT FUND[7]

The campaign for a global agency to aid economic development through grants and long-term loans has had more attention than any other item on the UN's economic agenda. By 1954 expert studies had confirmed the fact that the capital needs of the underdeveloped countries could not be met by the World Bank nor by private investment sources. The Assembly had already decided in principle that a UN development fund should be established,[8] and several industrialized European countries were ready to contribute to the Special UN Fund for Economic Development (SUNFED), as it was then called. But three major potential donors (the United States, the United Kingdom, and Canada) were opposed. In 1954 the Assembly set up an expert committee having a majority of five economically advanced Western countries of the potential donor category and a minority of four less developed countries. Then, following the admission of many new Members to the United Nations in 1955, the Assembly established a new sixteen-member committee, equally divided be-

tween less developed and advanced economies, with two Soviet bloc countries in the latter category. The less developed countries found it easy to concert their policies, but the potential donors were divided. The two Soviet bloc countries, previously lukewarm to SUNFED, had joined the less developed countries in support for it. The smaller Western countries on the committee had become convinced that SUNFED should be established in fact, not in principle only. But they avoided pressing their own preferences against the opposition of the large donor countries. The General Assembly, acting as a whole, refrained from pushing the matter to a divisive vote and was content for several years to keep attention focused on the need for a development fund.

The debate also produced other effects. The large potential donors had argued that the diversion of substantial resources to such a UN fund must await disarmament. And a small fund, they said, would be wasteful in view of the other agencies in the field. Yet United States initiative played an important role in the creation of three more agencies: the International Finance Corporation (IFC) in 1956, the UN Special Fund in 1958, and the International Development Association (IDA) in 1960.

The three last-named agencies show the effects of a powerful voice from the wings of the United Nations stage —domestic United States opinion as articulated in Congress, a voice which merits attention because the United States contributes about 40 per cent of the budgets of the UN assistance programs. The United States' belief that a major role in economic development should be given to private enterprise was taken into account in the creation of IFC. For both IFC and IDA, affiliates of the World Bank, decision-making procedures conformed to the United States view that contributing countries should retain an important

[7] See General Assembly Resolutions 822 (IX), December 11, 1954; 923 (X), December 9, 1955; 1219 (XII), December 14, 1957; 1317 (XIII), December 12, 1958; 1424 (XIV), December 5, 1959; 1521 (XV), December 15, 1960; 1706 (XVI), December 19, 1961; 1826 (XVII), December 18, 1962; and 1936 and 1945 (XVIII), December 11, 1963. See also UN Document E/CONF.46/L.28, Annex A, p. 94.

[8] General Assembly Resolution 520 (VI), January 12, 1952.

voice in organs administering economic aid.[9] (Although IDA is technically open to all, the Soviet bloc countries have not joined.) The Special Fund was limited to pre-investment activities.

Even though the Assembly's majority welcomed IDA, it continued to urge establishment of an agency more closely related to the United Nations, a UN capital development fund, as it was newly christened. The preference stemmed from the desire for a one-world agency including the East, the West, and the underdeveloped and from the desire that the agency be ultimately subject to the majority's rule in the Assembly.

In 1960 the Assembly decided "in principle" (once more) that a capital development fund "shall be established." [10] With important potential contributors dissenting or abstaining, the vote was 71 in favor, 4 opposed, with 10 abstentions. The Assembly President was asked to designate on the basis of equitable geographical distribution a 25-member committee which was to prepare for the actual establishment of the fund. Although the committee was geographically distributed between five regional groups of countries, the balance was definitely shifted in favor of the less developed nations by fifteen to ten. The committee was selectively loaded for both population and contributions; its 25 members in 1960 contributed about 80 per cent of the costs of the combined Expanded Program of Technical Assistance (EPTA) and the UN Special Fund. Yet the two countries which paid over half of the costs of these programs (the United Kingdom and the United States) were in the minority on this large committee, as indeed they

might be on any equal-voting committee of over four members.

Under the chairmanship of U Thant, then a delegate from Burma, the committee set to work in early 1961 and drafted a set of principles[11] governing the establishment and operations of a UN capital development fund in the light of which, the sixteenth Assembly decided,[12] the fund's statute should be prepared. Also involved in this decision was a concession to the industrialized countries' distaste for equal voting: the committee in drafting the statute was to take account of "the desirability of devising an arrangement for intergovernmental control and for voting such as to inspire the confidence of all members of the United Nations capital development fund. . . . " Despite this concession, important donor countries again dissented or abstained in plenary and later seven of these (Canada, Denmark, France, Japan, the Netherlands, the United Kingdom, and the United States) refused to participate in the committee's assigned task of drafting a statute. The seventeenth Assembly, nevertheless, commended the committee for formulating a statute and instructed it to propose measures to put the fund into operation. The next step, again without the blessing of the large potential donors, was a request made in 1963 by the committee and endorsed by the eighteenth Assembly that the Secretary-General study ways of converting the UN Special Fund into a capital development fund.

Inevitably, an item on the capital development fund was included in the agenda for the 1964 Trade and Development Conference. There the newly forged unity of the developing nations enabled them to roll up an overwhelming majority (90 votes in favor, 10 opposed, with 16 abstentions) for a recommendation that the fund be established soon, that it be financed by

[9] U.S. Congress, Senate, Committee on Banking and Currency, *Hearings, International Development Association,* 85th Congress, 2nd Session, 1958.

[10] General Assembly Resolution 1521 (XV), December 15, 1960.

[11] UN Document E/3514.

[12] General Assembly Resolution 1706 (XVI), December 19, 1961.

voluntary contributions, and that it emphasize projects in the field of industrialization.[13] This was one of a long series of "redistributive" resolutions in which the dissenting Western industrialized countries were asked to bear most of the burden of implementation.

UN CONFERENCE ON TRADE AND
DEVELOPMENT AND CONTINUING
MACHINERY [14]

While efforts to increase capital aid to the developing countries continued, UN economic reports concentrated more and more on another factor limiting economic growth, namely, the often unfavorable trade position of developing countries.

In 1961 the Assembly began to explore the possibility of holding an international trade conference to focus especially on primary commodities and the economic relations between developed and developing countries. The seventeenth Assembly decided definitely to convene UNCTAD and recommended that ECOSOC enlarge the preparatory committee for the Conference from eighteen to 30 members.[15] Specifications for the additional twelve included the usual due regard to "equitable geographical distribution" and also to "an adequate representation of developing and major trading countries." These recommendations were adopted by a vote of 91 in favor, none opposed, with 1 abstention, but the

[13] UN Document E/CONF.46/L.28, Annex A, p. 94.
[14] See General Assembly Resolutions 1707 (XVI), December 19, 1960; 1785 (XVII), December 8, 1962; and 1897 (XVIII), November 11, 1963. See also "Issues Before the Eighteenth General Assembly," *International Conciliation,* September 1963 (No. 544), p. 148; and UN Document E/CONF. 46/L.28 and Add. 1.
[15] General Assembly Resolution 1785 (XVII), December 8, 1962.

near unanimity was misleading since 33 countries, including most of the major trading nations, had abstained or dissented in the Second (Economic and Financial) Committee's vote. In response to an earlier feasibility inquiry seventeen countries, including most of the developed countries, had not replied favorably. However, a coalition of the Soviet bloc, Latin America, and most Asian and African states was actively in favor of holding the Conference, which was tentatively budgeted to cost $1,500,000 from the UN regular budget.

In early 1963, upon its own recommendation, the preparatory committee was augmented by two more members (Indonesia and Malaysia). The resulting committee of 32 had a composition representing all geographic regions, and it included four (all but China) of the Big Five (permanent Security Council members). It was divided by stage of development and regional grouping as follows: [*See table, p. 377.*] Thus, the developed countries were distinctly in a minority. They were also divided among themselves concerning trade policies, and some had serious problems of their own with regard to foreign exchange balances. The eighteenth Assembly promoted the forthcoming Conference with a unanimous resolution to which was appended the Joint Declaration of the Developing Countries stating the need for "special assistance and protection of the less developed parts of the world economy." [16] The significance of unanimity became clearer when UNCTAD convened in Geneva in March 1964 and began to wrestle with the very controversial items on its agenda.

The Trade Conference witnessed an ominous confrontation between two concepts of the proper distribution of decision-making power in the United

[16] General Assembly Resolution 1897 (XVIII), November 11, 1963.

PREPARATORY COMMITTEE FOR UNCTAD, 1963–1964

Regional Group	Industrial Countries, Including Major Traders [a]	Less Developed Countries [a]	Total
East Europe and Soviet Union	3	1	4
Asia	1	6	7
Africa	—	6	6
Latin America	—	6	6
West and Others	9	—	9
Total	13	19	32

[a] The classification used here is based on definitions later adopted by the General Assembly in Resolution 1885 (XVIII), October 18, 1963.

Nations: the developing countries' insistence on the principle of state equality in decision making, and the developed countries' emphasis on avoidance of decisions that could not be implemented.[17] At the Conference 77 developing countries, acting in concert, easily commanded a two-thirds majority for resolutions entirely dependent for their implementation on the often outvoted or abstaining minority. The delegates meeting in Geneva recommended to the nineteenth Assembly the establishment of the Conference on Trade and Development as a continuing subsidiary of the General Assembly, an organ which would be serviced by a permanent secretariat and governed by a 55-member Trade and Development Board. No final solution was reached on the question of voting and decision-making procedures in this continuing machinery. A special committee appointed by the Secretary-General would be charged with recommending methods which would preserve the principle of state equality

and which, at the same time, would establish conciliation procedures to precede voting on matters affecting the economic or financial interests of particular states.[18]

The proposed Trade and Development Board would include a larger *proportion* of all the advanced industrial countries than of all the developing countries. However, the latter would make up more than half the Board, which would make decisions by simple majority. The following tabulation shows the number and percentage of countries in each category used to allot seats: [*Top of p. 378.*]

The actions and trends shown by these two cases from the economic field lead to one conclusion: A subcommittee which is large enough to include all the factors claiming representation and whose members vote equally can give no assurance of responsible (implementable) decisions when the latter quality depends upon compliance by a very few countries. The adoption of qualified majority voting in suborgans would ameliorate but not remove the difficulty.

[17] See Sidney Weintraub, "After the U. N. Trade Conference: Lessons and Portents," *Foreign Affairs*, October 1964 (Vol. 43, No. 1), pp. 37–50.

[18] UN Document E/CONF.46/L.28, Annex A, pp. 128–139.

MEMBERS OF TRADE AND DEVELOPMENT ORGANS

Category	Conference	Board	Board Members as % of Conference Members
Asia, Africa, and Yugoslavia	61	22	36
Latin America	22	9	41
Western Market Economy Nations & Japan	29	18	62
Socialist Countries (East Europe and the Soviet Union)	9	6	67
Total	121	55	45

THE SPECIAL COMMITTEE OF
TWENTY-FOUR[19]

The powerful committee on colonialism, the Special Committee of Twenty-Four (more properly, the Special Committee on the Situation with Regard to the Implementation of the Declaration on the Granting of Independence to Colonial Countries and Peoples), was established in 1961. Originally composed of seventeen members, it was enlarged in 1962 to a total of 24 distributed as follows: [below]

SPECIAL COMMITTEE OF TWENTY-FOUR, 1962–1964

East Europe and Soviet Union	Asia	Africa	Latin America	West and Others
Bulgaria	Cambodia	Ethiopia	Chile	Australia
Poland	India	Ivory Coast	Uruguay	Denmark
Soviet Union	Iran	Malagasy Republic	Venezuela	Italy
Yugoslavia	Iraq	Mali		United Kingdom
	Syria	Sierra Leone		United States
		Tanganyika		
		Tunisia		

[19] See General Assembly Resolutions 1810 (XVII), December 17, 1962, and 1970 (XVIII), December 16, 1963; and C. W. A. Schurmann, "The Final Stage of Colonialism," *United Nations Review,* July 1961 (Vol. 8, No. 7), pp. 20–22.

Having a very broad mandate in the implementation of the above-mentioned Declaration, this Special Committee conducts field missions in dependent territories and negotiating missions in metropolitan capitals, and formulates many of the policies guiding the Fourth (Trusteeship) Committee. Formerly, the important committee in this area was the Committee on Information from Non-Self-Governing Territories, an organ whose membership was balanced with equal numbers of administering and nonadministering states. This Committee was dissolved in December 1963 and all its duties assigned to the Special Committee of Twenty-Four. An alliance of Soviet bloc countries with Asians and Africans makes it easy for the Special Committee to override the objections of its minority of administering powers and their sympathizers. The Special Committee of Twenty-Four is so largely made up of newly independent and strongly anticolonial countries that it has been difficult to get representatives of the viewpoint of countries still administering non-self-governing territories to serve on it. An approximate miniature of the whole, the Special Committee deals with a subject on which there is a broad consensus among an overwhelming majority of nations and people. Its existence and power are evidence of impatience with the progress made in the field under the "balanced" bodies that formerly had preeminent responsibility for decolonization, the Trusteeship Council and the Committee on Information from Non-Self-Governing Territories.

THE INTERNATIONAL LAW COMMISSION[20]

Turning now to the International Law Commission, the principal subsidiary organ that serves the Sixth (Legal) Committee and assists the Assembly in its Charter-imposed duty of encouraging "the progressive development of international law and its codi-

fication" (Article 13, paragraph 1[a]), one finds changes reflecting those in the UN's total membership. The Commission is composed of members elected to five-year terms by the Assembly from among those nominated by governments according to principles similar to those applicable for the International Court of Justice; i.e., they must as individuals have recognized competence in international law and must as a body represent the main forms of civilization and the principal legal systems of the world. The distribution of members by legal systems of the world before and after enlargements authorized in 1957 and 1961 are shown in the [tabulation on page 380]. It is evident that the changes have gone some way toward satisfying the demand that nonwestern countries should have a larger part in the development of international law.

Since the development and the codification of international law culminate in conventions binding only upon signatories, the distribution of influence in this subsidiary organ seems properly governed by the criteria mentioned above, a combination of expertise with knowledge of all relevant viewpoints. The successive enlargements of the Commission have conformed to the same criteria, reflecting successive changes in the United Nations itself. Proceeding with great deliberation, the Commission deals chiefly with those subjects deemed by itself and its parent body to be "ripe for codification," and some success has rewarded its efforts in less sensitive areas such as diplomatic immunities. Fortunately, the Cold War is muted in the UN's most influential legal bodies.[21]

[20] See General Assembly Resolutions 895 (IX), December 4, 1954; 1103 (XI), December 18, 1956; 1647 (XVI), November 6, 1961; and 1815 (XVII), December 18, 1962.

[21] For a critical evaluation of the Commission's work by representatives of different legal systems, see the report on the 56th annual meeting of the American Society of International Law in *The American Journal of International Law*, July 1962 (Vol. 56, No. 3), pp. 762–768.

INTERNATIONAL LAW COMMISSION, 1954–1964

Legal System[a]	1954	1959	1964
Common Law			
United States, United Kingdom and Canada	2	2	3
Africa and Israel	–	–	2
Roman Law			
West Europe	4	5	5
South America	4	4	4
East Europe	–	–	–
Balkans	–	1	1
Africa	–	–	2
Germanic Law	–	–	–
Islamic Law	1	3	3
Communist Law	2	2	2
Asian Law	2	4	3
Total	15	21	25

[a]The classification is adapted from that used to analyze the composition of the International Court by Shabtai Rosenne, *The World Court* (Leyden: A. W. Sythoff, 1962), p. 53. It is a rough classification since categories overlap somewhat. African states are here classed in the category of the former metropole, with subclasses added by the present writer to distinguish them.

Trends in Other Assembly Subsidiaries

If we designate the two extreme types of suborgans as the "microcosmic" and the "selectively loaded" types, we find many cases where, as in the above-described fields of aid, trade, and colonialism, the trend is toward the former type—the suborgan which is a smaller replica of the whole. Elements of selective loading are often present but they occur within a larger pattern usually determined by "equitable geographical distribution." They do not often shift decision-making power significantly toward countries with greater capacities and responsibilities in the areas of their concern. Many actions of the eighteenth Assembly in 1963 are evidence of this trend toward the microcosmic type of subsidiary.

Sometimes an agreed regional allocation of seats still leaves an *intraregional* imbalance, especially when the process is an elective rather than an appointive one. For example, a recent election by ECOSOC to fill seats on the Human Rights Commission resulted in a body with five Asians and only one African to represent the Afro-Asian group. Several responses are possible to this kind of situation: A further enlargement of the body or a more detailed stratification of seats (e.g., three for Asia and three for Africa) may be called for; or the electors may, as in the example cited, merely be exhorted to bear in mind the need for an equitable distribution.[22]

While competing claims to represen-

[22] General Assembly Resolution 1923 (XVIII), December 5, 1963.

tation have affected the structure of many UN organs, some others have remained largely unaffected for a variety of reasons. The two standing subcommittees in the budgetary area have changed very little in size or composition since the early years of the United Nations. Both include the Big Four (France, the Soviet Union, the United Kingdom, and the United States) and are small enough for negotiating procedures to take precedence over voting procedures. The Advisory Committee on Administrative and Budgetary Questions (which deals with appropriations) has twelve members, who often display a cleavage between large and small contributors, with the former group favoring economy while the latter group presses for a higher level of expenditures. An accommodation satisfactory at least to the large western contributors is usually reached although the Soviet Union (the second largest contributor to the regular budget) is often overridden in its attempts to economize on or eliminate programs of which it disapproves. The decisions of this body lean much further in the direction of economy than the whole Assembly would prefer, but the latter body in plenary nearly always accepts the suborgan's recommendations without amendment. The Committee on Contributions, a group of ten experts, sets assessment scales on the basis of fairly objective criteria, and it thus has little discretion to expose it to political controversy. Its recommendations are almost invariably accepted in plenary.[23]

Another UN organ that has long remained unaffected by pressures for seats is the United Nations Commission for the Unification and Rehabili-

tation of Korea (UNCURK). As a body made up entirely of Western allies and attempting to deal with a problem in dispute between East and West (how to unite Korea), its history is one of futility. A suggestion that the Commission be supplemented by the addition of some nonaligned states failed to be accepted in the eighteenth session.[24] A review of the annual debate on Korea recalls the warning made some years ago by Arthur N. Holcombe that such unbalanced bodies can serve only a propaganda function in political matters.[25] However, a heavy loading with Western powers does not necessarily cause frustration if there is an agreed basis for it. The UN Scientific Committee on the Effects of Atomic Radiation (UNSCEAR) is selectively loaded with states having competence in the field of its interest. Its fifteen scientist-members include only two from the "East Europe and Soviet Union" group and seven from the "West and allies" group (plus six other states). The same states were represented when UNSCEAR was first set up in 1955, and, while not entirely immune from political controversy, the Committee has functioned effectively in establishing and publicizing the facts about the effects of atomic radiation. Its lack of representational problems may be attributed in part to the universal fellowship of science stemming from its universal method and to the fact that the benefits of its work are indivisible. There is no "redistribution" involved.

In concluding this discussion of trends in the composition of UN organs, the historic action taken in the last hours of the eighteenth session, although it did not concern Assembly subsidiaries, deserves comment. The

[23] For background, see J. David Singer, *Financing International Organization: The U. N. Budget Process* (The Hague: Martinus Nijhoff, 1961); and John G. Stoessinger and others, *Financing the United Nations System* (Washington, D.C.: Brookings Institution, 1964).

[24] General Assembly *Official Records* (19th session), Supplement No. 1, p. 30.

[25] Arthur N. Holcombe, *Organizing for Peace in the Nuclear Age* (New York: New York University Press, 1959), pp. 50–116.

Assembly, for the first time, officially adopted certain amendments to the Charter.[26] If ratified by two-thirds of all Member States, including the permanent members of the Security Council, the revisions would increase the Security Council from eleven to fifteen members and the Economic and Social Council from eighteen to 27. Of the ten nonpermanent seats on the Security Council, states of Africa and Asia would be elected to five; eastern Europe to one; western Europe and Canada, Australia, and New Zealand to two; and Latin America and the Caribbean to two. Nine affirmative votes, including those of the five permanent members, would be needed for substantive decisions by the Security Council. A somewhat similar regional distribution would govern the election of the members of the enlarged ECOSOC; decisions in the Council would continue to be made by simple majority vote.*

These changes would bring these two principal UN organs closer to what we have labeled the "microcosm" type of organ. However, since the requirement for unanimity among the permanent members of the Security Council would be retained (while only four of the ten votes of the elective members would be required), substantive decision-making power would remain almost entirely in the hands of the Big Five in that organ. Still another way to achieve an indirect weighting of influence is the qualified majority rule which gives sizable minorities more power to block unwanted actions as seen, for example, in the previously mentioned United States proposal for a standing special committee on peacekeeping expenditures which would be governed by a two-thirds majority rule instead of the simple majority rule that

normally prevails in Assembly suborgans. Thus, not only the composition of UN organs but also the decision-making rules employed are of importance.

Conclusion

The above review of the experience of some important subsidiary organs of the General Assembly suggests that there are areas of decision making in which selectively loaded suborgans can provide an effective kind of indirect weighting which is not likely to be overruled by the parent body. Having achieved a satisfactory balance after long controversy, the Disarmament Committee and the Committee on the Peaceful Uses of Outer Space were able to make some progress in their respective fields. They are essentially patterned on the "troika" principle with ultimate decisions made between East and West being aided by the mediation of the nonaligned. Since the whole Assembly is only too grateful when East and West can reach even modest agreement in these areas, there is no problem of the whole body exercising restraint in accepting the results proposed by these subsidiaries. In other selectively loaded bodies, such as the UN Scientific Committee on the Effects of Atomic Radiation and the International Law Commission, the technical nature of the tasks mitigates the problems of representation and restraint.

On the other hand, for those subsidiaries whose functions entail redistributive decisions affecting *some* very differently than *others,* it is more difficult to set up an adequately balanced suborgan and to gain acceptance for the suborgan's decisions if they differ from what the equal-voting whole would prefer. As indicated by the cases in the field of trade and aid, the highly unsymmetrical division of the world into "have" and "have-not" nations makes it impossible to give the former a meas-

---

[26] General Assembly Resolution 1991 (XVIII), December 17, 1963.

* Editors' note. These amendments came into force on August 31, 1965.

ure of power in equal-voting subsidiaries commensurate with their power of implementation while at the same time keeping these bodies large enough for their communication and persuasion functions. Much the same is true in the area of colonialism except that the minority is a smaller one, fighting a holding action against history, rather than a powerful minority whose cooperation will long be needed by the majority. The tendency in the fields of aid, trade, and colonialism has thus been toward the microcosmic suborgan.

In the budgetary subsidiaries, which draft binding redistributive decisions rather than recommendations, it is especially important to have an effective balance of decision-making power since the alternative adjustive device of budgetary noncompliance threatens to disrupt the constitutional foundation of the Organization. Here too the distribution of assessments is too skewed to give adequate power to large contributors in equal-voting subsidiaries even though there is a disproportionate number of large contributors on these committees.

A question raised earlier is whether the whole Assembly exercises restraint in accepting elements of responsibility that are incorporated in the proposals of subsidiary organs reflecting different preferences than the whole body. The experiences reviewed above indicate that the question seldom arises. Those Assembly suborgans that deal with broadly redistributive matters (economic or political) have grown in size and increased in number, and the ubiquitous "equitable geographical distribution" clause keeps each structured largely as a General Assembly in microcosm. Thus, the hope that suborgans

in preliminary stages of decision making can correct the imbalance of the plenary body is a hope that must bravely face a contrary trend.

If this approach is finally found unavailing, there are several alternative methods by which greater compliance might be induced. One is to deal more forthrightly with questions concerning the legal competence of the Assembly (vis-à-vis the Security Council and domestic jurisdiction). This would take cognizance of the legal grounds upon which noncompliance with Assembly resolutions has often been based.

Another response would be to reallocate decision-making power in selected areas of subject matter through a direct weighting of plenary votes so that essential actors would have an incentive to participate rather than to defy.[27] While this is still widely regarded as impracticable, it may ultimately be found necessary. John Stuart Mill's remarks on representative government may be applicable also to a quasi-governmental organization like the United Nations. "The character of a representative government," he said, "is fixed by the constitution of the popular House. Compared with this, all other questions relating to the form of government are insignificant."[28] The "popular House" is the whole Assembly.

[27] See Catherine Senf Manno, "Weighted Voting in the United Nations General Assembly: A Study of Feasibility and Methods" (unpublished Ph.D. dissertation, The American University, 1964).

[28] John Stuart Mill, *On Liberty and Considerations of Representative Government,* ed. R. B. McCallum (Oxford: Basil Blackwell, 1948), p. 263.

21. The "Satisfied" and "Dissatisfied" States Negotiate International Law*

ROBERT L. FRIEDHEIM

PEACE will be achieved, virtually all Western leaders say upon issuing a general statement on foreign policy, when all men learn to obey a common law. The achievement of world peace through world law is a popular solution to the problems of world politics of our times. However, creating a viable international law that all or even most states are willing to obey has proved difficult.

An examination of the two United Nations Conferences on the Law of the Sea held in Geneva in 1958 and 1960 will help illuminate some of the difficulties in creating a law to which there is common consent—and therefore in employing law as the road to peace.

This article will address itself—by an analysis of the content of the debates at Geneva—to the different attitudes that representatives of states and bloc groups brought to the negotiating table. Because the difference in attitudes was so sharp, the conferences proved to be less successful than hoped for by advocates of world law. Not only were participants split on the question of the substantive content of the law, but they also differed on the nature of the international system, present and future, and on the proper means of negotiating law in a United Nations-sponsored conference, which is itself a special political area with distinctive characteristics.

I

The first set of attitudes to be considered is that of those states at the law

of the sea conferences who were dissatisfied with the legal status quo. They cannot all be labeled "new states," although most were. Although many were, not all were "revolutionary states" who felt compelled to "export their ideological impetus."[1] Nor can they be described as lacking an international-law tradition, because the Latin American states, which are included in this category, are very much in that tradition. Rather, the common factor was that these states were "have-not" states, most of whom were located in the southern half of the world, and most of whom believed that their interests were not served by present concepts of international law. This is not an unusual position for those who consider themselves underdogs to take. However, the verbal vehemence with which they expressed their revolt against the past trend of international law seemed to shock those participants in the conferences who were "satisfied" with international law. This antagonism resulted in a clash of wills on many important issues, with each side seemingly incapable of understanding the attitudes and modes of operation of the other.

The "dissatisfied" were heavily represented at the law of the sea conferences. The core of this category was composed of states that in the United Nations General Assembly are associated with the Asian-African, Arab, and Latin American caucusing groups and

* World Politics, Vol. XVIII, pp. 20–41. Reprinted by permission.

[1] Richard A. Falk, "Revolutionary Nations and the Quality of International Legal Order," in Morton A. Kaplan, ed., The Revolution in World Politics (New York 1962), 323.

the anticolonial common-interest group.[2] These constituted fifty-four of the eighty-six states represented at the first conference, and fifty-six of the eighty-eight at the second. In addition, some of the members of the underdeveloped common-interest group who were not also members of the regional and anticolonial groups felt discriminated against under present concepts of international law.[3]

The key attitude expressed by the dissatisfied states was a strong, conscious, and often expressed belief that the conference process was a *political* process. They clearly understood that their operations were to be guided by practices usually known collectively as parliamentary diplomacy. This meant bloc organization, bloc voting, bloc-sponsored proposals, bloc-sponsored candidates for the elective offices of the conferences, and bloc attempts to manipulate the rules of procedure. The groups of the dissatisfied were the most organized, evident, and self-conscious at the conferences. Mr. Ahmed Shu-

kairi, chairman of the Saudi Arabian delegation, was very outspoken in referring to the Arab states "attending the conference . . . as a voting group."[4] Other instances of frank references to blocs are too numerous to list. The dissatisfied took advantage of their numbers by frequently sponsoring multinational proposals.[5]

Probably the major reason why the dissatisfied considered the conference process as political and why a considerable number of representatives reflecting this position demonstrated great parliamentary skill was the large proportion of dissatisfied delegations which had as representatives men with recent General Assembly experience. Twenty of the dissatisfied states had at least one representative (five states had several) who was not only a "professional diplomat" but also—in Philip Jessup's phrase—a "professional parliamentarian."[6] Three other delegations had senior advisors who learned the art of parliamentary maneuver in the General Assembly.[7]

This is not to say that the dissatisfied controlled the conferences either by dominating a majority of the votes taken or by getting a majority of their

---

[2] Although the Soviet-bloc states are members of the anticolonialist group, a full discussion of their conduct must be omitted for reasons of space. However, it should be pointed out that the Soviet-bloc states should not be classified as "dissatisfied." Although often allied with the dissatisfied, the Soviet bloc did not participate in the all-out assault on law *per se* so characteristic of the dissatisfied states. The positions adopted by the Soviet Union (and her satellites) at the conferences were typical of a conservative revolutionary state ambivalently trying to accomplish two ends—on the one hand, export of revolutionary principles and harassment of cold-war enemies; on the other, a genuine attempt to negotiate commonly accepted legal principles in areas where important material interests would be protected if normative behavior could be enforced. For a discussion of conservative revolutionary states, see Falk, 315.

[3] The reader should not assume that the characteristics ascribed to a category of states created for purposes of analysis are wholly applicable to all states that generally fall into that category.

[4] United Nations Conference on the Law of the Sea, *Official Records,* Vol. 111, First Committee (A/CONF. 13/39), 4th meeting, par. 30. Hereafter all citations from the records, documents, or reports of both UN Conferences on the Law of the Sea will be made with the official UN document number.

[5] See, for example, A/CONF. 13/C.5/L.6 (19 "dissatisfied" sponsors), A/CONF. 13/-C.3/L.65, 66, 66/Rev. 1 (12 sponsors), A/-CONF. 19/C.1/L.2/Rev. 1 (18 sponsors), A/CONF. 19/C.1/L.6 (16 sponsors), A/-CONF. 19/L. 9 (10 sponsors), among many others.

[6] "International Negotiations under Parliamentary Procedure," *Lectures on International Law and the United Nations* (Ann Arbor, University of Michigan Law School, 1957), 419.

[7] These figures were compiled from the list of delegations to the Conferences on the Law of the Sea and to Sessions XII, XIII, XIV, and XV of the General Assembly.

proposals accepted. While the incidence of bloc voting was relatively high among the dissatisfied groups, so were the absence rates of members, which reduced the number of total votes the group cast. None of the dissatisfied except the underdeveloped group was among the groups that most frequently voted with the majority. But their evident, organized efforts constantly harassed their opponents, and frequently forced them either to water down or to withdraw proposals opposed by the dissatisfied bloc. Even more important was the ability of the dissatisfied groups to mobilize their numbers to dominate voting on key proposals. While their general record for effectiveness was not good, they could point with satisfaction to several successful attempts to block passage of the various United States proposals for a six-mile territorial sea and a twelve-mile contiguous fishing zone, and to force elimination from a British proposal of a fifteen-mile limit on the use of straight baselines. They could also point to more positive victories such as enlarging to twenty-four miles the baseline to be drawn from headland to headland in delimiting bays, forcing through an Indian proposal which gave the coastal state "sovereign" rather than exclusive rights over the continental shelf, and gaining majorities for several proposals sponsored jointly by Asian-African and Latin-American states which increased the authority of the coastal states over fishing in waters off their coasts.

The satisfied states were annoyed by the political strategy used by the dissatisfied. But they were profoundly shocked by the dissatisfied's analogous assumption—that the *subject matter* to be dealt with in the conferences should also be political. The dissatisfied made frequent reference to the General Assembly resolution that allowed political factors to be considered in formulating the law of the sea: "[The conferences] should take into account not only the legal but also the technical, biological,

economic, and political aspects of the problem." [8] These states early in the first conference made it evident that they understood this to mean carte blanche to fight for furthering what they conceived of as their own interests. While this motive was not uncharacteristic of most participating states and groups, the dissatisfied seemed more conscious of their interests and more outspoken in defending them.

A statement by the Vietnamese delegate, Mr. Buu-kinh, in a debate on the continental shelf, can scarcely be plainer: "His delegation would prefer to see the criterion of depth alone retained, particularly as the waters off its own shores were relatively shallow and did not reach a depth of 200 metres for more than 200 miles." [9] The Mexican delegate, Mr. Gomez Robledo, in discussing a Canadian proposal on reservations to any convention signed as a result of the conference, was equally candid: "Representatives wishing to permit reservations had been reproached for defending national interests; but they were attending the conference for that very purpose." [10] Or, as Mr. Caabasi of Libya flatly remarked about a United States proposal on the breadth of the territorial sea: ". . . His delegation had voted against the United States proposal because it contained provisions which were contrary to his country's interests." [11]

Since these dissatisfied states were so insistent and outspoken in asserting that the conference process was a political means of attaining their own national interest, they were no less definite in assigning to the states opposing them the same self-interested motives. For example, Dr. Alfonso Garcia Robles of Mexico, advocating a broad

[8] General Assembly Resolution 1105, XI Session, par. 2. For example, see A/CONF. 13/42, 19th meeting, par. 33.
[9] A/CONF. 13/42, 11th meeting, par. 14.
[10] A/CONF. 13/38, 9th plenary meeting, par. 34.
[11] *Ibid.*, 14th plenary meeting, par. 66.

belt of territorial sea, ascribed to the narrow-seas advocates the motive of sheer self-interest. He ignored entirely any reference to traditional historic and legal doctrines of freedom of the seas: "It had been suggested that the States whose fleets carried almost all the world's maritime transport should be asked why they opposed the extension of the breadth of the territorial sea to twelve miles. He could not see what would be the point in putting such a question. Gidel had given the answer when he had stated that a dominant factor in the dispute was the inequality of sea power; the greater a State's sea power, the more it would tend to limit the breadth of its territorial sea, for it had no need to look to international law for means to exercise special powers over a broad zone of sea adjacent to its coasts. Unfortunately, the maritime powers, which were usually also fishing powers, were not confining themselves to exercising special powers in the areas of sea adjacent to their coasts, but were only too often attempting to exercise them in the territorial sea of other countries, too." [12]

Just as these states saw the conference process in terms of politics and their own interests, so they regarded international law. They saw it as a cloak, a set of ideas used to camouflage self-interest, the domination by the few of the many. Nothing could be more candid than these remarks by Dr. Jorge Castaneda of Mexico: "Rigid adherence to the traditional rules of international law could prove disastrous to all concerned, for the traditional rules on the regime of the sea had been created by the great Powers for their own purposes before many major problems had arisen and before the birth of the new states which now formed the majority." [13]

The same theme was repeated again and again by delegates of many of the dissatisfied states. For example, Mr.

Ba Han, of Burma: ". . . In the past international law had been a body of rules and usages adopted by powerful states. However, the international situation had changed and new sovereign independent states had emerged, keenly conscious of their liberty." [14] Mr. Ulloa Sotomayor, of Peru: "Rules of international law had sometimes been unilaterally created in the interests of great powers; it was therefore reasonable for certain rules of law to be initiated by small States in their legitimate interests. . . . It was inadmissable that a sort of colonialism of the high seas should be allowed in the name of freedom of the seas." [15] Mr. Diallo, of Guinea: "With regard to 'historic rights,' . . . the concept was nothing other than a manifestation of the right of the strongest and a vestige of colonialism, which [Guinea] would oppose in all its forms. To perpetuate those rights would be a grave injustice to the young States that were struggling not only for political but also for economic independence." [16]

This attitude was not exclusive to the more vociferously dissatisfied anticolonial states, but also affected even friends and allies of the West. For example, Mr. Vu Van Mau of Vietnam observed that the purposes of the first United Nations law of the sea conference had been ". . . to single out from a mass of unilateral practices anarchically applied those which corresponded to rules of law, so that they could subsequently be adopted to the new needs of mankind and to the aspirations of emergent States." [17] And the Iranian delegate, Mr. Dara, said emphatically, "A great many delegations would not accept servitude to the large maritime Powers which wished to fish in the waters of the other States." [18]

[12] A/CONF. 19/8, 10th meeting, par. 12.
[13] A/CONF. 13/41, 13th meeting, par. 22.

[14] A/CONF. 13/39, 4th meeting, par. 6.
[15] Ibid., 5th meeting, par. 13.
[16] A/CONF. 19/8, 18th meeting, par. 6.
[17] Ibid., 3rd meeting, par. 6.
[18] A/CONF. 13/38, 20th plenary meeting, par. 70.

These views of the dissatisfied are, in effect, a denial of the entire history and body of international law. Several Latin American delegates did in fact deny that the great international-law writers of the past had ever had anything more in mind than protecting the interests of the states or organizations to which they owed allegiance. As Mr. Melo Lecaros of Chile put it, ". . . The rise and development of the law of the sea had been prompted by one single factor: interest. Political or economic interest had always prevailed in defining the law of the sea through the centuries. Grotius had not argued for the freedom of the seas simply as an intellectual concept, but to defend the interests of the Dutch East India Company. Selden's sole aim in refuting Grotius had been to defend England's interests. Things had changed very greatly since that time. The rule of law had been extended, but it was impossible to overlook the fact that the reason for the existence of law was interest. Law had been created by man for the use of man." [19] Mr. Llosa of Peru also felt it necessary to tilt against Hugo Grotius, the very "father of international law," who, he said, ". . . did not write a work on international law but a treatise to vindicate the claims of the Dutch East India Company, by whom he had been retained, to freedom of navigation and trade." [20] So international law had moved in the wrong direction from the outset!

The dissatisfied states were acutely aware of the factor of time in regard to international law. The new states among the group, those who often set its tone and behavioral pattern, were quite naturally very conscious of their own recent independence and separate national existence. They demanded that international law take them into account, and consider their interests and desires; they demanded participation and the right of consultation in formation of international law. Among innumerable statements of this attitude are the following two examples. Mr. Subardjo of the Philippines: ". . . The law of nations must take into account the fact that since the Second World War former dependencies and colonies in Asia and Africa had achieved the status of sovereign States." [21] And Mr. El Bakri of Sudan: "Those who had described the present conference as the third to codify the law of the sea, counting the Hague Codification Conference of 1930, had overlooked one of the major developments which had taken place since 1930, namely, the number of countries that had become independent and which, with their different outlook, had taken their rightful place in the international community. In considering the problem of the breadth of the territorial sea, full account must be taken of the changes in institutions and ideas that had supervened during the past thirty years, and the final solution would have to accord with the contemporary spirit of social and political progress." [22]

A close and perhaps necessary corollary of this extreme self-consciousness is that the new states and their allies did not recognize, and would not consider binding upon themselves, that law which was created before they became independent states. Expressions of this attitude at the conferences abound. Mr. Bocobo of the Philippines: ". . . The newer countries valued their freedom above all else and refused to accept certain rules of international law evolved before they had attained statehood." [23] Mr. Loutfi of the United Arab Republic: ". . . The majority of the new countries that had gained their independence since [the Hague Conference of 1930] had adopted a limit

[19] A/CONF. 19/8, 14th meeting, par. 13–14.
[20] A/CONF. 13/41, 23rd meeting, par. 11.
[21] A/CONF. 13/39, 7th meeting, par. 1.
[22] A/CONF. 19/8, 19th meeting, par. 14.
[23] A/CONF. 13/39, 50th meeting, par. 1.

in excess of three miles. Their argument that the three-mile rule constituted a principle of international law was thus devoid of substance." [24] Mr. Ba Han of Burma ". . . could not accept the suggestion that abandonment of the three-mile rule was a concession. That alleged rule had been established by others at a time when his own country, for one, was completely helpless under foreign rule." [25]

There was an impatience with, rather than a reverence for, age and tradition, a feeling that the old laws should be swept away or remolded so that the newer states could help create new laws for new conditions. In stating Afghanistan's position on the access of landlocked states to the sea, Mr. Tabibi remarked: "Besides, many of [the international instruments in question] were very old and an historic conference such as the present should replace them by others which would contribute to the development of international law, particularly since the signatories of the instruments relating to the rights of land-locked countries were mainly European countries." [26] Mr. Hekmert, explaining Iran's vote against a United States-proposed amendment to the International Law Commission draft, stated that he ". . . agreed with the arguments advanced against the proposed [amendments]. The International Law Commission, in whose proceedings he had taken part, had not forgotten the existence of the 1884 Conventions when it drew up articles 62 and 65. It had nevertheless felt that the provisions embodied in those articles were more in line with twentieth-century conditions. The group of Afro-Asian states now numbered more than thirty, whereas, in 1884 there had not been more than five or six independent states in that part of the world. In the days of the 1884 Convention international law had been largely a matter of concern to western countries. It was important that it should now be applicable and accepted on a world-wide basis." [27]

The keynote, the driving force, of this attitude was the need for change. Change for these states replaced history and tradition as a commander of respect. Symbolic were the remarks of the Korean delegate, Mr. Kim: "Several representatives had stressed how useful the three-mile limit had been in the past—at a time when it had been consistent with prevailing conditions. But those conditions had changed, and the three-mile limit was no longer adequate. Korea . . . earnestly hoped the Conference would adopt a principle better adapted to the varying conditions obtaining in the different parts of the world." [28] Consistent with their enthusiasm for change, the dissatisfied states were fond of calling those who were satisfied with the main aspects of international law "conservatives," while their own group was labeled "progressive."

Their devotion to change in international law was based on political, economic, and, particularly, technological changes in world conditions: "Legal rules had to develop at the same pace as modern technology"; and "existing rules might no longer be practical because of changed conditions." But it is clear that such statements were only a rationalization for a more profound sentiment. Without being fully aware of it, the dissatisfied states had returned to an older concept: law equated with justice, and further, with justice defined in relation to themselves. The older foundations of international law, having been established before the independent existence of these states, when they were "completely helpless under foreign rule," without regard for their welfare, could not be regarded as

[24] *Ibid.*, 21st meeting, par. 4.
[25] A/CONF. 13/38, 14th plenary meeting, par. 51.
[26] A/CONF. 13/43, 8th meeting, par. 32.

[27] A/CONF. 13/40, 31st meeting, par. 24.
[28] A/CONF. 13/39, 15th meeting, par. 14.

just; and since the law was unjust, it must be changed. Any change, in their view, was therefore a change for the better.

Justice to themselves was paramount, and it was elevated to the level of principle. But while they treated certain matters as principles, they rarely handled them in legal terms. They preferred to emphasize strictly political doctrines—coastal rights, wider areas of sea control—and to have these issues stated as vaguely as possible. In their practical, pragmatic, nonhistorical manner, they had no use for doctrine *qua* doctrine. Legal doctrine was for them political; they made no distinction in bargaining between legal matters and any other international problem. A speech by Mr. Quarshie of Ghana illustrates well the paradoxical concern for "principle" (justice) and disregard for law: "The African States, which had seen their continent divided among the great Powers without the consent of the populations concerned, found it difficult to understand the moral arguments now advanced against the division of the sea. That division was essentially a practical matter. The needs of shipping varied according to the region, and a 200-mile limit might be suitable in one place but unsuitable in another. Requirements also varied with time; for instance, the contiguous zone was now far more important than it had been in the past." [29]

The dissatisfied states, then, tended to use "doctrine" and "principle" not as bases for consistent legal philosophy, but, somewhat opportunistically, to attain their own political-economic ends, which they considered "justice." Frequently this resulted in absurd inconsistencies, but these states were not concerned with doctrinal purity—as U Mya Sein of Burma remarked characteristically, "There was an over-emphasis on legal niceties." [30] A good example of this was the position the dissatisfied states took on the issue of sovereignty.

Of all the juridical concepts developed in the long history of international law, the most meaningful to the dissatisfied states was sovereignty.[31] They defined the concept very rigidly so that no external political unit, nor any obligation made, could deprive them of their sovereign rights as they defined and understood them. Sovereignty to them was a symbol of their independence. The dissatisfied were not, however, concerned with the development of a logical theory about the symbol, but rather with the preservation of the facts for which the symbol stood. They pressed ardently for sovereignty over the continental shelf, for control of fisheries off their shores as an extension of their sovereignty, and for a wider belt of territorial sea in which to exercise their sovereignty. These states were also adamant opponents of any scheme that conveyed to an international court or arbitral group compulsory jurisdiction over questions touching upon a state's sovereignty. They were concerned with the preservation of their own sovereignty even at the risk of impinging upon the sovereignty of other states. Afghanistan, Bolivia, Ghana, Indonesia, Laos, Nepal, Paraguay, Saudi Arabia, Tunisia, and the UAR (among nineteen sponsors), all ardent supporters of an absolute theory of state sovereignty, were able to introduce with no qualms a proposal that would give a landlocked state an absolute right of transit across the territory of a coastal state, thereby possibly impairing the sovereignty of the latter.[32] India, a leading advocate of sovereignty of the coastal state over its continental shelf, making no attempt to explain away the seeming inconsistency

---

[29] A/CONF. 13/38, 21st plenary meeting, par. 21.

[30] A/CONF. 13/42, 19th meeting, par. 33.

[31] See the general debates of the Fourth Committee for views of the dissatisfied on sovereignty. A/CONF. 13/42, 1st meeting–29th meeting.

[32] UN Doc. A/CONF. 13/C.5/L.6.

of her position, introduced a proposal that would prevent the "sovereign" coastal state from "building military bases or installations [on] the continental shelf." [33] Thus sovereignty was not treated as a juridical idea to be developed so that the same legal rules would be applicable to all states equally; it was, instead, appropriated by the dissatisfied as a means of maintaining tactical freedom. This was typical of their opportunistic use of legal doctrine and principles.

The significance of the dissatisfied states' wholly *political* attitude toward international law was that these nations were unable to differentiate between political and legal reality. They assumed, incorrectly, that political reality was identical with legal reality. These states, firm opponents of the three-mile territorial sea, assumed and pronounced it politically "dead and buried" when "two of its traditional champions had withdrawn their support." [34] However, while it is probably true that the three-mile limit is no longer politically viable —that is, there is very little chance of its being accepted by states that do not already adhere to it—it is not true that it is dead and buried in legal terms. As long as states that had traditionally held to the three-mile rule continue to affirm it, it will be the rule applied by them off their coasts and in their courts. Moreover as Mr. André Gros, representative of France, pointed out, it "was the only rule that did not need express recognition by the international community." [35]

The dissatisfied states also tended to assume that a resolution, sponsored by ten of them, establishing a twelve-mile fisheries zone was already part of international law, without any conference

adoption. This presumption was based upon the willingness of opponents to consider the measure as a political possibility, a point for negotiation—that is, it was politically viable, but certainly not established international law. [36] On the other hand, at times the dissatisfied states were unwilling to recognize as international law that which had just been adopted by a majority of states. After a Swiss proposal on questions of landlocked countries had been adopted, the dissatisfied states, which had supported an unsuccessful nineteen-power proposal because it created new rights to overcome past injustices to landlocked states, claimed the contents of that defeated proposal to be "the existing rules of international law." [37] Thus, insistence upon the exclusively political nature of proposals which they wanted codified, led these states to a position in which communication with the more legally oriented nations was difficult and negotiation virtually impossible.

A few final characteristics of this attitude shoud be mentioned. The dissatisfied states displayed a typical "have-not" distrust of the expert. He was identified with the colonial powers, the West, and was therefore somewhat feared and resented. Mr. Quarshie of Ghana expressed the psychological reaction of the underdeveloped states to Western technical expertise: "Ghana feared the exploitation of its fishing resources and threats to its security; it sought a solution which would guarantee it a maximum freedom from exploitation and threats. Its fears could not be allayed by exhibitions of technical knowledge or outright dismissal of its views. In consultation, the main point often lay less in the validity of the argument itself than in the reaction to that argument." [38] The Mexican delegate, Mr. Gomez Robledo, also expressed

[33] UN Doc. A/CONF. 13/C.4/L.57.
[34] A/CONF. 13/39, 53rd meeting, par. 17. For other death pronouncements see *ibid.*, 54th meeting, par. 1 and 15; 55th meeting, par. 35; A/CONF. 19/8, 20th meeting, par. 26.
[35] A/CONF. 19/8, 20th meeting, par. 12.

[36] *Ibid.*, 12th plenary meeting, par. 24.
[37] A/CONF. 13/43, 25th meeting, par. 40–43.
[38] A/CONF. 19/1, 25th meeting, par. 22.

well the resentment of the learning and expertise of international-law specialists of older, and especially of European, states: ". . . Although the Mexican delegation had the greatest respect for recognized experts in international law, it should be remembered that the Conference was not a university but an assembly of sovereign states. Furthermore, every country in the world could now inform itself as to the true meaning of sovereignty and no state had a monopoly of learning on the matter." [39]

Along with their fear of the expert went an unwillingness to commit themselves to legal details on the exercise of rights and duties under consideration at the conferences. Legal detail was viewed by them as a trap for the inexperienced or the unwary. In part, the reason that they preferred vaguely general statements to more exact definitions of legal rights and obligations was their lack of technical expertise. The dissatisfied states constantly feared that their agreement to a detailed proposal would create obligations for them that their negotiators could not perceive. Moreover, agreement on detailed solutions to problems in the law would have reduced their tactical mobility, which they did not wish to have happen. Relatively weak in power terms, they saw as their main protection from the physically powerful states both the ability to avoid being permanently obligated to perform required acts and the ability to perform acts not yet sanctioned by law. They preferred that legal rights and obligations be no more than moral imperatives—broad legal obligations that should be fulfilled but whose enforcement is backed only by the sense of obligation of the affected state itself. Since their sense of obligation to the idea of law is weak, the law is weak. As a result of their preference for vagueness, many provisions spon-

[39] A/CONF. 13/38, 9th plenary meeting, par. 60.

sored by dissatisfied states embodied in the conventions, should they come into force, will present new ambiguities for states to continue to dispute.

II

Those states with an international-law tradition manifested a behavioral pattern very different from that of the dissatisfied states. This group included all states represented that had a Western European political tradition—some twenty-three states in all. The core of the category was composed of the Western European, Benelux, European Community, and Scandinavian caucusing groups, and the NATO common-interest group. Usually voting with these groups were the "White Commonwealth" states, five European states not represented in the General Assembly, and Israel. In addition, the votes of five United States cold-war allies—Japan, Pakistan, and the Republics of China, Korea, and Vietnam—could frequently be counted upon by the satisfied.

Although heavily outnumbered, the states in this category can be said statistically to have dominated the conferences. All the satisfied groups were able to command the votes of their members approximately eighty percent of the time on substantive issues. They also had an outstanding record of voting with the majority on both substantive and procedural issues. With additional votes coming from the five non-UN-member European states and the five United States cold-war allies, the satisfied voted with the majority on forty-three of sixty-six roll-call votes on substantive issues, and on ten of twelve votes on procedural issues. Another significant index of the "success" of the satisfied was the high percentage of proposals made by its members that were adopted by the conferences. Eighteen states each proposed more than two percent of the total number of amendments adopted. Of these states, fourteen were either in the satisfied category or were states such as Japan and Pakistan that ordinarily voted with the satisfied.

It should be noted, however, that statistics on the law of the sea conferences do not tell the whole story of the successes and failures of the satisfied. Although they controlled a majority of the votes taken, and proposed most of the amendments accepted, the satisfied failed to gain majorities for their proposals on *key issues* such as the breadth of the territorial sea and fishing rights in areas beyond the territorial sea. They failed here because they were unable to persuade the dissatisfied that the measures desired also guarded the interests of the dissatisfied. The failure can be laid in large part to the fact that the satisfied couched their arguments in terms of traditional law—which the dissatisfied did not recognize and would not accept—instead of in terms of more realistic political-economic bargaining. Although their political positions at the conferences were not uniform—ranging from flexibility on the part of the United States and the United Kingdom to extreme conservatism and legalism on the part of continental powers such as France and the Federal Republic of Germany—still they shared a common belief that international law exists, that it is fundamentally just, that it provides a hope for adjustment of interests as well as protection of interests. They showed clear agreement with the broad background of sea-law doctrine and its cornerstone, freedom of the seas. Many states showed great pride in their past roles as formulators of international law: the Dutch continually invoked Grotius and Bynkershoek; the Spanish, Vitoria; the French, their great international lawyers.

Naturally, the satisfied relied heavily upon technical experts to staff their delegations. Twenty satisfied states had one or more legal experts from their government legal departments, foreign offices, or leading universities as full representatives at the conferences. Eighteen of the satisfied also had as representatives men from their ministries of food, fisheries, transportation, navy, communications, and commerce. In addition, all of them brought to Geneva large delegations of advisers with legal or technical expertise. On the other hand, only five of the satisfied states—Australia, Canada, Greece, Italy, and Spain—had as representatives diplomats with recent experience in the political practices of the General Assembly.

Unfortunately the satisfied states' concept of law interfered with their understanding the process by which law must be negotiated in a contemporary international setting. They did not act as if they understood that the political process by which substantive questions are negotiated will itself help shape the results. In particular, many of the satisfied refused to admit that conferences with legal subjects on the agendas are political—that they provide forums in which agreements are forged by states when they believe that such agreements protect their mutual interests. Moreover, United Nations-sponsored conferences are legislative in nature. That is, they operate under the rules of parliamentary diplomacy, and decisions depend upon forming majorities. In such an arena, it is extremely difficult, and perhaps impossible, to create a majority that will vote for and be willing to be bound by what it believes to be an abstractly perfect legal or administrative formula. The satisfied tended to view the conferences as an opportunity to promulgate a legal code consistent with their international-law doctrine. They viewed apprehensively the possibility that past law and the international-law tradition were only two factors among many that would be considered in creating conventions to which a majority of states could agree politically. Such conventions would add to mere codification an element of progressive development—that is, the creation of new rules of international law

—which the satisfied delegates deplored.

The remarks of Swedish delegate, Mr. Sture Petren, illustrate precisely the reluctance of the satisfied to accept the notion of progressive development: "Mr. Petren . . . emphasized the difference between the 'progressive development' of international law and its 'codification.' In practice, the development of law and its codification could not easily be separated. . . . Any conventions which might be drafted by the Conference, whether they related to the codification or the development of law, would therefore be of a mixed nature, containing both old rules of law and new ones. These two kinds of law had not at all the same legal effect. The old rules, if they were based on customary law, bound all mankind independently of the new conventions to be concluded, whereas the new rules, which would come into being only through the conventions, would bind only those states which signed and ratified those conventions. Other states would not be bound to recognize or observe them. The Swedish delegation therefore felt that the Conference should proceed with caution, and should not depart too radically from existing law." [40]

The satisfied delegates were not averse to using political tactics at the conference; in fact they were quite skilled at forming voting groups, making bloc proposals, lobbying, and manipulating the rules of procedure. All the while they were publicly deploring the very use of such tactics by others and implicitly apologizing for finding it necessary to use them themselves. One after another satisfied delegate took the floor to excoriate blocs and bloc voting. They felt issues should be handled as ideas "on their merits." Typical was a British appeal to deemphasize national and bloc interests for "wider considerations." [41]

Another major blunder of the satisfied states was their failure to answer the charge of the dissatisfied that the former were interested in preserving the present law because it protected their own interests. It is true that their interests did coincide with their doctrinal views. Their key doctrine, freedom of the seas, while theoretically opening the seas to all, in practice can only be exploited by those who have existent navies and merchant fleets. The satisfied states are the biggest shippers, have the biggest surface fleets, have large, important trade and fishing interests. But the satisfied states could have answered this accusation in political and economic terms, and have declared that freedom of the seas is open-ended and in fact generous to small powers, since without it the powerful could physically control large areas of the sea.

Dumbfounded by the attack of the dissatisfied on what the satisfied regarded as a liberal concept, the latter fell back on rigid, legalistic defenses. At times this tactic was used politically simply to discourage change. But the evident dismay of many satisfied delegates indicated that they could not understand the need to answer this attack by different tactics and different language. All they could do was deplore the attack on the law of the sea. For example, Dr. Max Sorensen of Denmark felt that ". . . a trend which, over the past few decades, had weakened rather than strengthened the authority of the international law of the sea should be halted, and Denmark would cooperate wholeheartedly with other nations in restoring the authority of the law." [42]

There were exceptions. Occasionally one of the less powerful states with an international-law tradition such as New Zealand, Greece, Switzerland, Australia, or Sweden,[43] would defend the

---

[40] A/CONF. 13/39, 6th meeting, par. 1–2; see also par. 24–25; 18th meeting, par. 10.

[41] A/CONF. 13/39, 53rd meeting, par. 10.

[42] Ibid., 4th meeting, par. 10.

[43] Ibid., 9th meeting, par. 10, 18; 16th meeting, par. 18; 17th meeting, par. 11; 44th meeting, par. 11, respectively.

law of the sea not only as useful for the great seagoing powers, but also as valid for lesser and developing states. (Of course, these nations were themselves in the international-law tradition, and the law of the sea did serve their interests to some extent.) And, although they did not always act accordingly, both the United Kingdom and the United States occasionally recognized that explaining international-law doctrine in traditional terms did not appeal to the newer dissatisfied states, but only contributed to their suspicion and fear of the West.[44]

But these were only exceptions; the rule was a rather inflexible legalism and refusal to answer the dissatisfied states' political attack against the norms of traditional international law. The satisfied states had come to the conference not to adjust interests but to argue law. They did so to the detriment and sometimes to the exclusion of political-economic questions. The Federal Republic of Germany, for example, refused to recognize that fishery conservation was a problem and therefore refused to sign the convention on that subject.[45] Germany also consistently doubted the validity of the idea of the continental shelf in international law. Most of the satisfied states shared this belief. There is of course a legal case for this position; that is, the concept of the continental shelf is not of ancient lineage and is not therefore part of customary international law. In that case, they insisted, their consent was necessary to bring the concept of the shelf under law binding on them. But when they reluctantly did accept the idea of

the shelf, it seemed no compromise to the proponents of the shelf concept, since it had accumulated sixteen years of state practice by those states with an active interest in exploring or exploiting the shelf. By adopting a legally sound but extraordinarily conservative position, and then agreeing to no more than had been in practice for years, they gave their negotiating techniques an air of hollow unreality and empty legalism.

Too often delegates of satisfied states would not even concede any necessary relationship between law and politics. They saw law as an abstract perfectible entity, divorced from the compromises required by the politics of competing state interests. Consider the following remarks of Professor Paul de la Pradelle, the Monacan delegate: ". . . It was difficult to disentangle the law of the sea from the accretions imposed by national sovereignty. He hoped that one day the compromise formulae produced by the 'diplomacy of the sea' would give place to a true law of the sea, in harmony with the [United Nations] Charter."[46] Little wonder that the satisfied states were unable to cope with problems of negotiating legal subjects at a conference which was, after all, a political arena!

Just as the political emphasis of the dissatisfied states led them to fear detail in drafting and to eschew expert opinion and technical arguments, so the legal emphasis of the satisfied states led them to a firm reliance on just such techniques. Because these primarily Western states had interests in many diverse aspects of activities dealing with the sea, and had the necessary legal and technical resources, they submitted a large number of very detailed proposals. One difficulty for these states as a group was that there were often numerous competing proposals from states with similar outlooks. One of the many examples of very detailed pro-

[44] A/CONF. 13/43, 21st meeting, par. 40. See also Loftus Becker, "Some Political Problems of the Legal Advisor," *Department of State Bulletin,* xxxviii (May 19, 1958), 835; and U.S. Senate, Committee on Foreign Relations, *Conventions on the Law of the Sea,* Hearings, 86th Cong., 2nd sess. (Washington, January 20, 1960), 5.

[45] A/CONF. 13/38, 18th plenary meeting, par. 74–77.

[46] A/CONF. 19/8, 23rd meeting, par. 17.

posals is a Dutch revision of the International Law Commission Draft Article on the continental shelf. The original paragraph 2 read: "Subject to the provisions of paragraphs 1 and 5 of this article, the coastal state is entitled to construct and maintain on the continental shelf installations necessary for the exploration and exploitation of its natural resources, and to establish safety zones at a reasonable distance around such installations and take in those zones measures necessary for their protection." [47]

This sentence was expanded by the Dutch to read: "Subject to the provisions of paragraphs 1 and 5 of this article and within the limits mentioned in article 68, the coastal state is entitled to construct and maintain or operate installations and other devices in the said areas necessary for the exploration and exploitation of their natural resources. The said installations and other devices shall be surrounded by a safety zone of 50 metres radius prohibited for all vessels except exploration and exploitation craft. A group of such installations and devices shall be considered as one unit if the distances are less than half a nautical mile. Entrance into such units is forbidden for all ships of more than 1,000 registered tons, except exploration and exploitation craft. If such a unit is more than 10 nautical miles long, a fairway of one nautical mile wide shall be provided in the middle, and properly marked, without prejudice to paragraph 5. The area inside such units shall be a prohibited anchorage." [48] Like many other detailed proposals, the Dutch draft alienated several of the Netherlands' natural allies. In this case, the United Kingdom also proposed an amendment whose purpose was the same as the Dutch amendment, differing only in length and wording. The result was a quibble among states whose position was basically the same.

[47] UN Doc. A/3159.
[48] UN Doc. A/CONF. 13/C.4/L.22.

Submission of competing amendments to the same article, differing only in detail, was characteristic of the satisfied states at the conferences. Only infrequently would a legal specialist from one Western state agree that another's handling of details was technically correct and sufficiently comprehensive to cover all contingencies. This often meant that states of similar outlook which submitted proposals differing only in detail would maintain their competing proposals into the voting stage, instead of uniting to back one of the texts. As a result, it became difficult to get a detailed proposal adopted. When no agreement on details could be reached among these states, the committee or the conference adopted the most general proposal or the original International Law Commission text. While the desire of the legally sophisticated to write comprehensive codes is understandable, it would have been much more to the point to put greater effort into forming a consensus on basic issues. Without such a consensus, it is impossible to negotiate on details.

When the satisfied states tended to submit detailed proposals, their justifications and explanations for the proposals were of course complex legally and technically. These remarks were not, could not be, directed to the delegates from the dissatisfied states who most needed convincing. The dissatisfied delegates were never shown why certain proposals were not contrary to their interests and could indeed have been interpreted in the interest of all. Because the dissatisfied, suspicious of the satisfied states' position at the outset, were never sufficiently convinced by the arguments of the satisfied states' delegates, they tended automatically to oppose changes in the International Law Commission draft proposed by satisfied states. For example, it is difficult to see how a change requested by the United Kingdom in the definition of a pirate ship or aircraft should have been contrary to the interests of the dissatisfied. The International Law Commission draft had defined such craft by a clause of "intent"—that is, a craft was a pirate ship if "it is *intended* by the persons in dominant control to be used for the purposes of committing"[49] an act of piracy. The British desired to make the definition of fact; a pirate ship is one "which has been used to *commit* any acts of piracy."[50] Characteristically, another satisfied state, Italy, submitted another similar proposal.[51] Neither delegation clearly explained the legal difference between intent and act. Both proposals failed; the International Law Commission text was adopted.

The satisfied states placed reverent reliance upon expert opinion, particularly that of the great French expert on law of the sea, Gilbert Gidel, who was a delegate to the first conference. Great resentment was expressed by delegates of the satisfied states, the French in particular, when the dissatisfied states used a statement of Gidel's, taken out of context from a work written in 1934, to attack the three-mile limit: "La prétendue regle des trois milles a été la grande vaincue de la Conférence."[52] M. Gros, the chief French delegate, attacked the newer states for misquoting Gidel and mishandling expert opinion.[53] Furthermore, he informed them that, while expert opinion by its very nature is free of national or group bias, Gidel's opinion had the added authority of being practically synonymous with the position of the French Government.[54] Ironically, and sadly for those states who revered the opinion of

Professor Gidel and the experts, Gidel's proposed revision of the International Law Commission definition of the high seas, a masterpiece of drafting exactness, failed of adoption. This could not have eased the resentment felt at the "misuse and abuse" of expert opinion.

Another tendency of Western and international-law-minded states was, not surprisingly for those legally oriented, to re-argue decided cases in international law. In particular, the *Lotus Case* and the *Anglo-Norwegian Fisheries Case* were dissected by Western international lawyers at the first conference.[55] Politically, this was a waste of time. Legally, the differences between the respective positions were important, but no matter how the lawyers differed on the interpretation of the court's ruling, they and the states they represented felt bound by that ruling. The tendency to argue the legal niceties of the case often made them neglect the importance of convincing the dissatisfied of the basic validity of the court's ruling and its worthiness to be included in the draft articles on the law of the sea under negotiation.

III

From this article it may be concluded that the results achieved by the Conferences on the Law of the Sea, like those of any United Nations-sponsored international conference, were dictated by the willingness of the participating states to create essentially political agreements. States or groups of states which assume that a specialized subject matter such as international law should not be subject to the political rough-and-tumble associated with parliamentary diplomacy, but dealt with logically within the broad lines of its past development, are bound to be disappointed by results achieved in a conference.

[49] UN Doc. A/3159 (italics added).
[50] UN Doc. A/CONF. 13C.2/L.83 (italics added).
[51] UN Doc. A/CONF. 13/C.2/L.81.
[52] Gilbert Gidel, *Le Droit international public de la mer,* Vol. III, *La mer territoriale et la zone contiguë* (Paris 1934), 151.
[53] A/CONF. 13/39, 37th meeting, par. 16–20.
[54] A/CONF. 13/42, 17th meeting, par. 36.

[55] See, for example, A/CONF. 13/39, 5th meeting, par. 35; 9th meeting, par. 23; 17th meeting, par. 18; 28th meeting, par. 15.

Indeed, one conclusion that might be drawn from the study of attitudes of dissatisfied states at the law of the sea conferences is that future conferences would be useless for codifying and developing law because of the hostility of dissatisfied states toward international law, a remnant of their European and imperialist past. Their concern with sovereignty, their suspicion of legal details, their wholly political attitude—all make it unlikely that they will be willing to agree to universal norms. By characterizing international law as an institutionalization of the values of the "top dogs" of the European-centered past, the dissatisfied seemed to demonstrate that they could not conceive that states might value law for its normative quality. They could not acknowledge that states have in the past compromised in negotiating legal subjects in order to create a pattern of orderly relationships even though their interests might not be fully served by such norms, or even that order itself may be to the interest of a state.

This attitude of the dissatisfied bodes ill for the possibility of creating universality in the law in our time. If, however, this is to be an end actively sought, international conferences, or some other United Nations-sponsored device, will probably be necessary to gain consent of the dissatisfied.[56] And if conferences are to be used for this purpose, it must be recognized, and not merely ruefully as Mr. Petren of Sweden did, that "progressive development" is guided by political considera-

tions and that the results of a conference will be an undifferentiated mixture of "progressive development" and "codification." No purpose is served by deploring a "diplomacy of the sea" and distinguishing it from a true "law of the sea."

The course of attempting to achieve universality by means of conferences presents the satisfied with knotty problems. To avoid utter failure, the satisfied must alter their outlook on international law and on negotiating it.

The burden of responsibility for bringing conferences dealing with international law to successful conclusions rests with the states most devoted to international law. This does not mean that these states should make drastic changes in the law or sacrifice vital interests merely to foster agreement for agreement's sake. What is necessary is a recognition on the part of satisfied states that an international conference is a forum in which political negotiations must not be looked upon with distaste, and a determination on their part to find common interests, and to make real attempts to talk to other participants in terms which all understand. Such changes in attitude—if forthcoming—are no guarantee of success; indeed, they may only hasten failure by more clearly demonstrating the real reasons for disagreement. But a realistic appraisal of the conference process as a political process is the only approach which will make success even remotely possible.

---

[56] Alternative schemes, such as allowing the General Assembly to declare codes of customary law, or giving legislative power to an enlarged Security Council or to a special majority in the General Assembly, would not avoid those problems in negotiating that became obvious at the law of the sea confer-

ences. Legal rules under these schemes would still have to be negotiated under parliamentary diplomacy. For these schemes see Jorge Castaneda, "The Underdeveloped Nations and the Development of International Law," *International Organization,* xv (Winter 1961), 38–48; and Arthur N. Holcombe, "The Improvement of the International Law-Making Process," *Notre Dame Lawyer,* xxxvii, Symposium (1961), 16–23.

Chapter VI

INTEGRATION

VI. INTEGRATION

VI. Integration

URING the inter-war period, political scientists paid great and belated heed to nationalism. There was nothing surprising in this,
since nationalism had shaped European history through the nineteenth
century, had contributed to the outbreak of World War I, and had been
legitimized by Wilson's self-determination principle. In other words,
the political environment to some extent dictated research subjects. We
can now see a similar process with regard to political integration. Much
of the most interesting research and theory in contemporary political
science is directed at determining how and why large political units are
formed out of small ones. Over the long span of history, this is not a
unique phenomenon. Classical scholars have expanded much energy
on why the Greek city-states did *not* amalgamate. But insofar as political
science is concerned, the problems are novel and unexamined.

The reason for this is not far to seek. United Nations agencies have
spun a web of international cooperation quite without precedent. Regional organizations, pre-eminently the European Economic Community, have bound together nation-states in new, unanticipated ways.
Much of the literature talks about "supranational organizations"—an
awkward and imprecise term but one that has gained currency precisely because of the conceptual vacuum. "Sovereignty," the elusive but
pivotal abstraction of earlier analysis, becomes increasingly meaningless as decision-making is vested in international bodies. What can
"sovereignty" mean when these organizations may bind states and take
over functions previously performed at the state level? Indeed, an accurate political map of the world would have to include not only the
traditional state boundaries but numerous overlays describing the geographical and functional reach of multinational bodies.

As contemporary political science has extended its investigations of
integration, it has become clear that the integrative process is in fact
observable over a wide range of phenomena, ranging from the international to the metropolitan.[1] Significantly, such research has a strong
predictive component; it seeks to identify integrative trends long be-

[1] Phillip Jacob and James V. Toscano (eds.), *The Integration of Political Communities*
(Philadelphia: Lippincott, 1964).

fore integration itself is an accomplished fact. If we trace the fact of integration back from treaties and central institutions to less immediately visible indicators,[2] we find that integration seems to follow upon the accumulation of unofficial contacts. In other words, the closer the ties of all kinds among states, the more likely that they will eventually either amalgamate or at least set up central decision-making bodies in particular areas.

There are many such unofficial contacts and they have customarily not been of the kind that political scientists examine: for example, movements of labor and travelers, long-distance phone messages, mail flows, movements of capital and trade, the formation of associations with multinational memberships, and so on. Unfortunately, we are at a point where we can say that a web of transactions is a *necessary* condition for integration but not *sufficient*. The mere presence of transactions will not create in and of itself feelings of community and of shared fate. If transactions alone brought states together, how can we explain the violent antagonisms of recent European history, often between contiguous states such as France and Germany? But if we look farther back into the nineteenth century, we will find that small states sharing a common national group tended to combine into single integrated units; in that sense, Italy and Germany were supranational when viewed from the perspective of the early nineteenth century mosaics of Italian and German principalities. In other words, it is perfectly possible to talk about the unification of Germany and Italy as instances of international political integration, even though their present internal political patterns now fall within "domestic" or "internal" affairs.

What of international integration in the present? It can proceed according to either of two strategies. The goal can be immediate political integration, or political integration can be reached through the intermediate stage of functional integration. The term "political" here is a bit deceptive and imprecise, but what it connotes are those decisions that affect a state's ability to preserve its own identity, principally its ability to control the use of force within its own territory. The term is imprecise because, as we shall see, many aspects of functional integration have profound political consequences. In any case, political integration has been taken to mean something ranging from a loose federal system like Yugoslavia's or Switzerland's to complete amalgamation like the United States—except, of course, that the constituents would be presently existing states.

[2] Karl W. Deutsch, *et al.*, *Political Community and the North Atlantic Area* (Princeton: Princeton University Press, 1957).

Functional integration does not immediately seek to vest wide decision-making authority in new central institutions. Rather, only certain carefully defined decisions are reallocated. For example, states may agree to surrender their jurisdiction over allocation of radio frequencies or movement of international river traffic to a new international decision-making body. But that body's competence is limited solely to one aspect of international relations. The functional areas involved frequently are of an economic nature and often the decisions themselves involve a high degree of technical expertise. For these reasons, they are often thought of as "non-political," although a moment's reflection will suffice to show us their underlying political dimension. The opinions of technicians often contradict each other; the belief that experts can find the single correct answer is illusory. The economist's decision regarding development plans, the transportation engineer's concerning air routes, and the physicist's on nuclear weapons control are all ultimately political in nature despite the technical considerations. They intimately affect the power, prestige, and sense of security of states.

What is the significance of all of this for the United Nations system? First, simply by virtue of its existence, the United Nations implies the desirability of a certain degree of international political integration. The precise degree that is possible and/or desirable is a moot question. Second, the specialized agencies affiliated with the United Nations, as well as the UN itself, are themselves intimately involved in functional integration. Third, it is frequently suggested that these areas of functional integration have a "spill-over effect," that is, they inevitably lead to further integration in other areas, presumably with a greater manifest political content.

The UN system as a whole has not moved rapidly or in an unobstructed manner toward the direct creation of an integrated international political community. Organizational influence has waxed and waned, dependent upon such contingencies as the state of Great Power relationships and the forcefulness with which a Secretary-General is able to carry out his mandate, assuming he perceives himself to possess a mandate. In any event, the direct integrative potential of such organs as the General Assembly and the Security Council seems slight. The vesting of additional power in the General Assembly through the "Uniting for Peace Resolution" in the 1950s now seems more a brief episode than a future portent. Even the ideal of peacekeeping by a concert of Great Powers seems largely unrealizable.

But this represents only a single facet of the UN's integrative capa-

bilities. While the most prominent and the aspect most dwelled upon
in the early history of the organization, the linear path to international
political integration seems in what perspective we have to be far less
significant than functional integration. The specialized agencies, bolstered by a history running back in some cases to the nineteenth century and by the aura of technical competence, have proved moderately
successful and innovative in such areas as economic development and
public health. In effect, the specialized agencies divide among themselves those segments of interaction which states agree to be largely
non-political.

However, it has been suggested that functional integration in a sense
"primes the pump," creating conditions which lead to full-fledged political integration. This is an unanswered hypothesis. In Western Europe, for example, the Common Market seemed to be demonstrating
that economic integration could over time produce political consequences. The EEC has stopped short under Gaullist pressure, but
whether this disproves the spill-over hypothesis or merely represents a
brief digression remains to be seen. Similarly, the overall political effects, if any, of functional integration under UN auspices cannot properly be judged in the brief time period which we can observe.

Etzioni points out that integration consists of the pyramiding of
consensus. In other words, integration requires consensus within a
larger area than previously existed. All other things being equal, the
larger and more heterogeneous the area, the more difficult it is to attain consensus. This represents a built-in limitation on UN integrative
enterprises, since the organization is predicated upon universality of
members (even though at any given time some fairly significant states
are not members). The relatively greater success of regional integration stems no doubt from the smaller number of units and smaller
cultural differences with which they have to deal. Etzioni also observes
that the spill-over effect of functional integration is bound to be closely
tied to existing relationships between sectors of a society. For example,
the relatively isolated military sphere, Etzioni contends, is unlikely to
contribute greatly to political and social integration across boundaries
by reason of its general isolation *within* particular societies.

The integration literature serves as a measuring rod for Van Wagenen's assessment of the United Nation's first twenty years. He finds
grounds for a moderately high level of optimism, while making clear
that his evaluation is predicated upon a reading of future trends rather
than present accomplishments. The analysis of contemporary politics

inevitably takes place in the absence of adequate time perspective. The choice is either to avoid present-day events entirely or to acknowledge limitations and try to place controls on them. The juxtaposition of UN problems with the political science literature arising out of regional integration experiments is one way in which the distorting effects of the immediate environment can be held down. Then, too, what we know of the integrative process leads us to believe that in its early stages it is difficult to identify, since its components consist of trading relationships, attitude changes, and other interactions not always explicitly studied by political scientists.

The UN itself, as Gregg demonstrates, has been involved in regional integration, quite apart from separate regional organizations such as the OAS. Economic development proceeds differently in different geographical areas and hence it has been advantageous for the UN to decentralize economic planning through regional economic commissions. An examination of even the brief histories of the three commissions serving Africa, Asia, and Latin America shows strong interregional differences and consequently different integrative outputs. The outputs are seen to vary with combinations of five factors: ideological leadership, tangible initiatives, institutional legacies, personnel mobility, and regional image. While no commission has made a substantial contribution to the integration of its region, the Latin American commission (ECLA) has gone rather farther than the others.

Barkun examines the relationship between universal international organizations and independent regional integration experiments. The data available thus far indicates that the two are not necessarily mutually supportive; indeed, there is reason to believe that they may pursue incompatible courses. The origins of universal organizations like the Concert of Europe, the League of Nations, and the United Nations show them to be strongly tied to goals of stability, while political integration by definition upsets the status quo. The belief that both regional integration and simultaneous global integration will dovetail finds little support from diplomatic history.

22. The Dialectics of Supranational Unification*

AMITAI ETZIONI

THE application of several European Free Trade Association (EFTA) countries for membership in the Common Market (EEC) is viewed in Washington with great pleasure: the development of a United States of Europe is widely anticipated. Many observers have already calculated the combined manpower, economic resources, military power, etc. of the new union, and have pointed to the decisive advantage the United States, in coalition with this "third power," will have over the Soviet Union. Even the fact that the EEC and EFTA, if completely merged, would have 13 members is not considered unlucky: after all, the United States itself evolved out of a union of 13. It may, however, be premature to prepare a celebration for the birthday of the United States of Europe. The following theoretical excursion suggests that loading the EEC with new members may well reduce it to the level of a glorified customs union rather than forward it to a political federation. Moreover, I shall argue, political communities often unify not by increasing their membership, but in a dialectic fashion: two or more groups form; they appear to be moving in opposite directions until each is well integrated, then they are "synthesized" (not merged) in a superior union. That is, they form one encompassing union without dissolving the bonds that held together the units that composed a group before the larger unification. The earlier autonomous groups become sub-groups

in one union, adjusting to the new over-riding bond without being fused into one group that knows no internal divisions.

I. Consensus Formation in Heterogeneous Communities

The political process is one in which groups of citizens who differ in belief and interest work out a shared policy. The larger the number of participants in a unit, the greater the differences of belief and interest among them, the more difficult such a consensus becomes, to form or keep.[1] This holds for students in social relations laboratories, for executives in industrial conferences, and for politicians in national government. Increasing the number of participants in a group may cause it to become so heterogeneous that one of two things will happen: either the ability of the group to form consensus breaks down or a new structure for the formation of consensus is built. In this structure consensus is formed on two (or more) levels. On the first, participants are separated into sub-groups according to the relative affinity of their beliefs and interests. Each of these sub-

* The American Political Science Review, Vol. LVI, No. 4, 927–935. Reprinted by permission.

[1] Theoretically one can increase the number of participants without increasing heterogeneity by adding new participants who are just like the old ones; this is the common justification for immigration policies, e.g., that discriminate in favor of readily assimilable applicants for entry. In practice, I assume for the purpose of this discussion that heterogeneity increases with size. Note, though, that no one-to-one relationship is assumed. Actually, the marginal heterogeneity produced by increases in size probably declines.

groups forms consensus among its members, and sends a representative to the second level. The second level, composed of representatives only, establishes consensus for the whole unit. This differentiation can be extended to more than two levels.

Political systems differ in the way consensus formation is institutionalized. In some, the lower level is strictly informal, having no legal or organizational status, like the blocs in the United Nations. The recent Russian proposals, commonly referred to as the "troika" system, can be viewed as a suggestion to institutionalize a two-level structure in the UN. Three blocs would be recognized—a Communist, a Western, and a Neutral one. This would require each of the blocs to form consensus internally first, on a "lower" level.[2] In other systems, two or more levels are formally recognized. In the United States, for example, the state primaries serve as one level, national party conventions as another, and interaction between the parties and between the President and Congress (see below) as still another level.

In some systems, policies formulated on the top level, the most encompassing level, are brought before all the participants for final approval (e.g., the recent nomination of Burma's U Thant to be acting Secretary General of the UN was approved, but hardly worked out, by the plenum of the General Assembly). In other systems, approval by the representatives of the sub-groups is deemed satisfactory, as is the case in practically all bureaucratic structures.

II. On the National Level

All heterogeneous polities that effectively attain consensus have a multi-level consensus formation structure. The major national political systems

differ greatly, however, in their specific structures. In multi-party systems, as long as they work—a problem to which we will return—consensus is first formed in each faction; then the factions contained by each party reach a compromise (which all consensus formation involves). Inter-party consensus is then worked out among representatives of the parties, *not* the factions. The general outline of the consensus is worked out during the negotiations over the formation of a coalition, which follows the elections; more specific consensus is worked out daily in the parliament, expressed in legislation and motions supported by votes of confidence.

In some instances, the minority party or parties (the opposition) may be left out of the process; quite often, though, they affect the policies formed, by reason of the fact that the coalition parties take their positions into account, in bi-partisan policy (especially foreign policy), as well as through participation in other "governments." Often parties that are in opposition in the national government nevertheless participate in the national consensus formation process by joining a coalition with government-parties on the city or municipal level.[3] The effective operation of the multi-party system of consensus formation requires that the number of parties be limited, otherwise communication difficulties arise and the top level may become too heterogeneous for effective negotiations; it also requires that the parties be stable, at least to the degree that a consensus reached on the lower level will be maintained on

---

[2] The obvious disadvantages of this system for the UN are irrelevant to the present analysis.

[3] In Israel, many opposition parties share the leadership with the government leader, *Mapai* (Labor party), by joining the executive board of the Jewish Agency and the *Histadrut*, often referred to as the two other governments of Israel. On their functions and their effect on Israeli politics see my "Kulturkampf or Coalition: The Case of Israel" *Revue Française de Science Politique*, Vol. 8 (June 1958), pp. 311–331.

higher levels. If members of parliament maintain only a limited loyalty to their party once the parliament is elected, party representatives cannot negotiate in the name of its factions, and we are back to the state of many participants on one level. The French parliaments of the Third and Fourth Republics were at various times confronted with this type of stalemate.[4]

In two-party countries, more consensus formation takes place on the lower levels than in multi-party countries, because only two positions can compete on the top level. So, for instance, there are only two presidential candidates for national elections, but often more than two for one party's nomination. The British system differs from the American in that the minority party tends to be excluded from the top consensus formation level, except in periods of national crises and infrequent instances of bi-partisan foreign policy. In the United States, such exclusion is rare because the Congress and the Presidency are frequently not held by the same party, and because party ties sit more lightly than in England: witness the conservative Republican southern Democratic coalition. Moreover, in the United States, instances of a bi-partisan foreign policy —e.g., on Castro's Cuba—are common.

Totalitarian societies are not exempted from the need to form consensus, though they can rely to a greater degree on coercion and downward-produced consensus through the manipulation of the mass media, rituals, etc. The major upward consensus formation takes place within extra-political structures; first, in each major bureaucracy (e.g., the military, the economic planning agency, the party); then, among the bureaucracies. One might even speak, with caution, about coalitions of some bureaucracies against

others (e.g., Army and Party against the NKVD). In sum, while political systems differ in their consensus-formation structure, it is multi-level wherever it is effective.

III. In International Systems

An examination of the international scene from this viewpoint shows first, that the hypothesis that the formation of consensus within and among heterogeneous units requires differentiation, holds here too, though several additional variables have to be taken into account.

The United Nations is probably best characterized by lack of consensus because of the deep cleavages in interests and beliefs among many of its members. But when we review those infrequent decisions—limited in importance, to be sure—where an overall consensus was reached we see the same multi-level structure in operation. Representatives of various groups of nations "caucus" to work out their shared position; then, their unofficial spokesmen negotiate with those of the other caucuses or blocs, to work out a general compromise which in turn is brought, for discussion or approval by acclamation, to the UN floor.[5] Bloc decisions themselves are frequently reached in a two-level process of a similar sort. In this light one may wonder whether we do not exaggerate the monolithic nature of the Communist bloc. China seems to have "caucused" with Albanian, and evidently North Vietnamese and North Korean representatives also, before the Congress of Communist countries in Moscow, in October, 1961.[6] Khrushchev is reported to have conferred with East European Communist countries during his boat

[4] See Constantin Melnik and Nathan Leites, *The House Without Windows* (Evanston: Rowe Peterson, 1958).

[5] Private communication with UN officials, and participant-observation in a UNESCO Conference in Montreal, in 1959.

[6] Zbigniew K. Brzezinski, *Ideology and Power in Soviet Politics* (New York, 1962), pp. 150 ff.

trip to New York in 1959. The 1961 conference of twenty-five unaligned nations in Belgrade is reported to have comprised three factions: neutral-neutrals, pro-Western neutrals, and pro-Communist neutrals. The African "bloc" seems to have at least two groupings—though their degree of cohesion is as yet hard to assess—that of the Casablanca group and that of the Brazzaville group.[7] Although the latter is reported to have taken a more moderate, pro-Western line on the Congo issue, the two groups frequently vote *en bloc* in the UN.[8]

While blocs in international organizations such as the UN, and in particular conferences such as the Belgrade Conference, are highly fluid, sub-groupings of potential supranational communities seem to have a somewhat higher degree of permanency. Thus, the Benelux countries constitute such a sub-grouping in the EEC, though by no means with regard to all or even most issues. Australia and New Zealand seem to constitute such a sub-group in the British Commonwealth of Nations. The EEC and the EFTA play such a part in the General Agreement on Tariffs and Trade (GATT).[9]

So far, the process of forming consensus in international systems seems to be quite similar to the national one. Moreover, further examination of international consensus formation suggests that, there too, a multi-level structure is more effective than direct representation of all participants on the same level, and points to the process by which such a multi-level structure

tends to emerge. First, the lower level of consensus is attained by grouping a few states at a time; once the union of such groups solidifies, a more encompassing union—and a higher level of consensus—is produced. In the initial stage of the formation of this multi-level structure, there are seldom harmonious relations between two groups of nations (or unions). In fact, intense rivalry among them is more frequent. Such rivalry seems to help the integration of each group, preparing it for the next step, *i.e.,* the formation of higher level, more encompassing unions. Finally, to push an analogy further, if one group is seen as the thesis, the other as the anti-thesis, the emerging synthesis tends to include both unions. The original units are now *permanent* elements (though changed in character) of the union, acting as lower-level consensus formation units; the new union is not built on the atomization of the groups, but on their inclusion as "individual" members. The development of several unions will illustrate this hypothesis about the dialectics of unification.

The history of Benelux is enlightening from this viewpoint. Any historical development is affected by many factors; the degree to which a multi-level consensus-formation structure is erected is, of course, just one of them. Still, it is noteworthy that after centuries of shared rule under dukes of Burgundy and kings of Spain, the Low Countries—integrated into two groups, the northern and the southern provinces—were not ready when they tried to form one republic (1795–1814), or a *United* Kingdom (1814–1830). The effort failed, among other reasons, because all provinces were thrown together. The two unions of provinces were not recognized in the new structure; efforts were made to form all consensus on one level. In 1830, the southern provinces rebelled, and formed Belgium. The ensuing war between

[7] Immanuel Wallerstein, "Background to Paga-I," *West Africa,* July 29, 1961, p. 819.

[8] See Thomas Hovet, Jr., *Bloc Politics in the United Nations* (Cambridge, Mass.: Center for International Studies, M.I.T., 1958).

[9] The EEC is represented in certain GATT negotiations by the Economic Commission as one polity rather than six national polities. See W. W. Kitzinger, *The Challenge of the Common Market* (Oxford: Basil Blackwell, 1962), 3d ed., p. 27.

the north (the Netherlands) and the south (Belgium) helped the integration of each, but did *not* hinder the eventual union of the two, in a structure that does recognize the distinctiveness of the two regions, *i.e.,* in Benelux. This analysis suggests that if Benelux should ever attain complete supranational integration, it would be functional to maintain some degree of local governmental structure in units that are the present Belgium and the Netherlands. The inclusion of small Luxembourg was also not simply a matter of adding a nation to an existing union; the way was prepared, as far back as 1921, by a customs union (BELU) with Belgium, which is maintained as a sub-union of the present, larger union, just as Benelux itself is a viable part of the EEC.[10]

The 13 colonies that formed the United States were more or less autonomous societal units, with internal consensus-formation mechanisms. These societal units were not abolished with the federation, but found expression in the states' governments. They still have an important influence on the Federal government, both by carrying out some functions on the state level and through representation in the Senate. Moreover, groups of states—the South, East, Midwest, and West (sometimes smaller groupings, *e.g.,* the New England States or the Southwest) are still an important middle level of consensus formation informally recognized in Congress and in party conventions. The union here, as in Benelux, was completed only after a war between the South and the North, which did *not* eliminate either the South or the North or the states, as meaningful intermediary units in American politics. A similar analysis could be applied to the various Swiss cantons, and possibly even to their German and French-Italian groupings. Here too, civil wars,

one as late as the suppression of a rebellion of a Roman Catholic canton in 1847, preceded but did not prevent federation in 1848.[11] To return to the contemporary scene, the Organization of American States, which has 21 members, may well be too large for effective, one-level unification; recent efforts to form common markets have been made between five Central American countries and seven South American ones. The possibility of forming a more encompassing union later is explicitly recognized.[12] The strains that have re-asserted themselves in the last two years in the relations between the United States and western European powers, especially over the question of national nuclear deterrents, advance rather than retard the political unification of France and West Germany, and will not necessarily as often claimed, undermine the proposed Atlantic Union.[13]

It would be hasty, however, to conclude from the preceding discussion that the only or the best way to form a European Community is to integrate the EEC and the EFTA—as they are —in some super-system. Before the validity of other approaches can be assessed, some additional factors that affect supranational unification need to be examined. First, there is the question of the degree of integration a union aims at and the scope desired.

IV. Degree of Integration, and Scope

Political communities of nations differ from other international systems—

[10] See F. Gunther Eyck, *The Benelux Countries* (New York, 1959), Pt. I.

[11] Charlotte Muret, "The Swiss Pattern for a Federal Europe," in E. M. Earle, ed., *Nationalism and Internationalism* (New York, 1950), pp. 261 ff.

[12] Federal Reserve Bank of New York, "The Emerging Common Markets in Latin America," *Monthly Review,* September, 1960.

[13] *Cf.* Walter Lippmann, *Western Unity and the Common Market* (Boston, 1962), ch. 3.

such as alliances, blocs, international organizations—in having a "supranational" structure and not just an inter-governmental one. By definition they have one center of government that legitimately decrees and enforces decisions within its jurisdiction on matters that affect the member nations and their citizens; this requires a higher degree of consensus than the inter-governmental structure of other international systems. Since the decisions of inter-governmental bodies are not binding and collective international actions are under national control, consensus can often be worked out in an *ad hoc* manner, and on specific issues, even when general consensus is lacking. In short, supranationalism is a politically more integrated structure which requires correspondingly more consensus formation than typical inter-governmental organizations.[14] This is, though, a question of degree, not a "yes" or "no" proposition. NATO, for instance, has a supranational SHAPE, the European Coal and Steel Community (ECSC) its High Authority, and the European Economic Community, the Economic Commission; but all have also superior inter-governmental bodies, the various Councils of Ministers. They are, thus, part supranational, part inter-governmental.[15] Since the Council of Ministers has both formal and realistic superiority, these European bodies should be regarded as predominantly inter-governmental.

We would expect that the smaller a union is, all other things equal, the more homogeneous it could be, and the more integrated and "suprana-

tional."[16] This is in fact the case since, while many international organizations include almost all the states there are, from five continents and from all blocs (*e.g.,* 109 members of the UN), most supranational communities have less than ten members and are, comparatively homogeneous in their cultural, educational, economic, and political backgrounds. Hence, the question, whether the EEC and the EFTA should be merged and if merged should be preserved as sub-units, is in part dependent upon the degree of integration sought. A highly integrated union—a United States of Europe—is least likely to be formed by a large expansion of the membership of the EEC,[17] while a customs union—directed by an inter-governmental body—can readily accommodate a membership larger than that of the EEC and the EFTA combined. This conclusion, reached on the basis of studying the relationship between integration, heterogeneity and size, is reinforced by an examination of the relationship between integration and scope.

International systems differ in the number of societal sectors they pervade. Some, especially international organizations, are strictly mono-sectorial; they deal only with labor issues, or health issues, or postal services, or aviation; and as a rule only with some activities in these sectors, and not nec-

[16] See note 1, above, on the relationship between size and heterogeneity.

[17] The union of the United States, well "prepared" by 1789, took a hundred years and a civil war before it solidified, and yet was one of a highly homogeneous group: ". . . Providence has been pleased to give this one connected country to one united people—a people descended from the same ancestors, speaking the same language, professing the same religion, attached to the same principles of government, very similar in their manners and customs," John Jay, *The Federalist,* No. 2, cited by Gerard J. Mangone, *The Idea and Practice of World Government* (New York: Columbia University Press, 1951), p. 26, fn. 10.

[14] For a keen analysis of the difference between inter-governmental and supranational structures, see Ernst B. Haas, *The Uniting of Europe* (Stanford: Stanford University Press, 1958), pp. 520 ff.

[15] This point is elaborated in my "A Paradigm for the Study of Political Unification," *World Politics,* Vol. XV (October 1962), p. 44.

essarily the most central ones. Other international organizations penetrate into two or more sectors (as, for instance, the Nordic Council which serves political, economic, educational, and cultural needs of the member-nations). The larger the sectorial scope of a union, the more consensus is required; and hence the fewer the number of nations (or more precisely, the degree of heterogeneity) it can tolerate, and the more it will need two (or more) structural levels of consensus formation. Thus, it is not surprising that the typical mono-sectorial unions have many members, while typical multi-sectorial unions have only from 3 to 8 members: for instance, the Nordic Council has 5 members; the Eastern European Community (with two major organizations as tools, the Warsaw Treaty Organization and the Council for Mutual Economic Aid) has 8 members; the *Conseil de l'Entente* has 4, and Benelux has 3.

Even more important than the number of sectors encompassed is the nature of any particular sector to be integrated, in terms of its articulation with other sectors of the same society. Several authorities in the study of supranationalism have pointed out that integration in one sector tends to spill over into other sectors, *i.e.,* tends to trigger integration in them as well. Haas' study of the ECSC, for instance, shows how it spilled over into Euratom and the EEC.[18] He has also suggested that various societal sectors differ in their spill-over function.[19] On the basis of various sociological considerations that cannot be elaborated here,[20] I would order international organizations in various sectors with re-

spect to their spill-over tendencies— from low to high—as follows: (a) organizations that deal with services, such as postal services, allocation of radio frequencies, police cooperation, etc.; (b) organizations dealing with labor, health, and cultural exchange, *i.e.,* services to which "human values" are attached; (c) tariff agreements and military organizations; (d) economic unions or common markets.

The spill-over phenomenon points to the fact that societal sectors differ in the degree to which they are inter-related. Integrating some of them triggers unification tendencies in many other sectors; while integrating some other sectors has comparatively small repercussions. The military sector, for instance, is highly segregated and autonomous, unless industrial mobilization is involved. Military units of two nations can be integrated, their war plans coordinated, their navies participate in combined maneuvers, military information extensively exchanged, etc., without this having much effect on other societal sectors. Only when integration reaches the higher level of policy making is there a considerable spill-over into the political sector, and this because integration here requires some governmental integration, *e.g.,* of Defense Departments. Similarly, standardization of weapons and other equipment often has some repercussion on the economic sector. Economic integration, on the other hand, affects all societal groups—consumers, producers, management, labor, farmers, small business—and therefore tends to have extensive political repercussions. In contrast, tariff agreements, especially to the degree that they cover only some goods and concern only reduction but not abolition of tariffs, affect only some exporters and importers and a limited number of related industries. It is only as such unions become so broadly encompassing as to tend to affect the flow of capital, monetary policy, levels of employment, etc.,

---

[18] *Uniting of Europe, op. cit.*

[19] Ernest B. Haas, "International Integration," *International Organization,* Vol 15 (1961), pp. 366–392.

[20] See my "The Epigenesis of Political Community at the International Level," *American Journal of Sociology,* Vol. 68 (Jan. 1963).

in the countries involved, that they spill over into economic unions, *i.e.,* that they trigger integration of many other spheres.

In cases where the unification of a high spill-over sector has occurred and unification of other related sectors is blocked, an unbalanced state is created which generates pressures to "solve" the imbalance, either by removing the blocks or by reducing the degree of unification in the sector in which it was initiated. For instance, if furnishing nuclear weapons to NATO would require NATO to create a joint political authority to command their use (there would hardly be time to consult 15 governments if NATO is attacked nuclearly, and contingent decisions are unsatisfactory), and if for some reason the 15 nations are not "ready" for the required political integration, these would be two factors working against the acceptance of such weapons by NATO. The prospect that spill-over from the military into the political sector is blocked would work against military integration. [Integration, so to speak, proceeds in steps. There are several plateaus on which one can rest, but one cannot stand on two steps simultaneously; one has either to progress to more encompassing unification or retreat to a narrower one.]

What does the study of the scope of integration and spill-over add to our understanding of EFTA-EEC relations? The EEC is continuously growing closer to an economic union, above and beyond a mere tariff agreement. Such unions have high spill-over effects, as is evident in the EEC talks about federation and in the increased public and private support for a strong, political EEC.

In short, by 1962, the Europe of the Six was on the verge of an increasing spill-over into the political sector. Britain, on the other hand, though consistently interested in a European tariff agreement, or even in an economic one, was ambivalent if not negatively disposed toward a political union. This was one of the major reasons why England did not join the EEC in the first place and instead joined the EFTA, a free trade association with limited spill-over potentialities. By 1961 Britain had changed its position. EFTA clearly failed. Some of its members traded more across the tariff wall with EEC countries than with each other. While customs reductions within the EEC seemed to trigger a rapid rate of economic growth—better than six per cent a year—economic stagnation in Britain continued. The prospect of a fully integrated Western Europe became more and more real. Hence Britain's resolution, in the middle of 1961, to abandon EFTA, to weaken its ties to the Commonwealth if necessary, and to join the EEC on any reasonable conditions. Britain's interest in the EEC is, though, almost completely economic. British feelings against political unification with the continent have deep roots which include a long history of hegemony; a self-image of a big power, or even more painful, of an ex-big power, jealous of its remaining privileges, sensitive about its status, anxious to preserve its strong ties to the Commonwealth and to the United States. Many of these roots will have to be considerably weakened before the United Kingdom can genuinely participate in a political integration of Western Europe.

Last but not least, is the question of hegemony in the EEC. International communities seem to function best when one nation has clear hegemony;[21]

[21] *Cf.,* for instance, the period of hegemony in the British, Hapsburg, and German empires to the periods of dual or multi-leadership. See also Crane Brinton, *From Many One* (Cambridge: Harvard University Press, 1948). And compare the Communist bloc in the days when the Soviet Union had a clear hegemony to the later period of the Soviet-Chinese rift. See T. M. Mills, "Power Relations in Three Person Groups," *American Sociological Review,* Vol. 18 (1953), pp. 351–7; Georg Simmel, "The Number of

sometimes, two countries can share the leadership, especially when there is a third outside force against which they unite. This is the present situation in the EEC, where France and West Germany share the leadership. Systems with three leaders hardly ever stabilize.[22] There are too many latent and tempting benefits to be derived from the collusion or coalition of two against the third partner. On all these counts, Britain's entry into the EEC makes the completion of the spill-over from the economic to the political area quite unlikely. And this may mean that the EEC will not even remain an economic union, but instead will more likely regress to the level of a tariff agreement. This point requires some elaboration.

International unions of this type seem to have two stable stages: *low* integration with little or no spill-over, and *high* integration, where unification initiated in one sector spills over to many others, especially the political. Unions that try to maintain a medium-level integration, *e.g.,* economic only, or economic with a minimum of political integration, are unstable, not because they are likely to disintegrate but because their capacity to form consensus is out of balance with the need for it: they are likely to become more integrated or regress to a lower level of integration. The chances, in case England joins the EEC, favor regression rather than progression.

The fact that England and other EFTA members apply for membership in the EEC as individual countries, not *en bloc,* makes high integration of the EEC less, not more, likely, for it produces a merger rather than a synthesis on a higher level. One might

Members as Determining the Sociological Form of the Group," *American Journal of Sociology,* Vol. 8 (1902), pp. 45–6.
[22] See Miriam Camps, *Division in Europe,* Policy Memorandum No. 21, Center of International Studies (Princeton University, 1960).

therefore be inclined to favor the formation of a super-system, to include both the EFTA and the EEC as subunits. But this will not do because the units of an effective union, one that can maintain an adequate level of consensus, have to be fairly cohesive, stable units. One cannot build a second floor structure of consensus formation unless the first one has a firm foundation. While the EEC is already quite cohesive, and becoming more so, the EFTA is not. EFTA was formed, not out of any genuine commitment to a union, but to countervail the EEC; it was viewed as a temporary union, to be used to bargain with the EEC, hardly a morale-building feature. Austria and Switzerland, *e.g.,* trade more with EEC countries than with EFTA countries. In addition, the EFTA membership is highly heterogeneous: it includes NATO and non-NATO members; democracies and Portugal; Protestant countries and Austria.

The preceding discussion suggests that western Europe includes too many countries, is too heterogeneous, to form one union. It follows that two or more unions are needed, to form the units of a larger system. But it does not follow that the unification of any specific group of countries would be more conducive to European integration than any other, as long as cohesive unions serve as building blocs. One course toward unification is the expansion of the EEC to include a few more countries (though not all the members of the EFTA), such as some that are contiguous to the EEC and less competitive for its leadership than Britain. Austria and Switzerland are natural candidates. The fact that they are not NATO countries, and in the past have taken a neutral position in the inter-bloc strife, is not necessarily a barrier to their inclusion, probably first as associate members; and later as full members, to be included also in the political union. The neutrality of these nations is quite pro-Western and both France (since De Gaulle) and West Germany (since the inclusion of the Free Democrats in the government) move in the direction of a somewhat more "independent" foreign policy. [It is hard to see how the USSR could stop a gradual integration of Austria into the EEC.]

Another European union, the Scandinavian community, forms a core for a larger union. It has already grown from three to five members, adding Iceland and Finland to Sweden, Norway, and Denmark. Once European trade problems are solved in a large framework, as discussed below, Britain might find this union—which is democratic, Protestant and welfare-oriented —more appealing for political unification than the continental one. Portugal and Spain have been reported to have considered an Iberian union of their own.[23] Once the major requirements of small size and cohesion are satisfied, other possible combinations might emerge; the major question that remains is the type of super-system to which these unions can belong.

V. Kinds of Super-Systems

How encompassing could such a super-system be, in terms of the number of unions to be included? What could be the functions of the super-system, above and beyond those of the member unions? The major alternatives discussed seem to be a European super-system or an Atlantic one, the latter to include the United States and Canada in addition to the European countries (including either all western Europe or only NATO members).[24]

The following analysis suggests that a European super-system[25] will be more integrated and stable than an Atlantic one, as long as it will itself be a part of a third-level organization. The main reason for this is that the United States, as the leading Western power, has many commitments and functions in other international communities than the European ones, especially in Latin America, but also in the Far East, South East Asia, the Middle East, and to an increasing degree in Africa. Strong integration of the United States in a European union would impose sharp strains on these other American ties.

The optimal participation for the United States is on the third level of consensus formation, a structural level where super-systems—of several European unions, of several African ones, and of several Latin American ones, etc.—are integrated in a single super-super-system, already vaguely recognized as the "Free World." A three-level structure may perhaps seem too complicated to be attained; or if attained, to function effectively. It should therefore be pointed out that three-level structures are quite common. Most national governments and practically all large corporate enterprises have at least a three-level structure, and many of them are quite effective. Actually, the evolution of a third-level structure would not preclude active participation in the development of a fourth level, that of the United Nations.

The main problem is not the number of levels but the distribution of functions, powers and political loyalties among the various levels. The formal, legal and institutional differences between unions whose members are na-

[23] *Christian Science Monitor,* October 28, 1957, p. 6.
[24] Such a union has been advocated by Henry A. Kissinger, *The Necessity for Choice* (New York, 1960), pp. 165–8. See also Joseph Kraft, *The Grand Design* (New York, 1962). Some of the problems involved in its formation have been pointed out by Karl W.

Deutsch *et al., Political Community and the North Atlantic Area* (Princeton University Press, 1957).
[25] Not to be confused with a merger of nations as "individuals" in a European union, such as "revised" OEEC.

tions, and super-systems whose members are unions, is that representation in super-systems is in the hands of those who speak in the name of the unions (*e.g.,* the EEC), either in addition to or instead of national representatives. For the division of functions, we can consider two major possibilities: one is that the super-systems will be a replica of member-unions on a more encompassing level. Such a super-system is approximated (in limited spheres to be sure) in the relations between the EEC and the EFTA in the OEEC and in GATT. Each group, for instance, introduced some internal reductions of tariffs, then met in the wider arena of GATT to consider mutual tariff cuts—as well as small cuts for "third" countries, not members of either union. According to this plan the control of one specific function, in this case setting tariff rates, is divided between two levels beyond the national one: that of the unions and that of the super-system.

The second way to integrate unions into super-systems is to introduce a functional division of labor among the levels instead of a differentiation of authority. One such arrangement might take the form of leaving to the small, cohesive unions the economic and political functions; to the super-systems, the role of military integration; and to the third-level system (or bloc), the coordination of foreign policy, monetary policy (*e.g.,* through a revised International Monetary Fund), and tariff agreements.[26] This might also be the best level on which to coordinate aid to underdeveloped countries.

This specific division only illustrates the nature of inter-level division of functions; of course other arrangements can be worked out. It should,

though, be emphasized that the division outlined above takes into account the need to reserve to smaller, lower-level units those functions that require a high degree of consensus formation and hence of relatively strong supranationalism. The actual structure of the West approaches such a division with the smaller economic-political EEC and Nordic Council, the larger NATO, and the still more encompassing GATT, IMF, and OECD. The third-level system is still highly informal, and centered around trips of premiers to Washington, foreign tours of American representatives, and regional meetings—but no Free World ministerial conferences.

Which of the two types of inter-level division is optimal has yet to be determined. It seems that they differ in effectiveness with regard to different goals: functional division of labor seems better for short-run stability, and an inter-level division of control over each function the better for long-run integration of second- and third-level super-systems. This latter seems to be the case because here high spill-over functions are in part carried out by super-systems, and because the units which carry out high spill-over functions command more political loyalty than those which do not.

The long-run trend toward integration seems to be for functions, authority and loyalties to be transferred from smaller units to larger ones; from states to federations; from federations to supranational unions; and from these to super-systems. This transfer may progress without major upsets because a variety of processes tend to reduce the heterogeneity of the member-units—through industrialization, the spread of education, democratization, and the unification process—to lower-level units.[27] Hence the transfer of additional powers of decision to

[26] See Robert Trillon, *Gold and the Dollar Crisis* (New Haven: Yale University Press, 1961), ch. 4, and Alastair Buchan, *NATO in the 1960's* (London: Wiedenfeld & Nicolson, 1959), ch. 4.

[27] This point is elaborated in my *The Hard Way to Peace* (New York: Collier Books, 1962), ch. 8.

higher levels—those encompassing more members—need not undermine stabilization as long as the pace of upgrading function or authority does not overtake that of decreasing hetero-geneity. We close with the speculative, though not unimaginable possibility that eventually, in this way, the highest super-system, that of a global society, might develop.

23. The Concept of Community and the Future of the United Nations*

RICHARD W. VAN WAGENEN

It may be unthinkable, even unimaginable, that the United Nations could itself become a true "community" in the near future. It is *not* unthinkable that the UN may be pushing the present disarray a little closer to that goal. The popular press abounds with loose references to the "world community," but men who have thought deeply and hardheadedly about this prospect have also hinted in that direction, using various terms for the same thing. To quote only two, Lincoln P. Bloomfield calmly mentions "the universal society of which the United Nations is the forerunner"[1] and Richard N. Gardner believes that a "genuine world community is waiting to be born. . . ."[2]

In mid-1965 we are concerned on the surface with nothing more exalted than self-preservation. International Cooperation Year (ICY) dawned with the departure of the first Member ever to resign from the Organization, followed by the adjournment of a crippled General Assembly seeking to solve the greatest constitutional issue in the UN's history. Beneath the present political alignments, the world is in fact divided in a number of ways, as Secretary-General U Thant has pointed out: economically, racially, and ideologically.[3] Under these conditions the "concept of community" may seem to be a paradox.

This paradox needs to be examined in the light of the most advanced analysis available. In this brief space we have a choice of three approaches, only two of which are realistic here. One is to apply unstructured judgment on a straightforward premise that whatever seems to "strengthen" the UN is community building and will generate further integration. This runs into problems of definition right away. Another is to apply the findings of research on integration in certain other international contexts by using rough judgment and ignoring the fact that conditions underlying and surrounding the research in those other contexts are different and might render application to the UN unreliable. The

* *International Organization*, Vol. XIX, No. 3, 812–827. Reprinted by permission.

[1] *The United Nations and U.S. Foreign Policy: A New Look at the National Interest* (Boston: Little, Brown and Company, 1960), p. 233. He wisely warned that
> there is no evidence that purely "functional" interrelationships will lead by any natural or automatic process to political integration, or even that integration as such will eventually be the dominant trend.
(*Ibid.,* p. 230.)

[2] Richard N. Gardner, *In Pursuit of World Order* (New York: Frederick A. Praeger, 1964), p. 262.

[3] See U Thant's address to the Pacem in Terris Convocation, February 20, 1965 ("The UNITED NATIONS in a Changing World," *UN Monthly Chronicle*, March 1965 [Vol. 2, No. 3], pp. 41–46).

third is to develop a framework for the specific study of the integrative function of the UN system and then apply it to that system.

The last is the best, but it is impossible to accomplish in a short space. The first and second can be explored, the first very briefly because the wealth of concrete information and analysis in the preceding pages makes a longer treatment superfluous.

Looking at the record of the United Nations over the first twenty years and applying political judgment and common sense, we are likely to conclude that, on balance, the UN is a community-building institution. The line of reasoning is familiar. As the technology of transportation and other forms of communication squeeze the globe into a sphere that is a fraction of its former size, global institutions have been invented or have grown from regional functional institutions. They do not grow as fast as the need for them, but there is a new realization that many things which have to be done *cannot* be done on a less-than-global basis, among them the regulation of transport and communication, the control of outer space, the control of disease, and above all the control of massive armed conflict.

If the doctrine of functionalism is taken at face value, the next step is to reason that the performance of these tasks, especially the economic and social ones in which the UN is so deeply engaged, will strengthen the sense of community over wide areas. This will help to build institutions which in turn strengthen the consensus needed for political community. A benign spiral then carries that sense of community to a point where the institutions gradually grow strong enough to support enforceable law. Such authority, in turn, may be able to check war, the greatest of dangers to man at the present time. The UN is the nearest thing we have to a global political institution. Therefore,

to strengthen the UN in structure and function is to provide community-building authority.

There is probably a sound basis for this line of reasoning, but it still represents only a belief. We find it persuasive in the light of the many activities, most of them successful, which have been carried on by the UN in its first two decades. The situation is suggested by Adlai Stevenson, who gives the UN a large share of the credit:

The central trend of our times is the emergence of what, for lack of a better label, might be called a policy of cease-fire and peaceful change. I would suggest . . . that we may be approaching something close to a world consensus on such a policy. . . . Cease-fire and peaceful change may strike some as a curious way to describe a period so jammed by violence, by disorder, by quarrels among the nations—an era so lacking in law and order. But I do not speak wistfully; I speak from the record. It is precisely the fact that so much violence and so many quarrels *have not led to war* that puts a special mark on our times.[4]

Convinced as we may be, for reasons of good judgment and desperation in unequal parts, that the UN is most assuredly worth supporting, we

[4] Address at Princeton University, March 23, 1964, published in Andrew W. Cordier and Wilder Foote (ed.), *The Quest for Peace: The Dag Hammarskjöld Memorial Lectures* (New York: Columbia University Press, 1965), p. 57. For a differing estimate by another respected statesman, see Herbert Hoover in Raymond A. Moore, Jr. (ed.), *The United Nations Reconsidered* (Columbia: University of South Carolina Press, 1963), pp. 80–82. For a strong proposal for action on clearly functionalist lines but outside the UN, see the thoughtful speech, "Approaches to International Community," to have been delivered on March 6, 1965, at Pennsylvania State University by Senator J. W. Fulbright.

are left with a question: Did the UN really have much to do with the development of "cease-fire and peaceful change" or would this progress have come anyhow, swept forward by the facts of life? Indeed, does this alleged progress really exist? As analysts, we are uneasy until we have explored the intellectual basis—at least the underlying definitions and concepts—of the favorable assumption through social science research.

Premises and Considerations of Theory

In exploring the second approach, the first thing to note is that the concept of community is elusive and slippery. Any number of scholars, especially sociologists and political scientists, have tried to grip it. The variables involved are almost infinite. The concept is crucial at various levels from the village to the globe; understanding seems to vary inversely with the height of the level so that the international is the most opaque of all. We are not concerned with other levels except as theory developed for studying them is useful at the international level. We do not need to start, therefore, with a comprehensive framework.[5] Rather, we seek a theory which is limited in two respects: It speaks to the international level and it points to the minimal kind of community needed to maintain peace.

We are interested at this point in trying to learn how the existence and operation of the UN may contribute to its strength as an international peace-keeping agency. Is there any sign of UN "community building" as a basis for institutional strength? Is there any secular trend slanting upward or downward through the

pointed peaks and rounded valleys of UN crises, from the Iranian case of 1946 to the constitutional crisis of 1965? Does the UN itself have anything positive to do with that trend?

As to the "minimal or maximal" issue, it is a reasonable question whether those parts of the preamble calling for relief from the "scourge of war" and for the establishment of "conditions under which justice and respect for the obligations arising from treaties and other sources of international law can be maintained" are more basic than those parts reaffirming "faith in fundamental human rights" and encouraging "social progress and better standards of life in larger freedom." It is almost a cliché to say that peace is not merely the absence of war. But the absence of war is itself a valid overriding objective. What is specifically prohibited in the Charter is the unilateral use of force except in self-defense; if this is achieved, at least the "security" aim of the term "international peace and security" is realized.

To state a value premise, we believe that the war-prevention objective is the more fundamental because progress in the other elements of human welfare is impossible without this prerequisite. Yet the old question remains unanswered: Is a high level of welfare—economic and social and political—itself a prerequisite to a community cohesive enough to support institutions for keeping the peace? We take the minimal position: that where the object is peaceful change, the whole list of prerequisite or companion values is not necessary.

This drives us to the concept of security-community and integration as defined and elaborated some years ago in exploring "expanding community" as a focus for research.[6]

[5] Such as that of Philip Jacob and Henry Teune in the opening chapter of Philip E. Jacob and James V. Toscano (ed.), *The Integration of Political Communities* (Philadelphia, Penna.: J. B. Lippincott Company, 1964).

[6] Richard W. Van Wagenen, *Research in the International Organization Field: Some Notes on a Possible Focus* (Princeton, N.J.: Center for Research on World Political Institutions, 1952).

A *security-community* is considered to be a group which has become integrated, where *integration* is defined as the attainment of a sense of community, accompanied by formal or informal institutions and practices, sufficiently strong and widespread to assure peaceful change among members of a group with "reasonable" certainty over a "long" period of time.[7]

To avoid circularity, "sense of community" and "peaceful change" were further defined, leading to the necessity of handling also the classic legal and psychological problem of "authority."[8]

When applied to the UN, this set of definitions does not reveal the basis of authority for what the Organization does and the lack of authority for what it does not do. How can it push toward a security-community over as wide an area as possible? How can it promote the process of integration?[9] We are referring to what has been called the "ultimate task":

> to convert the world into a pluralistic society marked by a high adjustment potential—by the existence of component parts which are susceptible of regulation in their relationships with each other and with the whole, through the processes of political accommodation.[10]

We are thinking sociologically of

the possibility that the level of organization in the world may be raised, so to speak, so that a more inclusive social system comes to incorporate the national States.[11]

This would be incorporation to the minimum extent needed for a security-community, that is, for integration.

It is quite true, as a thoughtful scholar has put it, that

> the competition of states can be pursued by means short of violence but still far in excess of those used by even sharply opposed political parties which accept the basic constitutional order of a state.[12]

Yet it is the habit of this very pursuit short of violence that is the proximate and perhaps the ultimate goal we seek. Even though Stanley Hoffmann is correct in separating for purposes of analysis two different phenomena, the relations between individuals or groups across national boundaries ("transnational society") and competition and cooperation of states having no common authority above them,[13] the study of the integrative process seems to underlie both.

In the most thorough and sophisticated analysis of the doctrine of functionalism so far in print, Ernst Haas defines integration in a way not inconsistent with the definition we have just cited, provided both are used in the sense of process and not of condition:

> If the present international scene is conceived of as a series of interacting

---

[7] *Ibid.*, pp. 10–11.

[8] *Ibid.*

[9] The word is used to mean both the process and the condition.

[10] Inis L. Claude, Jr., *Power and International Relations* (New York: Random House, 1962), p. 284.

[11] Robert C. Angell, in *The Nature of Conflict* (Paris: United Nations Educational, Scientific and Cultural Organization, 1957), p. 205.

[12] Stanley Hoffmann, "Discord in Community: The North Atlantic Area as a Partial International System," *International Organization*, Summer 1963 (Vol. 17, No. 3), pp. 526–527.

[13] *Ibid.*, p. 525. There is room for disagreement that as a tool of analysis "the word *community* does more harm than good. . . ."

and mingling national environments, and in terms of their participation in international organizations, then integration would describe the process of *increasing* the interaction and the mingling so as to obscure the boundaries between the system of international organizations and the environment provided by their nation-state members.[14]

This is a more limited use of the word, but consistent especially when we note that Mr. Haas considers

modern nation-states as communities whose basic consensus is restricted to agreement on the *procedure* for maintaining order and settling disputes among groups, for carrying out well-understood functions.[15]

We are dealing with the United Nations as an organization. Concerning the outcomes of organizations, Mr. Haas identifies three types of decision-making processes or, as he calls them, recurrent patterns of outcomes. The least demanding is accommodation on the basis of the minimum common denominator, pleasing only the least cooperative bargaining partner. The other two are more demanding and carry the participants farther along the path toward integration: accommodation by splitting the difference and accommodation "on the basis of deliberately or inadvertently upgrading the common interests of the parties." Mr. Haas believes that

the proof of an organizational impact lies in the appearance of a new set of general interests that command respect among the members—in short, a new world task.

There are three specific indicators: institutional autonomy, authority ("grudging implementation bestowed on organizational acts"), and legitimacy. He believes that the position of the UN system could be summed up convincingly if the degree of its legitimacy could be specified.[16]

His pioneering studies exploring integration in the European setting are well-known.[17] It is quite a jump from a set of nuclear European politico-economic organizations to a single-purpose functional worldwide international organization (the International Labor Organization [ILO]) and from there to a general-purpose political organization (the UN). Ernst Haas' work lends encouragement to those who would like to make this second leap.

The other lead toward assessing the integrative possibilities of the UN comes from the indicators devised by Karl Deutsch[18] in order to apply the Princeton concept of integration and security-community[19] and to develop it for exploring the integration of the North Atlantic area.[20] Again there is a conceptual leap from the historical cases of integration to the North Atlantic area and from there to the UN.

In the Princeton study *dis*integrative conditions were not handled systematically except in the case of amalgamated security-communities in history[21]

[14] Ernst B. Haas, *Beyond the Nation-State: Functionalism and International Organization* (Stanford, Calif.: Stanford University Press, 1964), p. 29.
[15] *Ibid.*, p. 39.
[16] *Ibid.*, pp. 111, 131–133.
[17] Especially *The Uniting of Europe* (Stanford, Calif.: Stanford University Press, 1958) and *Consensus Formation in the Council of Europe* (Berkeley: University of California Press, 1960).
[18] *Political Community at the International Level: Problems of Definition and Measurement* (Garden City, N.Y.: Doubleday, 1954).
[19] See p. 420 above.
[20] Karl W. Deutsch and others, *Political Community and the North Atlantic Area: International Organization in the Light of Historical Experience* (Princeton, N.J.: Princeton University Press, 1957).
[21] Since the amalgamated security-community is beyond even the most visionary notions

so that we are unable to explore by this means whether the UN may be promoting some unknown disintegrative conditions at the same time it may be promoting integrative ones. Another of the many complications is the

essential difference between the relations among states (even peaceful and cooperative) that are not engaged in the process of integration toward "political community" in Haas' sense, and the relations among states that have joined (even partially) in such a process,

the main difference lying "in the conceptual framework suitable for the study of those two types of situations." [22]

We are concerned especially with functions that tend to *change* the system. As we have suggested elsewhere,

the criterion which has been generally overlooked is not the substantive result but the consensus-forming result of these international operations. This consensus-forming outcome might be considered not merely a by-product, but instead the most important single result from the standpoint of understanding the process of integration.[23]

Assessing Progress Toward Security-Community

Our second approach was to apply judgment to the observable facts, illuminated by the dim light issuing from the criteria we have just introduced.

Obviously the UN system as a whole is not a security-community

and perhaps it never will be. Some groups of its Members already constitute such communities. The United States and Canada provide the clearest example and there are many others. Some are at the other end of the scale, for example, Israel and Jordan. Most are in between. Does the UN system promote or deter the process of international integration among large groupings of at least its non-Communist membership?

Do the findings of the Princeton historical studies have any application here?

One of the three conditions that were found to be *essential but not sufficient* for attainment of a security-community was

a compatibility of the main values held by the relevant strata of all the political units involved; and with this condition there sometimes had to be also a tacit agreement to deprive any remaining incompatible values of their political significance.[24]

What can be construed as main values and relevant strata is wide open as far as the UN system is concerned. Values such as democracy and constitutionalism do not have equivalent meanings among many of the Members or among the relevant strata of society within Member States although they do have equivalent meanings among a majority of the Members having at least a bare majority of the population represented in the UN. Such broad values as social rights and economic welfare have a wide acceptance although the meaning of the terms is not identical everywhere. Prestige and independence are certainly among the main values of a nation-state, but they need referents: prestige in the eyes of whom, and independence from whom?

Our question is narrower, however, in two ways: (1) Integration does not

---

about the future of the UN, only those parts of the study found relevant to pluralistic security-communities will be applied here.

[22] Hoffmann, *International Organization,* Vol. 17, No. 3, p. 527.
[23] Van Wagenen, p. 43.

[24] Deutsch and others, p. 123.

ask congruence, only compatibility; peaceful coexistence, if it is genuine and permanent, is sufficient to uphold a security-community. (2) The present situation is not so much our concern as whether the UN promotes for the future any closer compatibility of values or the defusing of incompatible ones.

It is a temptation to decide that one value, an overwhelming desire to settle conflicts by peaceful (nonphysical) means, is more basic than any other in assessing progress toward a security-community. But this has not been proven, either as to its validity or as to its embodiment in national policies. Only two of the larger Members of the UN in 1964 or 1965 were on record with a policy of first-strike military force against another Member—the United Arab Republic (and its allies) and Indonesia—and by the end of the year one had resigned its membership. Two other Members came close to outright war in 1964 and it is not certain that they will avoid battle over Cyprus in the future. The availability of a UN alternative on the ground, which was not the case when three major Members of the UN undertook in 1956 to settle another problem by physical means, may have made some difference. The most that can be said about this indicator at present is close to simple assertion: Most students and observers of the UN system would probably judge that major national values are rendered slightly more compatible by constant exposure to each other in the UN system.

The second condition found to be essential was mutual responsiveness: mutual sympathy or loyalties, trust and consideration, at least some identification in terms of self-images and interests, and ability to predict behavior—a process of social learning.[25] Is there really much doubt that this

[25] Ibid., p. 129.

kind of learning goes on in the UN? Clearly the Organization serves as more than a magnifier of existing images, merely enhancing congruences and incongruities alike. It also helps to predict behavior. The perpetual attention to, communication of, and perception of needs are there, as is at least some identification in terms of self-images and interests. Constant communication is one of the advantages of parliamentary diplomacy most frequently celebrated.[26]

Even mutual sympathy or loyalties and probably increased consideration come out of the continuous friendly and unfriendly contact among representatives of governments at UN Headquarters.[27] But "trust" is a bigger word. This can develop on the individual level and also between certain governments, but in its full sense we cannot say that it is widespread. Yet we are not thinking of its full sense but only whether the existence of the UN causes any more trust or any more distrust among its Members than is already there. Nobody knows, but our own judgment is that a skeptical trust is fostered among those who are ideologically permitted such an adventure. Robert Osgood has pointed out that the Festinger principle of cognitive dissonance may have an application at the international level:

[26] Outside the formal agenda the General Assembly has become the world's greatest switchboard for bilateral diplomacy. . . . In New York last fall, in a period of 11 days, I conferred with the foreign ministers or heads of government of 54 nations.
(United States Secretary of State Dean Rusk, in Cordier and Foote, p. 74, referring to the fall of 1963.)
[27] "In many eyes, the personal relationships established at the UN have as much, if not greater, importance than the formal decisions which are reached." (John G. Hadwen and Johan Kaufmann, How United Nations Decisions Are Made [2nd rev. ed.; Dobbs Ferry, N.Y.: Oceana Publications, 1962], p. 58.)

When people are made to keep on behaving in ways that are inconsistent with their actual attitudes (e.g., as if they really trusted each other), their attitudes tend to shift into line with their behaviors. . . . [28]

There is also the only partially confirmed proposition arising from Chadwick Alger's close observation of General Assembly delegates to the effect that personal contacts with officials from other nations

> temper conflict with these officials, open new channels of communication with other nations, and keep them open when they might otherwise become closed.[29]

And how much permanent damage is avoided by depriving delegates of "opportunities for the solitary accumulation of anger"? [30]

The third condition found to be essential was

> a multiplicity of ranges of communication and transactions between the units involved, and also a fairly wide range of different functions and services, together with the organizations to carry them out.[31]

The same judgment applies to this criterion as to the one calling for mutual responsiveness. There seems little doubt that the operation of the far-flung UN system meets this condition even though these operations are

spread very thinly among the myriad contacts already flourishing outside that system—messages, face-to-face contacts, and especially trade. The operations are certainly pervasive.[32] But the question remains whether these are keeping up with the increasing number of participating people and units in the world. If not, the effect may be integrative but fail to be net integrative.

Of the eleven conditions that were found to be *helpful but not necessary* to integration, four are so irrelevant to the UN situation that they should be ignored.[33] Another is a nullity because neither it nor its opposite are taking place as a result of the UN system.[34] Space does not permit us more than to mention the other six. With regard to the two economic conditions,[35] the evidence is not conclusive. Another is military,[36] to the effect that for a considerable number of years war had to be "so unrespectable that it seemed fratricidal," a condition that we would judge to be closer to fulfillment because of the existence of the UN than it was before. The other three emphasize social communication of various forms.[37] Such evidence as we have, either through judgment about performance or through data such as Mr. Alger's,[38] gives the edge to the UN as making at least some net contribution toward integration.

---

[28] "Suggestions for Winning the Real War with Communism," *The Journal of Conflict Resolution,* December 1959 (Vol. 3, No. 4), p. 321.

[29] Chadwick F. Alger, "United Nations Participation as a Learning Process," *Public Opinion Quarterly,* Fall 1963 (Vol. 27, No. 3), p. 425.

[30] Hadwen and Kaufmann, p. 52. The crowded elevator described by the authors to make this point could be enlarged symbolically to include UN Headquarters as a whole.

[31] Deutsch and others, p. 144.

[32] "We must recognize that there is a United Nations angle, presently or prospectively, to every major subject of foreign policy." (United States Assistant Secretary of State Harlan Cleveland, in Francis O. Wilcox and H. Field Haviland, Jr. [ed.], *The United States and the United Nations* [Baltimore, Md.: The Johns Hopkins Press, 1961], p. 147.)

[33] Deutsch and others, pp. 133, 137, 139, 156.

[34] *Ibid.,* p. 158.

[35] *Ibid.,* pp. 141, 157.

[36] *Ibid.,* p. 155.

[37] *Ibid.,* pp. 148, 149, 151.

[38] Alger, *Public Opinion Quarterly,* Vol. 27, No. 3, especially pp. 422, 425.

To summarize, the most that can be said is that the UN system seems to promote some integrative conditions and to have an ambiguous effect on others.

Moving from indicators arising from the study of historical cases in limited geographical areas, we can ask what can be done with indicators arising from the study of a contemporary international organization performing a definite but limited function on an almost worldwide basis?

Those developed by Ernst Haas are of two kinds: (1) As to procedures, there should be a greater integrative effect as they move from minimum common denominator into accommodation by splitting the difference and still farther into upgrading the common interests of the parties. (2) If the result of the operations is increased autonomy, authority, or legitimacy for the organization, and especially legitimacy, there is an integrative effect.

Most decisions in the UN are doubtless of the "minimum common denominator" sort, with little compromise involved. These are found in many fields—gestures of condemnation against South Africa, the Kashmir dispute, a declaration of human rights in place of conventions, and the like. Most of these decisions are the ones that do not move from the corridors into the conference rooms because feelers have shown that an alternative has too little chance to survive. Compromise then takes the form of agreed inaction, sometimes quiet and sometimes noisy. Some of the noisy instances might be called the senatorial courtesy cases, where a matter that obviously concerns the UN is brought forward but laid aside after it is made clear that one Member would "take a walk" if pressed—the instances concerning Hyderabad, Goa, and Algeria, for example. Probably the greatest of these is the current constitutional crisis, where the will and wisdom to avoid confrontation on Article 19 have halted the General Assembly in its tracks. Even ILO, by far the most carefully studied agency in the UN system, usually operates on this basis of the minimum common denominator, according to Ernst Haas.[39]

There is ample evidence that the two more advanced procedures specified by Mr. Haas are also found frequently in the conduct of UN business. Compromising the final bargaining positions of Members is done each year when the budget tries to squeeze between the cutters and the spenders. It is also done in revising the scale of assessments and recently when the Committee of Experts on the Review of the Activities and Organization of the Secretariat revised the formula for geographical distribution of Secretariat members among the competing interests. The Secretary-General's mediation work, for example, the ground-breaking Beck-Friis mission to Cambodia and Thailand in 1959 and the mission to Laos later that year, might be considered in the third category, but to be conservative we can consider it here. The fact that these missions did not permanently solve the problems facing them (just as the mediation job in Cyprus has not yet succeeded) does not surprise those familiar with international politics or subtract much from the efficacy of such operations at the time. The "opting out" technique is an odd example of this procedure. By this we mean that the failure of certain members to buy UN bonds does not stop the sale of bonds to other Members, nor does the failure of some Members to pledge toward voluntarily supported programs such as the Expanded Program of Technical Assistance (EPTA) and the UN Children's Fund (UNICEF) veto those operations.

The third and most advanced procedure is naturally harder to identify

---

[39] Haas, *Beyond the Nation-State*, p. 445.

in the UN context, but two or three kinds of operations seem to involve upgrading the common interests of the parties. One is international military force authorized by a worldwide body, a "new world task" of recent times. Despite their distinctly different purposes, the UN Emergency Force (UNEF), the UN Operation in the Congo (ONUC), and the UN Peace-keeping Force in Cyprus (UNFICYP) are good examples. These are not simply the implementation of an existing will to peace, but a little bit more. Another kind of operation in this category is economic planning and execution on a multi-national scale, a task of large dimensions and poor co-ordination. Within the UN system the main agencies are the International Monetary Fund (IMF), the International Bank for Reconstruction and Development (IBRD) and its two affiliates, the other specialized agencies in the economic field, the Special Fund, EPTA, and the four regional economic commissions. Some of these operations mesh with each other, but that does not bring them very close to such regional non-UN organizations as the Inter-American Development Bank (IDB) of the Organization of American States (OAS) or the Development Assistance Committee (DAC) of the Organization for Economic Cooperation and Development (OECD). It is debatable whether the more successful these organizations become the more strongly they will give economic support to an existing political nationalism and hence have a disintegrative effect from the standpoint of the community as a whole. Yet they tend more and more to coordinate their efforts and at least some of them realize that not every country needs a steel mill.[40] It

is the national foreign aid programs that cater more to the desire for unwarranted self-sufficiency.

The personal factor may well be a strong catalyst leading toward an upgrading of common interests. One of Mr. Alger's conclusions was that "there is a remarkably extensive change being implemented in international society through the building of international organizations" [41] and that an

international organization such as the United Nations also permits the development of an international "interest group" that coalesces around a common desire to develop and strengthen the organization.[42]

We must not mistake this interest group for the whole international community, but even UN Headquarters is not an island. The delegations to the General Assembly normally include over a hundred members of parliaments, several hundred foreign office officials, and a number of high-status private citizens. It is undoubtedly true that both irritations and tolerations are renewed annually at the General Assembly, but we think most observers would agree that the latter outrun the former.

The "community of functional specialists," as Leon N. Lindberg calls it, is another kind of interest group which can be seen in some of the UN's activities. He analyzed the ministers of agriculture and other national officials in the agricultural sector of the Eu-

---

[40] Two recent publications of the UN illustrate this emphasis upon transnational approaches: *Possibilities of Integrated Industrial Development in Central America* (UN Document E/CN.12/683/Rev.1); and *The Economic Development of Latin America in the*

Post-War Period (UN Document E/CN.12/659/Rev.1). On the grand scale, the Mekong River program involves 25 countries within and outside the Economic Commission for Asia and the Far East (ECAFE) region plus twelve UN organs or units.

[41] Chadwick F. Alger, "Hypotheses on Relationships Between the Organization of International Society and International Order," *Proceedings of the American Society of International Law*, 57th annual meeting, Washington, D.C., April 25–27, 1963, p. 42.

[42] *Ibid.*, p. 45.

ropean Community.[43] The medical profession connected with the World Health Organization (WHO) also forms a transnational bond able to influence national policies through the ministries of health.

Turning to the factor of institutional autonomy mentioned by Mr. Haas, it may be noted first that the Secretary-General's authority has gone up and down.[44] Trygve Lie asserted more leadership than he is generally given credit for and achieved a considerable image of authority and autonomy before being turned upon by one of the major powers. Dag Hammarskjöld exhibited surefooted leadership, reaching a point where he was given political jobs to perform without specific instructions. This began with the United States flyers in Communist China (late 1954) and moved to the observation task in Lebanon (1958) and to the Congo operation in 1960. He went still further philosophically in his Oxford address shortly before his death.[45] It is doubtful that he would have been able to push that quite revolutionary stretching exercise, but his work may foreshadow a long-range trend in the direction of autonomy and authority if the Organization survives the present downdraft.

There is little doubt about the favorable effect of IBRD representatives and field missions in creating respect for the Bank, but the reluctance of staff members to advertise their connection with the UN makes it likely that no more than the outer rim of the Bank's halo touches the UN system as a whole. The halo seems to be stretching, however, as the Bank's new President brings the Bank closer to the UN and the other specialized agencies. Evidence of the influence of UN Resident Representatives is not scarce but has never been fully analyzed. As of 1964, their increasing utility has been noted, save in the task of country programming.[46] The impact of these 83 offices headed by either a Resident Representative or a Deputy, all engaged in economic and social activities of interest to the local population, varies from country to country and from situation to situation, but it is unknown in terms of their authority-building function. The same is true for Directors of UN Information Centers and indeed for the effect of the entire UN information program. However, in Gerard Mangone's judgment "all evidence seems to point to a proliferation of the responsibilities of the Resident Representative" and

the patterns of United Nations activities over the next decades . . . will shift from temporary, sporadic, and voluntary programs to permanent, continuous, and regular operations.[47]

Other on-the-spot contacts with representatives of UN functions at present, such as International Atomic En-

[40] "Decision Making and Integration in the European Community," *International Organization,* Winter 1965 (Vol. 19, No. 1), especially pp. 71–73; see also his interesting observations on penetration into national administrative structures (*ibid.,* pp. 73–74).

[44] See Charles Winchmore, "The Secretariat: Retrospect and Prospect," in Padelford & Goodrich (eds.), *The United Nations in the Balance* [New York: Praeger, 1965], pp. 258–275.

[45] He stated his belief that the Secretary-General could "resolve controversial questions on a truly international basis without obtaining the formal decision of the organs . . . ," since the

principles of the Charter are . . . supplemented by the body of legal doctrine and precepts that have been accepted by States generally, and particularly as manifested in the resolutions of UN organs.

(*The International Civil Servant in Law and in Fact* [Oxford: Clarendon Press, 1961], pp. 24–25.)

[46] Gerard J. Mangone, *The United Nations Resident Representative: A Case of Administrative Institution-Building* (unpublished paper, 1964), pp. 27, 79.

[47] *Ibid.,* p. 97.

ergy Agency (IAEA) inspectors and technical assistance experts of various kinds, plebiscite administrators, truce observers, officials of the program for the provision of Operational, Executive and Administrative Personnel (OPEX), and, in the future, arms control inspectors and outer space monitors cannot be judged to be integrative, disintegrative, or simply nonintegrative without closer study than anyone has yet given them.

The distinction Ernst Haas makes between authority and legitimacy is an important one from the standpoint of creating a real security-community,[48] yet one of these includes the other. It would be hard to imagine legitimacy without authority, but authority without legitimacy is commonplace.[49] If research could follow the suggestion Mr. Haas makes, we could learn something significant about integrative progress. He proposes that

> a rough measure of legitimacy can be provided by distilling from the historical material the situations in which member states invoke the purposes and principles of the UN to justify some item of national policy, such invocation being at the same time accompanied by an expansion of the global task.[50]

This index would be rough indeed, but if it sidestepped the trap of false cause-and-effect, it would be worth making.

Citing UN principles might be more of a justification than a true motive for something which a Member government wanted to do, seeking legitimation from the UN in the same way that battling troops seek the legitimation of God for their cause. Yet the mere fact that the blessing is sought would tend to build up the legitimacy of the blesser.

To our mind, the international military forces that have been authorized by the UN for various kinds of peacekeeping purposes would be prime subjects of study. Next best would be three prospective new tasks: governing atomic energy for peaceful international use, controlling the uses of outer space by whatever means are invented, and controlling military arms by focusing on inspection.

We could speculate at length about the effect that contact with the operations of the UN has upon Member States' attitudes toward the authority or legitimacy of the system. What might be called empirical speculation is more reliable:

> Central organizations themselves, although limited in ability to make authoritative decisions, may play crucial roles in building . . . a social structure by the learning experiences they provide for those playing organizational roles, and by the new linkages they provide between formerly isolated roles in individual units.[51]

This is exemplified by the change that occurs in Senators and Congressmen who serve a session on the United States delegation to the General Assembly, as observed by Francis O. Wilcox when he was on Capitol Hill and later when he was United States Assistant Secretary of State. Legislators, returning with greater knowledge,

[48] Legitimacy provides a presumption of "repetition or expansion of peaceful change procedures . . . ," whereas mere authority does not. (Hass, *Beyond the Nation-State*, p. 133.)

[49] For example, one would suppose that the UN Truce Supervision Organization (UNTSO) is a good case of at least some authority without legitimacy at present, asking again an old question: "What is the consensus-forming effect, not simply the immediate agreement-reaching effect, of the United Nations' mixed commissions in Palestine?" (Van Wagenen, p. 44.)

[50] Haas, *Beyond the Nation-State*, p. 133.

[51] Alger, *Public Opinion Quarterly*, Vol. 27, No. 3, p. 426.

were not transformed but were in every case changed in a direction more favorable to the UN. In committee discussions and elsewhere they enjoyed deference when UN matters came up; this helped to generate in them an especially responsible attitude toward the Organization and in turn either took the edge off prior hostile attitudes or sharpened already favorable ones.

The Escalation of Community

The conclusions are more suggestive than conclusive in response to our opening questions: Is there any sign of "community building"? Is there any secular trend slanting upward or downward? Does the UN itself have anything positive to do with that trend? While the UN undoubtedly does some disintegrative and many nonintegrative things, it also does many apparently integrative things in integrative ways. It is not too exuberant to say that the net direction seems to be integrative, tending toward the eventual building of a security-community broader than we have today.

There is no way to be sure of a security-community before time has delivered the pragmatic test. Yet it is likely that the work of the UN system and the personal contact which that work entails will help to grow more of what we have been calling pluralistic security-communities where they do not yet exist.[52] This conclusion, however, evades a crucial question: Is it more dangerous to have fewer and tighter communities on a less-than-global level than to leave things as they are? Also, we cannot forget that if evidence of a trend toward integration appears on the international political scene it is impossible to estimate how much credit is due to the UN system.

How can the integrative work of

the UN be strengthened? Activities should be undertaken which build muscle without the danger of hernia. These are activities that lead to the expansion of tasks that are successfully handled and that appear to increase the authority and later the legitimacy of the UN system.

In practical terms, this means that within the margins of maneuver open to Members the UN should be given jobs to do which (1) are conspicuously related to the UN, (2) have a good chance of success in a technical or administrative sense, (3) involve the lives of many influential people in several significant Member States, and (4) bring tangible rewards to Members, if possible including the prevention of expensive wars.

This simple formulation may seem self-evident enough in logic and unattainable enough in practice to invite concrete illustration. The most convincing examples are the normal activities of the specialized agencies, which are at present by no means conspicuous enough.[53] Greater use of the International Court of Justice would be helpful in cases where advisory opinions are certain to be accepted and where decisions are most likely to be executed. The field of human rights also offers an opportunity that may have been underrated.[54] Further practice is recommended in forming UN peacekeeping operations where they have a fair chance of being conspicuously successful in the eyes of many Members of the UN. Proposals for designating national contingents and for drafting logistical head starts and other plans are in this realm and have already begun. A greater use of UN

[52] Perhaps in Central America, parts of the Indian subcontinent and Southeast Asia, or some of the Arab states, for example.

[53] As with the reporting of public affairs at any level, the monotony of the unexciting brings about the monopoly of the exciting.

[54] See especially, Percy E. Corbett, *The Individual and World Society* (Princeton, N.J.: Center for Research on World Political Institutions, 1953), pp. 47–59; and Gardner, Chapter 10.

observers is also indicated. Arms control and outer space lie before us. The bed of the sea in some parts of the world is pregnant with resources and awaits community action to prevent fighting over their ownership. Indeed, the subtle "side effects" coming out of *any* operation bear close watching.

This brief inquiry into the concept of community has not shown us what it means to the future of the UN, but it may have given us a better idea of how to investigate over the next twenty years. We started with three choices of approach: to apply informed judgment to known facts, to use informed judgment in applying to known facts the findings that come from research in different contexts at the international level, or to develop and apply a framework for studying the integrative func-

tion of the UN system specifically. After a dip into the second, we recommend the first and the third.

The first is constantly employed; it is of course the best we currently have as a guide to national foreign policy in the UN. The reviews of UN experience brought out earlier in this volume are first-class testimony that educated insight and common sense have not been unhorsed. But it is time for someone brave enough to attack through the third approach—a colossal job. There is a good chance that

. . . the dry bones littered by the way
May still point giants toward their
    golden prey.[55]

[55] Stephen Vincent Benét, *John Brown's Body* (New York: Holt, Rinehart and Winston, 1941), Invocation.

24. The UN Regional Economic Commissions and Integration in the Underdeveloped Regions*

ROBERT W. GREGG

It is the purpose of this article to examine the role which the three regional economic commissions of the United Nations serving the developing world [1] play, whether consciously or unconsciously, in promoting integration within the regions which they serve. The emphasis is upon economic integration, not because it is more important than political union or federation or because it is a necessary antecedent to political integration. No attempt is made here to establish the thesis that

the relationship between economic and political integration is that of a continuum.[2] Any contribution which the UN regional economic commissions make to regional or subregional integration will almost certainly be in the economic area, given their terms of reference, the nature of their work programs, and the environmental conditions in which they operate. Economic integration resulting from ideas and initiatives originating in the re-

* *International Organization*, Vol. XX, No. 2, 208–232. Reprinted by permission.
[1] The Economic Commission for Latin America (ECLA), the Economic Commission for Asia and the Far East (ECAFE), and the Economic Commission for Africa (ECA).

[2] For a recent discussion of this relationship see Ernst B. Haas and Philippe C. Schmitter, "Economics and Differential Patterns of Political Integration: Projections About Unity in Latin America," *International Organization*, Autumn 1964 (Vol. 18, No. 4), pp. 705–737.

gional commissions *may* contribute to the evolution of political union.

In this context integration may be defined as the transformation of an international subsystem in a direction in which more weight is accorded to decisions and actions in the name of the aggregate of actors. In other words, the nation-state ceases to be an autonomous decision-making unit with respect to certain important policies; the locus of economic problem solving is to some extent shifted from the state to an intergovernmental or supranational body.[3]

The role of the regional economic commission in this process is difficult to assess. It is only one of several agents which may inspire integrative experiments; what it promotes could often more accurately be described as cooperation, which is clearly a much more modest relationship than integration. However, if the commission has a thrust which is regional in scope and emphasis and if it contributes to a way of thinking about economic problems which permits and encourages the delegation of more authority to some new and larger center, then the commission may be said to have an integrative output.

The UN Setting

Article 68 of the United Nations Charter provides for the creation of commissions under the aegis of the Economic and Social Council (ECO SOC) and suggests functional criteria for their establishment. The legislative history of the Charter reveals little interest in spatially as opposed to functionally defined institutions in the economic field.[4] However, it was not long after San Francisco that the UN embarked upon a policy of regionalization in the economic sphere, a step neither invited nor precluded by the Charter. The rationale for the creation of the first commission, the Economic Commission for Europe, was postwar reconstruction. In an early instance of UN coalition politics, however, the Asian and Latin American states engaged in some effective logrolling which led to the creation of commissions for each of those regions over the opposition of Western European and North American Members.[5] Thus, by March of 1948 the UN had created three regional economic commissions,[6] had laid the foundation for honoring the claims of other regions,[7] and had broadened the mission of these commissions from reconstruction to economic development.

[3] This definition is adapted from that employed by Haas, which focuses on political integration. See, for example, Ernst B. Haas, "International Integration: The European and the Universal Process," *International Organization*, Summer 1961 (Vol. 15, No. 3), pp. 366–367. See also the related definition, also derived from Haas, employed by Jean Siotis: *"Integration occurs when consensus formation tends to become the dominant characteristic of relations among actors in a system."* (Jean Siotis, "The Secretariat of the United Nations Economic Commission for Europe and European Economic Integration: The First Ten Years," *International Organization,* Spring 1965 [Vol. 19, No. 2], p. 178.)

[4] The question is probed in a recent book by Robert W. Macdonald, *The League of Arab States* (Princeton, N.J.: Princeton University Press, 1965), Chapter 1.

[5] For a description of debates and bargaining which led to the creation of ECE, ECAFE, and ECLA, see David Wightman, *Toward Economic Cooperation in Asia: The United Nations Economic Commission for Asia and the Far East* (New Haven, Conn.: Yale University Press, 1963), Chapter 2.

[6] ECE was established under ECOSOC Resolution 36 (IV) of March 28, 1947; ECAFE under ECOSOC Resolution 37 (IV) of March 28, 1947; and ECLA under ECOSOC Resolution 106 (VI) of February 25, 1948.

[7] The Economic Commission for Africa was established under ECOSOC Resolution 671 A and B (XXV) of April 29, 1958. Establishment of a commission for the Middle East has been considered and would almost certainly have been accomplished were it not for the enduring schism between the Arab states and Israel.

In effect, the regional economic commissions, while subsidiary organs of a universal international organization, are in a very real sense regional organizations with all that that fact implies with respect to relative environmental homogeneity. What is more, they are not regional replicas of the parent organization. They are more limited in purpose, embracing the economic and social tasks of the United Nations but not, in any direct fashion, its tasks in the fields of peace and security, self-determination, or human rights. Whereas the UN itself has been characterized by several historic phases,[8] a manifestation of environmental instability which has militated against integrative precedents, the regional commissions have been buffeted much less directly and obviously by the shifting winds of cold-war and colonial conflict. Although the commissions have not been guaranteed an integrative impact by their locations in the sheltered coves of relatively greater environmental stability, the absence of environmental phases, coupled with the exclusively economic and social content of their terms of reference, has facilitated comparatively stable agreement within the commissions on the tasks which are to receive primary attention.

Furthermore, the commissions enjoy a considerable amount of institutional independence from the parent organization. It is true that in a formal sense they are very much an integral part of the United Nations. Their budgets are a part of the UN budget; their staffs are part of the staff of the UN's Department of Economic and Social Affairs, subject to the same rules and regulations; their Executive Secretaries are selected by the Secretary-General. Their terms of reference, which are quite modest in scope, specify that they shall act within the framework of UN policies and under the general supervision of the Economic and Social Council.[9] But these limitations are deceptive. In practice the commissions have more discretion than their terms of reference suggest and consequently more capacity for taking initiatives, independently of New York, appropriate to the needs of the region. This independence should not be exaggerated. But it is an important fact, one which makes it possible to speak of the commissions as agencies which may have an ideology and a thrust of their own, shaped to some extent by their UN connection but not so inhibited by it as to deny them a distinct influence upon the regions they serve.

Although each commission has developed its own distinctive style and carved out its own areas of emphasis, all have experienced an expansion of tasks and a gradual strengthening of their positions within their respective regions. This shifting role was the theme of some remarks by Philippe de Seynes, Under Secretary for Economic and Social Affairs, which are quite revealing of the gulf between the thinking of headquarters and that of the regional centers.

So far as the regional commissions are concerned, we were more or less dominated, over a long period, by a way of thinking which doubtless originated in a desire to simplify and clarify matters. According to that way of thinking, the regional eco-

---

[8] For a discussion of these historic phases see Ernst B. Haas, "Dynamic Environment and Static System: Revolutionary Regimes in the United Nations," in Morton Kaplan (ed.), *The Revolution in World Politics* (New York: John Wiley & Sons, 1962), pp. 267-309.

[9] Their terms of reference may be found in annexes to the annual reports of the commissions to ECOSOC. For recently amended versions, see Economic and Social Council *Official Records* (37th session), Supplement No. 2, Annex III (ECAFE); Supplement No. 4, Annex III (ECLA); Supplement No. 7, Annex II (ECE); and Supplement No. 10, Annex III (ECA).

nomic commissions were organs which should devote themselves to research and study and which should be barred from what are termed operational activities.[10]

Intergovernmental study groups, serviced by secretariats performing research and conference machinery functions, would almost certainly not have been in a position to make much of an impact upon their regions. But the commissions, in every case but to varying degrees, have exceeded this minimalist level of involvement in the affairs of their respective regions. There are several explanations for their strength,[11] but in essence ECLA, ECAFE, and ECA have grown and assumed more importance both within the UN system and within their respective regions because they are a product of that system and perform an essential function within it.

This phenomenon is attributable to the environmental changes which have transformed the international system since the Korean War and the comparatively stark bipolarity of the UN's early years. The tacit agreement to encapsulate[12] the more destructive levels of cold-war conflict; the pronounced increase in the number of independent underdeveloped states; the emergence of a crude UN party system which is, to a very considerable extent, a multi-regional system; the evolution to paramountcy of the economic tasks on the UN's long agenda; the resultant increase in opportunities for bargaining among the UN's "parties"—all of these interrelated factors have contributed to the strengthening of the regional economic commissions. The recent campaign to decentralize authority for some UN economic and social programs from Headquarters to the regional commissions may be viewed as a natural culmination of these changes in the environment within which the UN system functions.[13] Regional groups have quite naturally tended to upgrade in importance those UN structures which are most conspicuously their own, whose secretariats have consciously been given a regional coloration, whose announced purposes correspond most closely with their own perceptions of the UN's most important tasks. The commissions have not only acquired a symbolic importance; they have also become vehicles whereby claims of developing states upon the UN could be articulated with the assistance of a professional secretariat attuned to the interests of the region. They are peculiarly agencies for action of the region, by the region, and for the region.

The Regional Setting

What each of the regional economic commissions has sought to accomplish and what it has achieved have been conditioned in large measure by the regional context in which it has had to work. Is there a tradition of thinking

---

[10] UN Document E/CN.12/572, March 5, 1961, pp. 1–2.

[11] One UN official, a long-time observer of the commissions, attributes it to the inclusive character of their membership within their respective regions; their tendency to act by agreement rather than by voting; a self-imposed discipline which induces them to behave in accordance with Charter principles and Assembly and ECOSOC resolutions; and a marked degree of regional consciousness and solidarity. See W. R. Malinowski, "Centralization and Decentralization in the United Nations Economic and Social Activities," *International Organization,* Summer 1962 (Vol. 16, No. 3), pp. 523–524.

[12] The term is Amitai Etzioni's. See his article "On Self-Encapsulating Conflicts," *Journal of Conflict Resolution,* September 1964 (Vol. 8, No. 3), pp. 242–255.

[13] For a more detailed discussion of decentralization, see the author's chapter "Program Decentralization and the Regional Economic Commissions" in a forthcoming book under the general editorship of Gerard J. Mangone to be published in 1966 by Columbia University Press.

about the region as a unit? Is the geographical scope of the region natural or artificial? What are the economic, social, and political conditions which prevail within the region? To what extent is it characterized by industrialization and economic diversification? How much functional similarity exists among units? What conditions prevail with repect to such variables as elite complementarity? All of these considerations enter into any assessment of the prospects for integration.[14]

The Economic Commission for Europe, for example, is distinguishable from the other commissions in that it serves a region which, for all the vicissitudes of European interstate relations, has traditionally been described as a community. As Jean Siotis has noted in a recent and perceptive essay on the role of ECE,[15] the central task for the Commission has been to prevent the disintegration of Europe into two implacably hostile and self-contained regions. The main element in the organizational ideology of the first Executive Secretary, Gunnar Myrdal, was his belief that ECE should be used as a bridge of functional cooperation between East and West, and that it should strenuously resist all efforts to institutionalize within ECE the rift between the two blocs. The Secretariat's problem was to find specific tasks which could fan the flickering flame of "Europe." The other three regional commissions, which are the primary concern of this article, have had a somewhat different problem. Fragmentation has, of course, accompanied decolonization, especially in Africa; but a sense of community had

[14] Conditions conducive to integration are discussed, *inter alia,* in Haas and Schmitter, *International Organization,* Vol. 18, No. 4, pp. 705–737; Haas, *International Organization,* Vol. 15, No. 3, pp. 366–392; and the recent book by Haas, *Beyond the Nation-State: Functionalism and International Organization* (Stanford, Calif.: Stanford University Press, 1964).

[15] Siotis, *International Organization,* Vol. 19, No. 2, pp. 177–202.

not been a characteristic of these areas, and so a principal task of the commissions has been to assist in the creation of such a sense of community, rather than to prevent the collapse of a previously existing one.

Moreover, these regions, quite aside from their lack of historical cohesiveness, are to varying degrees artificial in the geographic sense. Much the most arbitrary of the regions is Asia and the Far East. ECAFE's domain extends from Iran to Western Samoa and from Mongolia to New Zealand; Saudi Arabia and Israel have recently requested membership. Surely this is a single region in name only, appropriate perhaps for an administrative subdivision of the UN but not as a candidate for economic or political integration. The Economic Commission for Africa serves a region which looks more logical on the map but which is really an amalgamation of several regions, including the very dissimilar areas separated by the vast expanse of the Sahara. ECLA's domain, extending from the Rio Grande and the Straits of Florida to Tierra del Fuego, is also geographically arbitrary, a fact recognized by the division of the area into two subregions, with a main office in Santiago and a subregional office for Central America in Mexico City.

More significant than either the absence of a regional tradition or the presence of unwieldy regional boundaries are the economic, social, and political conditions prevailing in each region. The environmental conditions necessary for political integration are more exacting than those for economic union, but there would appear to be a relationship between successful economic integration and such factors, identified by Ernst Haas, as comparability of unit size and power and of pluralism plus elite complementarity and the rate of transaction among units. If recent experiences with integration yield any lesson, it is that urban-industrial societies with a relatively high level of economic diversification are better candidates for more rapid progress toward union than are underdeveloped, monocultural societies. Ironically, the integration movements in Europe, where optimal environmental conditions exist, are probably an important factor in spurring experimentation with economic unions in areas which otherwise fail to meet some of the criteria for integration. In spite of this incentive and that supplied by a shared state of underdevelopment and discouragingly slow progress toward overcoming it, the regions served by ECLA, ECAFE, and ECA do not present a profile conducive to economic union or even to very elaborately institutionalized co-operation. Some subregional clusters of states may constitute more promising laboratories for integration, but all are defective on one or more important counts. Although any generalization is differentially applicable among the regions, it is safe to state that the great majority of states within all three regions tend to be economically dependent upon a very few primary commodities and to trade predominantly with states outside the region.[16]

The Regional Economic Commissions

The environmental setting in which each of the three regional commissions exists would appear to be unpromising for economic, much less political, integration. This does not mean, however, that the commissions have not engaged in activities or promoted policies which may be described as integrative. It is

the function of the following analysis to identify the integrative output of ECLA, ECAFE, and ECA.[17]

Integrative output of a regional commission is shaped, to a very considerable extent, by the political and economic forces which operate upon that commission. Governments bring to the regional commissions different perceptions of national interest and different attitudes toward institutionalized forms of regional cooperation. Although a commission may pursue policies at variance with the preferences of some of its members, the integrative output of a commission is not likely to be significantly greater than the receptivity to integration of the commission's members. Integrative output is thus a product of national policy inputs, adapted by the commission with the vital assistance of an international secretariat which can articulate nascent interest in the idea of integration, synthesize diverse policies and proposals with an integrative content, and otherwise supply creative leadership. The focus here is primarily upon what the commissions, and more particularly their secretariats, do rather than on the policy inputs of member governments.

Several questions may be asked in order to facilitate judgment of the integrative output of the regional economic commissions.

(1) What has been the ideology of the leadership of the regional commission? Has it been significantly oriented toward economic problem solving at a level higher than that of the nation-state?

(2) What has been the degree of initiative assumed by the commission secretariat for skewing the work program of the commission in a regional direction?

[16] For statistical data on these and other indicators, see Bruce Russett and others, *World Handbook of Political and Social Indicators* (New Haven, Conn.: Yale University Press, 1964). For useful classification schemes, see Gabriel Almond and James S. Coleman, *The Politics of the Developing Areas* (Princeton, N.J.: Princeton University Press, 1960). For data on trade, see, *inter alia,* Robert M. Stern, "Policies for Trade and Development," *International Conciliation,* May 1964 (No. 548), and the sources cited therein.

[17] Many of the judgments made in the following sections are based upon interviews with UN Secretariat personnel at Headquarters and in the regional offices of ECLA in Santiago and Mexico City, ECAFE in Bangkok, and ECA in Addis Ababa.

(3) What has been the institutional legacy of the commission's activities? Is there a residue of organizations or programs with regional or subregional outlook which are thriving?

(4) What has been the flow of regionally minded commission secretariat personnel into positions of influence within individual states and especially into government posts with planning responsibilities?

(5) What has been the centripetal pull of the commission itself as a source of regional pride and purpose? Is there evidence of growth of respect for the commission secretariat as a kind of intellectual lodestone for the region?

The terms of reference of none of the regional economic commissions speak specifically of integration of the whole or of portions of their regions as one of their purposes, much less their paramount purpose. However, there is ample latitude for such an interpretation in authorizations to study regional economic and technical problems, to initiate measures for facilitating regional economic and social development, and to help formulate policies as a basis for practical action in promoting country and regional development. The problem is not whether the commission may or should be used as a fulcrum for transferring expectations for growth and development from the state to some larger unit; it is whether such an effort has been made or whether that has been the net result of activities undertaken by the commission.

It is very difficult to identify that component of the work of a regional economic commission which has a regional as opposed to a country orientation. There is very little to be gained by an attempt to factor out of the work program those activities which are concerned with the region as a whole or with some subregional grouping of states. Virtually all of the work carried on by a regional secretariat *may* be infused with the imperative of region-

alization or, conversely, none of it. What matters is not the frequency of such phrases as "regional programs of cooperation" or "development on a subregional or regional basis," phrases liberally sprinkled through descriptions of commission projects, but the extent to which the appearance of an integrative mission is supported by the appropriate mix of project significance and timeliness, the commitment of the secretariat, mutual reinforcement of various elements of the commission program, and governmental receptivity (or at least absence of active hostility).

ECLA

Of the three regional economic commissions serving the developing world, the Economic Commission for Latin America has made the most sustained and conscious effort to achieve a manner of thinking about economic problems of individual countries which would result in a shift of emphasis from decision making by and for the state to decision making by a collectivity of states for the economic benefit of the whole as well as each of the parts.

In part this is surely the consequence of a combination of environmental factors which produce a net political input more receptive to integration. There is the frequently cited evidence of comparatively greater cultural homogeneity; there is the fact of a much longer postcolonial history; there is statistical proof of a higher mean gross national product (GNP) per capita;[18] there is the history of common concern for the economic and geopolitical reality of the hemispheric hegemony of the United States; there is the relative absence of intraregional quarrels and of regional diversions from the task of economic growth and development. This does not mean that economic and political differences do not exist and are not reflected within ECLA. The United

[18] See Russett, especially Table 44, pp. 155–157, and Table B.2, pp. 294–298.

States has frequently been a dissenting member, taking exception to economic theories which have permeated Commission discussions and actions and occasionally placing a strain upon relationships among the Commission's Latin American members. The Cuban revolution has introduced a new ideological dimension into Commission debates.[19] There have been policy differences arising from different perceptions of advantage and disadvantage in specific ECLA program proposals. The case of Venezuelan reluctance to join the Latin American Free Trade Association (LAFTA) is a well-known example, one which conditioned ECLA's recommendations on the subject.[20]

But it has been the Secretariat of ECLA which has attracted the most attention and made the most conspicuous contributions to integration in Latin America. As Albert Hirschman remarks,

> The arresting feature of ECLA is that it possesses attributes not frequently encountered in large international organisations: a cohesive personality which evokes loyalty from the staff, and a set of distinctive beliefs, principles, and attitudes, in brief an ideology, which is highly influential among Latin American intellectuals and policymakers.[21]

ECLA's long-time Executive Secretary, Dr. Raúl Prebisch, supplied the ideology which infused the Secretariat with a sense of purpose and gave the Commission its sense of direction. There are many who will take issue with Dr. Prebisch's economics but none who will dispute the contention that his views have had an impact in Latin America, and indeed beyond that region.

The essence of the Prebisch-ECLA position has been that the economic difficulties of the developing countries are attributable to the prolonged and continuing deterioration in their terms of trade. To remedy this condition and overcome dependence of the periphery (developing states) upon the center (developed states), industrialization via the mechanism of a preferential regional market is proposed. To avoid a situation in which some states within Latin America would benefit from such a market at the expense of others, ECLA has promoted a doctrine of regionally balanced economic growth, with formulas for reciprocity and complementarity "to assure that everybody would be cut in on the deal, that nobody would gain disproportionately." [22]

The institutional embodiments of this philosophy and some of its subthemes are the Central American Economic Integration Program, the Latin American Free Trade Association,[23]

[19] Note that the Cuban application for membership in the Latin American Free Trade Association (LAFTA) was rejected. See Sidney Dell, *Trade Blocs and Common Markets* (New York: Alfred A. Knopf, 1963), p. 265.

[20] See the September 1960 statement of the Bank of Venezuela:

> Any common market or free trade area will leave us producing nothing but petroleum and iron ore, and importing everything else. Our textiles cannot compete with Brazilian textiles, our coffee cannot compete with Colombian coffee and our meat cannot compete with Uruguayan meat. For us a free trade area is utopian at the present time.

(Quoted in Dell, p. 274.)

[21] Albert O. Hirschman, "Ideologies of Economic Development in Latin America," in

Albert O. Hirschman (ed.), *Latin American Issues: Essays and Comments* (New York: Twentieth Century Fund, 1961), p. 13.

[22] Haas and Schmitter, *International Organization*, Vol. 18, No. 4, p. 730. For a recent, definitive statement of the ECLA-Prebisch theses see *Towards a Dynamic Development Policy for Latin America* (UN Document E/CVN.12/680/Rev.1), December 1963.

[23] The Central American Agreements embrace Costa Rica, El Salvador, Guatemala, Honduras, and Nicaragua. LAFTA includes Argentina, Brazil, Chile, Colombia, Ecuador, Mexico, Paraguay, Peru, and Uruguay. For a recent study of LAFTA, including the role of ECLA in its creation, see Miguel S. Wionczek, "Latin American Free Trade Association," *In-*

and, in a somewhat different sense, the United Nations Conference on Trade and Development (UNCTAD). ECLA-sponsored studies and negotiations, fed by ECLA research, led directly to the creation of the two subregional associations in Latin America. It is interesting to note that ECLA, alone of the four regional commissions, has not established an elaborate substructure of committees and other standing subsidiary bodies for its various fields of work. The only two exceptions are a Central American Economic Cooperation Committee and a Trade Committee, and it is no accident that the former played a key role in the evolution of the General Treaty on Central American Economic Integration (and its predecessors, the Agreement on Central American Integration Industries and the Multilateral Treaty on Central American Free Trade and Economic Integration) and that the latter performed a similar function with respect to the Treaty of Montevideo creating LAFTA.

This is not the place to evaluate either the Central American Economic Integration Program or LAFTA. Either or both may stagnate in the face of conditions which do not appear to be optimal for economic integration, much less politization. Haas argues that LAFTA in particular must experience a "creative crisis" and be blessed with the dynamic leadership of a reformmonger if this now weak and to a considerable extent untested economic union is to develop in the direction of political union.[24] However, the important point to be made in the context of this article is that while LAFTA and the Central American Agreements have now assumed the burden of serving as vehicles for integration, it is ECLA which played the catalytic role,

launching both experiments. Moreover, it has the continuing task of supplying creative leadership, indirectly through the force of ideas or directly through ECLA-trained personnel, with which to meet challenges requiring adaptation. The ECLA Secretariat has already displayed some aptitude for creative adaptation. As Hirschman notes, ECLA "has transferred the principal center of its activity from one area to another as it ran into difficulty or decreasing returns,"[25] but it has managed to do so without sacrifice of identity of its personality. The Commission, for example, spent a number of years urging upon Latin American governments the detailed programming of economic development; the shift to common market studies reflected, in part, frustration with the limited impact of its programming activity.

It may be that the Commission has been guilty on occasion of a utopian cast of mind or, conversely, that it has had more prosaic purposes than integration in mind, as Sidney Dell alleges with his observation that LAFTA was in part the product of a desire to observe General Agreement on Tariffs and Trade (GATT) ... st... achieve economic inte... s, pri... either case, ECLA has nonetheless contributed as has no other agency to a reexamination of economic, and hence political, relationships within and among Latin American states. As one observer remarks, Prebisch has been a "creator of enthusiasms and a destroyer of illusions."[27] He has made ECLA a force to be reckoned with in the western hemisphere. When policy decisions affecting economic development, industrialization, and trade are pending within a state, the outcome is likely to be affected by the Cassandra-like warnings of ECLA's annual reports, by the recommendations of one

---

ternational Conciliation, January 1965 (No. 551).

[24] Haas and Schmitter, *International Organization,* Vol. 18, No. 4, pp. 732 ff.

[25] Hirschman, p. 20.

[26] Dell, p. 264.

[27] Roberto de Oliveira Campos, quoted in Hirschman, p. 27.

of ECLA's economic development advisory groups, or by the very existence of an ECLA-fostered free trade machinery. Moreover, such decisions may be influenced by the presence within the government of economists who have held prominent positions on the ECLA staff.[28] More than in any of the other regions there is a significant flow of senior officials between the Commission Secretariat and the governments of member states.

Several years ago, one observer credited Prebisch with the feat of making ECLA into a kind of responsible political opposition in Latin America.[29] It is submitted that ECLA even has one foot in the government in some states. However, as Haas points out, the *técnicos* have an uneven influence throughout Latin America; his observation that they might be able to exert considerable influence in a number of the more advanced countries of the region "*if* their lines of rapport with major political groups were stable"[30] is illustrated by the exile of one of ECLA's more prominent "exports," Celso Furtado, from Brazil.

In spite of the recognized expertise in the ECLA Secretariat and the presence of ex-ECLA personnel in many governments, several UN officials have remarked that ECLA's impact is weakened by the preoccupation of its Secretariat with economic theory. Thus it has been alleged that ECLA underestimates the problems of negotiability; phrased another way, ECLA has been

accused of a reluctance to get its hands dirty with operational complexities. As one UN official observed, the ECLA Secretariat is probably the only agency in Latin America that could find the common denominators for implementing economic integration programs but does not possess the bent of mind necessary to do so.

In respects other than ideology, its translation into a work program with institutional results, and the interchange of senior economists, the Economic Commission for Latin America has not performed in a manner conspicuously different from that of ECAFE or ECA. What has distinguished ECLA's activities is that the integrationist ideology permeates the otherwise routine research and advisory services. For example, as a result of ECLA initiatives an Institute for Economic and Social Planning was established with UN Special Fund and Inter-American Development Bank (IDB) support in Santiago; Dr. Prebisch became the Institute's first Director General, and this prospectively influential training organ proceeded to assume responsibility for advisory groups which ECLA had pioneered, for the important economic development training program, and for research with respect to planning. The curriculum will not necessarily produce integrationists; but the close historical, physical, and personal links with ECLA suggest that the Institute may become an important training ground for regionally minded economists. Similar institutes have been created in Bangkok for Asia and the Far East and in Dakar for Africa, but while these bodies may relieve the regional economic commissions in those areas of in-service training responsibilities, the possibility is remote that they will in the near future serve as incubators for integrationists.

One final observation should be made concerning the political role of the Economic Commission for Latin

[28] Among the more prominent have been Victor L. Urquidi and Carlos Quintana in Mexico, Celso Furtado in Brazil, José A. Mayobre (now Executive Secretary of ECLA) in Venezuela, Hugo Trivelli in Chile, and Regino Boti in Cuba. Similarly, upon Juan Perón's overthrow, the government of Argentina requested Prebisch to make an economic survey of that country, his own.

[29] Andrew Shonfield, *The Attack on World Poverty* (New York: Random House, 1962), p. 49.

[30] Haas and Schmitter, *International Organization*, Vol. 18, No. 4, p. 731.

America. The recurrent conflict between the UN and the Organization of American States (OAS) in the peaceful settlement and enforcement fields[31] has had an interesting corollary in the competition between ECLA and the Inter-American Economic and Social Council (IA-ECOSOC) of the OAS. Although the Alliance for Progress has fostered formal structures for bringing activities of the two organizations into harmonious relationship,[32] the resultant coordination has been superficial and ECLA and IA-ECOSOC remain distinct and competing entities. It is not an exaggeration to state that the prestige within the region enjoyed by ECLA, an organization in which the United States has usually been a minor and dissenting participant, has been enhanced by the fact that the OAS is widely viewed as a United States-dominated institution. Regional pride in ECLA and a disposition to listen when ECLA prescribes for the region's ills may be inversely related to regional acceptance of the OAS machinery.

ECAFE

If the number of experiments in regional and subregional organization is any yardstick, Asia promises least progress of any of the developing regions toward economic, much less political, union. Reasons for Asian separatism are not hard to find. The litany of obstacles to cooperation has been cited many times: the region's geographic dispersion; its religious, cultural, and linguistic diversity; its deep political cleavages; the vast disparity in unit size. It is within this milieu that ECAFE operates.

Functional similarity is conspicuously lacking in this sprawling region. Two of ECAFE's territorial members (Australia and New Zealand) are "high mass-consumption" societies with a GNP per capita of more than $1,300; four (Afghanistan, Burma, Laos, and Nepal) are "traditional primitive" societies with a GNP per capita of less than $70; and only a handful, including only one major state, Japan, have a GNP per capita of as much as $200.[33] Clusters of states of roughly comparable size and power are divided by religious, ideological, and other deeply rooted animosities. If civil strife is divided into personnel wars, authority wars, and structural wars,[34] in Latin America such strife has usually been of the first two types, while in Asia it has frequently been structural; thus it has had much wider repercussions and has made it more difficult for the Commission to give undivided attention to economic development problems.

Among other inputs which have inhibited ECAFE's deliberations are the deep-seated suspicion of Japan's leadership, dating back to the days of the Coprosperity Sphere; anxiety about and some resentment of India's claims to leadership within the region and the Commission;[35] dissension introduced into the Asian scene by the creation and continued existence of the Southeast Asia Treaty Organization (SEATO); the presence within

---

[31] See Inis L. Claude, Jr., "The OAS, the UN, and the United States," *International Conciliation*, March 1964 (No. 547).

[32] An *Ad Hoc* Committee on Cooperation was established to guarantee coordination between the OAS, ECLA, and the Inter-American Development Bank (IDB). ECLA is also linked to the Inter-American Committee on the Alliance for Progress (CIAP), a committee of IA-ECOSOC, in an advisory capacity.

[33] Classification and data are from Russett, Table B-2, pp. 294–298.

[34] This typology is developed by James N. Rosenau, "Internal War as an International Event," in James N. Rosenau (ed.), *International Aspects of Civil Strife* (Princeton, N.J.: Princeton University Press, 1964), pp. 45–91.

[35] Figures supplied to the writer on a visit to ECAFE in 1964 revealed that as of that time India had as many professional staff serving on the Commission's Secretariat as Pakistan, Burma, Ceylon, Indonesia, and Iran combined.

ECAFE, alone of the three commissions, of both the United States and the Soviet Union; and the fact that mainland China is within the geographic scope of the Commission but that the Peking government, a brooding presence in all Asian affairs, is not a participant. In such an atmosphere economic progress is difficult, and no better or more enduring example can be found than Pakistan's lukewarm attitude toward the activities of ECAFE, a function of India's leadership of and stake in the Commission's affairs.

ECAFE has had no ideological thrust remotely comparable to that of ECLA. To say this is not to disparage the leadership of ECAFE but to record a fact. The impact of the Commission has simply been quite negligible. ECAFE's early years were characterized by the Commission's domination by non-Asian states. It was not until the Lahore Agreement of 1951 that the Asian states succeeded in converting the Commission into a body which could do what its Asian members wanted it to do without interference, and indeed blocking votes, from outside powers.[36] In the words of David Wightman, the Agreement "affirmed that ECAFE existed primarily to serve the interests of its Asian members." [37] This rudimentary triumph did not, of course, define those interests or guarantee that the Asian states and a secretariat consisting largely of their nationals would undertake a program with integrative purpose or potential.

Although it would be a mistake to underestimate the significance for Asia of the "Asianization" of the only important regional body in the entire continent, it must be noted that the subsequent performance of ECAFE has not created apprehension and dissatisfaction outside of the Commission comparable to that generated by ECLA. In other words, ECAFE is regarded as a relatively "safe" commission; the Lahore Agreement has not proved to be a Pandora's box. There has been little friction between ECAFE and the UN, which in this case means both the predominantly Western leadership within the Department of Economic and Social Affairs and the influential Western states on the Economic and Social Council and in the Second (Economic and Financial) and Third (Social, Humanitarian, and Cultural) Committees of the General Assembly. ECAFE may fairly be characterized as the most UN-minded of the regional commissions. The assessment implicit in this characterization, and one explicitly voiced by some UN staff members, is that the Secretariats in New York and in Bangkok are both cautious, slow to embrace new ideas, generally satisfied to perform routine tasks efficiently. Furthermore, a capacity for self-criticism, so necessary to continuing redefinition of tasks and the growth of influence, has been conspicuously lacking in ECAFE's leadership. ECAFE may do well those things that it does, but such an organization is unlikely to contribute significantly to the transformation of thinking either of

---

[36] See Wightman, pp. 50–52. A memorandum presented by the Executive Secretary, P. S. Lokanathan, at the 1951 session of the Commission catalyzed support for the following declaration by the Commission:

> Member governments feel, however, that the time has come when clearer recognition should be given to the principle that member countries belonging to the region should take their own decisions in the Commission on their own economic problems. . . . In pursuance of this principle the member countries of the Commission not in the region would be willing, as a general rule, to refrain from using their votes in opposition to economic proposals predominantly concerning the region which had the support of a majority of the countries of the region.

(See Economic and Social Council *Official Records* [13th session], Supplement No. 7, paragraph 341.)

[37] Wightman, p. 52.

economists or politicians within its member states.

Having stated that Asia is not Latin America and ECAFE not ECLA, it is necessary to scan the performance of the Commission for islands of impact in an unpromising sea. The first Executive Secretary, P. S. Lokanathan, had early indicated his determination not to preside over a mere study group.[38] Yet the Working Group of Experts on Regional Economic Co-operation for the ECAFE Region, in an important report submitted to the third Executive Secretary, U Nyun, in 1963, observed that

> increased regional cooperation as envisaged in this report requires the establishment of decision-making machinery, in contrast to the largely consultative machinery which ECAFE has provided for the past seventeen years.[39]

During ECAFE's long years as consultative machinery/study group, the ground was being laid for "joint efforts to secure the common or integrated development of basic facilities of natural resources" and, hopefully, for "those forms of co-operation which arise from the treatment of the region as a whole, or parts of it, as a single market." [40] The habit of consultation had to be instilled first; the economic map of the ECAFE region had to be charted. Both the map and the habit have been improved by ECAFE's existence and the list of ECAFE-inspired projects of regional or subregional import is beginning to lengthen. The roster includes the Mekong River Project, the Asian Highway, the Asian Institute for Economic Development and Planning, Intraregional Trade Promotion Talks, the Conference of Asian Planners, the Ministerial Conference on Asian Economic

nomic Cooperation, and the Asian Development Bank.

These frequently cited evidences of ECAFE's salutary role in that conflict-ridden region fall into two categories. The Mekong Project, the Highway, and the Institute are similar in that discussions have been followed by action in each case and in that they do not involve any sacrifice of the right of member countries to determine their own development and commercial policies. The Institute, as noted earlier, is comparable in form to one established through the initiative of ECLA, but its integrative potential will probably depend upon the development of a curriculum with a self-consciously regional viewpoint. The Asian Highway will no more lift the eyes of planners beyond the boundaries of nation-states than will the ECE-sponsored convention for transport of goods by roads under customs seal in Europe[41] although a comparison of the two projects underscores the rudimentary nature of ECAFE's task. However, the Asian Highway is symbolically important, "a modern revival of the ancient caravan routes along which traveled not only goods but peoples and ideas." [42] Unlike most highway projects, it is not a response to traffic but a promoter of it. The Highway, in other words, *may* in time help to create environmental conditions which are favorable to integration.

The other major project associated with ECAFE initiative is the development of the Mekong. Perhaps no other experiment in regional cooperation within the developing regions of the world has received more attention. Much has been made of the fact that under ECAFE's patient nurturing the Mekong Project has gone forward during periods of bitter political and even

---

[38] *Ibid.*, p. 286.
[39] UN Document E/CN.11/641, p. 69.
[40] *Ibid.*, pp. 53–54.

[41] See *Fifteen Years of Activity of the Economic Commission for Europe 1947–1962* (UN Document E/ECE/473/Rev.1), pp. 16, 81.
[42] Wightman, p. 221.

military conflict in the Southeast Asian subregion. By any standard ECAFE's performance has been a creditable one.[43] The Coordination Committee, a brainchild of the Commission's second Executive Secretary, C. V. Narasimhan, is a unique instrumentality in Asia, a body composed of representatives of the four riparian countries with authority to raise funds and approve programs for implementation. It was not intended to be a supranational body and it has not evolved in that direction, but under "the ECAFE umbrella"[44] the Committee has survived and registered tangible progress. Some of the most critical hurdles lie ahead, and the pattern of cooperation for decisions with respect to surveys and dam construction may not spill over into decision making with respect to costs, benefits, or modes of operation, not to mention other questions involving subregional development. Nevertheless, one is compelled to agree with Wightman that "the tinder of the ECAFE vision has been set alight."[45]

The second category of ECAFE initiatives includes those based upon the assumption

that the purpose of any major measures of intraregional co-operation must be to give the trade and production structure of the ECAFE countries a more regional orientation.[46]

This theme is not new, dating back at least to Lokanathan's aide-mémoire to the heads of delegations at a Tokyo session of the Commission in 1955;[47] but the ECAFE Secretariat approached the area of regional planning circumspectly for many years. Wightman takes the Secretariat to task for its failure to pursue the matter more vigorously, suggesting that "a touch of questing boldness on this theme would not have been amiss"[48] as long ago as 1955 and offering in mitigation the Secretariat's new preoccupation with the Mekong. Modest steps in the direction of regional cooperation in the field of trade and development were taken with the inauguration of Intraregional Trade Promotion Talks in 1959 and Conferences of Asian Planners, the first of which was held in New Delhi in 1961. Both were instituted only after strong opposition had been overcome and only with the constructive if belated leadership of the Secretariat. But periodic discussion is no substitute for joint action, and of the latter there has been very little to date. The discussions may be moving in the direction of limited action, however. Two groups of experts have rendered reports, the first in 1961 and the second in 1963, which not only urge cooperative regional action but also stress the need to establish machinery for the purpose.[49] The Manila Ministerial Conference on Asian Economic Cooperation used the second of these two reports as its principal working paper and resolved to pursue most of its objectives.[50] But except for the important agreement on establishment of an Asian Development Bank (which, in the recommendation of the Expert Group, would finance only regional projects), the level of commitment has been low, with emphasis still upon further *ad hoc* meetings of representatives

<hr/>

[43] See *ibid.*, pp. 183–202; and C. Hart Schaaf and Russell H. Fifield, *The Lower Mekong: Challenge to Cooperation in Southeast Asia* (Princeton, N.J.: D. Van Nostrand Co., 1963), especially Part II.
[44] The figure is Wightman's.
[45] Wightman, p. 197.
[46] UN Document E/CN.11/641, p. 57.
[47] See the discussion in Wightman, pp. 104–105, 292–294.

[48] *Ibid.*, p. 297.
[49] Consultative Group of Experts on Regional Economic Cooperation in Asia (1961) and Working Group of Experts (1963). See UN Documents E/CN.11/615, February 13, 1963, and E/CN.11/641, Appendix V, Annex 2.
[50] The Ministerial Conference's resolution on Asian economic cooperation appears in UN Document E/CN.11/641, pp. 2–3.

and expert groups. The institutional equivalent of LAFTA, not to mention the European Economic Community (EEC), is still over the horizon.

Unlike ECLA, ECAFE has had no appreciable impact upon its member states through the placement of regionally minded officials from the Commission Secretariat in important government posts. Not only has there been a less coherent gospel of regionalism to carry back to the service of individual governments, but there has also been a much lower turnover among senior officials. There is less enthusiasm for new blood in the ECAFE Secretariat than in any of the other commissions. The result has been the perpetuation of the tradition of caution and a failure to build useful bridges between the Secretariat and the ministries concerned with development questions. In general, the recommendations and activities of the ECAFE Secretariat seem to occupy no very prominent place in the discussion of policy within governments.

ECA

The Economic Commission for Africa is still the least developed and hardest to categorize of the commissions, as one might expect of an organization which is less than eight years old and more than half of whose members have been independent states no more than six years. Every effort has been made to give the Commission parity with ECLA and ECAFE, however, and in UN circles there are those who insist that the real meaning of ECA is "every cent for Africa." In its relatively brief life ECA has overtaken the other commissions in size of staff,[51]

in the volume of UN regional technical assistance projects,[52] and in the number of subregional offices.

In spite of all this activity, and some would say in part because of it, ECA has not yet developed a distinctive style of operation or an identifiable sense of direction. Most of its membership lived until recently as colonies either of France or of the United Kingdom, and economically most ECA members still remain within the orbit of the former metropolitan power. The preferential treatment accorded countries in the French Community by the EEC and countries of the British Commonwealth by the United Kingdom is "a disintegrating factor in Africa, and tends to perpetuate the cleavage between the British and French areas of the continent." [53] Furthermore, the political boundaries make even less economic sense on this badly fragmented continent than they do in other areas. The number of states involved in any regional or subregional negotiations looking to economic union would necessarily be large if negotiations are to be economically meaningful, and yet the larger the number of participants the more difficult the task of mutually satisfactory negotiation.

Nor are the fragmentation of Africa and the fact of distinctive areas of residual British and French influence the only significant forces acting upon the Commission. The Pan-African leadership aspirations of some African states are viewed with suspicion by others;

---

[51] Professional staff as of April 1 in each of several recent years:

	1960	1962	1964
ECAFE	78	75	87
ECLA	87	87	103
ECA	34	70	102

(Figures supplied by the Administrative Man-

agement Service of the UN Secretariat and by the individual commission secretariats.)

[52] In 1965 the UN was executing agency for regional projects in Africa under the Expanded Program of Technical Assistance (EPTA) and its own regular program totaling approximately $1,520,000; most of the projects were decentralized to ECA. This is to be compared with the figures for Asia ($1,010,000) and Latin America ($1,000,000). (UN Document E/4075, June 14, 1965, p. 24.)

[53] Dell, p. 286.

there are latent problems in the relationship between the Arab members of ECA, especially the United Arab Republic, and the sub-Saharan African states; there has been competition over the location of subregional offices. Of singular importance has been the continuing struggle for self-determination of the indigenous African population in the southern quarter of the continent. This issue, which unites African states as does no other, has also distracted ECA from its economic tasks. Although ECOSOC "resolved" the problem in 1963 by expelling Portugal from membership in ECA[54] and suspending South Africa until conditions for constructive cooperation had been restored by a change in that country's racial policies,[55] in the larger sense ECA functions at less than full effectiveness because the primary preoccupation of many of its member governments remains the colonial and racial issues.

Another issue which has preempted the attention of the Commission is the Africanization of the ECA Secretariat. ECA is the only one of the three commissions serving the developing world the majority of whose professional staff is not indigenous to the region. But the talent pool in Africa is still shallow, a stubborn fact which has made it difficult to Africanize the Commission's Secretariat. The effort to do so continues, however, with the result that ECA's staff, in spite of some areas of considerable skill, is not yet either particularly effective or stable. Nor was there stable leadership at the top during the critical early years. The first Executive Secretary, Mekki Abbas, had only a brief tenure, and the second, Robert K. A. Gardiner, spent his first year in the post on assignment in the Congo (Leopoldville). Political considerations have dictated that there be a French-speaking African Deputy Ex-

ecutive Secretary, and the result seems to have been to smuggle the continent's divisions into the Secretariat rather than to ameliorate the problem. As a result of uncertain leadership, staff deficiencies, lack of experience, and the imperatives of Africanization, ECA has had to move with "deliberate speed."

Although ECA has been plagued by the existence of barriers not of its making, it has been spared some other problems which could have complicated its efforts to establish itself as an effective force in Africa. In the first place, neither the United States nor the Soviet Union is a member although it was originally assumed that both would be; this has partially removed from ECA the propensity, often noticeable in ECAFE, to substitute ideological argument for more pragmatic discussion of hard issues. In the second place, the Organization of African Unity (OAU) had not yet been launched when ECA was created in 1958. Had the order been reversed, ECA might have failed, its role preempted by another organization, prospectively stronger because its participants are foreign ministers rather than economic and finance ministers. On the other hand, the relatively late establishment of the Economic Commission for Africa meant that the conference habit, dating back to Bandung in 1955, was built into ECA as it had not been in the case of ECAFE.

Like ECLA, ECA has had to compete with other regional organizations; and like ECLA, ECA has benefited in this competition from its "regional purity." ECA's principal strength, however, derives from the simple fact that it has survived while other African organizations have folded. The Organization of African Unity is, of course, very much alive; but the OAU has come to depend upon the ECA Secretariat to do its economic and social work, a relationship which the Commission has encouraged and which is

[54] ECOSOC Resolution 974 D III (XXXVI), July 24, 1963.

[55] ECOSOC Resolution 974 D IV (XXXVI), July 30, 1963.

facilitated by the location of both organizations in Addis Ababa.

In the final analysis, there is probably not now in Africa a disposition to
see economic problems as the most
critical ones. This takes pressure off
ECA, but it also deprives ECA of some
of its prospective importance and suggests that African political leaders will
probably not for a time tolerate the
emergence of strong leaders within the
ECA Secretariat. The prospect, therefore, is for a further development of
Secretariat strength; continued leadership in such areas as the development
of statistical standards through the
Conference of African Statisticians;
the gradual assumption of more operational responsibilities under the decentralization program; an expansion of
advisory and training services through
the African Institute for Economic Development and Planning in Dakar; and
the further elaboration of an economic
profile for the continent. The impact
of the EEC, the example of LAFTA,
and participation in planning for
UNCTAD are making the ECA Secretariat more integration conscious. It
has prepared preliminary documenta-
tion on the subject of an African common market,[56] helped to launch an
African Development Bank, worked
with a group of experts in the preparation of a report on an African payments union,[57] organized industrial
coordination missions to several subregions in Africa, and laid the ground-
work for a standing Conference of
African Planners. This list of activities
could be expanded. There is obviously
a great deal of ferment within ECA,
but the fact remains that virtually
every one of these programs is still on
the drawing board. What is more, the
plans are still fuzzy and Commission
discussions still deal in generalities, as
evidenced by the following excerpt

from the summary of discussions during a recent ECA session: "The creation of an African common market
was a generally accepted goal. What
remained to be determined, was the
best way of going about it." [58]

It may be that the most significant
impact of the Commission upon national political systems will be registered through the subregionalization
of ECA's structure and work program.
One UN official likens the subregional
aspects of ECA's activity to the sub-
merged portion of an iceberg. Although
the iceberg analogy may seem climati-
cally out of place in a discussion of
African affairs, it is true that ECA has
created subregional offices for West
Africa in Niamey, for East Africa in
Lusaka, for North Africa in Tangier,
and for Central Africa in Leopoldville;
that it has curtailed the number of
large meetings in favor of small, specialized subregional meetings in such
fields as trade, energy, industry, and
transport; that many of the regional
technical assistance projects proposed
and implemented by ECA are organized subregionally (such as the Regional Center for Demographic Research and Training in Cairo, serving
Algeria, Libya, Morocco, the Sudan,
Tunisia, and the United Arab Republic, and the subregional statistical training centers which serve different clients
from such points as Yaoundé, Accra,
Rabat, and Addis Ababa). This emphasis upon the subregion is made explicit in a recent statement of the Executive Secretary of ECA, who noted
that if there was to be economic progress in the foreseeable future,

each country would have to determine its development strategy and
each subregion its machinery for
cooperation. Groups of countries
should decide on criteria for sharing

[56] See UN Document E/CN.14/261 and
Corr. 1.
[57] UN Document E/CN.14/262.

[58] Economic and Social Council *Official
Records* (37th session), Supplement No. 10,
paragraph 234 (c).

out new industries, and conferences should be superceded by closer negotiations between countries.[59]

By focusing its studies increasingly upon subregional groupings of states and giving its industrial coordination missions subregional assignments, the Secretariat has sought to translate this appeal into state policy. The talk of an African common market has a region-wide flavor, and the Secretariat is trying to develop an integrated African telecommunications network with the help of the International Telecommunications Union (ITU), to nationalize African air transport in cooperation with the International Civil Aviation Organization (ICAO), and to promote a trans-Sahara road link, all objectives which transcend any one subregion. However, the principal thrust of ECA is today subregional, suggesting that the Commission is coming to terms with some of the geographical and linguistic realities of Africa.

Recapitulation and Some Tentative Conclusions

The foregoing paragraphs constitute a *tour d'horizon,* a necessarily brief and limited inquiry into the nature of the momentum, if any, imparted by ECLA, ECAFE, and ECA to the regions which they serve. Hopefully they

[59] *Ibid.,* paragraph 109.

offer a few benchmarks for further study of the extent to which the commissions have assumed an integrative function.

Earlier in the article five questions were raised relative to the performance of the commissions. They concerned the ideological leadership of the Executive Secretary; the tangible initiatives taken by the commission, as reflected in the work program; the institutional legacy of the commission at the regional or subregional level; the flow of regionally minded personnel from commission secretariat to positions of influence within states; and the image of the commission within the region. Although it is difficult to measure leadership and initiative or to pin down such an elusive commodity as image, a very rough scale of integrative output can be constructed, ranging from nil through marginal, low, modest, and substantial to high, for each of the five areas. A net evaluation should then be possible.

ECLA has had the highest integrative output. Certainly the environmental conditions in that region are more conducive to this kind of thrust than those in Asia or Africa, but ECLA could easily have fallen into the rut of a more limited role. Instead, its leadership has been characterized by an ideology which, while short of supranationalism, has nonetheless been instrumental in focusing attention on re-

	ECLA	ECAFE	ECA
Ideological leadership	Substantial	Low	Marginal
Tangible initiatives	Substantial	Modest	Marginal
Institutional legacies	Modest	Low	Marginal
Personnel mobility	Modest	Marginal	Marginal
Regional image	Modest	Marginal	Low
Net evaluation of integrative output	Modest	Low	Marginal

gional approaches to problems previously deemed domestic. Its initiatives have given meaning to that ideology, putting it to work in a program which has given to the region several modest but pioneering projects, some of which may yet acquire supranational traits. Alone of the commissions it has a record of senior staff mobility, a phenomenon which spreads ECLA's ideas and prestige and which reflects at least some willingness to entertain some of those ideas. The Commission has a strong image although it is predictably controversial; at least it is paid the compliment of attention.

ECAFE, on the other hand, has been handicapped by the vastness and variety of its region, by the shadow of Communist China, by fear of domination by India and Japan, by a protracted quest for identity, and by an uncritical attitude toward its own performance. No organizational ideology or comprehensive program for regional growth and development has been put forward by the Commission's leadership. In this case, the *ad hoc* initiatives of the Commission have anticipated the development of an ideology, and one or two of these, e.g., the Mekong Project, are monuments to ECAFE's creativity and perseverance. Although the Commission has been called extravagantly an economic parliament for Asia, there is little evidence that this wish, if wish it is, will become father to the fact. ECAFE's integrative output has been low.

The third commission in the developing world, ECA, is even weaker than ECAFE in every respect except image. This is not surprising, given its relative newness and growing pains. That its image in Africa exceeds its accomplishments is due to a variety of factors, including the importance attached to international organization generally on that continent. Otherwise, it is too early to make a judgment about ECA, except to say that to date its integrative output is low, buoyed

only by the growing consciousness of a common cause among all African peoples from which ECA benefits and to which it may in time contribute.

In all three cases the judgment as to integrative output is based upon the complete record. If one were to look only at the current situation, it is doubtful if ECLA would stand out so far above ECAFE. Some veteran observers at the UN think they detect signs of stagnation in Santiago, while ECAFE is coming to life. A flurry of excitement has attended the launching of the Asian Development Bank; on the other hand, the slow progress of LAFTA has eroded some of ECLA's enthusiasm, and continued uncertainty about the viability of the Alliance for Progress appears to have contributed to a state of suspended animation in ECLA. But these observations may only suggest that what distinguishes the regional commissions may be less important than what they have in common. If ECLA is in a less creative phase, it may be that it has simply encountered some of the boundaries imposed by environmental conditions, while ECAFE may be discovering in the midst of regional conflict that it can do more, that the very urgency of the political situation may generate pressure for functional cooperation.

The performance of the commissions indicates that each of them, like water seeking its level, will in time but at a differential rate produce some common institutions and policies. ECLA has frequently pioneered, although action by ECAFE and ECA has often had an independent genesis. Thus, the creation of an Asian Development Bank means that each region now has both a regional planning institute and a development bank. Neither is an instance of economic union, of course, but both reflect a capacity to cooperate in launching institutions of continuing utility to the region as a whole. If neither promotes integration directly, they will at least afford an opportunity for nationals of several states from within the region to cooperate in managing programs of regional scope, and they will hopefully contribute to a reshaping of national views about integration and national capacities to approach the subject seriously.

Similarly, recent measures of decentralization from UN Headquarters to the commissions and attendant efforts to strengthen the latter's secretariats should provide more opportunities for the commissions to identify themselves with specific, concrete tasks of regional proportions. Although decentralization is primarily a movement to transfer UN decision making in the economic field from the hands of Europeans and North Americans to persons from the developing countries, not a movement to transfer decision making within the region from the state to some subregional or regional organization, it has the effect of focusing attention upon agencies of regional scope and upon projects of a regional rather than a country-by-country nature inasmuch as it is regional projects which have been decentralized.[60]

Another institutional development in which all three commissions share and one which may have a profound impact upon their direction and function is the United Nations Conference on Trade and Development. The Secretariats of ECLA, ECAFE, and ECA served as research staff for the several groups of developing countries which joined forces to form the surprisingly cohesive and effective "77" at Geneva. There is every reason to believe that they will continue to perform in the capacity of "secretariat for the poor," a role which the commissions have explicitly been invited to play. Dr. Prebisch has carried his economic doctrines from ECLA, where he made Santiago the most vital of the regional

centers, to UNCTAD. Just as the commission secretariats helped to make the first Geneva Conference a success, so should the UNCTAD connection logically contribute to a broader, regional outlook within the commissions.

Although the subregional approach has been made most explicit in the case of ECA, all three commissions have been characterized by this kind of pragmatic response to the challenge of political and economic diversity within their regions. In spite of the concern of each commission for a whole region, many of the important instances of commission initiative, such as the Central American Agreements and the Mekong Project, have a subregional focus; the broader scope of LAFTA and the Asian Highway does not conceal the fact that both are primarily programs of a subregional nature, at least for the present. It would seem fairly safe to assert that the commissions will continue to explore the possibilities of subregional cooperation. If the commissions are less ambitious with respect to the geographic scope of their projects, they can perhaps afford to be more ambitious with respect to their integrative content.

All of this activity underscores the vitality of the commissions, but it does not mean that economic policy is about to be made at any level higher than that of the nation-state. Certainly the regional commissions themselves have no such mandate or the faintest prospect of acquiring one, and the evidence that ideas and initiatives emanating from the commissions will foster supranational decision making is fragmentary and on the whole disappointing. To date we have only LAFTA and the Central American Agreements as modest examples of economic union. Cooperation, not federation, has been the high-water mark reached by the commissions, and much of the cooperation is still in a rudimentary stage.

Integrative output of the commissions, we may conclude, is related

---

[60] For the most recent official statements on the status of decentralization see UN Documents A/6114, November 23, 1965, and E/4075, June 14, 1965.

closely to environmental conditions and resultant receptivity of member states to ideas and initiatives of the commissions and their secretariats. One of the principal functions of the commissions has been to increase the awareness of member states of the possibilities for cooperative economic behavior within the limits set by those conditions and to help devise schemes for mobilizing energies which will carry members to those limits. Hopefully, conditions and attitudes will be modified in the process, thereby removing some of the limitations upon cooperative action within the region. In any event, whether the commissions will play a role of increasing consequence within their respective regions depends upon their ability to increase their integrative output by overcoming environmental impediments and to sustain their impact by creative adaptation in the face of inevitable environmental changes.

25. Integration, Organization, and Values*

MICHAEL BARKUN

THIS is a time of changing international political forms. The state, once the only significant international political actor both in law and in fact, retains pride of place but must share the international arena with a host of new arrivals. Some, like "systems," are the constructs of observers and in principle can be projected onto any period.[1] Others, however, are clearly discernible elements of the real world. We will be examining two in particular which vie with the state itself as the paradigmatic form of future international relations: the universal political organization, of which the United Nations is the most recent example; and the embryonic "supranational community," most vividly present in the Common Market but evident in other regional groupings as well. A number of assumptions tie the two together on the levels of both fact and value. First, the former is presumed to further the latter. That is,

universal political organizations are presumed to assist the development of integrated political communities. Second, political integration is presumed to offer policy advantages which existing nation-states do not.

The comments that follow examine the nature of the linkage between universal political organizations and newly integrated political communities and attempt to trace out some of the value implications inherent in the hypothesized line of development between them.

The international political organizations we shall examine here are the Concert of Europe, the League of Nations, and the United Nations. The three share criteria by which we can set them apart from other international actors: First, they have some pretensions of universality, thus separating them from regional associations. This is true even of the Concert of Europe, the career of which coincided with European hegemony in the world generally. Second, they are all broadly concerned with threats to peace and stability, thus demarcating them from narrowly technical organizations. Third, they possess relatively long life-

* This essay is based on a paper delivered at the Annual Meeting of the New York State Political Science Association in Albany, N.Y., March 25–26, 1966.

[1] E.g., Richard N. Rosecrance, *Action and Reaction in World Politics,* Boston: Little, Brown (1963).

spans, setting them apart from meetings called once and never reconvened.[2] Finally, they have some institutional expression, be it the periodic congresses of 19th-century diplomacy or the complex organs of the United Nations.[3a]

Of what does political integration consist? It is characterized by a sense of community on the part of those within a territory, coupled with expectations of peaceful change and means for achieving it.[3] Integration has his-

[2] Even this is sometimes a difficult distinction to make. The Conference of Versailles lasted two years. The negotiations that eventuated in the Peace of Westphalia were fixed for 1643, actually met in 1644, began work seriously the next year, while the treaties were not signed until near the end of 1648. As to the Concert of Europe, however, conferences from 1815 on were *ad hoc* only to the extent that each was invoked by a separate contingency, but the membership, procedures, and overriding purposes remained essentially constant.

[3a] It is worthwhile quoting in full the definition offered by Karl W. Deutsch, *et al.*, in *Political Community and the North Atlantic Area*, Princeton, N.J.: Princeton University Press (1957).

A SECURITY COMMUNITY is a group of people which has become "integrated."
By INTEGRATION we mean the attainment, within a territory, of a "sense of community" and of institutions and practices strong enough and widespread enough to assure, for a "long" time, dependable expectations of "peaceful change" among its population.
By SENSE OF COMMUNITY we mean a belief on the part of individuals in a group that they have come to agreement on at least this one point: that common social problems must and can be resolved by processes of "peaceful change."
By PEACEFUL CHANGE we mean the resolution of social problems, normally by institutionalized procedures, without resort to large-scale physical force. (Authors' emphasis.)

[3] The League of Nations retained some vestige of structure until World War II and did not formally dissolve itself until 1946, but its most useful work was already completed by the end of the 1920's. The Concert of Eu-

torically appeared around some kind of interactional core,[4] an area within which frequent interchanges of persons, messages, and goods and services take place. The lists of variables related to the achievement of integration have a significant feature in common: they all include substantial numbers of factors that cannot be described as overtly political. Data on trade patterns, mass communications, and personal mobility figure prominently, yet they fall far outside traditional notions of the political. The search for significant variables in integration has seemed to

rope enjoyed a strikingly similar curve of growth and decline. It worked with maximum efficacy from 1814 to 1822 and by mid-century it, too, survived more by dint of inertia than as a result of functional necessity. Rosecrance, *op. cit.,* 73, 99, 118. In general, then, the continuity of international organizations is relative, encompassing a decade or two of effective operation followed by the survival of inert forms.

[4] Karl W. Deutsch, "The Growth of Nations," *World Politics,* V (January, 1953), 168–195. Jacob and Teune isolate ten factors presumptive of political integration: geographical proximity; homogeneity; transactions, or interactions, among persons or groups; knowledge of each other; shared functional interests; the "character" or "motive" pattern of a group; the structural frame or system of power and decision-making; the sovereignty-dependency status of the community; governmental effectiveness; previous integrative experiences. Philip E. Jacob, and Henry Teune, "The Integrative Process: Guidelines for Analysis of the Bases of Political Community," in Jacob and James V. Toscano (eds.), *The Integration of Political Communities,* Philadelphia: Lippincott (1964), 1–45.

Deutsch has supplied a list of thirty-two potentially significant "ranges of transaction," of which only the major sub-headings need detain us here: political; public finance; private finance; personal mobility; distribution of commodities; direct communications; mass communications; and indirect and informal communications. Karl W. Deutsch, *Political Communities at the International Level,* Garden City, N.Y.: Doubleday (1954), 70.

greatly subordinate the directing role of political organizations.

The primary implication of these studies is that political institutions are an effect rather than a cause of political integration. On this basis, they would seem to have little role to play in the integrative process. Indeed, if highly visible political institutions really are manifestations of scarcely visible and marginally political activities, international organizations emerge as useful indicators but hardly as directing forces. Yet many still argue their primary role in initiating the process. Thus Kenneth Carlston asserts:

> . . . international organizations may soon reach that degree of interdependency in which the establishment of each new organization directed toward a new goal so varies the functional relationships of existing organizations with one another as to make the changed pattern of relationships the basis for establishing still another organization, which will in turn create a new pattern of interrelationships that will promote further growth and integration of the international systems.[5]

This line of argument has an aesthetic appeal but retains the drawback that it lumps together organizations concerned primarily with threats to the peace, with the so-called "specialized agencies" whose province is that of technical expertise. The latter's ability, first of all, to survive the demise of affiliated universal organizations attests to different sources of support.[6] Sec-

ond, there is no compelling body of evidence to indicate the kind of "snowball" effect once predicted. The assumption that the integrative function of international political organizations is embodied in their capacity to act as nuclei for further integration has not been borne out by events. On the surface at least, the great integrative movements of history have gone on in seeming isolation from attempts to consciously construct universal political institutions.

If international political organizations on the global level can serve an integrative function, their role must surely be less direct and less visible than was once thought, for their promised catalytic effect has not materialized. Where in the sequence of integration does the international organization make its presence felt? If, as Etzioni asserts, integration requires a point of "take-off," it may be worthwhile inquiring into the circumstances that determine where that point occurs.

> The central variable for the "take-off" of supranational authority [Etzioni writes] is the amount of international decision-making required. This, in turn, is determined largely by the amounts and kinds of flows that cross international borders (e.g., tourists, mail) and the amounts and kinds of shared international activities (e.g., maintaining an early-warning system).[7]

Political integration thus turns out to hinge upon a web of transactions and

---

[5] Kenneth S. Carlston, *Law and Organization in World Society,* Urbana, Ill.: University of Illinois Press (1962), 114.

[6] Specialized agencies, like their domestic counterparts, federal regulatory agencies, have led notoriously independent lives. The older specialized agencies are not creatures of the United Nations but are tied to it through bilateral agreements. These agencies arose out of industrialization and the ensuing tech-

nological imperatives. Gerald J. Mangone, *A Short History of International Organization,* New York: McGraw-Hill (1954), 67–90. They have at various times intersected with the League and the UN, yet their separate development, remarkable persistence, and carefully demarcated goals suggest a separate phenomenon, to be separately dealt with.

[7] Amitai Etzioni, "The Epigenesis of Political Communities at the International Level," *The American Journal of Sociology,* LXVIII (January, 1963), 407–421

shared activities largely non-political in nature. At least they are perceived to be so. Hence, as technical matters they may be entrusted to the care of safe, non-political experts.

We find ourselves engaged in further regression through time, back from the fact of integration itself to its take-off point; beyond that to the transactional web that made take-off possible; and now one step further, to the preconditions that allow the transactions and shared activities to persist in the first place. The transactions and shared activities constitute what we may call the infrastructure upon which visible political institutions may later be built, and as such they have a relatively enduring, repetitive quality. Consequently, anything that interrupts or breaks down patterned behavior prevents the integrative infrastructure from being realized. The mundane but essential transactions across borders thrive in some environments and fragment and disappear in others. Eventual political integration depends upon their continuous undisturbed character, for the integrative process occurs over long periods of time, traversing a shadow area between separation and integration rather than a neat and clear-cut threshold.[8]

To what extent do international political organizations support or undercut this environmental requirement? In order to adequately examine this question, we must first take a look at the function such organizations are supposed to perform. The Concert of Europe, the League, and the United Nations have been pre-eminently concerned with threats to the peace. In seeking to manage conflict on an international scale, they have sought, with some few exceptions,[9] to include the widest group of relevant actors. Further, an examination of the aims surrounding these organizations at their foundings clearly demonstrates their preoccupation with conflict resolution.

Nineteenth century Europe saw the development of procedures principally aimed at avoiding a repetition of the Napoleonic wars,[10] and as long as the memories of that conflict remained vivid, these procedures were relatively effective. The League of Nations looked back with nostalgia to the golden age of the pre-War Concert, which seemed placid indeed compared to the war Europe had just endured. Both the League and the UN were the Concert reborn,[11] both having been based upon the supposition that the failure of Great Power consensus had allowed the scourge of war to fall.

The experience of severe deprivation quite naturally engenders the strong drive to prevent its recurrence,[12] and universal political organizations born out of conflict are dedicated at their foundation to a new era of order. Frequently the immediate circumstances

---

[8] Jacob and Teune, in Jacob and Toscano (eds.), *op. cit.*

[9] The principle anomaly here, of course, is the absence of Communist China, the Germanies, and Japan. Despite these limitations on access, the consensus of the San Francisco Conference was that universal membership should be posited as an organizational goal. Leland Goodrich and Edvard Hambro, *The Charter of the United Nations, Commentary and Documents,* Boston: World Peace Foundation (1946), 77.

[10] Those wars that did not give birth to some search for order were those which left the combatants too exhausted to pursue a constructive peace or left the issue in such doubt as to make another round of combat inevitable. The Peloponnesian War ended in political chaos. Adda B. Boseman, *Politics and Culture in International History,* Princeton, N.J.: Princeton University Press (1960), 505-513. The Thirty Years War, although its toll has been exaggerated, nevertheless destroyed the very resources that might otherwise have been directed towards political and social reconstruction. C. V. Wedgwood, *The Thirty Years War,* Garden City, N.Y.: Doubleday (1961), 485-506.

[11] Rosecrance, *op. cit.,* 187-205.

[12] Henry Teune, "The Learning of Integrative Habits," in Jacob and Toscano (eds.), *op. cit.,* 247-282.

out of which they arise are the victorious wartime alliances and/or the peace conferences that follow the cessation of hostilities. One need only recall the juxtapositions of the Congress of Vienna and the Concert of Europe, the Conference of Versailles and the League, the Grand Alliance and the UN. The organizations in question became the chosen instruments for the preservation of the postwar settlements. They acted as its custodians, with the victors given sufficient authority over the levers of organizational action to insure speedy and effective intervention.

In short, then, through circumstances that attended their foundings, these organizations have been oriented towards the status quo, insofar as postwar settlements and alignments defined it. Under their aegis, the distribution of power, location of boundaries, and occasionally the ideological bases of regimes serve to limit the direction and tempo of legitimate change. Any forces which seek to break through these limitations threaten the very purposes for which the international organizations were established. They were constructed as buffers against rapid change rather than as its vehicle.

The Concert of Europe openly and actively opposed forces of social revolution. The League of Nations foundered on its inability to assimilate and control opponents of the status quo.[13] The United Nations at this juncture stands or falls on its ability to draw in and socialize revolutionary regimes.[14] Now there is no denying the enormous variation in the value systems represented by these threats, and in this sense the threats are incomparable. Yet there is

a parallelism among the nationalisms of the nineteenth century; German, Italian, Japanese, and Soviet expansionism in the 1930s; and European integration and the restiveness of the new nations of Asia and Africa: for all seek to break through the constraining conditions that the respective international organizations set down.

Even given the possibility of channeling some change-producing forces, there is little in the past history of international political organizations to indicate that they can easily be transformed into substantial agents of change. In any case, their attachment to the status quo stems not from a direct ideological commitment *per se* but, rather, from the structure of events and relationships of power at the times they were founded.

What relationships may then be said to exist between organizational purpose and the integrative process? First, to the extent that such organizations fulfill their primary function, they establish an environment within which the infrastructure of integration may be built. Patterned behavior must precede institutions. The paths of trade, travel, and communication must be free to develop, for without their growth overtly political development faces insuperable obstacles. Since global political organizations have given first priority to the regulation and, ideally, to the supression of violent international conflict, their purpose meshes with the designs of integration in its early stages.

The movement from peace to war is a shift in the mode of interaction[15] and hence is likely to disrupt existing interactional flows.[16] To the extent that

[13] Ernst B. Haas, "Dynamic Environment and Static System: Revolutionary Regimes in the United Nations," in Morton A. Kaplan (ed.), *The Revolution in World Politics*, New York: Wiley (1962), 267–309.

[14] Richard A. Falk, "Revolutionary Nations and the Quality of International Legal Order," *ibid.*, 310–331.

[15] Raymond W. Mack and Richard C. Snyder, "The Analysis of Social Conflict—toward an overview and synthesis," *Conflict Resolution, 1* (June, 1957), 212–248.

[16] It is also true that in certain circumstances war furthers integration. Particularly within the confines of a political unit that has already achieved a partially integrated

it does so, it spells an end for existing sequences of political development. Political stability, while it cannot in and of itself stimulate interactional flows, can at least aid in their preservation. The equilibration universal political organizations seek may seem an admirable end in itself, but, more importantly, it serves as a necessary condition for laying the foundations of political integration. The beginnings of political integration are more likely to flourish under the protective cover of such organizations than in their absence. While universal political organizations may not in themselves contain the seeds of future political communities, they serve to produce the environment in which such seeds may grow.

This notion of organizational purpose also serves to set universal political organizations apart from the so-called "specialized agencies." The latter, like their domestic counterparts, concern themselves with such functional segments as transportation, communications, labor, health, and economic growth. Although they can aid all member states in improving the basic conditions of life, of more particular concern from the standpoint of integration is the obvious relationship between the agencies and the infrastructure of integration. For many of the agencies support the growth of pre-

cisely those variables associated with political integration. The overtly non-political nature of their work makes them particularly vulnerable to the disruptive forces of war, since it almost certainly cuts across agency memberships.[17] In any case, it is worthwhile effecting an analytical separation between global political organizations like the United Nations, primarily concerned to maximize political stability, and specialized agencies like the International Telecommunications Union, which seek to set and meet standards in their areas of expertise.

It is precisely at the point of intersection of questions of political stability and matters of technical expertise that we find the problem of organization and integration most vividly posed. For it is at that point that technical issues become politicized, that hitherto non-political activities take on political shape. From an organizational standpoint, the intersection does not involve a specialized agency itself, for the agency serves only to support activities under other, indigenous auspices. Rather, the intersection involves the universal political organization and whatever new political community is about to arise out of the matrix of interactions.

What appear to social scientists as initial stages in the profoundly political process of integration remain quite extra-political (hence rarely subjects of great controversy) for participants. The regulation of river traffic or the transmission of long-distance telephone messages are not ordinarily matters freighted with heavy political overtones. Rather, the conjunction of perceptions of mutual self-interest with the absence of immediately foreseeable political consequences allows them to

---

form conflict is apt to result in further cohesiveness. The necessary mobilization of resources and the polarization of attitudes into "we" and "they" components turn a society in upon itself. Quincy Wright, *A Study of War*, Chicago: University of Chicago Press (1942), ii, 1013–1021. To a lesser extent, the cohesiveness of alliances demonstrates the integrative potential of war. The tendency of international political organizations to arise out of alliances indicates the longevity of war-forged relationships. However, as noted earlier, these organizations do not themselves develop into full-fledged political communities. Further, when conflict cuts across already existent transactional flows it jeopardizes and may destroy a political community in process of development.

[17] The wartime meetings of the International Civil Aviation Conference and the International Labor Organization show their remarkable persistence, but their work was necessarily at a standstill for the duration: Mangone, *op. cit.*, 222, 226.

go forward unimpeded. Such matters are customarily left in the hands of experts until time and circumstances transmute them into the stuff of politics.

At this point, however, the role of universal organizations undergoes a crucial change; for should the preceding transactions eventuate in a new political community, the status quo is imperiled. Political integration thus runs counter to the primary purpose of the organizations. The inherently discordant relationship between them has historically been obscured by two factors.

First, the degree of political integration that in fact emerges tends to be less than had originally been hoped for by proponents of integration. New political units have from time to time been suggested by publicists, but more often than not what reaches the light of day is a newly expanded state, but a state still markedly smaller than what was initially anticipated. However, this ought not to obscure the fact that the new boundaries do increase territory and/or cohesion and do extend the state beyond earlier limits.

Second, the issue of nationalism has confused an understanding of integration by virtue of the stereotype of inevitable "Balkanization." As the term implies, the fragmenting effects of national consciousness derive from specific sets of historical circumstances. At least insofar as Europe is concerned, nationalism proved to be integrative in the late nineteenth century and disintegrative in the early twentieth.[18] Over the long span of history, a sense of nationhood has produced not only divisions within existing polities but has brought tribes, towns, and feudatories together into new, more comprehensive groupings.

The development of enlarged political units, then, operates at potential cross-purposes with universal political organizations. The former represent change, the latter seek stability. Having been brought to birth in the equilibrated environments these organizations may be capable of providing, the new polities then operate to destroy and restructure the status quo the organizations are bent on preserving. This disruptive potential results from a latent function of a universal organization: it produces the conditions under which the ground for integration may be prepared; but when the integration has been accomplished, the very organization which helped bring it about is jeopardized.

Now let us turn from general consideration to an examination of two sets of specific historical circumstances: integration and the fate of the Concert of Europe (1850–1870) and integration and the crisis of the League of Nations (1931–1939). Both have the obvious advantage, which the United Nations lacks, of being sufficiently removed in time to be examined in their entirety. The evidence being readily accessible, contours of growth and decline appear clearly and political consequences have run their course.

Robert Binkley, a particularly perceptive student of the late nineteenth century, in an effort to break free of "sovereignty" as the touchstone of political analysis, coined in 1935 the term "federative polity." He cast into his new category all the political arrangements which seemed important to him, yet which escaped then-current concepts of state sovereignty: the Concert of Europe, the German Confederation, the British Commonwealth of Nations, and the League of Nations.[19] In seek-

[18] E. H. Carr, *Conditions of Peace*, New York: Macmillan (1943), 39–69.

[19] Robert C. Binkley, *Realism and Nationalism*, New York: Harper (1963), 157–163. In order to appreciate Binkley's contribution, we must separate his analysis from his evaluation. He not only seized upon federative polity as an analytic tool, he elevated it into a preferred form of political organization, and measured actual polities against it. On

ing the pivot point around which the history of late nineteenth century Europe revolved, Binkley chose this anomalous political form, midway in the movement from old autonomous states to new, larger, fully integrated units.

Hence Binkley saw in the years 1857–58 the "crisis of federative polity," a period coinciding with the swift decline of the Concert of Europe. The outbreak of the Crimean War in 1854 meant that

> For the first time since 1815, the Concert had failed to prevent a war among the major powers, and now it could only deal with the results. For fourteen years afterward the Concert not only failed to prevent war, it did not even ratify the evil which war had caused.[20]

From the 1850's to 1870 federative arrangements proposed or begun failed the test of political survival: the German and Italian Confederations, the Balkan Confederation, the Scandinavian Alliance, and the Austrian Federalist Diploma. Notwithstanding the failure of these grandiose plans, however, the map of Europe did alter; and new sets of boundaries were drawn over most of the continent. The new boundaries did not always match the expectations held at midcentury and states existed where loose, federal arrangements had been planned, but these departures from the ideal ought not to obscure the fact that integration was the rule. The Kingdom of Norway and Sweden replaced the Kingdoms of Norway and Sweden; a unified Italy encompassed the old set of principalities; Rumania joined together

what had previously been the United Principalities of Moldavia and Wallachia; the German Empire supplanted the Confederation; the precarious position of Austria, expelled from the German Confederation, was solidified into the Dual Monarchy.

These developments at once represented the amalgamation of political units and the demise of any effective Concert of Europe. The relative tranquillity that obtained during the optimal functioning of the Concert paradoxically allowed the very marshalling of resources and the establishment of interactions that were later to cripple the Concert. The preservation of the post-Vienna norms fostered the development of the very situation the norms were meant to prevent. During the crucial mid-century years, it was clear that the Concert was at cross purposes with the trend toward larger, more integrated states.

To what extent was this true also of the League of Nations? The League, through its inheritance of defunct empires and by its commitment to national self-determination, seemed destined to preside over the division rather than the amalgamation of territories. Commitments arising out of Versailles were in fact executed with a modicum of effectiveness for about a decade. An *a priori* notion of self-determination survived even the quite equivocal plebiscite results of the Twenties.[21] In retrospect, during this early period the League performed tolerably well as executor and caretaker for the peace treaties.

The end of the decade of "normalcy" can effectively be placed at 1931, when Japan invaded Manchuria. From then on international politics altered according to a new logic of national self-aggrandizement. The 1930's saw the ex-

---

this basis, Europe's political history was regressive, indeed, not to mention centralizing tendencies already evident in this country. Notwithstanding this normative component, Binkley's work stands as a sophisticated study far ahead of its time.

[20] Rosecrance, *op. cit.,* 117.

[21] Carr (1943), *op. cit.,* 47–48. In general, language statistics were predictive of plebiscite results in German, Danish, and French-speaking areas, but inaccurate in Polish and southern Slavic speaking regions.

pansion of frontiers by Japan, Italy, Germany, and the Soviet Union. Nineteen thirty-one, E. H. Carr notes, proved to be a watershed not because it marked any "return to power politics" *per se,* but because it "was, in fact, the termination of the monopoly of power enjoyed by the *status quo* powers." [22] The founders of the League envisaged a world in which traditional concentrations of power would provide the political underpinning for the peace treaties, but once this distribution was broken up and reconstituted, the treaties ceased to appear automatically enforceable.[23]

The instances of political integration during the Thirties were very nearly all attempts to reassert past authority, and they were no less integration for being ratified by force of arms.[24] Japan, which had struggled with Russia over Manchuria since the previous century, took this opportunity to renew the competition. Italy, with previous colonial ties to North and East Africa, chose to re-establish them and, in the case of Ethiopia, to overcome an earlier defeat. Germany, always ready to rationalize its actions in terms of the Versailles settlement, worked toward the political realization of pan-Germanism, although the dispersion of German minorities throughout Europe promised grave consequences. The Soviet Union, finally, made good some of the losses suffered at Brest-Litovsk and in general extended its perimeter toward the limits of the Romanoff empire.

Now, clearly, the disruptions of the the 1930's proceeded from a number of sources, of which the amalgamation of polities was only one. Then, too, the stability of the 1920's was at best a relative matter. Nonetheless, insofar as it is possible to determine at this vantage point in time, the Twenties, thanks in part to the League, provided the respite during which the infrastructure could be built. The following decade saw the political results of this respite body forth, shattering the League in the process.

The foregoing, necessarily abbreviated discussion carries with it some disturbing value implications. For every age there are two languages of political discourse, the language of events and the language of aspirations; everyday counterparts to the categories of empirical and normative. The nineteenth century achieved the peculiar distinction of a congruence between the two, for the nation-state held both spiritual and for the most part actual hegemony. In our own time, the supranational community has been elevated to a high place in the language of political aspiration. Wide currency has been given to the view that the nation-state is an anachronism.[25] It has been widely hoped that universal political organizations would, by some teleological necessity, move towards supranationality; and that supranationality would make up the presumed moral deficiencies of the contemporary nation-state. The evidence, as we have noted, points in another direction. The purposes of international political or-

---

[22] E. H Carr, *The Twenty Years' Crisis, 1919–1939,* London: Macmillan (1939), 133.

[23] Wright (1954), *op. cit.,* 67, 72–73.

[24] For the connection between the implementation of integration and force, see Wright (1942), *op. cit.,* ii, 1038–1042. The frequent conjunction of integration and force in the implementation of a new polity in no way invalidates the negative relationship between war and the integrational infrastructure.

[25] Even the curiosity with which Americans receive Gaullist rhetoric is a measure of their alienation from the nation-state era. "The traditional grant of sovereign discretion rested upon a relative condition of national independence on a factual level. We now live in a contrasting world of predominant national interdependence, thereby making any nation's independent power to decide appear deeply arbitrary." Richard A. Falk, *Law, Morality, and War in the Contemporary World,* New York: Praeger (1963), 52–53.

ganizations tied to the past and supranational communities newly emerged into the present are profoundly contradictory.

Integration may well have performed prodigies of economic reconstruction in post-war Europe.[26] European integration, moreover, has cut across some of the intra-European animosities that made the nation-state world seem such a threat to peace. The even more recent and tentative experiments in Latin American, African, and Asian integration seem to confirm "supranationality" as an apt vehicle for economic development. In short, American policy has looked with favor upon the growth of larger international units beginning at the level of economies, but holding the promise of political union. The readiness with which social scientists have applied themselves to the study of integration itself is a barometer of environmental changes.

Integration does not, however, exhibit any necessary affinity for what we may choose to regard as social progress. The value systems and historical circumstances bound up with it have been too many and too varied to make for the realization of a single set of policy objectives. The periods 1850–1870 and 1931–1939 manifest, if nothing else, the moral neutrality of political integration, the extent to which it is productive of no single distribution of values. If the past is any guide, the goals of universal political organizations and of political integration may well collide. Political integration, no matter what more specific values in advances, seeks to do violence to the status quo by altering the distribution of power through changes in the number and kinds of actors. Political movements to which the greatest opprobrium has attached at a given time

[26] This is a moot point and posed as a choice between the beneficent effects of integration and what would have been accomplished without it, untestable as well.

have frequently included those most clearly involved in the furtherance of integration; for in the eyes of states enmeshed in the existing distribution of power, new actors represent a threat. It is completely plausible that integration might stem from values different than those which underlie the universal organization. But it is also possible that the institutionalization of particular values in the organization may build in a potential for the subsequent polarization of values. In other words, any initial discrepancy between organizational values and those of the emerging polity is apt to widen with time. For political developments that violate the status quo may well impel the violators toward a wholesale rejection of the dominant value system. While incremental change takes place within a value consensus, the introduction of new international actors can constitute a qualitative change in existing arrangements. Hence, the contradiction of organizational purpose and integration may produce changes not simply at the level of power distribution but at the level of ideology as well. Integration, to the extent that it ruptures the status quo, sets in motion a process of the polarization of values: on the one hand, the norms of the universal organization, hitherto dominant; on the other, the mirror-image norms of the *parvenu* state.

The integrative movements of our own time that have so captured the imaginations of thoughtful men have thus far coexisted well with the United Nations. Yet it is only fair to point out that current experiments have not proceeded much past the establishment of the infrastructure. The ability of the United Nations to tolerate this level of change is considerable. When, however, overt political manifestations show themselves, the problem will have taken a different turn. The ability of the UN to survive profound alterations in the political landscape depends upon its ability to socialize new or presumptive members.[27] Yet the relationship cannot be one of imposed values alone, but must entail the organization's transcending the limitations of its founding. Socialization itself can aspire only to modest objectives if the state to be socialized constitutes, by its very existence, a threat to the prevailing order. The fruitful meshing of organization and change, to the extent that it is a live option, depends upon the readiness of the organization to modify and if need be renounce its original purposes, turning itself into a new instrument direct towards new ends.

[27] The most complete discussion of the UN and socialization is William D. Coplin, *Functions of International Law*, Chicago: Rand McNally (forthcoming).